DISCOVERING
PSYCHOLOGY

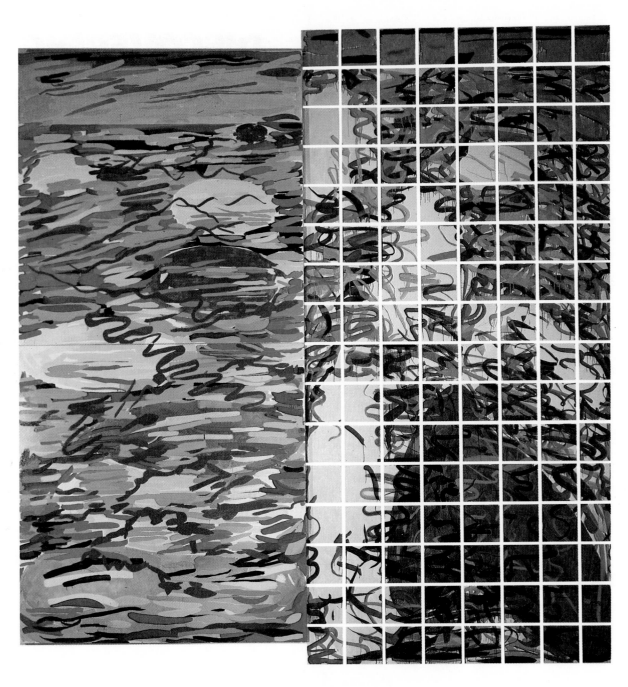

Jennifer Bartlett
Swimmers Atlanta: Seaweed   1979
Courtesy Paula Cooper Gallery
Commissioned by the Art in Architecture Program
    of the General Services Administration

DISCOVERING PSYCHOLOGY

Neil R. Carlson

THE UNIVERSITY OF MASSACHUSETTS

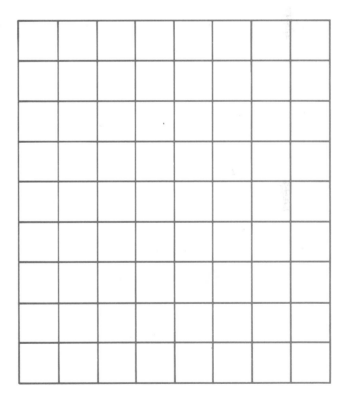

Allyn and Bacon, Inc.

Boston ▪ London ▪ Sydney ▪ Toronto

Developmental Editor   Allen Workman

Cover Administrator   Linda Dickinson

Manufacturing Buyer   Bill Alberti

Library of Congress Cataloging-in-Publication Data

Carlson, Neil R., 1942–
    Discovering psychology / Neil R. Carlson.
        p.   cm.
    Bibliography: p.
    Includes index.
    ISBN 0-205-11401-6
    1. Psychology.   I. Title.
BF121.C34 1988   87-33334
150—dc19   CIP

Printed in the United States of America

10 9 8 7 6 5 4 3 2   92 91 90 89 88

PHOTO CREDITS

Chapter 1

Page 3 © Ted Kaufman/The Stock Market; page 4 © Mike Yamashita 1985/Woodfin Camp & Associates;   page 5 The Granger Collection;   page 6 The Bettmann Archive;   page 7 Culver Pictures;   page 8 The Granger Collection;   page 9 The Bettmann Archive;   page 10 Culver Pictures;   page 12 © Frank Fournier 1982/Contact Stock Images/Woodfin Camp & Associates;   page 13 Photo News/Gamma-Liaison; page 15 (left) © Charles Gupton 1986/The Stock Market; page 15 (right) Ellis Herwig/The Picture Cube;   page 17 Leonard Freed/Magnum Photos;   page 21 © Jeff Lowenthal 1982/Woodfin Camp & Associates;   page 23 © John Launois 1982/Black Star;   page 24 UPI/Bettmann Newsphotos.

Chapter 2

Page 49 Manfred Kage/Peter Arnold, Inc.;   page 50 Lefton, Psychology, Third Edition, © 1985 by Allyn and Bacon, Inc.;   page 51 Science Source/Photo Researchers;   page 53 © David Madison 1985/Duomo;   page 56 Paul Sequeira/ Photo Researchers;   page 57 Lefton, Psychology, Third Edition, © 1985 by Allyn and Bacon, Inc.;   page 58 Catherine Ursillo/Photo Researchers;   page 65 Science Source/Photo Researchers;   page 70 Ethan Hoffman/Archive Pictures, Inc.;   page 72 © David L. Johnson 1986/Action Images Sportschrome;   page 74 Ed Ballotts/South Bend Tribune.

Chapter 3

Page 82 © Bob Krist 1986/Black Star;   page 85 Courtesy of Douglas G. Mollerstuen, New England Medical Center; page 90 Courtesy of Munsell Color Corporation;   page 92 Photo Courtesy of GATF;   page 95 Courtesy of American Optical Corporation;   page 98 © c/o Cordon Art—Baarn— Holland;   page 105 Paul Solomon/Wheeler Pictures;   page 106 (left) L. Goldman/Visions;   page 106 (right) Andy Caulfield/The Image Bank;   page 114 Marcia Rules/*Sports Illustrated;*   page 116 John P. Cavanagh/Archive Pictures, Inc.

Chapter 4

Page 122 © Howard Sochurek 1983/Woodfin Camp & Associates;   page 124 (top) Petit Format/Nestle/Science Source/

(Continued on page 585)

Contents

PART A

FOUNDATIONS AND DEVELOPMENT OF HUMAN BEHAVIOR *38*

vi

Chapter 4   **120**

Child Development

PART B

LEARNING AND COGNITION   *176*

Chapter 7   210

Memory

Chapter 8   240

Language

Chapter 9   270

Intelligence

PART C

MOTIVATION, EMOTION, AND CONSCIOUSNESS   *302*

Chapter 10   306

Consciousness

Chapter 11   334

Motivation

Chapter 12   360

Emotion

PART D

SOCIAL PROCESSES
384

Chapter 13
388

Social Psychology: Attitudes and Attribution

Chapter 14
412

Social Psychology: Influence and Attraction

Chapter 15   440

Personality

PART E

PSYCHOLOGICAL DISORDERS AND THEIR TREATMENT 472

Discovering Psychology is a text aimed at introducing students to the science of psychology through its most important theories and research. The book has two main purposes: to create interest in how people discover what we know about psychology, and to encourage a basic understanding of psychology's fundamental topics through a compact, balanced presentation and useful learning aids.

One of the first priorities in my teaching and textbook writing has always been to give students a realistic appreciation for the scientific discovery process that takes place in the laboratory or in the field. I have made an effort to bring to the textbook the fascination and excitement of the pursuit of knowledge that I try to convey in my lectures. In addition, I have put renewed emphasis on describing the process psychologists use to discover and test what we know about the causes of behavior, while also summarizing conclusions on important topics.

Discovering Psychology grew out of my successful textbook, *Psychology: The Science of Behavior*, 2nd Edition. Both books present psychology as a valid experimental science and strive to involve students in the critical thinking behind the experimental method.

The organization of this text into seventeen chapters represents an effort to give students both a balanced view of our field and a clearly focused idea of its key scientific findings. This format allows ample space for important findings in the developmental, social, clinical, and psychometric areas (8 chapters) as balanced against coverage of the basic physiological, behavioral, and cognitive topics (8 chapters). It also provides 25 to 35 page chapters which are broken into subsections or "chunks" that students can review easily. As a framework for learning the material, the opening of each chapter presents an organizing outline and a preview of the scientific issues that emerge in the chapter. Each subsection of text is followed by thought-provoking questions which link ideas together and provide students with a way to check their learning of key concepts. To help students in reviewing, key terms are highlighted throughout the text, while numbered summaries and chapter glossaries appear at the end of each chapter.

This book contains no "boxes." I find them to be distracting, and so do my students. They often interrupt one's reading of the main text. If something is worth saying, it is worth integrating into the continuing discussion. In addition, I have included coverage of statistical methods in the first chapter of the text, not in an appendix, because statistics is such an important part of the experimental method.

Throughout the text I have tried to show some of the motives as well as the reasoning behind scientific attempts to explain behavior. To emphasize that explaining behavior has important consequences for our lives, there is a featured discussion at the opening of each part and chapter which focuses on a contemporary research topic of importance in everyday behavior. These topics all draw attention to our need to evaluate research in psychology as it impacts our daily lives.

Discovering Psychology presents new research and up-to-date material that has not appeared in any of my other texts. Discussions on such topics as moral development, sex role development, death and dying, coping with stress reactions, attitude change and persuasion, and the effectiveness of therapy are newly incorporated into the text.

Supplements

A series of questionnaires, reviews, and focused discussion groups were used to guide the development not only of this text, but also of its supplements. Consequently, the entire teaching package has been carefully correlated with the text. The Instructor's Manual has been developed to serve as a guide to the topical coverage and includes learning objectives for the text. It is also a resource for finding creative material for demonstration and class activities.

A systematic learning framework for text and supplements is provided by a list of Learning Objectives incorporated into all the supplements. These objectives appear as a numbered list in the Instructor's Manual and Study Guide. They serve as reference points for topical coverage in the text (closely paralleled by the text's subsection questions) and for topical groupings of Test Bank questions. At the same time they provide a learning structure for students as they use the Study Guide. The result is a highly integrated teaching, testing, and studying system.

A reliable Test Bank of approximately 2000 class-tested items has been prepared by experienced test developers and teachers, and is available in convenient printed and computerized formats. The Study Guide has two functions: (1) to aid students in an active learning process to master text concepts and review for exams; and (2) to provide interesting "discovery" demonstrations—actually short desk-top experiments—that students can run to illustrate and help recall important principles in the text. Study Guide users will learn terms through unique "concept cards" while using the short and long-answer study questions and Self-Tests to master each of the Learning Objective concepts.

Acknowledgments

As a writer I tend to think of the book as "mine," but it also reflects the work of many other people. I acknowledge their contributions and thank them. The plan for this book was developed by Sandi Kirshner, Diana Murphy, and Nancy Forsyth of Allyn and Bacon's Special Projects Group; Bill Barke, Editor-in-Chief; and my editor, John-Paul Lenney. Developmental Editors Allen Workman and Susan Sanderson were instrumental in the preparation of this text. Cynthia Newby and her staff at Curriculum Concepts, Inc., coordinated production for this book. Few realize the amount of labor that goes into producing books like this, but I do, and I thank these people.

I also want to thank the many people who reviewed this manuscript as well as those who prepared the original ancillary material. Eric Carlson (no relation), Madeleine Leveille, and my wife, Mary Carlson, wrote the Study Guide; Clint Anderson and Steve Miscovich wrote the Instructor's Manual; the test items were written by Charles Hinderliter, Gail Ditoff, and a team from the University of Minnesota—including Sheryll Mennicke, Laurie Dunn, Jon Koerner, Nancy Lawroski, David Lubinski, Cynthia Thompson, and Kara Witt. All of these ancillary materials were adapted for *Discovering Psychology* by the Allyn and Bacon Special Projects Group.

Finally, I thank my family for tolerating my spending so much time on the book and for putting up with my grouchiness when work seemed to be going slowly.

If you would like to have input into the next edition of this text, please write to me at the Department of Psychology, Tobin Hall, University of Massachusetts, Amherst, MA 01003. I hope to hear from you.

DISCOVERING
PSYCHOLOGY

The Science of Psychology

Can we ever really understand ourselves? Some people would say that we cannot; we humans are just too complex, too individualistic, and too unpredictable for our behavior to be successfully understood through scientific analysis. True, people *are* complex, and a thorough understanding of the causes of human behavior is one of the most formidable tasks that we can contemplate. But it is also one of the most important tasks, and perhaps the most interesting.

What are some of the ways psychologists study human behavior? The earliest psychologists tried to understand human behavior by looking inward. They attempted to be detached self-observers, carrying out a systematic analysis of their own thoughts and perceptions. The attempt failed; with each person examining his or her own mental processes, how could their observations be compared? How could people know that they were examining the same phenomena, and making comparable judgments? Although the attempt failed, it provided enough information to get the next generation of researchers started on the right track: observing the behavior of others and applying the rules of the scientific method to these observations.

What does the scientific method provide that less rigorous methods of study do not? As you will see, it provides researchers with a common set of rules to follow when investigating natural phenomena, such as human behavior. The rules are clear and reasonable, and can be applied to everyday problems that interest us all: What are the effects of daycare on a child's physical, psychological, and social development? How accurate are our memories? Do men and women have different needs in regard to love and work? What causes depression? How is it best treated? Psychologists use the scientific method to study these and other interesting questions about human behavior.

In this chapter, you will learn about the history of psychology and the way the scientific method is applied to the study of human behavior. You will learn about the use of statistics, and will probably be pleasantly surprised to learn that statistics need not be esoteric and complicated; in fact, they can be straightforward. What you learn will help you evaluate which statements about the causes of behavior have a valid scientific foundation, and which do not stand up under close scrutiny. This chapter will show you what it means to be a scientist, and why psychology is a science.

Introduction

In this book we will study the science of psychology. The primary emphasis is on discovering the causes of human behavior. I shall describe the applications of these discoveries to treating mental disorders and improving society, but the focus will be on the way in which psychologists discover what could be the explanations for human behavior.

EXPLAINING BEHAVIOR

The major goal of psychology as a science is to understand human behavior: to explain why people do what they do. As more and more psychologists have come into the field, they have become interested in different kinds of behaviors and different levels of explanation.

How do psychologists "explain" behavior? In general, we discover its causes—those events that are responsible for its occurrence. If we can describe the events that caused the behavior to occur, we have "explained" it. Each type of psychologist looks for certain types of **causal events.** Some look inside the organism for physiological causes, such as the activity of nerve cells or the secretions of glands. Others "look inside" the organism in a metaphorical sense, explaining behaviors in terms of hypothetical mental states, such as anger, fear, or a need to achieve. Still others look only for environmental events that cause behaviors to occur.

Research psychologists differ from one another in two principal ways: in the types of *phenomena* they investigate and in the *causal events* they analyze. That is, they explain different types of behaviors, and they explain them in terms of different causes. For example, two psychologists might both be interested in the same psychological phenomenon of memory, but they might attempt to explain memory in terms of different types of causal events. But all types of explanations are subjected to a critical analysis by other researchers. The evidence must be gathered in accordance with the scientific method described later in this chapter, and the explanations based on the evidence must prove themselves useful in predicting behav-

ior. Psychology is both a scientific discipline and a profession. Psychologists are probably the most diverse group of people in our society to share the same title. According to the 1980 census, there are 119,000 people in the United States employed as psychologists. They engage in research, teaching, counseling, and psychotherapy; they advise industry and governmental agencies about personnel matters, the design of products, advertising and marketing, and legislation; they also devise and administer tests of personality, achievement, and ability. Psychologists study a wide variety of phenomena, including physiological processes within the nervous system, genetics, environmental events, mental abilities, and social interactions. And yet psychology is a new discipline. The first person to call himself a psychologist (Wilhelm Wundt) was still living in 1920, and by far the majority of people who have done work in psychology are still at work today.

THE DEVELOPMENT OF PSYCHOLOGY

Although philosophers and other thinkers have been concerned with psychological issues for a long time, the science of psychology is comparatively young; it started in Germany in the late nineteenth century. But in order to understand how this science came into being, we must first trace its roots back through philosophy and the natural sciences, because these disciplines provided the methods we use to study human behavior. These roots took many centuries to develop. Let us examine them now and see how they set the stage for the emergence of the science of psychology in the late nineteenth century.

Philosophical Roots of Psychology

Each of us is conscious of our own existence. This consciousness is a private experience; we cannot directly experience the consciousness of another person. But by extension, we attribute consciousness to our fellow human beings and assume that they are like us. Philosophers have long thought about the origins and nature of human consciousness.

The seventeenth-century mathematician René Descartes was one of the first thinkers to attempt a systematic study of human consciousness and behavior. Descartes has been called the father of modern philosophy and the originator of a biological tradition that led to the development of modern physiological psychology. As a philosopher and scientist, Descartes said that one should study nature by gathering evidence with the senses and applying human reasoning.

Descartes developed a systematic theory of the human mind and behavior on the assumption that all reality can be divided into two distinct entities: the soul or mind belonged to the nonmaterial realm, and the body belonged to the material realm. He reasoned that in humans the mind and body must somehow interact, or else how could the mind control the acts of the body? He believed (wrongly) that the interaction occurred in a part of the brain called the pineal gland; the mind caused the pineal gland to move in various directions, which caused fluid to be pumped through the nerves into the muscles, making them inflate and move the body. Although his explanation was wrong, it focused attention on the workings of the body, and on the ways that sensations gave rise to reactions, in the form of movements. He believed that the human mind was a nonphysical structure contrasted with his conception of the body as a machine; later philosophers and scientists began regarding the mind as a part of that machine, not as its controller.

The work of the English philosopher John Locke completed the trend toward conceiving of the world as a mechanical operation. Locke did not exempt the mind from the mechanical laws of the material universe. Descartes's *rationalism* (pursuit of truth through reason) was supplanted by **empiricism**—pursuit of truth through observation and experience. Locke rejected the notion that ideas were innately present in an infant's mind. Instead, all knowledge must come through experience. It is empirically derived. (In Greek, *empeirā* means "experience.") His model of the mind was a tablet of soft clay, smooth at birth and ready to accept the writings of experience upon it.

Locke believed that our knowledge of complex experiences was nothing more than linkages of simple, primary sensations: simple ideas combined to form complex ones. In contrast, the Irish philosopher and mathematician George Berkeley believed that our knowledge of events in the world did not come simply from direct experience but instead was the result of inferences based upon the accumulation of past experiences. In other words, we must learn how to perceive. For example, our visual perception of depth involves several elementary sensations, such as observing the relative movements of objects as we move our heads and the convergence of our eyes (turning inward toward each other or away) as we focus on near or distant objects. Although our knowledge of visual depth seems to be immediate and direct, it is actually a secondary, complex response constructed from a number of simple elements. Our perceptions of the world can also involve integrating the activity of different sense organs, such as when we see, hear, feel, and smell the same object.

As you can see, the philosophers Locke and Berkeley were grappling with the structure of the human mind and the way in which people acquire knowledge. They were dealing with the concept of learning. (In fact, modern psychologists are still concerned with the issues that Berkeley raised.) As philosophers, they were trying to fit a nonquantifiable variable—reason—into the equation.

Psychology is the science of behavior; the task of psychologists is to understand and explain behavior.

Biological Roots of Psychology

The mechanical view of the human body that Descartes developed—showing behavior as the product of a complex physical system—inspired later thinkers and scientists to investigate the physical aspects of behavior. Pioneering studies in the eighteenth century were often performed by people interested in isolated phenomena, such as the electrical aspects of nerve impulses, hypnosis, and other curiosities. But by the early nineteenth century the work of the German physiologist Johannes Müller brought a careful, systematic, experimental approach to the physiology of behavior.

Müller was a forceful advocate of applying experimental procedures to the study of physiology. According to him, biologists should do more than observe and classify; they should remove or isolate various organs, test their responses to chemicals, and manipulate other conditions in order to see how the organism worked. His most important contribution to what would become the science of psychology was his **doctrine of specific nerve energies.** He noted that the basic message sent along all nerves was the same—an electrical impulse. And the impulse itself was the same, regardless of whether the message concerned, for example, a visual perception or an auditory one. What, then, accounts for the brain's ability to distinguish different kinds of sensory information? That is, why do we see what our eyes detect, hear what our ears detect, and so on? After all, the optic nerves and auditory nerves both send the same kind of message to the brain.

The answer is that the messages are sent over different channels. Because the optic nerves are attached to the eyes, the brain interprets impulses received from these nerves as visual sensations. You have probably already noticed that rubbing your eyes causes sensations of flashes of light. When you rub your eyes, the pressure against them stimulates visual receptors located inside. The brain then interprets these messages as sensations of light.

Müller's doctrine had important implications. If the brain recognizes the nature of a particular sensory input by means of the particular nerve that brings the message, then perhaps the brain is similarly specialized, with different parts having different functions. In other words, if the messages sent by the nerves are anatomically distinct, then those regions of the brain that receive these messages must also be anatomically distinct. Müller's ideas have endured, forming the basis for investigations into the functions of the nervous system. For centuries, thinking or consciousness had been identified as the distinguishing feature of the human mind and had been localized as a function of the brain. Now the components of the nervous system were being identified and their means of operation were being explored.

The brain distinguishes between visual and auditory stimuli.

The person to apply this logic more specifically to human behavioral capacities was Paul Broca, a French surgeon. In 1861 Broca performed an autopsy on the brain of a man who had had a stroke several years previously; the stroke had caused him to lose the ability to speak. Broca discovered that part of the cerebral cortex on the left side of the man's brain was damaged. He suggested that this region of the brain is a center for speech.

Although subsequent research has found that speech is not controlled by a single "center" in the brain, the area that Broca identified is indeed necessary for speech production to occur. The comparison of postmortem anatomical findings with a patient's behavioral and intellectual deficits has become an important means of studying the functions of the brain. Psychologists can operate on the brains of laboratory animals, but they obviously cannot operate on the brains of humans. Instead, they must study the effects of brain damage that occurs from natural causes.

In 1870 the German physiologists Gustav Fritsch and Eduard Hitzig introduced the use of electrical stimulation as a tool for mapping the functions of the brain. The results of this method complemented those produced by the experimental destruction of nervous tissue and provided some answers that the methods of experimental surgery could not. For example, Fritsch and Hitzig discovered that applying a small electrical shock to different parts of the cerebral cortex caused movements of different parts of the body. In fact, the body appeared to be "mapped" on the surface of the brain, as we shall see in the next chapter.

In Germany, Ernst Weber began work that led to the development of ways to measure the magnitude of human sensations. Weber, an anatomist and physiologist, investigated the ability of people to discriminate between pairs of various kinds of stimuli and discovered a principle that held true for all sensory systems: the **just-noticeable difference (jnd).** For example, when he presented subjects with two metal objects and asked them to say whether they differed in weight, he found that people reported that the two weights felt the same unless they differed by a factor of at least 1 in 40; that is, a person could just barely distinguish a 40-gram weight from a 41-gram weight or a 400-gram weight from a 410-gram weight. Different

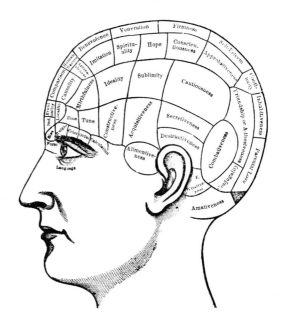

During the early nineteenth century, phrenologists claimed to have mapped the location of personality characteristics and abilities in the brain. Scientists later showed through experiments that these speculations were incorrect.

senses had different ratios; for example, the ratio for detecting differences in the brightness of white light is approximately 1 in 60. These ratios came to be called Weber fractions.

Gustav Fechner, another German physiologist, used Weber's concept of just-noticeable difference to measure the magnitude of people's perceptions. This concept was revolutionary; previously, most scientists and philosophers had believed that characteristics of the mind could not be measured. Assuming that the just-noticeable difference was the basic unit of perceptual experience, he used it to measure the absolute magnitude of a perception.

The Development of Psychological Science

Psychology as a unique science began in Germany in the late nineteenth century with Wilhelm Wundt. Wundt was the first person to call himself a psychologist. He shared the conviction of other German scientists that all aspects of nature, including the human mind, could be studied scientifically. His book *Principles of Physiological Psychology* was the first textbook of psychology.

Wilhelm Wundt (1832–1920) founded the first psychological laboratory in Leipzig in 1879. As a psychologist, he used introspective methods to study the contents and structure of the human mind.

Structuralism

Wundt defined psychology as the "science of immediate experience." His approach was called **structuralism.** Its subject matter was the *structure* of the mind, built from the elements of consciousness, such as ideas and sensations. Its raw material was supplied by trained observers who described their own experiences. The observers were taught to engage in **introspection** (literally, "looking within"). They observed stimuli and described their experiences. Wundt and his associates made inferences about the nature of mental processes by seeing how changes in the stimuli caused changes in the verbal reports of their trained observers.

Wundt was particularly interested in the problem that had intrigued George Berkeley: how did basic sensory information give rise to complex perceptions? His trained observers attempted to ignore complex perceptions and report only the elementary ones. For example, the sensation of seeing a patch of red is an immediate and elementary one, whereas the perception of an apple is a complex one.

Wundt was a very ambitious and prolific scientist who wrote many books and trained many other scientists in his laboratory. Although structuralism has been supplanted, Wundt's contribution must be acknowledged. He established psychology as an experimental science, independent of philosophy. He trained a great number of psychologists, many of whom established their own laboratories and continued the evolution of the new discipline.

Ebbinghaus: Pioneer in Research on Human Memory

Most of the pioneers of psychology founded **schools,** groups of people with a common belief in a particular theory and methodology. (In this context, the word *school* refers to a branch of a particular academic discipline, not a building or institution. For example, structuralism was a school of psychology.) The exception to this general trend was provided by Hermann Ebbinghaus. In 1876, after having received his Ph.D. in philosophy but still unattached to an academic institution, Ebbinghaus came across a second-hand copy of a book by a contemporary of Weber's, Gustav Fechner, which described a mathematical approach to the measurement of human sensation. Intrigued by this research, Ebbinghaus decided to apply similar methods in an attempt to measure human memory—the process of learning and forgetting.

Working alone—both as experimenter and as subject of the experiment—Ebbinghaus devised methods to measure memory and the speed with which forgetting occurred. He realized that he could not compare the learning and forgetting of two prose passages or two poems, because some passages would undoubtedly be easier to learn than others. Therefore, he devised a relatively uniform set of materials—nonsense syllables, such as *juz, bul,* and *gof.* He printed the syllables on cards and read through a set of them, with the rate of presentation controlled by the ticking of a watch. After reading the set, he paused a fixed amount of time then read the cards again. He recorded the number of times he had to read the cards to be able to recite them without error. He measured forgetting by trying to recite the nonsense syllables on a later occasion—minutes, hours, or days later. The number of syllables he remembered was an index of the percentage of memory that had been retained.

Ebbinghaus's approach to memory was entirely empirical; he devised no theory of why learning occurs and was interested only in gathering facts through careful, systematic observation. However, despite the lack of theory, his work made important contributions to the development of the science of psychology. He introduced the principle of eliminating **variable errors** by making observations repeatedly on different occasions (using different lists each time) and calculating the average of these observations. (Examples of variable errors include those caused by random differences in the subject's mood or alertness or by uncontrollable changes in the environment.) He constructed graphs of the rate at which the memorized lists of nonsense syllables were forgotten, which provided a way to measure mental contents across time. As we will see in Chapter 7, Ebbinghaus's research provided a model of systematic, rigorous experimental procedures that modern psychologists still emulate.

Functionalism

After structuralism, the next major trend in psychology was **functionalism.** This approach, which began in the United States, was in large part a protest against the structuralism of Wundt. While structuralists were interested in what they saw as the components of consciousness (ideas and sensations), the functionalists focused on the process of conscious activity (perceiving and learning). Functionalism grew from the new perspective on nature supplied by Charles Darwin and his followers. They pursued the idea that human behaviors, like other biological characteristics, could best be explained by understanding their roles, or functions, in human adaptation to the environment. Proponents of functionalism stressed the biological significance (the purpose or *function*) of natural processes, including behaviors. The emphasis was on overt, observable behaviors, and not on private mental events.

The most important psychologist to embrace functionalism was William James. As James said, "My thinking is first, last, and always for the sake of my doing." That is, thinking was not

an end in itself; its function was to produce useful behaviors.

James was a brilliant writer and thinker. Although he did not produce any important experimental research, his teaching and writing influenced those who followed him. His theory of emotion is one of the most famous and durable psychological theories. It is still quoted in modern textbooks of psychology. Psychologists still read James's writings; he supplied ideas for experiments that still sound fresh and new.

Unlike structuralism, functionalism was not supplanted; instead, its major tenets were absorbed by its successor, behaviorism. One of the last of the functionalists, James Angell, described its basic principles: (1) Functional psychology is the study of mental *operations* and not mental *structures*. (For example, the mind remembers; it does not contain a memory.) It is not enough to compile a catalog of what the mind does; one must try to understand what the mind accomplishes by this doing. (2) Mental processes are not studied as isolated and independent events but as part of the biological activity of the organism. These processes are

---

William James (1842–1910) set up the first psychological laboratory in America at Harvard University, in 1875. Founder of the functionalist school, James believed psychologists should study the functions of the mind.

aspects of the organism's adaptation to the environment and are a product of its evolutionary history. The fact that we are conscious implies that consciousness has adaptive value for our species. (3) Functional psychology studies the relation between the environment and the response of the organism to the environment. There is no meaningful distinction between mind and body, they are part of the same entity.

■ How did Locke's empiricism and Descartes's rationalism differ in their view of the role of the human mind?

■ What did Wundt and Ebbinghaus contribute to the study of behavior as a science?

■ What basic principles of functionalism are still observed by some modern psychologists?

Sigmund Freud (1856–1939) was the first to employ psychoanalytic methods in his treatment of patients. In doing so, he successfully treated illness that seemed to have no apparent organic explanation.

Freud's Psychodynamic Theory

While psychology was developing as a fledgling science, an important figure was formulating a theory of human behavior that would greatly affect psychology and psychiatry and radically influence intellectuals of all kinds. Sigmund Freud began his career as a neurologist, so his work was firmly rooted in biology. He soon became interested in behavioral and emotional problems and began formulating his psychodynamic theory of personality, which would evolve over his long career. Although his approach was based on observation of patients and not on scientific experiments, he remained convinced that the biological basis of his theory would be established someday.

Freud and his theory are discussed in detail in Chapter 15; I mention him here only to mark his place in the history of psychology. His theory of the mind included structures, but his structuralism was quite different from Wundt's. He devised his concepts of ego, superego, id, and other mental structures through talking with his patients, not through laboratory experiments. His hypothetical mental operations included many that were unconscious and hence not available to introspection. And unlike Wundt, Freud emphasized function; his mental structures served biological drives and instincts and reflected our animal nature.

Behaviorism

The next major trend in psychology, **behaviorism,** directly followed from functionalism. It went further in its rejection of the special nature of mental events, denying that unobservable and unverifiable mental events were properly the subject matter of psychology. Psychology was the study of observable behaviors, and mental events, because they could not be observed, were outside the realm of psychology.

Edward Thorndike was an American psychologist who studied the behavior of animals. His studies of the behavior of cats while they learned a task led him to formulate the **law of effect.** He placed cats in a cage that was equipped with a latch. The cats, who were hungry, had to operate the latch in order to leave the cage and eat the food that was placed in a dish outside. Thorndike observed that the cats' restless activity eventually resulted in their accidentally operating the latch. On subsequent trials the cats' behavior became more and more efficient, until they operated the latch as soon as they were placed into the cage. He called the process "learning by trial and accidental success."

Thorndike noted that some events, usually those that one would expect to be pleasant, seemed to "stamp in" a response that had just occurred. Other, apparently noxious events, seemed to "stamp out" the response, or make it less likely to occur. (Nowadays, we call these processes *reinforcement* and *punishment*.)

The law of effect is certainly in the functionalist tradition. It observes that the consequences of a behavior act back upon the organism, affecting the likelihood that the behavior that just occurred will occur again. The cat accidentally presses the latch, and the consequences of this act (being able to leave the cage and eat) make pressing the latch become more likely the next time the cat is put into the cage. This process is very similar to the principle of natural selection; just as organisms that successfully adapt to their environment are more likely to survive and breed, behaviors that cause useful outcomes become more likely to recur.

Although Thorndike insisted that the subject matter of psychology was behavior, his explanations contained somewhat mentalistic terms. For example, in his law of effect he spoke of "satisfaction," which is certainly not a phenomenon that can be directly observed. Later behaviorists threw out terms like "satisfaction" and "discomfort" and replaced them with more objective terms, that reflected the behavior of the organism rather than any feelings it might have.

Another major figure in the development of the behavioristic trend was not a psychologist at all but a Russian physiologist. Ivan Pavlov studied the physiology of digestion. In the course of studying the stimuli that produce salivation, he discovered that hungry dogs would salivate at the sight of the attendant who brought in their dish of food. Pavlov found that a dog could be trained to salivate at completely arbitrary stimuli, such as the sound of a bell, if the stimulus was quickly followed by the delivery of a bit of food into the animal's mouth.

Ivan Pavlov (1849–1936) won a Nobel Prize for his study of digestion. His accidental discovery of the conditioned reflex is one of those happy occurrences in which research reveals a valuable, though unsought, result.

Pavlov's discovery had profound significance for psychology. His principles showed that through experience an animal could learn to make a response to a stimulus that had never caused this response before. This ability could explain how organisms learn cause-and-effect relations in the environment. In contrast, Thorndike's law of effect suggested an explanation for the adaptability of a person's behavior to its particular environment. Two important behavioral principles had been discovered.

Behaviorism as a formal school of psychology began with the publication of a book by John B. Watson, *Psychology from the Standpoint of a Behaviorist.* Watson was a professor of psychology at Johns Hopkins University. He was a popular teacher and writer and was a very convincing advocate of behaviorism. Even after being fired from his position at Johns Hopkins and embarking on a highly successful career in advertising, he continued to lecture and write magazine articles about psychology.

According to Watson, psychology was a natural science whose domain was restricted to observable events: the behavior of organisms. He believed that the elements of consciousness studied by the structuralists were too subjective to lend themselves to scientific investigation. He defined psychology as the objective study of stimuli and the behaviors they produced. Even thinking was reduced to a form of behavior—talking to oneself.

> Now what can we observe? We can observe *behavior—what the organism does or says*. And let us point out at once: that saying is doing—that is, *behaving*. Speaking overtly or to ourselves (thinking) is just as objective a type of behavior as baseball. (Watson, 1930, p. 6)

Behaviorism is still very much alive today in psychology. Its advocates include B.F. Skinner, whose name is undoubtedly familiar to you. Behaviorism has given birth to the technology of teaching machines (which have since been replaced by computers), the use of behavior modification in instructing the mentally retarded, and the use of behavior therapy to treat mental disorders. Research on the nature of the basic principles that were discovered by Thorndike and Pavlov still continues.

John B. Watson (1878–1958) sought to make psychology a purely objective experimental branch of natural science by restricting it to the study of relations between environmental events (stimuli) and behavior (responses).

Reaction Against Behaviorism: The Cognitive Revolution

The emphasis on behaviorism restricted the subject matter of psychology to observable behaviors. For many years such concepts as consciousness were considered to be outside the domain of psychology. As one psychologist put it, ". . . psychology, having first bargained away its soul and then gone out of its mind, seems now . . . to have lost all consciousness" (Burt, 1962, p. 229). During the past two decades many psychologists have protested against the restrictions of behaviorism and have turned to the study of consciousness, feelings, dreams, and other private events. Much of *cognitive psychology* uses an approach called **information processing;** information received through the senses is "processed" by various systems of neurons in the brain. Some systems store the information in the form of memory, and other systems control behavior. Some systems operate automatically and unconsciously, while others are conscious and require effort on the part of the individual. Because the information-processing approach was first devised to describe the operations of complex physical systems such as computers, the modern model of the human brain is, for most cognitive psychologists, the computer.

Although cognitive psychologists now study mental structures and operations, they have not gone back to the introspective methods that were employed by structuralists like Wundt. They still use objective research methods, just as behaviorists do.

For example, several modern psychologists have studied mental imagery. Because we cannot observe what is happening within a person's head, the concept of mental imagery is a hypothetical one. However, experiments can measure aspects of people's behavior that strongly suggest that they are using mental images. For example, Kosslyn (1973, 1975) showed pictures to people and then asked them questions about what they had seen. If he told them to imagine that they were looking at one part of the picture and then asked them a question about another part, they answered quickly if the second part was nearby, but took longer if it was far away. That is, they appeared to have to "scan" the image in their head, jut as they would have to scan a real image with their eyes.

Although the explanation for the results of such experiments is phrased in terms of a private mental event (an image), the behavioral data (the time taken to give an answer) are empirical and objective. Thus the experimental and behavioral traditions are used to investigate mental structures in current cognitive research.

- How did Freud's theory integrate structuralism and functionalism?
- How did the work of Thorndike and Pavlov lead to Watson's behaviorism?
- How does modern cognitive psychology compare to structuralism?

TYPES OF PSYCHOLOGISTS

This book emphasizes the science of psychology, and its main concern is the basic research that underlies how we as psychologists try to discover the causes of human behavior. The professional knowledge of all psychologists, including those whose work is mostly solving everyday problems, must focus on this basic research as a foundation. And yet psychologists come in many varieties, as you can tell from the way the science has developed. Some are pure research scientists; others are clinical practitioners helping people with problems or mental disorders. Some work on commercial projects for marketing and advertising firms; others design educational or research testing instruments. Because this book can deal only indirectly with many of these applied fields, I would like to describe briefly the important work of the different types of psychologists and the problems they study.

Physiological psychologists study almost all behavioral phenomena that can be observed through the physiology of humans and non-human animals. They study such topics as learning, memory, sensory processes, emotional behavior, motivation, sexual behavior, and sleep. They look for causal events in the organism's physiology, especially the nervous system and its interaction with glands that secrete hormones. Physiological psychologists mostly experiment with animals because physiological experiments cannot ethically be performed with humans.

Psychophysiologists generally study human subjects. They measure people's physiological reactions, such as heart rate, blood pressure, electrical resistance of the skin, muscle tension, and electrical activity of the brain. These measurements provide an indication of a person's degree of arousal or relaxation. Most psychophysiologists investigate phenomena like stress and emotions. A practical application of their techniques is the lie detector test.

Comparative psychologists, like physiological psychologists, mostly study the behavior of animals other than humans. The behavioral phenomena they study are also similar to those of physiological psychologists. However, comparative psychologists explain behavior in terms of adaptation to the environment; thus, they are the direct descendants of the functionalist tradition in psychology. They are more likely than most other psychologists to study inherited behavioral patterns, known as **species-typical behaviors,** such as courting and mating, predation, defensive behaviors, and parental behaviors.

In the past the term **experimental psychologist** described a very large group of scientists in the mainstream of the behavioristic tradition. Today this term is usually applied to those psychologists who are interested in the general principles of learning, perception, motivation, and memory. Some experimental psychologists investigate the behavior of animals, but most of them study human behavior. The causal events that they study are nearly all environmental.

Cognitive psychologists almost exclusively study humans, although investigators have begun to study animal cognition as well. They study complex processes like perception, memory, attention, and concept formation. To them, the causal events consist of functions of the human brain in response to environmental events, but most of them do not study physiological mechanisms. Their explanations involve characteristics of inferred processes or structures of the mind, such as imagery, attentional processes, and language mechanisms.

Experimental neuropsychologists are closely allied with both cognitive psychologists and physiological psychologists. They are generally interested in the same phenomena that are studied by cognitive psychologists, but they attempt to discover the particular brain mechanisms responsible for cognitive processes. One

Social psychologists are psychologists who study the effects of people on people. At this mass wedding ceremony, Rev. Sun Myung Moon joined 2500 couples in holy matrimony.

differences in temperament and patterns of behavior. They look for causal events in a person's past history, both genetic and environmental. Some personality psychologists are closely allied with social psychologists; others work on problems related to adjustment to society and hence study problems of interest to clinical psychologists.

Psychometricians devise ways to measure human personality and ability. Psychometricians develop psychological tests, some of which you have taken during your academic career. These tests are used by school systems, counselors, clinical psychologists, and employers. In general, psychometricians are interested in the practical issues of measurement, and most of them do not seek causes in a person's hereditary or environmental history. However, their tests are often used by other psychologists to investigate the causes of behavior.

Most **clinical psychologists** are practitioners who attempt to help people solve their problems, whatever the causes. Others are scientists who do research. They study **psychopathology** (mental disorders) and problems of adjustment. They look for a wide variety of causal events, including genetic factors, physiological factors, and environmental factors such as parental upbringing, interactions with siblings, and other social stimuli.

Besides clinical psychology, the applied areas of psychology include counseling, educational psychology, school psychology, industrial and organizational psychology, and engineering psychology. Psychologists who specialize in **counseling** help people with minor problems of everyday life and assist them with vocational and academic guidance. **Educational psychologists** often conduct basic research, but most attempt to apply the principles discovered by experimental, cognitive, social, and developmental psychologists to the task of education. **School psychologists** are counselors within elementary and secondary school systems. **Industrial and organizational psychologists** are usually employed in industry, where they advise management about the application of psychological principles to running a business. In addition, many industrial and organizational psychologists are scientists who do basic research in academic institutions. **Engineering psychologists** assist in the design of products so that they can most quickly, accurately, and comfortably be used by humans.

of their principal research techniques is experimental surgery, which I described earlier; they study the behavior of people whose brains have been damaged by natural causes.

Developmental psychologists study physical, cognitive, emotional, and social development, especially of children. Some of them study phenomena of adolescence or adulthood, in particular the effects of aging. The causal events they study are as comprehensive as all of psychology: physiological processes, cognitive processes, and social influences.

Social psychologists study the effects of people upon people. The phenomena they explore include perception (of oneself as well as others), cause-and-effect relations in human interactions, attitudes and opinions, interpersonal relationships, and emotional behaviors, such as aggression and sexual behavior.

Personality psychologists study individual

THE SCIENTIFIC METHOD

Psychologists attempt to explain behavior—to understand its causes. As scientists, we believe that behaviors, like other natural phenomena, are subject to objective investigation. Like other scientists, psychologists must follow the procedures and principles of the scientific method.

The scientific method permits a person to discover the causes of a natural phenomenon, including an organism's behavior. The scientific method has become the predominant method of investigation for a very practical reason: *it works better than any other method we have discovered.* The generalizations obtained by following the scientific method are the ones that are most likely to survive the test of time. What you learn here can be applied to everyday life. Knowing how a psychologist can be fooled by the results of an improperly performed experiment can help us all avoid being fooled by more casual observations.

Following the steps of the scientific method does not guarantee that the results of an experiment will be important. Not all properly performed experiments are worthwhile; some studies are trivial or have no relevance to the natural environment. All the scientific method promises is that the question being asked of nature will be answered. If a scientist asks a trivial question, nature returns a trivial answer.

Human behavior is complex; the task of the psychologist is to determine the variables that influence it. At this World Cup Soccer game in Brussels, Belgium, a riot broke out between fans of opposing teams. Objective investigation of group behavior is one task of the psychologist.

It is important to note that no area of psychological investigation is inherently more "scientific" than any other. For example, the physiological analysis of hunger is not inherently more scientific than an investigation of the social factors affecting a person's willingness to help someone else. A scientist is a person who follows the scientific method while investigating natural phenomena. He or she does not necessarily need a laboratory, or any special apparatus. Depending on the question being asked, a scientist might need no more than a pad of paper and a pencil, and some natural phenomenon (like another person's behavior) to observe.

What can a scientist hope to accomplish, and what rules must be followed? As we will see, a scientist attempts to discover *relations* among events, and to phrase these relations in language that is precise enough to be understood by others but general enough to apply to a wide variety of phenomena. As we have seen, this language takes the form of "explanations," which are general statements about the events that cause phenomena to occur. But what is the nature of these general statements? The answer should become clear as we see how psychologists use the scientific method.

The **scientific method** consists of four major steps, listed below. Some new terms are introduced here without definition, but they will be described in detail later in this chapter.

1. Identify the problem and formulate hypothetical cause-and-effect relations among variables. This step involves classifying *variables* (different behaviors and different environmental and physiological events) into the proper categories and describing the relations among variables in general terms. An example might be the following *hypothesis:* "Humiliation increases a person's susceptibility to propaganda." This statement describes a relation between two events—humiliation and susceptibility to propaganda—and states that an increase in one causes an increase in the other.

2. Design and execute an experiment. This step involves manipulating *independent variables* and observing *dependent variables*. For example, if we wanted to test the hypothesis I just suggested, we would have to humiliate people (the independent variable) and see whether that experience altered their susceptibility to propaganda (the dependent variable). But how would we humiliate them, and how would we measure susceptibility to propaganda? Both variables must be *operationally defined*, and the independent variable *controlled* so that definitive conclusions can be made.

3. Determine the truth of the hypothesis by examining the data from the experiment. Do the results support the hypothesis, or do they suggest that the facts are otherwise? This step often involves special mathematical procedures to determine whether an observed relation is *statistically significant*.

4. Communicate the results. Once a psychologist has learned something about the causes of a behavior from an experiment or observational study, he or she must tell others about the new information. In most cases, this communication is accomplished by writing an article that includes a description of the procedure and results and a discussion of their significance. The article is sent to one of the many journals that publish results of psychological experiments. Thus, other psychologists will be able to incorporate these findings into their own thinking and hypothesizing.

Now that I have presented an overview of the scientific method, let me describe its components and the rules that govern it.

Hypotheses

A **hypothesis** is the starting point of any experiment. It is an idea, phrased as a general statement, that the scientist wishes to test in an experiment. In the original Greek, *hypothesis* means "suggestion," and the word still conveys the same meaning. When a scientist forms a hypothesis, he or she is simply suggesting that a relation exists among various phenomena (like one that might exist between humiliation and a person's susceptibility to propaganda). Thus, a hypothesis is a *tentative statement about a relation between two or more events*.

Hypotheses do not spring out of thin air; they occur to a scientist as a result of research or scholarship. Experiments breed experiments. That is, worthwhile research does not merely answer questions; it suggests new questions to be asked—new hypotheses to be tested. Productive and creative scientists formulate new hypotheses by thinking about the implications of experiments that have been performed.

Psychological studies can be conducted in informal settings, such as the supermarket survey being conducted at left, or in formal laboratories, such as the one in the photograph on the right.

Theories

A **theory** is an elaborate form of hypothesis. In fact, a theory can be seen as a way of organizing a system of related hypotheses to explain some larger aspect of nature. In addition, good theories fuel the creation of further hypotheses. (More accurately, a good scientist, contemplating a good theory, thinks of more good hypotheses to test.) For example, Einstein's theory of relativity states that time, matter, and energy are interdependent. Changes in any one will produce changes in the others. The hypotheses that were suggested by this theory revolutionized science; the field of nuclear physics largely rests on experiments arising out of Einstein's theory.

Within psychology, the most influential people have been those who suggested a new way of looking at nature—a way that organized previously unrelated facts and hypotheses into a cohesive theoretical framework. Sigmund Freud's theory of personality certainly changed the way scientists looked at human behavior. It even affected novelists, playwrights, artists, historians, and political scientists. In fact, even though much of Freud's theory has not been

verified, it is so comprehensive, and provides an "explanation" for so much of human behavior, that it continues to exert considerable influence today.

Much research in psychology is based on frameworks that are larger in scope than hypotheses but smaller in scope than full-fledged theories. A psychologist might publish an article that seems to pull together the results of many previous experiments on a particular topic. For example, the frustration-aggression hypothesis, which you will learn about in a later chapter, suggests that organisms have a tendency to become aggressive when they do not achieve a goal that they have become accustomed to achieve in a particular situation. This hypothesis is less comprehensive than Freud's theory of personality, but it makes a prediction that might fit a wide variety of situations. Indeed, many experiments have been performed to test this hypothesis under different conditions. Even though the frameworks that most psychologists construct fall short of constituting a theory, they serve a similar function by getting researchers to think about old problems in new ways, and by showing how findings that did not appear to be related to each other can be

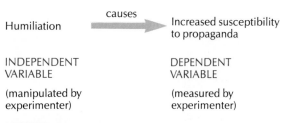

FIGURE 1.1

Independent and dependent variables.

explained by a single concept. There is even a scientific journal (*Psychological Reviews*) that is devoted to articles that the authors hope will have theoretical significance.

Variables

The hypothesis that I proposed earlier—"Humiliation increases a person's susceptibility to propaganda"—describes a relation between humiliation and susceptibility to propaganda. Scientists refer to these two components as **variables:** things that can vary. Variables are quantities, characteristics, or phenomena that a scientist either measures or manipulates when performing an experiment. **Manipulate** literally means "to handle," from *manus,* "hand." Psychologists use the word to refer to setting the value of a variable for experimental purposes. The results of this manipulation determine whether the hypothesis is true or false.

To test the "humiliation" hypothesis in an experiment, we would set the value of people's humiliation at a high level and then measure their susceptibility to propaganda. The first variable—the one that the experimenter manipulates—is called the **independent variable.** The second one, which the experimenter measures, is the **dependent variable.** An easy way to keep them straight is to remember this: a hypothesis always describes how a dependent variable *depends* on the value of an independent variable. For example, susceptibility to propaganda (the dependent variable) depends on the level of a person's humiliation (the independent variable). (See Figure 1.1.)

As we saw, hypotheses are expressed in general terms. This means that the variables that hypotheses deal with are also general rather than specific. That is, we want to understand the behavior of people in general, not just one particular person in one particular situation. Thus, variables are *categories* into which various behaviors are classified. For example, if a person hits, kicks, or throws something at someone else, we could label all of these behaviors as "interpersonal aggression." Presumably, they would have very similar causes. Therefore, a psychologist must know enough about a particular type of behavior to be able to classify it correctly.

Although one of the first steps in psychological investigation involves naming and classifying behaviors, we must be careful to avoid committing the **nominal fallacy.** The nominal fallacy refers to the erroneous belief that one has explained an event simply by naming it. (*Nomen* means "name.") However, classifying a behavior does not explain it; it only prepares the way toward discovering the events that cause it. For example, suppose that we see a man frown and shout at other people without provocation, criticize their work when it is really acceptable, and generally act unpleasantly toward everyone around him. Someone says, "Boy, he's really angry today!" Does this statement explain his behavior?

It does not; it only *describes* it. Instead of saying he is angry, it might be better to say he is "engaging in angry or hostile behaviors." That statement does not pretend to explain why he is acting the way he is. To say he is angry suggests that an internal state is responsible for his behavior; that is, that anger is causing his behavior. But all we have observed is his behavior, not his internal state. Even if he is experiencing feelings of anger, these feelings still do not explain his behavior. What we really need to know is *what events made him act the way he did.* Perhaps he has a painful toothache. Perhaps he just learned that he missed out on an important promotion that he expected to earn. Perhaps he had a terrible fight with his wife. Perhaps he just read a book that advised him to be more assertive. Events like these are causes of both the behavior and the feelings, and unless they are discovered we cannot say that we have explained his behavior.

Of course, a large number of events precede any behavior. Many of these events are completely unrelated to the observed behavior.

When I get off the train, it is because the conductor announces my stop and not because one person coughs, another turns the page of her newspaper, another crosses his legs, or another looks at her watch. The task of a psychologist is to determine which of the many events that occurred before a particular behavior caused that behavior to happen.

Operational Definition

Hypotheses are phrased in general terms, but experiments (step 2 of the scientific method) require that something *particular* be done. In order to humiliate the subjects in our proposed experiment, the experimenter must arrange a particular situation that causes humiliation. Similarly, the experimenter must measure the subjects' susceptibility to propaganda in a particular way, perhaps by testing their opinion on a certain topic, then showing them a film that promotes a point of view on the topic, and finally testing their opinion again. In other words, generalities such as "humiliation" and "susceptibility to propaganda" must be translated into specific operations.

This translation of generalities into specific operations is called an **operational definition:** independent variables and dependent variables are defined in terms of the operations an experimenter performs to set their values or measure them. Here is an example of an operational definition of an independent variable:

> "Humiliation" was produced by having the subjects (college students) spend 15 minutes working on an insoluble task and then informing them—contemptuously—that their performance was so poor that they should consider quitting school, because most below average students can do much better than they did.

The operational definition of the dependent variable "susceptibility to propaganda" would include a description of the opinion test that was used and the propaganda film that the subjects watched.

Validity of an Operational Definition

The question of the "correctness" of an operational definition of a variable brings us to the issue of **validity.** Everyone knows the meaning

If we attribute this person's behavior to anger, we are committing the nominal error. To understand the behavior we must ask what caused it.

of the word *valid*: well-grounded, fit, appropriate. Thus, the validity of an operational definition refers to how appropriate it is—how accurately it represents the variable whose value it sets or measures. Obviously, validity is very important; if an operational definition is not valid, an experiment that uses it cannot provide meaningful results.

How can the validity of an operational definition be determined? Unfortunately, there is no simple answer. Various techniques have been used, but none is foolproof. To begin with, an investigator examines the **face validity** of the operations. This is just a fancy way of saying that he or she thinks about them and decides whether they make sense: on the *face* of it, do the operations appear to manipulate or measure the variables in question? My earlier definition of humiliation—having someone fail at a task that the experimenter says is a simple one—makes sense (at least to me), so it has some face validity. When a psychologist tries to decide how to test a particular hypothesis, he or she uses common sense to arrive at operations that have face validity.

Given enough time, the validity of an operational definition will emerge (or so we hope). Investigators will compare the results of their experiments with those of others and will see whether they are compatible. If the results are compatible, the operational definition gains some **construct validity.** *Construct,* as a noun (pronounced *CON-strukt*), is defined as "something assembled from simple elements, especially a concept." In the case of construct validity, the elements are the pieces of evidence, obtained from a number of studies, that show that the operational definition works—that the results of experiments that use it make sense. Validity is *constructed,* piece by piece.

Reliability of an Operational Definition

Having carefully designed an experiment, the psychologist must then decide how best to conduct it. This brings us to the second part of step 2 of the scientific method: execute the experiment. The psychologist must decide what subjects will be used, what instructions will be given, and what equipment and materials will be used. He or she must ensure that the data that are collected will be accurate; otherwise, all effort will be in vain.

If the procedure that is described by an operational definition gives consistent results under consistent conditions, the procedure is said to be **reliable.** Note, however, that it may or may not be *valid.* For example, suppose that I operationally define "susceptibility to propaganda" as the length of a person's thumb; the longer the person's thumb, the more susceptible he or she is to propaganda. Even though this measurement could be made accurately and reliably it would still be nonsensical. (Of course, most examples of reliable but invalid operational definitions are more subtle than this one.) It is usually much easier to achieve reliability than validity; reliability is mostly a result of care and diligence on the part of the experimenter.

Let us look at an example. Suppose you want to measure people's reading speed. You select a passage of prose and see how much of it each person can read in five minutes. This operational definition of reading speed certainly has face validity, so long as you choose a passage that is reasonably easy for a normal adult to understand. But suppose you test people in a building that is located under the flight path of an airport. At times, the noise of planes flying overhead creates a terrible din. At other times,

all is quiet. If people are tested when planes are roaring overhead, the distracting noise might very well disrupt their reading, producing low scores. The on-again, off-again noise would affect the accuracy of the measurement. It would lower its reliability.

An alert, careful experimenter can control most of the extraneous factors that could affect the reliability of his or her measurements. Conditions throughout the experiment should always be as consistent as possible. For example, the same instructions should be given to each person who participates in the experiment, all mechanical devices should be in good repair, and all assistants hired by the experimenter should be well trained in performing their tasks. Noise and other sources of distraction should be kept to a minimum.

Often experimenters attempt to measure variables that cannot be specified as precisely as reading speed. For example, suppose a psychologist wants to count the number of friendly interactions that a child makes with other children in a group. This measurement would require someone to watch the child and count the number of times a friendly interaction occurs. But it is difficult to be absolutely specific about what constitutes a friendly interaction and what does not. What if the child looks at another child and their gazes meet? One observer might say that the look conveyed interest in what the other child was doing, so it should be scored as a friendly interaction. Another observer might deny that anything passed between them and say that a friendly interaction should not be scored.

The solution in this case is, first of all, to try to specify as precisely as possible the criteria for scoring a friendly interaction. Then two or more people should watch the child's behavior and score it independently. That is, each person should not be aware of the other person's ratings. If their ratings agree, we can say that the scoring system has high **interrater reliability.** If they disagree, interrater reliability is low, and there is no point in continuing the experiment. Instead, the rating system should be refined, and the raters should be trained to apply it consistently. Any investigator who performs an experiment that requires some degree of skill and judgment in measuring the dependent variables must be sure that interrater reliability is sufficiently high.

■ What are the four major steps of the scientific method?

■ What difference is there between theories and hypotheses?

■ How do psychologists manipulate variables to study the causes of behavior?

■ What are operational definitions?

Control of Independent Variables

A hypothesis, you will recall, makes a tentative statement about a possible relation between two or more variables. An experiment is the procedure for testing the hypothesis to determine whether these variables *are* related. A scientist performs an experiment by altering the value of the independent variable (such as the degree of humiliation) and then observing whether this change affects the dependent variable (in this case, susceptibility to propaganda). If an effect is seen, we can conclude that there is a cause-and-effect relation between the variables. That is, changes in the independent variable cause changes in the dependent variable.

In designing an experiment, the experimenter must be sure that the procedure alters the value of the independent variable, and *only* the independent variable. In most experiments we are interested in the effects of a small number of independent variables (usually, just one) on a dependent variable. For example, if we want to determine whether noise has an effect on people's reading speed, we must choose our source of noise carefully. If we use the sound from a television set to supply the noise and find that it slows people's reading speed, we cannot conclude that the effect was caused purely by "noise." We might have selected a very interesting program (as unlikely as that may seem), thus distracting the subjects' attention from the material they were reading. If we want to do this experiment properly, we should use noise that is neutral and not a source of interest: noise like the *sssh* sound that is heard when an FM radio is tuned between stations.

In the example I just described, the experimenter intended to test the effects of an independent variable (noise) on a dependent variable (reading speed). By using a television to provide the noise, the experimenter was inadvertently testing the effects of other variables besides noise on reading speed. The experimenter had introduced extra, unwanted independent variables.

Confounding of Independent Variables

One of the meanings of the word *confound* is "to fail to distinguish." This is precisely the meaning that applies here. If an experimenter accidentally manipulates more than one independent variable, it is impossible to distinguish the effects of any one of them on the dependent variable. There are many ways in which **confounding of variables** can occur. The best way to understand the problems that can arise is to examine some of the mistakes that an experimenter can make.

Let us look at an example of an extra, unwanted independent variable intruding into an experiment. Suppose we want to determine whether watching violence on television increases a child's aggressiveness. We would select two television shows, one violent and the other nonviolent. We would show the violent program to one group of children and the nonviolent one to another group and would then observe the behavior of both groups. We might place the children in a room full of toys and count the number of destructive acts they commit (such as knocking down towers of blocks, banging toy trucks into the furniture and walls, or fighting with other children). We would train our observers well and make sure that the inter-rater reliability of the measurement was high.

The design of this experiment is simple and straightforward, but to be able to conclude that watching the violent program affected the children's aggressive behavior we must be sure that the treatment of both groups is identical in every way except for the amount of violence they see. But how can we select, from the programs available on television, two that are identical except for the amount of violence they contain? Obviously we cannot. And the differences could be very important. Suppose that the children who watched the violent program found it to be very interesting but the children who watched the nonviolent one found it to be extremely dull and boring. We might expect a group of angry and hostile children to emerge from watching the nonviolent program, having been forced to undergo such a tedious experience.

If these events occurred, the results of our study might suggest that watching a violent program *reduced* the frequency of aggression in children. Of course, we would really have proved nothing of the kind. The higher level of violence in the group of children who watched the nonviolent program was caused by their having been forced to watch a program that bored them.

What solutions are there to this problem? First, we should add another group of children, who would not watch a television program at all. This group is called a **control group.** A control group is a "no treatment" group; it is used to contrast the effects of manipulating an independent variable with no treatment at all. If we had used such a group, perhaps we would have seen that the children who watched the nonviolent program were more violent and aggressive than the children who did not watch television at all, and we would realize that something was wrong. We would see that watching a nonviolent program was not the neutral experience we had thought it would be. (See Figure 1.2.)

Ideally, we would want to consider producing our own television shows. That way, we could keep them as similar as possible, having them differ principally in the amount of violence they portrayed. This task would obviously be a challenge; the programs would have to be equally lively, interesting, and plausible, but only one would contain violence.

Confounding of Subject Variables

My example so far has dealt with the confounding of independent variables, which are manipulated by the experimenter. But there is another source of confounding: variables that are inherent in the subjects whose behavior is being observed. Here is an example of a study with confounded subject variables: Suppose a professor wants to determine which of two teaching methods works best. She teaches two courses in introductory psychology, one that meets at 8 A.M. and another that meets at 4 P.M. She uses one teaching method for the morning class and another for the afternoon class. At the end of the semester she finds that the final-examination scores were higher for her morning class. Therefore, she concludes that from now on she will use that particular teaching method for all of her classes.

What is the problem? The two groups of subjects for the experiment are not equivalent. People who sign up for a class that meets at 8 A.M. are likely to be somewhat different from those who sign up for a 4 P.M. class. It is possible that the school schedules some kinds of activities (like long laboratory courses or athletic practice) late in the afternoon, which means that some students will not be able to enroll in the 4 P.M. class. In addition, people's learning efficiency might vary at different times of the day. For a variety of reasons, the students in the two classes will probably not be equivalent.

FIGURE 1.2

Possible outcome of an experiment testing the effects of watching a violent television program. This design includes a control group.

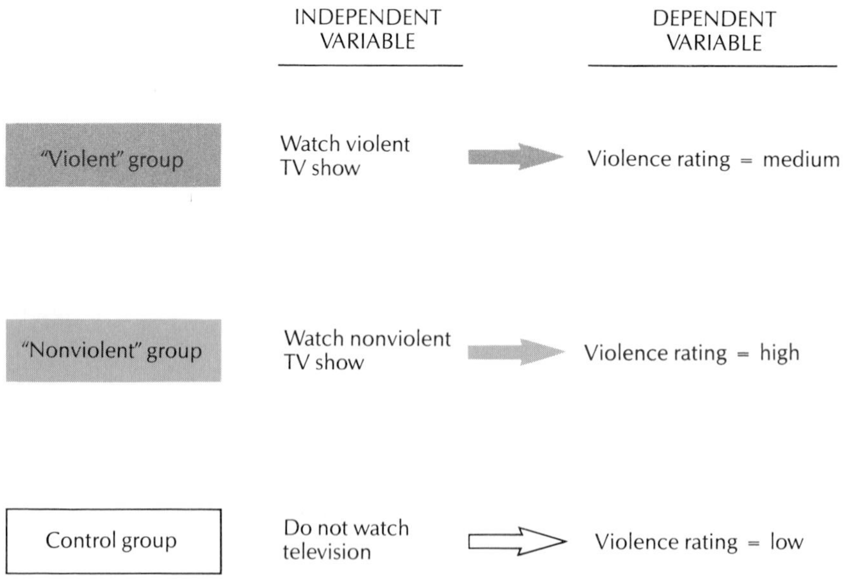

	INDEPENDENT VARIABLE	DEPENDENT VARIABLE
"Violent" group	Watch violent TV show	Violence rating = medium
"Nonviolent" group	Watch nonviolent TV show	Violence rating = high
Control group	Do not watch television	Violence rating = low

Therefore, we cannot conclude that the differences in their final-examination scores were solely a result of the different teaching methods.

Subjects must be carefully assigned to the various groups used in an experiment. The usual way to assign them is by **random selection.** One way to accomplish this is to assemble the names of the available subjects and then toss a coin for each one, to determine their assignment to one of two groups. (More typically, the assignment is made by computer or by consulting a list of random numbers.) We can expect people to have different abilities, personality traits, and other characteristics that might affect the outcome of the experiment. But if they are randomly assigned to the experimental conditions, the composition of the groups should be approximately the same.

The Problem of Subjects' Expectations

When subjects take part in an experiment, they are not simply passive participants whose behavior is controlled solely by the independent variables selected by the experimenter. The subjects know they are being observed by a psychologist, and this knowledge is certain to affect their behavior in some way. In fact, some subjects may try to outwit the psychologist by acting in a way that is opposite to what they think is expected. However, most subjects will try to cooperate because they do not want to ruin the experiment for the investigator. In fact, they may even try to figure out what question is being asked so that they can act accordingly. Because the study is being run by a psychologist, some subjects are unlikely to take what he or she says at face value and will look for devious motives behind an apparently simple task. Actually, most experiments are not devious at all; they are what they appear to be. An experimenter must always remember that his or her subjects do not merely react to the independent variable in a simple-minded way.

Single-Blind Studies. Suppose we want to study the effects of a stimulant drug, such as amphetamine, on a person's ability to perform a task that requires fine manual dexterity. We would administer the drug to one group of subjects and leave another group untreated. (Of course, the experiment would have to be supervised by a physician.) We would determine

Psychologists study a sample of the population and generalize results to a larger population.

how many times subjects in each group could thread a needle in a ten-minute period (our operational definition of manual dexterity). We would then see whether taking the drug had any effect on the number of needle-threadings.

But there is a problem. For us to conclude that a cause-and-effect relation exists, the treatment of the two groups must be identical except for the single variable that is being manipulated. In this case, the *mere administration* of a drug might have effects on behavior, independent of any pharmacological effects. If subjects know that they have just taken an amphetamine pill, their behavior is very likely to be affected by this knowledge, as well as by the drug circulating in their bloodstream.

The answer, of course, is to give pills to the members of both groups. People in one group would receive amphetamine, while those in the other group would receive an inert pill—a **placebo.** (The word comes from the Latin *placēre,* "to please." A physician sometimes gives a placebo to hypochondriacal patients, to placate them.) Subjects would not be told which pill they received. Using this improved experimental procedure, we can infer that any observed differences in the needle-threading ability of the two groups were produced by the pharmacological effects of amphetamine. The procedure is called a **single-blind** study; the subjects do not know what kind of pill they are taking.

Double-Blind Studies. Let us look at another example, in which it is important to keep the experimenter, as well as the subjects, in the dark. Suppose we believe that if patients with mental disorders take a particular drug, they will be easier to talk with. We give the drug to some patients and administer a placebo to others. We talk with all of the patients afterward and rate the quality of the conversation. But "quality of conversation" is a difficult dependent variable to measure, and the rating is therefore likely to be at least somewhat **subjective**—a matter of personal judgment. (In contrast, **objective** measurements are those that everyone agrees on and that do not rely on personal judgment.) The fact that we, the experimenters, know which patients received the drug means that we may tend to give higher ratings to the quality of conversation with those patients. Of course, we would not intentionally cheat, but even honest people tend to perceive results in a way that favors their own preconceptions.

The solution to this problem is simple. Just as the patients should not know whether they are receiving a drug or a placebo, neither should the experimenter in this case. Someone else should administer the pill, or give the experimenter a set of identical-looking pills in coded containers, so that both experimenter and patient would be unaware of the nature of the contents. Now the ratings cannot be affected by experimenter bias. We call this method the **double-blind** procedure.

Observational Studies

There are some variables, especially subject variables, that a psychologist cannot manipulate. For example, a person's sex, income, social class, and personality are determined by factors not under the psychologist's control. Nevertheless, these variables are often of interest. Because they cannot be altered by the psychologist, they cannot be investigated in an experiment, which is the only means by which a cause-and-effect relation can be proved. Therefore, a different approach is used; an **observational study** is performed.

The basic principle of an observational study is very simple: in each member of a group of people, measure two or more variables as they are found to exist, and determine whether the variables are related. Studies like this are often done to investigate the effects of personality variables. For example, we might ask whether shyness (a personality variable) is related to daydreaming. We would decide how to assess a person's shyness and the amount of daydreaming that he or she engages in each day and would then take the measure of these two variables for a group of people. If shy people tended to daydream more (or less) than people who were not shy, we would conclude that the variables were related.

Suppose we found that shy people spent more time daydreaming. Such a finding would not permit us to make any conclusions about cause and effect. Shyness might have caused the daydreaming, or excessive daydreaming might have caused the shyness, or perhaps some other variable that we did not measure caused both shyness and an increase in daydreaming.

A good illustration of this principle is provided by an observational study that attempted to determine whether membership in the Boy Scouts would affect a person's subsequent participation in community affairs (Chapin, 1947). The investigator compared a group of men who had once been Boy Scouts with a group who had not. He found that the men who had been Boy Scouts tended to join more community-affairs groups later in life.

The investigator wanted to conclude that the experience of being a Boy Scout increased a person's tendency to join community organizations. However, this conclusion is not warranted. All we can say is that people who join the Boy Scouts tend to join community organizations later in life. It could be that people who, for one reason or another, are "joiners" tend to join the Boy Scouts when they are young and community organizations when they are older. To determine cause and effect, we would have to make some boys join the Boy Scouts and prevent others from doing so and then see how many organizations they would voluntarily join later in life. Because we cannot interfere in people's lives in such a way, this is a question we cannot answer.

When attempting to study the effects of a variable that he or she cannot alter (such as sex, age, socioeconomic status, or personality characteristics), a psychologist uses a procedure called **matching.** Rather than select subjects randomly, the experimenter will *match* the subjects in each of the groups on all of the relevant variables except the one being studied. For instance, if a psychologist wants to study the effects of shyness on daydreaming, he or she might gather two groups of subjects, shy and "nonshy." The subjects would be selected in such a way that the effects of other variables would be minimized. The average age, intelligence, income, and personality characteristics (other than shyness) of the two groups would be the same.

If, after following this matching procedure, the investigator found that shyness was still related to daydreaming, we could be somewhat more confident that the relation was one of cause and effect. (However, the matching procedure still does not help us decide which is the cause and which is the effect. Shyness could cause daydreaming, or daydreaming could cause shyness.) The weakness in the matching procedure is that a psychologist might not know all the variables that should be held constant. If the two groups are not matched on an important variable, then the results will be misleading.

Generality

When we carry out an experiment, we are usually not especially interested in the particular subjects whose behavior we observe. Instead, we probably assume that our subjects are representative of the larger population. In fact, a group of subjects is usually referred to as a **sample** of the larger population. (The words *sample* and *example* have the same root.) If we study the behavior of a group of five-year-old children, we probably want to make conclusions about five-year-olds in general. That is, we want to be able to **generalize** our specific results to the population as a whole—to conclude that the results of our study tell us something about human nature in general, and not simply about our particular subjects.

Many psychology experiments recruit their subjects from introductory courses in psychology. Thus, the results of experiments that use these students as subjects can be generalized only to other groups of students who are recruited in the same way. In the strictest sense, the results cannot be generalized to students in

other courses, or to adults in general, or even to all students enrolled in Introductory Psychology—after all, students who volunteer to serve as subjects might be very different from those who do not. Even if we used truly random samples of all age groups of adults in our area, we could not generalize the results to people who live in other geographical regions. If our ability to generalize is really so limited, it would hardly seem worthwhile to do the experiments at all.

But we are not so strict, of course. Most psychologists assume that a relation among variables that is observed in one group of humans will also be seen in other groups, so long as the relation is a relatively strong one and the sample of subjects is not an especially unusual one. (For example, we might expect that data obtained from prisoners will have less generality than data obtained from college students.) Generalization from a particular sample of subjects to a larger population is one of those cases in which scientific practice usually does not rigorously follow scientific law.

The problem of generalizing occurs in observational studies just as much as it does in experiments. In one famous case, the limitations of generalizing were demonstrated with a vengeance. During the United States presidential campaign of 1948, poll takers predicted, from a sampling of the populace, that Dewey would easily defeat Truman. Of course, they

One difficulty in research is choosing a sample representative of the population. The findings of a study of these Amish girls, for example, would not necessarily apply to the general population.

were wrong—embarrassingly so. The subjects in the sample group had been drawn from telephone directories. In 1948, a smaller percentage of Americans had telephones than today, and those who did have telephones tended to be wealthier than those who did not. A much higher proportion of this second group (people without telephones) voted for Truman; hence, the samples drawn by poll takers were not representative of the population to which they wanted to generalize—United States voters.

Case Studies

Not all investigations make use of groups of subjects. **Case studies** investigate the behavior of individuals, and for some phenomena this method is very effective.

Psychologists often take advantage of "experimental manipulations" that occur because of events outside their control. For example, some colleagues and I studied a woman who had sustained a serious skull fracture in an automobile accident (Margolin, Marcel, and Carlson, 1985).

Animal rights activists displaying their concern about the use of primates in research.

The damage to her brain made it impossible for her to read, although her vision was almost normal. We gave her lists of words like these: "rose, violet, carrot, petunia, daffodil" and asked her to choose the one that did not belong with the others. She would point to the word "carrot" even though she could not read it and had no idea why she chose the one she did. Her performance proves that people can have some idea of the meaning of words that does not depend upon their "saying the words to themselves."

Obviously, we cannot fracture the skulls of a group of people to study phenomena like this experimentally. Instead, we carefully study patients whose brains have been damaged by accident or disease and then, if possible, form hypotheses that can be tested with groups of normal people.

Case studies are also performed by clinical psychologists, who observe the behavior of their clients and listen to what they have to say about their lives. Often, the psychologist tries to correlate events that occurred in the client's past (perhaps in childhood) with the client's present behavior and personality. Studies like these are called **retrospective** ("backward looking"), and their validity depends heavily on the client's memory for past events. Because recollections are often faulty, one must be cautious about accepting the conclusions of retrospective studies whose results cannot be independently verified.

ETHICS

Unlike some other scientists, psychologists must study living subjects. This means that a psychologist must obey ethical rules as well as scientific ones. Psychologists who use animal subjects must be sure that the animals are adequately fed and comfortably housed, and they must not be subjected to unnecessary pain. Rules for the case and treatment of animals have been established by such societies as the American Psychological Association.

Much more care is needed in the treatment of human subjects, not only because they are members of our own species, about whom we care the most, but also because it is possible to hurt people in very subtle ways. For example, let us consider (for the last time) the hypothetical experiment on humiliation and susceptibility to propaganda. For the experiment to be scientifically valid, we must actually humiliate someone. But does a psychologist have the right to do so, even in the interest of science? Suppose that some of the subjects feel *very* humiliated and suffer a real loss of self-esteem?

In the United States, federal regulations state that all departments of psychology that engage in federally funded research must have a committee that reviews the ethics of all experiments that use humans as subjects. The committee must review the experiments before they can be performed, to ensure that subjects will be treated properly. In addition, the American Psychological Association has its own ethical guidelines for human research. Review committees are in everyone's interest; both the experimenters and their subjects can be confident that the experimental procedures are unlikely to produce harm.

- What are the advantages and disadvantages of experimental versus observational studies?
- What problems do researchers encounter when they attempt to control independent variables? How do they solve these problems?
- What problems do researchers encounter when they attempt to control subject variables, and how do they solve those problems?
- What differences are there between single-blind and double-blind experiments?
- Why are ethical rules necessary for psychologists?

DESCRIPTIONS OF OBSERVATIONS

In most of the examples I have cited so far, the behavior of a number of subjects was observed. I implied that the data obtained from them would be combined in some way to represent a particular value of a variable. This means, of course, that a single number will be used to represent the results of several observations.

There is nothing novel about such a procedure. For example, I am sure that all of you know how to calculate the average of a set of numbers; an average is a common measure of central tendency. You might be less familiar with measures of variability, which tell us how groups of numbers differ from one another, or with measures of relations, which tell us how closely related two sets of numbers are.

These measures, which describe the results of experiments, are called **descriptive statistics.** They are used for two reasons. First, the investigator calculates them and uses their values to determine if the hypothesis is true (step 3 of the scientific method). Second, the investigator uses these values to communicate the results of the experiment accurately and succinctly (step 4 of the scientific method).

Measures of Central Tendency

Mean

When we say that the average weight of an adult male in North America is 173 pounds or that the average density of population in the United States is 63.9 people per square mile, we are using a **measure of central tendency,** a statistic that represents a number of observations. The most common measure of central tendency is the average, which psychologists and statisticians usually refer to as the **mean.** As everyone learns in elementary school, the mean is calculated by adding the individual values of the sample and dividing by the number of observations. The mean is the most frequently used measure of central tendency in reports of psychological experiments.

Median

Although the mean is usually selected to measure central tendency, it is not the most precise measure of that characteristic. When we want to choose a measure for descriptive purposes that is the most representative of a sample of numbers, we should use the **median,** not the mean. For this reason we usually read "median family income" rather than "mean family income" in newspaper or magazine articles.

Let us see why the median is a more representative measure than the mean. The median is defined as "the midpoint of a set of values arranged in numerical order." The median of the set of values listed in Table 1.1 is 5, because that number is at the midpoint of the list. The mean, however, is 8, because $2 + 3 + 5 + 14 + 16 = 40$, and $40/5 = 8$. (See Table 1.1.)

TABLE 1.1

Mean and median of a sample of five scores
2
3
5 ←*median*
14
<u>16</u>
Total: 40
Mean: 40/5 = 8

How can we assess the accuracy with which a measure of central tendency represents a sample of several numbers? We first calculate the difference between each score and the measure of central tendency and add these differences up. We then divide this total figure by the number of scores, thus obtaining the **average deviation** of each score from the measure of central tendency. The measure of central tendency that deviates the least, on the average, from the individual scores in the sample can then be regarded as the most representative. (See Table 1.2.)

We find that the average deviation of each score from the mean is 5.6; the average deviation of each score from the median is 5.0. Therefore, the median can be said to represent

the sample better than the mean does. To take an example that makes more intuitive sense than a set of five numbers, consider a small town that contains 100 families. Ninety-nine of the families, all of whom work in the local textile mill, make between $15,000 and $20,000 per year. However, the income of one family is $2 million per year. This family consists of a novelist and her husband. The mean income for the 99 families who work in the mill is $17,500 per year. The mean income for the town as a whole, considering the novelist as well as the mill workers, is $37,325 per year. In contrast, the median income for the town is $17,500 per year. Clearly, this figure represents typical family income better than $37,325.

Why, then, would we ever bother to use the mean rather than the median? There are three reasons: (1) The mean is easier to calculate when the sample is large; it is easier to add up a large set of numbers than it is to arrange them in numerical order. (2) Most samples are not like my example of ninety-nine low values and one very high one; in most cases the mean and median are not very different. (3) As we will see later in this chapter, the mean is used to calculate other important statistics and has special mathematical properties that make it more useful than the median.

Measures of Variability

Many experiments produce two sets of numbers, consisting of the scores of subjects in the experimental and control groups. If the mean scores of these two groups differ, then the experimenter can conclude that the independent

TABLE 1.2

Calculation of average deviation		
Scores	Difference Between Score and Median (5)	Difference Between Score and Mean (8)
2	3	6
3	2	5
5	0	3
14	9	6
16	<u>11</u>	<u>8</u>
Total:	25	Total: 28
Average deviation: 25/5 = 5.0		Average deviation: 28/5 = 5.6

variable had an effect. As we will see in a later section of this chapter, the psychologist must decide whether the difference between the two groups is larger than what would probably occur by chance. To make this decision, he or she calculates a measure of variability, against which difference in means can be compared.

Range

Two samples can have the same measure of central tendency and still be very different. For example, the mean and median of both sets of numbers listed in Table 1.3 are the same, but the samples are clearly different. The scores in sample B are more disparate. (See Table 1.3.)

One way of stating the difference between the two samples is to say that the numbers in sample A range from 8 to 12 while the numbers in sample B range from 0 to 20. To put it another way, the range of sample A is 4 (12 − 8 = 4) and the range of sample B is 20 (20 − 0 = 20).

The **range** is especially easy to calculate for small samples: simply subtract the lowest score from the highest score. However, this measure of variability is not used very often to describe the results of psychological experiments because another measure of variability—the variance—typically has more useful mathematical properties.

Variance and Standard Deviation

In an earlier example I calculated the average deviation from the mean and median for a set of five numbers. The average deviation is, of course, a measure of the degree to which scores differ from one another. However, this measure is almost never used, except for demonstrations like the one I presented. What is used is the **variance,** which is defined as "the average of the squared deviation of each score from the mean." To calculate this measure, you square each deviation score (multiply it by itself). Then you calculate the mean of these values. (See Table 1.4.)

The number most often used to report the amount of variability is the **standard deviation,** which is simply the square root of the variance. The square root of 34 is 5.83, so the standard deviation of our sample is 5.83. (See Table 1.4.) If you look back at the earlier example (Table 1.2), in which I used the same set of numbers to calculate how closely the mean and median represented the scores, you will find that the

TABLE 1.3

Two samples with the same mean and median but different ranges

Sample A	Sample B
8	0
9	5
10 ← median	10 ← median
11	15
12	20
Total: 50	Total: 50
Mean: 50/5 = 10	Mean: 50/5 = 10
Range: 12 − 8 = 4	Range: 20 − 0 = 20

TABLE 1.4

Calculation of variance and standard deviation

Scores	Difference Between Score and Mean (Deviation Score)	Squared Difference Between Score and Mean (Squared Deviation Score)
2	6	36
3	5	25
5	3	9
14	6	36
16	8	64
Total: 40		Total: 170
Mean: 40/5 = 8		Variance: 170/5 = 34
		Standard deviation: $\sqrt{34}$ = 5.83

average deviation of the scores from the mean was 5.6. That is close to the standard deviation of 5.83. For most samples of numbers, these two measures will be almost the same. It is only because of special mathematical properties of the standard deviation that we use it instead of the average deviation. These properties concern the assessment of statistical significance, which I will discuss in a later section of this chapter.

Measurement of Relations

In many studies—especially observational studies—the investigator wants to measure the degree to which two variables are related. For example, suppose that a psychologist has developed a new aptitude test and wants to sell the test to college admissions committees to use for screening applicants. Before they would consider buying the test, the psychologist would have to show that a person's score on the test was related to his or her subsequent success in college. The psychologist would give the test to a number of freshmen entering college and would later obtain their average grades. The psychologist would then measure the relation between test scores and grades. But how does one measure a relation?

Let us suppose that we gave the test to ten students entering college and later obtained their average grades. We would have two scores for each person, as shown in Table 1.5.

TABLE 1.5

Test scores and average grades of ten students

Student	Test Score	Average Grade*
A.C.	15	2.8
B.F.	12	3.2
G.G.	19	3.5
L.H.	8	2.2
R.J.	14	3.0
S.K.	11	2.6
P.R.	13	2.8
A.S.	7	1.5
J.S.	9	1.9
P.V.	18	3.8

*0 = F, 4 = A

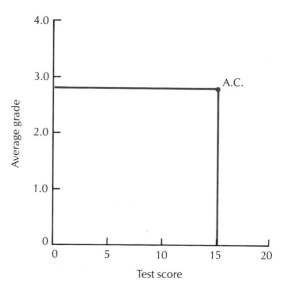

FIGURE 1.3

An example of the graphing of one data point: the test score and average grade of student A.C.

We can examine the relation between these variables by plotting the scores on a graph. For example, student A.C. received a test score of 15 and earned an average grade of 2.8 (B minus). We could represent this student's score as a point on the graph shown in Figure 1.3. The horizontal axis represents the test score, and the vertical axis represents the average grade. A point is placed on the graph that corresponds to the score of student A.C. on both of these measures. (See Figure 1.3.)

We can construct a graph that contains the scores of all ten students and then look at the distribution of scores to determine whether they are related. (See Figure 1.4.) This graph, called a **scatter plot,** shows that the points are not randomly distributed; instead, they tend to be located along a diagonal line that runs from the lower left to the upper right.

The data shown in Figure 1.4 indicate that a rather strong relation exists between a student's test score and average grade. High scores are associated with good grades, low scores with poor grades. However, the psychologist who developed the test would want a more convenient way to communicate the strength of the relation than showing scatter plots, so he or she would probably calculate the **correlation coefficient.** A calculation of this statistic for the two sets of scores in my example gives a correlation of +.9 between the two variables. (I will not bother you with the details of how this measure

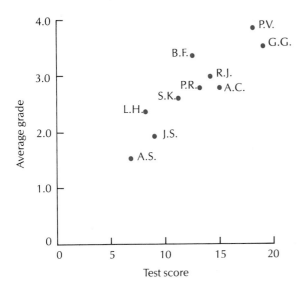

FIGURE 1.4

A scatter plot of the test scores and average grades of ten students.

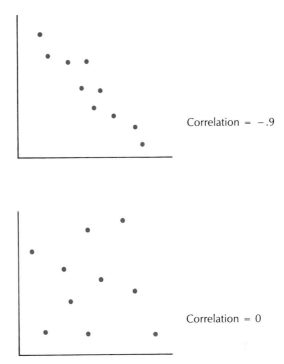

Correlation = −.9

Correlation = 0

Correlation = +.4

FIGURE 1.5

A variety of scatter plots, indicating several different correlations.

is calculated.) A correlation this high is indeed a strong one, and a psychologist would be delighted to have developed a test whose scores correlated with college grades this well. The value of a correlation coefficient can vary from 0 (no relation) to 1.0 (perfect relation). A perfect relation means that if we know the value of a person's score on one measure then we can determine precisely what his or her score will be on the other. Thus, a correlation of +.9 is very close to perfect; the hypothetical aptitude test of our example is indeed an excellent indicator of how well a student will do in college.

I should note that correlations can be negative as well as positive. A **negative correlation** indicates that high values on one measure are associated with low values on the other, and vice versa. An example of a negative correlation would be the relation between the average score of a professional golfer and the amount of money he or she wins in a year. Because low golf scores indicate more skill, players with the lowest scores will tend to win the most money, and those with the highest scores will win the least.

For purposes of prediction, a negative correlation is just as good as a positive one. A correlation of −.9 is an almost-perfect relation, but in this case high scores on one measure predict low scores on the other. Examples of scatter plots for high and low correlations, both positive and negative, are shown in Figure 1.5.

ASSESSING THE SIGNIFICANCE OF RELATIONS

Scientific investigations, whether they consist of experiments or observational studies, are concerned with relations. Sometimes the investigator calculates the relation directly, by computing a correlation coefficient. Other times (for example, in an experiment) the investigator selects two or more values of the independent variable and measures the dependent variable.

The results, usually expressed as means and standard deviations, indicate whether the independent variable had an effect on the dependent variable—that is, whether the mean values for the dependent variable differed from one another. The next step is to decide whether the difference observed between the group means reflects a real effect of the independent variable, or whether the results are due to chance.

Statistical Significance

When we perform an experiment we select a sample of subjects from a larger population—the one to which we want to generalize. In so doing, we hope that the results will be similar to those we might have obtained had we used all members of the population in the experiment. We assign the subjects to groups in an unbiased manner (usually by random selection), alter only the relevant independent variables, and measure the dependent variable with a valid method. In other words, we put into practice the procedures I have outlined in this chapter. After we have completed the experiment we must decide whether our results indicate a relation exists between independent and dependent variables; that is, we must decide whether the results are **statistically significant.**

The concept of statistical significance is not an easy one to grasp, so I want to make sure you understand the purpose of this discussion. Suppose we want to determine whether the presence of other people affects the speed at which a person can solve simple arithmetic problems. We would test members of the experimental group with other people watching them; members of the control group would work alone. We would then calculate the mean number of problems that were solved by each group. If the means were different, we would conclude that the presence of an audience does affect the rate at which a person can solve arithmetic problems.

But how different is different? Suppose we tested two groups of people, *both* of whom performed alone. Would the mean scores by precisely the same? Of course not. By *chance*, they would be at least slightly different. Now back to our experiment. Suppose we found that the mean score for the group that worked in the presence of an audience was lower than the mean score for the group that performed alone. How much lower would it have to be before we could conclude that the presence of an audience disrupted our subjects' performance? In other words, how do we go about determining whether the difference between the mean scores is greater than could be accounted for by chance? These are the kinds of questions that every psychologist must ask after an experiment is over.

Assessment of Differences Between Samples

The obvious way to determine whether two group means differ significantly is to look at the size of the difference. If it is large, then we can be fairly confident that the independent variable had a significant effect. If it is small, then the difference is probably due to chance. What we need are guidelines to help us determine when a difference is large enough to be statistically significant.

The following example will explain how these guidelines are constructed. A few years ago, I distributed cards to students in one of my classes to collect some data that I could analyze to explain some statistical concepts. I will use the data I collected for that purpose here, too.

There were seventy-six students in the class. Their average height was 67.2 inches. I performed an observational study to test the following hypothesis: People whose first names end in a vowel will, on the average, be shorter than people whose first names end in a consonant. (I will tell you later why I expected this hypothesis to be confirmed.)

I divided the subjects into two groups: those whose first names ended in a vowel and those whose first names ended in a consonant. Table 1.6 contains a listing of these two groups. Indeed, the means for the two groups differed by 4.1 inches.

A difference of 4.1 inches seems large, but how can we be sure that it is not due to chance? What we really need to know is how large a difference would there be if the means had been calculated from two groups that were randomly selected, and not chosen on the basis of a variable that might be related to height. For comparison, I divided the class into two random groups. To do this I shuffled the cards

TABLE 1.6

Height (in inches) of selected sample of students

Name Ends in Consonant		Name Ends in Vowel
65	61	67
67	68	68
71	70	62
72	65	63
73	73	62
65	60	64
74	70	60
74	72	63
67	63	61
69	67	69
68	73	63
75	66	65
72	71	69
71	72	71
65	64	69
66	69	65
70	73	70
72	75	63
72	72	63
71	66	64
62	71	65
62	68	63
80	70	66
	75	62
Total: 3257		72
Mean: 3257/47 = 69.3		65
		66
		65
		65
		Total: 1890
		Mean: 1890/29 = 65.2

Difference between means: 69.3 − 65.2 = 4.1

TABLE 1.7

Height (in inches) of a random division of the class into two groups

Group A		Group B	
65	71	63	62
72	63	62	63
72	74	70	65
69	72	70	75
61	71	65	71
69	65	64	80
66	71	75	71
70	67	63	68
66	72	70	71
65	66	75	73
66	72	67	62
65	73	65	72
64	63	68	65
72	69	63	72
63	62	69	66
65	60	67	73
62	70	68	65
67	68	60	73
	69		61
	64		74
Total: 2561		Total: 2586	
Mean: 67.4		Mean: 68.1	

Difference: −0.7

TABLE 1.8

Mean heights (in inches) of five random divisions of the class into two groups

Group A	Group B	Difference
67.6	67.9	−0.3
68.1	67.4	0.7
67.8	67.6	0.2
67.9	67.5	0.4
68.0	67.4	0.6

with the students' names on them and then dealt them out into two piles. Then I calculated the mean height of the people whose names were in each pile. The difference between the means was 0.7 inch. (See Table 1.7.)

I divided the class into two random groups five more times, calculating the means and the difference between the means each time. The differences ranged from 0.2 inch to 0.7 inch.

(See Table 1.8.) It began to look as though a mean difference of 4.1 inches was bigger than what one would expect by chance.

Next I divided the class into two random groups 1000 times. (I used my computer to do the chore.) *Not once in 1000 times was the dif-*ference between the means of the two randomly chosen groups greater than 3.0 inches. Therefore, I can conclude that if the class is divided randomly into two groups, the chance that the means of their heights will differ by 4.1 inches is much less than one time in a thousand, or 0.1 percent. Thus, I can safely say that when I divided the students into two groups according to the last letter of their first names, I was dividing them on a basis that was somehow related to their height. The division was *not* equivalent to random selection; a person's height *is* related to the last letter of his or her first name.

Figure 1.6 presents a **frequency distribution** of the differences between the means of the two groups for 1000 random divisions of the class. The height of a point on the graph represents the number of times (the frequency) that the difference between the means fell into that particular range. For example, the difference between the means fell between −0.2 inch and +0.2 inch 170 times.

Suppose the difference between the means in our observational study had been smaller than 4.1 inches. Suppose it had been only 2.3 inches. Would we conclude that the difference represented a real relation, or would we decide that the difference was due to chance? Figure 1.6 would help us decide.

We can see that only 15 out of 1000 times (1.5 percent) will the difference between the means of the two groups be as large as or larger than 2.3 inches: $11 + 4 = 15$. (See Figure 1.6.) Therefore, if we obtained a difference of 2.3 inches between the means of the groups and concluded that people whose first names end in vowels tend to be shorter than people whose first names end in consonants, *the likelihood of our being wrong is 1.5 percent.* The calculations show that we will obtain a difference of at least 2.3 inches between the means purely by chance only 1.5 percent of the time. Because 1.5 percent is a small likelihood, we would probably conclude that the relation was statistically significant.

The method I used to determine the significance of my original findings from the group of seventy-six students (a difference of 4.1 inches) employs the same principles that a psychologist uses to determine whether the results observed in a given experiment represent a real difference or are just due to chance. In my example we considered two possibilities: (1) the difference in the means was due to chance and (2) the difference in the means occurred because the last letter of a person's first name is related to his or her height. We found that a difference of 4.1 inches would be expected less

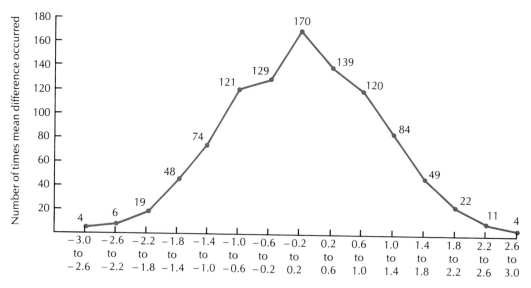

FIGURE 1.6

A frequency distribution that illustrates the number of occurrences of various ranges of mean differences in height. The group of 76 people was divided randomly into two samples 1,000 times.

"Tonight, we're going to let the statistics speak for themselves."

Drawing by Koren; © 1974 The New Yorker Magazine, Inc.

than one time in a thousand. Therefore, we rejected alternative 1 and concluded that alternative 2, my original hypothesis, was correct.

Ordinarily, psychologists who conduct experiments or observational studies like this one would not use their computers to divide their subject's scores randomly 1000 times. Instead, they would calculate the mean and standard deviation for each group and consult a table that statisticians have already prepared for them. The table (which is based upon the special mathematical properties of the mean and standard deviation that I have alluded to) will tell them how likely it is that their results could have been obtained by chance. If the likelihood is low enough, they will conclude that the results are statistically significant. Most psychologists consider a 5 percent probability to be statistically significant but are more comfortable with 1 percent or less.

Statistical tests help us decide whether results are representative of the larger population, but not whether they are *important*. Questions of importance must be determined by other means. For example, suppose a school system decided to perform an experiment to try a new teaching method. They found that the test scores of students who were taught by the new method were significantly higher than those of students who were taught by the old method. However, the difference was very small: the students who learned from the new method did only slightly better. (A small difference can be statistically significant if the variability within the groups is low enough, or if the groups of subjects are very large.) Because it would be very expensive to change to the new method, the school system would probably decide to continue with the present one.

I should now tell you why I originally hypothesized that the last letter of a person's first name is related to his or her height. Females are more likely than males to have first names that end in a vowel (Paula, Angela, Anna, etc.). Because females tend to be shorter than males I expected that a group of students whose first names end in vowels would be shorter, on the average, than those whose first names end in consonants. The data proved me correct.

- What are the uses of the two most common measures of central tendency?
- How do researchers use the three most common measures of variability?
- How can the strength of relations be indicated by use of scatter plots or correlation coefficients?
- Why do psychologists assess the statistical significance of their results?

CHAPTER SUMMARY

1. René Descartes attempted a systematic study of human consciousness, using the evidence of the senses and human reasoning. Descartes's rationalism (pursuit of the truth through reason) was supplanted by empiricism (pursuit of truth through observation and experience).

2. Psychology as a unique science began in the late nineteenth-century Germany. Wilhelm Wundt established psychology as a discipline independent of philosophy. Ebbinghaus contributed important methods for objectively measuring learning and forgetting. Wundt's approach to psychology, called structuralism, was replaced by functionalism, which grew out of Darwin's theory of evolution with its stress on the adaptive value of biological phenomena. Functionalism gave rise to the objectivity of behaviorism, which still dominates psychological research today. Cognitive psychology goes beyond the restrictions of behaviorism (limited to observable behaviors) to study the consciousness, feelings, dreams, and other private events of people.

3. Psychologists are interested in explaining the causes of behavior. Some psychologists are pure research scientists; others are clinical practitioners who deal with mental disorders, and still others work in the business world or in educational systems.

4. The scientific method of inquiry allows psychologists to determine the causes of natural phenomena. Scientists form hypotheses and experiment by manipulating independent variables and measuring dependent variables. Operational definitions clarify the meaning of the hypothesis to other psychologists. Procedures must be reliable, producing consistent results from consistent conditions. High reliability requires independent observers (or scorers) to have a high interrater reliability (agreement). Low interrater reliability requires a redefinition of the criteria for scoring or rating.

5. Problems in an experiment may involve confounded variables. An extra independent variable may be introduced and have an effect on the dependent variable. Subject groups in experiments should be chosen either by random selection or by matching to exclude all but one variable to be tested. Subjects' expectations as to the purpose of the experiment can affect their behavior. To overcome this, a single-blind (subject does not know) procedure should be followed. Experimenters hope that results from any study can be generalized to a larger population.

6. For accurate and concise communication of experimental results, psychologists employ three kinds of descriptive statistics: measures of central tendency, variability, and relations. The most common examples of these measures are the mean or median, the standard deviation, and the correlation coefficient. To determine whether the observed difference between two groups of subjects is greater or less than expected, we must decide whether the results are statistically significant. Most psychologists consider 5 percent probability statistically significant but prefer 1 percent or less.

KEY TERMS

average deviation The difference from the measure of central tendency of both the mean and median.

behaviorism A movement in psychology that asserts that the only proper subject matter for scientific study in psychology is observable behavior.

case study The observation of the behavior of particular individuals, as opposed to studies of groups; primarily encountered in studies of people with mental or neurological disorders.

causal event An event that causes another event to occur.

clinical psychology The branch of psychology devoted to the investigation and treatment of abnormal behavior and mental disorders.

cognitive psychology A branch of psychology that deals with perception, learning and memory, concept formation, verbal behavior, and problem solving, especially of humans. Unlike behaviorism, cognitive psychology deals with unobservable mental processes that presumably are composed of particular brain functions.

comparative psychology The branch of psychology that studies the behaviors of a variety of organisms, in an attempt to understand the adaptive and functional significance of the behaviors and their relation to evolution.

confounding of variables Inadvertent alteration of more than one independent variable during an experiment. The results of an experiment with confounded independent variables permit no valid conclusions about cause and effect.

construct validity Proof gathered from a number of studies that an operational definition works.

control group A comparison group used in an experiment, the members of which are exposed to the naturally occurring or zero value of the independent variable.

correlation coefficient A measurement of the degree to which two variables are related. A correlation of zero indicates no relation; perfect relations is ±1.0. A negative correlation indicates that large values of one variable are associated with small values of the other one.

counseling psychology The branch of psychology devoted to helping people with everyday problems of life, and to providing vocational and academic guidance.

dependent variable The event that is observed in an experiment. Manipulation of independent variables demonstrates whether or not they affect the value of dependent variables.

descriptive statistics Mathematical procedures for organizing collections of data, such as the mean, median, range, variance, and correlation coefficient.

developmental psychology The branch of psychology that studies the changes in behavioral, perceptual, and cognitive capacities of organisms as a function of age and experience.

doctrine of specific nerve energies Johannes Müller's observation that different nerve fibers convey specific information from one part of the body to the brain, or from the brain to one part of the body.

double-blind method An experimental procedure in which the subjects and experimenter do not know the value of the independent variable for a particular subject.

educational psychology A branch of psychology devoted to understanding the variables that determine how people learn in an academic setting.

empiricism The philosophical view that all knowledge is obtained through the senses.

engineering psychology A branch of psychology that assists in the design of products to facilitate quick, accurate, and comfortable use.

experimental neuropsychology A branch of psychology allies with both cognitive psychology and physiological psychology with emphasis on determining which brain mechanisms are responsible for cognitive processes.

experimental psychology A branch of psychology dealing with the general principles of learning, perception, motivation, and memory.

face validity The appearance that a method of measuring or manipulating a variable is valid; a measure of "reasonableness," rather than one that can be objectively determined.

frequency distribution The distribution of the number of times that the differences between the means of various groups fall within a range.

functionalism The strategy of understanding a species' structural or behavioral features by attempting to establish their usefulness with respect to survival or reproductive success.

generalize To draw a general conclusion that applies to all human nature from a specific study.

hypothesis A statement, usually designed to be tested by an experiment, that expresses a tentative causal relationship between variables.

independent variable The variable that is manipulated in an experiment as a means of determining causal relations; manipulation of an independent variable demonstrates whether or not it affects the value of the dependent variable.

industrial and organizational psychology A branch of psychology involved in industry that advises management about the application of psychological principles to running a business.

information processing An approach used by cognitive psychologists to describe how information is processed through the senses by neurons in the brain into memory and to control behavior; based on the variable for experimental purposes.

interrater reliability The degree to which two

or more independent observers agree in their ratings of another organism's behavior, expressed in terms of a correlation coefficient.

introspection Literally, "looking within," in an attempt to describe one's own memories, perceptions, cognitive processes, or motivations.

just-noticeable difference (jnd) The smallest change in a stimulus that is reliably perceived.

law of effect Thorndike's observation that stimuli that are contingent on a response can increase (through reinforcement) or decrease (through punishment) response frequently.

manipulate To set the value of the variable for experimental purposes.

matching A procedure in which an experimenter matches subjects in study groups on all relevant variables except the one being studied.

mean A measure of central tendency; the sum of a group of values divided by their number; the arithmetical average.

measure of central tendency A statistic showing the average or mean.

median A measure of central tendency; the midpoint of a group of values arranged numerically.

negative correlation An inverse relation between two variables; large values of one measure are associated with small values of the other.

nominal fallacy The false belief that one has explained the causes of a phenomenon by identifying and naming it; for example, one does not explain lazy behavior by attributing it to "laziness."

objective Something that everyone agrees on and that does not rely on personal judgment.

observational study Observation of two or more variables in the behavior or other characteristics of a group of people. Observational studies can reveal correlations but not causal relations among variables; the latter can be revealed only by experiments.

operational definition The specification of a measurement or of the manipulation of a variable in terms of the operations that the experimenter performs to measure or manipulate it.

personality psychology A branch of psychology that studies individual differences in temperament and patterns of behavior.

physiological psychology The branch of psychology that studies the physiological basis of behavior.

placebo An inert substance that cannot be distinguished from a real medication by the patient or subject; used to please anxious patients or as the control substance in a single-blind or double-blind experiment.

psychometrics A branch of psychology devoted to the development of tests of personality and mental abilities.

psychopathology A division of clinical psychology that studies psychological disorders and problems of adjustment.

psychophysiology The measurement of peripheral physiological processes, such as blood pressure and heart rate, to infer changes in internal states, such as emotions.

random selection Selection of subjects for the various groups of an experiment by random means, assuring comparable groups.

range The difference between the highest score and the lowest score of a sample.

reliability The repeatability of a measurement; the likelihood that if the measurement were made again it would yield the same value. See *validity*.

retrospective method A research technique that requires subjects to report what happened in the past.

sample A group of items selected from a larger population; can refer to subjects, stimuli, or behaviors.

scatter plot A coordinate graph that contains all the variables of one study and which should show the correlation of those variables.

school A group of people with a common belief in a particular theory and methodology.

school psychology A division of educational psychology that counsels within the elementary and secondary school systems.

scientific method Process of identifying a problem, formulating an hypothesis, experimenting to prove or disprove and communicating the results.

single-blind method An experimental method in which the experimenter but not the subject knows the value of the independent variable. See also double-blind method.

social psychology A branch of psychology devoted to the study of the effects people have on each other's behavior.

species-typical behavior A behavior that is seen in all or most members of a species, such as nest building, special food-getting behaviors, or reproductive behaviors.

standard deviation A statistic that expresses the variability of a measurement.

statistical significance The likelihood that an observed relation or difference between two variables is not due to chance factors.

structuralism Psychology concerned with the structure of the mind, dealing with conscious elements such as ideas and sensations.

subjective Involving personal judgment.

theory An elaborate form of an hypothesis, even a system of related hypothesis.

validity The degree to which a test or measurement is related to the variable it is designed to measure; a valid test is a perfect reflection of the psychological trait that it purports to measure.

variable Things that can vary; quantities, characteristics, or phenomena that a scientist either measures or manipulates when performing an experiment.

variable error Within experimental procedures, those factors caused by random differences such as the subject's mood or changes in the environment.

variance The average of the squared deviation of each score from the means.

who had to be out of the home no longer had to be fearful and guilt-ridden.

. . . Professional caregiving seems to offer more to parents and society than to infants . . .

New controversies arose, however, when researchers moved beyond the high-quality daycare settings represented in the early studies, which often were conducted at universities, and began to apply the same techniques in more typical settings. The strange-situation test, for example, was interpreted differently by researchers who focused on the child's reaction to the *mother* rather than to the stranger. Compared with children reared at home, those in daycare remained somewhat anxious and even avoided their mothers when they returned. In 1986 Belsky changed his mind about the efficacy of daycare and argued that infants under age one who spend more than twenty hours a week with nonmaternal caregivers may become less securely attached to their mothers. During their early school years, they seem more likely to be aggressive and uncooperative. Other researchers questioned whether a child's reaction to a strange situation is a valid measure of emotional security in the first place, especially since children in daycare meet strangers regularly. Those who defend the earlier studies say that the central issue is the *quality* of a child's care, not where the care is given or who the caregiver is. In 1987 the quality issue was investigated at Michael Reese Hospital in Chicago by Peter Barglow and associates, who concluded that high-quality care by others even within the home runs the risk of weakening attachment during the first year of an infant's development.

Evaluating Research: A Critical Component

Back and forth the pendulum swings. Now, four decades after Bowlby gave it a push with his study of orphans, it seems to have returned with the message that professional caregiving seems to offer more to parents and society than to infants, at least during some still-indefinite critical period immediately following birth. But how long is that? Some cautious researchers believe that a baby is best left in the care of one person, preferably a parent, for the first several months of life. No doubt most parents would prefer to do so. After that, however, if daycare is necessary, the quality of care should be considered carefully; a ratio of about three infants to one adult seems best. The overall size of the group is also important, at least for two-year-olds, who do better in groups of only ten children or so.

The issues and results of specific research are not isolated phenomena. In the study of human development they are a few pieces in the puzzle and must be fit into a context whose pattern and overall shape no one knows. Informed curiosity, common sense, and enthusiasm are about all we have to go on as we spread the pieces on the table.

The point is apparent: We must look critically at research and must evaluate it in combination with other available information. Part A explores the foundations of human development and behavior, from the biological, perceptual, and cognitive processes that make it possible for us to experience the world, to the social influences that shape our experience of the world.

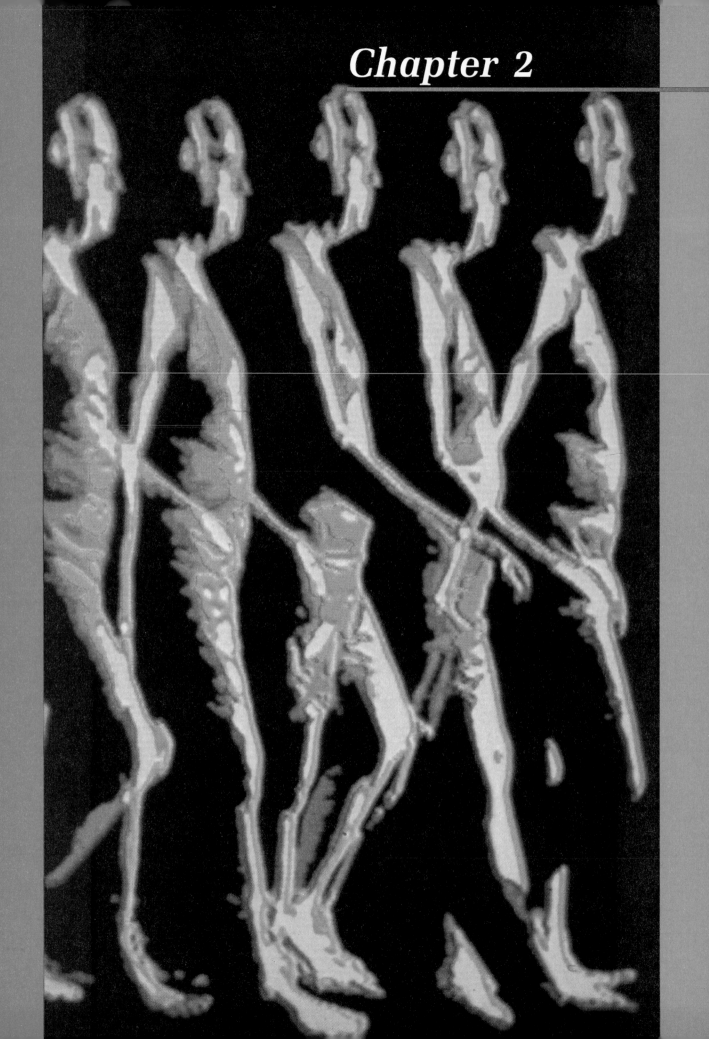

Biology of Behavior

The last frontier of modern science lies within us. The human nervous system—the most complex piece of machinery in the world—is at the center of our existence. It receives information from our sense organs and controls the movements of our muscles. It is responsible for our perceptions, thoughts, memories, feelings, and actions. Thus, its study occupies many of today's most talented scientists.

How does one find out how the brain works? Anatomists study the structure of the nervous system: the location, shape, and interconnections of the nerve cells of which the brain is composed. Physiologists and biochemists study the functions of individual nerve cells: how they detect events in the environment, how they communicate with each other, how they make decisions, and how they control the muscles and thus produce behaviors. Pharmacologists study the ways that drugs interact with the chemical processes of nerve cells, thus affecting brain functions. And psychologists look at the big picture; they try to find out how the brain perceives what is happening in the environment, how it remembers what it has perceived in the past, and how it decides what course of action to take.

How do psychologists make discoveries about the brain? Many psychologists study laboratory animals, applying biological and behavioral techniques. Others study humans who have lost the functions of some part of their brain because of a stroke, an injury, or a disease. By studying what people can and cannot do after part of their brain is damaged, they try to infer the normal function of the missing part.

Thanks to the scientific investigations of biologists and psychologists we have learned much about the neural systems responsible for perceiving, learning, thinking, planning, talking, reading, and writing. Of course, the quest has just begun; the complexity of the human nervous system will keep scientists busy for many years to come. But we can learn a lot by looking at what they have discovered so far. This chapter addresses questions such as: What is the overall structure of the brain? What are the basic functions of its most important parts? What are the basic operations of the nerve cells? How do the brain, the body, and the nervous system work together to produce behavior? In subsequent chapters you will learn more about the role the brain plays in perceptions, memories, language abilities, and emotions.

INVESTIGATIONS OF THE BIOLOGY OF BEHAVIOR

The efforts of scientists in many different fields contribute to our understanding of the biology of behavior. For example, various types of biologists study the structure of the nervous system, explore the functioning of its cells, investigate how nerve cells transmit information, research the chemistry of the nervous system, and use drugs to uncover its functions. These scientists provide the basic tools that others use to study the biology of behavior. The research performed by neurologists, physiological psychologists, and neuropsychologists has the most relevance to psychology.

Neurologists are physicians (M.D.s) who specialize in diseases of the nervous system. Most neurologists are involved in treatment, not research. Yet these physicians were the first to study the role that the nervous system plays in human behavior. They observed that damage to different portions of the human brain produced different kinds of disorders; this finding suggested that different parts of the brain have different functions. Today neurologists use this information in making their diagnoses. For example, if a patient loses sensation to pain in the right leg, loses sensation to touch in the left leg, and has difficulty making accurate, rapid movements of either arm and hand, a neurologist can be almost certain that a particular region of the left side of the lower part of the brain has been damaged.

The studies that began with the efforts of neurologists in the last century and the early part of this century have been continued and extended by **neuropsychologists,** who try to learn how the nervous system organizes and controls human behavior. Neuropsychologists study patients who have sustained damage to some portion of the nervous system through injury or disease. They use their assessment skills to determine which sensory, motor, or cognitive abilities have been disrupted by the injury. On the basis of their findings, they draw inferences about the psychological functions that are performed by various parts of the nervous system.

Basically, neuropsychologists use the following logic to draw their inferences: if damage to a particular part of the nervous system (structure A) impairs a person's ability to perform a particular function (function B), we can infer that structure A plays a role in the execution of function B. For example, if a person can no longer see after the back part of the brain is destroyed, we can be fairly certain that the back part of the brain plays a role in vision. Much of what we know about the functions of various parts of the brain was obtained by using this inferential strategy. The logic of this strategy comes from the method of *experimental surgery*. Of course, neuropsychologists do not *produce* the brain damage; the damage occurs through injury or disease.

Physiological psychologists use a wider range of research techniques, which are described in the next section. These scientists perform most of their investigations with laboratory animals. Unlike neuropsychologists, who assess the behavior of patients whose nervous systems have been damaged by injury or disease, physiological psychologists can operate on their animals and produce damage to any structure of the brain. They can also insert wires to stimulate the brain with electricity or to record the electrical activity that the brain produces. They can inject drugs or remove pieces of tissue for chemical analysis. Although the animals they study lack many of the abilities that humans possess (such as speech), physiological psychologists can use animals to conduct investigations that cannot be performed with humans.

Research Methods of Physiological Psychology

The most common research method used by physiological psychologists is the one that neuropsychologists also use: correlation of a behavioral deficit with the location of damage to the nervous system. But instead of looking for patients who have accidentally suffered damage to a particular part of the brain, the physiological psychologist operates on a laboratory animal in order to produce that damage. This technique is called lesion production. (A *lesion* is an injury.) The investigator produces the injury in a particular part of the brain and then studies the effects of the lesion on the animal's behavior.

To produce a brain lesion, the researcher anesthetizes an animal and prepares it for surgery, drills a hole in the skull, and destroys part of the brain. In most cases, the region under investigation is located in the depths of the brain, so the investigator must use a special device called a stereotaxic apparatus. *Stereotaxic* means "solid arrangement"; it refers to the ability to manipulate an object in three-dimensional space. A stereotaxic apparatus permits a physiological psychologist to insert a fine wire into a precise location in the brain. The researcher then passes electrical current through the wire, which destroys a small portion of the brain around the tip of the wire. After a few days, the animal recovers, and the researcher can assess its behavior.

A stereotaxic apparatus can also be used to insert wires for recording the electrical activity of nerve cells in particular regions of the brain. The wire is inserted into the brain and attached to an electrical connector cemented to the animal's skull, and the scalp is sewed together. The connector is later attached to a wire leading to electronic devices that record the electrical activity of the brain while the animal is performing various behaviors. (See Figure 2.1.) As we will see later in this chapter, nerve cells transmit information from place to place by means of electrical charges; the wire in the brain detects these charges.

A wire placed in an animal's brain can be used to lead electrical current *into* the brain as well as out of it. The electrical connector on the animal's skull is attached to an electrical stimulator, and current is sent to a portion of the animal's brain. The experimenter then assesses the effects of this artificial stimulation on the animal's behavior. One example of an experiment that uses this technique is shown in Figure 2.2.

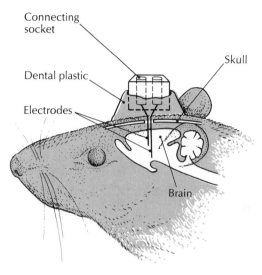

FIGURE 2.1

A permanently attached set of wires (electrodes) in an animal's brain, with a connecting socket cemented to the skull.

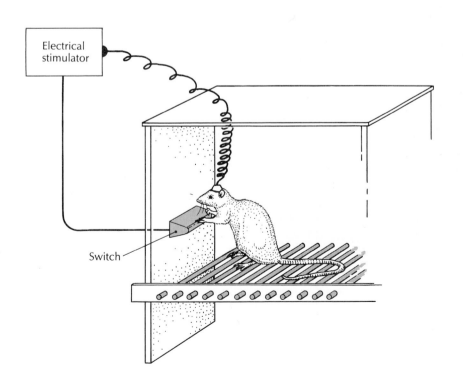

FIGURE 2.2

When the rat presses the switch, it receives a brief pulse of electricity to its brain, through wires like those shown in Figure 2.1.

A rat presses a lever attached to an electrical switch that turns on a stimulator. The stimulator sends a brief pulse of electricity through a wire placed in the rat's brain. If the tip of the wire is located in certain parts of the brain, the animal will press the lever again and again. This finding suggests that these parts of the brain play a role in reward mechanisms.

Different drugs affect different types of nerve cells of the brain in different ways, and many of the hormones that are produced by the glands of the body affect behavior by stimulating nerve cells. Therefore, physiological psychologists often use these chemicals in their investigations, in order to determine how their behavioral effects are produced.

Although physiological psychologists regularly use many other techniques, lesion production, electrical recording, electrical stimulation, and the administration of drugs and hormones are the ones most frequently used.

Human Brain Damage as a Key to Assessing Behavior

Physiological psychologists know the location of the lesions in the brains of their laboratory animals because they placed them there. In addition, they can confirm the precise location of the lesions by examining slices of the animals' brains under a microscope after the behavioral testing is completed.

Neuropsychologists have a more difficult task. Their subjects are human beings, whose brains can be directly examined only when they die, and then only if the patient's family gives permission for an autopsy. Sometimes the brain damage was caused by surgical removal of a tumor or diseased region of the brain; in such cases the neurosurgeon can provide the neuropsychologist with drawings of the parts that were removed. However, the majority of human brain lesions are the result of natural causes, such as stroke. Most strokes occur when a blood clot obstructs an artery in the brain and blocks the supply of oxygen and nutrients to a particular region, causing that region to die. No surgery takes place, so a neurosurgeon's report is not available.

Until recently, it was not possible to determine the location of brain lesions until the patient died and an autopsy was performed. Now, however, several diagnostic machines are available to assist neuropsychological research. The one commonly used is the CAT scanner.

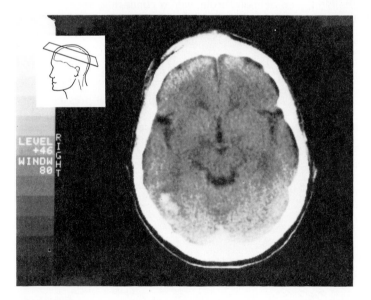 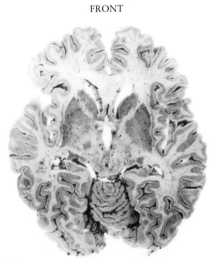

FIGURE 2.3

An image from a CAT scan (left) and a photograph of an actual slice of a brain (right) cut in approximately the same plane. (CAT scan courtesy of Dr. J. McA. Jones, Good Samaritan Hospital, Portland, Oregon. Photograph from DeArmond, S.J., Fusco, M.M., and Dewey, M.M. *Structure of the Human Brain: A Photographic Atlas*, 2nd ed. New York: Oxford University Press, 1976.)

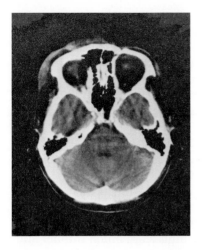

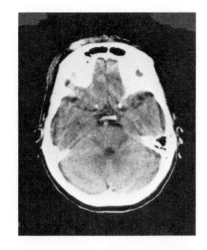

FIGURE 2.4

A set of CAT scans from a patient with a lesion in the right occipital-parietal area. Note that left and right are reversed, and the lesion is clearly visible in the lower corner of the last scan. (Courtesy of Dr. J. McA. Jones, Good Samaritan Hospital, Portland, Oregon.)

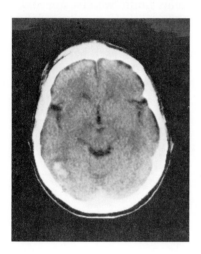

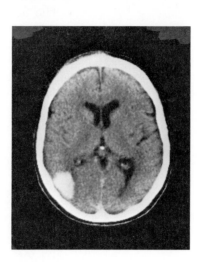

CAT stands for **computerized axial tomography.** *Axis,* meaning "a line around which something rotates," refers to the circular movement of the X-ray tube and detector around the person's head; *tomos,* meaning "cut," describes the fact that the picture looks like a slice. A CAT scanner sends a narrow beam of X rays through a person's head. A detector measures the amount of radiation that gets through to the other side. The beam is moved around the patient's head, and a computer calculates the amount of radiation that passes through at various points along each angle. The result is a two-dimensional image of a "slice" of the person's head, parallel to the top of the skull. Figure 2.3 shows a picture produced by a CAT scanner (left) and a photograph of the corresponding slice through a human brain (right). (See Figure 2.3. on the facing page.)

Although it was developed to assist neurologists and neurosurgeons to see tumors, regions destroyed by strokes, and other abnormalities within the brain, the CAT scanner has become an indispensable tool for neuropsychological research. Now the investigator can determine the approximate location of a brain lesion while the patient is still alive. Knowing the results of behavioral testing and the location of the brain damage, the neuropsychologist can compare them and make inferences about the normal function of the missing brain tissue. Figure 2.4 shows a set of CAT scans from a person who has difficulty perceiving and drawing pictures of three-dimensional objects. You will have no trouble spotting the lesion in the scan in the lower right corner. It appears as a white spot in the lower left-hand corner of that scan. (See Figure 2.4.)

STRUCTURE AND FUNCTION OF NERVOUS SYSTEM

The anatomy of the brain is very complex. We now know a great deal about the structure of different regions of the brain. We also know the pathways of the nerve fibers that connect them, and, as you shall see later in the chapter, we also know much about the operations of the building blocks of the nervous system: the neurons. However, because the human brain is so complex and its capabilities are so vast, we have only an elementary knowledge about the specific functions performed by each of these regions.

Central Nervous System

The brain and spinal cord are the most protected organs of the body. The brain is encased in the skull, which consists of a very tough set of bones; the spinal cord runs through the middle of a column of hollow bones, the *vertebrae*. (See Figure 2.5.) Both the brain and the spinal cord (which together are referred to as the **central nervous system**) are surrounded by a set of three membranes called the **meninges.** (*Meninges* is the plural of *meninx*, the Greek word for "membrane." You have probably heard of *meningitis*, which is an inflammation of the meninges.) Three different sets of meninges encase the brain. The outer one is a thick, tough, unstretchable wrapping, rather like soft parchment. When operating on a person's brain, a neurosurgeon must cut it with scissors. The inner two meninges are much thinner and more fragile.

The average human brain weighs approximately 1200 to 1500 grams (approximately 3 pounds). It is extremely soft and fragile. Because of its great delicacy, and because we often move our heads around, the brain is provided with a cushioning device: **cerebrospinal**

FIGURE 2.5

The central nervous system: brain and spinal cord.

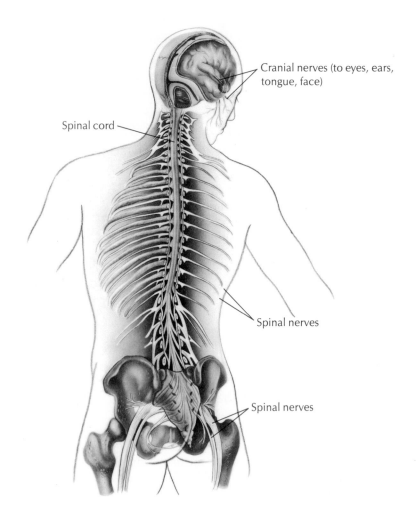

Cranial nerves (to eyes, ears, tongue, face)

Spinal cord

Spinal nerves

Spinal nerves

fluid (CSF). Cerebrospinal fluid is similar to blood plasma, the clear liquid that remains when the red and white blood cells are removed from blood. This fluid is produced continuously by specialized blood vessels located in hollow chambers of the brain that are called **ventricles.**

Cerebrospinal fluid flows out of the ventricles into the space between the two inner (delicate) meninges, providing a liquid cushion around the entire brain. As a result, the brain floats within this cushioned space instead of resting directly against the base of the skull. Because an object weighs less when it is submerged in liquid, the effective weight of the brain is reduced from well over a kilogram to less than 80 grams (2.8 ounces). Without the cushioning effect of CSF, the brain would be bruised and injured by any rapid movement of the head.

Peripheral Nervous System

The business of the brain is to control the movements of the muscles—to produce appropriate behaviors in appropriate situations. Of course, we use our brains for thinking as well as for moving, but if we could not perceive the world or move our muscles in response to our perceptions, we would have nothing to think about. Thus a brain is useful only if it can receive sensory information and exert control over the muscles. These processes require the peripheral nervous system.

The **peripheral nervous system** consists of the nerves that connect the central nervous system with sense organs, muscles, and glands. The sense organs detect changes in the environment and send signals through the peripheral nerves to the central nervous system. The brain makes appropriate responses by sending signals out through the peripheral nerves to the muscles (causing behavior) and glands (producing adjustments in internal physiological processes).

Nerves are bundles of many thousands of individual nerve fibers, all wrapped in a protective set of meninges, just like the brain. Under a microscope, nerves look something like telephone cables. Like bundles of individual wires in a telephone cable, nerve fibers transmit messages through the nerve, from sense organ to brain, or from brain to muscle or gland.

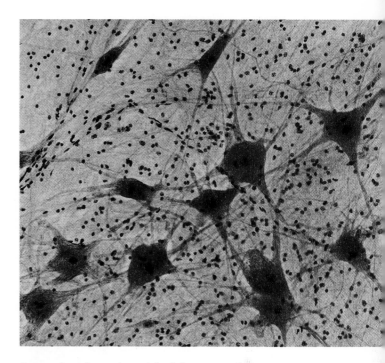

A greatly enlarged model of the types of interconnections that occur among neurons in the brain.

Some nerves are attached to the spinal cord. These **spinal nerves** serve all of the body below the neck, conveying sensory information from the skin and carrying messages to muscles and glands. (Look at Figure 2.5.) For example, if you stub your toe, the pain you feel comes from sensory receptors at the ends of nerve fibers in your toe. These fibers run through nerves attached to the lower part of the spinal cord. The information is sent up to the brain through bundles of nerve fibers that run the length of the spinal cord. Other nerves are attached directly to the base of the brain; these **cranial nerves** serve muscles and sense receptors in the neck and head. For example, when you taste food, the sensory information gets from your tongue to your brain through one set of cranial nerves, and when you chew the food, the message to chew reaches your jaw muscles through another set of cranial nerves. (See Figure 2.6.)

- What four experimental methods are most common in physiological psychology?
- What are the basic structural features and functions of the central nervous system?
- What are the functions of the peripheral nervous system?

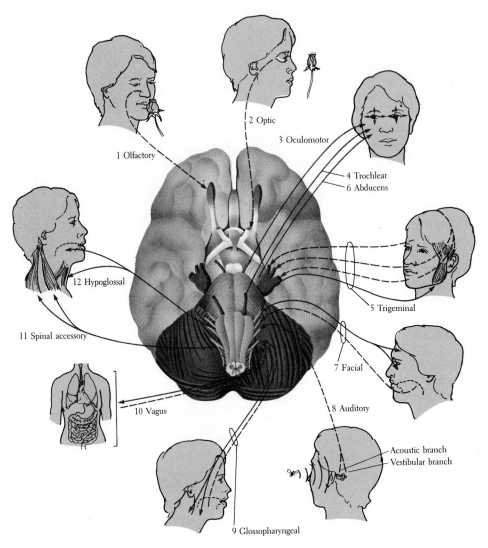

FIGURE 2.6

The twelve pairs of cranial nerves and the regions they serve.

Sensory Input to the Brain

Cerebral Cortex

We perceive information from the environment when messages about events that occur there are sent from sensory receptors to the central nervous system, through nerve fibers in spinal or cranial nerves. Sensory information goes to many locations within the brain, but the most important of these locations (so far as conscious perception is concerned) is the **cerebral cortex.** The word *cortex* means "bark." The cerebral cortex consists of a thin layer of tissue approximately 3 millimeters thick that con-

tains billions of nerve cells. It is here that perceptions take place, memories are stored, and plans are formulated and executed.

The cerebral cortex covers the surface of the *cerebrum,* which is divided into two **cerebral hemispheres.** These two large masses form the greatest bulk of the human brain. Figure 2.7 shows two views of the human brain and illustrates the extent of the cerebral cortex. The gray shading is appropriate, because the cerebral cortex is often referred to as the brain's **gray matter.** The drawing on the left shows how the brain looks from the side, with the front of the brain at the left. The drawing on the right shows the brain sliced through the middle,

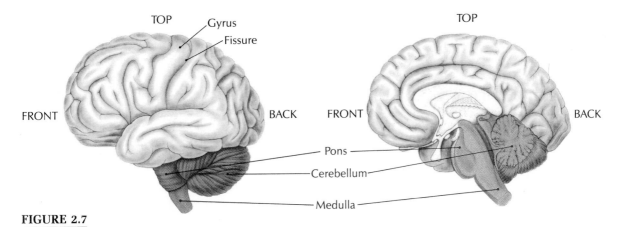

FIGURE 2.7

Side views of the human brain: intact (left) and sliced through the middle from front to back (right). The cerebral hemispheres are shown in gray.

from front to back, with the left half of the brain cut away. The figure shows the inner surface of the right side of the brain.

The human cerebral cortex is very wrinkled; it is full of bulges separated by grooves. The bulges are called **gyri** (singular, gyrus), and large grooves are called **fissures.** Fissures and gyri serve to increase the amount of surface area of the cortex. If the surface of the brain were smooth (as it is in most other animals), the total surface area of the cerebral cortex would be much less. Figure 2.8 shows a slice through the cerebral hemispheres; note how the cerebral cortex follows the grooves.

Thalamus

All sensory information (except for olfaction, the sense of smell) is sent to the **thalamus** before it reaches the cerebral cortex. If you stripped away the cerebral cortex, you would find a layer of nerve fibers that connect the cortex with the rest of the brain. These fibers are referred to as **white matter** because of the shiny white appearance of the substance that coats and insulates them. If you stripped away the white matter, you would reach the thalamus.

Almost all parts of the brain come in pairs: a left portion and a right portion, one in each hemisphere. Thus the thalamus has two parts, one on each side of the brain. Each part looks rather like a football, with the long axis oriented from front to back. (See Figure 2.9 on the next page.) Nerve fibers from the various sensory systems enter the thalamus from below, and other sets of fibers exit from the top of the

thalamus and travel to specific regions of the cerebral cortex. The thalamus has been referred to as the "relay station" of the brain because it passes information from the sensory systems along to the cerebral cortex.

Sensory Areas of the Cerebral Cortex

We become aware of events in our environment by means of the five major senses: vision, audition, olfaction, gustation (taste), and the

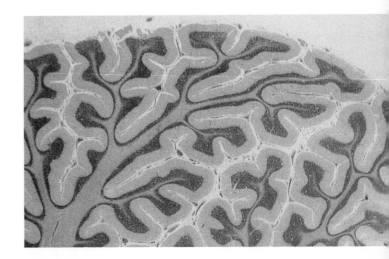

FIGURE 2.8

A slice through the cerebellum, stained with a special dye. The cerebral cortex looks pale pink, and the white matter looks medium pink and purple.

somatosenses (touch, pain, and temperature). Three areas of the cerebral cortex receive the sensory information relayed by the thalamus. The **primary visual cortex,** which receives visual information, is located at the back of the brain, mostly hidden from view on the inner surfaces of the cerebral hemispheres. The **primary auditory cortex** is also mostly hidden from view on the surface of a deep fissure in the side of the brain. The **primary somatosensory cortex,** a vertical strip near the middle of the cerebral hemisphere, receives information from the body senses: touch, pain, and temperature (*soma* means "body"). Different regions of the primary somatosensory cortex receive information from different regions of the body. In addition, the base of the somatosensory cortex receives information concerning taste. (See Figure 2.10.)

■ What are the three basic areas of research in behavioral biology?

■ What four common experimental research methods are used in physiological psychology? How do psychologists use CAT scans?

■ What are the basic structural features and functions of the central nervous system? Of the peripheral nervous system?

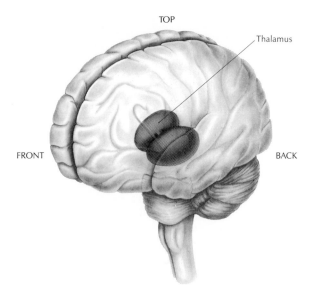

FIGURE 2.9

The thalamus.

Motor Output from the Brain

As I mentioned earlier, the brain is the organ that controls behavior; that is, it moves the muscles. Muscular movement is referred to as *motor activity.* (The word *motor* is used in its

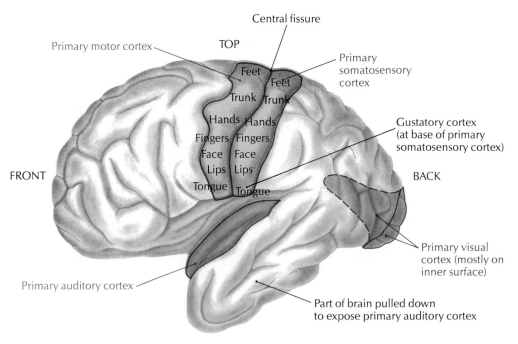

FIGURE 2.10

Primary sensory and motor areas of the human brain.

original sense, referring to movement, not mechanical engines.) Many different motor systems control our behavior. The movement of the eyes, the hands and fingers, the arms and legs, the trunk, and the muscles used for speech all appear to have separate control mechanisms within the brain (which interact and cooperate with each other, of course).

The region of the cerebral cortex most directly involved in the control of movement is the **primary motor cortex,** located just in front of the primary somatosensory cortex. (Refer to Figure 2.10.) The actual commands to make movements are initiated elsewhere in the cerebral cortex (to be described shortly). These commands produce activity in nerve cells within the primary motor cortex. Control of hand and finger movement is accomplished by means of nerve fibers that travel from the primary motor cortex directly to the spinal cord. There, information is transmitted out through spinal nerves to the muscles that perform the movements. Control of arm, leg, and body movements is accomplished by connections between the primary motor cortex and structures located within the depths of the brain. As Figure 2.10 shows, nerve cells in different parts of the primary motor cortex control movements of muscles in different parts of the body. A useful analogy is to think of the strip of primary motor cortex as the keys of a piano, with each key controlling a different movement. We will encounter the "player" of this piano in the next section.

Movement of different parts of the body uses separate control mechanisms in the brain.

One structure deserves special mention with respect to motor activity: the **cerebellum** ("little brain"). The cerebellum is well named; Figure 2.11 shows you that the cerebellum indeed looks like a miniature brain, nestled beneath the overhanging back part of the cerebral hemispheres. (See Figures 2.8 and 2.11.) The cerebellum receives information from the various motor systems of the brain and provides an important degree of coordination among them. It smooths out movements, especially those that involve rapid changes in direction. It monitors information regarding posture and balance and keeps us from falling down when we stand or walk. It also plays an important role in the control of eye movements.

Association Areas of the Cortex

The primary sensory and motor cortex constitute only a small fraction of the total area of the

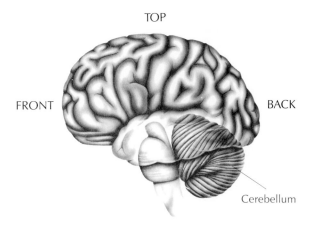

TOP

FRONT　　　　　　　　　　　　　　BACK

Cerebellum

FIGURE 2.11

The cerebellum.

cerebral cortex. The rest of the cerebral cortex accomplishes what is done between sensation and action: perception, concept formation, memory, planning, and all the rest. These processes take place in the *association areas* of the cerebral cortex. The term comes from early theories of brain function that assumed that elements of perception and movement were linked together (associated) here. To understand these processes better, we must examine the anatomy and functions of other subdivisions of the cerebral cortex.

The **central fissure** provides an important dividing line between the front part of the cerebral cortex and the posterior (back) regions. All the primary sensory areas lie in back of the central fissure, and the primary motor area lies in front of it. The remaining areas of these two regions of the cortex perform similar functions. The front part of the cerebral cortex is involved in movement-related activities, such as planning and initiation of behavior. The posterior part is important for perception, concept for-

mation, and storage of most memories.

The cerebral cortex is divided into four areas, or *lobes*, named for the bones of the skull that cover them: the frontal lobe, parietal lobe, temporal lobe, and occipital lobe. (Of course, the brain contains two of each lobe, one in each hemisphere.) The **frontal lobe** includes everything in front of the central fissure except the tip of the temporal lobe, which projects forward beneath it. The **parietal lobe** lies behind the central fissure, in back of the frontal lobe. The **temporal lobe** lies beneath both the frontal lobe and the parietal lobe. The **occipital lobe** lies at the very back of the brain, behind the parietal and temporal lobes. Thus, the primary motor cortex is in the frontal lobe, the primary somatosensory cortex is in the parietal lobe, the primary auditory cortex is in the temporal lobe, and the primary visual cortex is in the occipital lobe. (See Figure 2.12.)

Each primary sensory area of the cerebral cortex sends information to adjacent areas of the cortex, called **sensory association cortex.**

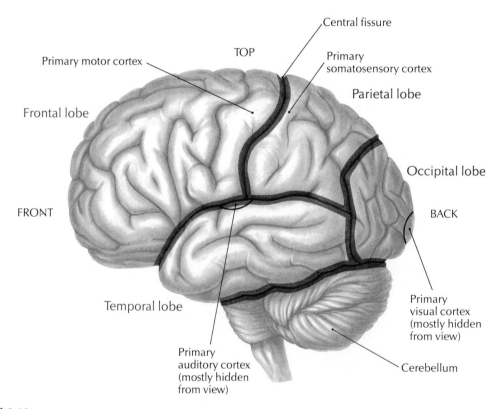

FIGURE 2.12

The four lobes of the cerebral cortex.

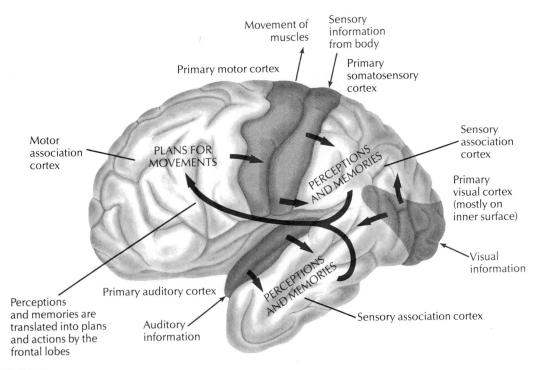

FIGURE 2.13

The relation between primary sensory and motor cortex and association cortex.

The sensory association cortex performs perceptual analyses of the information received from the primary sensory cortex, and memories related to the information are stored there. The regions of sensory association cortex located closest to the primary sensory areas receive information from only one sensory modality. Thus, we can speak of the visual association cortex, the somatosensory association cortex, and the auditory association cortex. Other regions of sensory association cortex, located farther from the primary sensory areas, receive information from more than one sensory modality. These regions include the borders between the temporal, parietal, and occipital lobes. (See Figures 2.12 and 2.13.)

The regions of association cortex that receive information from more than one sensory modality perform higher-order analyses of sensory information and represent abstract information in ways that are independent of the individual sensory modalities. For example, when you think about a tree, you can picture a visual image of a particular tree, you can remember how the bark of various trees feels, you can imagine the sound of wind rustling some leaves, or you can think about the wood products that can be made from lumber. You can

also think about the sound of the word *tree*, a drawing that might represent it, or the visual appearance of the letters t-r-e-e. These thoughts can be started by the sight of an actual tree, by the sound of the word, or by the printed words you have just read.

Just as regions of the posterior association cortex provide the location for sensory images and memories, the frontal association cortex is involved in the planning and execution of movements. Thus, this area can be referred to as the **motor association cortex.** Some regions of the frontal association cortex have rather specific functions; in particular, one region is necessary for the production of proper speech. (It will be described in Chapter 8.) The association cortex of the frontal lobes receives information from the sensory association areas in the posterior part of the brain and integrates this information into plans and actions. In terms of my piano analogy, the motor association cortex serves as the "piano player," receiving advice about what to play from the areas of sensory association cortex and then pressing the appropriate keys. (See Figure 2.13.)

I will say more about the sensory and motor association cortex when I describe the complex functions of the cerebral cortex.

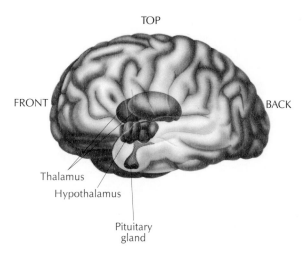

FIGURE 2.14

The hypothalamus and the pituitary gland.

■ What are the functions of the thalamus and sensory areas of the cerebral cortex?

■ What major neural structures control motor activity?

■ What are the functions of the different areas of association cortex?

Structures Within the Cerebral Hemispheres

So far I have described three important regions of the brain: the cerebral cortex, thalamus, and cerebellum. Several other brain structures, located within the cerebral hemispheres, are important enough to warrant attention here.

Hypothalamus

Hypo- means "less than" or "beneath," and as its name suggests, the **hypothalamus** is located below the thalamus, at the base of the brain. (See Figure 2.14.) The hypothalamus is a small region, consisting of less than one cubic centimeter of tissue. Its relative importance far exceeds its relative size.

The hypothalamus participates in two major functions: homeostasis and control of species-typical behaviors. **Homeostasis** (from the root words *homoio,* "similar," and *stasis,* "standstill") refers to the maintenance of a proper balance of physiological variables such as temper-

ature, concentration of fluids, and the amount of nutrients stored within the body. **Species-typical behaviors** are those exhibited by most members of a species that are important to survival, such as eating, drinking, fighting, courting and mating, and caring for offspring.

The hypothalamus receives sensory information, including information from receptors inside the body; thus, it is informed about changes in the organism's physiological status. It also contains specialized sensors that monitor various characteristics of the blood that flows through the brain, such as temperature, nutrient content, and amount of dissolved salts. In turn, the hypothalamus controls the **pituitary gland,** which is located on the end of a stalk attached directly to the base of the hypothalamus. (See Figure 2.14.)

The pituitary gland has been called the "master gland" because it controls the activity of the rest of the **endocrine glands,** which secrete hormones. Thus, by controlling the pituitary gland the hypothalamus exerts control over the entire endocrine system. Figure 2.15 lists some of the

---

The hypothalamus is responsible for the "fight or flight" reaction we experience in frightening situations.

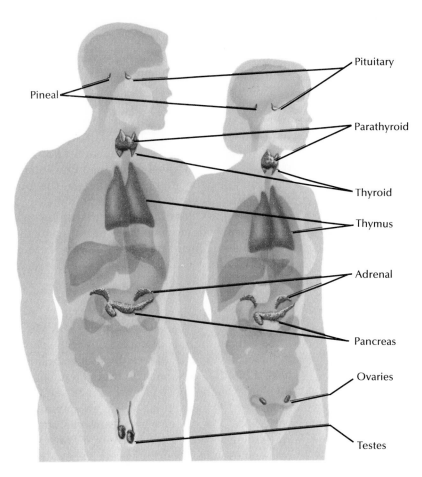

FIGURE 2.15

The major endocrine glands: their location, the hormones they secrete, and their principal functions.

TABLE 2.1

Major functions of the autonomic nervous system

	Effect of Activity of Autonomic Nerve Fibers	
Organ	Sympathetic	Parasympathetic
Adrenal medulla	Secretion of epinephrine and norepinephrine	
Bladder	Inhibition of contraction	Contraction
Blood vessels		
Abdomen	Constriction	
Muscles	Dilation	Constriction
Skin	Constriction or dilation	Dilation
Heart	Faster rate of contraction	Slower rate of contraction
Intestines	Decreased activity	Increased activity
Lacrimal glands	Secretion of tears	
Liver	Release of glucose	
Lungs	Dilation of bronchi	Constriction of bronchi
Penis	Ejaculation	Erection
Pupil of eye	Dilation	Constriction
Salivary glands	Secretion of thick, viscous saliva	Secretion of thin, enzyme-rich saliva
Sweat glands	Secretion of sweat	
Vagina	Orgasm	Secretion of lubricating fluid

Circuits of neurons in the brain stem, including the reticular formation, regulate our level of sleep and wakefulness.

endocrine glands and the functions they regulate. Some of these hormones have important effects on behavior and will be discussed in later chapters.

The hypothalamus also controls much of the activity of the **autonomic nervous system.** This division of the peripheral nervous system consists of nerves that control motor functions other than those performed by the skeletal muscles, such as sweating, shedding tears, salivating, secreting digestive juices, changing the size of blood vessels (which alters blood pressure), and secreting some hormones. The autonomic nervous system has two branches, the **sympathetic branch** and the **parasympathetic branch.** The sympathetic branch directs activities that involve the expenditure of energy, whereas the parasympathetic branch controls quiet activities such as digestion of food. (See Table 2.1.) Psychophysiologists monitor many of the responses produced by these two branches; in so doing, they can measure autonomic nervous system activity and its relation to psychological phenomena such as emotions. For example, when a person is angry, his or her heart rate and blood pressure rise. The "lie detector" works in a similar manner.

The homeostatic functions of the hypothalamus can involve either nonbehavioral physiological changes or overt behaviors. Nonbehavioral changes include regulation of temperature

by sweating or by increasing the metabolic rate. Overt behaviors include putting on or taking off a coat, turning the thermostat up or down, and adding another log to the fire. Damage to the hypothalamus can cause impaired regulation of body temperature, changes in food intake, sterility, or stunting of growth. Obviously, the hypothalamus is a very important structure.

The hypothalamus exerts a great deal of control over species-typical behaviors. Physiological psychologists often refer to them as the *four Fs*: feeding, fighting, fleeing, and "mating." However, this classification omits other species-typical behaviors that are controlled by the hypothalamus: drinking, nest-building, care of offspring, and various behaviors that conserve or get rid of body heat.

Brain Stem

If the human brain is dissected out of the skull, it looks as though the cerebral hemispheres have a handle, or stem. The **brain stem** constitutes one of the most primitive regions of the brain, and its functions are correspondingly basic ones. The brains of some animals, such as amphibians, consist primarily of a brain stem and a simple cerebellum. (See Figure 2.16.)

The upper part of the brain stem, located just behind the thalamus, is called the **midbrain.**

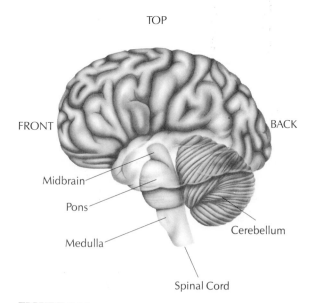

FIGURE 2.16

The brain stem: midbrain, pons, and medulla.

Several important structures in the motor system are located within the midbrain, including structures that control movements of the eyes and that control independent limb movements. The midbrain also contains circuits of nerve cells that control the complex movements that constitute species-typical behaviors. Although the hypothalamus plays a major role in determining *when* an animal fights, feeds, flees, or performs other species-typical behaviors, the hypothalamus does not directly control the patterns of muscular movements that produce these behaviors. It does so indirectly, by sending messages to structures in the brain stem, including several in the midbrain.

The **pons** is a large bulge in the brain stem, located just below the midbrain. *Pons* means "bridge"; it received its name from the prominent bundles of nerve fibers that pass through it. (See Figure 2.16.) The pons contains circuits of nerve cells with functions related to sleeping and alertness, attention, and movement.

The **medulla** ("marrow") is the lowest part of the brain, located just above the spinal cord. (See Figure 2.16.) The medulla is vital for life; a very small lesion located in a critical region of this structure will cause immediate death.

The medulla controls the so-called vital functions: heart rate, blood pressure, and respiration. The medulla also plays an important role in other physiological activities, such as vomiting, coughing, and sneezing. The medulla receives sensory information directly from receptors within the body and exerts its effects through nerve fibers that travel out through the cranial and spinal nerves. In addition, the medulla receives information from the hypothalamus, which exerts some of its control over the autonomic nervous system by influencing the activity of this structure.

An important structure occupies the central core of the brain stem, from the medulla up to the midbrain. This structure, the **reticular formation,** consists of a tangle of nerve cells and fibers. (*Reticulum* means "net" and refers to this tangle.) Some parts of the reticular formation control movements or physiological functions. For example, the nerve cells of the medulla that control the vital functions are located within the reticular formation. Other parts increase our alertness during times of danger or excitement. Still others cause us to sleep and regulate such activities as dreaming (which

involve nerve cells located in the cerebral hemispheres, especially in the cerebral cortex). Control of wakefulness and sleep is accomplished by means of nerve fibers that connect the reticular formation with the thalamus and cerebral cortex.

COMPLEX FUNCTIONS OF THE CEREBRAL CORTEX

As we saw earlier, the central fissure divides the brain in two regions, a front part (the frontal lobe) and a back part (the parietal, occipital, and temporal lobes). The area in front of the central fissure is concerned with motor functions, the area behind it with sensory functions. This section describes the types of deficits that are produced by damage to particular areas of the human cerebral cortex and the inferences that have been made about their functions on the basis of this damage. As we saw earlier in this chapter, much of what we know about the functions of the human brain comes from observations of the behavior of people whose brains were damaged; the missing functions are presumably what the damaged parts previously did. Now I will describe some of these observations, and the conclusions derived from them.

Lateralization of Function

Although the two cerebral hemispheres cooperate with each other, they do not perform identical functions. Some functions are *lateralized*— located primarily on one side of the brain. In general, the left hemisphere participates in verbal functions and in the *analysis* of information—the extraction of the elements that make up the whole of an experience. This ability makes the left hemisphere particularly good at recognizing serially ordered events—that is, events whose elements occur one at a time. In contrast, the right hemisphere is specialized for *synthesis;* it is particularly good at putting isolated elements together to perceive things as a whole.

Some of the most interesting information about the lateralization of function in the cerebral hemispheres comes from people whose

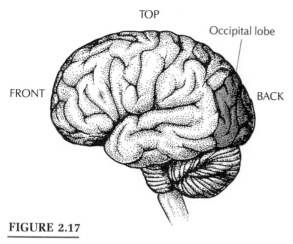

FIGURE 2.17

The occipital lobe.

hemispheres have been surgically disconnected in order to control a severe form of epilepsy. In these cases, the two hemispheres can operate independently, each controlling the part of the body on the opposite side and being aware of sensory information on that side. A section of Chapter 10 describes these people, and the relation of the disconnection to consciousness.

In almost all people the left hemisphere is specialized for speech, but in some, especially those who are left-handed, the *right* hemisphere performs this role. Thus, in later descriptions, functions of the left and right hemispheres would be reversed for these people.

Occipital Lobe

The primary business of the occipital lobe is seeing. (See Figure 2.17.)

Extensive damage to the primary visual cortex produces blindness on that side, but a small lesion in the primary visual cortex only produces a "hole" in the field of vision. A person with such a lesion can move his or her eyes around and eventually see everything in the environment. (Imagine looking at the world through a cardboard tube that you have to move around in order to see everything.) In contrast, damage to the visual association cortex (which includes parts of the parietal and temporal lobes as well as the occipital lobe) does not impair the primary sensory functions; no blindness results. However, such damage impairs the ability to recognize objects by sight. This deficit is called **visual agnosia** (*a-*, "without"; *gnōsis*, "knowledge").

As I mentioned earlier, the left hemisphere is specialized for analysis of the elements of something being perceived. Damage to the visual association cortex of the left hemisphere produces deficits in the ability to recognize the elements of a visual scene: angles, curves, and line segments. Depending on the location of the damage, the person may lose the ability to read and write. On the other hand, damage to the visual association cortex of the right hemisphere produces deficits in visual recognition of familiar objects; the person will be able to walk around without bumping into things and to point to objects that an experimenter holds up but might be unable to name the objects or identify their functions.

Temporal Lobe

The principal sensory function of the temporal lobe is hearing, but this lobe is also involved in vision, memory, and functions related to personality and social behavior. (See Figure 2.18.)

Damage to the temporal lobe results in a variety of symptoms, depending on which region is destroyed and whether the left or right lobe is affected. The primary auditory cortex is located on the inner surface of the temporal lobe. The auditory association cortex is located on the sides of the temporal lobes, back toward the

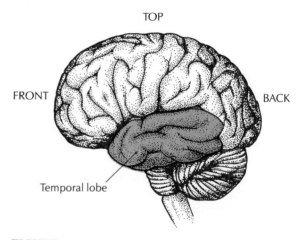

FIGURE 2.18

The temporal lobe.

occipital lobes. Damage to the left auditory association cortex causes severe language deficits. These people are no longer able to comprehend speech, presumably because they have lost the nerve cells that decode speech sounds. However, the deficit is more severe than that; they also lose the ability to read, and although they can still talk, their speech becomes a meaningless jumble of words. I will say more about language deficits produced by brain damage in Chapter 8.

Damage to the auditory association cortex in the right hemisphere does not seriously affect speech perception or production, but it does affect the ability to recognize nonspeech sounds, including patterns of tones and rhythms. The damage can also impair a person's ability to perceive the location of sounds in the environment. As we will see later in this chapter, the right hemisphere is very important in perception of space. The contribution of the right temporal lobe to this function is to participate in perceiving placement of sounds.

Bilateral damage to the temporal lobes (that is, damage to both sides) usually results in severe loss of memory. In some cases, the patient has a relatively good memory for events that occurred before the injury but becomes almost totally incapable of learning anything new. This disorder is discussed in Chapter 7.

Damage to various portions of the temporal lobes can affect social behavior and emotional reactions. For example, a person with damage to a temporal lobe (especially the right one) sometimes becomes a compulsive talker who harangues any available listener, even if the listener shows no sign of interest in what is being said. This finding suggests that the right temporal lobe normally plays a role in evaluating the appropriateness of thoughts and speech; when it is damaged, people no longer perform such evaluations. People with abnormally functioning temporal lobes are often egocentric, suspicious, and preoccupied with religious issues.

Sexual behavior also appears to be at least partly under the control of the temporal lobes. A particular kind of epilepsy is caused by abnormal activity of nerve cells in one of the temporal lobes. Some (but certainly not all) patients who have this form of epilepsy show a lack of interest in sexual activity. If a portion of the defective temporal lobe is removed, sexual interest usually increases to a normal level.

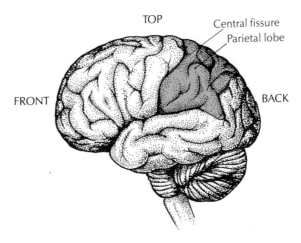

FIGURE 2.19

The parietal lobe.

Parietal Lobe

The principal sensory function of the parietal lobe is somatosensory perception, but this part of the brain does much more than mediate our awareness of what is happening in the body and on its surface. The functions of the parietal lobe overlap with those of the occipital and temporal lobes. Thus, the back and lower parts of the parietal lobe are concerned with visually and acoustically related functions. In addition, the parietal lobe is very important in perceiving space and being aware of the location of one's own body in space. (See Figure 2.19.)

Damage to the left parietal lobe (and its junction with the temporal and occipital lobes) can result in a variety of disorders, including loss of the ability to read or write. These disorders are discussed with the other language disorders in Chapter 8.

Damage restricted to the parietal lobe itself usually impairs a person's ability to draw. When the left parietal lobe is damaged, the primary deficit seems to be in the person's ability to make his or her hand go where it should. In contrast, the primary deficit produced by damage to the right parietal lobe is perceptual; the person can analyze the picture into its constituent parts but has trouble integrating these parts into a consistent whole.

Figure 2.20 shows two drawings of a bicycle by patients who both had suffered damage to one parietal lobe. The drawing on the left, by a person with left parietal lobe damage, is in relatively good proportion, but it is clumsily

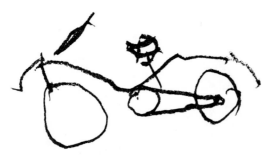

FIGURE 2.20

Drawing of a bicycle by patients with damage to the left hemisphere (left) and the right hemisphere (right). (From Lezak, M.D. *Neuropsychological Assessment*. New York: Oxford University Press, 1976.)

drawn, as if it were done by a young child. The drawing lacks detail. (See Figure 2.20, left.) In contrast, the drawing on the right, by the patient with right parietal lobe damage, is smoothly executed and shows good detail, but the parts are not all placed appropriately. (See Figure 2.20, right.)

There is another peculiarity in the right-hand drawing. Look at the drawing again to see whether you notice it.

The patient with right parietal lobe damage exhibited a common symptom of this disorder: **sensory neglect.** He did not attempt to draw the spokes in the left part of the wheels or the teeth on the left half of the gear around the pedals. People with damage to the right parietal lobe tend not to notice objects that are located toward their left, and they neglect the left side of

objects they are attending to. For example, a person with such damage who is given a pancake for breakfast may eat only the right half, ignoring the portion on the left half of the plate. The spokes are missing from the drawing of the bicycle because the patient was not even aware of the existence of the left sides of the wheels. Figure 2.21 shows this phenomenon even more graphically; this picture of a clock was drawn by a person who had sustained damage to the right parietal lobe. (See Figure 2.21.)

Sometimes people with damage to the right parietal lobe even fail to be aware of the left side of their own body. For example, a person might dress only one half of the body, putting a shirt or coat on only the right arm. A man might shave only the right side of his face. If someone calls the person's attention to his or her left arm, the person will see it and recognize it as an arm but may say it belongs to someone else.

Most neurologists and neuropsychologists believe that the left parietal lobe plays an important role in our ability to keep track of the location of the moving parts of our own body, whereas the right parietal lobe helps us keep track of the space around us. People with right parietal lobe damage usually have difficulty with tasks related to space, such as reading a map. People with left parietal lobe damage usually have difficulty with parts of their body; for example, when asked to point to their elbow, they may actually point to their shoulder.

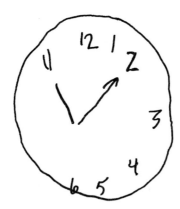

FIGURE 2.21

Drawing of a clock by a patient with damage to the right parietal lobe. (From Kaplan, E., and Velis, D.C. *The Neuropsychology of 10 after 11.* Paper presented at the International Neuropsychological Society Annual Meeting, 1983.)

Frontal Lobe

The principal function of the frontal lobe is motor activity; the primary motor cortex is located in the back of the frontal lobe, just ahead of the central fissure. (See Figure 2.22.) However, the frontal lobe does much more. Its functions seem to be related to planning, changing strategies, self-awareness, attention to emotionally related stimuli, and the spontaneity of behavior.

For many years, neurologists and anatomists thought the frontal lobes were the "seat of the human intellect." After all, they are by far the largest lobes of the cerebral cortex, and they are proportionately larger in humans than in any other species. Because we regard ourselves as the most intelligent species of animal, the conclusion that the frontal lobes are responsible for our intellectual capacities seems reasonable.

This conclusion is wrong. Damage to the frontal lobes—even very extensive damage—does not make a person stupid. The effects of frontal lobe damage are severe, but they cannot be characterized as intellectual deterioration. Many studies have shown that if a person with frontal lobe damage can be properly motivated, the person will often perform just as well on standard intelligence tasks as before the brain damage occurred. Thus, the ability to think and reason is not dependent on the frontal cortex.

The general deficits produced by destruction of the front part of the frontal lobes are the following: (1) *slowing* of thoughts and behavior, (2) *perseveration* (that is, continuing with a strategy that used to work even though it no longer does), (3) *loss of self awareness* and changes in emotional reactions, and (4) *deficiencies in planning*. In addition, damage to a particular region of the posterior right frontal

lobe leads to a speech disorder, and damage to the primary motor cortex, or to the motor association cortex located just adjacent to it, leads to problems in the control of movements.

Except for speech functions (discussed in Chapter 8), the association cortex of the frontal lobes shows less of a right-left difference in function than any other region of association cortex. A person with extensive frontal lobe damage shows a great deal of behavioral inertia; he or she may sit still, staring vacantly into the distance. In addition, various reflexes that are otherwise seen only in infants are easily triggered. These include sucking on an object placed near the mouth and tightly grasping an object placed against the palm. Presumably the frontal lobes in normal adults suppress these responses, which are produced by neural circuits located in the depths of the brain.

Loss of spontaneity also accompanies frontal lobe damage. When a person with such damage is asked to say or write as many words as possible, he or she will have great difficulty coming up with more than a few, even though there is no problem in understanding words or identifying objects by name. In addition to this loss of spontaneity, patients with this disorder have difficulty changing strategies. If given a task to solve, they may solve it readily, but they fail to abandon this strategy and learn a new one if the problem is changed (that is, they show perseveration).

People with damaged frontal lobes often have rather bland personalities. They react with indifference to events that would normally be expected to affect them emotionally. For example, they may show no signs of distress at the death of a close relative, even though they obviously understand what has happened. They have little insight into their own problems and are uncritical of their performance on various tasks. They are even indifferent to pain, although they may report that they feel the pain just as much as they did before the damage occurred.

In terms of daily living, the most important consequences of damage to the frontal lobes are probably lack of foresight and difficulty in planning. A person with frontal lobe damage might perform fairly well on a test of intelligence but be unable to hold a job. Presumably, planning is related to the general motor functions of the region in front of the central fissure. Just as we can use the occipital, temporal, and

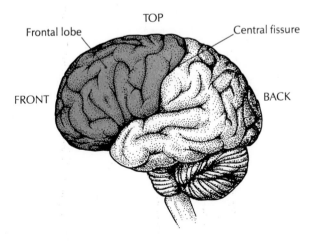

FIGURE 2.22

The frontal lobe.

parietal regions of the brain to imagine something we have perceived, we can use the frontal region to imagine something we might do. Perhaps we test various possible actions by imagining ourselves doing them and guessing what the consequences of these actions might be. When people's frontal lobes are damaged, they often do things or say things that have unfavorable consequences because their ability to plan their actions is lost.

■ What are the functions of the hypothalamus?
■ What are the functions of the midbrain, pons, medulla, and reticular formation?
■ How is lateralization of brain functions involved in behavior?
■ What are the functions of the occipital lobe, temporal lobe, parietal lobe, and frontal lobe?

NEURONS

A tour of the brain and central nervous system gives a "map" of where some of the critical behavioral functions may take place, though the limited state of our knowledge makes this a very crude overview diagram. In fact, understanding where and how our behavior is regulated is not a simple matter of "filling in" gaps in a map; it is more like trying to trace incredibly complex possible relationships in a wiring network in terms of very small-scale electric impulses and chemical processes. At the most basic level of the wiring system, physiological psychologists know a great deal about the "building block" elements of the nervous system; from this they can try to learn more about how the whole system seems to work—or to get short-circuited, as we shall see in the last section of this chapter.

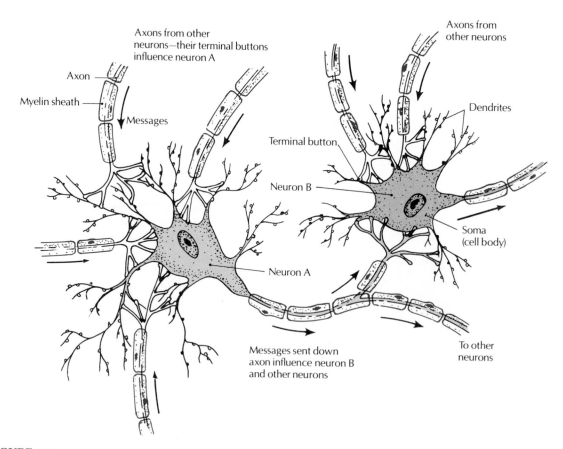

FIGURE 2.23

Synapses between several neurons. (Redrawn from Carlson, N.R. *Physiology of Behavior,* 3rd ed. Boston: Allyn and Bacon, 1986.)

Structure

Neurons, or nerve cells, are the elements of the nervous system that bring sensory information to the brain, store memories, reach decisions, and control the activity of the muscles. A neuron is shown in Figure 2.23. It has four principal parts.

1. The **soma,** or cell body, is the largest part of the neuron and contains the mechanisms that control the metabolism and maintenance of the cell. The soma also receives messages from other neurons. (See Figure 2.23.)

2. The **dendrites,** or treelike growths attached to the soma, function principally to receive messages from other neurons. They transmit the information that they receive down their "trunks" to the soma. (See Figure 2.23.)

3. The **axon** carries messages away from the soma toward the cells with which the neuron communicates. An axon is usually much longer than the illustration shows—up to tens of thousands of times longer than the diameter of its soma. (See Figure 2.23.) The message carried by the axon involves an electrical current, but it does not travel down the axon the way electricity travels through a wire. For one thing, electricity travels through a wire at the rate of 186,000 miles per second (the speed of light), or almost 300 million meters per second.

A useful analogy in understanding the nature of the message carried by the axon is that of a fuse used for explosives. When one end of such a fuse is lit, the flame travels to the opposite end, where the explosive is located. Similarly, when an axon is stimulated at one end, it sends an electrical message called the **action potential** down to the other end. (Of course, there is no explosion at the end.) Unlike an explosive fuse, the axon is reusable; messages can be sent down it repeatedly.

4. The **terminal buttons** are located at the ends of the "twigs" that branch off the axons. (See Figure 2.23.) Terminal buttons secrete a chemical called a **transmitter substance** whenever an action potential is sent to them down the axon. The transmitter substance affects the activity of the other cells with which the neuron communicates. Thus, the message is conveyed from one neuron to another (or from a neuron to a muscle or gland) by a chemical.

Most drugs that affect the nervous system (and hence alter a person's behavior) do so by affecting these chemical transmissions of messages from cell to cell.

Many axons, especially long ones, are insulated with a substance called *myelin.* The white matter on the outer part of the spinal cord and beneath the cerebral cortex gets its color from the **myelin sheaths** around the axons that travel through these areas. Myelin, part protein and part fat, is produced by special cells that individually wrap themselves around segments of the axon, leaving small bare patches of the axon between them. (See Figure 2.23.) The principal function of myelin is to insulate axons from each other and prevent the scrambling of messages. Its importance is illustrated by the effects of multiple sclerosis, in which a loss of myelin produces disturbances in sensory functions and motor control.

Synapses

Neurons communicate by means of **synapses.** A synapse is the conjunction of a terminal button of one neuron with the somatic or dendritic

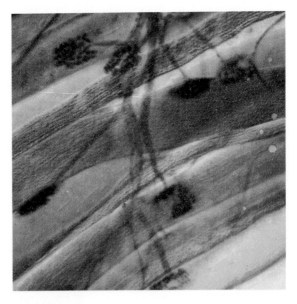

FIGURE 2.24

A photograph taken through a microscope of individual muscle fibers (running horizontally) and individual axons (thin dark lines) that serve them. The synapses the axons make with the muscle fibers appear as grapelike clusters.

membrane of another. (See Figure 2.23.) There are many terminal buttons forming synapses with a single neuron, and this neuron in turn forms synapses with many other neurons. The drawing is considerably simplified; an individual neuron can have tens of thousands of synapses on it.

Figures 2.24 (page 65) and 2.25 illustrate the relation between a **motor neuron** and a muscle. A motor neuron is one that forms synapses with a muscle. When its axon transmits a message, all the muscle fibers with which it forms synapses contract with a brief twitch. A muscle consists of thousands of individual muscle fibers. It is controlled by a large number of motor neurons, each of which forms synapses with different groups of muscle fibers. The strength of a muscular contraction, then, depends on the number of motor neurons whose axons are transmitting messages at a given time.

Effects of Synaptic Transmission

There are basically two types of synapses: **excitatory synapses** and **inhibitory synapses.** Excitatory synapses do just what their name implies. When they are activated by an action potential, they release a transmitter substance that excites the neurons upon which they synapse. The effect of this excitation is to make it more likely that these neurons (called **postsyn-** aptic neurons) will "fire," that is, send an action potential down their axons. (The neuron that synapses with—sends messages to—the postsynaptic neuron is called the **presynaptic neuron.**)

Inhibitory synapses do just the opposite. When they are activated, they lower the probability that the axon of the postsynaptic neuron will fire. Thus, the rate at which a particular axon fires is determined by the activity of the synaptic inputs to the dendrites and soma of the cell. If the excitatory synapses are more active, the axon will fire at a high rate. If the inhibitory synapses are more active, it will fire at a low rate, or perhaps not at all. (See Figure 2.26.)

The contest between excitatory and inhibitory synapses is the neural mechanism that takes place during decision making. The importance of this contest will be demonstrated later in the discussion of reflexes.

Mechanisms of Synaptic Transmission

Terminal buttons excite or inhibit postsynaptic neurons by releasing transmitter substances. These chemicals are stored within small round containers called **synaptic vesicles.** (*Vesicle* means "small sac.") Figure 2.27 shows the sequence by which the vesicles release their transmitter substances.

FIGURE 2.25

Synapses between terminal buttons of the axon of a motor neuron and a muscle.

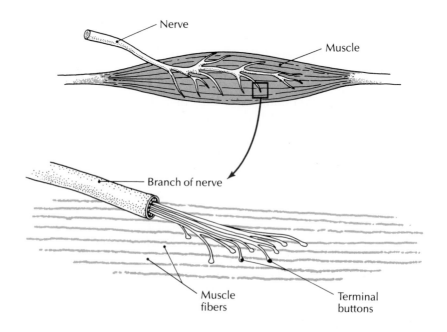

Nerve

Muscle

Branch of nerve

Muscle fibers

Terminal buttons

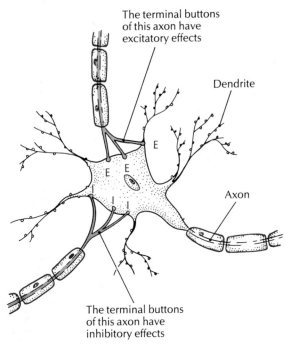

FIGURE 2.26

Synapses that excite (E) or inhibit (I) the postsynaptic neuron.

When an axon fires, the action potential travels to all its terminal buttons. The arrival of an action potential at a terminal button causes some of the synaptic vesicles located closest to the presynaptic membrane to attach and adhere to it, and then to break open, spilling their contents into the fluid-filled space between the terminal button and the membrane of the postsynaptic cell—the **synaptic cleft.** (See Figure 2.27.) The transmitter substance causes reactions in the postsynaptic neuron that either excite or inhibit it. These reactions are triggered by special submicroscopic protein molecules embedded in the postsynaptic membrane that are called **receptors.**

A molecule of transmitter substance acts upon a receptor like a key upon a lock. When a terminal button releases a transmitter substance, molecules find their way to the receptors and activate them. In turn, the receptors produce excitatory or inhibitory effects on the postsynaptic neuron. (See Figure 2.27.) Many drugs produce effects on behavior by stimulating or blocking postsynaptic receptors.

The excitation or inhibition produced by a synapse is brief; the effects soon pass away,

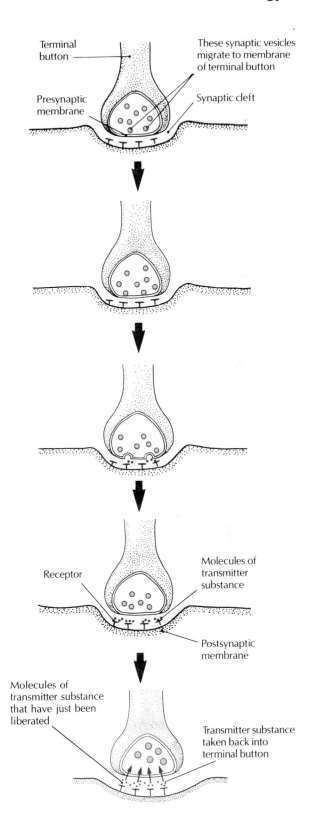

FIGURE 2.27

The release of a transmitter substance from a terminal button followed by re-uptake (*bottom*).

usually in a fraction of a second. The two mechanisms that terminate these effects are chemical deactivation and re-uptake. In chemical deactivation, the transmitter substance is actually destroyed by an enzyme. The more common process is **re-uptake.** Most transmitter substances are recycled by the terminal buttons through this mechanism. The chemical is released by the terminal button and is quickly taken up again, so that it has only a brief time to stimulate the postsynaptic receptors. (See Figure 2.27.) The transmitter substance is then reused; newly formed synaptic vesicles, manufactured in the terminal button, are filled with the recycled chemical. The rate at which the terminal button takes back the transmitter substance obviously determines how prolonged the effects of the chemical on the postsynaptic neuron will be. As we will see, some drugs affect the nervous system by altering the rate of re-uptake.

REFLEXES

The interconnections of the billions of neurons in our central nervous system provide us with the capacities for perception, decision making,

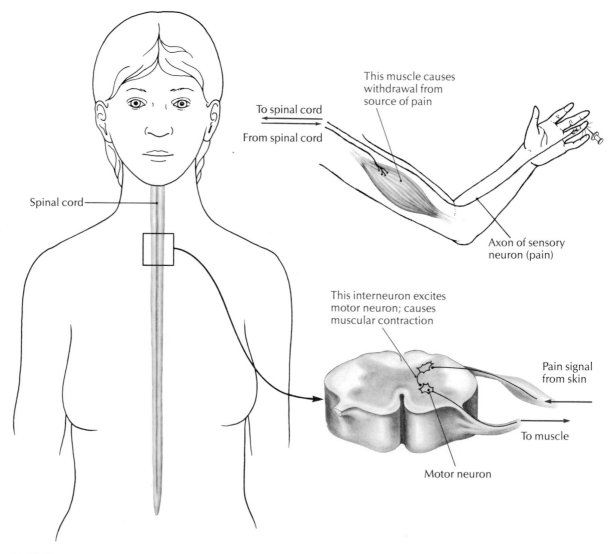

FIGURE 2.28

A schematic representation of the elements of a withdrawal reflex.

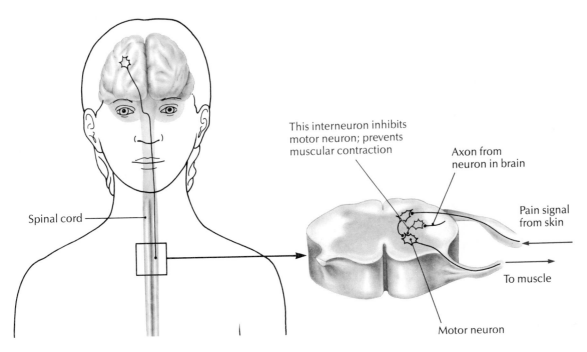

This interneuron inhibits motor neuron; prevents muscular contraction

Axon from neuron in brain

Spinal cord

Pain signal from skin

To muscle

Motor neuron

FIGURE 2.29

A schematic representation of a withdrawal reflex being inhibited by the brain.

memory, and action. Although it is impossible to draw a "neural wiring diagram" for such complex functions, we can do so for some of the simpler reflexes that are triggered by certain kinds of sensory stimuli. For example, when your finger is pricked by a pin, your hand withdraws. When your eye is touched, you close your eyes and draw your head back. When a baby's cheek is touched, it turns its mouth toward the object, and if the object is of the appropriate size and texture, the baby begins to suck. These activities occur quickly, without requiring thought. Their usefulness is obvious.

A simple withdrawal reflex, which is produced by a noxious stimulus (such as a pinprick), requires three types of neurons. **Sensory neurons** detect the noxious stimulus and convey this information to the spinal cord. **Interneurons** receive the sensory information and in turn stimulate the motor neurons that cause the appropriate muscle to contract. (See Figure 2.28.) The sequence is simple and straightforward. A noxious stimulus applied to the skin produces a burst of action potentials in the sensory neurons. Their axons fire, releasing an excitatory transmitter substance that stimulates the interneurons. This stimulation causes the

interneurons to fire, exciting motor neurons, which in turn cause the muscle fibers with which they form synapses to contract. (See Figure 2.28.)

The next example adds a bit of complexity to the circuit. Suppose you have removed a hot casserole from the oven. As you start over to the table to put it down, the heat begins to penetrate the rather thin potholders you are using. Because of the withdrawal reflex, this noxious stimulus excites the motor neurons that control the muscles that open your hands. And yet you manage to get the dish to the table without dropping it. How is this accomplished?

As we saw earlier, the activity of a neuron depends on the relative activity of the excitatory and inhibitory synapses on it. The hot object increases the activity of a number of excitatory synapses on the motor neurons that control the muscles that open your hands, but this excitation is counteracted by inhibition from another source—your brain. Figure 2.29 shows an axon from a neuron in the brain that forms a synapse with an interneuron, which in turn forms a synapse with a motor neuron that causes the hand to open. The effect of the interneuron is inhibitory; when this neuron is active

The activity of neurons in the brain can inhibit the withdrawal reflex.

its terminal buttons inhibit the firing of the motor neuron and thus prevent your hand from opening. This example illustrates the usefulness of the contest between excitation and inhibition; the activity of some neurons in the brain prevents the withdrawal reflex from causing you to drop the dish.

- How do neurons communicate by means of synapses?
- What two basic effects do synapses have on postsynaptic neurons?
- How does the process of synaptic transmission work?
- What is the basic circuit involved in a withdrawal reflex?

PHARMACOLOGY OF NEURONS

Although the action potential consists of an electrical charge, most of the important events that take place within the nervous system are chemical in nature. Communications between neurons, between sensory receptor and neuron, and between neuron and muscle take place chemically; a terminal button secretes a transmitter substance, which has an excitatory or inhibitory effect on another cell. There are many different kinds of transmitter substances in the brain, and various drugs affect their production or release, mimic their effects on the receptors, block these effects, or interfere with their re-uptake once they are released. Through these mechanisms, a drug can alter the perceptions, thoughts, and behaviors that are controlled by a particular transmitter substance. In this section we will study the ways in which drugs can affect the nervous system, and hence behavior.

Production of Transmitter Substances

Transmitter substances are produced by neurons from raw ingredients present in the fluid that bathes them. The production of some transmitter substances can be facilitated by administering the appropriate raw ingredient. Parkinson's disease, a serious motor disorder, is caused by the death of a particular kind of neuron located in a motor system in the depths of the brain. These neurons secrete a transmitter substance called **dopamine.** They produce dopamine from L-DOPA, an amino acid. When a person with Parkinson's disease is given some L-DOPA, his or her surviving dopamine-secreting neurons produce more dopamine than usual and hence are able to release more of the transmitter substance. The increased release of dopamine partially compensates for the loss of dopamine-secreting neurons, thus reducing the symptoms of Parkinson's disease.

Release of Transmitter Substances

Some drugs cause the terminal buttons to release their transmitter substance; thus these drugs duplicate the effect of firing the axons to which the terminal buttons are attached. Other drugs prevent the terminal buttons from releasing their transmitter substance, even when the axon fires. The effects of most of these drugs are more or less specific to one transmitter substance. Therefore, because different classes of

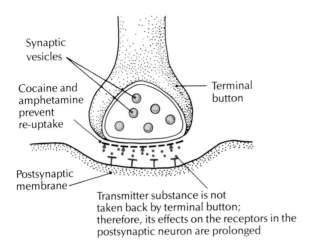

FIGURE 2.30

Cocaine and amphetamine prevent re-uptake of certain transmitter substances, thus prolonging their effect on the postsynaptic neuron.

neurons release different transmitter substances, only a selected set of neurons is affected by a drug that facilitates or inhibits the release of a particular transmitter substance. An example of a stimulating drug is the venom of the black widow spider, which causes the release of **acetylcholine,** an important transmitter substance. In contrast, botulinum toxin, a poison that is sometimes present in improperly canned food, completely blocks the release of acetylcholine. An extremely small amount— less than one millionth of a gram—can kill a person.

Postsynaptic Receptors

Transmitter substances produce their effects by stimulating postsynaptic receptors, which in turn excite or inhibit the postsynaptic neurons. Some drugs duplicate the effects of particular transmitter substances by directly stimulating particular kinds of receptors. For example, nicotine stimulates one class of acetylcholine receptors (there are two different kinds) and thus serves as a potent poison. Other drugs block receptors, making them inaccessible to the transmitter substance and thus inhibiting synaptic transmission. For example, curare is a poison that was discovered by South American Indians, who use it on the darts of their blowguns. This drug blocks the same class of acetyl-

choline receptors that nicotine stimulates, many of which are located on muscles. The curare prevents synaptic transmission in muscles, causing paralysis. The victim is unable to breathe and consequently suffocates.

Some medically useful chemicals work by blocking receptors. For example, chlorpromazine alleviates the symptoms of a mental disorder called *schizophrenia*, apparently by blocking receptors in the brain that are normally stimulated by dopamine. (Chlorpromazine and related drugs are discussed in more detail in Chapters 16 and 17.)

Inhibition of Re-Uptake

Most transmitter substances are taken back into the terminal buttons soon after they are released. Re-uptake thus keeps the effects of synaptic transmission brief. Some drugs inhibit the process of re-uptake so that molecules of the transmitter substance remain in the synaptic cleft for a longer time and continue to stimulate the postsynaptic receptors. Therefore, inhibition of re-uptake *increases* the effect of the transmitter substance. The excitatory effects of cocaine and amphetamine are produced by their ability to inhibit the re-uptake of certain transmitter substances, including dopamine. (See Figure 2.30.)

POPULAR DRUGS

A number of drugs are taken not for any therapeutic use but rather for the pleasurable effects they give the user. We might call them "recreational drugs," although people who become addicted to them and have to organize their lives around procuring them can hardly be said to be having fun.

This section explains only the pharmacological effects of these drugs on the nervous system, not why a person becomes an addict. First, I will describe the effects of some stimulant drugs—cocaine and amphetamine. Another much-used stimulant, caffeine, is less potent pharmacologically than the others. Although the nicotine in tobacco is very potent as a stimulant, the user receives only a small dose.

Len Bias, star University of Maryland basketball player, was killed by an overdose of cocaine.

Then, I will describe drugs that generally depress the system—alcohol and barbiturates—as well as the opiates, heroin, and morphine.

Stimulants

Many drugs stimulate the nervous system; the ones most frequently used recreationally are amphetamine and cocaine. These drugs have remarkably similar effects: they facilitate the release and retard the re-uptake of two transmitter substances, dopamine (which I have already discussed) and **norepinephrine** (a related

substance). Thus, they increase the activity of dopamine-secreting and norepinephrine-secreting synapses. In addition, cocaine is a potent local anesthetic that blocks the transmission of action potentials in axons. It is still the drug of choice for anesthesia of the eye and its associated membranes during surgery. Cocaine's effect on axons, which occurs only at very high concentrations, is not related to its effect on synapses.

Cocaine is usually injected, smoked, or sniffed into the mucous membranes of the nasal passages. The initial effects are an intense euphoria and a feeling of abundant energy. The euphoria is probably produced by the effects of the drug on dopamine, and the increased energy by its effects on norepinephrine. As the high wears off, the user typically takes another dose of the drug. After a while, a high becomes more difficult to sustain, and the side effects of the drug (muscular pain, severe teeth-grinding, tremors, and feelings of paranoia) intensify. The user then stops taking the drug and "crashes," sleeping for a day or so. Sometimes, the user will take a depressant drug, such as alcohol or heroin, to take the edge off the unpleasant feelings the drug has produced. Upon awakening, the user feels depressed and anxious and often begins to take the drug again to eliminate these symptoms and to regain the pleasurable high.

Cocaine is an intensely reinforcing and strongly addictive drug. It appears to activate neural circuits in the brain that are normally triggered by reinforcing events such as eating or sexual contact; thus, the drug artificially provides some of the pleasurable aspects of these activities. Around the turn of the century, cocaine was available from the corner drugstore, without prescription. In fact, Sigmund Freud was a user for a while; he praised the delights of this drug until some users began to die from its effects.

Long-term, heavy use of cocaine and amphetamine has serious effects; chronic, heavy users suffer psychotic reactions (symptoms of mental disorders) that often cannot be distinguished from true schizophrenia. (Chapter 16 discusses the physiology of schizophrenia, including its relation to cocaine or amphetamine psychosis.) The availability of a particularly potent form of cocaine ("crack") has increased the risk of addiction and has caused several deaths. In high doses (or even in moderate doses, in suscepti-ble individuals), cocaine can destabilize the rhythm of the heartbeat, causing heart failure. The potential for addiction and the serious side-effects of crack make it one of the most dangerous drugs available.

Depressants

Alcohol

Although we know that alcohol depresses neu-rons, especially those in the cerebral cortex, we do not really know how it does so. Alcohol is a powerful drug; most people experience intoxi-cation with a blood alcohol content of approxi-mately 0.12 percent, which is equal to five 1.5-ounce shots of 80-proof (40 percent) alcohol. However, there are large individual differences in people's susceptibility to alcohol.

Use of alcohol unquestionably can produce addiction. A person who abruptly stops drink-ing after severe and prolonged intoxication will suffer profound withdrawal symptoms: fevers, restlessness, nausea, and the hallucinations of *delirium tremens*. These effects can be very severe; sometimes they even cause death. Other depressants, such as tranquilizers, can be ad-ministered to ease withdrawal from alcohol. Unlike a heroin addict, who can safely take an amount of the drug that would kill someone who does not use it, chronic alcoholics do not have a higher tolerance than nonaddicts; that is, they cannot safely tolerate larger doses of alcohol than nonaddicts can.

When used in moderate doses, alcohol is often regarded as a stimulant. Most of this ef-fect probably results from depression of brain mechanisms that normally inhibit behavior. When released from this inhibition, many peo-ple do and say things they normally would not. (How many people recall with regret what they did or said at a party the previous evening?)

Prolonged and heavy use of alcohol can have disastrous effects. Chronic alcoholics usually lack a well-balanced diet because they con-sume many hundreds of calories from alcohol each day and consequently eat less food. Fur-thermore, alcohol interferes with absorption of B vitamins from the intestinal tract. These two effects of alcohol consumption increase the

likelihood of suffering a vitamin deficiency. The result of a prolonged vitamin B deficiency is brain damage; in particular, many chronic alcoholics suffer from a severe memory deficit. For example, institutionalized patients suffer-ing from such a memory deficit cannot find their way around the grounds without assist-ance, and upon questioning may report that they arrived at the institution only a few days before, while in fact they have been there for many years.

Barbiturates, Tranquilizers, and Aromatic Solvents

Other drugs also depress the central nervous system. Barbiturates (sometimes used in sleep-ing pills) and aromatic solvents (such as the volatile constituents of substances like airplane glue and paint thinner) are similar in effect to alcohol. Tranquilizers vary in their specific mode of action, but their general effect is to depress the activity of neurons. They are gener-ally safer than the other depressants—few peo-ple die from tranquilizer overdose.

When two or more depressant drugs are taken together, the effects are additive; a nonle-thal dose of alcohol and a nonlethal dose of bar-biturates, taken together, can kill. Chronic bar-biturate addicts suffer withdrawal symptoms when they cease taking the drug, and the reac-tion can be severe. Chronic use of barbiturates is less likely to produce long-term damage than chronic use of alcohol, because no calories are supplied by the drug, so that the addict is more likely to maintain a well-balanced diet.

Opiates

Opium, derived from a sticky resin produced by the opium poppy, has been eaten and smoked for centuries. Morphine, one of the nat-urally occurring ingredients of opium, is some-times used as a painkiller but has largely been supplanted by synthetic opiates. Heroin, a compound produced from morphine, is the most commonly abused opiate.

Recently, the effects of opiates have become better understood. Researchers have discov-ered the presence of **opiate receptors,** similar to the postsynaptic receptors that respond to transmitter substances, on neurons in the brain.

While some people use opiates to dim their awareness of pain, others are willing to endure pain if they believe something worthwhile is being accomplished. Heat and humidity were so severe after this race that a fire truck was sent to hose down the runners.

These receptors exist because the brain produces its own opiates, called **endorphins,** or "inner morphines." During times of stress or during sexual activity, fighting, or other behaviors that are important to species survival, specialized neurons release endorphins into the fluid that bathes the cells of the brain. The endorphins then diffuse throughout the brain and stimulate the opiate receptors. The effect of such stimulation is to produce **analgesia,** or lessening of pain. This lessening of pain undoubtedly serves to prevent an animal from running away if it is hurt during fighting or mating. The analgesic effect appears to be mediated principally by neurons in the midbrain, which contain many opiate receptors.

When injected into a vein, heroin and other opiates produce a "rush" that the user finds intensely pleasurable. So, too, do the endorphins, leading neuroscientists to speculate that these naturally produced chemicals are important in regulating mood.

When opiates are used over a period of time, physiological tolerance and addiction occur; that is, progressively more of the drug must be injected to produce the rush, and withdrawal symptoms occur when the chronic user stops taking the drug. The chief symptoms of opiate withdrawal are nausea, abdominal pain (cramps), and restlessness. In North America today, the symptoms of opiate withdrawal are likely to be much less severe than they were twenty-five or thirty years ago, because street heroin nowadays is usually no stronger than 2 percent pure. An addict with a typical eight-to-ten-bag-per-day habit simply does not take enough of the drug to cause dangerously severe withdrawal symptoms. Thus, addicts are "protected" from more severe symptoms by high price and low quality.

Authoritative sources (such as Hofmann, 1975) state that the symptoms of opiate withdrawal are often no worse than those of a severe cold. In fact, addicts who are undergoing medically supervised withdrawal may exaggerate their symptoms in order to obtain a larger dose of the drug being used to ease their symptoms. When the cost of their habit becomes too high, many addicts voluntarily go "cold turkey" for several days so they can obtain a high from smaller, cheaper doses. Several days of abdominal cramps, retching, and nausea cannot be called pleasant, but withdrawal from opiates is less traumatic than the popular media imply.

Chronic use of opiates is unlikely to produce long-term damage that can be attributed *directly* to the drug. For example, addicted dentists and physicians (who can obtain pure drugs) can usually manage to continue their practice. However, the majority of addicts do not observe aseptic techniques when they inject the drug into a vein. As a result, heroin addicts have a high incidence of hepatitis (a liver disease), endocarditis (inflammation of the membrane that lines the interior of the heart), and other infectious diseases. Furthermore, the illicit manufacturers and distributors of heroin take little care in its production and dilution. Quinine, milk sugar, and talc are commonly used to "cut" (dilute) the drug, and many deaths that are attributed to overdose probably occur because of a reaction to impure adulterants.

In addition to drugs that block postsynaptic receptors and hence inhibit synaptic transmission, there are drugs that block opiate receptors. These drugs, called **opiate antagonists,** have saved many lives in the emergency room, where they are used to treat drug overdoses. However, they are not of much use in controlling heroin addiction itself. The most effective of these drugs (naloxone) must be injected, and none of the opiate antagonists is effective for more than a few minutes. Furthermore, they are expensive and produce varying degrees of unpleasant side effects. The best hope in preventing addiction is to determine the factors that predispose an individual to use drugs and then develop ways to help this type of individual avoid their use.

■ What are the four basic mechanisms by which drugs may alter normal synaptic activity?
■ What are the physiological and behavioral effects of the major stimulant drugs, cocaine and amphetamine?
■ What are the physiological processes and behavioral effects of opiates?

CHAPTER SUMMARY

1. One basis for the study of human behavior is an understanding of the structure of the brain and its functions. Neuropsychologists study people who have sustained brain damage, correlating the person's behavioral deficits with the location of the lesion, usually determined by a CAT scan. Physiological psychologists experiment on the brains of animals to study the effects of lesions or electrical stimuli on brain functions and on behavior.

2. The central nervous system (brain and spinal cord) is protected by heavy bones and by the meninges. In addition, the brain floats in cerebrospinal fluid. The peripheral nervous system includes the spinal nerves and cranial nerves. The cerebral hemispheres are wrinkled by fissures and gyri and are covered by the cerebral cortex.

3. Information from our senses is received and processed by our brain along different sensory pathways. Sensory receptors are stimulated by the sight, sound, taste, smell, or touch of an object. This stimulation is transmitted through nerve fibers in the optic or auditory nerves (two pairs of the twelve pairs of cranial nerves) or by spinal nerves to the spinal cord in the case of the somatosenses (touch, pain, temperature), then to the thalamus, and finally to the primary visual, auditory, gustatory, or somatosensory cortex. Smell is the one sense that is not relayed through the thalamus to the brain but instead through the olfactory nerves (another pair of cranial nerves) and then to various locations in depths of the brain as well as directly to the cerebral cortex.

4. The integration of all the information from our senses is accomplished by connections between the regions of the cerebral cortex that analyze the individual sensory components.

5. Movement is controlled by the primary motor cortex. Commands are sent from the motor association cortex in the frontal lobe. One cerebellum, beneath the back part of the cerebral hemispheres, receives information from various motor systems of the brain and provides an important degree of coordination among them, especially in balance and in rapid, skilled movements.

6. As well as sensory and motor activities, two major functions are directed by the hypothalamus. These are homeostasis (the maintenance of physiological variables such as temperature, concentration of fluids, and the amount of nutrients stored in the body) and control of species-typical behavior (such as eating, drinking, fighting, courting and mating, and the care of offspring). The hypothalamus controls the pituitary gland, which regulates the activity of the rest of the endocrine glands. It also controls much of the activity of the autonomic nervous system, consisting of the sympathetic branch, which directs activities involving the expenditure of energy, and the parasympathetic branch, which controls quiet activities such as digestion.

7. The brain stem consists of a midbrain (with important structures of the motor system and, with the hypothalamus, controls the execution of species-typical behavioral movements), the pons (containing circuits of nerve cells with functions related to sleeping and alertness, attention, and movement), and the medulla (controls the vital functions of heart rate, blood pressure, and respiration). The reticular formation of the brain stem, a tangle of nerve cells and fibers, controls attention and, in conjunction with nerve cells located in the cerebral hemispheres, regulates our wakefulness and sleep.

8. The central fissure divides the cerebral cortex into two major regions. The frontal lobes are concerned with motor functions, including planning and formulation of strategies. The three lobes behind the central fissure are generally concerned with sensation: somatosenses in the parietal lobe, vision in the occipital lobe, and audition in the temporal lobe. The other functions of these lobes are related to these sensory processes; for example, the parietal lobe is concerned with perception of space as well as knowledge about the body.

9. The right and left hemispheres are somewhat specialized. The left hemisphere is mostly concerned with details of perception and with events that occur one after the other, such as the series of sounds that constitute speech. The right hemisphere is mostly concerned with the general form and shape of things, such as putting isolated elements together to form a whole.

10. The basic element of the nervous system is the neuron, with its soma, dendrites, axon, and terminal buttons. One neuron communicates with another (or with muscle or gland cells) by means of synapses. A synapse is the junction of the terminal button of the presynaptic neuron with the membrane of the postsynaptic neuron. This communication is chemical in nature; when an action potential travels down an axon, it causes a transmitter substance to be released from synaptic vesicles located in the terminal buttons. Molecules of the transmitter substance stimulate the receptors on the postsynaptic neuron; the receptors then either excite or inhibit the firing of the postsynaptic neuron. The combined effects of excitatory and inhibitory synapses on a particular neuron determine its rate of firing. The reflex is the simplest element of behavior, and it serves to illustrate the contest between excitation and inhibition.

11. The nervous system contains neurons that release a wide variety of transmitter substances, many of which participate in several different functions. For example, acetylcholine is involved in memory and in control of muscles, dopamine is involved in motor control and in mechanisms of reward (and hence produces pleasurable feelings), and norepinephrine is involved in alertness and attentiveness.

12. Drugs can facilitate or interfere with synaptic activity. Facilitators include drugs that cause the release of a transmitter substance itself (such as nicotine), drugs that cause the release of a transmitter substance (such as the venom of the black widow spider), drugs that provide the raw material out of which transmitter substances are produced (such as L-DOPA, used to treat Parkinson's disease), and drugs that inhibit the re-uptake of a transmitter substance (such as amphetamine and cocaine). Drugs that interfere with synaptic activity include those that block receptors (such as curare, which paralyzes the muscles), and those that inhibit the release of a transmitter substance (such as botulinum toxin).

13. Many chemicals found in nature have pleasurable effects, and many more have been synthesized in the laboratory. Alcohol, barbiturates, tranquilizers, and aromatic solvents depress the activity of the central nervous system, whereas amphetamine and cocaine stimulate it. The opiates duplicate the effects of chemicals the brain itself produces, causing analgesia and an intensely enjoyable "rush." Probably, the brain's own opiates (the endorphins) are involved in mood as well as in reducing pain while the animal engages in important behaviors such as fighting and mating.

KEY TERMS

acetylcholine A transmitter substance that is released by the terminal buttons of some neurons in the brain and peripheral nervous system. Acetylcholine is the transmitter substance that causes muscles to contract, and acetylcholine-secreting neurons in the brain appear to be involved in memory.

action potential A brief electrochemical event that is carried by an axon from the cell body of the neuron to its terminal buttons, which in turn release a transmitter substance, stimulating or inhibiting the neurons with which the terminal buttons form synapses.

analgesia Literally, complete loss of the sensation of pain, but the term usually refers to partial loss.

autonomic nervous system The part of the nervous system that controls the internal organs, blood vessels, sweat glands, and endocrine glands.

axon A long, thin process of a neuron that divides into a few or many branches, ending in terminal buttons. See also *action potential.*

brain stem The "stem" of the brain, including the medulla, pons, midbrain, and diencephalon (thalamus and hypothalamus). The cerebral hemispheres and cerebellum are not part of the brain stem.

central fissure Dividing line between the front part of the cerebral cortex and the posterior regions.

central nervous system The brain and spinal cord.

cerebellum A pair of hemispheres resembling the cerebral hemispheres but much smaller and lying beneath and in back of them; controls posture and movements, especially rapid ones.

cerebral cortex The outer layer of the cerebral hemispheres of the brain. Specialized areas include the primary sensory and motor cortex, the association cortex, and regions that are necessary for speech comprehension and production.

cerebral hemispheres Two large masses, left and right, of the cerebrum.

cerebrospinal fluid (CSF) A fluid similar to blood plasma that fills the hollow ventricles of the brain and in which the brain and spinal cord float.

computerized axial tomography or **CAT scanner** A device that uses a special X-ray machine and a computer to produce images of the brain that appear as slices taken parallel to the top of the skull.

cranial nerve One of twelve pairs of nerves that are directly attached to the brain.

dendrite A treelike part of a neuron on which the terminal buttons of other neurons form synapses.

dopamine A transmitter substance that is released by the terminal buttons of some neurons in the brain. Dopamine is apparently important in reinforcement and control of movement. Dopamine-secreting neurons may be involved in producing schizophrenia.

endocrine gland   A gland that secretes a hormone into the blood supply; for example, the adrenal gland and pituitary gland.

endorphin   A chemical secreted by neurons in the brain that produces analgesia and has reinforcing effects. The action of these chemicals is simulated by opiates such as morphine and heroin.

excitatory synapse   A synapse that excites the post-synaptic neuron, making it fire at a faster rate.

fissure   A large groove in the surface of a cerebral hemisphere.

frontal lobe   The front portion of the cerebral cortex, including Broca's speech area and the motor cortex. Damage impairs movement, planning, and flexibility in behavioral strategies.

gray matter   The portions of the central nervous system that are abundant in cell bodies of neurons rather than axons. See also *white matter*.

gyrus   A bulge in the surface of the cerebral hemispheres; located between adjacent grooves (fissures or sulci).

homeostasis   The process by which important physiological characteristics (such as body temperature and blood pressure) are regulated so that they remain at their optimum level.

hypothalamus   A region of the brain located just above the pituitary gland; controls the autonomic nervous system and many behaviors related to regulation and survival, such as eating, drinking, fighting, shivering, and sweating.

inhibitory synapse   A synapse that inhibits the post-synaptic neuron, making it fire at a slower rate.

interneuron   Neuron that receives sensory information and stimulates motor neurons.

medulla   The part of the brain stem that attaches to the spinal cord; contains part of the reticular formation and neural circuits that control respiration, heart rate, blood pressure, and other vital functions.

meninges   A set of three membranes that en-

case the central nervous system. (Singular is meninx.)

midbrain   Part of the brain stem just behind the diencephalon (thalamus and hypothalamus) and just above the pons.

motor association cortex   Frontal section of the cerebral cortex involved in planning and executing movement.

motor neuron   A neuron whose terminal buttons form synapses with muscle fibers. When an action potential travels down its axon, the associated muscle fibers will twitch.

myelin sheath   The insulating material that encases most large axons in the nervous system.

neurologist   A physician who treats disorders of the nervous system.

neuropsychologists   Psychologists who study the nervous system and its influence on behavior.

neuron   The most important cell of the nervous system; consists of a cell body with dendrites, and an axon whose branches end in terminal buttons that synapse with muscle fibers, gland cells, or other neurons.

norepinephrine   A transmitter substance that is liberated by the terminal buttons of some neurons. In the brain it appears to play a role in arousal and control of REM sleep.

occipital lobe   The rearmost portion of the cerebral cortex; contains the primary visual cortex.

opiate antagonist   A drug that blocks opiate receptors, making them insensitive to opiates.

opiate receptor   A receptor on a neuron that is activated by opiates, including the natural endorphins.

parasympathetic branch   Part of the autonomic nervous system that controls quiet activity such as food digestion.

parietal lobe   The region of the cerebral cortex behind the frontal lobe and above the temporal lobe; contains the somatosensory cortex; is involved in spatial perception and memory for and planning of the execution of motor sequences.

peripheral nervous system   The cranial and spinal nerves and their associated structures; that part of the nervous system peripheral to the brain and spinal cord.

pituitary gland   An endocrine gland attached to the hypothalamus at the base of the brain.

pons   Large bulge in tthe brain stem, located below the midbrain.

postsynaptic neuron   A neuron with which the terminal buttons of another neuron forms synapses and that is excited or inhibited by that neuron.

presynaptic neuron   A neuron whose terminal buttons form synapses with and excite and inhibit another neuron.

primary auditory cortex   The region of the cerebral cortex that receives information directly from the auditory system; located in the temporal lobes.

primary motor cortex   The region of the cerebral cortex that directly controls the movements of the body; located in the back part of the frontal lobes.

primary somatosensory cortex   The region of the cerebral cortex that receives information directly from the somatosensory system (touch, pressure, vibration, pain, and temperature); located in the front part of the parietal lobes.

primary visual cortex   The cerebral cortex region that receives information directly from the visual system; located in the occipital lobes.

receptor   A special protein molecule located in the membrane of the postsynaptic neuron that responds to molecules of the transmitter substance. Receptors such as those that respond to opiates are sometimes found elsewhere on the surface of neurons.

reticular formation   A structure in the core of the brain stem that contains neurons important in the control of sleep, attention, arousal, and vital functions such as heart rate, respiration, and blood pressure.

re-uptake   The process by which a terminal button retrieves the molecules of transmitter substance that it has just released; terminates the effect of the transmitter substance on the receptors of the postsynaptic neuron.

sensory association cortex   Areas of the cerebral cortex that perform perceptual analyses of information received from the primary sensory cortex; memories related to information are stored here.

sensory neglect   A neurological disturbance in which a person fails to notice or pay attention to stimuli that he or she is physically able to perceive; often caused by damage to the parietal lobe in the right hemisphere.

sensory neuron   Detects various stimuli and conveys this information to the spinal cord.

soma   Cell body of the neuron; contains mechanisms that control metabolism and maintenance of the cell.

species-typical behavior   A behavior that is seen in all or most members of a species, such as nest-building, special food-getting behaviors, or reproductive behaviors.

spinal nerve   A nerve that is attached to the spinal cord.

sympathetic branch   Part of the autonomic nervous system that directs activities involving the expenditure of energy.

synapse   The junction between the terminal button of one neuron and the membrane of the postsynaptic neuron, which contains receptors that respond to the transmitter substance released by the terminal button.

synaptic cleft   The space between a terminal button and the membrane of the postsynaptic neuron.

synaptic vesicle   A submicroscopic sac located in a terminal button and containing the transmitter substance.

temporal lobe   The portion of the cerebral cortex below the frontal and parietal lobes and containing the auditory cortex. Damage produces deficits in audition, speech perception and production, sexual behavior, visual perception and/or social behaviors.

terminal button   Rounded swelling at the end of the axon of a neuron; releases transmitter substance. See also *action potential*.

thalamus   A region of the brain near the center of the cerebral hemispheres. All sensory information except smell is sent to the thalamus and then relayed to the cerebral cortex.

transmitter substance   A chemical released by the terminal buttons that causes the postsynaptic neuron to be excited or inhibited. See also *action potential*.

ventricle   One of the hollow chambers in the brain that is filled with cerebrospinal fluid.

visual agnosia   The inability of a person who is not blind to recognize the identity or use of an object by means of vision; usually caused by damage to the brain.

white matter   The portions of the central nervous system that are abundant in axons rather than cell bodies of neurons. The color derives from the presence of the axons' myelin sheaths. See also *gray matter*.

Chapter 3

Sensation and Perception

All of our experiences come to us through our senses. Our feelings, our thoughts, and our actions are all evoked by our perceptions. Our sense organs tell us about the shapes, colors, sounds, smells, and movements of things in the world around us; they tell us about the texture, weight, and temperature of things near us; they tell us about the taste of things we eat or drink; they even tell us about the location and position of our own body. Our sense organs provide us with the pleasures of life: the sight of a beautiful sunset, the sound of our favorite music, the smell of a rose, the touch of a lover's hand. In a very real sense, the world for us is nothing more than what we can perceive.

But can we safely assume that each of us sees and hears the same thing? Is it possible we each pick up a unique and specialized view? We know that for some color-blind people the contrasting red and green signals of a stoplight do not exist as they do for others. All humans miss some of the high frequency sounds or light waves that can be picked up by other animals. The task of science has been to discover the many sensory phenomena that are widely shared, and these will be described in this chapter. Yet all of them have had to be described and confirmed by reference to an independent source. In this way the sensory psychologists were among the first to confront the problem of objectivity in a human science. What one person's senses may or may not detect had to be discovered by outside evidence, such as special measuring equipment or by observing the reactions of others.

But if we all share much the same sensory capacity, why do people seem to differ so much in the way they notice things? One reason is that our ability to receive information through the senses is very much affected by our past experience. Thus, because different people have different experiences, not everyone perceives the world the same way. Most of our perceptions involve *memories*: a new perception matches, to a certain extent, memories of previous experiences. Our eye gathers an image of a shape consisting of a complex arrangement of colors, and our brain perceives, say, a young woman with short brown hair and brown eyes wearing a white blouse and a blue skirt. We may never have seen her before, but because of our memories of what people look like, we clearly recognize the shape as that of another human being.

As you will see in this chapter, psychologists who study sensation and perception are confronted with two tasks: discovering the sensory phenomena that we all share, and understanding how the experiences unique to each person affect his or her perception of the world.

A Word on Sensation and Perception

Experience is traditionally divided into two classes: sensation and perception. Most psychologists define **sensation** as the awareness of simple properties of stimuli, such as brightness, color, warmth, or sweetness, and **perception** as the awareness of more complex characteristics of stimuli. However, neither behavioral nor physiological research has been able to establish a clear boundary between "simple" sensations and "complex" perceptions. Indeed, research has shown that experience is essential to the development of some of the most elementary features of sensory systems. Therefore, in this chapter I will use the term *perception* to refer to all sensory experience.

SENSORY PROCESSING

Sense organs can respond directly to the environmental stimuli of light, sound, odor, taste, or touch, but the brain cannot. Sensory information must be introduced to the brain through neural impulses—action potentials along axons in sensory nerves. To serve as an effective stimulus, an environmental event must cause a unique pattern of neural activity that

To appreciate the wonders of nature we often need to call on more than one of our senses.

the brain can distinguish from all other patterns. The process of *transduction* transforms sensory events into neural activity. It is basic to the ways in which we perceive the world.

Transduction

Transduction (literally, "leading across") is the process by which the sense organs convert energy from environmental events into neural activity. Each sense organ responds to a particular form of energy given off by an environmental stimulus and translates that energy into neural firing to which the brain can respond. The means of transduction are as diverse as the kinds of stimuli we can perceive. In most senses, specialized **receptor cells** release chemical transmitter substances that stimulate neurons, thus altering the rate of firing of their axons. In the body senses, neurons respond directly to physical stimuli, without the intervention of specialized receptor cells. Figure 3.1 illustrates these two processes schematically.

Sensory Coding

As we saw in Chapter 2, nerves are bundles of axons, each of which can do no more than transmit action potentials. These action potentials are fixed in size and duration; they cannot be altered. Yet our sense organs must respond differently to a multitude of stimuli, and therefore the nerves conveying the information to the brain must carry distinctive messages. For example, we are capable of discriminating among approximately 7.5 million different colors, if we were permitted to examine them side by side. We can recognize touches to different parts of the body, and we can further discriminate the degree of pressure involved and the sharpness or bluntness, softness or hardness, and even the temperature of the object touching us. Because the action potentials themselves cannot be altered, differences in stimuli must be encoded by other means.

A code is a system of symbols or signals representing information. Spoken English, written French, semaphore signals, magnetic fields on a recording tape, and the electrical zeroes and ones in the memory of a computer are all codes. So long as we know the rules of a code, we can convert a message from one medium to another

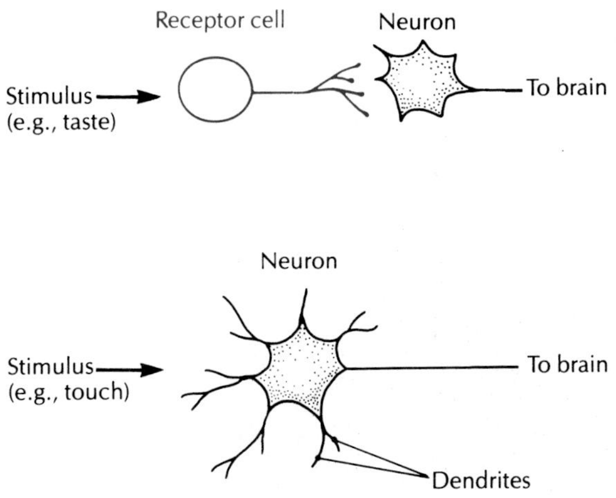

Receptor cell   Neuron

Stimulus ➞
(e.g., taste)   ➞ To brain

Neuron

Stimulus ➞
(e.g., touch)   ➞ To brain

Dendrites

FIGURE 3.1

Two general types of receptors.

without losing any information. Although we do not know the precise rules used by the sensory systems to transmit information to the brain, we do know that they take two general forms: anatomical coding and temporal coding.

Anatomical Coding

Since the early 1800s, when Johannes Müller formulated his doctrine of specific nerve energies (discussed in Chapter 1), we have known that the brain learns what is happening through the activity of specific sets of neurons. Sensory organs are located in different places in the body and send their information to the brain through different nerves. Because the brain has no direct information about the physical energy impinging on a given sense organ, it uses **anatomical coding;** that is, it interprets the location and type of sensory stimulus according to which incoming nerve fibers are active. For example, if you rub your eyes and thus mechanically stimulate their light-sensitive receptors you will see stars and flashes. Experiments performed during surgery have shown that electrical stimulation of the nerves that convey taste produces a sensation of taste, electrical stimulation of the auditory nerve produces a buzzing noise, and so forth.

We use forms of anatomical coding to distinguish not only among the sense modalities themselves but also among stimuli of the same sense modality. Obviously, sensory coding for

the body surface is anatomical: different nerve fibers innervate different parts of the skin. Thus, we can easily discriminate a touch on the arm from a touch on the knee. As we saw in Chapter 2, the primary somatosensory cortex contains a neural "map" of the skin. In addition, the primary visual cortex maintains a map of the visual field.

Temporal Coding

Temporal coding is the transmission of information in terms of time. The simplest form of temporal code is *rate*. By firing at a faster or slower rate according to the intensity of a stimulus, an axon can communicate quantitative information to the brain. Thus the firing of a particular set of neurons (an anatomical code) tells *where* the body is being touched; the rate at which these neurons fire (a temporal code) tells *how intense* that touch is. So far as we know, all sensory systems use rate of firing to encode the intensity of stimulation.

- How would you describe the transduction process?
- What are the two types of sensory coding?

VISION

We experience the world through our senses. Our knowledge of the world stems from the accumulation of sensory experience and subsequent learning. All sensory experiences are the result of energy from events that is transduced into activity of receptors, which are either specialized cells or dendritic endings of neurons.

The Eye and Its Functions

The eyes are important organs. Because they are delicate, they are well protected. Each eye is housed in a bony socket and can be covered by the eyelid to keep dust and dirt out. The eyelids are edged by eyelashes, which help keep foreign matter from falling into the open eye. The eyebrows prevent sweat on the forehead

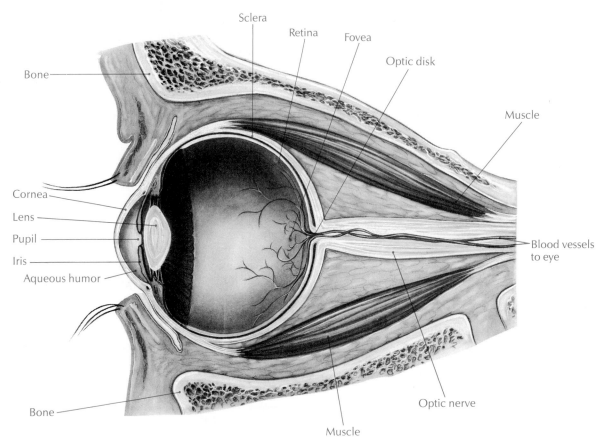

FIGURE 3.2

A cross-section of the human eye. (Adapted from Carlson, N.R. *Physiology of Behavior,* 3rd ed. Boston: Allyn and Bacon, 1986.)

from dripping into the eyes. Reflex mechanisms provide additional protection: the sudden approach of an object toward the face or a touch on the surface of the eye causes automatic eyelid closure and withdrawal of the head.

Figure 3.2 shows a cross-section of a human eye. The transparent **cornea** forms a bulge at the front of the eye and admits light. The rest of the eye is coated by a tough white membrane called the **sclera** (from the Greek *sklēros,* "hard"). The **iris** consists of two bands of muscles that control the amount of light admitted into the eye. The brain controls these muscles and thus regulates the size of the pupil, constricting it in bright light and dilating it in dim light. The space immediately behind the cornea is filled with **aqueous humor,** which simply means "watery fluid." This fluid is constantly produced by tissue behind the cornea that filters the fluid out of the blood.

The curvature of the cornea and of the **lens,** which lies immediately behind the iris, causes images to be focused on the back inner surface of the eye. The shape of the cornea is fixed, but the lens is flexible; a special set of muscles can alter its shape so that the eye can obtain images of either nearby or distant objects.

The **retina,** which lines most of the inner surface, performs the sensory functions of the eye. Embedded in the retina are over 130 million **photoreceptors**—receptor cells that transduce light into neural activity. The information from the photoreceptors is transmitted to neurons that send axons toward one point at the back of the eye—the **optic disk.** All axons leave the eye at this point and join the *optic nerve,* which travels to the brain. (See Figures 3.2 and 3.3.) Because there are no photoreceptors directly in front of the optic disk, this portion of the retina is blind. If you have not located your own *blind spot,* try the demonstration in Figure 3.4.

Photoreceptors respond to light and pass the information on by means of a transmitter substance to the bipolar cells with which they synapse. Bipolar cells transmit this information to the ganglion cells, neurons whose axons travel across the retina and through the optic nerves. Thus, visual information passes through a three-cell chain to the brain: photoreceptor → bipolar cell → ganglion cell → brain.

A single photoreceptor responds only to light that reaches its immediate vicinity, but a ganglion cell can receive information from many different photoreceptors. The retina also contains neurons that interconnect both adjacent photoreceptors and adjacent ganglion cells. (See Figure 3.5.) The existence of this neural circuitry indicates that some kinds of information processing are performed in the retina.

The human retina contains two general types of photoreceptors: 125 million **rods** and 6 million **cones.** The **fovea,** a small pit in the back of the retina, approximately one millimeter in diameter, contains only cones. (Look back at Figure 3.2.) Because most cones are connected to only one ganglion cell apiece, the fovea is responsible for our finest, most detailed vision. When we look at a point in our visual field, we move our eyes so that the image of that point falls directly upon the cone-packed fovea. Thus the fovea provides us with our greatest visual acuity. (*Acuity* derives from the Latin *acus*, meaning "needle." We use the same concept

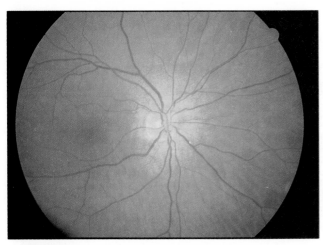

FIGURE 3.3

A view of the back of the eye, showing the retina, with the optic disk and blood vessels. The fovea is located to the left of the optic disk, midway to the edge of the photograph. (Courtesy of Douglas G. Mollerstuen, New England Medical Center.)

Figure 3.5 shows a cross section of the retina, with its three principal layers. Light passes successively through the **ganglion cell** (top) layer, the **bipolar cell** (middle) layer, and the photoreceptor (bottom) layer. Early anatomists were surprised to find the photoreceptors in the bottom layer, rather than in the top. As you might expect, the cells that are located above the photoreceptors are transparent.

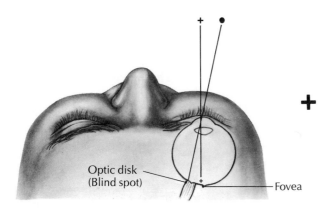

FIGURE 3.4

A test for the blind spot. With the left eye closed, look at the + with your right eye and move the page back and forth, toward and away from yourself. At about 20 centimeters the black circle disappears from your vision because its image falls on your blind spot. (From Carlson, N.R. *Physiology of Behavior*, 3rd ed. Boston: Allyn and Bacon, 1986.)

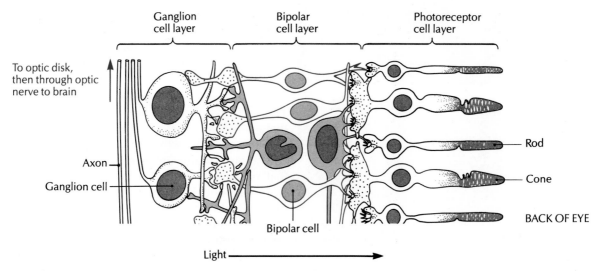

FIGURE 3.5

The cells of the retina. (Redrawn by permission of the Royal Society and the authors from Dowling, J.E., and Boycott, B.B., *Proceedings of the Royal Society (London).* 1966, Series B, *166*, 80–111.)

when we say that someone has "sharp eyes"; we mean he or she can see extremely small details.) Cones are also responsible for our ability to see colors.

Farther away from the fovea the number of cones decreases and the number of rods increases. Up to 100 rods may converge on a single ganglion cell. A ganglion cell that receives information from so many rods is sensitive to very low levels of light; a small quantity of light falling on many rods can thus effectively stimulate the ganglion cell on which their information converges. Rods are therefore responsible for our sensitivity to very dim light but provide poor acuity.

Transduction of Light by Photoreceptors

Although light-sensitive sensory organs have evolved independently in a wide variety of animals—from insects to fish to mammals—the chemistry is essentially the same in all species: A molecule derived from vitamin A is the central ingredient in the transduction of the energy of light into neural activity. (Carrots are supposed to be good for vision because they contain a substance that the body easily converts to vitamin A.) In the absence of light, this molecule is attached to another molecule, a protein.

The two molecules together form a **photopigment.** The photoreceptors of the human eye contain four kinds of photopigments (one for rods and three for cones), but their basic mechanism is the same. When a **photon** (a particle of light) strikes a photopigment, the photopigment splits apart into its two constituent molecules. This event starts the process of transduction. The splitting of the photopigment causes a series of chemical changes that stimulate the photoreceptor and cause it to send a message to the bipolar cell with which it forms a synapse. The bipolar cell sends the message to the ganglion cell, which sends it on to the brain. (See Figure 3.6.)

Intact photopigments have a characteristic color. For example, **rhodopsin,** the photopigment of rods, is pink (*rhodon* means "rose" in Greek). However, once the photopigments are split apart by the action of light, they lose their color—they become bleached.

After light has caused a molecule of photopigment to become bleached (split), energy from the cell's metabolism causes the two molecules to recombine, and the photopigment is ready to be bleached by light again. Each photoreceptor contains many thousands of molecules of photopigment. The number of intact molecules of photopigment in a given cell depends upon the relative rates at which they are being split by light and being put back together

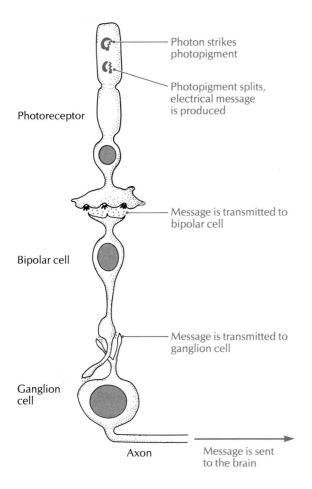

- Photon strikes photopigment
- Photopigment splits, electrical message is produced

Photoreceptor

- Message is transmitted to bipolar cell

Bipolar cell

- Message is transmitted to ganglion cell

Ganglion cell

Axon — Message is sent to the brain

FIGURE 3.6

Transduction of light into neural activity and the transmission of information to the brain.

by the cell's energy. The brighter the light, the more bleached photopigment there is. But this leads us to the topic of the next section.

Adaptation to Light and Dark

The easiest way to introduce the phenomenon of visual adaptation is to ask you to remember how difficult it is to find a seat in a darkened movie theater. If you have just come in from the bright sun, your eyes do not respond well to the low level of illumination. However, after a few minutes you can see rather well—your eyes have adapted.

In order for light to be detected, the photons must bleach (split) molecules of rhodopsin (or the other photopigments). When high levels of illumination strike the retina, the regeneration

of rhodopsin falls behind the bleaching process. With only a small percentage of the rhodopsin molecules intact, the rods are not very sensitive to light. If you enter a dark room after being in a brightly lit room or in sunlight, there are too few intact rhodopsin molecules for your eyes to respond immediately to dim light. The probability that a photon will strike an intact molecule of rhodopsin is very low. However, after a while the regeneration of rhodopsin overcomes the bleaching effects of the energy of light. The rods become full of unbleached rhodopsin, and a photon passing through a rod is likely to find a target. The eye has undergone **dark adaptation.**

Figure 3.7 shows the results of the dark-adaptation experiment by Hecht and Schlaer (1938). Each point on the vertical axis indicates the intensity of light necessary to produce a sensation as a person adapts to darkness. (Note that the scale on the vertical axis is logarithmic; a log value of 8 is 100,000 times greater than a log value of 3.) The figure shows clearly that the process of dark adaptation is not smooth and continuous; a break occurs after about seven minutes in the dark.

The discontinuity in the dark-adaptation curve is called the **rod-cone break.** The function is really two curves, not one. Cones, which are less sensitive than rods, complete their regeneration of photopigments in five to seven minutes. The part of the curve before the break represents their activity. Rods are slower to regenerate rhodopsin, but they are more sensitive to light, so we see the effect of their adaptation only after the cones are completely dark adapted.

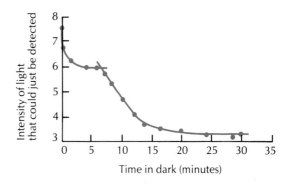

FIGURE 3.7

A dark-adaptation curve showing a rod-cone break. (From Hecht, S., and Schlaer, S. *Journal of the Optic Society of America*, 1938, *28*, 269–275.)

Eye Movements

Our eyes are never completely at rest, even when our gaze is fixed upon a particular place (the *fixation point*). Three types of movements can be observed: (1) Fast, aimless, jittering movements occur, probably similar to the fine tremors that are seen in the hands and fingers when we attempt to keep them still. (2) Superimposed on these random tremors are slow, drifting movements that shift the image on the retina a distance of approximately twenty cone widths. (3) These slow drifts are terminated by quick movements that bring the image of the fixation point back to the fovea.

Although the small, jerky movements that the eyes make when at rest are random, they appear to have a definite purpose. Riggs, Ratliff, Cornsweet, and Cornsweet (1953) devised a way to project **stabilized images** on the retina using a special contact-lens device. A stabilized image is one that remains in one location on the retina. The image that the experimenters projected always fell on precisely the same part of the retina despite the subject's eye movements. Under these conditions, details of visual stimuli began to disappear. At first the image was clear, but then a "fog" drifted over the subject's field of view, obscuring the image. After a while, some images could not be seen at all.

These results suggest that elements of the visual system are not responsive to an unchanging stimulus. The photoreceptors or the ganglion cells, or perhaps both, apparently cease to respond to a constant stimulus. The small, involuntary movements of our eyes keep the image moving and thus keep the visual system responsive to the details of the scene before us.

The eyes also make three types of "purposive" movements: conjugate movements, saccadic movements, and pursuit movements. **Conjugate movements** are cooperative movements that keep both eyes fixed upon the same target or, more precisely, that keep the image of the target object on corresponding parts of the two retinas. If you hold up a finger in front of your face, look at it, and then bring your finger closer to your face, your eyes will make conjugate movements toward your nose. If you then look at an object on the other side of the room, your eyes will rotate outward, and you will see two separate blurry images of your finger. As you will learn later in this chapter, conjugate

eye movements are very important in the perception of distance.

When you scan the scene in front of you, your gaze does not roam slowly and steadily across its features. Instead, your eyes make jerky **saccadic movements**—you shift your gaze abruptly from one point to another. When you read a line in this book, your eyes stop several times, moving very quickly between stops. You cannot consciously control the speed of movement between stops; during each *saccade* the eyes move as fast as they can. Only by performing a **pursuit movement**—say, by looking at your finger while you move it around—can you make your eyes move more slowly.

- How do photoreceptors transduce light into neural activity?
- What is the process of light and dark adaptation?
- What are the categories of involuntary and voluntary eye movements and how would you explain their functions?

Color Vision

Among mammals, only primates have full color vision. A bull does not charge a red cape; he charges what he sees as an annoying gray object being waved at him. Among nonmammals, many birds and fishes also have excellent color vision; the brightly colored lure may really appeal to the fish as much as to the angler who buys it.

Experiments have shown that there are three types of cones in the human eye, each containing a different type of photopigment. Each type of photopigment is most sensitive to a particular **wavelength** of light; that is, light of a particular wavelength most readily causes a particular photopigment to split. Thus, different types of cones are stimulated by different wavelengths of light. Information from the cones enables us to perceive colors.

To understand color vision we must know something about the physical nature of light. Wavelength is an important physical characteristic of light. Light from an incandescent source, such as the sun, consists of radiant energy similar to radio waves and contains a mixture of many frequencies. Because the speed of radiant energy is always constant—186,000 miles per second—the frequency of vibration determines the wavelength of the energy. The faster the vibration, the shorter the wavelength. (See Figure 3.8.)

The wavelength of visible light ranges from 380 through 760 **nanometers (nm).** (A nanometer is a billionth of a meter.) Ultraviolet radiation, X rays, and gamma rays are also forms of radiant energy but have shorter wavelengths. Infrared radiation, radar, radio waves, and AC circuits have longer wavelengths. The entire range of wavelengths is known as the *electromagnetic spectrum.* (See Figure 3.9.)

Wavelength is related to color, but the terms are not synonymous. For example, the **spectral colors** (the colors we see in a rainbow, which

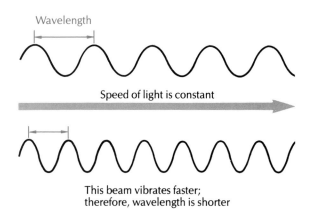

FIGURE 3.8

Because the speed of light is constant, faster vibrations produce shorter wavelengths.

FIGURE 3.9

The electromagnetic spectrum.

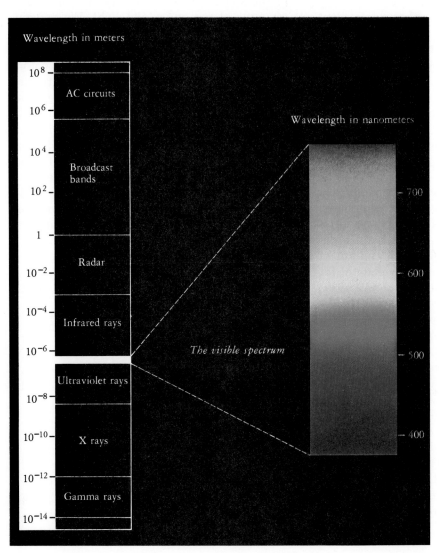

TABLE 3.1

Physical and perceptual dimensions of color

Perceptual Dimension	Physical Dimension	Physical Characteristics
Hue	Wavelength	Frequency of oscillation of light radiation
Brightness	Intensity	Amplitude of light radiation
Saturation	Purity	Intensity of dominant wavelength, relative to total radiant energy

contains the entire spectrum of visible radiant energy) do not include all colors that we can see, such as brown, pink, and the metallic colors silver and gold. The fact that not all colors are found in the spectrum means that differences in wavelength alone cannot account for the differences in the colors we can perceive.

The Dimensions of Color

Most colors can be described in terms of three physical dimensions: wavelength, intensity, and purity. Three perceptual dimensions corresponding to these physical dimensions describe what we see. (See Table 3.1.) The **hue** of most colors is determined by wavelength; for example, light with a wavelength of 540 nm is perceived as green. A color's **brightness** is determined by the intensity, or degree of energy, of the light that is being perceived, all other factors being equal.

The third perceptual dimension of color is **saturation.** Saturation is roughly equivalent to purity. A fully saturated color consists of light of only one wavelength; the spectral colors of the rainbow are all fully saturated. If white light (light containing a mixture of all wavelengths) is mixed with light of a particular wavelength, the result will be a desaturated color. For example, when red light (700 nm) is added to white light, the result is pink light. Pink is thus a less saturated version of red. Fig-

ure 3.10 illustrates how a color with a particular dominant wavelength (hue) can vary in its brightness and saturation. Figure 3.11 illustrates a series of fully-saturated colors of different hues. (See Figures 3.10 and 3.11.)

Color Mixing

The outer rim of the circle shown in Figure 3.11 demonstrates the fact that not all hues can be specified by wavelength; some hues are not found in the visual spectrum. There is a gap between red (700 nm) and violet (380 nm), but psychologically no gap exists. The colors blend, and there do not appear to be any sudden shifts in hue. (See Figure 3.11.) The colors on the circle between red and violet are not part of the spectrum; they are mixtures of various amounts of red and violet light. We perceive these mixtures as individual colors, intermediate in hue to the colors that produce them. We do not see the original two component colors.

Vision is a *synthetic* sensory modality; that is, it synthesizes (puts together) rather than analyzes (takes apart). When two wavelengths of light are present we see an intermediate color rather than the two components. (In contrast, the auditory system is *analytical*. If a high note and a low note are played together on a piano we hear both notes instead of a single, intermediate tone.) The addition of two or more lights of different wavelengths is called **color**

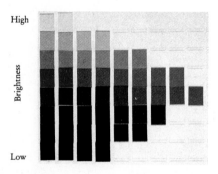

FIGURE 3.10

These colors have the same dominant wavelength (hue), but different saturation and brightness. (Courtesy of Munsell Color Corporation.)

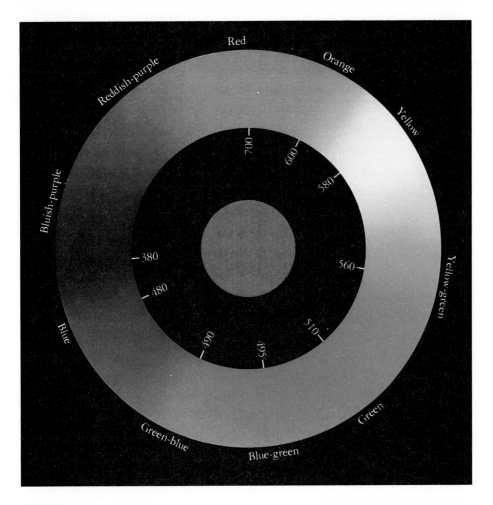

FIGURE 3.11

A color circle showing fully saturated hues of different wavelengths. The reddish-purple hues between 380 and 700 nanometers are not part of the spectrum, but consist of mixtures of these two wavelengths. Pairs of hues on opposite sides of the circle are complementary; when added together they produce a colorless gray.

mixing. This procedure is very different from paint mixing, and so are its results. If we pass a beam of white light through a prism we break it into the spectrum of the different wavelengths it contains. If we recombine these colors by passing them through another prism, we obtain white light again. (See Figure 3.12.)

When we mix paints we are subtracting colors, not adding them together. Mixing two paints always yields a darker result: mixing blue paint with yellow paint yields green paint, which looks darker than yellow. But mixing two beams of light of different wavelengths always yields a brighter color. For example,

when red and green light are shone together on a piece of white paper, we see yellow. In fact, we cannot tell a pure yellow light from a synthesized one made of the proper intensities of red and green light. To our eyes, both yellows appear identical.

To reconstitute white light, we do not even have to recombine all the wavelengths in the spectrum. If we shine a blue light, a green light, and a red light together on a sheet of white paper and properly adjust their intensities, the position at which all three of the beams overlap will look perfectly white to us. (See Figure 3.13 on the next page.)

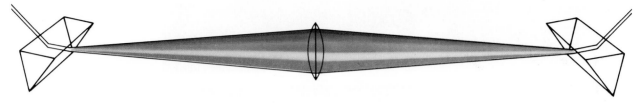

FIGURE 3.12

White light can be split into a spectrum of colors with a prism and recombined through another prism.

Color Coding in the Retina

Experiments in recent years have shown that the cones in the human eye contain three types of photopigments, each of which preferentially absorbs light of a particular wavelength: 420, 530, and 560 nm. Although these wavelengths actually correspond to blue-violet, green, and yellow-green, most investigators refer to these receptors as blue, green, and red cones. To simplify this discussion I will pretend that the three cones respond to pure blue, green, and red. Red and green cones are present in about equal proportions, but there are far fewer blue cones. Figure 3.14 shows a hypothetical arrangement.

Figure 3.15 will help explain the principle by which the three types of cones in the retina analyze the colors in a scene. The left photograph shows a color television screen displaying a white cross against a gray background. The right photograph shows a close-up of the center of the screen. You can see that the white cross is made of bright blue, green, and red spots of light, whereas the surrounding gray background is made of dimmer spots. The screen contains absolutely no white spots. (See Figure 3.15.) When the screen displays various colors, it does so by varying the intensity of the spots. For example, in a patch of red, only the red spots will be illuminated.

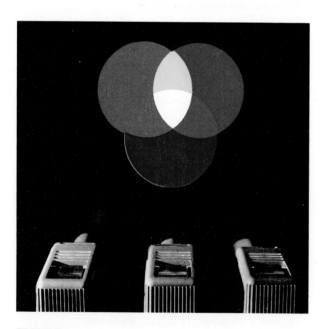

FIGURE 3.13

Additive color mixing and paint mixing. When blue, red, and green light of the proper intensity are all shone together, the result is white light. When red, blue, and yellow paints are mixed together, the result is a dark gray. (Photo courtesy of GATF.)

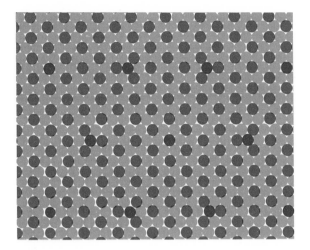

FIGURE 3.14

A possible arrangement of blue, red, and green cones in the human retina, based on the model proposed by Walraven (1974).

The eye uses the principle of the color television screen, but in reverse: instead of displaying colors it analyzes them. If a spot of white light shines on the retina, all three types of cones are stimulated equally, and we perceive white light. If a spot of pure blue, green, or red light shines on the retina, only one of the three classes of cones is stimulated, and a pure color is perceived. If a spot of yellow light shines on the retina, it stimulates red and green cones equally well, but has little effect on blue cones.

(You can see from Figure 3.11 that yellow is located midway between red and green.) Stimulation of red and green cones, then, is the signal that yellow light has been perceived.

Two types of ganglion cells encode color vision: red/green and yellow/blue. Both types of ganglion cells fire at a steady rate when they are not stimulated. If a spot of red light shines on the retina, the red/green ganglion cells will begin to fire at a high rate, and, conversely, if a spot of green light shines on the retina, the cells will begin to fire at a slow rate. Thus, the brain learns about the presence of red or green light by the increased or decreased rate of firing of axons attached to red/green ganglion cells. Similarly, yellow/blue ganglion cells are excited by yellow light and inhibited by blue light. Because red and green light, and yellow and blue light, have opposite effects on the rate of axon firing, this coding scheme is called an *opponent process*. (See Figure 3.16.)

The retina contains red/green and yellow/blue ganglion cells because of the nature of the connections between the cones, bipolar cells, and ganglion cells. The brain detects colors by comparing the rates of firing of the axons in the optic nerve that signal red or green, and yellow or blue. Now you can see why we cannot perceive a reddish green or a bluish yellow: an axon that signals red or green (or yellow or blue) can either increase or decrease its rate of firing; it cannot do both at the same time.

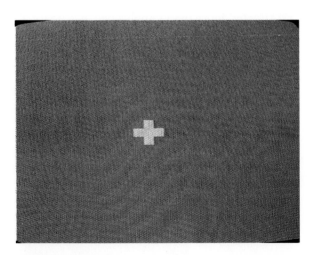

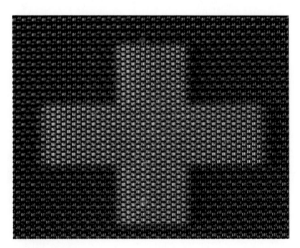

FIGURE 3.15

The television screen demonstrates—in reverse—the principle of color coding by the three types of cones in the retina. The right photograph is an enlargement of the plus sign shown in the left photograph. Note that the right photograph contains only red, blue, and green spots of light.

FIGURE 3.16

Opponent process: the effect of various hues of light on the activity of yellow/blue and red/green ganglion cells.

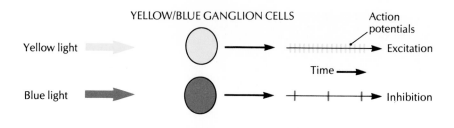

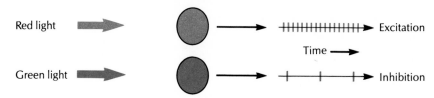

Negative Afterimages

The figures in Figure 3.17 demonstrate an interesting property of the visual system: the formation of a **negative afterimage.** Stare at the dot in the center of the lefthand circle (the one with the patches of color) for approximately 30 seconds. Then quickly look at the dot in the center of the blank gray circle to the right. You will have a fleeting experience of seeing four colors that are **complementary,** or opposite, to the ones on the left. Complementary items are those that go together to make up a whole. In this context, complementary colors are those that make white (or shades of gray) when added together. To me, complements of the blue, red, green, and yellow of the left-hand figure are orangish yellow, pale blue, magenta, and purple.

The most important cause of negative afterimages is bleaching of photopigments. When cones in one region of the retina are stimulated with color of a particular hue, some are stimulated more than others, and their supply of photopigment becomes more bleached out. For

example, the patch of blue in Figure 3.17 bleaches out some of the photopigment in blue cones. When this region of the retina is stimulated with the neutral-colored light reflected off the gray-colored paper, the red and green cones respond more vigorously. Because stimulation of red and green cones leads to the perception of yellow, we see a yellow afterimage.

Defects in Color Vision

Approximately one in twenty males has some form of defective color vision. These defects are sometimes called *color blindness,* but this term should probably be reserved for the very few people who cannot see any color at all. Males are affected more than females because many of the genes for producing photopigments appear to be located on the X chromosome. Because males have only one X chromosome (females have two of them), a defective gene there will always be expressed.

There are many different types of defective color vision. Two of the three described here

FIGURE 3.17

A negative after-image. Stare for approximately 30 seconds at the dot in the center of the left figure; then quickly transfer your gaze to the dot in the center of the right figure. You will see colors that are complementary to the originals.

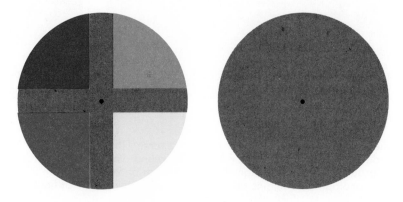

involve the red/green system. People with these defects confuse red and green. Their primary color sensations are yellow and blue; red and green both look yellowish. Figure 3.18 shows one of the figures from a commonly used test for defective color vision. A person who confuses red and green will not be able to see the 5 or the 7. (See Figure 3.18.) The most common defect, called **protanopia** (literally, "first-color defect"), appears to result from a lack of the photopigment for red cones. The fact that people with protanopia have relatively normal acuity suggests that they do have red cones, but that these cones are filled with green photopigment (Nathons, Piantanida, Eddy, Shows, and Hogness, 1986). To a protanope, red looks much darker than green. The second form of red/green defect, called **deuteranopia** ("second-color defect"), appears to result from the opposite kind of substitution: green cones are filled with red photopigment.

The third form of color defect, called **tritanopia** ("third-color defect"), involves the yellow/blue system and is much rarer: it affects fewer than 1 in 10,000 people. Tritanopes see the world in greens and reds; to them a clear blue sky is a bright green, and yellow looks pink. Unlike protanopia and deuteranopia, the faulty gene that causes tritanopia is not carried on a sex chromosome; therefore, it is equally common in males and females. This defect appears to involve loss of blue cones, but because there are far fewer of these than of red and green cones to begin with, it is not possible to determine whether the cones are missing or filled with one of the other photopigments.

- What are the three physical dimensions of color and their corresponding perceptual dimensions?
- How would you compare synthetic and analytic sensory systems?
- What are the two kinds of color coding that occur in the cones and ganglion cells of the retina?
- How do negative afterimages occur?

Brain Mechanisms of Vision

Although the eyes contain the photoreceptors that detect areas of different brightnesses and colors, perception takes place in the brain. As

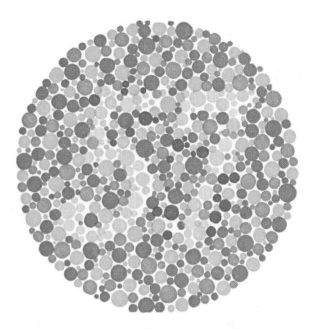

FIGURE 3.18

A figure commonly used to test for defective color vision. People with red/green color blindness will fail to see the 5 or the 7. (Courtesy of American Optical Corporation.)

we saw in Chapter 2, the optic nerves send visual information to the thalamus, which relays the information to the primary visual cortex, located in the occipital lobe. In turn, neurons in the primary visual cortex send visual information to the visual association cortex.

Visual perception by the brain is often described as a hierarchy of information processing. According to this scheme, circuits of neurons analyze particular aspects of visual information and send the results on to another circuit, which performs further analysis. At each step in the process, successively more complex features are analyzed. Eventually, the process leads to the perception of the scene, and of all the objects in it. The higher levels of the perceptual process interact with memories: the viewer recognizes familiar objects and learns the appearance of new, unfamiliar ones.

There are many pieces of evidence that contradict this general scheme. For example, even the "lowest" levels of the hierarchy can be modified by learning, and anatomical studies have shown that the flow of information is not strictly hierarchical but often goes both ways.

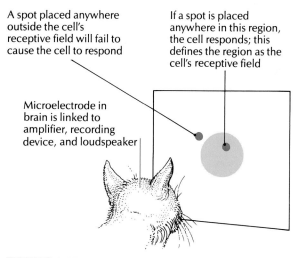

A spot placed anywhere outside the cell's receptive field will fail to cause the cell to respond

If a spot is placed anywhere in this region, the cell responds; this defines the region as the cell's receptive field

Microelectrode in brain is linked to amplifier, recording device, and loudspeaker

FIGURE 3.19

Locating a neuron's receptive field.

However, the principle provides a useful, if simplified, overview of the brain mechanisms of perception.

Our knowledge about the characteristics of the earliest stages of analysis has come from investigations of the activity of individual neurons in the thalamus and primary visual cortex. For example, David Hubel and Torsten Wiesel have inserted **microelectrodes,** extremely small wires with microscopically sharp points, into various regions of the visual system of cats and monkeys to detect the electrical disturbances that accompany the action potentials of individual neurons (Hubel and Wiesel, 1977, 1979). The signals that are detected by the microelectrodes are electronically amplified and sent to a recording device so that they can be studied later. They are also sent to a loudspeaker, where the action potentials are converted into easily recognizable crackling noises.

After positioning a microelectrode close to a neuron, Hubel and Wiesel presented various stimuli on a large screen in front of the anesthetized animal. The anesthesia makes the animal unconscious but does not prevent neurons in the visual system from responding. The researchers moved a stimulus around on the screen until they located the point where it had the largest effect on the neuron. Almost always, the neuron responded to stimuli in a limited portion of the visual field. Next, they presented various shapes, to learn which stimulus produced the greatest response from the neuron.

They found that neurons in the thalamus, along with those in the primary visual cortex that are stimulated directly by them, changed their firing rate most when a spot of light was shone on a very small circular region of the screen. This region is called the neuron's **receptive field.** If they moved the spot of light just outside the receptive field, the neuron stopped responding, and its neighbors began responding instead. (See Figure 3.19.)

From their experiments Hubel and Wiesel concluded that the geography of the visual field is retained in the primary visual cortex. That is, they observed a point-by-point relation between the real world and the surface of the primary visual cortex. However, this "map" on the brain is distorted, with the largest amount of area given to the center of the visual field, which projects on the fovea.

The primary visual cortex, like other areas of the cerebral cortex, is composed of several layers, like a sandwich. The neurons that receive information directly from the thalamus are located in the middle layer. These neurons send information to those located in other layers. Neurons in the layer just above the middle layer have somewhat larger receptive fields, and they respond to lines of a particular orientation. For example, one might respond to a vertical line, another to a line rotated 10 degrees from the horizontal. Hubel and Wiesel call neurons that respond in this way **simple cells.** (See Figure 3.20.)

Other layers of the primary visual cortex contain **complex cells.** Like the simple cells, these neurons respond to lines of a particular orientation. However, they have somewhat larger receptive fields, and, unlike simple cells, they respond best to lines that are moving at right angles to their angle of orientation. (See Figure 3.21.)

Hubel and Wiesel noted that although neurons in the primary visual cortex appear to analyze successively more complex forms of stimuli, each neuron has information about only a restricted area of the visual field. Therefore, the primary visual cortex cannot analyze shape and form; higher levels of perceptual analysis must take place elsewhere. To understand better why this is so, consider this analogy. Imagine a large group of people, each of whom is examining a small part of a visual scene with a telescope mounted on a tripod. Each telescope

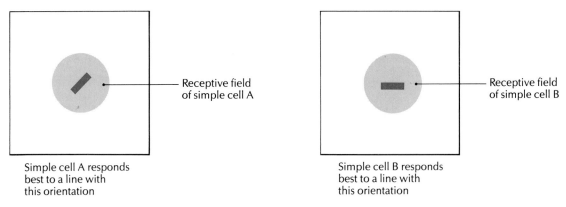

Receptive field
of simple cell A

Receptive field
of simple cell B

Simple cell A responds
best to a line with
this orientation

Simple cell B responds
best to a line with
this orientation

FIGURE 3.20

The kind of stimulus that produces the best responses in simple cells in the primary visual cortex.

is aimed at a different part of the scene, and none can be moved. Obviously, none of the people can describe what is happening in the scene in front of them. They can report spots, lines, colors, and movements from a small part of the scene, but they cannot perceive the whole. If the people could talk with each other, they could share their information and possibly make some inferences about what was going on in front of them. Or they could report what they are seeing to someone else, who would put all the reports together and come up with a perception of the scene. We know that neurons in the primary visual cortex share their information only with their immediate neighbors, so the first possibility is ruled out. However, the

neurons *do* send reports to the visual association cortex, where the analysis of information from particular parts of the visual field is put together to form perceptions of complex shapes.

Investigations of neurons in the visual association cortex have shown that many of these cells respond to complex stimuli, presented anywhere in the visual field. For example, Gross, Rocha-Miranda, and Bender (1972) found one particular neuron that responded vigorously when they presented a picture of a monkey's hand. The results suggest that these neurons are located at the top of the hierarchy, putting together the information received from lower levels of analysis.

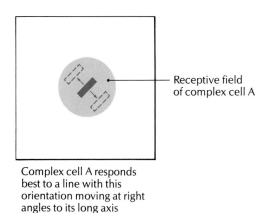

Receptive field
of complex cell A

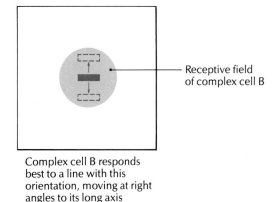

Receptive field
of complex cell B

Complex cell A responds
best to a line with this
orientation moving at right
angles to its long axis

Complex cell B responds
best to a line with this
orientation, moving at right
angles to its long axis

FIGURE 3.21

The kind of stimulus that produces the best responses in complex cells in the primary visual cortex.

This painting evokes interest because of its ambiguity with respect to figure and ground. *Heaven and Hell,* M.C. Escher

VISUAL PERCEPTION

The visual system performs many remarkable tasks. The brain receives fragments of information from approximately one million axons in each of the optic nerves and combines and organizes them into the perception of a scene—objects with different forms, colors, and textures, residing at different locations in three-dimensional space. Even when our eyes move, exposing the photoreceptors to entirely new patterns of visual information, our perception of the scene before us does not change. We see a stable world, not a moving one, because the brain keeps track of the constantly changing patterns of neural firing.

If you can conveniently do so, take a break from your reading now and go for a short walk—even if it is only around the room. Think of what you are seeing—shapes, figures, background, shadows, areas of light and dark—as you move and as your eyes move. Your knowledge of the objects and their relative location is extensive, and you have a good idea of what they will feel like, even if you have not touched them. If the lighting suddenly changes (if lamps are turned on or off or if a cloud passes in front

of the sun), the amount of light reflected by the objects in the scene changes too, but your perception of the objects remains the same—you see them as having the same shape, color, and texture as before. Similarly, you do not perceive an object as increasing in size as you approach it, even though the image it casts upon your retina does get larger. These perceptions of form, movement, and space are the topics of this section.

Perception of Light and Dark: Brightness Constancy

Experiments have shown that people can judge the whiteness or grayness of an object very well, even if the level of illumination changes. If you look at a sheet of white paper in either bright sunlight or in shade, you will perceive it as being white, although the intensity of its image on your retina will vary. If you look at a sheet of gray paper in sunlight, it may in fact reflect more light to your eye than a white paper located in the shade, but you will still see the white paper as white and the gray paper as gray.

This phenomenon is known as **brightness constancy.** Katz (1935) demonstrated brightness constancy by constructing a vertical barrier and positioning a light source so that a shadow was cast to the right of the barrier. In the shadow he placed a gray square card on a white background. In the lighted area on the left of the barrier he placed a number of shades of gray and asked subjects to choose one that would match the gray square in the shadow. (See Figure 3.22.) His subjects matched the grays not in terms of the light that the cards actually reflected, but in terms of the light they *would have* reflected if both had been viewed under the same level of illumination. In other words, the subjects compensated for the dimness of the shadow. The match was not perfect, but it was much closer than it would have been if perception of brightness were made solely on the basis of the amount of light that fell on the retina.

The perception of white and gray, then, is not a matter of absolutes; rather, they are perceived relative to the surrounding environment. For example, you perceive a ceiling painted a rather dark off-white color as pure white unless a piece of white paper is placed next to it for comparison. Furthermore, you see the white of a ceiling or wall as white even where it is in shadow. In fact people often do not even see shadows unless they specifically look for them.

Perception of Form: Figure and Ground

If you look at the scene in front of you, you will observe that most of what you see can be categorized as either object or background. Objects appear as things and have a particular location in space; they have *form*. The background, essentially formless, serves mostly as a texture behind the objects. The distinction between object and background is not rigid; a picture hanging on a wall can appear as an object or as part of the background, depending on whether you pay specific attention to it. If you are looking at the picture, it is an object; if you are looking at a person standing between you and the wall, it is part of the background. Sometimes we receive ambiguous clues about what is object and what is background; for example, does Figure 3.23 illustrate two faces or a wine goblet?

Psychologists use the terms **figure** and **ground** to label an object and its background, respectively. Even without three-dimensional cues, we tend to organize what we see in terms of figure and ground.

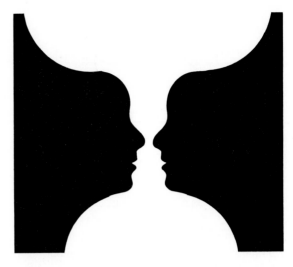

FIGURE 3.23

A drawing in which figure and ground can be reversed. You can see either two faces against a background or a wineglass against a dark background.

What rules determine which parts of a scene we perceive as figure, and which parts as ground? If the pattern of stimulation is that of a well-known object, it will almost certainly be seen as a figure, but so will an unfamiliar, meaningless form such as the one you see in Figure 3.24. Therefore, although familiarity is important for perception of form, it is not necessary. If it were, we would have difficulty perceiving objects we had never seen before.

One of the most important aspects of form perception is the existence of a *boundary*. If the visual field contains a sharp and distinct change in brightness, color, or texture, an edge is perceived. If this edge forms a continuous boundary, the space enclosed by the boundary will probably be perceived as a figure. The form you saw in Figure 3.24 is perceived as such because of its distinct border. But the presence of an actual line is not necessary for the perception of form. Figure 3.25 shows that when small elements are arranged in groups, we tend to perceive them as larger figures.

The tendency to perceive elements as belonging together has been recognized for many years. Earlier this century, a group of psychologists organized a theory of perception called **Gestalt psychology.** *Gestalt* means "form," but Gestalt psychologists use the term to mean more than that. Their essential thesis is that the whole, in perception, is more than the sum of

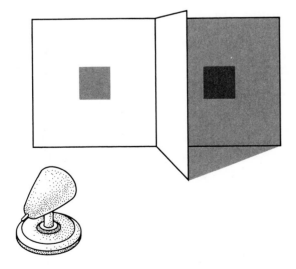

FIGURE 3.22

The experiment by Katz (1935), which demonstrated brightness constancy.

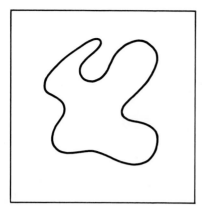

FIGURE 3.24

We immediately perceive even an unfamiliar figure when the outline is closed.

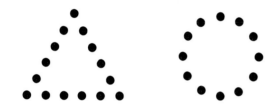

FIGURE 3.25

We tend to perceive a group of smaller elements as a larger figure.

its parts. Visual perception cannot be understood simply by analyzing the scene into its elements, because what we see depends on the *relations* of these elements to one another.

Organizational Laws of Gestalt Psychology

Elements of a visual scene can combine in various ways to produce different forms. Gestalt psychologists have observed that several principles can predict the combination of these elements.

The law of **proximity** states that elements that are closest together will be perceived as belonging together. Figure 3.26 demonstrates this principle. The pattern on the left looks like four vertical columns, whereas the one on the right looks like four horizontal rows.

The law of **similarity** states that elements that look similar will be perceived as part of the

same form. It is easy to see the diamond inside the square in Figure 3.27.

Good continuation refers to predictability or simplicity. Which of the two sets of colored dots best describes the continuation of the line of black dots in Figure 3.28? If you see the figure the way I do, you will choose the colored dots that continue the curve down and to the right. It is simpler to perceive the line following a smooth course than suddenly making a sharp bend. Figure 3.29 illustrates a similar principle. It is possible to see two complex lines that do not cross each other, but it is simpler to describe the figure as a straight line superimposed on a wavy line, and most people tend to perceive it this way.

The law of **closure** states that we often supply missing information to close a figure and separate it from its background. For example, Figure 3.30 looks a bit like a triangle, but if you cover the gaps with a pencil the figure undeniably looks like a triangle.

In Figure 3.31, the nonexistent—but still very apparent—triangle looks brighter than the background. Apparently our visual system, in perceiving a figure against a ground, emphasizes the figure and makes it more vivid.

FIGURE 3.26

The Gestalt principle of proximity. Different spacing of the dots produces four vertical or four horizontal lines.

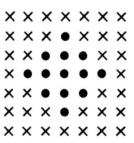

FIGURE 3.27

The Gestalt principle of similarity. Similar elements are perceived as belonging to the same form.

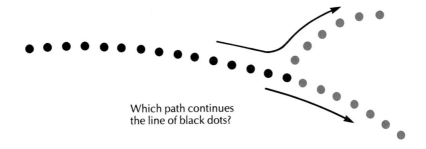

FIGURE 3.28

The Gestalt principle of good continuation. It is easier to perceive a smooth continuation than an abrupt shift.

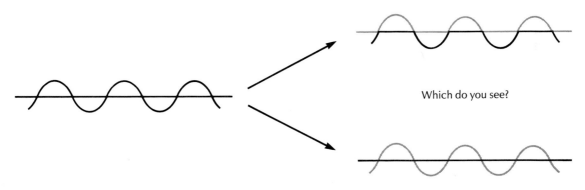

FIGURE 3.29

The Gestalt principle of good continuation. Which do you see?

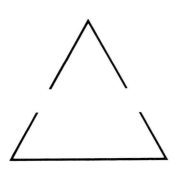

FIGURE 3.30

The Gestalt principle of closure. We tend to supply missing information to close a figure and separate it from its background. Lay a pencil across the gaps and see how strong the perception of a complete triangle becomes.

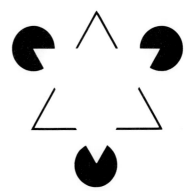

FIGURE 3.31

Even when boundaries are not present, we can be fooled into seeing them. The triangle with its point down looks brighter than the surrounding area. (From Rock, I. *An Introduction to Perception*. New York: Macmillan, 1975.)

The final Gestalt law of organization relies on movement. The law of **common fate** states that elements that move in the same direction will be perceived as belonging together and forming a figure. In the forest, an animal is camouflaged if its surface is covered with the same elements that are found in the background—spots of brown, tan, and green—because its boundary is obscured. There is no basis for grouping the elements on the animal. As long as the animal is stationary, it remains well hidden. However, once it moves, the elements on its surface will move together, and the animal's form will quickly be perceived.

■ How does the phenomenon of brightness constancy affect our perception of white or grey?

■ What are some features that contribute to our perception of form?

■ What are the five organizational laws of Gestalt psychology?

Effects of Experience

It has been known for some time that the lack of a stimulating visual environment can prevent normal development of the visual system. In fact Hubel and Wiesel received a Nobel prize in 1981 for discovering that neurons in the primary visual cortex will never respond to stimulation of both eyes unless the animal has had experience with binocular vision early in life.

Previously, most investigators believed that innately determined neural connections produced the responses of the simpler elements of the visual system. But Hirsch and Spinelli (1971) showed that experience can alter the responses of even the simplest elements, which suggests that the neural connections can be affected by what an organism sees. They raised kittens in the dark from birth to the age of 3 weeks, then fitted them with a pair of goggles and allowed them to run about in the light for a time each day. The goggles presented very special stimuli to each eye. The right eye saw only vertical lines; the left only horizontal lines.

After several weeks of training Hirsch and Spinelli recorded the responses of neurons in the cats' visual cortex and found cells there that previous investigators had never before seen. These cells responded best to vertical lines shown to the right eye and to horizontal lines shown to the left eye. Thus, the features detected by neurons in the visual cortex are at least partially affected by the animal's early visual environment.

A study by Ball and Sekuler (1982) suggests that the feature detectors can be modified even in the visual system of adults. The experimenters trained people to detect extremely small

FIGURE 3.32

Size constancy. Although the retinal image of the apple is larger when the apple is nearer, we tend to perceive it as being the same size whether it is near us or far away.

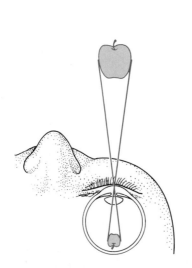
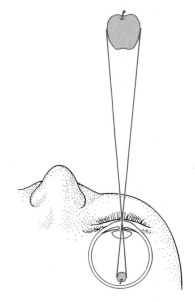

movements. Each subject sat in front of a display screen. A series of dots would appear, scattered across the face of the screen, and would either all move an extremely small distance or all remain stationary. The dots always moved in the same direction, but the direction was different for each person in the experiment. After several sessions, the experimenters assessed the subjects' sensitivity to detecting movements of the dots. They found that each person was especially good at detecting movement only in the direction in which he or she had been trained; the training did not increase their detection of movements in other directions. The effect was still present when the subjects were tested again ten weeks later.

The fact that the subjects learned to detect a small movement in a particular direction, and not small movements in general, suggests that their visual systems were modified at a rather elementary level. Possibly, they acquired new sets of feature detectors that responded to movement in a particular direction. As yet we have no way of knowing where these hypothetical detectors may be.

Perception of Space: Form Constancy

Besides being able to perceive the forms of objects in our environment, we are able to judge their relative location in space quite accurately. Furthermore, when we approach an object or when it approaches us, we do not perceive it as getting larger. Even though the image of the object on the retina gets larger, we perceive this change as being due to a decrease in the distance between ourselves and the object. Our perception of the object's size remains relatively constant. (See Figure 3.32.)

The unchanging perception of an object's size and shape when it moves relative to us is called **form constancy.** (People also refer to *size constancy,* but size is simply one aspect of form.) In the nineteenth century, Hermann von Helmholtz suggested that form constancy was achieved by **unconscious inference.** We know the size and shape of a familiar object; therefore, if the image it casts upon our retina is small, we perceive it as being far away. If the image is large, we perceive it as being close. In

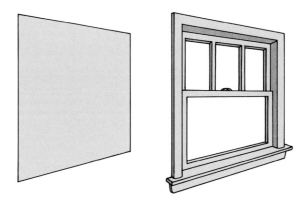

FIGURE 3.33

Form constancy. The left-hand figure can be perceived as a trapezoid, but because we recognize the right-hand figure as a window we perceive its shape as rectangular.

either case, we perceive the object itself as being the same size. Form constancy also works for rotation. The left-hand drawing of Figure 3.33 could be either a trapezoid or a rectangle rotated away from us. However, the extra cues clearly identify the right-hand drawing as a window, and experience tells us that windows are rectangular; thus, we perceive it as such. (See Figure 3.33.)

Perception of Distance

We perceive distance by means of two kinds of cues: binocular ("two-eye") and monocular ("one-eye"). Only animals with eyes on the front of the head (such as primates, cats, and some birds) can obtain binocular cues. Monocular cues are potentially available to any species with good form vision.

Binocular Cues

Convergence. An important cue about distance is supplied by **convergence.** You will recall that the eyes make conjugate movements so that both look at (*converge* on) the same point of the visual scene. If an object is very close to your face, your eyes are turned inward. If it is farther away, they look more nearly straight ahead. Thus, the eyes can be used like range finders;

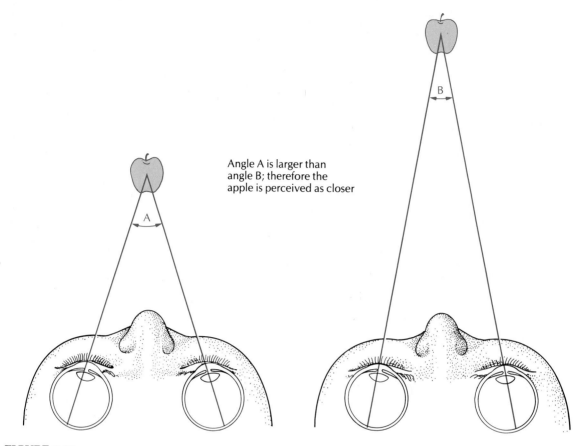

Angle A is larger than angle B; therefore the apple is perceived as closer

FIGURE 3.34

When the eyes converge on a nearby object the angle between them is greater than when they converge on a distant object. The brain uses this information in perceiving the distance of an object.

the brain controls the extraocular muscles, so it knows the angle between them, which is related to the distance between the object and the eyes. (See Figure 3.34.)

Retinal Disparity. An even more important factor in the perception of distance is the information provided by **retinal disparity.** If you hold your finger up in front of you and look past it into the distance you will see a double image of your finger. Because your eyes are now directed toward objects in the distance, and not toward your finger, the image of your finger falls on different portions of the retina in each eye. The degree of retinal disparity provides an important clue about an object's distance.

The perception of depth from retinal disparity is called **stereopsis.** A *stereoscope* is a device that shows two slightly different pictures, one to each eye. When you look through a stereoscope, you see a three-dimensional image. An experiment by Julesz (1965) demonstrated that retinal disparity is what produces the effect of depth. Using a computer, he produced two displays of randomly positioned dots in which the location of some dots differed slightly. If the differing dots were placed properly, the two displays gave the impression of depth when viewed through a stereoscope.

Electrical recordings of individual neurons in the visual system of the brain have found a class of cells that respond only when there is a slight disparity between the image of an object on both retinas. (This is the effect that would occur if an object was not quite at the convergence point of the gaze of the eyes.) Thus, it appears that some neurons at this level compare the activity of neurons with corresponding receptive fields for both eyes and respond when there is a disparity. Obviously, these neurons participate in stereopsis.

Monocular Cues

Good Form. Just as the Gestalt law of good continuation plays a role in form perception, the principle of **good form** affects our perception of the relative location of objects: we perceive the object with the simpler border as being closer. Figure 3.35 contains two drawings that can be seen either as complex two-dimensional figures or as two simple objects, one in front of the other. Because we tend to resolve an ambiguous drawing according to the principle of good form, we almost always see two objects.

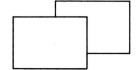

FIGURE 3.35

Use of the principle of good form in the perception of depth. The objects are perceived as identical pairs, but the one on the left in each pair looks closer than the one on the right.

Perspective and Texture. Figure 3.36 shows two columns located at different distances. The drawing shows **perspective:** the tendency for parallel lines that recede from us to converge at a single point. Because of perspective we perceive the columns as being the same size even though they produce retinal images of different sizes. (See Figure 3.36.) On the right side are

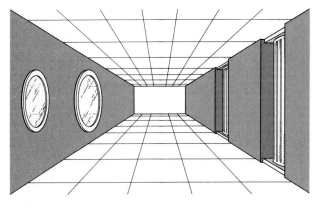

FIGURE 3.36

Although the two mirrors (at left) are drawn to the same size, perspective makes one look smaller.

Because of our experience with seeing reflections of objects, we know that the left-hand side of this cloud, not the cloud itself, is a reflection.

objects that produce retinal images of the same size, but the one toward the rear is perceived as larger.

Texture, especially the texture of the ground, provides another cue we use to perceive the distance of objects sitting on the ground. A coarser texture looks closer, while a finer texture looks more distant. The earth's atmosphere can also supply texture. Parts of the landscape that are farther away become less distinct because of haze in the air. Figures 3.37 and 3.38, located on the following page, illustrate these points.

Information from Head and Body Movements. The information derived from our movements relative to other objects also helps us perceive distance. If you focus your eyes on an object close to you and move your head from side to side, your image of the scene moves back and forth behind the nearer object. If you focus your eyes on the background while moving your head from side to side, the image of the nearer object passes back and forth across the background. Head and body movements cause the images from the scene before us to change; the closer the object, the more it changes, relative to the background. The information contained in this relative movement helps us perceive distance.

Figure 3.39 (on the facing page) illustrates the kinds of cues that are supplied when we move with respect to features in the environment. The top part of the figure shows three objects at different distances from the observer: a man, a house, and a tree. The lower part shows the views that the observer will see from five different places ($P_1 - P_5$). The changes in the relative locations of the objects provide cues to their distance from the observer.

FIGURE 3.38

Variation in detail, owing to fog, produces an appearance of distance.

Perception of Movement

The Gestalt law of common fate, mentioned earlier, states that elements that move together are perceived as being part of the same figure and therefore give rise to the perception of form. This phenomenon enables us to detect moving objects quickly and easily. The eyes also make their own movements, and the brain can compensate for eye, head, and body movements. This compensation enables us to determine whether parts of the visual field are stationary or in motion.

Interpretation of a Moving Retinal Image

Besides perceiving absolute movements, we perceive the movements of objects relative to one another. Sometimes we can be fooled. You may have sat in an automobile at a stoplight

FIGURE 3.37

Variations in texture can produce an appearance of distance.

when the vehicle next to you started to move forward. For a moment you were uncertain whether you were moving backward or the other vehicle was moving forward. Only by looking at nonmoving objects such as buildings or trees could you be sure.

In general, if two objects of different size are seen moving relative to each other, the smaller one is perceived as moving and the larger one as standing still. We perceive people at a distance moving against a stable background, and flies moving against an unmoving wall.

Perception of movement can even help us perceive three-dimensional forms. Johansson (1973) demonstrated just how much informa-

tion we can derive from movement. He dressed actors in black and attached small lights to several points on their bodies, such as their wrists, elbows, shoulders, hips, knees, and feet. He made movies of the actors in a darkened room while they were performing various behaviors, such as walking, running, jumping, limping, doing pushups, and dancing with a partner who was also equipped with lights. Even though observers who watched the films could only see a pattern of moving lights against a dark background, they could readily perceive the pattern as belonging to a moving human, and could identify the behavior the actor was performing. Subsequent studies (Kozlowski

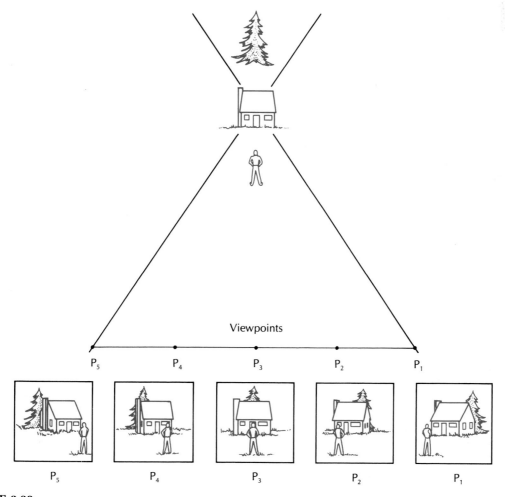

FIGURE 3.39

As we move, we make inferences about distance from the relative positions of objects in the environment. (From Haber, R.N., and Hershenson, M. *The Psychology of Visual Perception*. New York: Holt, Rinehart and Winston, 1973.)

and Cutting, 1977; Barclay, Cutting, and Kozlowski, 1978) showed that people could even tell, with reasonable accuracy, the sex of the actor wearing the lights. The cues appeared to be supplied by the relative amounts of movement of the shoulders and hips as the person walked.

Perception of Movement in the Absence of Motion

If you sit in a darkened room and watch two small lights that are alternately turned on and off, your perception will be that of a single light moving back and forth between two different locations. You will not see the light turn off at one position and then turn on at the second position; if the distance and timing are just right, the light will appear to stay on at all times, quickly moving between the positions. This response is known as the **phi phenomenon.** Theater marquees and "moving" neon signs make use of it.

This characteristic of the visual system accounts for the fact that we perceive the images in motion pictures and on television as continuous rather than separate. The images actually jump from place to place, but we see smooth movement.

- Can you describe three types of monocular cues for perception of distance?
- What are the factors that contribute to visual perception of movement?
- How does experience with objects affect perception of size and shape?

AUDITION

Vision involves the perception of objects in three dimensions, at a variety of distances, and with a multitude of colors and textures. These complex responses may involve a single point in time or an extended period; they may also involve an unchanging scene or a rapidly changing one. The other senses analyze much simpler stimuli (such as an odor or a taste) or depend upon time and stimulus change for the development of a complex perception. For example, to perceive a solid object in three dimensions by means of touch we must manipulate it—turn it over in our hands or move our hands over its surface. The stimulus must change over time for a full-fledged perception of form to emerge. The same is true for audition: we hear nothing meaningful in an instant.

Most people consider the sense of hearing second in importance only to vision. In some ways, it is *more* important. A blind person can converse and communicate with other people almost as well as a sighted person. Deafness is much more likely to produce social isolation; a deaf person cannot easily join in the conversation of a group of people. Although our eyes can transmit much more information to the brain, our ears convey some of our most important forms of social communication.

The Stimulus

Sound consists of rhythmical pressure changes in air. As an object vibrates, it causes the air around it to move. When the object is in the phase of vibration in which it moves toward you, it compresses molecules of air; as it moves away, it pulls the molecules farther apart. As a pressure wave arrives, it bends your eardrum in. The following wave of negative pressure (when the molecules are pulled farther apart) causes your eardrum to bulge out. (See Figure 3.40.)

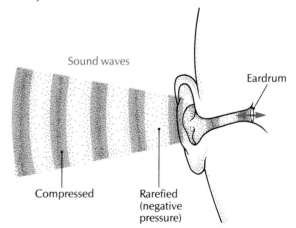

FIGURE 3.40

Changes in air pressure from sound waves move the eardrum in and out.

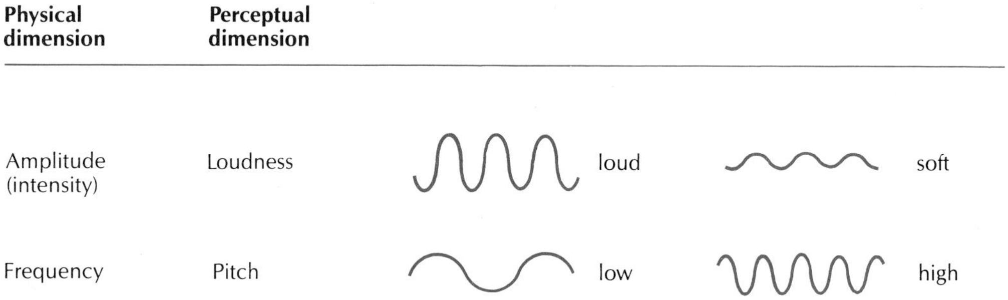

Physical dimension	Perceptual dimension				
Amplitude (intensity)	Loudness	$\bigvee\!\bigvee\!\bigvee$	loud	$\sim\!\sim$	soft
Frequency	Pitch	$\frown\!\smile\frown$	low	$\bigvee\!\bigvee\!\bigvee\!\bigvee$	high

FIGURE 3.41

The physical and perceptual dimensions of sound waves.

Sound waves are measured in frequency units of cycles per second called **hertz (Hz).** The human ear perceives vibrations between approximately 30 and 20,000 Hz. Sound waves can vary in **intensity** and **frequency.** These variations produce corresponding changes in perception of **loudness** and **pitch.** (See Figure 3.41.) However, the relation is not perfect; if a pure tone is increased in intensity, the perceived pitch rises slightly.

Structure and Functions of the Auditory System

When people refer to the ear they usually mean what anatomists call the **pinna**—the flesh-covered cartilage attached to the side of the head. (*Pinna* means "wing" in Latin.) But the pinna performs only a small role in audition; it helps funnel sound through the *ear canal* toward the middle and inner ear, where the business of hearing gets done. (See Figure 3.42.)

The *eardrum* responds to sound waves and passes the vibrations on to the receptor cells in the inner ear. The eardrum is attached to the first of a set of three middle ear bones called the **ossicles** (literally, "little bones"). The three ossicles are known as the *hammer,* the *anvil,* and the *stirrup,* because of their shapes. These bones act together, in lever fashion, to transmit the vibrations of the eardrum to the fluid-filled structure of the inner ear that contains the receptive organ.

The bony structure that contains the receptive organ is called the **cochlea.** (*Kokhlos* means "snail," which accurately describes its shape—see Figure 3.42.) A chamber attached to the cochlea (the *vestibule*) contains two openings, the **oval window** and the **round window.** The last of the three ossicles (the stirrup) presses against a membrane behind the oval window and transmits sound waves through it into the fluid inside the cochlea. The cochlea is divided into two parts by the **basilar membrane.** As the footplate of the stirrup presses back and forth against the membrane behind the oval window, pressure changes in the fluid above the basilar membrane cause it to vibrate back and forth. Because the basilar membrane varies in its width and flexibility, different frequencies of sound cause different parts of the basilar membrane to vibrate. High-frequency sounds cause the end near the oval window to vibrate, medium-frequency sounds cause the middle to vibrate, and low-frequency sounds cause the tip to vibrate.

In order for the basilar membrane to be able to vibrate freely, the fluid in the lower chamber of the cochlea must have somewhere to go—unlike gases, liquids cannot be compressed. Free space is provided by the round window. When the basilar membrane flexes down, the displacement of the fluid causes the membrane behind the round window to bulge out; in turn, when the basilar membrane flexes up, the membrane behind the round window bulges in. Some people suffer from a middle ear disease that causes the bone to grow over the round window. Because their basilar membrane cannot easily flex back and forth, these people have a severe hearing loss. However, their hearing can be restored by a surgical procedure called *fenestration,* or "window making," in which a tiny hole is drilled in the bone where the round window should be.

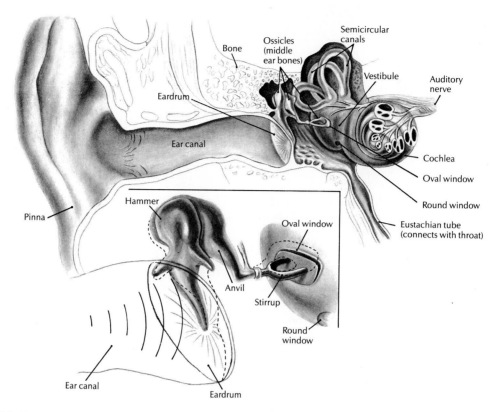

FIGURE 3.42

Anatomy of the auditory system. (From Carlson, N.R. *Physiology of Behavior*, 3rd ed. Boston: Allyn and Bacon, 1986.)

As Figure 3.43 illustrates, sounds are detected by special neurons known as **auditory hair cells.** Auditory hair cells transduce mechanical energy caused by the flexing of the basilar membrane into neural activity. These cells possess hairlike protrusions called **cilia** ("eyelashes"). The ends of the cilia are embedded in a fairly rigid shelf (the **tectorial membrane**) that hangs over the basilar membrane like a balcony. When sound vibrations cause the basilar membrane to flex back and forth, the cilia are stretched. This pull on the cilia is translated into neural activity.

When a mechanical force is exerted on the cilia of the auditory hair cells, the electrical charge across their membrane is somehow altered. The change in the electrical charge causes a transmitter substance to be released at a synapse between the auditory hair cell and the dendrite of a neuron of the auditory nerve. Then, the release of the transmitter substance at the synapse excites the neuron, which transmits messages through the auditory nerve to the brain.

Perception of Pitch

Scientists originally thought that the neurons of the auditory system represented pitch by firing in synchrony with the vibrations of the basilar membrane. However, they subsequently learned that axons cannot fire rapidly enough to represent the high frequencies that we can hear. A good, young ear can hear frequencies of more than 20,000 Hz, but axons cannot fire more than 1000 times per second. Therefore, high-frequency sounds, at least, must be encoded in some other way.

As we saw, high-frequency and medium-frequency sounds cause different parts of the basilar membrane to vibrate. Thus, sounds of different frequencies stimulate different groups of auditory hair cells located along the basilar membrane. We know that at least for high-frequency and medium-frequency sounds, the brain is informed of the pitch of a sound by the activity of different sets of axons from the auditory nerve.

Two basic types of evidence indicate that pitch is detected in this way. First, direct observation of the basilar membrane has shown that the region of maximum vibration depends on the frequency of the stimulating tone (von Békésy, 1960). Second, experiments have found that damage to specific regions of the basilar membrane causes loss of the ability to perceive specific frequencies. The discovery that some antibiotics damage hearing (for example, deafness is one of the possible side effects of an antibiotic used to treat tuberculosis) has helped auditory researchers investigate the anatomical coding of pitch.

Although high-frequency and medium-frequency sounds are detected because they cause different regions of the basilar membrane to vibrate, low-frequency sounds are detected by a different method. Frequencies lower than 200 Hz cause the very tip of the basilar membrane to vibrate in synchrony with the sound waves. Neurons that are stimulated by hair cells located there are able to fire in synchrony with these vibrations, thus firing at the same frequency as the sound. The brain "counts" these vibrations (so to speak) and thus detects low-frequency sounds. As you may have recognized, this process is an example of temporal coding.

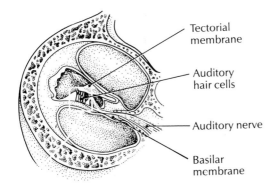

FIGURE 3.43

The transduction of sound vibrations in the auditory system.

■ What are the physical properties of sound and their corresponding perceptual dimensions?
■ What are the major structures of the outer and inner ear?
■ How are low and high frequency sounds detected?

TASTE AND SMELL

We obtain most of our information about distant events in the world from the senses of vision and hearing. However, except for our ability to smell distant odors, the other senses are devoted primarily to objects or events that are near to us, such as things we eat, touch, or feel from the movement of our own bodies.

Gustation

Taste, or **gustation,** is the simplest of the sense modalities. We can perceive only four qualities of taste: *sourness, sweetness, saltiness,* and *bitterness.* Taste is not the same as flavor, which depends on odor as well as taste. The surface of the tongue is differentially sensitive to taste. The tip is most sensitive to sweet and salty substances; the sides to sour substances; and the back of the tongue, the back of the throat, and the soft palate overhanging the back of the tongue to bitter substances. (See Figure 3.44 on p. 112.) The physical properties of the molecules that we taste determine the nature of the taste sensations. Different molecules stimulate different types of receptors.

Receptors

The tongue has a somewhat corrugated appearance, being marked by creases and bumps. The bumps are called **papillae** (from the Latin meaning "nipple"). Each papilla contains a number of *taste buds* (in some cases as many as 200). A taste bud contains a number of receptor cells, each of which is shaped rather like a segment of an orange. The cells have hairlike projections called **microvilli** that protrude through the pore of the taste bud into the saliva that coats the tongue and fills the trenches of the

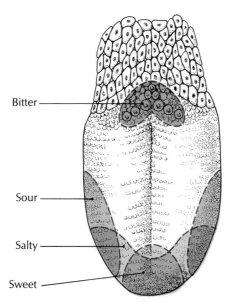

FIGURE 3.44

Different regions of the tongue are especially sensitive to different tastes.

papillae. Molecules of chemicals dissolved in the saliva stimulate the receptor cells, probably by interacting with special receptors on the microvilli that are similar to the postsynaptic receptors found on other neurons. The receptor cells form synapses with dendrites of neurons that send axons to the brain through three different cranial nerves.

Olfaction

The sense of smell—**olfaction**—is one of the most interesting and puzzling of the sense modalities. Odors have a powerful ability to evoke old memories and feelings, even many years after an event. At some time in their lives, most people encounter an odor that they recognize as having some childhood association, even though they cannot identify it. The phenomenon may occur because the olfactory system sends information to the limbic system, a part of the brain that plays a role in emotions and memories. (Functions of the limbic system will be discussed in Chapters 11 and 12.)

Anatomy of the Olfactory System

Figure 3.45 shows the anatomy of the olfactory system. The receptor cells lie in the **olfactory**

mucosa. These one-inch-square patches of mucous membrane are located on the roof of the nasal sinuses, just under the base of the brain. The receptor cells send axons up through small holes in the bone above the olfactory mucosa. The axons synapse on neurons in the **olfactory bulbs,** which are enlargements at the ends of the stalklike olfactory nerves. We do not yet know how olfactory receptor cells detect odors. The most widely accepted hypothesis is that the interaction between odor molecule and receptor is similar to that of transmitter substance and postsynaptic receptor on a neuron. Thus, similar mechanisms may detect the stimuli for taste and olfaction.

In contrast to our knowledge of the four taste dimensions, we do not know how many odors people can identify, but the number is very large. It seems unlikely that we have separate receptors for each odor. Such a requirement would involve a phenomenal number of different receptors, and it undoubtedly takes more than a single receptor cell to produce a sensation. Moreover, it would not explain the fact that we can smell and learn to identify new, synthetic chemicals that were not in existence while our olfactory system was evolving. It

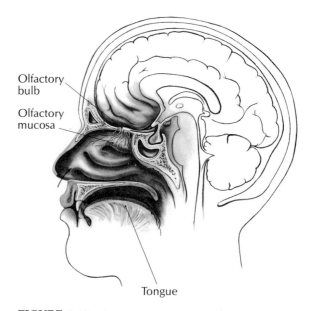

FIGURE 3.45

The olfactory system.

does not seem likely that we possess unique olfactory receptors for every new odor that exists or is yet to be synthesized by chemists.

The problem is to determine how many "odor primaries" there might be. Amoore (1970) studied the words that chemists used to describe the odors of chemicals and was able to reduce the descriptive adjectives to a list of seven: camphoraceous, ethereal, floral, musky, pepperminty, pungent, and putrid. Perhaps, he reasoned, the fact that people find these seven adjectives necessary means there are seven odor primaries, just as there are four taste primaries.

Amoore also hypothesized that there were receptors on the cilia of the olfactory cells with specific shapes to accommodate odor molecules with particular three-dimensional configurations. According to this hypothesis, a particular molecule might fit the pepperminty receptors fairly well, the floral receptors a little less well, the ethereal receptors even less well, and the others not at all. Thus, the brain would receive signals of an odor that was strongly pepperminty, moderately floral, and slightly ethereal, combining these dimensions to produce the perception of a unique odor. Unfortunately, there is not enough evidence to evaluate this or any other hypothesis that has been proposed about the dimensions of odor. Whatever the mechanism of odor reception is, the answer appears to be a long way off.

- How does the transduction of gustatory stimuli work?
- What are the four categories of taste and where are the regions of the tongue that detect each of them?
- What are the main anatomical features of the olfactory system?

THE SOMATOSENSES

The body senses, or **somatosenses,** include our ability to respond to touch, vibration, pain, warmth, coolness, limb position, muscle length and stretch, tilt of the head, and changes in the speed of head rotation. The number of sense modalities represented in this list depends on one's definition of a sense modality. However, it does not really matter whether we say that we respond to warmth and coolness by means of one sense modality or two different ones; the important thing is to understand how our bodies are able to detect changes in temperature.

The Skin Senses

The entire surface of the human body is innervated (supplied with nerve fibers) by the dendrites of neurons that transmit somatosensory information to the brain. Cranial nerves convey information from the face and front portion of the head (including the teeth and the inside of the mouth and throat); spinal nerves convey information from the rest of the body's surface. All somatosensory information is detected by the dendrites of neurons; the system uses no separate receptor cells. However, some of these dendrites have specialized endings that modify the way in which they transduce energy into neural activity.

Temperature

There is general agreement that different sensory endings produce the sensations of warmth and coolness. Detectors for coolness appear to be located closer to the surface of the skin. If you suddenly place your foot under a stream of rather hot water, you may feel a brief sensation of cold just before you perceive that the water is really hot; this sensation probably results from short-lived stimulation of the coolness detectors located in the upper layers of the skin.

Our temperature detectors respond best to *changes* in temperature. Within reasonable limits, the air temperature of our environment comes to feel "normal." Temporary changes in temperature are perceived as warmth or coolness. Thus, our temperature detectors adapt to the temperature of our environment. This adaptation can easily be demonstrated. If you place one hand in a pail of hot water and the other in a pail of cold water, the intensity of the sensations of heat and cold will decrease after a few minutes. If you then plunge both hands into a pailful of water that is at room temperature, it will feel hot to the cold-adapted hand, and cold to the hot-adapted hand. It is mainly the change in temperature that is signaled to the brain. Of course, there are limits to the process of adaptation. Extreme heat or cold will continue to feel hot or cold, however long we experience it.

Pain is caused by damaged tissue in the body.

Pressure and Pain

Sensory psychologists speak of touch and pressure as two separate senses. They define *touch* as the sensation of very light contact of an object with the skin, and *pressure* as the sensation produced by more forceful contact. Sensations of pressure occur only when the skin is actually moving, which means that the pressure detectors respond only while they are being bent. Just how the motion stimulates the neurons is not known. If you rest your forearm on a table and place a small weight on your skin, you will feel the pressure at first, but eventually you will feel nothing at all, if you keep your arm still. You fail to feel the pressure not because your brain "ignores" incoming stimulation; your sensory endings actually cease sending

impulses to your brain. Studies that have measured the very slow, very minute movements of a weight sinking down into the skin have shown that sensations of pressure cease when the movements stop. With the addition of another weight on top of the first one, movement and sensations of pressure begin again (Nafe and Wagoner, 1941). A person will feel a very heavy weight indefinitely, but the sensation is probably one of pain rather than pressure.

Pain is a complex sensation involving not only intense sensory stimulation but also an emotional component; a given sensory input to the brain might be interpreted as pain in one situation and as pleasure in another. For example, when people are sexually aroused, they become less sensitive to many forms of pain and often even find such intense stimulation pleasurable.

Painful stimuli are detected by neurons in the skin and internal organs that detect the presence of chemicals released by cells that have been injured. However, physiological and behavioral evidence suggest that the *sensation* of pain is quite different from the *emotional reaction* to pain. Opiates such as morphine diminish the sensation of pain by stimulating opiate receptors on neurons in the brain; these neurons block the transmission of pain information to the brain. In contrast, some tranquilizers (such as Valium) depress neural systems that are responsible for the emotional reaction to pain but do not diminish the intensity of the sensation. Thus, people who have received a drug like Valium will report that they feel pain just as much as they did before, but that it does not bother them much.

The Internal and Vestibular Senses

Nerves in our internal organs, bones and joints, muscles, and in the vestibular apparatus of our inner ear allow us to perceive the location of our limbs and the balance and orientation of our heads and bodies. We have sensory endings, especially at the joints or junctions between muscles, tendons, and bones, that give information about the amount of force the muscle is exerting and inhibit excessively forceful muscular contractions. In the muscle itself are stretch-detecting receptors called **muscle spindles.** These, with receptors from our joints, give the brain messages concerning the location of parts of the body and the muscular contraction needed for control.

Our "sense of balance" involves these sensations and also our vision, but of central importance to help us remain upright is the **vestibular apparatus** in the inner ear. Among the critical parts of this are the **semicircular canals,** three loops at right angles to each other and oriented to detect the three dimensional movements of the head. With rotation of the head, a liquid inside these loops flows past nerve fibers to give information about head orientation.

Another set of inner-ear organs, the **vestibular sacs,** contain calcium carbonate crystals whose weight shifts within the sacs to detect head movement. These sacs are involved in a reflex movement with the eyes, which enables us to see clearly even when the head is jarred. The vestibular sacs detect undulating motion to produce motion sickness in susceptible individuals.

■ What sensations are detected by the somatosensory system?
■ What information is detected by our internal and vestibular senses?

CHAPTER SUMMARY

1. Our knowledge of the world stems from the accumulation of sensory experience and subsequent learning. All sensory experiences are the result of energy from events that is transduced into activity of receptors, which are either specialized cells or the dendritic endings of neurons. This transduction causes changes in the activity of axons of sensory nerves and informs the sensory mechanisms of the brain about the environmental event. The information received from the receptors is transmitted to the brain by means of two coding schemes: anatomical coding and temporal coding.

2. The cornea and lens cast an image of the scene on the retina, which contains photoreceptors: rods and cones. The energy from light is transduced into neural activity when a photon strikes a molecule of photopigment, splitting it into its two constituents. This event causes the photoreceptor to send information to the ganglion cells, by means of the bipolar cells. Adaptation to light and dark depends on the relative number of split and intact photopigment molecules in the photoreceptors. Rods are more sensitive to light but provide poor acuity; cones are less sensitive to light but provide excellent acuity and color vision.

3. The eyes have a repertoire of movements that function for visual perception. Research experiments with stabilized images demonstrate that the small, involuntary movements keep the image moving across the photoreceptors, thus preventing them from adapting to a constant stimulus. We use other eye movements as well, including conjugate movements, saccadic movements, and pursuit movements.

4. When an image is cast upon the retina, each part of the image has a specific hue, brightness, and saturation. The red, blue, and green cones respond in proportion to the amount of each of these wavelengths contained in the light striking them. The encoded information is transmitted through red/green and yellow/blue ganglion cells, which send axons to the brain. The amount of activity in the red/green and yellow/blue axons from each part of the retina gives rise to the perception of an image, complete with color. Staring at a particular color for a while causes a negative afterimage to form, which contains the complementary color. Defects in color vision include two red/green confusions, in which red or green cones contain the wrong photopigment, and a blue/yellow confusion, caused by the absence of functioning blue cones.

5. Studies of the electrical activity of single neurons in the brain have shown that cells in the thalamus respond to spots of light in their receptive field and that there is a point-by-point correlation between the visual field and the surface of the primary visual cortex. In addition, both simple cells and complex cells in the primary visual cortex respond to lines of a particular orientation; the receptive field of complex cells is larger, and they respond best when the lines move. Cells in the visual association cortex analyze information they receive from the primary visual cortex and respond to complex stimuli presented almost anywhere in the visual field.

6. Rules govern the way in which we see our world. Most phenomena of visual perception depend on relations among different elements of the scene before us. We perceive the brightness of an object relative to the brightness of objects around it; thus, objects retain a constant brightness under a variety of conditions of illumination. The Gestalt organizational laws of proximity, similarity, good continuation, closure, and common fate describe some ways that we distinguish figure from ground.

7. Experience, too, has an effect on visual perception. Although it was thought that simple features were analyzed by innate neural connections in the visual system, research has shown that visual deprivation early in life prevents some mechanisms from developing properly, while a special visual experience early in life causes the development of novel feature detectors.

8. Because the size and shape of a retinal image vary with the location of an object relative to the eye, accurate form perception requires perception of an object's location in space. Binocular cues (from convergence and retinal disparity) and monocular cues (from the principle of good form, perspective, texture, and the effects of head and body movements) help us perceive distance.

9. Because our bodies might be moving while we visually follow something, the visual system keeps track of the commands to the eye muscles and compensates for the direction in which the eyes are pointing. Movement is perceived when objects move relative to one another. In particular, the smaller object is likely to be perceived as moving across the larger one. Movement is also perceived when our eyes follow a moving object, even though its image remains on the same part of the retina.

10. The phi phenomenon describes our tendency to see an instantaneous displacement of an object from one place to another as movement of that object.

11. The physical dimensions of sound— amplitude, frequency, and complexity—are translated into the perceptual dimensions of loudness and pitch for sounds ranging from 30 to 20,000 Hz. Sound pressure waves put the process in motion by setting up vibrations in the eardrum, which are passed on to the ossicles. Vibrations of the stirrup against the membrane behind the oval window create pressure changes in the fluid within the cochlea that cause the basilar membrane to flex back and forth. This vibration causes the auditory hair cells on the basilar membrane to move relative to the tectorial membrane. The resulting pull on the cilia of the hair cells stimulates them to secrete a transmitter substance that excites neurons of the auditory nerve. This process informs the brain of the presence of a sound.

12. Two different methods of detection enable the brain to differentiate the multitude of sounds that can be produced. Different high-frequency and medium-frequency sounds are perceived when different parts of the basilar membrane vibrate in response to these frequencies. Low-frequency vibrations are detected when the tip of the basilar membrane vibrates in synchrony with the sound, which causes the axons in the auditory nerve to fire at the same frequency.

13. Both gustation and olfaction are served by cells with receptors that respond selectively to various kinds of molecules. Taste buds have four kinds of receptors, responding to molecules that we perceive as sweet, salty, sour, or bitter.

14. Olfaction is a remarkable sense modality. We can distinguish countless different odors and can even recognize smells from childhood, although we cannot remember when or where we encountered them.

15. The somatosenses gather several different kinds of information from different parts of the body through the skin senses (temperature, touch and pressure, vibration, and pain), the internal senses (involving control of joints and muscles), and the vestibular senses (balance, which involves the vestibular apparatus of the inner ear).

KEY TERMS

anatomical coding A means of representing information by the nervous system; different features are coded by the activity of different neurons. For example, in the auditory system, each pitch of moderate-to-high frequency is represented by the activity of a different set of neurons.

aqueous humor Watery fluid behind the cornea that is filtered out of blood.

auditory hair cell Neurons that detect sound within the cochlea.

basilar membrane A membrane that divides the cochlea of the inner ear into two compartments. The receptive organ for audition resides here.

bipolar cell layer The layer of neurons in the retina that receives information from photoreceptors and passes it on to the ganglion cells, from which axons proceed through the optic nerves to the brain.

brightness A perceptual dimension of color, most closely related to the intensity or degree of radiant energy emitted by a visual stimulus.

brightness constancy The tendency to perceive objects as having constant brightness even when they are observed under varying levels of illumination.

cilia Hairlike protrusions of auditory hair cells.

closure The tendency to see incomplete or partially obscured forms as complete and whole.

cochlea A snail-shaped chamber set in bone in the inner ear, where audition takes place. See also *basilar membrane*.

color mixing The perception of two or more lights of different wavelengths seen together as light of an intermediate wavelength.

common fate The tendency to perceive elements that move together in the same direction as belonging to the same figure in the foreground.

complementary colors Colors that, when mixed, will produce a neutral hue (white or shades of gray). A negative afterimage is complementary to the color to which the eye was exposed.

complex cells Neurons of the primary visual cortex that respond best to lines moving at right angles to the angle of orientation.

cone One of the photoreceptors in the retina; responsible for acute daytime vision and for color perception. See also *rod*.

conjugate movement The cooperative movement of the eyes, which ensures that the image of an object falls on identical portions of both retinas.

convergence Binocular cue that involves conjugate eye movement to perceive distance.

cornea The transparent tissue covering the front of the eye.

dark adaptation The process by which the eye becomes capable of distinguishing dimly illuminated objects after going from a bright region to a dark one. This process involves chemical changes in the photoreceptors of the retina.

deuteranopia A form of hereditary anomalous color vision, resulting from defective "green" cones in the retina.

figure Within a picture or scene, the object rather than its background.

form constancy The tendency to perceive objects as having a constant form, even when they are rotated or moved farther from or closer to the observer.

fovea A small pit near the center of the retina, containing densely packed cones; responsible for the most acute and detailed vision.

frequency The speed of a periodic event, especially of sound vibrations. Frequency is closely related to pitch, a perceptual dimension of sound.

ganglion cell layer The layer of neurons in the retina that receive information from photoreceptors by means of bipolar cells, and from which axons proceed through the optic nerves to the brain.

Gestalt psychology The study of perception that deals with the relation of elements to one another, that the whole in perception is greater than the sum of its parts.

good continuation Gestalt principle that refers to the predictability of simplicity; a simple pattern is seen more readily than a complex pattern.

good form Gestalt principle of the relative location of objects; an object with a simple border is perceived as being closer.

ground Within a picture or scene, the background of an object rather than the object itself.

gustation   The sense of taste.

hertz (Hz)   The primary measure of the frequency of vibration of sound waves; cycles per second.

hue   A perceptual dimension of color, most closely related to the wavelength of a pure light. The effect of a particular hue is caused by the mixture of lights of various wavelengths.

intensity   Amplitude of a physical stimulus; in audition, the intensity of a sound is closely associated with its loudness (a perceptual dimension); in vision.

iris   Two bands of muscles that control the amount of light admitted into the eye.

lens   Behind the iris, the lens focuses images on the back inner surface of the eye.

loudness   A perceptual dimension of sound, most closely associated with intensity (amplitude).

microelectrodes   Extremely small wires with microscopically sharp points that detect electrical disturbances that accompany the action potentials of individual neurons.

microvilli   Hairlike projections on receptor cells of a taste bud.

muscle spindles   Stretch-detecting receptors in the muscle.

nanometer (nm)   One billionth of a meter, or one millionth of a millimeter.

negative afterimage   The image that is seen after a portion of the retina is exposed to an intense visual stimulus; a negative afterimage consists of colors complementary to those of the physical stimulus.

olfaction   The sense of smell.

olfactory bulb   Enlargements at the ends of olfactory nerves.

olfactory mucosa   One-inch-square patches of mucous membrane on the roof of the nasal sinuses.

optic disk   Point at the back of the eye at which axoms leave the eye and join the optic nerve; this portion of the retina is blind.

ossicles   The three bones of the middle ear (known as the hammer, anvil, and stirrup) that transmit acoustical vibrations from the eardrum to the membrane behind the oval window of the cochlea.

oval window   An opening in the bone surrounding the cochlea that permits the footplate of the stirrup to transmit acoustical vi-

brations to the receptive organ inside the cochlea.

papilla   Bump on the tongue containing taste buds.

perception   Awareness of the more complex characteristics of stimuli.

perspective   Tendency of parallel that recede from the viewer to converge at a single point.

phi phenomenon   The perceived movement that is caused by the running on of two or more lights, one at a time, in sequence; often used on theater marquees; responsible for the apparent movement of images in movies and television.

photon   A particle of electromagnetic energy, including light.

photopigment   A protein dye that is bonded to a substance derived from vitamin A; when struck by light it bleaches and stimulates the membrane of the photoreceptor in which it resides.

photoreceptor   A receptive cell in the retina; rods and cones are photoreceptors.

pinna   The flesh-covered cartilage attached to the side of the head, commonly known as the ear.

pitch   A perceptual dimension of sound, most closely associated with frequency.

protanopia   A form of hereditary anomalous color vision, caused by defective "red" cones in the retina.

proximity   Gestalt principle that elements closest together will be perceived as belonging together.

pursuit movement   The movements that the eyes make to maintain an image upon the fovea.

receptive field   The portion of the visual field in which stimuli elicit responses in a neuron or group of neurons in the nervous system.

receptor cell   A neuron that directly responds to a physical stimulus, such as light, vibrations, or aromatic molecules.

retina   The tissue at the back inside surface of the eye that contains the photoreceptors and associated neurons.

retinal disparity   Factor in the perception of distance that refers to the double image of a near object when focusing on a far object.

rhodopsin   The photopigment contained by rods.

rod   A photoreceptor that is very sensitive to

light but cannot detect changes in hue. See also *cone*.

rod-cone break The discontinuity in the dark-adaptation curve.

round window An opening in the bone surrounding the cochlea of the inner ear. A membrane behind the round window bulges in and out in response to pressure changes exerted by the footplate of the stirrup on the membrane behind the oval window.

saccadic movement The rapid movement of the eyes that is used in scanning a visual scene, as opposed to the smooth pursuit movements used to follow a moving object.

saturation A perceptual dimension of color, most closely associated with purity of a color.

sclera Tough, white membrane that coats the eye, except for the cornea.

semicircular canals A set of organs in the inner ear that respond to rotational movements of the head.

sensation Awareness of simple properties of stimuli.

similarity Gestalt principle that similar-looking elements will be perceived as part of the same form.

simple cells Neurons in the primary visual cortex that respond to line of a particular orientation.

somatosenses Body senses including skin, internal, and vestibular senses.

spectral color A color that can be found in the visual spectrum (rainbow).

stabilized image Remains in one location on the retina.

stereopsis Device used to show each of a pair of eyes a slightly varying image.

tectorial membrane Rigid shelf holding cilia in the middle ear.

temporal coding A means of representing information by the nervous system; different features are coded by the pattern of activity of neurons. For example, in the auditory system, pitches of low frequency are represented by the rate of firing of a particular set of neurons.

transduction The conversion of physical stimuli into electrical events in cells of sensory organs.

tritanopia "Third color defect," in which people see the world in reds and greens; caused by loss of cones in the retina that are sensitive to light of short wavelengths ("blue" cones).

unconscious inference Theory that explains form constancy of an object whether it is small and far or large and near.

vestibular apparatus The receptive organs of the inner ear that contribute to balance and perception of head movement.

vestibular sacs A set of two receptor organs in each inner ear that detect changes in the tilt of the head.

wavelength The distance between adjacent waves of radiant energy; in vision, most closely associated with the perceptual dimension of hue.

Child Development

All human life is characterized by growth and change. Some of the changes are rapid and momentous; others are so slow that we do not notice them until we look back and see how different we are from the way we once were. Infancy and childhood are certainly times of rapid change. Developmental psychologists study these changes and attempt to identify optimal conditions for growth.

How do physiological and environmental factors interact to facilitate human development? Psychologists know that physical development of the nervous system depends on an infant's interaction with the environment. If the child does not actively explore the environment, development of the nervous system may be adversely affected. At the same time, however, a child's ability to actively explore the environment depends on a certain degree of physical and perceptual development. Time-tables for activities such as walking and talk-ing, for example, are regulated in large part by neurological growth. As you will see, physiological and environmental factors interact; a child needs to grow up in a responsive and varied environment so that physiological development can occur at the right times in the maturational process.

In this chapter, you will read about attempts developmental psychologists have made to understand the many factors that influence child development. How do infants perceive the world? Do all children pass through a series of predictable stages of cognitive development? Is there a critical period for attachment between infants and parents? How important is interaction with peers to a child's social development? While psychologists have made many discoveries about many of the factors that influence child development, the complexity of the field continues to challenge the developmental psychologist.

CONCEPTION AND BIRTH

Chromosomes and Genes

Our bodies consist of many trillions of cells, all descendants of a single fertilized egg that must contain the information necessary to construct a human being. This information resides in the nucleus of the cell in twenty-three pairs of chromosomes, and in the course of our physical development, copies of these chromosomes will be included in each of these trillions of cells. This must certainly be the most efficient means of information storage found anywhere in nature; a set of human chromosomes can easily fit on the point of a pin. (See Figure 4.1.)

The functional unit of the chromosome is the **gene**; every chromosome consists of many thousands of genes, each of which contains the instructions necessary to produce a particular protein. Through their ability to direct the kinds and amounts of proteins that are manufactured, genes control an organism's development. In this regard, the most important proteins are called enzymes.

When a pregnant woman eats, she ingests complex molecules in the form of animal or plant tissue and then proceeds to break these molecules down to simple ones. Her body provides these simple nutrients to the cells of her developing offspring; each cell then combines these simple molecules into the complex ones it requires. This process is controlled by enzymes. **Enzymes** act as biological catalysts; they determine the kinds of chemical reactions that occur, without themselves becoming part of the final product. Thus, the types of enzymes present in a cell determine which complex molecules are produced by that cell and hence control the cell's structure and function.

Production of Gametes

Fertilization requires the production of ova (eggs) and sperms. Approximately 500,000 ova are present in the female's body from birth. Because these ova contain different assortments of chromosomes, they represent an enormous potential for genetic diversity among her offspring. After puberty, one of a woman's ovaries will produce a ripe ovum each month, which is released and picked up by one of her fallopian tubes. (This discharge of the ovum is called **ovulation**.) The fallopian tube conveys the ovum toward the woman's uterus. An ovum is the largest cell of the human body; it is approximately the size of the head of a pin. It has a yolk that contains nutrients to sustain its growth for a few days. Sperms are small cells that swim by lashing their long tails back and forth. They are produced daily in a man's testes and are carried in a fluid called semen. Over the course of a man's life his testes produce billions of sperms.

Ova and sperms are collectively referred to as **gametes** (from the Greek *gamos*, meaning "marriage"). They are produced by the division of special cells in the ovaries and testes. This division is special because it results in cells that have only half the normal number of chromosomes. Instead of twenty-three *pairs* of chromosomes, sperms and ova contain twenty-three *single* chromosomes—one member of each pair.

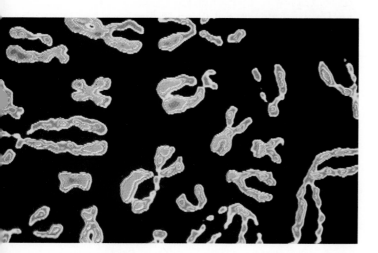

FIGURE 4.1

Human chromosomes contain genes, which are found in the nucleus of every cell in the body. At conception, the twenty-three unpaired chromosomes of the egg unite with the twenty-three unpaired chromosomes of the sperm to form a complete cell.

Fertilization

Once a man ejaculates semen into a woman's vagina, the sperms begin their journey into the uterus and up the fallopian tubes. Fertilization occurs if a sperm meets and unites with an ovum traveling downward through one of the

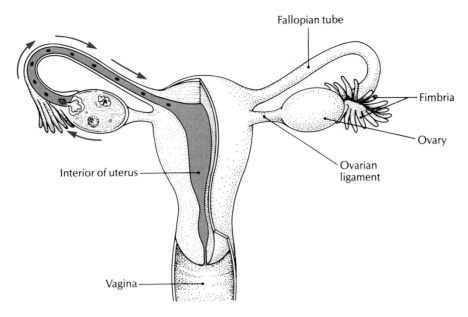

FIGURE 4.2

After ovulation, the ovum is swept into a fallopian tube by the fimbria and travels toward the uterus. If fertilization occurs, it takes place in the fallopian tube.

fallopian tubes. (See Figure 4.2.) Sperms and ova contain twenty-three single chromosomes—one member of each pair. When an ovum is fertilized, the pairs are reconstituted in a single cell called a **zygote,** with one member of each new pair coming from each parent. In this way, each parent contributes half of a child's genetic material. (See Figure 4.3.)

A single ejaculation of semen contains hundreds of millions of sperms and thus might appear to be a wasteful expenditure of genetic material, because only one sperm unites with the ovum. But the trip through the woman's reproductive system is so arduous that only a few of the millions of sperms ever get near the ovum. Furthermore, biologists believe that sperms release a chemical that breaks down a barrier surrounding the ovum, permitting one of them to enter and fertilize it. Thus, although only one sperm contributes its genetic material to the beginning organism, fertilization requires the presence of many sperms.

A fertilized human egg is nothing more than a very large cell containing the twenty-three pairs of human chromosomes. This cell divides and redivides, with each division doubling the previous number of cells. Just before a cell divides, it duplicates all of its parts; it produces a duplicate set of chromosomes, with one set going to each of the two new cells. At first the

exact same cell is replicated, creating a mass of identical cells. Then, according to a special internal mechanism, the cells produced in this sequence of divisions undergo **differentiation.** In this process, the various cells "specialize" by acquiring certain distinct features. A single cell develops into a complex organism consisting of thousands of *different* kinds of cells.

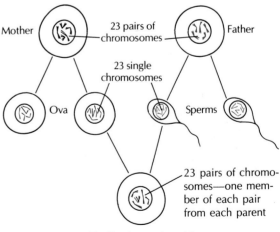

Fertilized ovum (zygote)

FIGURE 4.3

Each parent contributes one half of his or her child's chromosomes through the sperm or ovum.

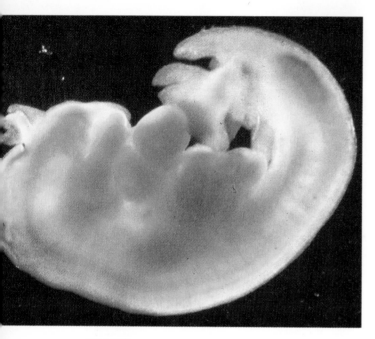

FIGURE 4.4

A human embryo 28 days after fertilization. Most of the primitive organ systems are formed and the embryonic heart is beating. The embryo's curved appearance is due to the symmetrical growth of the brain.

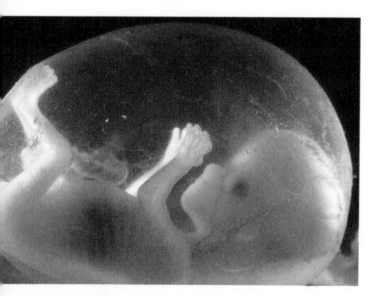

FIGURE 4.5

A human fetus at 14 weeks. The fetus is now recognizable as an infant although the head is still proportionately large. Facial features are evident, the upper limbs are further developed than the lower ones, and sexual differentiation has occurred.

The factors that control the development of a human organism are incredibly complex. For example, the most complicated organ—the brain—consists of many billions of neurons (nerve cells), all of which are connected to other neurons. In addition, many of these neurons are connected to sensory receptors, muscles, or glands. During development, these billions of neurons must establish the proper connections, so that the eyes send their information to the visual cortex, the ears send theirs to the auditory cortex, and the neurons controlling movement connect with the right muscles.

Experiments have shown that as the axons of developing neurons grow, they thread their way through a tangle of other growing cells, responding to physical and chemical signals along the way, much as a salmon swims upriver to the tributary in which it was spawned. During this stage of development, differentiating cells can be misguided by false signals. For example, if a woman contracts German measles during early pregnancy, toxic chemicals produced by the disease virus may adversely affect the development of the fetus. Sometimes these chemicals can misdirect the interconnections of brain cells and produce mental retardation. Thus, although development of a human organism is programmed genetically, environmental factors can affect development even before a person is born.

Development in the Uterus

The fertilized ovum, sustained by its yolk, travels down the fallopian tube, dividing and redividing. When the developing organism reaches the uterus, it attaches itself to the wall of the uterus and begins to grow tendrils that intertwine with the rich supply of blood vessels located there. The mass of dividing cells begins to differentiate into various kinds of tissues. At this moment, when the cells begin to specialize, the organism becomes an embryo.

The embryo develops an **amniotic sac,** a membrane that completely encases it in a watery fluid. It also develops a **placenta,** which draws nourishment from the mother and passes waste products to her to be excreted. These transfers are conveyed by blood vessels in the umbilical cord, which connects the fetus to the placenta. (See Figures 4.4 and 4.5.)

By the time the embryo becomes a fetus (in approximately eight weeks) it is unmistakably human in appearance. When it is four months old, the mother can feel its movements. In another month it is capable of responding to the environment; it can swallow some of the amniotic fluid in which it floats, and sometimes it even develops hiccups. The sucking reflex is well established before birth; pictures taken of fetuses by means of sonar have caught them in the act of sucking their thumbs.

As we saw, some chemicals can have disastrous effects on fetal development. There is some evidence that even a single alcoholic "binge" during a critical stage of pregnancy can cause permanent damage to the fetus. One of the most common drug-induced abnormalities, the **fetal alcohol syndrome,** is seen in many offspring of women who are chronic alcoholics. The children are much smaller than average, have characteristic facial abnormalities, and more significantly, are mentally retarded.

Genetic Abnormalities That Harm Development

Many different types of genetic abnormalities can harm development. Some of the abnormalities result in brain damage and consequent mental retardation. The best-known example is **Down's syndrome.** This disorder was previously called *mongolism*, because of the slight facial resemblance of these children to people of Mongolian origin. It is usually produced by a chromosomal abnormality consisting of an extra twenty-first chromosome, so that there are three, rather than a pair. Researchers do not yet know how the extra chromosome produces its harmful effects. Although the disorder is *genetic*, it is not caused by a faulty gene and is therefore not *hereditary*. The incidence of Down's syndrome is related to the mother's age and, according to some researchers, possibly the father's as well.

Children with Down's syndrome are typically affectionate, loving, and cheerful. Some of them are only moderately retarded; some score as well on tests of intelligence as people considered normal. Therefore, many such children remain with their families instead of living in an institution for mentally retarded children. However, children with Down's syndrome are

more susceptible than normal children to a variety of physical disorders and therefore have a shorter life expectancy.

A second genetic disorder, **phenylketonuria (PKU),** is caused by a pair of faulty genes that fail to produce a particular enzyme. The enzyme normally causes one amino acid (phenylalanine) to be converted into another (tyrosine). In a baby with PKU, the unconverted phenylalanine accumulates in the blood and damages the brain cells, causing mental retardation.

Fortunately, PKU can be treated. A special diet containing very little phenylalanine keeps the blood level of this amino acid low and allows the nervous system to develop normally. Once it is mature enough, the nervous system builds barriers that protect it from excessive levels of phenylalanine in the blood, and the dietary restriction can be relaxed somewhat.

Early treatment is vital, because the brain damage is permanent. After the first twenty-five weeks of postpartum life, it is too late to prevent mental retardation. Reliable,valid tests for PKU are now available, and many countries require that all newborn infants be tested for the disorder.

■ What are the roles of chromosomes, genes, and proteins (including enzymes) in human development?

■ How are gametes produced? How would you describe the processes of fertilization and differentiation?

■ What development takes place in the uterus?

■ What are the causes and prognosis of Down's syndrome and phenylketonuria (PKU)?

PHYSICAL AND PERCEPTUAL DEVELOPMENT OF THE INFANT

The word *infant* means "unable to speak." By general agreement, the newborn baby is called an infant until two years of age, even though normal infants begin to speak during their second year. A newborn human infant is a helpless creature, absolutely dependent on adult care. But recent research has shown that newborns do not passively await the ministrations of their caretakers; they very quickly develop skills that shape the behavior of the adults with whom they interact.

Motor Development

At birth, the infant's most important movements are reflexes—automatic movements in response to specific stimuli. The most important reflexes are **rooting, sucking,** and **swallowing** responses. If a baby's cheek is lightly touched, the baby will turn its head so the object reaches the lips (the rooting response). If the object is of the appropriate size, texture, and temperature, the baby will open its mouth and begin to suck. When the milk enters the mouth, the baby will automatically make swallowing movements. Obviously, these reflexes are important for the baby's survival. As we will see later in this chapter, these behaviors, along with cuddling, looking, smiling, and crying, are important for an infant's social development as well.

Newborn infants can also respond to noxious stimuli by withdrawing, but this reflex tends to be rather diffuse. Older children will pull their arm back if their hand strikes a hot or sharp object, but a baby's withdrawal reflex lacks such precision—the entire body participates in the movement. Because the baby's own organized movements are so limited, he or she must depend on adult intervention for protection from harm and for provision of food.

Normal motor development follows a distinct pattern, which appears to be dictated by maturation of the muscles and the nervous system. For example, Shirley (1933) carried out a careful, thorough study of the stages of development of the ability to walk. Although individual children progress at different rates, their development follows the same basic pattern. Figure 4.6 shows her results.

Two general trends stand out in the development of motor control: **cephalocaudal development** and **proximodistal development** (Appleton, Clifton, and Goldberg, 1975). *Cephalocaudal* ("head to tail") refers to the fact that an infant learns to control the movements of the upper part of the body first. In fact, a newborn baby has good control of eye movements, and the presence of the rooting, sucking, and swallowing responses demonstrates control of some movements of the head, mouth, lips, tongue, and throat. *Proximodistal* ("near to far") refers to the fact that a baby can control

Infants expend much energy learning how to walk.

0 month
Fetal posture

1 month
Chin up

2 months
Chest up

3 months
Reach
and miss

4 months
Sit with
support

5 months
Sit on lap,
grasp object

6 months
Sit on high
chair, grasp
dangling object

7 months
Sit alone

8 months
Stand
with help

9 months
Stand holding
furniture

10 months
Creep

11 months
Walk when led

12 months
Pull to stand
by furniture

13 months
Climb stair steps

14 months
Stand alone

15 months
Walk alone

FIGURE 4.6

Milestones in a child's motor development. (From Shirley, M.M. *The First Two Years,* vol. 2, *Intellectual Development.* Minneapolis: University of Minnesota Press, 1933.)

the arms long before he or she can control the hands and fingers.

Development of motor skills requires two ingredients: maturation of the child's nervous system and lots of practice. Development of the brain is not complete at birth; a great deal of growth occurs during the first several months (Dekaban, 1970). In fact, some changes are still taking place in early adulthood. Particular kinds of movements must await the development of the necessary neuromuscular systems. But motor development is not merely a matter

of using these systems once they develop; instead, physical development of the nervous system depends, to a large extent, on the baby's own movements while interacting with the environment. The infant's movements greatly affect the development of the nervous system.

Normal infants in stimulating and nonrestrictive environments will practice their developing motor skills. This often means hard work; young children have to put real effort into mastering new skills. For example, infants expend much energy while learning how to

Studies have shown that a stimulating environment encourages infants' perceptual development.

walk. By the end of the first year of life, babies can get from place to place very efficiently by crawling. However, they soon begin to struggle with standing upright and taking a few steps. When trying to get somewhere fast, a baby will drop to all fours and crawl. But when exploring in a more leisurely fashion, the baby will try to walk, even though this means of locomotion is slow, tedious, and punctuated by frequent falls. For an infant, mastery of the skill of walking seems to serve as its own reward.

Studies have shown that children who have spent their infancy lying on their backs in cribs in institutional nurseries do not develop the normal motor skills of children who are raised in homes or in institutions that provide more stimulation and opportunity for movement and exploration (Dennis, 1960). Crawling and walking are among the skills that can be severely retarded. Fortunately, normal motor skills will develop in a wide range of environments; only the most restrictive ones will produce severe motor impairments.

Perceptual Development

Almost everyone who has watched a newborn baby has wondered how infants perceive the world. What can they see? What can they hear? Until a few years ago, we could only speculate about the answers to these questions.

If we want to study how older children or adults perceive the world, we can simply ask them about their experiences. We can determine how large an object must be for them to see it, or how loud a sound must be for them to hear it. But we cannot talk to infants and expect to get any answers; we must use their nonverbal behavior as an indicator of what they can perceive.

It has been clear for a long time that a newborn baby's senses function at least to a certain extent. We know that the auditory system can detect sounds, because the baby will show a startle reaction when presented with a sudden, loud noise. Similarly, a bright light will elicit eye closing and squinting. A cold object or a pinch will produce crying, so the sense of touch must be present. If held firmly and tilted backward, a baby will stiffen and flail his or her arms and legs, so we must conclude that babies have a sense of balance.

Research indicates that even an unborn fetus has a sense of taste. When a pregnant woman accumulates too much amniotic fluid, the condition can be corrected by injecting a sugar solution into the fluid. The fetus obviously detects the sweet taste, because it usually swallows enough fluid to eliminate the excess (Bookmiller and Bowen, 1967). The swallowed fluid enters the bloodstream of the fetus and is then transported through the placenta to the mother, who excretes it in her urine.

1-month-old

2-month-old

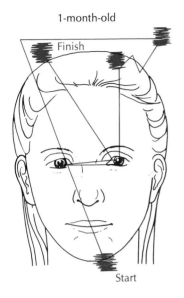

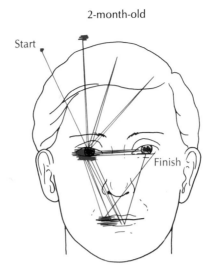

FIGURE 4.7

The scanning sequence used by children viewing actual faces. (From Salapatek, P. In *Infant Perception: From Sensation to Cognition*, vol. 1, *Basic Visual Processes*, edited by L.B. Cohen and P. Salapatek. New York: Academic Press, 1975.)

Beyond these simple demonstrations, most recent investigations of the perceptual abilities of newborn infants have taken advantage of cephalocaudal development—the fact that babies have good control of movements of their head, eyes, and mouth.

Perception of Patterns

Most investigations of infant perception have concentrated on vision, probably because it is such an important sense for humans. No careful observer ever doubted that a baby's eyes can respond to light; newborn infants will close their eyes and screw up their faces if the level of illumination is too high. But what about their ability to perceive objects?

A clever technique, first reported by Stirnimann (1944) and later developed by Fantz (1961), takes advantage of a young infant's good control over eye movements. The baby lies on his or her back a few inches beneath a plywood screen, and various stimuli are placed on this ceiling. Through a small peephole above the screen, Fantz observed and recorded the baby's eye movements. He discovered that as early as four days after birth, babies looked longer and more often at a facelike object than at a same-sized object with a scrambled face pattern. Fantz concluded that newborn infants have an innate preference for human faces.

Subsequently, investigators employed modern technology to refine Fantz's technique (Haith, 1969, 1976; Salapatek, 1975). A harmless spot of infrared light, invisible to humans, is directed onto the baby's eyes. A special television camera, sensitive to infrared light, records the spot and superimposes it on an image of the display that the baby is looking at. The technique is precise enough to determine *which parts* of a stimulus the baby is scanning. For example, Salapatek (1975) reported that a one-month-old infant tends not to look at the inside of a figure; instead, the child's gaze seems to be "trapped" by the edges. However, by the age of two months, the baby scans across the border to investigate the interior of a figure. Figure 4.7 shows a computer-drawn reconstruction of the paths followed by the eye scans of infants of these ages. (The babies looked at *real* faces, not the drawings in Figure 4.7.)

Haith (1976) suggested that the rule governing an infant's visual exploration is the following: maximize the activity of the visual system. This hypothetical rule accounts for the preferences that babies show for one pattern over another; they spend more time looking at patterns with the highest amount of contrast. Perhaps the strategy of keeping the activity of the visual system as high as possible is an innate behavioral tendency that makes children participate in their own visual development.

Perception of Space

The ability to perceive three-dimensional space comes at an early age. Gibson and Walk (1960) placed six-month-old babies on what they called a *visual cliff*—a platform containing a checkerboard pattern. The platform adjoined a glass shelf mounted several feet over a floor, which was also covered by the checkerboard pattern. Most babies who could crawl would not venture onto the glass shelf. They acted as if they were afraid of falling. (See Figure 4.8.)

As we saw in Chapter 3, one of the most important sources of binocular cues is stereopsis. Stereoscopic vision occurs after neurons in the visual cortex become connected with ganglion cells from both eyes. Hubel and Wiesel (1970) showed that these connections depend on visual experience. They found that if one or the other of an animal's eyes are alternately covered so that it can use only one eye at a time, the connections never occur—the animal never acquires stereoscopic vision. Thus, there is a critical period for the development of these connections; once it is over, they cannot be established. (Hubel and Wiesel won a Nobel Prize in 1981 for this discovery.)

This critical period for depth perception has important implications for human development. If an infant's eyes do not move together properly, so they both are directed toward the same place in the environment, the infant never develops stereoscopic vision, even if the eye movements are later corrected by surgery on the eye muscles. Banks, Aslin, and Letson (1975) studied infants whose eye-movement

deficits were later corrected surgically. Their results show that the critical period ends sometime between one and three years of age; if surgery occurs later, stereoscopic vision will not develop.

- How would you describe infant motor development?
- What are the methods used to study infants' perceptions? What results have these methods produced?
- What does current research suggest about the development of depth perception during infancy?
- What implications for human development does the concept of a critical period for depth perception have?

COGNITIVE DEVELOPMENT

The Importance of a Responsive Environment

As children grow, their nervous systems mature and they undergo new experiences. Perceptual and motor skills develop in complexity and competency. Children learn to recognize particular faces and voices, begin to talk and respond to the speech of others, and learn how to solve problems. In short, their cognitive capacities develop.

Cognition means "to get to know." The cognitive development of infants is therefore the process by which they get to know things about themselves and their world. Evidence suggests that one of the first steps in cognitive development is learning that events in the environment are often contingent on one's own behavior. Thus, the most stimulating environment—that is, the environment that is most effective in promoting cognitive development—is one in which the infant's behavior has tangible effects.

In an experiment testing this hypothesis, Watson and Ramey (1972) presented three groups of infants with a mobile ten minutes per day for fourteen days. A pillow containing a pressure-sensitive switch was placed under the baby's head, and the mobile was suspended

FIGURE 4.8

In experiments using the visual cliff, most infants do not crawl out onto the glass shelf. (From a study conducted by Nancy Rader and Associates.)

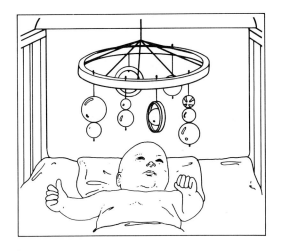

	First condition	**Later condition**
Group A	Head turning causes mobile to move. *Babies learn to move head.*	Head turning causes mobile to move. *Babies continue to move head.*
Group B	Mobile remains stationary.	Head turning causes mobile to move. *Babies do not learn to move head.*
Group C	Mobile intermittently moves on its own.	Head turning causes mobile to move. *Babies do not learn to move head.*

FIGURE 4.9

The procedure and results of the experiment by Watson and Ramey (1972).

above the baby's face. For one group, the mobile automatically rotated whenever the infant moved his or her head and activated the switch. For another group, the mobile remained stationary. For the third group, the mobile intermittently moved on its own (*not* in response to head movement).

Several weeks later the babies were tested again. Those who had learned the contingency between head turning and mobile movement continued to turn their heads. In contrast, when the babies in the second and third groups were later given the opportunity to make the mobile move by turning their heads, they did *not* learn to control it. It was as if they had learned that nothing they could do would affect the movements of the mobile. (See Figure 4.9.)

These results may have implications for infant-rearing practices. In some tragic cases, babies have been raised in unresponsive, unstimulating institutions (Goldfarb, 1955). In the worst institutions, nothing the children did

had any effect on what happened to them. Crying did not result in handling or feeding; the babies were fed and changed on a rigid schedule. The cribs were plain and often visually isolated from each other. Movements made by the babies had no effect on the environment, because there was nothing to manipulate.

Many babies reared in such environments simply stop trying to affect anything in their environment. A six-month-old baby who has been institutionalized from birth is generally passive and apathetic. In contrast, a home-reared child of the same age is much more active and responsive to the environment (Lewis and Goldberg, 1969). Clearly, a responsive environment is very important for an infant's cognitive development. As we will see later in this chapter, the normal social interactions that parents engage in with their infants follow this principle; most parents play a "contingency game" with their babies that promotes early cognitive development.

The Work of Jean Piaget

The most influential student of child development was Jean Piaget, a Swiss psychologist. Piaget formulated the most complete and detailed description of the process of cognitive development that we now have. Perhaps even greater, however, was his role as a catalyst for the study of cognitive processes within the discipline of psychology. Piaget's theory is essentially a cognitive theory; it is concerned with explaining how the structure of the mind develops. His research and writings focused attention on the importance of cognitive processes in a way no other psychologist had done. His theoretical framework provided a basis for much additional research and will undoubtedly continue to do so for years to come.

Jean Piaget (1896–1980) was this century's most influential student of cognitive development. His conclusions were based on his observations of children as shown in this photo.

Piaget's conclusions were based on his observations of the behavior of children—first, his own children at home and later other children at his Center of Genetic Epistemology in Geneva. He noticed that children of similar age tend to engage in similar behaviors and to make the same kinds of mistakes in problem solving. He concluded that these similarities are the result of a sequence of development that is followed by all normal children. Completion of each period, with its corresponding abilities, is the prerequisite for entering the next period.

According to Piaget, a child's cognitive development consists in the acquisition of **cognitive structures,** rules that are used for understanding and dealing with the world, for thinking about and solving problems. The two principal types of cognitive structures are schemas and concepts. A **schema** is a set of rules that define a particular category of behavior—how the behavior is executed and under what conditions. For example, the cognitive structure of an infant includes sucking schemas, reaching schemas, and looking schemas.

Piaget suggested that a child acquires knowledge of the environment by developing mental structures called **concepts.** Concepts are rules that describe properties of environmental events and their relations with other concepts. For example, concepts about the existence of various objects include what the objects do, how they relate to other objects, and what happens when they are touched or manipulated. Thus, the cognitive structure of an infant includes concepts of such things as rattles, balls, crib slats, hands, and other people.

Infants acquire the rules that constitute their schemas and concepts by interacting with their environment, a process that Piaget called **assimilation.** Infants assimilate new classes of stimuli (concepts) to their behavioral schemas; that is, the stimuli begin to elicit the behaviors. For example, the *object concept* is assimilated to the *reaching schema;* the infant first learns to perceive visual stimuli with certain properties as objects, then learns to control arm and hand movements, and finally learns to reach for an object that is within the field of vision.

The assimilation of a concept to a behavioral schema leads to **accommodation;** that is, the behavioral schema is adjusted as the infant learns about the properties of the concept. For example, once infants have learned to reach for objects, they learn how to adjust opening and

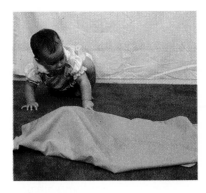

FIGURE 4.10

In stage 4 of Piaget's sensorimotor period, children learn that "out of sight" is not "out of mind." A hidden object continues to exist even though it is not in view.

closing their hands to grasp objects of different sizes and shapes. As they learn more about various classes of objects (that is, as they develop more concepts), they also develop new behavioral schemas—dropping schemas, banging schemas, and so on—through discovering the properties of these objects. Assimilation of new stimuli to behavioral schemas leads to accommodation of new behaviors, which leads to the assimilation of new stimuli, and so on. Interaction with the environment teaches a child what it needs to know in order to learn new things.

Piaget's Four Periods of Cognitive Development

Although development is a continuous process, the cognitive structures of children vary enough from age to age to permit inferences about the rules used by children of certain ages to understand their environment and control their behavior. Piaget has divided cognitive development into four periods.

The Sensorimotor Period

The **sensorimotor period** lasts for approximately the first two years of life. During this period, cognition is closely tied to external stimulation. An important feature of the sensorimotor period is the development of the **object concept.** At first, the child appears to lose all interest in an object that disappears from sight; the proverb "out of sight, out of mind" seems appropriate. In addition, cognition consists entirely in behavior. Thinking is doing.

Piaget subdivided the sensorimotor period into six stages, on the basis of the rules that make up the schemas and concepts at each stage. According to Piaget, the best way to investigate an infant's object concept is to see what the child does when an object disappears or is hidden. Piaget's observations include many descriptions of what his children did when he hid an interesting object.

Stage 1 (0–2 Months). At this stage, infants do not appear to have a concept for objects. They can look at visual stimuli and will turn their head and eyes toward the source of a sound, but hiding an object elicits no particular response.

Stage 2 (2–4 Months). Infants now become able to follow moving objects with their eyes. If an object disappears behind a barrier, the infant will continue to stare at the place where the object disappeared but will not search for it. If the object does not soon reappear, the infant seems to lose interest. Piaget called this phenomenon **passive expectation,** because the baby appears to expect the object to reappear but does not actively search for it.

Stage 3 (4–6 Months). The infant can now grasp and hold objects. If an object is completely hidden under a cloth, the infant will not attempt to retrieve it. However, a child at this stage will reach for an object that is at least partly visible.

A stage 3 infant can also anticipate the future position of a moving object. If a moving object passes behind a screen, the infant turns his or her eyes toward the far side of the screen; the child appears to anticipate the reappearance of the object on the other side.

Stage 4 (6–12 Months). The infant grasps objects, turns them over, and investigates their properties. By looking at an object from various angles, the infant learns that it can change its visual shape and still be the same object. In addition, if an object is hidden, the infant will actively search for it; the infant's object concept contains the rule of **permanence.** For a stage 4 infant, a hidden object still exists. "Out of sight" is not "out of mind." (Look back at Figure 4.10 on p. 133.)

The behavioral schemas for dealing with hidden objects are still not fully developed. Even though the child can retrieve a hidden object, he or she has difficulty in shifting the strategy for searching. If the infant has been permitted to uncover an object hidden in the same place several times, he or she will persist in looking for the object in the same place even if it is hidden in a new place. Here is Piaget's description:

> At [ten months, eighteen days] Jacqueline is seated on a mattress without anything to disturb or distract her (no coverlets, etc.). I take her parrot from her hands and hide it twice in succession under the mattress, on her left. . . . Both times Jacqueline looks for the object immediately and grabs it. Then I take it from her hands and move it very slowly before her eyes to the corresponding place on her right, under the mattress. . . . Jacqueline watches this movement but at the moment when the parrot disappears . . . she turns to her left and looks where it was before. . . . (1964, p. 51)

Stage 5 (12–15 Months). By early in the second year infants will search for a hidden object in the last place they saw it hidden; they no longer persist in looking in a place where they had previously succeeded in finding the object. However, infants at this stage can only keep track of changes that they can see in the hiding place. For example, if an adult picks up an object, puts it under a cloth, drops the object while his or her hand is hidden, closes the hand again, and removes it from the cloth, the infant will look for the object in the adult's hand. When the child does not find the object there, he or she looks puzzled or upset and does not search for the object under the cloth.

Stage 6 (15–18 Months). According to Piaget, the infant begins to think during this stage. Thought is closely tied to motor schemas and

concepts of the properties of objects, but the beginnings of symbolic representation are evident. The following quotation from Piaget illustrates how his sixteen-month-old daughter Lucienne used a motor schema to solve a problem—an early example of thinking. While playing with his daughter, Piaget hid a watch chain inside an empty match box.

> I put the chain back into the box and reduce the opening to 3 mm. It is understood that Lucienne is not aware of the functioning of the opening and closing of the match box and has not seen me prepare the experiment. She only possesses two preceding schemas: turning the box over in order to empty it of its contents, and sliding her fingers into the slit to make the chain come out. It is of course this last procedure that she tries first: she puts her finger inside and gropes to reach the chain, but fails completely. A pause follows during which Lucienne manifests a very curious reaction. . . .
>
> She looks at the slit with great attention; then, several times in succession, she opens and shuts her mouth, at first slightly, then wider and wider!
>
> [Then] . . . Lucienne unhesitatingly puts her finger in the slit, and instead of trying as before to reach the chain, she pulls so as to enlarge the opening. She succeeds and grasps the chain. (1952, pp. 337–338)

At this stage of development, the object concept is rather mature. Permanence is complete, and the infant can infer which movements an object makes while it is out of sight. If a hand containing an object goes into a hiding place and comes out empty, the child immediately looks for the object in the hiding place.

Other cognitive structures develop by the end of the sensorimotor period. The infant begins to differentiate self from other objects in the environment and gains an appreciation of time and space. The child actively experiments with objects and discovers the consequences of these experiments. For example, the infant may learn what happens when a light switch is moved or when the knob of a television is turned. By the end of this period the infant has a good start acquiring language ability. The child knows the meaning of several dozen words and can say a number of his or her own.

The Preoperational Period

Piaget's second period of cognitive development, the **preoperational period,** lasts from approximately age two to age seven. This period is characterized by rapid development of language ability and of the ability to represent things symbolically—the **symbolic function.** The child arranges toys in new ways to represent other objects (for example, a row of blocks can represent a train), begins to classify and categorize objects, and starts learning to count and to manipulate numbers.

Piaget asserted that development of the symbolic function actually begins during the sensorimotor period, when an infant starts imitating events in his or her environment. For example, when Lucienne imitated the opening of the match box by opening her mouth, she was representing a concept symbolically by means of a behavioral schema that she possessed. Similarly, a child might represent a horse by making galloping movements with the feet or a bicycle by making steering movements with the hands. Symbolic representations like these are called **signifiers:** the motor act represents (signifies) the concept because it resembles either the movements the object makes or the movements the child makes when interacting with the object. Even a very young infant demonstrates the beginnings of this function; babies will often make shaking movements with their hand when they see a rattle.

Concepts can also be represented by words, which are symbols that have no physical resemblance to the concept. (Piaget referred to such abstract symbols as **signs.**) Signifiers are personal, derived from the child's own interactions with objects. Therefore, only the child and perhaps members of the immediate family will understand the child's signifiers. In contrast, signs are social conventions understood by all members of society. A child who is able to use words to think about reality has made an important step in cognitive development.

Piaget's work demonstrated quite clearly that a child's representation of the world is different from that of an adult. For example, most adults realize that a volume of water remains constant when poured into a taller, narrower container, even though its level is now higher. However, early in the preoperational period, children will fail to recognize this fact; they will say that the taller container contains more water. The ability to realize that an object retains mass, number, or volume when it undergoes various transformations is called **conservation;** the

1. Conservation of mass

The experimenter presents two balls of clay.

The experimenter rolls one ball into a "sausage" and asks the child whether they still contain the same amount of clay.

2. Conservation of length

The experimenter presents two dowels.

The experimenter moves one dowel to the right and asks the child whether they are still the same length.

3. Conservation of number

The experimenter presents two rows of poker chips.

The experimenter moves one row of chips apart and asks the child whether each row still contains the same number.

FIGURE 4.11

Various tests of conservation. (Adapted from Lefrancois, G.R. *Of Children.* Belmont, Calif.: Wadsworth, 1973.)

transformed object *conserves* its original properties. (See Figure 4.11.)

Challenges to Piaget's Theory. Piaget concluded that the abilities to perceive the conservation of number, mass, weight, and volume are attributes of increasing development; his studies showed number to be conserved by age six, whereas conservation of volume did not occur until age eleven. However, subsequent evidence suggested that a child's ability to conserve various physical attributes occurs earlier than Piaget had supposed. Part of the problem might be in the child's understanding of words like *more* and *larger.* For an adult, the word *more* means "containing a greater number." But suppose a child's concept of *more* is less restrictive than that of an adult. Perhaps *more,* for a young child, refers to a general concept of larger, longer, or occupying more space. If this is so, the response may then suggest that the child cannot conserve a particular property when in fact he or she actually can.

Gelman (1972) found that when the appropriate task is used, even three-year-old children are able to demonstrate conservation of number. She showed children two toy platters, each containing a row of toy mice. Instead of using the word *more*, Gelman called the platter with a larger number of mice the "winner," while she called the one with a smaller number of mice the "loser." The children were invited to play a game. They watched the experimenter hide the platters under two cans and then move the cans around the table. Each child had to point to the can that contained the "winner," which was then uncovered. If the uncovered plate contained the original number of mice,

the children were satisfied that it was still the "winner," even if the experimenter tricked them by lengthening or shortening the row of mice. The children noticed that the mice had been moved but still identified the plate as the "winner." However, if mice were removed from the plate containing the larger number, the children were disturbed and asked where the missing mice were.

Clearly, the children were able to respond to the concept of number and recognized that a larger number of mice was still a larger number of mice even if the row was lengthened or shortened. It thus seems likely that children learn to conserve number before they learn the adult meaning of the word *more*. We must recognize that an estimate of a child's cognitive ability can be substantially affected by the testing method.

The Period of Concrete Operations

The **period of concrete operations** spans approximately ages seven to twelve. It is characterized by the emergence of the ability to perform logical analysis, by an increase in the ability to empathize with the feelings and attitudes of others, and by an understanding of more complex cause-and-effect relations. The child becomes much more skilled at the use of symbolic thought. For example, during most of the period of concrete operations children can arrange a series of objects in order of size and can compare any two objects and say which is larger. However, if they are told that A is larger than B, and B is larger than C, they cannot infer that A is larger than C. During the later part of this period and the beginning of the next (the period of formal operations) children become capable of this type of reasoning.

Other psychologists have suggested that the increases in children's cognitive abilities are not due solely to basic changes in the structure of the cognitive processes, but also to increased memory capacity. For example, if a child cannot simultaneously remember that A is larger than B and that B is larger than C, then it is impossible to reason that A is larger than C.

An important form of growth during the period of concrete operations is the transition from **egocentrism** to the ability to understand another person's point of view. In this context *egocentrism* does not mean selfishness; it refers

During Piaget's period of formal operations, children use logic to solve problems.

to a child's belief that others see the world in precisely the way that he or she does. For example, a child who is explaining a story or sequence of events to another person is likely to omit many important details, apparently because of the belief that other people know and understand what the child does. A child often uses pronouns without considering that another person might not understand to whom or what they refer.

The Period of Formal Operations

The final stage of cognitive development, the **period of formal operations,** begins at twelve years of age and includes the use of an essentially adult form of logic and symbolic representation; that is, in solving problems, the child learns to formulate a set of alternatives and to test these alternatives against reality. For example, the adolescent learns to reason with inductive and deductive logic and to consider several possible alternatives to a problem-solving situation and decide which is the most appropriate. Not everyone reaches this stage of cognitive development; in fact, an investigation by Graves (1972) found that many adults do not even conserve volume. This final period of cognitive development takes the child into the realm of adult abilities.

Why does a child pass from one stage of cognitive development to the next? What motivates a child to change his or her way of reasoning and perceiving? According to Piaget, the important principle is **cognitive disequilibrium** (*disequilibrium* means "lack of balance"). Disequilibrium is produced when children encounter unexpected feedback from the environment as their developing ability to explore brings them in contact with new concepts that they cannot easily assimilate to their existing behavioral schemas. This disequilibrium requires the child to acquire new concepts and new behavioral schemas. For example, when an infant encounters another infant for the first time, he or she meets an object that is interesting to touch and grasp but can also move and do unexpected things, such as touch and grab. The infant must develop a concept for this new object and learn new ways of dealing with it.

In addition, if children who are at a particular stage of cognitive development observe an adult or older child solving a problem by rules that belong to another stage, they are put off balance by the fact that the other person's solution is different from their own. This disparity is motivating; the child seeks to reduce it by learning the new rules. A child who is sufficiently mature will learn to imitate the older model and will begin to pass on to the new stage. Thus, children can learn new concepts and behavioral schemas socially, by observing the behavior of other people.

Although Piaget's work has dominated twentieth-century child psychology, not all of his conclusions have been uncritically accepted. Perhaps the major criticism is that Piaget did not always define his terms operationally; consequently, it is difficult for others to interpret the significance of his generalizations. Many of his studies lack the proper controls that were discussed in Chapter 1. Thus, much of his work is not scientific, in that there is no way to identify cause-and-effect relations among variables. And as we saw, Gelman's research indicates that adults must not assume that young children use words the way we do; careful study indicates that conservation of number actually occurs at an earlier stage of cognitive development than Piaget had proposed. Nevertheless, Piaget's meticulous and detailed observations have been extremely important in the field of child development and have had a great influence on educational practice.

MORAL DEVELOPMENT

One psychologist who has been strongly influenced by the work of Piaget is Lawrence Kohlberg. Kohlberg (1969) developed a theory of moral development based on Piaget's theory of cognitive development. Kohlberg believes that moral development progresses through stages in much the same way cognitive development occurs. Through research in which individuals were asked to make moral decisions, Kohlberg has identified six stages of moral development. (See Table 4.1.)

At the lowest or **preconventional** level, moral judgments are made to avoid punishment or to gain personal rewards. Individuals then progress to the **conventional** level where

TABLE 4.1

Kohlberg's Stages of Moral Development

Stage	Moral reasoning
Level 1: Preconventional morality	
Stage 1	Avoid punishment
Stage 2	Gain reward
Level 2: Conventional morality	
Stage 3	Gain approval or disapproval of others
Stage 4	Defined by rigid codes of law and order
Level 3: Postconventional morality	
Stage 5	Defined by a social contract, for the public good
Stage 6	Based on abstract ethical principles that become internalized

Adapted from Kohlberg, L. *Stage and Sequence: The Cognitive-Developmental Approach to Socialization,* In *Handbook of Socialization Theory of Research,* edited by D.A. Goslin. Chicago: Rand-McNally, 1969.

moral decisions conform to society's definition of right and wrong. Finally, some individuals move on to the **postconventional** level. At this level, decisions are based on internalized universal moral principles and a belief in human equality. An often cited example of someone with postconventional morality is Martin Luther King, Jr., who believed that securing the rights of individuals was more important than upholding existing governmental laws (Kohlberg, 1981).

While Kohlberg suggests that all individuals fit into one of these six stages of moral development, Gilligan (1982) has argued that Kohlberg's stages are based on a male definition of morality. She is critical of the research on which Kohlberg based his theory, citing the fact that only boys between the ages of ten and sixteen were used as subjects. According to Gilligan, men and women have different notions of what constitutes morality. Men, Gilligan suggests, apply somewhat abstract ethics and universal principles to make decisions on moral issues. Women, on the other hand, judge moral decisions according to a more personal standard, taking into consideration interpersonal relationships and responsibilities to other people. This concern for other people results in women being rated at Kohlberg's conventional level of moral development, while men's concern with universal ethics and principles results in them being rated at the postconventional level. Gilligan believes that women's social perspective on moral issues is an equal yet different view which complements the male notion of morality.

■ How would you describe the differences between each of four periods of development Piaget observed?

■ How does Piaget explain progression from one period of development to the next? What do you see as the strengths and weaknesses of his theory?

■ What are Kohlberg's three levels of moral development? How would you describe the moral reasoning used at each level of development?

SOCIAL DEVELOPMENT DURING INFANCY

Development of Attachment

Normally, the first adults with whom an infant interacts are the child's parents. In most cases, one parent serves as the primary caregiver. As many studies have shown, a close relationship called **attachment** is extremely important for the infant's social development. Because both parent and child are involved, the interactions must work both ways, with each of the participants fulfilling certain needs of the other. Formation of a strong and durable bond depends on the behavior of both people in the relationship.

Newborn infants are completely dependent upon their parents (or other caregivers) to supply them with nourishment, to keep them warm and clean, and to protect them from harm. But to most parents, the role of primary caregiver is much more than a duty; it is a source of joy and satisfaction. Nearly all parents anticipate the birth of their child with the expectation that they will love and cherish the child. And when the child is born, most of them do exactly that. As time goes on, and as parent and child interact, they become strongly attached to each other. What factors cause this attachment? As we will see, the most important factors come from the behavior of the child.

Behaviors of the Infant That Foster Attachment

Evidence suggests that human infants are innately able to produce special behaviors that shape and control behavior of their caregiver. The most important of these are sucking, cuddling, looking, smiling, and crying.

Sucking

A baby must be able to suck in order to obtain milk. But not all sucking is related to nourishment. Piaget (1952) noted that infants often suck on objects even when they are not hungry. Nonnutritive sucking appears to be an innate behavioral tendency in infants that serves to inhibit a baby's distress. The behavior is not unique to humans; a young monkey often holds onto its mother's nipple with its lips even when it is not feeding. This behavior is undoubtedly important in forming the attachment between a mother monkey and her baby. In modern society a human mother covers her breasts between feedings or feeds her baby with a bottle, so that a baby's nonnutritive sucking must involve inanimate objects or the baby's own thumb. In the Ganda society in Uganda, mothers were observed to give their babies access to a breast when they were fussy, just as mothers in other cultures would give them a pacifier (Ainsworth, 1967).

Cuddling

The infants of all species of primates have special reflexes that encourage front-to-front contact with the mother. For example, a baby monkey clings to its mother shortly after birth. This clinging leaves the mother free to use her hands

and feet. Human infants are carried by their parents and do not hold on by themselves. However, infants do adjust their posture to mold themselves to the contours of the parent's body. This response plays an important role in reinforcing the behavior of the caregiver. Some infants, perhaps because of hereditary factors or slight brain damage, do not make the cuddling response and remain rigid in the adult's arms. Adults who hold such infants tend to refer to them as being not very lovable (Ainsworth, 1973).

One of the earliest explanations for the phenomenon of attachment was the so-called *cupboard theory*. This theory is based on the fact that the mother provides food when her infant is hungry, warmth when the child is cold, dryness when he or she is wet and uncomfortable. In other words, the mother serves as a virtual "cupboard" of supplies for her child. Through association, she herself becomes a positive stimulus. (This phenomenon is called *conditioned reinforcement* and is described in more detail in Chapter 6.) As a result of this process,

The sucking reflex is one of the infant's inborn survival responses.

Parents and children readily form durable attachments.

---

the baby clings to her and shows other signs of attachment. However, a series of experiments by Harry Harlow, the late director of the primate laboratory at the University of Wisconsin, showed unequivocally that the cupboard theory cannot account for signs of attachment behavior in monkeys; instead, clinging to a soft, cuddly form appears to be an innate response (Harlow, 1974). Harlow and his colleagues isolated baby monkeys from their mothers immediately after birth and raised them alone in a cage containing two mechanical **surrogate mothers** (*surrogate* means "substitute"). One surrogate mother was made of bare wire mesh but contained a bottle that provided milk. The

other surrogate was padded and covered with terry cloth but provided no nourishment. (See Figure 4.12.)

If the cupboard theory were valid, the babies should have learned to cling to the model that provided them with milk. However, they did not; the babies preferred to cling to the cuddly surrogate and went to the wire model only to eat. If they were frightened, they would rush to the cloth-covered model for comfort. (See Figure 4.13.) These results indicate that close physical contact with a cuddly object is a biological need for a baby monkey, just as hunger and thirst are. A baby monkey clings to and cuddles with its mother because the contact is innately reinforcing, not simply because she also provides it with food. Undoubtedly, physical contact with a soft object is also inherently reinforcing for human infants.

Looking

Vision is not a passive sensory system; it is coupled with the behavior of looking. The eyes see best what is at the center of the gaze, so it is necessary to move them in order to see important visual features of the environment. Wolff (1966) showed that infants can control their eyes well enough to pursue a moving object visually within one day of birth.

FIGURE 4.12

A cuddly surrogate mother. (Harry F. Harlow, University of Wisconsin Primate Laboratory.)

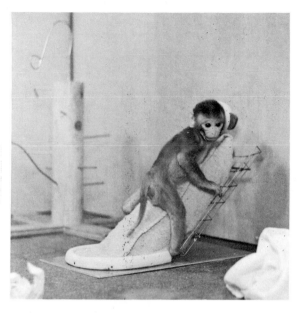

FIGURE 4.13

An isolated infant monkey clings to its cuddly surrogate mother if it is frightened by novel stimuli. (Harry F. Harlow, University of Wisconsin Primate Laboratory.)

Looking is more than an adjunct to vision; it serves as a signal to the parent. Even a very young infant seeks eye-to-eye contact with the parents. If a parent does not respond when eye contact is made, the baby usually shows signs of distress. Tronick, Als, Adamson, Wise, and Brazelton (1978) observed face-to-face interactions between mothers and their infants. When the mothers approached their babies, they typically smiled and began talking in a gentle, high-pitched voice. In return, they received a smile and an outreach of arms and legs from the infants. The mothers poked and gently shook their babies, making faces at them. The babies responded with facial expressions, wiggles, and noises of their own.

To determine whether the interaction was really two sided, the experimenters had each mother approach her baby while keeping her face expressionless, or masklike. At first the infant made the usual greetings, but when the mother did not respond, the infant turned away. (See Figure 4.14 on the next page.) From time to time the infant looked at her again, producing a brief smile but again turning away when the mother continued to stare without changing her expression. These interactions were recorded on videotape and were scored by

raters who did not know the purpose of the experiment, so the results were not biased by the experimenters' expectations.

Each mother found it difficult to resist her baby's invitation to interact; in fact, some of the mothers broke down and smiled back. Most of the mothers who managed to hold out (for three minutes) later apologized to their babies, saying something like "I am real again. It's all right. You can trust me again. Come back to me" (Tronick, et al., 1978, p. 10).

This study made it clear that the looking behavior of an infant is an invitation for the mother to respond. If she does not, the infant is disturbed and avoids further visual contact.

Smiling

For almost any human, but especially for a parent, the smile of an infant is an exceedingly effective reinforcer. For example, the day after reading an article about imitation of facial expressions by newborn infants I had a conversation with a woman who was holding her two-month-old daughter. The baby was alert, actively looking at the people around her. For approximately five minutes she made no particular facial expression. Then I remembered the article and mentioned it to the baby's father, who was also present. He suggested I see whether his daughter would imitate my facial expression. I stuck out my tongue, and immediately the baby smiled, made a noise, and stuck out her tongue. I can still feel the delight that her smile gave me.

The smiling of a human infant seems to be an innate behavior. Babies can produce smiles within a few hours after birth. Although parents are often told that early smiles are not smiles at all but merely grimaces caused by the discomfort of intestinal gas, in fact, infants rarely smile when they are uncomfortable. Even blind infants smile early in life (Izard, 1971). Parents of these babies must deliberately reinforce this behavior by making noises or touching them, or the smiling soon disappears. Normally, parents' facial responses reinforce and maintain the smiling of sighted infants.

Wolff (1963) studied the development of smiling in infants and observed the stimuli that elicited it. During the first month the sound of a voice, especially a high-pitched voice, can elicit smiles. Moreover, people appear to recognize this fact; when they approach a baby and

FIGURE 4.14

Reaction of an infant to the mother's expressionless face. Although each
panel shows mother and infant side by side, they actually faced each other.
The infant greets the mother with a smile and, getting no response,
eventually turns away from her. (From Tronick, E., Als, H., Adamson, L.,
Wise, S., and Brazelton, T.B. *Journal of the American Academy of Child
Psychiatry*, 1978, *17*, 1–13.)

talk to him or her, they tend to raise the pitch of
their voice (Tronick et al., 1978).

By the time an infant is five weeks old, visual
stimuli begin to dominate as elicitors for smiling. A face (especially a moving one) is a more
reliable elicitor of a smile than a voice is; even a
moving mask will cause an infant to smile.
Later (at approximately three months of age),
specific faces—those of people to whom the
infant has become attached—will elicit smiles.
The significance of these facts should be obvious. An infant's smile is very rewarding. Almost every parent reports that parenting be-

comes a real joy when the baby starts smiling as
the parent approaches; the infant is now a "person." Once the infant begins smiling on seeing
the parent's face, the parent becomes eager to
spend more time with his or her infant.

At around three months, infants also begin to
smile at the effects of their own activities. In
particular, they tend to smile when they detect
events that are produced by their own behavior. Watson (1973) observed that that soon after
two-month-old infants in the experiment by
Watson and Ramey (1972) had learned to move
their heads in order to make a mobile turn, they

began to smile as soon as the mobile turned. In contrast, control subjects did *not* smile when the mobile moved independently of their head turning. Thus, it was not the movement of the mobile that made the infants smile; it was the fact that the mobile moved *in response to their own behavior*. (See Figure 4.15.)

Watson also studied the interactions between parents and babies and concluded that a considerable amount of time is spent playing what he called the "contingency game." (In this context, a *contingency* is the cause-and-effect relation between two events.) For example, each time an infant opens his or her mouth, the parent pokes the baby's abdomen; whenever the baby stretches his or her arms out, the parent touches the baby's nose. In this game, the parent's response is *contingent* on some behavior produced by the infant. Infants appear to take great delight in games like this one; whenever the contingent response (such as touching or poking) is produced by the parent, the baby smiles, wiggles, makes cooing or gurgling sounds, and otherwise indicates his or her pleasure. The effect of these behaviors is, of course, to reinforce game playing by the parent.

Playing the contingency game is undoubtedly an important part of an infant's cognitive development. Detection of contingencies appears to be innately reinforcing for infants; it produces smiling and other behaviors that reinforce the parental behavior that brought about the contingency, making it more likely that the parent will repeat the behavior. Thus, an infant reinforces parental behaviors that provide the child with important cognitive exercise.

Crying

For almost any adult, the sound of an infant's crying is intensely irritating. A young infant usually cries only when he or she is hungry, cold, or in pain (Wolff, 1969). In these situations, only the intervention of an adult can bring relief. The stimulus that most effectively terminates crying is being picked up and cuddled. Because picking up the baby stops the crying, the parent learns to pick up the infant when he or she cries. Thus, crying serves as a useful means for a cold, hungry, or wet child to obtain assistance.

Everyone knows that children can be "spoiled"; when things are made too easy for them, they come to believe that their every

whim will be (and should be) gratified. But research has made it clear that a parent's attention does not "spoil" a very young infant.

In the first few months of a baby's life, a parent should respond promptly when the baby cries. Bell and Ainsworth (1972) found that babies whose caregivers responded quickly to crying during the first three months actually cried *less* during the last four months of their first year than did infants with unresponsive caregivers. Instead of becoming spoiled, these babies learned to cry only when they needed attention from their caregiver. The infants with responsive caregivers also learned to communicate effectively by means of behaviors other than crying, such as prespeech sounds and facial gestures. Just as it is important for parents to play the contingency game with their infants, it is important for babies to learn that their communicative behaviors (such as crying) can affect the behavior of other people.

The Critical Period for Attachment

For many species there is a critical period in which attachment must occur, or it will fail to develop. For example, many young birds are able to move about and feed themselves very soon after hatching. Because these birds must follow their mother around in order to survive, it is important for them to become attached to

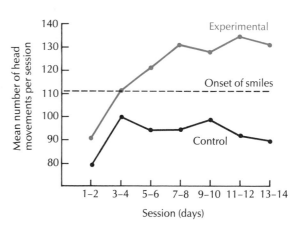

FIGURE 4.15

A contingency between movement of the mobile and head turning leads to increased head turning and also to smiling. (From Bower, T.G.R. *Perception in Infancy*, 2nd ed. San Francisco: W.H. Freeman, 1972, after Watson, 1973.)

Konrad Lorenz was the first moving object these young geese saw after they hatched, so they became imprinted to him.

her. This form of attachment is called **imprinting** (Lorenz, 1957); a baby bird learns to follow the first moving object that it encounters—normally its mother—within the first day or two of life. If it is kept isolated during this time, it will fail to become imprinted; it will never learn to follow its mother (or any other moving object, for that matter).

Evidence suggests that there is also a critical period, though a much longer one, for the development of attachment between human parents and their infants (Ainsworth, 1973). Most infants become attached to their parents by six to nine months of age. Once the attachment is formed, infants become very disturbed if they are separated from their primary caregivers, and they do not readily accept substitutes. (As we will see later, babies do form secondary attachments to people other than their primary caregivers, but this is a different matter.)

Infants who are raised in an institution or who otherwise lack primary caregivers in the early months of life can form a normal attachment if they are adopted soon after their first birthday (Gardner, Hawkes, and Burchinal, 1961). Infants older than eighteen months do not readily form attachments with foster parents (Provence and Lipton, 1962).

Some studies have shown that a particular aspect of attachment may occur very early in life. In some mammalian species, mothers will accept and care for their infants only if they are able to see and smell their offspring during the first day of life. For example, if a lamb is removed from its mother immediately after birth and is brought back a day later, the mother will reject it. However, if a ewe is in contact with her lamb for just a few minutes after birth, she will accept it and take care of it when it is given back to her the next day (Klopfer, Adams, and Klopfer, 1964).

A few studies have suggested that a similar phenomenon occurs in humans; a mother experiences **bonding** with her newborn infant if the baby is placed naked against her skin. For example, Klaus, Jerauld, Krieger, McAlpine, Steffa, and Kennell (1972) performed an experiment with mothers who were having their first child. The control group experienced what was then the usual hospital procedure, seeing their babies for a short time at birth and feeding them (by bottle) five times a day. The other mothers (the extended-contact group) received their babies for an hour soon after birth and for five hours each afternoon on the next three days. Thus, these mothers were in contact with their babies for sixteen hours more than the mothers in the control group. A month later the mothers were interviewed during their infants' one-month checkups. The mothers in the extended-contact group acted more concerned about their babies, holding and fondling them more than the mothers in the control group. Differences in the behavior of the two groups of mothers were still present two years later.

This study, then, suggested that mothers and babies should be together as much as possible during the first few days of life. Indeed, as a result of such studies, many hospitals have changed their procedures to ensure that a mother becomes "bonded" to her infant; the newborn baby is placed against the mother's abdomen so that skin-to-skin contact occurs.

Although these studies are interesting, their conditions were not sufficiently controlled to prove that a maternal bond develops this early. The mothers in the experimental groups were aware that they were being treated differently, because they had their babies with them longer than other mothers who shared their rooms. In addition, nurses may have inadvertently communicated to these mothers that it was important to spend more time with their infants. Thus, if several months later these mothers were observed to interact with their babies slightly more, either of these variables may have accounted for the result. Recent research conducted under more carefully controlled conditions has failed to confirm the results of the earlier studies. For example, Svejda, Campos, and Emde (1980) first made sure that the mothers who received extended contact with their babies did not perceive themselves as "special." These investigators found that extended contact had no effect on interactions between mothers and their infants later in life.

The Role of Attachment in an Infant's Environmental Interaction

To develop normally, infants must learn to explore and interact with their environment, exercising their own power of locomotion. Because the environment contains many dangers, it is advantageous for infants to be frightened by unfamiliar stimuli and seek contact with their parents. This tendency makes it more likely that the parents will be able to prevent harm to their baby.

The presence of a primary caregiver provides a baby with considerable reassurance when he or she first becomes able to explore the environment. Although the unfamiliar environment produces fear, the parent provides a **secure base** that the infant can leave from time to time to see what the world is like. Two studies have demonstrated the effectiveness of this reassurance (Rheingold, 1969; Rheingold and Eckerman, 1970). Ten-month-old infants were placed one at a time in a large, strange room. If the infant's mother was present, the child explored and played with toys. If the mother was absent, the infant cried and showed other signs of distress. The child did not explore the room. However, if an infant was brought by the mother into an adjoining room, he or she was likely to leave the mother and enter the large room alone, explore the room, and play with toys, apparently secure in the knowledge that the mother was available nearby. Most of these infants crawled back and forth between the rooms during the observation.

Other researchers have made similar observations in studies of baby monkeys. For example, as I discussed, Harlow and his colleagues found that an infant monkey who has been raised in isolation forms an attachment to a cuddly surrogate (Harlow, 1974). In unfamiliar

situations the presence of this surrogate can provide reassurance; if the surrogate is present, the baby monkey will explore happily. However, if the monkey is alone in the cage, or if only the wire surrogate is present, the baby will retreat in fear and huddle in a corner.

In fact, a baby monkey will be reassured by the cuddly surrogate even if the behavior of the surrogate is the *source* of the infant's distress. Harlow and his colleagues constructed cuddly surrogates that were capable of rather nasty behaviors. One kind would periodically shake so violently that the infant would be flung off. The other contained a series of blunt brass spikes that would protrude from time to time, pushing the baby off. Both behaviors caused fear and distress in the baby monkeys, but as soon as the models stopped shaking or the

Does extended contact between newborn infants and parents promote bonding?

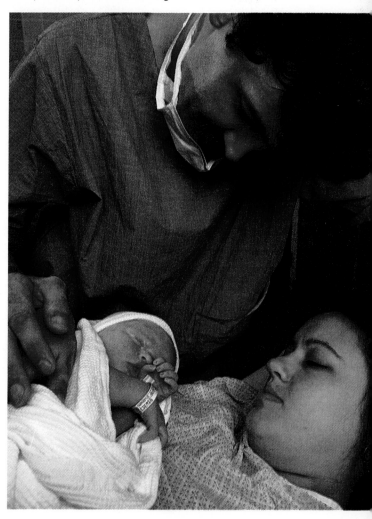

brass spikes were retracted, the babies ran back and desperately clung to them.

This phenomenon is probably related to one that is seen in humans. Most people are shocked by the fact that battered and abused children are often very closely attached to the parents who mistreat them. It is not unusual for a severely injured child to resist being separated from a parent who has just beaten him or her. The child needs consolation after the distressing experience and, as soon as the beating is over, turns to the parent (who is now usually remorseful) for comfort. The parent holds and comforts the child, thus reinforcing the child for coming back. A pathological attachment such as this is especially tragic.

Interactions with Peers

Although the attachment between an infant and its primary caregiver is the most important social interaction in early life, a child's social development must also involve other people. A normal infant develops attachments with other adults and with older siblings, if there are any. But interaction with peers is especially important to social development.

Studies by Harlow and his colleagues (Harlow, 1974) have shown that social contact with peers is essential to an infant monkey's social development; in fact, these interactions appear to be even more important than interactions with its mother. An infant monkey that is raised with only a cuddly surrogate mother can still develop into a reasonably normal adult. However, an isolated monkey that does not interact with other juveniles before puberty shows severe deficits. When a previously isolated adolescent monkey is introduced to a colony of normally reared age mates, it will retreat with terror and huddle in a corner in a desperate attempt to hide.

Apparently, social interaction helps young monkeys learn how to respond to each other—how to cope with fear, when to be dominant, and when not to challenge a more powerful and aggressive playmate. Young monkeys, like human children, engage in play, and this play appears to teach them what they need to know in order to form adult relationships.

Subsequent studies from Harlow's laboratory (such as Suomi and Harlow, 1972; Novak and Harlow, 1975) have shown that it is possible to eliminate the pathological fearful behavior shown by a monkey that was raised in isolation. If there is a critical period during which monkeys learn to interact with peers, it does not seem to be an absolute one. The important variable seems to be the abruptness with which a formerly isolated monkey is brought into social situations. If it is first placed with a younger, not-so-threatening "therapist" monkey, it can gradually learn how to interact normally with older monkeys. Regardless of the stage of development at which socialization occurs, learning to cope with a strange environment must be a gradual process.

An experiment by Fuhrman, Rahe, and Hartup (1979) demonstrates that research with nonhuman primates can have important implications for the understanding of human development. These researchers used the "juvenile therapist" technique that Harlow and his associates discovered to improve peer interactions among socially withdrawn children, ages two-and-one-half to six-and-one-half years. The children appeared to be relatively isolated from their peers, spending less than a normal amount of time with them. Each child was paired with a partner for a series of ten play sessions of twenty minutes each. The partner was another child of the same age or twelve to twenty months younger. Interactions with peers were observed before, during, and after the play session. The play sessions were successful; they increased the amount of time that the isolated children spent with their peers. Furthermore, children paired with younger "therapists" showed the greatest change. Control subjects, who did not participate in play sessions with another child, showed no change over the four-to-six week periods.

■ How do behaviors such as sucking, cuddling, looking, smiling, and crying shape and maintain attachment between infants and their primary caregivers?

■ Does research support the idea that attachment between infants and primary caregivers must occur during a critical period?

■ What does the research with humans and monkeys say about the importance of interactions with peers?

CHAPTER SUMMARY

1. Fertilization of an ovum by a sperm determines the genetic blueprint for an individual. The eventual expression of this blueprint involves a complex interaction between the developing organism and its environment that begins long before the child is born. The importance of this interaction is underscored by the existence of genetically and environmentally produced defects, such as Down's syndrome or fetal alcohol syndrome.

2. Genetically, an infant has the potential to develop skills that coincide with the maturation of its nervous system. But in order for this potential to be realized, the infant's environment must supply the opportunity to test and practice these skills. If an infant is deprived of the opportunity to practice them at crucial times, these skills may fail to develop, which will affect his or her performance as an adult.

3. The first step in children's cognitive development is learning that many events are contingent on their own behavior. Jean Piaget divided a child's cognitive development into four periods, determined by the joint influences of the child's experiences and the maturation of the child's nervous system. They consist of the sensorimotor period, the preoperational period, the period of concrete operations, and the period of formal operations.

An infant's earliest cognitive abilities are closely tied to the external stimuli in the immediate environment; objects exist for the infant only when they are present. Gradually infants begin to differentiate themselves from other objects in the environment and learn that objects exist even when hidden. The development of object permanence leads to the ability to represent things symbolically, which is a prerequisite for the use of language. Next, the ability to perform logical analysis and to understand more complex cause-and-effect relations develops. Around the age of twelve a child develops more adultlike cognitive abilities—abilities that may allow the child to solve difficult problems by means of abstract reasoning.

4. Lawrence Kohlberg developed a theory of moral development with these stages: precon-

ventional morality in which judgments are made to avoid punishment or to gain reward; conventional morality in which decisions conform to society's definition of right or wrong; and postconventional morality in which decisions are based on internalized universal moral principles and a belief in human equality. Kohlberg has been criticized for a male-oriented definition of morality.

5. The development of attachment between parent and infant is crucial to the infant's survival. A baby has the innate ability to shape and reinforce the behavior of the parent. Infant and parent reinforce each other's behavior, which facilitates the development of a durable attachment. In humans, the time for bonding is not restricted to a few hours after birth.

6. Some of the behaviors that babies possess innately are sucking, cuddling, looking, smiling, and crying. These behaviors promote parental responses and are instrumental in satisfying physiological needs. In the case of smiling, the behavior develops as the child matures; the baby first smiles spontaneously, then in response to a high-pitched voice, next in response to visual stimuli (especially the caregiver), and eventually in response to his or her own activities, particularly those that produce reactions in the environment. Thus, smiling encourages caregivers to arrange a responsive environment (that is, to play the "contingency game"), which in turn facilitates the baby's cognitive development.

7. Harlow's studies with monkeys have shown that clinging, one of the important behaviors in attachment, is an innate tendency and does not have to be reinforced by food or warmth. Infant humans and monkeys are normally afraid of novel stimuli, but the presence of their caregiver (or cuddly surrogate) provides a secure base from which they can explore a new environment.

8. Development also involves the acquisition of social skills. Interaction with peers is probably the most important factor in social development. Research with monkeys has shown that deprivation of contact with peers has even more serious effects than deprivation of contact with the mother.

KEY TERMS

accommodation According to Jean Piaget, the process by which a child's behavioral schemas are altered by interaction with the environment.

amniotic sac A membrane filled with amniotic fluid that surrounds and protects the mammalian fetus.

assimilation According to Jean Piaget, the process by which a new concept comes to elicit a child's behavioral schema.

attachment The process by which parent (or caregiver) and child form a mutually reinforcing system.

bonding An attachment between mother and offspring of some species that occurs within a few hours after birth, stimulated primarily by the odor of the infant; not conclusively demonstrated in humans.

cephalocaudal development The tendency for an infant's control of the upper (cephalic) parts of the body to develop sooner than control of the lower (caudal) parts.

cognition To get to know; process by which infants learn about themselves and their world.

cognitive disequilibrium Piaget principle describing that stage at which children encounter unexpected feedback that requires the child to acquire new concepts and new behavioral schemas.

cognitive structures According to Piaget, the rules used to understand and deal with the world, to think about and solve problems, in a child's cognitive development.

concepts In Piaget's theory of child development, rules that describe properties of environmental events and their relations with other concepts.

conservation The tendency to perceive quantities, mass, and volume as remaining constant even if elements are moved or the shape of the substance is changed. According to Jean Piaget, this is an important cognitive concept.

conventional morality According to Kohlberg, one level of moral development in which a person's moral decisions conform to society's definition of right and wrong.

differentiation The process by which the cells of a developing organism begin to differ and give rise to the various organs of the body.

Down's syndrome A disorder caused by the presence of an extra twenty-first chromosome, characterized by moderate to severe mental retardation and often by physical abnormalities; previously called mongolism.

egocentrism The tendency of young children to perceive the world solely in terms relative to themselves.

enzyme A protein that serves as a biological catalyst, breaking certain molecules apart or causing certain molecules to be joined together.

fetal alcohol syndrome A disorder that adversely affects an offspring's brain development; caused by the mother's alcohol intake during pregnancy.

gamete A germ cell; a sperm or ovum.

gene The functional unit of the chromosome; contains the information that cells need to produce proteins, which serve structural purposes or operate as enzymes. Genes encode the instructions for development of an organism and for control of its maintenance and functions.

imprinting The tendency of an infant to follow any large, moving object (usually the mother) that is encountered during the first day or two of life; seen especially in precocial birds, which can walk soon after hatching.

object concept The beliefs and expectancies that children have about physical objects; an important part of Piaget's theory of cognitive development.

ovulation The release of a ripe ovum, which can subsequently be fertilized.

passive expectation In Piaget's stages of cognitive development, a phenomenon of the sensorimotor period in which infants expect an object that has disappeared to reappear but do not actively search for it.

period of concrete operations Within Piaget's stages of cognitive development, this spans approximately ages seven to twelve and is characterized by the emergence of the ability to perform logical analysis, an increase in the ability to empathize with others, and greater understanding of cause and effect.

period of formal operations In Piaget's stages of cognitive development, the final period (beginning around age twelve) in which adult forms of logic and symbolic representation are adopted.

permanence The concept that objects and people continue to exist even when they are hidden from view; develops during infancy.

phenylketonuria (PKU) A hereditary disorder caused by the absence of an enzyme that converts the amino acid phenylalanine to tyrosine. The accumulation of phenylalanine causes brain damage unless a special diet is implemented soon after birth.

placenta A structure that unites the fetus to the mother's uterus and draws nourishment for the fetus and passes waste products to the mother to be excreted.

postconventional morality In Kohlberg's theory of moral development, the final stage (not always attained) in which a person's decisions are based on internalized universal moral principles and a belief in human equality.

preconventional morality In Kohlberg's theory of moral development, the first stage in which a person makes moral judgments to avoid punishment or gain personal rewards.

preoperational period Piaget's second period of cognitive development (approximately ages two to seven), characterized by rapid development of language and of the ability to represent things symbolically.

proximodistal development The tendency for an infant to be able to control its arms before its hands and fingers.

rooting Reflex of the infant to turn the head in response to a light touch on the cheek so that the object reaches the lips.

schema In the theory of Jean Piaget, the set of rules that define a behavioral sequence. See also *accommodation*.

secure base The presence of a primary caregiver (such as a parent) who gives reassurance to the child in exploring the environment.

sensorimotor period In Piaget's theory of cognitive development, the first stage in the first two years of life in which the child's cognition is closely tied to external stimulation.

signs According to Piaget, abstract symbols such as words that have no physical resemblance to the concept.

signifiers According to Piaget, personal symbolic representations learned from the child's own interactions with objects.

sucking Reflex of an infant to open its mouth and suck if an object touches the lips and is the right size, texture, and temperature.

surrogate mother Substitute mother, used in monkey experiments to show that contact with a soft object is innately reinforcing.

swallowing Survival reflex of an infant that causes it to swallow when sucking.

symbolic function According to Piaget, the child's ability during the preoperational period to represent things symbolically.

zygote A fertilized ovum, from which a multicellular organism develops.

Chapter 5

Adolescent and Adult Development

The study of human development does not end with childhood. Adolescence is a time of change, as biological and psychological factors interact to accelerate development and open up new horizons. Adulthood also holds new discoveries: becoming independent, beginning a career, and establishing an intimate relationship are just a few of its milestones.

Perhaps none of the discoveries that occur during adolescence is as powerful or as important as that of sexuality and the ability to become a parent. Although biological sex is determined at conception, our sense of masculinity or femininity is strongly influenced by social factors. How do we learn to behave in masculine or feminine ways? Most psychologists agree that society reinforces behaviors that are deemed appropriate for each sex. But some boys act more masculine than other boys, and some girls act more feminine than others. Are these differences the result of the social environment, or does prenatal exposure of the fetus to sex hormones influence the development of masculinity or femininity? Psychologists attempt to answer these questions by applying scientific methods to the study of sex role development.

Developmental psychologists are also studying the cognitive, physical, and behavioral changes associated with aging. The question that has received the most attention is whether cognitive abilities must inevitably decline with advancing age, or whether the decline can be avoided if a person maintains an active and stimulating existence. Once again, psychologists are faced with the difficult task of evaluating the relative contribution of the physiological and environmental factors responsible for the changes that occur at the beginning and at the end of our lives. This is what makes the field of psychology so exciting—psychologists themselves are still "discovering" answers to many interesting and complex questions about human behavior.

BIOLOGICAL ASPECTS OF SEXUAL DEVELOPMENT

Sexual identity is an aspect of our self-image that begins to be established at a very early age. We are treated as males or females right from the time of birth. When someone announces the birth of a baby, most of us immediately ask "Is it a boy or a girl?" And once we find out the baby's sex, we interact with the child in subtly different ways.

Chromosomal Determination of Sex

A person's genetic sex is determined by the father's sperm at the time of fertilization. You will recall from the last chapter that each parent contributes one member of each of the twenty-three pairs of the offspring's chromosomes. When the chromosomes of the sperm and ovum unite, the pairs are joined together. Twenty-two of these pairs are **autosomes** ("independent bodies"); they determine the organism's physical development independent of its sex. The last pair consists of two **sex chromosomes,** which determine whether the offspring will be a boy or a girl.

There are two types of sex chromosomes: *X chromosomes* and *Y chromosomes.* Females have two X chromosomes (XX); thus, all the ova that a woman produces will contain an X chromosome. But males have an X and a Y chromosome (XY). When a man's sex chromosomes divide, half the sperms contain an X chromosome and the other half a Y chromosome. A Y-bearing sperm produces an XY fertilized ovum, and therefore a male. An X-bearing sperm produces an XX fertilized ovum, and therefore a female. (See Figure 5.1.)

Development of the Sex Organs

Through the fourth week of prenatal development, male and female fetuses are identical. Both sexes have a pair of identical, undifferentiated **gonads,** which can develop into either testes or ovaries. The determining factor appears to be a single gene on the Y chromosome. If it is present, the undifferentiated gonads become testes. If the gene is not present, the gonads develop into ovaries.

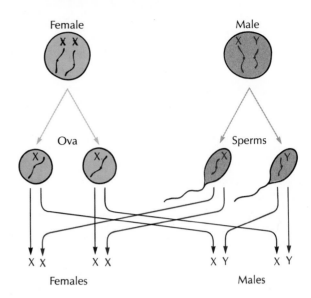

FIGURE 5.1

Determination of gender.

The rest of sexual development is determined by the presence of testes or ovaries. By the time the undifferentiated gonads develop into ovaries or testes, the embryo contains two sets of internal sex organs, both male and female. Only one of these primitive sets of organs will develop. The female system develops into the fallopian tubes, uterus, and inner two-thirds of the vagina; the male system develops into the epididymis, prostate, seminal vesicle, and sperm duct.

Unlike the internal sex organs, the external sex organs (the genitalia) develop from a single set of primitive organs. The undifferentiated phallus becomes the glans penis (males) or the clitoris (females). The genital swelling becomes the scrotum (males) or the outer labia (females). The genital tubercle becomes the shaft of the penis (males) or the inner labia (females).

The factor that determines whether the sex organs will be male or female is the presence or absence of a single class of sex hormones, known as **androgens.** (*Andros* means "man"; *gennan* means "to produce.") In males, once the undifferentiated gonads develop into testes, they secrete androgens, the most important of which is **testosterone.** Androgens cause the development of the male internal sex organs and of the penis and scrotum. Development of female sex organs does not need to be stimulated by a hormone. We know that this is true because a particular genetic disorder, **Turner's syndrome,** prevents the gonads from developing, so that the fetus has neither testes nor ovaries. Nevertheless, the female internal and external sex organs develop. In the absence of sex hormones from the gonads, an individual will develop as a female. This fact has led to the dictum "Nature's impulse is to create a female."

Experiments with laboratory animals have confirmed the conclusion made from observations of people with Turner's syndrome. Jost (1969) removed the testes from a male rabbit fetus while it was still in its mother's uterus. As a result of this surgery the female system, and not the male system, developed; the animal was born with fallopian tubes, a uterus, and a vagina. (Of course, the animal was unable to reproduce, because it did not have ovaries.) In addition, many studies have shown that if androgens are given to female fetuses, male sex organs will develop. Thus, the norm is a female, and only the intervention of androgens produces a male. Many different genetic disorders can cause syndromes in which androgen secretion is abnormal; some disorders interfere with androgen secretion in males, while others cause secretion to occur in females, and still others prevent cells in males from responding to androgens. These syndromes result in the development of abnormal sex organs. People with some of these disorders can receive corrective surgery.

Further Sexual Development at Puberty

Puberty (from the Latin *puber,* meaning "adult") marks the beginning of the transition from childhood to adulthood. Many physical events occur during this stage: people reach their ultimate height, develop secondary sex characteristics (including breasts, increased muscle size, and body hair), and become capable of reproduction. There is also a change in social role. As a child, a person is dependent on parents, teachers, and other adults; as an adolescent, he or she is expected to assume more responsibility. Relations with peers also suddenly change; members of one's own sex become potential rivals for the attention of members of the other sex.

The internal sex organs and genitalia do not change much for several years after birth, but they begin to develop again at puberty. When boys and girls are about eleven to fourteen, their ovaries or testes secrete hormones that begin the process of sexual maturation. This activity of the gonads is initiated by the hypothalamus, the part of the brain to which the pituitary gland is attached. The hypothalamus stimulates the **anterior pituitary gland** to secrete **gonadotropic hormones.** *Gonadotropic* ("gonad-changing") describes the effects of the hormones: They stimulate the gonads to secrete sex hormones. These sex hormones act on various organs of the body and initiate the changes that accompany sexual maturation.

The sex hormones secreted by the gonads cause growth and maturation of the external genitalia and of the gonads themselves. In addition, these hormones cause the maturation of ova and the production of sperms. All of these developments are considered **primary sex characteristics.** The sex hormones also stimulate the development of **secondary sex characteristics**—the physical changes that distinguish a male from a female. Before puberty boys and girls look much the same. If they have similar hair styles and clothing, it is difficult to determine their gender without looking at their genitalia. At puberty, young men's testes begin to secrete testosterone. This hormone causes

Although one of the tasks of adolescence is to develop an independent identity, most teenagers are susceptible to peer pressures to conform to the group.

their muscles to develop, their facial hair to grow, and their voices to deepen. Young women's ovaries secrete **estradiol,** which is the most important **estrogen,** or female sex hormone. Estradiol causes women's breasts to grow and their pelvises to widen, and produces changes in the layer of fat beneath the skin and in the texture of the skin itself.

This last change explains why older women, whose ovaries no longer secrete hormones, often use skin creams that contain estrogens. In one unusual case, a six-year-old girl who had begun to show signs of puberty was found to have been eating her grandmother's skin cream. The cream contained enough estrogen to stimulate the changes that normally occur several years later.

The effects of sex hormones on the internal sex organs and external genitalia are sex-specific; for example, testosterone can cause maturation of the penis and scrotum only in a male, because only a male possesses these structures. But both males and females can develop many secondary sex characteristics; when stimulated by the appropriate hormones, both males and females can grow breasts, a beard, or wider hips or can develop strong muscles or a deep voice.

- What is the role of chromosomes in determining gender?
- How would you describe the prenatal development of the sex organs?
- How would you describe the sexual development that occurs during puberty?

Effects of Hormones on Human Social Behavior

As we have seen, a fetus will become physically female, unless its sex organs are exposed to androgens. Androgens also appear to affect behavior, presumably by altering the development of the brain. This section addresses the possible role of prenatal sex hormones in human social behavior. The possible role of these hormones in sexual behavior and sexual orientation is addressed in a later section.

There is no doubt that sex hormones can affect the development of the brains of various species of laboratory animals. Many studies

have shown that some neural circuits develop differently if androgens are present (Goy and McEwen, 1980). Anatomical differences are also seen in some areas of the human brain (Wada, Clarke, and Hamm, 1975; de Lacoste-Utamsing and Holloway, 1982). However, no research has shown that particular regions of the human brain control a person's interests in "masculine" or "feminine" behaviors.

The following evidence, though still inconclusive, suggests that prenatal androgens, through their organizational effects on the developing brain, can influence human social behavior. However, this influence is not very strong. Normally, a female human fetus is not exposed to considerable amounts of androgens, so her body develops female characteristics. However, several years ago a number of female fetuses were inadvertently exposed to a chemical that partially androgenized them. Their mothers, who had had a history of spontaneous abortions (miscarriages), were given a synthetic hormone to support their pregnancies. Unfortunately, this drug had an unexpected side effect: it caused partial masculinization of female fetuses. The effect of the drug was noticed in the infant's external sex organs, which appeared somewhat masculine. In addition to this group of infants, another group has been studied. These infants have a disorder called the **adrenogenital syndrome,** which causes the adrenal glands to secrete large amounts of androgens before and after birth. This disorder, too, causes masculinization of female fetuses. It is treated by removing the adrenal glands and administering proper amounts of the other hormones these glands produce. In both cases, masculinization of external genitalia can be corrected surgically and usually does not cause problems.

Money and Ehrhardt (1972) studied girls who had been masculinized prenatally by the drug or by their own adrenal glands to determine whether their early exposure to an androgenizing hormone had any effect on their subsequent behavior. Perhaps androgenization was not restricted to external genitalia; perhaps it also affected development of the brain.

The investigators compared the interests of both groups with the interests of a control group of normal girls. Normal children show a wide range in interests; some boys and girls have mostly "masculine" interests, others have mostly "feminine" interests, and still others are in between. The sample of girls in the control group showed a considerable variation in interests. In contrast, both groups of girls who had received androgens before birth displayed behavior on the "masculine" side of the continuum; for example, they referred to themselves as "tomboys," they preferred vigorous athletic sports to quiet play, and they did not like to wear "feminine" clothing. They also preferred to play with boys rather than with other girls.

There was nothing unusual about these children as individuals. All were happy to be girls and accepted their gender identity as female. Their social behavior was not abnormal; after all, many girls are bored by dolls and prefer to play very active games. And today many girls in North America prefer pants to skirts and dresses. But the fact that *as a group* the androgenized girls differed significantly from the control group suggests that the androgens had an effect on their brains, and thus on their behavior. Perhaps the prenatal androgens simply increased their tendency to be active. This tendency would account for their preference for boys as playmates, because they shared their interests in vigorous games.

The case of the prenatally androgenized girls does not provide conclusive evidence that androgens have organizational effects on behavior. The girls' parents knew that the infants had been affected by the drug or the adrenal hormone, because their external genitalia were somewhat masculinized. Possibly as a result of this knowledge they treated their daughters somewhat differently, and this treatment affected their behavior. However, it seems more likely that the parents would instead emphasize their daughters' identities as girls.

Laboratory research with other primate species has supported the conclusion that prenatal exposure to androgens affects social behavior. Young male rhesus monkeys are much more likely than females to initiate periods of play, to engage in rough-and-tumble play, and to make playful threat gestures. Males also tend to mount other juvenile monkeys in a way that mimics adult male sexual behavior, whereas females tend to present their hindquarters, as an adult female would. Goy and Goldfoot (1973) administered androgens to pregnant rhesus monkeys; when female babies were born, they isolated these infants from their mothers,

Normal children have a wide range of interests. Many girls prefer active sports to quiet activities, such as this girl playing on her high school football team.

so that the mothers would not notice their daughters' masculinized genitalia and somehow behave differently toward them. The androgenized females acted much like males. Their play behavior was more aggressive than that of normal females, and they were more likely to mount other monkeys.

Social Influence on Prenatal Hormone Exposure

Although it is possible that sex-role behaviors are strongly biased by prenatal sex hormones, most gender-related behaviors are undoubtedly learned through socialization.

One famous study suggested that socialization can not only reinforce the effects of a person's prenatal hormone exposure but even reverse them. Money and Ehrhardt (1972) reported the case of a seven-month-old baby boy born in 1963 who was brought to a physician for circumcision (removal of the fold of skin that covers the glans penis). The skin was to be cut with a cautery, a special surgical instrument that cuts with a spark of electricity. Unfortunately, the device was turned up too high, and when the physician applied it, the boy's penis burned up in a flash of smoke. Ten months later, after much consultation and soul-searching, the parents decided to raise their son as a girl. They renamed the child and undertook the first in several stages of plastic surgery. The mother reported later: "I started dressing her not in dresses, but, you know, in little pink slacks and frilly blouses . . . and letting her hair grow" (Money and Ehrhardt, 1972, p. 119). The child apparently accepted the sex reassignment well, taking on characteristics that she perceived as feminine. She became neat and tidy. According to her mother, "She likes for me to wipe her face. She doesn't like to be dirty, and yet my son is quite different. I can't wash his face for anything. . . . She seems to be daintier. Maybe it's because I encourage it. . . . One thing that really amazes me is that she is so feminine" (pp. 119–120).

For a decade this study was taken as evidence that socialization can undo the effects of prenatal androgenization. However, Diamond (1982) provided evidence that the child's later social development was not as smooth as it had appeared earlier. The young woman was teased by other children and called "cavewoman," apparently because of her masculine gait. She did not appear to be happy; she had difficulty making friends and found it hard to accept her gender identity as a female.

Of course, the facts of this case do not necessarily prove that socialization *cannot* reverse the effects of prenatal androgenization. After all, there can be many reasons for a person's unhappiness and difficulty in making friends. But this outcome weakens the conclusion that socialization can undo the effects of prenatal androgenization. The case has some practical implications, too. It suggests that if an infant boy's penis is destroyed (this does happen occasionally, primarily through injury), perhaps this damaged boy should not be raised as a girl.

■ What does research say about the effects of hormones on social behavior?
■ What effect does socialization have on prenatal androgenization?

SOCIAL INFLUENCES ON SEXUAL DEVELOPMENT

We have seen how a person's biological sex is determined by chromosomes. However, a person's sense of his or her own maleness or femaleness—what psychologists call **gender identity**—is determined by more than biological factors. In this section, we explore the role that socialization plays in influencing gender identity, and the complex interaction between biological and environmental factors.

Gender Roles

People are justifiably sensitive to statements that behavioral differences are biologically determined, because these alleged differences have been used to justify the exclusion of women from position of status and power in

Traditional gender roles are changing. However, it is still more common to see a woman taking care of home and children than a man.

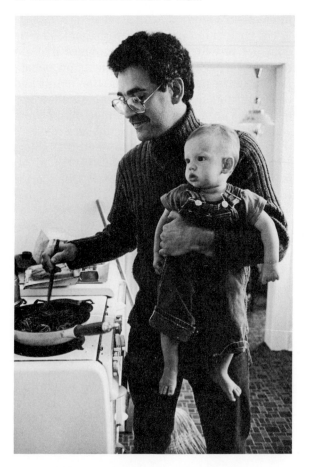

society. Most cultures, including our own, have some degree of bias against women's achievement in professions that society defines as masculine. Although cultural stereotypes are changing, **gender roles,** the behaviors society expects of males and females, still exist. Young boys, for example, still play roughly and actively; young girls still tend to play more quietly. Gender roles also exist for adults. Despite their entry into male-dominated professions, women are still expected to perform most household tasks and to assume primary responsibility for meeting their children's needs. They are expected to express their emotions and to be submissive. Men, on the other hand, are expected to be breadwinners and to limit their display of emotion. Where do these differences come from?

Despite the remarkable similarities of newborn males and females, they are treated differently from birth onward (Condry and Ross, 1985). Mothers spend more time in close physical contact with daughters than sons. Fathers spend more time talking to daughters while they play more often with sons. Comments

Many women are choosing careers that were previously regarded as suitable only for men.

Studies indicate that fathers spend more time playing with their sons than with their daughters.

about newborn babies tend to be sex-stereotyped: Observers talk about the masculine appearance and behavior of male babies and the feminine appearance and behavior of female babies (Oakley, 1972). Children constantly hear comments such as "Boys will be boys" or "Girls don't do that," and adults encourage them to play with particular kinds of toys. Television programs, advertisements, and stories (including fairy tales read to very young children) convey the information that males and females are different in interests and behavior. With such powerful and pervasive social stimuli, it should not be surprising that children become sex-typed at a very early age. **Gender-typing** refers to the "acquisition of sex-appropriate preferences, skills, personality attributes, behaviors and self-concepts" (Bem, p. 181). Gender-typed behavior, then, refers to behavior that is appropriate for only one sex.

Theories of Gender-Typing

Several different theories have been proposed to explain the process of gender-typing—how a female becomes feminine and how a male becomes masculine. Three theories are especially influential: psychoanalytic theory (Freud,

1959), social-learning theory (Mischel, 1970) and cognitive-developmental theory (Kohlberg, 1966).

According to psychoanalytic theory, gender-typing occurs because of the child's identification with the same-sex parent. Through the process of identification, children unconsciously model themselves after their same-sex parent, trying to become like them. In doing so, they acquire aspects of personality and behavior that are appropriate for their sex.

While Freudian theory emphasizes unconscious processes and minimizes the role of people other than the same-sex parent in gender-typing, social-learning theory emphasizes the role of the social environment in shaping individual behavior. Social-learning theorists suggest that children learn gender-appropriate behaviors by observing the behavior of others. In addition, children are positively reinforced by adults, older children, and peers for the display of gender-appropriate behaviors and punished for the display of gender-inappropriate behaviors. In other words, girls are rewarded for acting like girls, and boys are rewarded for acting like boys.

In contrast to social-learning theory, cognitive-developmental theory shifts the focus back to the world of the child and places gender-typing within the larger context of cognitive development (which was discussed in Chapter

Social learning theory suggests that children learn gender-appropriate behaviors by modeling behaviors of an adult of the same sex.

4). The theory suggests that children form self-concepts that include information on whether they are male or female. Once children become aware of their own gender identity, they actively seek models who show them how to behave in gender-appropriate ways. Thus, exhibiting gender-appropriate behavior becomes a way of confirming one's own self-concept.

Gender-Typing and Mental Health

Traditionally, gender-typing was seen as necessary for psychological well-being. Females were expected to behave in feminine ways; males were expected to behave in masculine ways. Deviance from gender-appropriate behaviors was believed to result in maladjustment. In the mid-seventies, Sandra Bem (1974) introduced a radically different perspective. She suggested that traditional gender-typing limits the freedom and individuality of both sexes by restricting the range of behaviors that can be displayed. For example, a gender-typed woman would only exhibit behaviors the culture defines as appropriate for females, such as gentleness, sensitivity, warmth, and passivity. A gender-typed woman would not act in ways the culture defines as masculine: strong, dominant, forceful, and courageous. Bem argued that if gender roles were abolished, men and women would be psychologically healthier, since they would be free to choose from a wider range of behaviors. She suggested an ideal of **psychological androgyny**—a person who is not gender-typed, and who instead can choose from among both masculine and feminine characteristics and behaviors. Since 1974, over 100 studies have been conducted to explore how androgynous individuals compare with gender-typed individuals on a range of psychological dimensions.

Most of the research has focused on two major areas: behavioral flexibility and psychological well-being. According to the Bem's theory, androgynous individuals should exhibit greater behavioral flexibility because they can choose from a wider range of behaviors—both masculine and feminine. Conversely, gender-typed individuals would exhibit less adaptability because they have a more limited range of behavioral choices. In fact, studies have shown that androgynous individuals do display a broader range of behaviors (Bem, 1977; Orlofsky and Windle, 1978). Androgynous individuals are more effective in situations calling for the display of both gender-appropriate and gender-inappropriate behaviors. They seem to choose the most effective behavior, regardless of whether it is perceived as masculine or feminine. In contrast, gender-typed individuals perform less well in situations that require them to engage in behaviors more appropriate for the opposite sex.

Studies of androgyny and psychological well-being have not been as convincing. The individuals who reported the greatest feelings of well-being were gender-typed as masculine, not as androgynous. Masculine traits have been associated more strongly with numerous correlates of personal and social well-being, including self-esteem, identity, capacity for pleasure, and freedom from anxiety and depression. (Adams and Sherer, 1982; Bassoff and Glass, 1982; Cook, 1985; Whiteley, 1983; Lubinski, Tellegen and Butcher, 1981; Jones, Chernovetz and Hansson, 1978)

Individuals gender-typed as feminine, on the other hand, report greater enjoyment of social interactions and greater satisfaction with their interpersonal relationships. Antill (1983) discovered that marital satisfaction was reported to be much higher among couples in which at least one of the members possessed feminine traits, such as sensitivity, nurturance, or gentleness. Couples with both partners androgynous or both masculine-typed were less satisfied with their marriages. As we have seen, however, feminine traits do not have the same degree of significance for individual adjustment and well-being as do masculine traits. Thus, according to Bem, research has shown that it is psychological masculinity—not androgyny—that is associated with positive mental health in both men and women (Bem, p. 190).

Gender Schema Theory

More recently, Bem (1981, 1985) has proposed a theory of gender-typing that is based on elements of cognitive-developmental and social-learning theory. She suggests that children form cognitive structures called schemas—

A gender schema for "male" might specify that it is inappropriate for men to cry in public. When Wade Boggs cried in the dugout after the Boston Red Sox lost the 1986 World Series, he attracted much attention because his behavior was "inappropriate."

frameworks for organizing and guiding perceptions—which they use to make sense out of a complex world. According to Bem, masculinity and femininity are powerful schemas children use to process and categorize incoming information. Having learned the meaning of masculinity and femininity from society, children place themselves in the appropriate gender category. Gender-typing occurs as children compare their behavior to their schemas for masculinity and femininity, and modify their behavior to fit the gender-appropriate schema.

■ How do the three theories of gender-typing explain the process by which females become feminine and males become masculine?

■ What is psychological androgyny? What does the research say about the relationship between androgyny and mental health?

INFLUENCES ON SEXUAL BEHAVIOR

When people reach puberty, the effects of sex hormones on their maturing bodies and on their brains increase their interest in sexual activity. The motivation to engage in sexual behavior can be very strong.

Development of Sexual Orientation

As sexual interest increases, most people develop a special interest in members of the other sex—they develop a heterosexual orientation. Why does this occur? And why does the opposite sometimes occur? Why do some people develop a homosexual orientation?

Homosexual behavior (engaging in sexual activity with members of the same sex; from the

---

The prevalence of homosexual behavior makes it difficult to classify it as "unnatural." Many homosexuals lead fulfilling lives.

Greek *homos,* meaning "the same") is seen in male and female animals of many different species. The widespread occurrence of homosexual behavior makes it difficult to refer to it objectively as "unnatural." However, humans are apparently the only species in which some members regularly exhibit *exclusive* homosexuality. Other animals, if they are not exclusively heterosexual, are likely to be **bisexual** (engaging in sexual activity with members of both sexes), rather than exclusively homosexual. In contrast, the number of men and women who describe themselves as exclusively homosexual exceeds the number who describe themselves as bisexual.

There is no evidence that homosexuality is a disorder. The problems that many homosexuals have in adjustment reflect the fact that our society at large treats them differently. Therefore, even if we observe more neuroses in homosexuals, we cannot conclude that their maladjustment is directly related to their sexual orientation. In a society that was absolutely indifferent to a person's sexual orientation, homosexuals might be as well adjusted as heterosexuals. In fact, a large number of homosexuals are well adjusted and happy with themselves (Bell and Weinberg, 1978), suggesting that homosexuality is not always associated with emotional difficulties.

Possible Social Origins of Homosexuality

Some researchers have suggested that homosexuality is an emotional disturbance caused by faulty child rearing. For example, one study suggested that male homosexuals tend to be only children, youngest children, or youngest males in their families (Westwood, 1960). Others have reported that fathers of homosexuals tend to be cold and unaffectionate or even hostile (Evans, 1969; Siegelman, 1974) and that their mothers tend to be domineering and physically intimate (Bieber et al., 1962). Many clinicians have concluded that these boys lack an adequate male figure on which to model their behavior and continue to need the male affection that they never received from their fathers.

Much of the data in these studies were gathered from people who went to a psychiatrist or clinical psychologist for help with emotional problems. Therefore, they were not necessarily typical of all homosexuals, and we cannot know whether their homosexuality was caused by an unhappy childhood, whether their unhappy childhood was caused by early manifestations of homosexual tendencies, or whether their emotional instability and homosexual orientation were purely coincidental.

An ambitious project reported by Bell, Weinberg, and Hammersmith (1981) studied a large number of male and female homosexuals, most of whom had not sought professional psychological assistance. The researchers obtained their subjects by placing advertisements in newspapers, approaching people in gay bars and bookstores, and by asking known homosexuals to recommend friends. The study took place in San Francisco, where homosexuals form a large part of the population.

The subjects were asked about their relationships with their parents, siblings, and peers and about their feelings, gender identification, and sexual activity. The results provided little or no support for traditional theories of homosexuality.

The major conclusions of the study were as follows:

1. Sexual orientation appears to be determined prior to adolescence and prior to homosexual or heterosexual activity. The most important single predictor of adult homosexuality was a self-report of homosexual feelings, which usually occurred three years before genital homosexual activity. This finding suggests that homosexuality is a deep-seated tendency. It also tends to rule out the suggestion that seduction by an older person of the same sex plays an important role in the development of a homosexual orientation.

2. Most homosexual men and women have engaged in some heterosexual experiences during childhood and adolescence but, in contrast to their heterosexual counterparts, found these experiences unrewarding. This pattern is also consistent with the existence of a deep-seated predisposition prior to adulthood.

3. There is a strong relation between gender nonconformity in childhood and the development of homosexuality. Gender nonconformity is characterized by an aversion in boys to "masculine" behaviors and in girls to "feminine" behaviors. For example, among the male sub-

Research studies designed to discover why some people develop a homosexual orientation have thus far proved inconclusive.

jects, only 11 percent of the homosexuals, compared with 70 percent of the heterosexuals, reported having enjoyed boys' activities very much. In contrast, 46 percent of the homosexuals reported having enjoyed girls' activities, compared with 11 percent of the heterosexuals. The same pattern held true among the women: 62 percent of the homosexuals described themselves as having been masculine during childhood, compared with 10 percent of the heterosexuals.

4. Poor relationship with the father is a modest but significant predictor of homosexuality in *both males and females*. However, a person's relationship with his or her mother does not seem to predict later sexual orientation. This finding contradicts earlier theories of homosexuality that suggested that a boy's relationship with his mother is of paramount importance in the development of homosexuality.

Moreover, the fact that a poor relationship with the father was associated with homosexuality gives no indication of cause and effect; that is, a distant or hostile father might drive a child to homosexuality, or a child whose behavior did not conform to his or her gender might antagonize or distress the father and thus lead to a bad relationship.

Possible Biological Origins of Homosexuality

As the researchers admit, the results of the study are consistent with the hypothesis that homosexuality is at least partly determined by biological factors. That is, biological variables may predispose a child to behavior that is more typical of the other sex and eventually to sexual arousal by members of his or her own sex.

Is there evidence for what these biological causes of homosexuality may be? We can immediately rule out the suggestion that male homosexuals are deficient in testosterone or have excessive levels of female sex hormones in their blood. Although some studies have found evidence of androgen deficiencies in male homosexuals, it is well known that stress can affect production of these hormones (Rose, Bourne, Poe, Mougey, Collins, and Mason, 1969). Tests of homosexuals who have difficulty accepting their own sexual orientation or who feel harassed by society are likely to show that homosexuals have lower testosterone levels than most heterosexuals. However, it appears that well-adjusted male homosexuals have normal levels of testosterone (Tourney, 1980).

Another possible biological cause of male homosexuality is inadequate prenatal androgenization of the brain, which might result in a preference for the sexual partner that a woman would normally prefer—namely, a man. Prenatal androgens have two effects on sexual behavior: masculinization and defeminization. Masculinization refers to the development of neural circuits necessary for male sexual behavior, and defeminization refers to suppression of the development of neural circuits necessary for female sexual behavior. It is conceivable that prenatal exposure of the male human brain to androgens accomplishes two different effects: masculinization (establishment of a tendency to perceive females as sex-ual partners) and defeminization (suppression of the tendency to perceive males as sexual partners). If this hypothesis is correct, it would predict that most males would be exclusively heterosexual, because their brains would be masculinized and defeminized. However, if some factor (such as maternal stress or a genetic abnormality) interfered with the secretion of androgens during prenatal development, some males would be bisexual (their brains would be masculinized but *not* defeminized), and some would be exclusively homosexual (their brains would be neither masculinized nor defeminized).

Perhaps some genes are associated with sexual orientation; a certain percentage of homosexuals might be said to "inherit" their orientation. Attempts to identify a genetic role in homosexuality have provided strong but not conclusive evidence. For example, Kallman (1952) studied a large number of genetically identical twins and found that all had the same sexual orientation; if one was homosexual, so was the other. Heston and Shields (1968) studied a remarkable family of fourteen children that contained three pairs of male identical twins. Two of the pairs were homosexual and one pair was heterosexual. No environmental factor could be found to explain why two of the pairs, but not the third, became homosexual. Identical male twins of different sexual orientation (one homosexual, the other heterosexual) are apparently rare; Zuger (1976) found only nine cases in the scientific literature.

The possible biological causes of female homosexuality have been studied far less than those of male homosexuality. One study with rats suggested that the prenatal environment may play a role. Clemens (1971) found that the probability of malelike mounting behavior in female rats was related to the number of brothers in the litter. Presumably, when a female fetus shares the uterus with a number of brothers, her brain is affected by their androgens, and her behavior is slightly masculinized.

Our knowledge of the factors that influence sexual orientation remains indefinite. The study by Bell, Weinberg, and Hammersmith (1981) suggests that future research should focus on the gender-related behavior of children and try to determine the factors—biological and environmental—that influence its development.

Responses to Erotic Imagery

Men and women respond in basically the same way to visual and tactile sexual stimuli, but they appear to differ in the kinds of stimuli, imagery, and fantasies they consider erotic. Sigusch, Schmidt, Reinfeld, and Wiedemann-Sutor (1970) and Schmidt and Sigusch (1970) studied the attitudes and sexual responses of fifty men and women toward sexual stimuli. They measured sexual arousal by monitoring penile erections or vaginal lubrication with electronic sensing equipment.

The subjects looked at pictures of couples in romantic situations, showing affection and kissing, and in explicitly sexual situations, engaging in intercourse. The women reported finding the pictures of romantic situations sexually arousing, and physiological measurements confirmed their statements. However, most of them reported finding the sexually explicit pictures distasteful. Presumably, women learn this distaste from their culture; many women are taught that it is not proper to show an interest in erotic materials. Thus, some women are likely to avoid these materials, even though they can become as stimulated by them as men. The men reported the pictures of sexual behavior to be arousing (and the physiological measurements agreed), but, unlike the women, they were not aroused by the romantic pictures.

Men and women find different kinds of stimuli and fantasies erotic.

Money and Ehrhardt (1972) described the kinds of stimuli to which men and women respond. If a man responds sexually to a picture of an attractive woman, he tends to imagine her as a sex object; figuratively, he takes her out of the picture and uses her. A woman might also respond to an erotic picture of another woman, but in this case she imagines herself in the woman's situation. On the other hand, a picture of a naked man is generally not arousing to heterosexual men *or* women.

TABLE 5.1

The most prevalent types of sexual fantasies, by sex and sexual preference

Males	Females
Heterosexual	
1. Replacement of established partner	1. Replacement of established partner
2. Forced sexual encounter with female	2. Forced sexual encounter with male
3. Observation of sexual activity	3. Observation of sexual activity
4. Homosexual encounter	4. Idyllic encounter with unknown male
5. Group sex experience	5. Lesbian encounter
Homosexual	
1. Imagery of male sexual anatomy	1. Forced sexual encounter
2. Forced sexual encounter with male	2. Idyllic encounter with established partner
3. Heterosexual encounter	3. Heterosexual encounter
4. Idyllic encounter with unknown male	4. Recall of past sexual experience
5. Group sex experience	5. Sadistic imagery

Adapted from Masters, W.H. and Johnson, V.E. *Homosexuality in Perspective*. Boston: Little, Brown, 1979.

Masters and Johnson (1979) interviewed heterosexual and homosexual men and women and found that the subject matter of their sexual fantasies bore striking similarities, although the gender of the sex partner in the fantasies differed according to the person's orientation. (See Table 5.1 on the preceding page.)

Effects of Sex Hormones on Behavior

Effects of Androgens

As we saw, testosterone is necessary for sexual behavior of males, including humans. During prenatal development, the testes of male fetuses secrete testosterone, which causes the male sex organs to develop and also affects the development of the brain. These effects are called **organizational effects** because they alter the organization of the sex organs and the brain. Studies with laboratory animals have shown that if the organizational effects of androgens on brain development are prevented, the animal later fails to exhibit male sexual behavior. In addition, the ability of males to have an erection and engage in sexual intercourse depends on the presence of testosterone in adulthood, either from functioning testes or from injections of the hormone. These effects are called **activational effects** because the hormone activates sex organs and brain circuits that have already developed.

Davidson, Camargo, and Smith (1979) performed a carefully controlled double-blind study of the activational effects of testosterone on the sexual behavior of men whose testes failed to secrete normal amounts of androgens. The men were given monthly injections of a placebo or one of two different dosages of a long-lasting form of testosterone. Compared with the performance of controls, the effect of the testosterone on the total number of erections and attempts at intercourse during the month following the injection was large and statistically significant, and the larger dosage produced more of an effect than the smaller dosage. Thus, we may conclude that testosterone definitely affects male sexual performance.

If a man is castrated (has the testes removed), his sex drive will inevitably decline. Usually he first loses the ability to ejaculate, then the ability to achieve an erection (Bermant and Davidson, 1974). But studies have shown that some men lose these abilities soon after castration, whereas others retain at least some level of sexual potency for many months. Injections or pills of testosterone quickly restore potency. It is possible that the amount of sexual experience prior to castration affects performance afterward. Rosenblatt and Aronson (1958) found that male cats who had copulated frequently before castration were able to perform sexually for much longer periods of time after the surgery. Perhaps the same is true for men.

Environment can affect testosterone levels: sexual activity raises the level, and stress lowers it. Even the *anticipation* of sexual activity can affect testosterone secretion. One careful observer (Anonymous, 1970) worked on a remote island, far from any women, and measured his beard growth every day by shaving with an electrical razor and weighing the clippings. Just before his periodic trips to the mainland his beard grew faster. Because the rate of beard growth depends upon the testosterone level, it appears that the anticipation of sexual activity resulted in an increase in the observer's testosterone production.

Testosterone affects sex drive, but it does not determine the object of sexual desire. A homosexual man who receives injections of testosterone will not suddenly become interested in women. If the testosterone has any effect, it will be to increase his interest in sexual contact with other men.

Although the evidence shows clearly that testosterone affects men's sexual performance, we humans are uniquely emancipated from the biological effects of hormones in a special way. Not all human sexual activity requires an erect penis. A man does not need testosterone to be able to kiss and caress his partner or to engage in other noncoital activities. Men who have had to be castrated and who cannot receive injections of testosterone for medical reasons report continued sexual activity with their partners. We must remember that for humans, sexual activity is not limited to coitus.

It appears that androgens activate sex drive in women as well as men. Waxenberg, Drellich, and Sutherland (1959) observed that women whose adrenal glands had been surgically removed because of cancer showed a decline in sexual activity and desire. The adrenal glands secrete a variety of hormones, including androgens. Of course, factors other than loss of the adrenal glands may have caused this decline. However, Schon and Sutherland (1960) confirmed the importance of the adrenal hormones. They observed that removal of the pituitary gland, which causes a decrease in the hormonal output of the adrenal glands, also diminishes women's sex drive.

There is other evidence that women's androgen levels are correlated with their sexual desire. Salmon and Geist (1943) reported that testosterone has a stimulating effect on sexual desire and on the sensitivity of the clitoris to touch. Persky, Lief, Strauss, Miller, and O'Brien (1978) studied the sexual activity of eleven married couples ranging in age from twenty-one to thirty-one. The subjects kept daily records of their sexual feelings and behavior, and the experimenters measured their blood levels of testosterone twice a week. Couples were more likely to engage in intercourse when the woman's testosterone level was at a peak. In addition, the women reported finding intercourse more gratifying during these times.

Effects of Progesterone and Estrogen

In most species of mammals, the hormones estradiol and progesterone have strong effects on female sexual behavior. The levels of these two sex hormones fluctuate during the menstrual cycle of primates and the **estrous cycle** of other female mammals. (The difference between these cycles is primarily that the lining of the primate uterus—but not that of other mammals—builds up during the first part of the cycle and then sloughs off at the end.) A female mammal of a nonprimate species—for example, a laboratory rat—will receive the advances of a male only when the levels of estradiol and progesterone in the blood are high. This condition occurs around the time of ovulation, when copulation is likely to make her become pregnant. During this time, the female will stand still while the male approaches her. If he attempts to mount her, she will arch her back and move her tail to the side, giving him access to her genitalia. In fact, an estrous female often does not wait for the male to take the initiative: she engages in seductive behaviors such as hopping around and wiggling her ears. These behaviors usually induce sexual activity by the male (McClintock and Adler, 1978).

Romantic settings can play a role in arousing sexual desire.

A female rat whose ovaries have been removed is normally nonreceptive—even hostile—to the advances of an eager male. However, if she is given injections of estradiol and progesterone to duplicate the hormonal condition of the receptive part of her estrous cycle, she will receive the male or go after him. In contrast, women and other female primates are unique among mammals in their sexual activity: they are potentially willing to engage in sexual behavior at any time during their reproductive cycle. Some investigators have suggested that this phenomenon has made monogamous relationships possible; because the male can look forward to his mate's receptivity at any time during her menstrual cycle, he is less likely to look for other partners. However, some

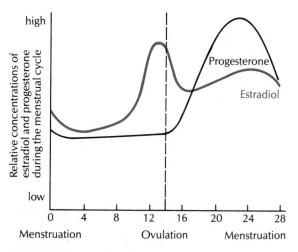

FIGURE 5.2

Hormonal changes during the menstrual cycle.

species form monogamous-pair bonds even though they mate during only one season of the year. Most primate species, in contrast, are promiscuous in nature.

As we saw in the previous section, androgens appear to be the most important class of hormones in stimulating a woman's sexual desire. However, the hormonal fluctuations in estradiol and progesterone during the menstrual cycle have an effect, too, though not to the same degree in all women. The estradiol level in women rises to a peak at midcycle, when ovulation occurs. After ovulation, progesterone begins to dominate, but some estradiol is still present. Toward the end of the cycle, the levels of both estradiol and progesterone fall, and menstruation begins. (See Figure 5.2.)

Many women report having two periods of peak sexuality: at midcycle (around the time of ovulation) and just before and during menstruation. They also report two different kinds of sexual desire at these times; at midcycle they feel a need to be occupied sexually—to be possessed. Around the time of menstruation they feel more sexually aggressive; they want to envelop and ``capture'' the penis (Money and Ehrhardt, 1972).

Adams, Gold, and Burt (1978) provided clear evidence for the midcycle peak in a woman's sexuality. Women who were not taking birth control pills were more likely to masturbate or to initiate sexual activity with their partners around the time of ovulation. In contrast,

women who took birth control pills, which prevent ovulation, did not show the same midcycle peak.

An interesting study by Van de Castle and Smith (1971) found that women's dreams tend to vary during the menstrual cycle in ways related to changes in sexual desire. During the menstrual phase (the time when women tend to feel more sexually aggressive), the women had more dreams of aggression directed toward men, but not toward women, and of friendly advances toward both men and women. During the nonmenstrual phase, they had more dreams of experiencing aggression from men, but not from other women, and of many more encounters—aggressive or not—with men than with women. These results support the conclusion that hormonal changes during the menstrual cycle have an effect on a woman's sexuality.

Unlike that of most other female mammals, women's sex drive does not depend on the presence of ovarian hormones. During menopause, when the ovaries suddenly cease to secrete hormones, women experience various uncomfortable symptoms, such as hot flashes, headaches, and depression, which can temporarily interfere with sex drive. The loss of estradiol tends to make the walls of the vagina thinner, and the decrease in vaginal secretions can make intercourse somewhat painful. However, with the use of a lubricant jelly, intercourse can be just as satisfying as it was before the ovaries ceased to function. Masters and Johnson (1966) reported that frequent intercourse itself tends to retard the effects of menopause on the vagina. In fact, with pregnancy no longer a possibility, many women report an *increase* in desire for sexual activity.

■ What are the hypotheses put forth to explain the development of sexual orientation? What does the research say about the development of a homosexual orientation?

■ Do males and females respond in similar ways to erotic imagery?

■ What role do androgens play in human sexual responses?

■ What role do progesterone and estrogen play in human sexual responses?

ADULT DEVELOPMENT

We will now leave the topic of sexual development and turn our attention to other important aspects of adult development: psychosocial development, physical development, and intellectual development. Mental and emotional changes during adulthood are more closely related to individual experience than to age. Some people achieve success and satisfaction with their careers, while some hate their jobs, and some marry and have happy family lives, while others never adjust to the role of spouse and parent. Crises occur at different times for different people, and they do not come in the same order. No one description of adult development will fit everyone.

Thus, we can note only some general trends. Physically we decline after early adulthood, although the decline need not be rapid; a healthy, active person can retain his or her vitality for many years. Sexual performance may decline with age, but the rate of decline is closely related to a person's activity and attitudes. Intellectual changes are also variable and are particularly difficult to assess.

Stages of Adult Development

One theorist who has attempted a description of lifelong human development is Erik Erikson, a psychoanalyst who studied with Anna Freud, Sigmund Freud's daughter. Erikson's theory, which was based on his observations of patients in his psychoanalytical practice, divides human development into eight stages. As we shall see in Chapter 15, Freud believed that the important stages of development centered on changes in sexuality, and thus were largely complete when a person reached young adulthood. In contrast, Erikson proposed that people encounter a series of crises in their social relations with other people. The ways in which people resolve these crises determine the character of their personality. Thus, Erikson's theory is one of **psychosocial development.** Because the nature of people's social relations changes through life, their psychosocial development does not end when they become adults.

Table 5.2 on the next page lists Erikson's eight stages of development, the nature of the psychosocial crises, social relationships involved in these crises, and possible consequences—favorable or unfavorable—of these crises.

Erikson's theory of lifelong development has been very influential. In fact, the term *identity crisis,* which he coined, has become a familiar phrase in modern society. However, because the theory is phrased in global terms, it is difficult to make specific predictions from it that can be tested experimentally; thus, the theory has little empirical support.

In the 1970s, several other stage theories of adult development became popular. (Levinson, 1978; Gould, 1978). On the basis of in-depth interviews with 40 men, Levinson suggested that adult males progress through a series of predictable stages from early adulthood through late adulthood. The orderly progression is characterized by a period of crisis followed by a period of stability. Gould also studied adult males and found evidence for stages of adult development. Despite their popularity, stage theories of adult development have received little empirical support (Datan, Rodeheaver, & Hughes, 1987).

Others have argued that adult development does not occur in predictable and ordered ways. One longitudinal study reported that personality traits were relatively stable throughout adulthood (McCrae & Costa, 1984). However, the results of a different longitudinal study found that while some personalities are stable and enduring, others are susceptible to change (Shanan, 1985).

The debate over whether adult development is characterized by stability or change is not over yet. However, psychologists have begun to realize that to account for the full complexity of human development throughout the lifespan, more rigorous study of both continuity and change is required.

Physical Changes

Unlike the rapid physical changes that occur during prenatal development, childhood, and adolescence, the changes that occur during adulthood—except for sudden changes caused by accident or disease—are gradual. People are

TABLE 5.2

Erikson's stages of psychosocial development

Life Crisis	Favorable Outcome	Unfavorable Outcome
First Year Trust—mistrust	Hope. Trust in the environment and the future.	Fear of the future; suspicion
Second Year Autonomy—shame, doubt	Will. Ability to exercise choice as well as self-restraint; a sense of self-control and self-esteem leading to good will and pride.	Sense of loss of self-control or sense of external overcontrol; the result is a propensity for shame and doubt about whether one willed what one did or did what one willed.
Third through Fifth Years Initiative—guilt	Purpose. Ability to initiate activities, to give them direction, and to enjoy accomplishment.	Fear of punishment; self-restriction or overcompensatory showing off.
Sixth Year through Puberty Industry—inferiority	Competence. Ability to relate to the world of skills and tools, to exercise dexterity and intelligence in order to make things and make them well.	A sense of inadequacy and inferiority.
Adolescence Identity—confusion about one's role	Fidelity. Ability to see oneself as a unique and integrated person and to sustain loyalties.	Confusion over who one is.
Early Adulthood Intimacy—isolation	Love. Ability to commit oneself, one's identity, to others.	Avoidance of commitments and of love; distancing of oneself from others.
Middle Age Generativity—stagnation	Care. Widening concern for what has been generated by love, necessity, or accident; for one's children, work, or ideas.	Self-indulgence, boredom, and interpersonal impoverishment.
Old Age Integrity—despair	Wisdom. Detached concern for life itself; assurance of the meaning of life and of the dignity of one's own life; acceptance that one will die.	Disgust with life; despair over death.

H. Gardner, *Developmental psychology* (2d ed.). Boston: Little, Brown, 1982, p. 51.

unlikely to notice these changes until they try to do something they have not done for several years and find it more difficult than it used to be, such as playing a sport that they have not practiced since their college days.

Most physical functions decline during adulthood. As people grow older, their muscles become weaker, their bones become brittle through loss of calcium, their lungs become less efficient, and the walls of their blood ves-sels lose some elasticity and may become coated with atherosclerotic plaques, which increase the risk of heart attack or stroke. As their bodies lose their resilience people find it harder to recover from the stress of illness or injury. Physical stress that would be relatively minor in a young adult has much more serious consequences in an older person.

The effects of *looking* old can be more devastating than the purely physical effects on a person's functional capacity. For example, the sex life of a person who is viewed as sexually unattractive because of age will suffer even if he or she is physiologically capable of vigorous sexual performance. Similarly, the intellectual and physical skills of an older person will go untested if he or she is regarded as "too old for the job." These age-related effects are purely social; they depend on people's attitudes toward older people.

Aging brings with it an increased chance of developing senile or presenile dementia—a class of diseases characterized by the progressive loss of cortical tissue and a corresponding loss of mental functions. (*Senile* means "old," *dementia* literally means "an undoing of the mind.") The distinction between senile and presenile dementia is not important, because the disease process is the same in both cases. The most prevalent form of dementia is **Alzheimer's disease.** People with this disorder rapidly lose the gray matter of the cerebral cortex. The cause of the degeneration is not known, and there is no useful medical treatment. The disease progresses from disruption of memory to decline in language functions to loss of physical control and finally to death.

An even more important cause of mental deterioration in old age is depression, a psychological disorder. Many people find old age an unpleasant condition: they are declining physically; they no longer have jobs or family-related activities that confirm their usefulness to other people; and many old friends have died, are infirm, or have moved away. With this strong sense of loss or deprivation, older people become depressed; they lose their appetite for food and for living in general, appear sad and confused, have trouble concentrating, and suffer losses in memory. Too often these symptoms of depression are diagnosed as dementia. Yet unlike dementia, depression is treatable with psychotherapeutic and pharmacological methods, as we will see in Chapters 16 and 17.

Although it is easy to measure a decline in the sensory systems (such as vision or hearing), older people often show very little *functional* change in these systems. Most of them learn to make adjustments for their sensory losses, using additional cues to help them decode sensory information. For example, people with a hearing loss can learn to attend more carefully to other people's gestures and lip movements; they can also profitably use their experience to infer what was said.

Many of these physical changes appear to be related to lifestyle. People who are active both physically and intellectually are likely to continue to be active and productive in old age. With a flexible attitude, individuals can accommodate their interests and activities to the inevitable changes in physical abilities. There is no reason why a reasonably healthy person of *any* age should stop enjoying life.

As more and more older adults find time for exercise, differences in physical abilities between younger and older adults may lessen.

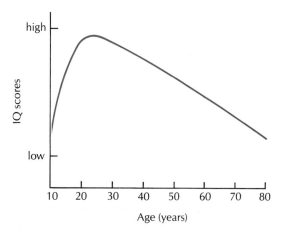

FIGURE 5.3

A traditional graph showing that IQ inevitably declines with age. (From Jones, H.E., and Kaplan, O.J. In *Mental Disorders in Later Life,* 2nd ed., edited by O.J. Kaplan. Stanford, Calif.: Stanford University Press, 1956.)

Intellectual Changes

One of the topics of adult development that has received the most attention is intellectual development. Psychologists have studied the effects of education and experience on intellectual abilities and have questioned whether intelligence inevitably declines with age. Most of us can conceive of a future when we can no longer run as fast as we do now or perform well in a strenuous sport, but we do not like to think of being outperformed intellectually by younger people. And in fact research indicates that people can get old without losing their intellectual skills.

Intelligence and Age: Problems of Interpretation

As we get older, our joints will get stiff, and our muscles and ligaments will become less flexible and resilient. Is the same true for our brain? Will we start to lose our memory, find it difficult to reason, and generally become a little fuzzy about everything? The graph presented in Figure 5.3 supposedly shows how intelligence changes with age. The downward slope depicted there does not look very promising.

However, the studies suggesting that intelligence declines with age have used methodologies that are open to challenge.

There are several obstacles to obtaining an accurate and unbiased estimate of the relation between age and intelligence. The first is the fact that age is usually correlated with other variables. You will recall from Chapter 1 that we can assess the effects of one variable upon another only when all other variables are held constant. Suppose we perform a **cross-sectional study**—a slice through the various age layers of society. We obtain a sample of healthy twenty-year-olds, thirty-year-olds, and so on, up to age eighty. We administer various intelligence tests to all our subjects and then compare the performances of the various age groups. Would we be justified in saying that the results represent the effects of age on intellectual functions?

We would not. Many variables besides age may have affected the performance of the various age groups. For one thing, the people of different ages may have had very different environments; for example, the twenty-year-old people in our sample will all have received their education recently, whereas the eighty-year-old people will have been educated early in this century, when educational norms and requirements were very different: Far fewer people went to college, many did not even finish high school, and those who did went to schools that were very different from high schools today. Furthermore, the health care that the older people's mothers received during pregnancy and their own health care during childhood will probably not have been as good as the care that children and pregnant women receive now.

Given that the cross-sectional method cannot yield accurate estimates of the effects of aging in times during which the environment is changing (and this certainly applies to our century), what method would provide more accurate results? At first glance, the ideal method would seem to be a **longitudinal study**—that is, observation of the intellectual performance of the same group of people throughout their lives. Because the various age groups would consist of the same sample of people, age would not be confounded with environmental factors. But this method introduces other problems. Some problems are practical in nature.

For instance, a longitudinal study is expensive and depends on a long-term commitment of resources, whereas most granting agencies limit their funding commitments to three years. Because the investigator might not live as long as his or her subjects, a team of people must carry out the study, adding younger recruits from time to time. And because the person who begins such a study might not be able to participate in its completion, there is less incentive to perform a longitudinal study. Cross-sectional studies, which provide immediate results, are much more common.

Besides the expense, difficulty, and delay of gratification, there are methodological problems inherent in longitudinal studies. Perhaps people from poor families received poor nutrition and health care and an inadequate education; we would expect them to score less well on intelligence tests. If, because of chronic poor health, these people die sooner than those with a good history of health care, the mean intelligence of the long-lived group will rise, because it contains only healthy survivors. Thus, the method may provide *inflated* estimates of the mean intellectual ability of older people, relative to younger ones.

Research has shown that, indeed, group composition changes in the course of a longitudinal study. People who score poorly on intelligence tests tend not to be available for later testing. For example, in 1956 Riegel, Riegel, and Meyer (1967) tested 380 German men and women between the ages of fifty-five and seventy-five. Five years later only 202 were available for testing; the others had died, were in poor health, or were simply reluctant to be tested again. Five years after that, the sample was reduced still further. An analysis showed the people who remained were those who had originally scored best on the intelligence tests. Such changes in the composition of a group make it impossible to obtain a pure measure of the effect of age on intellectual performance.

Because of the problems inherent in the cross-sectional and longitudinal methods, the results of such studies must be viewed with some skepticism. For example, the shape of the curve relating age to intellectual performance may not be accurate. Both methods indicate a decline in performance with age, but longitudinal studies show the decline beginning later in life—not until the fifties.

Specific Abilities and Age

Whatever the true shape of the curve may be, studies have shown clearly that aging affects different intellectual abilities to different degrees. Cattell (1971) divided these abilities into two major categories. In general, old people in good health do well on tests of **crystallized intelligence**—abilities that depend on knowledge and experience—until they die. Vocabulary, the ability to see similarities between objects and situations, and general information are all aspects of crystallized intelligence.

Fluid intelligence, or the capacity for abstract reasoning, appears to decline with age (Baltes and Schaie, 1974; Horn, 1976). The ability to solve puzzles, to memorize a series of arbitrary items such as unrelated words or letters, to classify figures into categories, and to change problem-solving strategies easily and flexibly are aspects of fluid intelligence.

The fact that older people excel in crystallized intelligence and younger people excel in

Old age can be a time of great artistic expression. Artist Georgia O'Keeffe painted until she was in her eighties. When her vision became impaired, and painting was no longer possible, she expressed her creativity through sculpture.

Theodore White chronicled American cultural and social history. His greatest intellectual contributions were made in later life, lending support to Cattell's notion that older adults excel in crystallized intelligence.

fluid intelligence is reflected in the kinds of intellectual endeavors that the two age groups seem to be best suited for. For example, most great mathematicians make their most important contributions during their twenties or early thirties; apparently the ability to break out of the traditional ways of thinking and to conceive of new strategies is crucial in such achievements. In contrast, great contributions to literature and philosophy, in which success depends heavily on knowledge and experience, tend to be made by older people.

At least three reasons may account for older people's apparent decline in fluid intelligence: (1) The abilities that constitute fluid intelligence may be especially sensitive to the inevitable deterioration in the brain that accompanies aging. (2) People's previous experience may cause them to adhere rigidly to particular problem-solving strategies, even when a more flexible approach would be more effective. In this case, the decline would be due to experience rather than to a real loss of intellectual capacity. (3) People may learn so much and see so many relations among variables that they have difficulty focusing on the simple answer.

In support of the third suggestion, Kogan (1973) compared the strategies used by college students and members of a senior citizens club (average age seventy-three) to classify a number of objects and photographs. The older people were more likely to classify the items according to functional relations. For example, they might group pipes with matches. Younger people were more likely to classify objects according to physical characteristics (such as having handles) or according to a common general concept (such as kitchen utensils). Kogan attributed the difference to experience; the older subjects used a more subtle and less conventional scheme. Kogan noted that children who are rated as more creative also tend to classify according to functional relations rather than by type or physical characteristics. Thus, the behavior of the older people could be taken as evidence of a higher stage of cognitive development, and not as evidence of their intellectual deterioration.

Many studies have shown that older people learn lists of words more slowly than younger people do. However, some studies have shown that crystallized intelligence can sometimes facilitate new learning (Canestrari, 1966; Lair, Moon, and Kausler, 1969). Both younger people and older people were given lists of words arranged in pairs. Some pairs were frequently associated ones (such as *chair* and *table*), while others were unrelated. The older people learned the frequently associated pairs (but not the unrelated pairs) faster than the younger people did.

Another aspect of intellectual ability is speed. Older people have difficulty responding and performing quickly. When time pressures prevail, their performance is worse than that of younger people. However, when time requirements are relaxed, the performance of older people improves much more than that of younger people (Arenberg, 1973; Botwinick and Storandt, 1974).

Part of the age-related decline in speed can be attributed to deterioration in sensory functions and to difficulty in changing strategies to meet new demands. But another important reason for decreased speed is caution; older people appear to be less willing to make mistakes. In some endeavors this caution is valuable. In many societies, important decision-making functions are reserved for older people because they are less likely to act too hastily. A study by Leech and Witte (1971) illustrates the effect of caution on performance. The investigators found that older people who were paid for each response they made—correct or incorrect—learned lists of pairs of words faster than older people who were paid for only correct responses. The payment for incorrect responses increased their willingness to make a mistake, and this relaxation of their normal caution paid off in an increased speed of learning.

In a review of human abilities, Horn (1976) summarized the features of aging as follows:

> In general . . . the findings suggest that if one lives long enough he will experience difficulties, relative to his skills at an earlier age, in organizational thinking, perceiving relationships, forming hypotheses, making integrations, and shifting from one learning or thinking task to another. . . . But some intellectual changes with age in adulthood reflect changes in styles of thinking which are not indicative of decreased abilities to cope but instead indicate increased capacities. (p. 470)

DEATH AND DYING

Kübler-Ross (1969), as a result of interviews with terminally ill patients, identified five stages which people go through when confronting death. In the first stage, denial, individuals do not want to acknowledge they are dying. The second stage brings anger and resentment: Why is this happening to me? Eventually the anger lessens, and the bargaining stage begins. People accept the fact that they are dying, but also try to bargain for more time. Depression, the fourth stage, is accompanied by sorrow and sadness. In the final stage, acceptance, individuals make peace with the idea that they are going to die.

While Kübler-Ross' ideas were well-received and influential in determining how the dying should be treated, psychologists have pointed out a number of flaws in her research. First, she did not use scientific methods in her study of the terminally ill. Her observations were not systematically carried out and her sample consisted of only people with long-term illnesses. On this basis, researchers have questioned whether the stages she identified can be generalized to all people facing death. Kastenbaum and Costa (1977) argue that peoples' reactions to death are unique and personal. Others have suggested that young people facing an untimely death, such as those afflicted with AIDS, may be less likely than older adults to reach Kübler-Ross' final stage of acceptance.

■ What physical and psychological changes occur during adulthood?
■ Why is it difficult to assess the effects of aging on intellectual abilities?
■ How do the specific intellectual abilities of younger and older adults compare?
■ According to Kübler-Ross, what are the five stages (or attitudes) through which terminally ill persons typically pass? On what basis has her theory been criticized?

CHAPTER SUMMARY

1. Early prenatal development of males and females is identical until a gene on the Y chromosome of males causes the undifferentiated gonads to develop as testes. Females lack a Y chromosome, so the undifferentiated gonads become ovaries. In males, the fetal gonads secrete testosterone, which causes the male reproductive system to develop. Females do not produce androgens, so the female reproductive system develops instead. Fetuses that do not have either ovaries or testes (such as individuals with Turner's syndrome) develop as females; thus it is nature's impulse to create a female.

2. Puberty is the final phase of sexual maturation. It is initiated by the hypothalamus, which causes the anterior pituitary gland to secrete the gonadotropic hormones, which in turn stimulate the ovaries or testes to produce estradiol or testosterone. The sex hormones cause the internal sex organs and external genitalia to assume their adult form and function and promote the development of secondary sex characteristics.

3. The effects of sex hormones on the development of the brain mechanisms responsible for sexual behavior are similar to the effects of these hormones on the development of the sex organs; that is, androgens such as testosterone cause behavioral masculinization and defeminization. No sex hormone is necessary for the development of the brain mechanisms responsible for female behavior.

Studies of human females who were exposed to androgens during prenatal development have shown that the hormones have a small effect on gender-related social behaviors, perhaps through an effect on the person's physical activity.

4. Social factors influence a person's sense of his or her own maleness or femaleness—what psychologists call gender identity. Individuals acquire gender-appropriate behaviors through the process of gender-typing. Three theories have been put forth to explain how gender-typing occurs: psychoanalytic theory, social learning theory, and cognitive-developmental theory.

Psychological androgyny refers to a person who is not gender-typed as masculine or feminine. Such individuals can choose both masculine and feminine characteristics and behaviors, depending on the appropriateness of the situation.

5. The development of sexual orientation appears to have its roots early in life—perhaps even in prenatal development. A large-scale study of homosexuals failed to find evidence that particular child-rearing practices fostered homosexuality. Instead, the findings were consistent with the hypothesis that genetic factors or some events that occur during pregnancy may reduce or eliminate the masculinization and defeminization of neural circuits that play a role in the later development of preference for a sexual partner of a particular gender. However, this hypothesis must be regarded as speculative.

6. Men and women respond in similar fashion to erotic stimuli although they find different kinds of stimuli erotic. Social factors can have strong influences.

7. The sexual behavior of female mammals with estrous cycles depends on estradiol and progesterone, but these hormones have only a minor effect on women's sexual behavior. Their sexual desire, like that of men, is much more dependent on androgens. Testosterone has two major effects on male sexual behavior: organizational and activational. In the fetus, testosterone organizes the development of male sex organs and of some circuits in the brain, while in the adult, testosterone activates these structures and permits erection and ejaculation to occur.

8. Aging brings with it a gradual deterioration in people's sensory capacities and changes in physical appearance that many people regard as unattractive. The effects of these changes can be minimized by vigorous participation in life's activities.

9. Although older people are more likely to develop dementing illnesses such as Alzheimer's disease, severe intellectual deterioration is often caused by depression, which can usually be treated successfully. Rather than sudden intellectual deterioration, older people are more likely to exhibit gradual changes, especially in abilities that require flexibility and learning new behaviors. Intellectual abilities that depend heavily on an accumulated body of knowledge are much less likely to decline.

10. Studies related to age and intelligence may be cross-sectional or longitudinal. One problem related to cross-sectional studies (those that investigate various age layers of society) is the inability to limit the variables. Longitudinal studies (observations of the same group throughout the lifespan) require great funding, strong incentives for both the researcher and subjects, and involve those difficulties that occur when the time period is many years long. The results from either method are somewhat inaccurate.

11. Kübler-Ross proposed five stages people go through when confronted with knowledge that their own death is near. However, her research has drawn criticism because of her lack of experimental and methodological rigor. Others have suggested that peoples' reactions to death are unique and personal, and that they may differ depending on the person's age at the time of death and a number of other factors.

KEY TERMS

activational effect (of hormone) The effect of a hormone on a physiological system that is already developed, as contrasted with an organizational effect, which influences prenatal or early postnatal development. Examples include breast growth, beard growth, and facilitation of sexual arousal and performance.

adrenogenital syndrome Masculinization of a female, caused by excessive secretion of androgens by the adrenal gland.

Alzheimer's disease A degenerative illness in which neurons of the cerebral cortex die. The result is loss of memory and other cognitive processes and ultimately death.

androgen The primary class of sex hormones in males. The most important androgen is testosterone.

androgenization An organizational effect of androgens that causes a fetus to differentiate as a male.

anterior pituitary gland Within the endocrine system, that part of the "master gland" that secretes gonadotropic hormones.

autosomes Twenty-two of the twenty-three pairs of chromosomes formed when sperm and ovum unite; determine the organism's physical development independent of its sex.

bisexual behavior Sexual activity with members of both sexes.

cross-sectional study Observation of the behavior of people of different ages at approximately the same time. See also *longitudinal study*.

crystallized intelligence According to Raymond Cattell, that part of a person's intellectual abilities that accumulates through experience. See *fluid intelligence*.

estradiol The primary estrogen in mammals.

estrogen The principal class of sex hormones in females.

estrous cycle The ovulatory cycle in mammals other than primates; the sequence of physical and hormonal changes that accompany the ripening and disintegration of ova.

fluid intelligence According to Raymond Cattell, the component of general intellectual ability that determines how likely a person is to profit from experience (that is, to develop crystallized intelligence).

gender identity A person's sense of his or her own maleness or femaleness.

gender roles Behaviors society expects of males and females.

gender typing The acquisition of sex-appropriate preferences, skills, personality attributes, behaviors, and self-concepts for either males or females.

gonad An organ that produces gametes; an ovary or testis.

gonadotropic hormone A hormone secreted by the anterior pituitary gland that has activational effects on the ovaries or testes.

homosexual behavior Sexual activity with members of the same sex.

longitudinal study Observation of the behavior of one group of people at several different stages of development.

organizational effect (of hormone) An effect of a hormone that usually occurs early in development, producing permanent changes that alter the development of the organism.

primary sex characteristics Sex organs such as genitalia, gonads, and related organs.

psychological androgyny According to Bem, a gender role free from gender-typing, allowing a person to choose among both masculine and feminine characteristics.

psychosocial development The lifelong process of encountering and resolving social crises that determine a person's character and personality.

puberty The beginning of the transition from childhood to adulthood, characterized by physical changes in height, the development of secondary sex characteristics, and reproductive ability.

secondary sex characteristics External distinguishing features of a mature male or female, such as facial hair or breasts.

sex chromosomes The X and Y chromosomes, which determine an organism's gender. Normally, XX individuals are female, and XY individuals are male.

testosterone The principal androgen, or male sex hormone, secreted by the testes.

Turner's syndrome A condition caused by the presence of only one sex chromosome, an X chromosome. The person has no ovaries or testes and is morphologically female, but puberty must be induced by the administration of sex hormones.

LEARNING
AND COGNITION

Our survey of physical and psychological factors and how they interact over the lifespan should have persuaded you that human beings are marvelously complex and adaptable. Part B will examine the characteristics that make us unique— our mental processes. The abilities to learn, to remember, to communicate—to *think*—are generally seen as the basis for human progress and civilization. As far as we know, no other species has developed the technology to travel to the moon, or the vocabulary and desire to describe such an event to its cohorts, or the vision to attempt doing the "unthinkable" in the first place. If we were less complex or less adaptable, we might still be performing rituals to influence and appease whichever deities we thought governed the moon.

Central to our cognitive abilities is memory. Without that, it seems doubtful that we could learn, or speak, or think about things—at least not in the sociable way required to achieve a landing on the moon. Without memory, our internal lives would be isolated and remote even to ourselves, for there would be no way to label and organize our "thoughts," no "language" by which to share them. Our "learning" would be fixed by rote biological processes, as we believe it is for most other organisms. There would be no shared shot at the moon, for we could not amass the technology, vocabulary, and imagination to attempt it. Our ability to *adapt* through learning, language, and thinking would be severely limited.

Dependent as we are on memory, both as a species and as individuals, it is far less accessible to us than we commonly think. Like the other aspects of cognition, memory is an unobservable mental process that presumably results from particular brain functions. We say that we "have" a specific memory of something, and we think of that memory as an object—as something that was definite and real in the past,

even if it no longer exists. But was it ever as definite and real as we remember it, or are our memories unreliable, distorted fabrications? The question is extremely important, for we depend on our memories to store the information by which we learn.

Among the most intriguing of popular ideas is the one that we can remember anything if we just concentrate hard enough—that our complete life experiences lie coiled in the convolutions of our brains, awaiting release. Many people expect to relive their entire lives in a split second on their deathbed. Police and attorneys press witnesses for one more detail of evidence; patients in analysis strain to recall (or repress) the memory of what "really happened." But *what* are we remembering? Are we dealing with "just the facts" when we recount some cherished memory or successfully snare a long-lost one? Do we deliberately distort our memories the way we might embellish a favorite story, or is memory serving some purpose we know little about and don't acknowledge?

Memories of Life

Lee Robbins, of Washington University in St. Louis, is one researcher who thinks that people do color their memories to create a picture that fits with their current self-image, forgetting and changing details selectively. In one study of adults who had been troubled children and had received treatment thirty years earlier, those who were now well-adjusted had relatively few painful memories of childhood compared with those whose lives were still troubled emotionally. Yet both groups, as children, had experienced poverty and had lived in homes for foster children and delinquents. Robbins also probed the memories of depressed and alcoholic patients and compared them with the memories of similarly aged siblings. In this case the *kind* of childhood memory apparently influenced the degree to which it was colored in adulthood. The rate of agreement between siblings was 71 percent on questions of fact (such as, Did your family move?), but it dropped to only 47 percent when the question involved the frequency of such an event; when the siblings were asked to make value judgments (Were your parents hard on the children?), they agreed only 29 percent of the time.

The finding that these subjects agreed so much more often about the fact of a matter than about its frequency or interpretation is significant. When we talk about a memory, we are really referring to several aspects of memories. One type of memory consists of information about specific experiences (such as whether one's family moved); another type consists of conceptual information (such as whether one's parents were "hard" on the children). One can say *when* a *specific* memory was formed, because, by nature, it places perceptions within the context of time—the family moved in 1983. Some memories, however, involve meanings that usually are formed over time, not on one specific occasion, and so we usually cannot pinpoint exactly when they were formed. People who remember their parents as being stern (or loving) may illustrate their claim by relating a series of specific examples. But these memories are the means by which they learned to *think* of their parents as stern or loving. The memory of stern or loving parents is a concept that resulted from their thinking. Over time, individuals think about factual episodes in different ways, analyzing and combining the information with other information. As a result, individuals form different concepts. Thus, family members may experience the same things, but they process them differently, and so their memories also differ.

We think about, or "process" information,

and we store it as memories. Relatively superficial processing as well as deeper analysis of information make up our *long-term memory,* from which we can retrieve facts and concepts, once we learn them, without a great deal of thought. Before we learn anything, however, we must perceive it, recognize what it is, and organize it into meaningful information. First our senses very briefly store a perceptual stimulus—light, sound, taste, touch, smell—until we decide whether or not to attend to it. If we are interested, we name and recognize the stimulus (or are confused by it) in our *short-term memory,* the seat of awareness. By retrieving facts and concepts already held in long-term memory, we convert the short-term data into information that can be made meaningful.

Because perceptions constantly flood our awareness and must be screened and compared with what we already know, short-term memory is necessarily limited. As new data arrive, they assume priority for a moment and force other perceptions out of awareness. This is all to the good if the newest stimulus is the honk of a car's horn when you had stopped in the street to pick up a penny. But the limits of short-term memory can be maddening, too.

Apparently, "everyday life" is so ordinary that we forget most of it very quickly . . .

The task of memorizing a list—as when studying for a vocabulary test in French—reveals the limits of short-term memory. Most people find it more difficult to remember the words in the middle of the list than those at the beginning or the end. This makes sense, when you consider that the first words have been rehearsed longer, and the last words are the most recent. Since storage space is limited, the less significant words in the middle tend to get squeezed out. Until recently it was thought that the order and significance of data influence only short-term memory. Now there seems to be evidence that long-term memory, too, may be affected by similar factors.

In a study at the University of Illinois, psychologist William Brewer asked students to carry beepers with them and to record what they were thinking and doing whenever the beepers sounded. One week later the students could recall about 80 percent of what they had been doing—but only if they were first reminded of what they had been thinking. When they were simply told the date and time of their notations, they could remember only one-third of what happened. Two months later, even prompted by their notes, they had forgotten half of the events; and without the prompts they remembered only 15 percent. Apparently, "everyday life" is so ordinary that we forget most of it very quickly. If something exciting or unusual happens, however, it is more likely to make an impression and be remembered.

Some surprising results came from a series of studies by David Rubin at Duke University. Over the lifespan people seem to remember more distant periods better than more recent times, and this pattern of memories seems to hold true for everyone beginning with middle age. At seventy, for instance, people remember their twenties and thirties best; for fifty-year-olds, the late teens and early twenties are most memorable. Recollections from childhood diminish and are lost as the years pass. Rubin suggests that this pattern of personal memory results from the significance of such events as choosing a mate and establishing a career and family. Life becomes more stable after that and thus less memorable.

If memory is far less reliable and far less accessible than we like to think, it also is far more significant than we can yet grasp. Normal, *fallible* memory has made human cognition so extraordinary that we can set our sights not only on the moon but on ourselves as well.

Learning

We are what we are because of our history—both our ancestors' history and the history of our own lives. The evolution of our species was shaped by the process of natural selection: mutations introduced variability, and those changes that produced favorable consequences were maintained. Our behaviors are similarly selected: Behaviors that produce favorable consequences are repeated, while those that produce unfavorable consequences tend not to recur. In other words, we learn from our experiences.

Learning refers to relatively long-lasting changes in an individual's behavior that are produced by environmental events. The word *behavior* is essential, because evidence of learning comes to us from changes in behavior. The process is an adaptive one, in that the changes in behavior are the result of interactions with the environment.

Most of our knowledge about the principles of learning has come from carefully controlled laboratory experiments. This model of study depends on the systematic identification of reliable reinforcers so we can predict behavior change. Which rewards produce the strongest change in behavior? For a child, the smile of a parent can be a powerful reinforcer. Which punishers are most effective? Studies indicate that pain is not the only effective punisher.

Can we learn something without directly experiencing it? According to social learning theory, we can learn by observing and imitating the behavior of others. In fact, it may actually be easier to learn certain things by watching rather than by doing. Most of us first learned how to play baseball by watching others with experience play the game. By observing what other people do and what happens to them as a result, we can learn new responses without directly performing the behavior ourselves. This chapter presents the general principles of learning, as they apply to humans and other animals.

HABITUATION

There are many events that cause us to react automatically. For example, a sudden, unexpected noise causes an **orienting response**—we become alert and turn our head toward the source of the sound. However, if the noise occurs again and again, we gradually cease to respond to it—we eventually ignore it. **Habituation,** learning *not* to respond to an event that occurs repeatedly, is the simplest form of learning. Even animals with very primitive nervous systems are capable of habituation. For example, if we tap the shell of a land snail with the point of a pencil, it will withdraw its body into its shell. After half a minute or so it will extend its body out of its shell and continue with whatever it was doing. If we tap it again, it will again withdraw, but this time it will stay inside its shell a shorter time. Another tap will cause it to withdraw again, but for even less time.

Habituation refers to the fact that we learn to ignore certain stimuli in the environment which we recognize as inconsequential.

Eventually it will stop responding to the tap. The withdrawal response will have habituated.

From an evolutionary perspective, habituation makes sense. If a once-novel stimulus occurs again and again without any important result, the stimulus has no significance to the organism. Obviously it is a waste of time and energy to keep responding to a stimulus that has no importance. Consider what would happen to a land snail in a rainstorm if its withdrawal response never habituated. And consider how distracting it would be to have your attention diverted every time a common household noise occurred.

The simplest form of habituation is temporary, known as **short-term habituation.** Suppose we tap a snail's shell until the withdrawal response habituates. If we tap it again the next day we will find that it withdraws into its shell again and continues to do so for several more taps. It takes just as long for habituation to occur as it did the day before. And if we repeat our experiment every day afterward, the same thing will happen; the snail does not "remember" what happened previously.

Animals with more complex nervous systems are capable of **long-term habituation.** For example, a hunting dog may be frightened the first few times it hears the sound of a shotgun, but it soon learns not to respond to it. This habituation carries across from day to day, or even from one hunting season to the next.

Certainly, habituation is the least interesting form of learning, but it is a useful one: it permits us to get more important things done, relatively free from distraction by petty events.

CLASSICAL CONDITIONING

In contrast to habituation, which occurs when nothing important happens, **classical conditioning** occurs when an organism encounters an unimportant, unexpected stimulus followed by an important one that is capable of causing an automatic reaction. The pairing of the unexpected stimulus with the important stimulus causes the reaction to become conditioned to the unexpected stimulus.

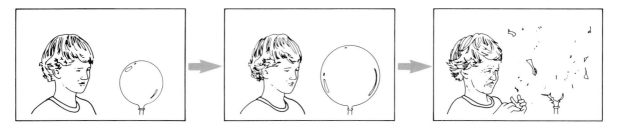

FIGURE 6.1

Classical conditioning: the child watches the balloon grow large until it bursts, which causes a defensive startle reaction.

Many of your behaviors have been shaped by this learning process. For example, suppose you are seated in a small room with a balloon located directly in front of your face. Someone starts inflating the balloon with an electric pump until the rubber begins to look very thin and taut. What are you likely to do? It is a pretty safe bet that at the very least, you are grimacing and squinting through partly closed eyelids, and your head is hunched down. Why?

You know that the balloon is ready to burst, and when it does, it will make a very loud noise. You undoubtedly learned about balloons early in childhood; in fact you probably cannot remember your first encounter with one. But let us analyze how a person learns to flinch defensively at the sight of a thinly stretched balloon. Suppose we inflate a balloon in front of a young boy who has never seen one before. The child will turn his eyes toward the enlarging balloon, but he will not flinch. When the balloon finally explodes, the noise and the blast of air will cause a defensive startle reaction: the subject will squint, grimace, raise his shoulders, and suddenly move his arms toward his body. A bursting balloon is an undeniably important stimulus, one that causes a defensive reaction.

Figure 6.1 presents a schematic diagram of what I have discussed so far.

We will probably not have to repeat the experience many times until our subject reacts the way you do—by flinching defensively before the balloon actually bursts. Perhaps one experience will be enough. A previously neutral stimulus (the overinflated balloon), followed by an important stimulus (the explosion that occurs when the balloon bursts), can now trigger the response. The defensive flinching response has been *classically conditioned* to the sight of an overinflated balloon. (See Figure 6.2.)

The Work of Ivan Pavlov

Ivan Pavlov, a Russian physiologist, carried out the pioneering studies in classical conditioning. (He performed such an impressive and authoritative series of experiments over his long career that this form of learning is called "classical" out of respect for his work. It is sometimes also referred to as *Pavlovian conditioning*.) Pavlov's research interest was originally in the physiology of the digestive process, and not in behavior. His interest led him to study

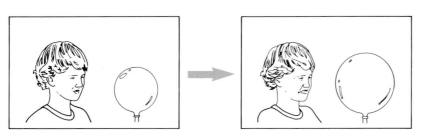

FIGURE 6.2

After the child's first experience with a bursting balloon, the mere sight of an inflating balloon elicits a defensive reaction.

FIGURE 6.3

Pavlov's original procedure for classical conditioning. The experimenter strikes the tuning fork and then presents the food. Saliva is collected in the tube.

the neural control of salivation and secretion of digestive juices in dogs. He inserted a small tube in a duct in the animal's mouth and collected drops of saliva as they were secreted by the salivary gland.

During his studies Pavlov noticed that after a dog had participated in an experiment for a while, it would begin to salivate as soon as he or one of his assistants entered the room. He had expected salivation to occur when the dogs received their food during the course of the experiment; he was surprised that it began earlier than that. At first, Pavlov regarded this anticipatory secretion of saliva as an annoying complication. However, he soon realized that the phenomenon had important implications. He knew that both dogs and humans begin to salivate at the beginning of a meal, even before food enters their mouth: the sight of the food itself is sufficient to stimulate salivation. Previously, scientists believed that this salivation was nothing more than an automatic, reflexive response. But obviously Pavlov's dogs had *learned* to salivate when they saw him or one of his assistants. Therefore, it seemed possible that the salivation that normally occurs at the beginning of a meal is also learned.

Pavlov devised a new apparatus to investigate this phenomenon, which he called "psychic secretion." He struck a tuning fork to make a sound, and half a second later he gave the dog some food. He found that salivation very quickly became conditioned to the tone. (See

Figure 6.3.) In later studies, he used an electrical bell as a noise source and varied the time interval between the presentation of the sound and the food. Conditioning occurred only when the food followed the sound within a short time. If there was a long delay between the sound and the food, or if the sound *followed* the food, the animal never learned to salivate to it. Thus, the sequence and timing of events are important factors in classical conditioning. Presumably, these conditions are dictated by the characteristics of the neural circuits that are responsible for the learning.

It is important to understand that classical conditioning is adaptive learning, in which an already existing stimulus-response relation is modified. In classical conditioning, a response that is automatically produced by one stimulus becomes linked to another stimulus. (Remember that Pavlov was originally studying reflexive reactions when he made his discovery.) The process is illustrated in Figure 6.4.

The eliciting stimulus upon which the learning depends is referred to as the **unconditional stimulus (US).** The response it elicits, which occurs naturally before learning occurs, is called the **unconditional response (UR).** Conditioning occurs when a neutral, noneliciting stimulus, called the **conditional stimulus (CS)** is paired with the unconditional stimulus (and thus with the unconditional response). Once learning occurs, the conditional stimulus produces the response by itself, and the response is now called the **conditional response (CR).** (See Figure 6.4.)

If you think about it, the terms make sense. The unconditional stimulus automatically produces the unconditional response; no conditions have to be met. Once the conditions of pairing have been met, the conditional stimulus elicits what is now called the *conditional response.* The basic form of the response in both instances is the same; what differs is the stimulus that elicits it. (Because of an error in the original translation of Pavlov's writings into English, many people use the terms *unconditioned* and *conditioned*, but the terms *unconditional* and *conditional* are more appropriate.)

The Significance of Classical Conditioning

Many different types of responses can be classically conditioned to previously neutral stimuli. These responses include both overt, directly observable behaviors and internal physiological responses. For example, consider a behavior such as the attack of a male dog on a rival that intrudes upon its territory. A number of reflexes accompany the attack. The dog's pupils dilate, its eyes widen, its adrenal glands secrete hormones that increase its heart rate and raise its blood pressure, and the fur on the back of its neck stands up. All these responses can be classically conditioned. Or consider a more pleasant behavior: eating. Eating is accompanied by reflexes such as salivation, se-

cretion of digestive juices, and release of insulin into the bloodstream. These reflexes, too, can be classically conditioned.

In the laboratory, a response may be conditioned to an arbitrary stimulus. For example, salivation may be conditioned to the sound of a bell. The only reason the sound of the bell precedes the food is that the experimenter has arranged the sequence of these events. However, in everyday life, most conditional responses are made to conditional stimuli that bear a cause-and-effect relation to the unconditional stimuli that originally elicited the responses. For example, the sight of lightning and the sound of thunder are causally related. In fact they are different sensory aspects of a single event: the lightning heats the air and produces a sudden explosion of sound. It is only because sound travels more slowly than light that the two stimuli occur at different times. Through classical conditioning, someone who is frightened by the sound of thunder is likely to show signs of distress to a sudden flash of light from the sky even before hearing the thunder.

We are unaware of some of the physiological responses that become classically conditioned; for example, we cannot feel the secretion of insulin. However, we *can* feel other physiological responses, such as a pounding heart, trembling, or the queasy feeling caused by adrenalin secretion. The classically conditioned responses that we are able to perceive play an important role in feelings of emotion. For instance, if your employer (or parent or spouse or teacher) addresses you in a particular tone of voice (conditional stimulus), you may get a queasy feeling

CONDITIONING PROCEDURE

Neutral stimulus (bell) + Eliciting stimulus (food) ⟶ Elicited response (salivation)
Unconditional stimulus (US)   Unconditional response (UR)

AFTER CONDITIONING

Previously neutral stimulus (bell) ⟶ Response (salivation)
Conditional stimulus (CS)   Conditional response (CR)

FIGURE 6.4

The process of classical conditioning.

in your stomach (conditional response) because that tone of voice was followed by unpleasant scenes in the past (unconditional stimuli). People, tones of voice, objects, and places can all serve as conditional stimuli for unpleasant conditional responses—and consequently, unpleasant emotions—such as the queasy feeling.

Pleasant reactions that lead to positive emotions can also be classically conditioned. A person may feel a warm wave of remembrance (conditional response) upon hearing a song (conditional stimulus) that was associated with a happy romance during which there were many unconditional stimuli. Even the pleasure received from the sight of a loved one is partly a result of classical conditioning: the presence of that person has been associated with enjoyable events. The topic of emotion is discussed in more detail in Chapter 12.

You might ask *why* classical conditioning takes place. What is its utility? In general, it permits an organism to prepare for events that will soon occur. For example, it is useful to have learned to duck your head when you hear the buzz of a wasp near your ear. Similarly, your digestive system can do its job more easily if you have learned to salivate before food enters your mouth, and if your stomach secretes digestive juices before you swallow your food.

Classical conditioning has another function, which is even more important: once responses have become classically conditioned to new stimuli, those previously neutral stimuli can shape the behavior of the organism. Because a neutral stimulus becomes desirable when it is associated with a desirable stimulus, or undesirable when it is associated with an undesirable one, our behavior can be modified by these stimuli. For example, money has meaning for us because it has been associated with desirable commodities. (You will learn more about such conditioned reinforcers and conditioned punishers later in this chapter.)

- What is habituation? What is its functional significance?
- How would you describe the process of classical conditioning?
- What is the functional significance of classical conditioning?

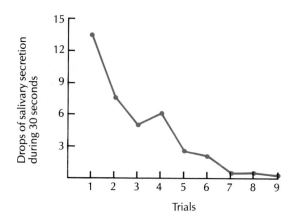

FIGURE 6.5

Extinction of a classically conditioned salivation response. (From Hall, J.F. *An Invitation to Learning and Memory.* Boston: Allyn and Bacon, 1982. Based on data from Pavlov, 1927.)

Extinction

The pairing of a neutral stimulus with an eliciting stimulus leads to classical conditioning; the previously neutral stimulus becomes a conditional stimulus that produces the conditional response. However, classical conditioning is not necessarily permanent. Although the response will occur when the conditional stimulus is presented by itself, the unconditional stimulus must occur occasionally, or the conditional stimulus will lose its ability to elicit the response.

For example, suppose we train a dog to salivate (conditional response) to the sound of a bell (conditional stimulus) by following the sound with a squirt of food (unconditional stimulus) into the dog's mouth. Soon the sound of the bell will elicit salivation even when no food is squirted. Now suppose that we permanently disconnect the device that squirts the food into the dog's mouth but continue to ring the bell every few minutes. For a while, the dog will salivate whenever the bell is rung, but eventually it will secrete less and less saliva; finally, the dog will stop responding. **Extinction** has taken place. The response has been *extinguished.* (Note that responses, not organisms, are extinguished. In exams or papers, students sometimes write that "the animal was extinguished." Obviously, an extinguished animal is a dead one.)

Figure 6.5 presents data obtained for one of Pavlov's dogs during extinction. The dog had previously been trained to salivate in response to a noise. Pavlov then presented the noise (CS) every three minutes without the food (US) and counted drops of saliva (CR). By the ninth presentation of the noise alone, the response was completely extinguished, as is illustrated by the graph.

Extinction is usually not permanent. Given a rest period after a series of presentations of the conditional stimulus alone, the organism will once again emit the conditional response when the conditional stimulus is presented. This phenomenon is appropriately called **spontaneous recovery.** However, unless the unconditional stimulus is also presented, the response will extinguish even more quickly than it did the first time.

Classical Conditioning and Abnormal Reactions to Stimuli

Many people are troubled by behaviors that they wish they could stop doing or by thoughts and fears that trouble them. One way or another, most of these undesirable responses are learned. Just the existence of two extreme forms of such responses—phobias and fetishes—provides ample evidence that classical conditioning does indeed have an effect on emotions and behaviors.

Phobias are unreasonable fears of specific objects or situations, such as spiders, automobiles, or enclosed spaces. Presumably, at some time early in life, the person was exposed to the now-fearsome object in conjunction with a stimulus that elicited pain or fear. For example, a person stuck in a hot, overcrowded elevator with fellow passengers who are sweating, screaming, and vomiting might be expected to develop a strong distrust of elevators afterward and perhaps even to produce a full-fledged phobia.

Fetishes are abnormal sexual attachments to objects, such as articles of clothing. It is probable that they occur because of the prior association of some stimulus that most people find neutral with sexual stimuli, which most people do *not* find neutral. One possible scenario might involve a teenage boy looking at sexually arousing pictures of women wearing high-heeled shoes. His arousal could become conditioned to the shoes worn by the women, and the boy would subsequently become a shoe fetishist. However, fetishism cannot be that simple; there must be other factors operating, too. Some people are undoubtedly more susceptible than others to developing fetishes. For example, women very rarely develop them. Nevertheless, there is good laboratory evidence that both fear and sexual arousal can be conditioned to neutral stimuli.

If classical conditioning is responsible for the development of phobias and fetishes, then perhaps a knowledge of the principles of learning can be used to eliminate them. In fact, therapists have devised procedures to do so, which will be discussed in Chapter 17.

■ How are classically conditioned responses extinguished?
■ How can classical conditioning processes generate unusual behavior patterns?
■ How can classical conditioning play a role in maintaining phobias?

Most phobias, such as fear of heights, are learned through classical conditioning. Earlier, the now-feared object was experienced in conjunction with an unpleasant stimulus. Psychologists use learning principles to help people overcome their fears.

INSTRUMENTAL CONDITIONING

Just as habituation and classical conditioning play a part in shaping behavior, so too does **instrumental conditioning.** The principle behind instrumental conditioning is already familiar to you: when an organism is rewarded for a particular action, its tendency will be to repeat that action; conversely, when an organism is punished for a particular action, its tendency will be to avoid repeating that action. Having read Chapter 1, you may recognize this principle as Thorndike's law of effect.

The essence of instrumental conditioning is the occurrence of a rewarding or punishing stimulus immediately after an organism performs a particular behavior. The occurrence of the stimulus is said to be *contingent* upon the organism's behavior. (A **contingency** is another name for a cause-and-effect relation; in this case it refers to the fact that the stimulus occurs only when the behavior does.) The effect of the stimulus is to increase or decrease the probability that the organism will perform that behavior again. In a general sense, instrumental conditioning is a description of the ways in which the consequences of an organism's actions cause its behavior to adapt to its environment.

Reinforcement and Punishment

Because it has fewer connotations, most psychologists prefer to use the term **reinforcement** rather than *reward*. A stimulus that increases the probability of a response that precedes it is called a **reinforcing stimulus,** or simply a **reinforcer.** In common usage the term *reward* implies that an organism has done something "good" and deserves a special treat. The neutrality of the process of reinforcement becomes clear when we think of it as the natural consequence of a behavior. Sometimes we deliberately set up a contingency between response and reinforcer (for example, when we train a pet to do a trick by giving it some food especially likes). But many reinforcement contingencies are unintentional. Suppose that a large, friendly dog jumps up on a small child with a candy bar who is playing in a park. The child takes fright, drops the candy bar, and runs away. The dog sees the candy bar and eats it. Suppose further that the dog now tends to jump up on small children playing in the park. We would conclude that the first child inadvertently reinforced the dog's behavior by dropping the candy bar. However, we would not want to say that the child intended to *reward* the dog for its behavior.

The behaving organism, and not the agent that delivers the stimulus, determines whether or not a particular stimulus is reinforcing. Suppose a mother decides to punish her child's whining. Every time the child whines, she says sternly, "stop whining!" and delivers a lecture on the subject. Unfortunately, the child continues to whine several times a day and in fact seems to do so even more frequently than before the mother began the course of "punishment." Without intending to do so, the mother has actually reinforced whining. Although the rebuke was meant to punish the child's behavior, the attention she gave the child was apparently reinforcing enough to increase the frequency of whining.

The term *instrumental conditioning* reflects the fact that the behavior of the organism is *instrumental* in determining whether the reinforcing or punishing stimulus occurs. This type of learning involves a stimulus change that is contingent upon a response. Please note the use of the term *stimulus change* rather than simply *stimulus*; a behavior may be reinforced or punished by the *removal* of some stimuli, as well as by the administration of others. The stimulus change can thus involve either an **appetitive stimulus** (one that an organism tends to approach) or an **aversive stimulus** (one that an organism tends to avoid).

Suppose you have to walk barefoot across a large asphalt parking lot on a hot, sunny day. As you walk, your feet get hotter and hotter. The pain becomes intense, and you look around for some relief. You see a puddle of water in a patch of shade provided by a large truck. You step into the puddle and find it to be delightfully cool on your feet. This stimulus change—removal of an aversive stimulus—is certainly reinforcing.

The type of reinforcement I just described—in which the behavior is reinforced by removal of an aversive stimulus—is called **negative reinforcement.** (The other form of reinforcement—in which the behavior is reinforced by the occurrence of an appetitive stimulus—is some-times called *positive reinforcement*, but most psychologists simply call it *reinforcement*, as I do in this book.) Many people confuse negative reinforcement with punishment, but the terms refer to entirely different phenomena. The most common use of the term **punishment** refers to the suppressing effect on behavior of an aversive stimulus that occurs right after the particular behavior. In contrast, negative reinforcement is a particular kind of reinforcement; it refers to the reinforcing effect caused by terminating an aversive stimulus immediately after a particular behavior. These contingencies are clearly different: punishment causes a behavior to decrease, whereas negative reinforcement causes a behavior to increase.

Just as the termination of an aversive stimulus is reinforcing, the termination of an appetitive stimulus is punishing. Suppose you meet a person to whom you find yourself attracted. You engage the person in conversation and enjoy the friendly attention that you receive. You talk for a while and are pleased to find that the other person also seems to be attracted to you. Then you make a disparaging remark about a well-known politician, and your new friend's smile disappears. You quickly change the subject and never bring it up again. The behavior (disparaging remark) is followed by removal of an appetitive stimulus (a warm, friendly smile). The removal of the smile punishes the behavior.

This type of punishment is called **response cost**; a particular response (behavior) costs the organism the loss of a reinforcing stimulus. Just as negative reinforcement involves the removal of an aversive stimulus, punishment (in the form of response cost) involves the removal of an appetitive stimulus. Thus, there are four types of instrumental conditioning—two kinds of reinforcement and two kinds of punishment—caused by the administration or termination of appetitive or aversive stimuli. (See Figure 6.6 on page 190.)

Immediacy of Reinforcement and Punishment

Reinforcement and punishment occur only when a stimulus *immediately* follows the behavior, within a second or two. It may occur to you that many organisms—particularly hu-

The aversive stimulus (noise) provided by this saw can be partially removed by the wearing of headphones. Thus, the removal of an aversive stimulus can be reinforcing.

mans—can tolerate a long delay between their work and the reward they receive for it. This ability appears to contradict the principle that reinforcement must occur immediately. However, the apparent contradiction can be explained by a phenomenon called *conditioned reinforcement*, which I will discuss later in the next section.

An experiment by Logan (1965) illustrates the importance of the immediacy of reinforcement. Logan trained hungry rats to run through a simple maze in which a single passage led to two corridors. At the end of one corridor the rats would find a small piece of food. At the end of the other corridor they would receive much more food, but it would be delivered only after a delay. Although the most intelligent strategy would be to enter the second corridor and wait for the larger amount of food, the rats chose to take the small amount of food that was delivered right away. Immediacy of reinforcement took precedence over quantity.

Obviously, the reason that our behaviors are capable of being punished or reinforced by certain stimuli is that our brains contain neural circuits that are capable of being changed. And because causes and effects usually occur one right after the other, only stimuli that occur immediately before a behavior can reinforce or punish the behavior. But there are some events that produce effects that occur hours later. For example, if a rat eats some food that contains a poison, it will not become sick for an hour or two. If it survives the illness, it will not eat that food again. Thus, an aversive stimulus (nausea, cramping, and other unpleasant effects of the poison) is able to punish a behavior that occurred a relatively long time ago.

It is certainly to a rat's advantage to be able to learn about the relation between a particular taste and an illness that occurs later. Thus, the evolutionary process has selected for the neural circuits that can detect such a relation. In fact, different neural circuits appear to be involved in different types of learning. For example, Garcia and Koelling (1966) found that rats would learn to avoid a particular taste that was followed by illness or to avoid a particular noise that was immediately followed by a shock to the feet. However, they did not learn to avoid a

Advertisers frequently use interesting characters, hoping that people will pay attention to their products.

REINFORCEMENT

Appetitive stimulus — Positive reinforcement

onset reinforces response

Aversive stimulus — Negative reinforcement

termination reinforces response

PUNISHMENT

Appetitive stimulus — Response cost

termination punishes response

Aversive stimulus — Punishment

onset punishes response

FIGURE 6.6

Reinforcement and punishment produced by the onset or termination of appetitive or aversive stimuli.

particular taste followed by a shock, or a particular noise followed by illness. The results make good sense; after all, the animal has to *taste* the food that makes it sick, not *hear* it.

Humans are also capable of the same kind of learning. Bernstein (1978) gave ice cream with an unusual flavor to cancer patients who were about to receive a session of chemotherapy that produces nausea. Several months later, 75 percent of the patients refused to eat ice cream with this flavor, whereas control subjects who did not taste it before their chemotherapy said that they liked it very much.

Conditioned Reinforcement and Punishment

Some reinforcers and punishers have obvious biological significance; they are important to an individual's survival or to the survival of its species. For example, food, warmth, and sexual contact are reinforcing, and stimuli that cause pain are punishing. These stimuli are called **primary reinforcers** or **primary punishers.** Other classes of reinforcers and punishers are not so obvious. For humans, stimuli like money, admission tickets, the smell of delicious food, or parking tickets can serve as reinforcers or punishers, but only if the person has learned something about them. These stimuli are called **conditioned reinforcers** and **conditioned punishers.** (Sometimes they are called *secondary reinforcers* and *secondary punishers,* to contrast with primary reinforcers and primary punishers.)

A stimulus becomes a conditioned reinforcer or punisher by means of classical conditioning. That is, if a neutral stimulus occurs regularly just before an appetitive or aversive stimulus, then the neutral stimulus itself becomes an appetitive or aversive stimulus. If *this* stimulus in turn occurs immediately *after* a behavior, it serves to reinforce or punish that behavior. For example, because money (initially a neutral stimulus) is regularly associated with appetitive stimuli (those things that money will buy), eventually money itself becomes an appetitive stimulus, which can then serve as a conditioned reinforcer. In contrast, the sight of a flashing light on top of a police car serves as a conditioned punisher to a person who is driving too fast, because such a sight precedes an unpleasant set of stimuli: a lecture by a police officer and a speeding ticket. The ticket itself is also a conditioned punisher, because it signals the loss of an appetitive stimulus: money.

The distinction between primary and secondary (conditioned) reinforcers and punishers cannot always be made with certainty. For example, given the fact that food is considered to be a primary reinforcer, then a caterpillar would have to be said to be a primary reinforcer for a member of one of several South American tribes. However, few North Americans would consider a caterpillar to be food. Experience in the two cultures has determined which items are considered to be food. Mother's milk is undoubtedly a primary reinforcer, but a caterpillar is probably a conditioned reinforcer.

The phenomena of conditioned reinforcement and punishment are extremely important. They permit an organism's behavior to be affected by stimuli that are not biologically important in themselves but that are regularly associated with the onset or termination of

To a person who has been speeding, the sight of flashing lights on a police car is a conditioned punisher, because seeing the lights precedes an unpleasant set of events.

biologically important stimuli. Indeed, stimuli can even become conditioned reinforcers or punishers by being associated with *other* conditioned reinforcers or punishers. (The speeding ticket is just such an example.) If an organism's behavior could only be controlled by primary reinforcers and punishers, then that behavior would not be very flexible. The organism would never learn to perform behaviors that had only long-range benefits; instead, its behavior would be controlled on a moment-to-moment basis. Conditioned reinforcers and punishers make it possible for behavior to be altered by a wide variety of contingencies.

- How does instrumental conditioning affect behavior?
- How would you compare reinforcement and punishment procedures?
- Why are immediate consequences important in conditioning procedures?
- How can conditioned reinforcers affect behavior?

The Nature of Reinforcement: The Premack Principle

Some stimuli—food to a hungry animal, water to a thirsty one, warmth to a cold one—are obviously reinforcing. Other stimuli, not related to survival, are not so easy to predict. Sometimes, when trying to teach children or to change people's behavior, it is important to identify an effective reinforcer. Premack (1965) has suggested that an animal's own preference can be used to determine whether a stimulus will serve as a reinforcer or punisher.

Sometimes an organism surprises us with its choice. Countless numbers of children have participated in learning experiments that required them to work a knob on a device resembling a pinball machine in order to receive an M&M candy (Premack, 1965). In other words, a response was reinforced with the delivery of M&Ms. (M&Ms, sugar-coated chocolate candies, are widely used because they are of a small, uniform size and can easily be dispensed, one at a time, by an automatic dispensing machine.) Premack found that some children, if given the choice, would play with the knob rather than eat an M&M: it was more fun to play the "game" than to eat an M&M. Premack turned the contingency around; he offered these children an M&M, and if they ate it they got a chance to play with the knob for a while. The children quickly learned to eat M&Ms so that they could get a chance to play. Again, it is clear that the *subject*, and not the *experimenter*, determines which stimuli will serve as reinforcers.

The first part of the **Premack principle** states that an organism has different preferences for performing different behaviors. A large list of behaviors can be assembled, ranked in order of preference from low to high. (Such a list is called a **preference hierarchy**.) Some behaviors are very high on the list, some are neutral, and some are so low on the list that they will be avoided. (Screaming in response to the pain caused by having one's foot pounded by a sledge hammer is a behavior that is low on most people's list.) The second part of the Premack principle states that an organism will perform a behavior that is low in the hierarchy in order to gain the opportunity to perform a preferred behavior. Thus, if a child prefers playing with the knob to eating M&Ms, he or she can be trained to eat M&Ms if this behavior is reinforced by the opportunity to play with the knob.

Stimuli, then, are reinforcing when they permit a particular behavior to occur, and each organism has its own set of preferences for engaging in a particular behavior. And preferences can change from moment to moment, as we get bored with a particular behavior or as our physiological state changes.

I should note that although the practical value of the Premack principle is unassailable, several learning theorists have discovered qualifications to it and conditions under which it does not work. Nevertheless, the concept of a preference hierarchy is an important one, and the Premack principle reminds us that reinforcers and punishers are effective to the extent that they cause us to engage in behaviors.

Conditioning of Complex Behaviors

Most of our behaviors are products of conditioned reinforcers. Consider the behavior of a young girl who is learning to print letters. She sits at her school desk, producing long rows of letters. What maintains her behavior? Why is she devoting her time to a task that appears to involve so much effort? The answer is that her behavior produces stimuli (the printed letters) that are reinforcing. In other words, the effects of her behavior serve to reinforce that very behavior. In previous class sessions, the teacher has demonstrated how to print the letters and has praised (reinforced) the girl for printing them herself. The act of printing has been reinforced, and thus the printed letters that this act produces come to serve as conditioned reinforcers. The child prints a letter, sees that it looks approximately the way it should, and her behavior is reinforced by the sight of the letter. *Doing something correctly*, or making progress toward that goal, can provide effective reinforcement of behavior.

This fact is often overlooked by people who take a limited view of the process of reinforcement, thinking that it has to resemble the delivery of a small piece of food to an animal being taught a trick. Some people even say that because reinforcers are rarely delivered to humans immediately after they perform a behavior, instrumental conditioning must not play a major role in human learning. Perhaps we psychologists who teach introductory psychology must take some of the blame for this misunderstanding. We often illustrate an explanation of instrumental conditioning with examples taken from the laboratory, so that when students think of instrumental conditioning, they often think only of rats pressing levers or running through mazes.

It is true that most of the phenomena of instrumental conditioning have been discovered in experiments with nonhuman animals, but the process of reinforcement in real life is similar to what is observed in the laboratory. Psychologists sometimes unintentionally emphasize *procedures* rather than processes; they say that a reinforcer is *delivered* because in the controlled circumstances of experiments psychologists do deliver reinforcers to their subjects. However, the overwhelming majority of reinforcers are not delivered by another agent; they are *obtained* by the organism that is doing the behaving. The reinforcement occurs as a natural consequence of the behavior. Only in the laboratory, in some social situations, or in the classroom does a person *deliver* a reinforcer to another person. Most reinforcers are a direct result of a person's behavior.

A good synonym for the conditioned reinforcement that shapes and maintains our behavior when we perform a behavior correctly is *satisfaction*. Usually, we work hard at some task because it "gives us satisfaction." An artist who produces a fine painting gains satisfaction from the image that emerges as she works on it and receives even stronger satisfaction from looking at the finished product. This satisfaction derives from a lifetime of experience. The artist has learned to recognize good pieces of art, and when she produces one herself she delivers her own conditioned reinforcer.

Shaping

Laboratory experiments have shown the importance of conditioned reinforcers in the instrumental conditioning of behaviors. You already know that reinforcement increases the probability that a particular response will occur again. But suppose you want to train an animal to perform a completely new response—one that you have never seen it make. How can you do so, when a behavior must occur before it can

be reinforced? The answer lies in the procedure of **shaping,** which consists in reinforcing a succession of responses that are increasingly similar to the one you want the animal to perform.

Psychologists who study instrumental conditioning often use hungry rats as subjects and require them to press a small lever attached to a wall in order to obtain food. They use an apparatus called an **operant chamber.** (See Figure 6.7 on p. 194.) (The term comes from **operant conditioning,** which many psychologists use synonymously with *instrumental condition-*

As Martina Navratilova knows after winning her eighth Wimbledon singles' title, doing something well can become a conditioned reinforcer.

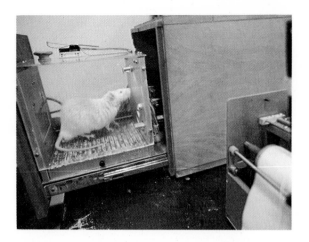

FIGURE 6.7

A rat in an operant chamber. When the rat presses the lever, the device at the right records the animal's activity.

ing, although some make a distinction that need not concern us here.) The device is also referred to as a **Skinner box,** after B.F. Skinner of Harvard University, who invented it and pioneered the modern study of instrumental conditioning. (However, Skinner himself dislikes the term "Skinner box.")

The lever on the wall of the chamber is attached to an electrical switch wired to electronic control equipment or a computer. A mechanical dispenser can automatically drop molded pellets of food, about the size of a very small pea, into a dish in the chamber. Thus, the delivery of a food pellet can be made contingent upon the rat's pressing the lever. In most operant chambers, both visual and auditory stimuli can be presented. (See Figure 6.7.)

If we put a hungry rat into the apparatus, the animal will explore the chamber and may even depress the lever, perhaps while attempting to climb the wall. But we would probably have to wait a long time for the lever-pressing behavior to be reinforced by the delivery of the food. Reinforcement must be *immediate,* and unless the rat finds the food right after pressing the lever, some other behavior, not lever pressing, will be reinforced. Most likely, the delivery of the food pellet after an accidental lever press will reinforce the rat's approach to the dish, so the animal will tend to remain in its vicinity.

The solution is to deliver a reinforcer that has an immediate effect. To do so, we establish an auditory stimulus as a conditioned reinforcer. An auditory stimulus is best for our purpose because the rat will perceive it from any part of the cage. In this particular case, a buzzer or other noise-making device is not necessary, because the pellet dispenser makes a noise of its own when it delivers a piece of food. So to begin with, we operate the pellet dispenser and let the rat find the pellet. After it eats the food, we deliver a few more pellets while the rat is in the vicinity of the food dish, until the noise of the pellet dispenser itself becomes an appetitive stimulus. Then we wait until the rat leaves the food dish and turns in the direction of the lever. As soon as the animal turns toward the lever, we operate the dispenser. The rat hears the noise and returns to the dish to eat the piece of food. Because the noise, now a conditioned reinforcer, was presented immediately after the turning movement, the turning movement is reinforced. The rat soon turns away from the food dish and toward the lever, and we activate the dispenser again.

Once the behavior of turning away from the food dish and toward the lever is firmly established, we reinforce a behavior that more closely resembles lever pressing. We wait until the rat turns even farther away from the dish and almost touches the lever before we activate the dispenser. (It is still the *noise,* not the food, that reinforces the behavior. The food simply serves to maintain the noise as a conditioned reinforcer.) Soon the rat is rapidly shuttling between lever and food dish. Now we wait until it touches the lever with any part of its body—most commonly, with its nose. Next, we require it to put its front feet on the lever, and finally we activate the dispenser only when the rat actually presses the lever down hard enough to operate the switch. Now we can connect the switch to the dispenser and let the device operate automatically.

The formal name for shaping is the **method of successive approximations.** A reinforcer (almost always a conditioned reinforcer) is delivered immediately after responses that at first only approximately resemble the response that is to be conditioned (the **target behavior**). Successive responses must resemble the target behavior even more closely to be reinforced, until the goal is reached.

The method of successive approximations can be used to train an animal to perform just about any response that it is physically capable of doing. The tricks of performing dolphins and trained seals are developed by reinforcing a succession of responses that are increasingly similar to the desired one. The trainers usually reinforce the animals' behavior by producing a noise (such as the sound of a whistle) that has been paired with the delivery of food.

Shaping is a formal training procedure, but something like it also occurs in the real world. A teacher praises poorly formed letters produced by a child who is just beginning to print, but as time goes on, only more accurately drawn letters bring approval. The method of successive approximations can also be self-administered. Consider the acquisition of skills through trial and error. To begin with, you must be able to recognize the target behavior—that is, the behavior displayed by a person with the appropriate skill. Your first attempts produce behaviors that vaguely resemble those of a skilled performer, and you are satisfied by the results of these attempts. In other words, the stimuli that are produced by your behavior serve as conditioned reinforcers for that behavior. As your skill develops, crude approximations to the final behavior become less reinforcing; you are satisfied only when your behavior improves so that it more closely resembles the target behavior. Your own criteria change as you become more skilled. This process is perfectly analogous to the use of changing criteria in training an animal to perform a complex behavior.

Aversive Control: Escape and Avoidance Responses

Through negative reinforcement, organisms learn an **escape response.** As you will recall, negative reinforcement is the termination of an aversive stimulus that is contingent upon a specific behavior; thus, the organism escapes from the aversive stimulus by performing the appropriate response. (In this context the organism does not necessarily have to run away in order to "escape" the aversive stimulus.) Under some conditions, the organism can do more than escape the aversive stimulus—it can learn to produce a response that will *prevent* the occurrence of the aversive stimulus. This type of response is known as an **avoidance response.**

Let me give an example. Suppose you meet a man at a party who backs you against the wall and subjects you to the most tedious and tiresome conversation you have ever experienced. This obnoxiously and aggressively boring person clearly delivers aversive stimuli. You experience a great sense of relief when you finally manage to break away from him. A few days later you attend another party. You are having a good time until you see your tormenter from the earlier party heading your way. The gleam in his eyes foretells another long harangue. You suddenly remember that you have business elsewhere, make your excuses to your host, and leave. You do not want to repeat your earlier experience, so you behave in such a way as to avoid it entirely.

The behavior that brings about the termination of an aversive stimulus is called an *escape response.* The behavior that prevents another aversive stimulus from occurring is called an *avoidance response.* Clearly, leaving the second party before the boring person could get to you is an avoidance response. Psychologists disagree about what produces and maintains avoidance responses, but most would probably support the following explanation. The sight of your tormenter at the second party serves as a conditioned aversive stimulus, because the sight of him was paired with the boring conversation. Once you go out the door you can no longer see him, so leaving the party (the avoidance response) is reinforced by the termination of the conditioned aversive stimulus.

- What is the Premack principle? What is its importance to instrumental conditioning?
- How would you describe the process of shaping? What is its role in reinforcing infrequent or unusual behaviors?
- How would you compare escape and avoidance behaviors? Why is aversive control often not as effective as positive reinforcement?

Extinction

We have seen how responses may be reinforced by their consequences. When a response produces a reinforcing stimulus, that response becomes more frequent. But sometimes the environment changes, so that the contingency between response and reinforcement no longer exists. If this happens, there is no reason to continue to respond. In fact, if a reinforcer no longer follows the response, the organism will eventually stop responding. This phenomenon, referred to as *extinction,* was described earlier in the discussion of classical conditioning.

Extinction takes place only when the organism is actually given the opportunity to make the response that was formerly reinforced. Suppose a rat is trained in an operant chamber to press a lever for food pellets. If the animal is taken out of the chamber for a few days, its behavior will not extinguish—it will continue to respond when it is placed into the operant chamber again. For extinction to occur, the animal must press the lever and *not* receive food for doing so.

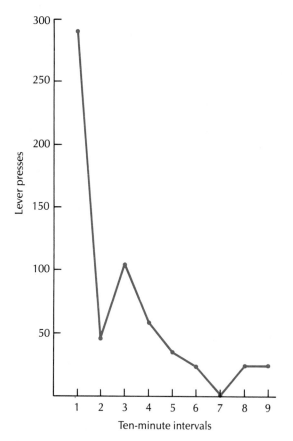

FIGURE 6.8

Extinction of an instrumentally conditioned lever-pressing response in a rat. (Based on data from Reynolds, G.S. *A Primer of Operant Conditioning.* Glenview, Ill.: Scott Foresman, 1968.)

When an animal's behavior is no longer reinforced, its rate of responding will usually increase at first. The increase is soon followed by a slow-down, and finally by a long pause in responding. Periodically, at irregular intervals, the animal will respond again, usually in bursts. Finally, responding will cease. The behavior has been extinguished. Figure 6.8 illustrates the extinction in a rat of a lever-pressing response that was formerly reinforced by food pellets.

Suppose we train a rat to press a lever for food reinforcement and allow the animal to respond, one hour each day, for several days. Then we turn off the food dispenser so that the response will become extinguished. After a while, the animal ceases to respond. We take the animal out of the operant chamber and put it back in its cage. The next day we again put the rat in the operant chamber. We find that it quickly runs to the lever and begins responding once more. This phenomenon is called *spontaneous recovery:* after an interval without any opportunity to respond, the animal's rate of responding recovers spontaneously. However, unless the animal's behavior is reinforced again, it does not respond very long; the response soon extinguishes. (You will recall from the section on classical conditioning that extinguished conditional responses also show spontaneous recovery.)

Extinction makes good sense in a natural environment. If a response no longer "works," there is no point in persisting in making it; doing so expends energy unnecessarily and keeps the organism from discovering a different response that *will* work. Similarly, spontaneous recovery makes good sense. Perhaps conditions have changed again, and the response will produce the reinforcer once more. It is certainly worth a try.

You can probably think of several examples of extinction of human behavior. For instance, suppose an angler catches a lot of fish in one place and hence comes back to try it again. Even if no more fish are ever caught there, he or she will probably still try the spot a few more times, spending less time there on each subsequent visit. While the behavior in this example was extinguished by a change in the natural environment, other instances of extinction are deliberately produced. Sometimes social reinforcers are withheld in order to extinguish another person's behavior. If you do not enjoy someone's company, you will probably stop smiling, nodding, and showing the signs of interest that serve as social reinforcers.

Extinction of a previously reinforced response does more than reduce the probability of that response; it also increases the probability of other responses, especially aggressive ones. For example, a pigeon subjected to the frustration of extinction will learn to peck at a plastic disk that opens a door enabling it to attack another pigeon (Azrin, 1964). The frustration of extinction appears to cause a variety of behaviors. Chapter 11 covers this topic further.

Intermittent Reinforcement

So far we have considered situations in which a reinforcing stimulus is presented after each response (or, in the case of extinction, not at all). But in the world outside the laboratory, not every response is reinforced. Sometimes a kind word is ignored, sometimes it is appreciated. Not every fishing trip is rewarded with a catch, but some are, and that fact is enough to keep a person trying. In this section I will describe the effects of various patterns of **intermittent reinforcement.**

Intermittent Reinforcement and Resistance to Extinction

Imagine that you have been locked up in a room that is empty except for a refrigerator stocked with food. After exploring your room, you decide to have a bite to eat. You get some food out of the refrigerator and begin eating. As you are eating, you realize that you have nothing to drink and find that there are no beverages in the refrigerator. You notice a recess in the wall that contains a small cup set under a metal spout. A push button is located on the wall beneath the recess. You press the button, and the spigot dispenses a small amount of water into the cup. You drink the water, replace the cup, and press the button again. You repeat the process until you get as much water as you want.

Suppose you spend several days in the room, obtaining food from the refrigerator and water from the dispenser mounted in the wall. Then one day the dispenser suddenly stops working.

Behaviors that are reinforced intermittently, such as fishing, are slow to disappear. Once we catch one fish, we will wait a long time for another bite even if no fish are caught in the interim.

You press the button several times, but nothing happens. What would you do next? You would probably pound on the wall, hit the button several times, and start pacing around the room. (You would be displaying the aggressive responses produced by the frustration of extinction.) Every now and then you would come back to try the dispenser, but you would not work long at pressing the button. You would probably become upset and agitated, but the total number of times that you would press the button would not be very large. Your response would rather rapidly be extinguished.

Suppose, however, that your original experience with the water dispenser had been different. The first time you pressed it, water was delivered, but you had to press it twice before it would make it work, and at other times it required a hundred presses or more.

Now suppose that, unknown to you, the dispenser is permanently turned off. The next time you become thirsty, you approach and begin pressing the button. Nothing happens. You keep pressing and pressing—many more times than you did in the first example. You begin to get desperate, and perhaps you begin to bang and kick the wall, but you keep working away at the button. Finally you leave, perhaps pacing around the room, but you return now and then to the button, pressing it many times before you leave.

Your behavior follows the rule that a response that has been reinforced intermittently is resistant to extinction; in other words, *it takes longer to extinguish a response that has been reinforced intermittently.* The more responses you have had to make for each reinforcement, the longer you will respond during extinction. And I am sure the reason is obvious to you. In the first example, you immediately noticed when extinction began—the dispenser went from one squirt of water per press to no water at all. You probably said to yourself, "Oh, no! This thing is broken!" In the second case, you were accustomed to making many responses per reinforcement, so that it would take many more responses before you decided that the dispenser was not working anymore. I doubt whether an animal other than a human would *decide* that the dispenser was broken, but the behavior of rats, pigeons, monkeys, and humans would be the same under these conditions—even to the extent of pacing around and banging on the wall.

Here is the most common explanation for the effects of partial (intermittent) reinforcement on extinction: continuous reinforcement (that is, reinforcement after every response) is quite different from extinction; the very first nonreinforced response signals the fact that conditions have changed. In contrast, intermittent reinforcement and extinction are much more similar. A nonreinforced response is not a novel event to an organism whose behavior has been reinforced intermittently; it has had much experience making nonreinforced responses. Thus, the organism cannot readily detect the fact that responses are no longer being reinforced. Only after many responses have gone unreinforced can the organism detect that the reinforcement contingencies have changed. Therefore, because an organism that has been

trained with intermittent reinforcement is accustomed to making nonreinforced responses, the behavior extinguishes more slowly.

Schedules of Reinforcement

B.F. Skinner, who pioneered the field of instrumental conditioning, invented procedures for administering intermittent reinforcement. These procedures are called **schedules of reinforcement.** There are two types of schedules: response-dependent schedules and response-and-time-dependent schedules.

Response-Dependent Schedules of Reinforcement. If an animal receives a reinforcer for each response, the ratio of responses to reinforcers is one to one. We call this form of **response-dependent schedule** a **continuous reinforcement (CRF) schedule.** If a reinforcer follows every second response (that is, two responses per reinforcer) the schedule is a **fixed-ratio (FR) schedule** of two, or *FR-2*. One reinforcer after every third responses is called FR-3, and so on. Fixed-ratio schedules of up to several hundred responses per reinforcer can be used to keep an animal responding, but it is necessary to start at an easy schedule and then gradually increase the work required. If the schedule is increased too quickly, the response may extinguish.

An animal working on a long fixed-ratio schedule (say, FR-75) will usually pause for a while after obtaining a reinforcer, then start in again at a steady rate until the next reinforcer is delivered. The more responses that are required per reinforcement, the longer the pause before the animal gets back to work. This phenomenon is called (appropriately enough) a **postreinforcement pause.**

People rarely encounter fixed-ratio schedules in real life. A possible example might be the harvesting of crops when a person is paid for each container filled—such as a basket of apples or a box of tomatoes. Of course, payment is not made each time a container is filled but is deferred until the end of the day or week. However, the immediate reinforcer is the satisfaction provided by filling the container (and the anticipation of receiving payment for doing so).

Variable-ratio (VR) schedules are slightly more complicated but are much more common in life outside the laboratory. When working on a VR-10 schedule of reinforcement, an animal receives, *on the average*, one reinforcer for every ten responses, although a particular reinforcer might be obtained after as few as two or as many as twenty responses. The point is that the *mean* number of responses per reinforcer on a VR-10 schedule is ten. Figure 6.9 illustrates fixed-ratio and variable-ratio schedules of reinforcement.

The behavior of an animal on a variable-ratio schedule of reinforcement is different from that of one on a fixed-ratio schedule. On a variable-ratio schedule, responding is generally steady and is not marked by pauses after each reinforcement, unless the ratio is very high. The animal gets right back to work again after a rather brief pause. What accounts for this difference in postreinforcement pausing? The answer is that the pauses are actually controlled by the work that is to come, not the work that was just completed. That is, the pause *anticipates* the number of responses that will have to be made before the next reinforcer is received. If the animal is facing a short bout of responding, it gets to work right away. However, if it faces a long bout of responding, it pauses for a while. Thus, the postreinforcement pause

should really be called a "preresponding pause." In this case of a variable-ratio schedule, the animal has no way of knowing how many responses will be required before the next reinforcer is delivered; therefore, it tends to begin responding more quickly than it would on an equivalent fixed-ratio schedule.

In real life we often encounter variable-ratio schedules of reinforcement. Any skilled activity that requires an attempt (response) that can be scored as successful or unsuccessful will be reinforced according to a variable-ratio schedule. The average number of responses per reinforcer is determined by the person's skill. If you go bowling and get a strike 25 percent of the time, you are on a VR-4 schedule: an average of one strike (reinforcer) for every four attempts made (responses). A traveling sales representative who manages to make a sale to 10 percent of the people visited is on a VR-10 schedule.

There is even an apparatus that automatically dispenses reinforcers on a variable-ratio schedule: a slot machine. Some percentage of the pulls of the handle will be reinforced with a payoff. The owner of the machine sets the probability of a payoff and thus determines the value of the ratio of responses to reinforcers,

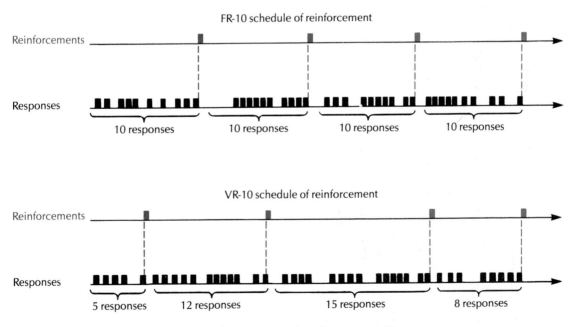

FIGURE 6.9

Fixed-ratio (FR) and variable-ratio (VR) schedules of reinforcement.

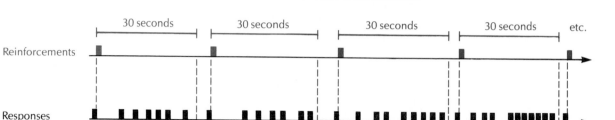

FIGURE 6.10

Fixed-interval-30-second (FI-30-second) schedule of reinforcement.

keeping it high enough to produce a good profit, but low enough to maintain a steady rate of responding from the customer. Variable-ratio schedules produce a high rate of responding; after all, the next response could bring the pay-off. Furthermore (to the delight of the person who owns the machine), responding that has been reinforced on a variable-ratio schedule is very resistant to extinction.

Response-and-Time-Dependent Schedules of Reinforcement. In **response-and-time-dependent schedules,** reinforcement is not contingent on the number of responses produced, but on the amount of time that has elapsed since the last reinforcer was delivered. After receiving a reinforcer, an organism will not get a chance to receive another one until a predetermined interval of time elapses. When that time is up, the next response will be reinforced.

Let us first examine a **fixed-interval (FI) schedule** of reinforcement. Suppose a rat is pressing a lever for food pellets that are being delivered on an FI-30-second schedule of reinforcement. The rat receives a food pellet (from the previous response), and a timer is started. The animal eats the food and starts pressing the bar again, but nothing happens. Finally the timer gets to thirty seconds. The next time the rat presses the lever the food dispenser delivers another pellet of food. The timer is reset to zero and begins measuring another thirty-second interval. Note that no matter how rapidly the rat presses the lever, the minimum time between deliveries of food pellets is thirty seconds. It is the first response that occurs *after* the elapsed time that gets the pellet. (See Figure 6.10.)

The behavior of an animal that is being reinforced on a fixed-interval schedule is similar to that of most students working on a term paper: a long pause during which nothing is done, then a frantic burst of activity as the deadline approaches. Although there is no deadline for the rat and no food pellet for the student, their patterns of responding are similar. The rat working on an FI-30-second schedule learns that a response made soon after receiving a food pellet is never reinforced and stops responding then. Time passes, and the rat approaches the lever. The animal starts pressing—slowly at first, then steadily faster. As you might expect, an animal will pause longer after each reinforcement on a FI-2-minute schedule than it will on an FI-30-second schedule.

A **variable-interval (VI) schedule** bears the same relationship to a fixed-interval schedule that a variable-ratio schedule does to a fixed-ratio schedule. For example, on a VI-30-second schedule the opportunity for reinforcement occurs, *on the average,* every thirty seconds. Sometimes the organism will receive a reinforcer for a response made a few seconds after the last reinforcer. At other times, two or three minutes must elapse. After each reinforcement a timer is started, and responses are ignored until the timer gets to the end of the interval, which is set to vary. Once the time is up, the next response will be reinforced.

When an organism's behavior is reinforced by a variable-interval schedule, it responds at a steady, even pace. The next opportunity for reinforcement may be very near, or it may be far away, so there is no point in working *too* hard. Psychologists use variable-interval schedules of reinforcement more than any other type. The organism's rate of responding is very stable and is sensitive to changes in motivation (such as hunger) and to other variables that affect its physiological state. For example, researchers in the pharmaceutical industry often administer a drug to rats that are responding on a variable-interval schedule in order to determine whether the drug affects their rate of responding. Sedatives will slow the response rate; stimulants will raise it.

My favorite example of a variable-interval schedule in real life is fishing. One form of fishing consists in casting a lure into the water and retrieving it in such a way that it resembles a minnow. If no fish are present, none will be caught. Even if one is present it may not bite. Every now and then, a hungry, eager-to-bite fish will come by. If a lure is moving through the water at the same time, the angler may get a fish. After a fish is caught, another may come by soon, or not for a long time. The only way to find out is to cast the lure. Because intermittent reinforcement produces resistance to extinction, catching a fish now and then will keep the angler's behavior going through long periods during which no fish are caught. You never know—that next cast might hook the big one.

- How are instrumentally conditioned behaviors extinguished?
- What is the relation between intermittent reinforcement and resistance to extinction?
- What are the characteristics and behavioral effects of response-dependent reinforcement schedules?
- How would you describe the characteristics and behavioral effects of response-and-time-dependent schedules?

Discrimination

Most of my descriptions of instrumental conditioning so far have involved responses and reinforcing or punishing stimuli. But other kinds of stimuli also play an essential role in instrumental conditioning. Suppose you own a dog and want to teach it to bark whenever you say "Speak!" First, you would probably get a few pieces of food that the dog likes. Then you would attract its attention and say, "Speak!"

while waving a piece of food in front of it. The dog would begin to show signs of excitement at the sight of food and would finally let out a bark. Immediately, you would feed it. After it had finished eating, you would bring out another piece of food and again say "Speak!" This time the dog would bark a little sooner. After several trials, the dog would bark whenever you say "Speak!" even if no food is visible.

You would not reinforce barking whenever it occurred but only when you had first presented the stimulus "Speak!" At all other times barking would be under an extinction schedule. In this way, the dog would learn to **discriminate** between the two conditions and to respond appropriately. The command "Speak!" would serve as the **discriminative stimulus.**

Every instance of instrumental conditioning involves discriminative stimuli, even if they are not explicitly delivered like the command "Speak!" If you have been reinforced for telling funny jokes, you will do so only when there are other people present; you will not tell jokes in an empty room. The presence of other people serves as the discriminative stimulus for telling jokes. Similarly, a rat that has been trained to press a lever for food pellets will not make pressing movements with its paws unless there

Through discrimination, we learn to share different thoughts with different people.

is a lever to push. And an angler will not cast a lure into a swimming pool. We all learn that there are some conditions under which responding is worthwhile, and some conditions under which it is useless.

Discrimination tasks are common in real life. For example, we usually talk about different things with different people. We learn that some friends do not care for sports, so we do not talk about this topic with them, because we will receive few reinforcers (such as nods or smiles). Instead, we discuss topics that have interested them in the past. A person with good social skills is one who is particularly adept at observing signs of interest in someone he or she has just met, and who selects topics of conversation, and even conversational styles, that elicit signs of interest. That is, the person is alert to discriminative stimuli in the behavior of other people.

Discrimination in classical conditioning involves making conditional responses to some stimuli but not to others. For example, if one elevator in the building where you work sometimes makes frightening lurches when it stops at a floor, you may feel uneasy while riding in it but not while riding in the other elevators, which always travel smoothly; your response discriminates between that elevator and the others. Discriminations can even be made on the basis of complex stimuli; for example, compare how you might feel if you are approached by an unsavory character who asks you for the time under two conditions: a busy sidewalk full of other pedestrians and a deserted street at night.

Generalization

No two stimuli are precisely alike. If you say "Speak!" many times, the sounds you produce will be very similar, but careful analysis of recordings would show that each time the word is pronounced somewhat differently. However, once your dog is trained it responds by barking every time you say the word, ignoring these slight differences. In other words, your dog does not discriminate among the slightly different sounds. Instead, it shows **generalization.**

The word *general* comes from the Latin *generalis,* meaning "belonging to a kind or species." The definition fits precisely. Once an

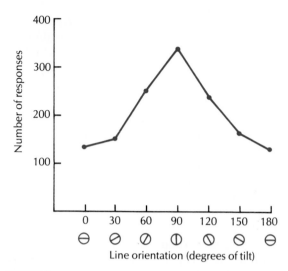

FIGURE 6.11

A generalization gradient. The pigeon was originally trained to peck at the disk when it contained a vertical line (90°). (From Honig, W.K., Boneau, C.A., Burstein, K.R., and Pennypacker, H.C. *Journal of Comparative and Physiological Psychology,* 1963, *56,* 111–116.)

organism has learned to respond to a particular discriminative stimulus, it is said to be *generalizing* when it responds in the same manner to stimuli that are similar to the original one.

Let me give a more typical example of generalization. Honig, Boneau, Burstein, and Pennypacker (1963) trained pigeons to peck at a translucent plastic disk. When the disk contained a vertical line (projected onto the back of the disk), pecking was reinforced on a VI-60-second schedule. When the disk did not contain a line, responses were not reinforced (an extinction schedule was in effect). After several sessions the pigeons learned the discrimination task: to peck when a line was present, not to peck when it was absent. Then they were tested for generalization: lines with different orientations were projected onto the disk and the animals' responses were counted.

Figure 6.11 shows the results. The circles below the horizontal axis illustrate the orientation of the line. Note that the birds made the most responses when the vertical line was present and responded less and less when they saw lines tilted progressively farther away from the vertical. They responded according to the similarity between the original training stimulus and the test stimulus.

Generalization is not restricted to laboratory demonstrations; it includes some of the most complex behaviors that we can perform. For example, in **concept formation** a person learns a strategy (that is, a complex pattern of behavior) that solves a particular problem (that is, provides a reinforcer—probably a conditional reinforcer such as satisfaction). When that person encounters a situation that shares some elements with the original one, he or she is likely to *generalize* the strategy to the new situation. Of course, merely identifying the process of concept formation as a form of generalization does little to explain it. We still have to find out how people are able to learn the complex behaviors required to solve the problem, and how they detect the common elements in similar situations. But perceiving the process in these terms helps outline an approach for research on this phenomenon.

Generalization operates in both instrumental conditioning and classical conditioning. For example, if the first bursting balloon that you experience is blue, you will nevertheless flinch at the sight of a red balloon that is about to explode; your response will generalize to other conditional stimuli. Similarly, the process of conditional reinforcement makes a *class* of stimuli serve as reinforcers. For example, social reinforcers are probably established through contact with a few people (such as members of your immediate family) very early in life. Your behavior is then reinforced by smiles and nods from other people whom you had not met earlier. The reinforcing effect of these gestures has thus generalized to similar gestures made by different people.

- What is discrimination?
- What is generalization? Describe its relationship to concept formation.
- How would you compare discrimination and generalization in classical conditioning?

OBSERVATIONAL LEARNING

We learn from experience; our behavior is reinforced or punished by its consequences. But we can also learn by a less direct method: observing the behavior of others. Video game ma-

chines usually have instructions printed on them and often flash instructions on the screen. But it is much easier to learn how to play the game by first watching someone who has had experience with it. Likewise, one of the best ways to improve your tennis game (besides taking lessons) is to spend some time watching the experts play.

Humans are not the only animals who learn by imitation. A pigeon that watches another bird performing a complex operant task will learn the task much more quickly than one that has not had this opportunity. Why do organisms learn to imitate the behavior of others? Is this tendency innate?

There are clear examples from nature that imitation does seem to be an innate tendency. Many species of birds must learn to sing their characteristic song; if they are raised apart from other birds they will never sing, or they will sing a peculiar song that bears little resemblance to that of normally raised birds. However, if they hear the normal song played over a loudspeaker, they will sing it properly when they become adults. They have learned the song, but clearly there were no external reinforcement contingencies; nothing in the envi-

Many things are readily learned by observing others. While these teenagers could read the instructions on the video screen to learn how to play, it is much easier to learn by observation.

ronment reinforced their singing of the song. (This phenomenon is an excellent example of the distinction between learning and performance. A baby bird hears the proper song but does not sing it until adulthood. The changes that take place in its brain do not manifest themselves in behavior for many months.)

Under normal circumstances, learning by observation may not require external reinforcement; in fact, there is strong evidence that imitating the behavior of other organisms may be reinforcing in itself. However, in some cases in which this ability is absent, it can be learned through reinforcement. Baer, Peterson, and Sherman (1967) studied three severely retarded children who had never been seen to imitate the behavior of other people. When the experimenters first tried to induce the children to do what they themselves did, like clap their hands, the children were unresponsive. Next, the experimenters tried to induce and reinforce imitative behavior in the chidren. An experimenter would look at a child, say "Do this," and perform a behavior. If the child made a similar response, the child was immediately praised and given a piece of food. At first the children were physically guided to make the

response; if the behavior to be imitated was clapping, the experimenter would clap his or her hands, hold the child's hands and clap them together, then praise the child and give him or her some food.

The procedure worked. The children learned to imitate the experimenters' behaviors. But even more important, the children had not simply learned to mimic a specific set of responses; they had acquired the *general tendency to imitate.* When the experimenters performed new behaviors and said "Do this," the children would imitate them.

Obviously, teaching retarded children is much more effective when they pay attention to their teachers and imitate their behaviors when requested to do so. The procedure I just described has proved to be extremely useful for teaching retarded children behaviors that will help them lead useful lives. But the theoretical significance of this demonstration is also important. The experiment indicates that imitation, as a general tendency, is subject to reinforcement (and presumably also to punishment). An organism can learn more than a particular response to a particular stimulus; it can learn a strategy that can be applied to a variety of situations.

Social Learning Theory

For humans (and probably for many other animals) there is a class of conditioned reinforcers known as **social reinforcers,** as well as a complementary class known as **social punishers.** These stimuli consist of behaviors of other people, especially those behaviors that indicate approval or rejection. A smile, a nod, or a frown can serve as a potent reinforcer or punisher. The special significance of social reinforcement and punishment to human behavior is emphasized by the development of *social learning theory,* based on the principles outlined in this chapter.

Social learning theory differs from classical and instrumental conditioning in the role assigned to the process of reinforcement in learning. According to classical and instrumental conditioning, reinforcement (or punishment) is crucial for learning; without it learning does not occur. Social learning theorists agree that reinforcement is very important, but they

---

The behaviors of people important to us can be very powerful social reinforcers. Social learning theory emphasizes the role of social behaviors in the learning process.

FIGURE 6.12

Top. Aggressive behavior of the model. *Middle and bottom.* Imitative behavior by children. (From Bandura, A., Ross, D., and Ross, S.A. *Journal of Abnormal and Social Psychology*, 1961, 66, 3–11.)

assert that learning can sometimes take place without it. Bandura (1977) says that much social learning takes place through observation; people see what other people do and what happens as a result, and they learn new responses by watching this process take place. They do not have to engage in overt behaviors or to experience reinforcement or punishment directly.

A classic series of experiments reported by Bandura (1973) distinguished between the role of observation in learning a response and the role of reinforcement in determining whether the child performed it. In one set of experiments an adult attacked a large, inflated clown doll ("a Bobo doll"). One group of children witnessed the attack in person; others watched it on television. The control group watched the adult engage in innocuous behaviors. Later, the children were allowed to play in the room where the doll was kept.

All the children who had seen the adult beat Bobo, either in person or on television, imitated the adult's behavior, giving the doll a savage beating. The children who had watched innocuous behaviors did not display aggression toward the doll. It was also clear that the children's aggressive behavior was modeled on that of the adult. Those who had seen the adult kick the doll, use a hammer to hit it, or sit on top if it and pound its face did the same. Figure 6.12 shows the model behavior of the adult (top) and the imitative behavior of the children.

In other experiments, children watched a film of a person engaging in aggressive behavior and being subsequently rewarded or punished. Children who saw the person being rewarded were more aggressive, whereas those who watched the person being punished made fewer attacks on the Bobo doll. When the experimenter later offered the children a reward for imitating the model, *both groups* started beating Bobo. Thus, it is clear that all the children had learned the aggressive response through observation. However, the sight of the model being punished had inhibited the children's experession of the learned behaviors, so that they did not act out what they had learned until direct reinforcement of these behaviors removed the inhibition.

- What are the conditions under which observation and imitation are likely to occur?
- How do observational and social learning differ from classical and instrumental conditioning?

CHAPTER SUMMARY

1. Four forms of learning help shape behavior: habituation, classical conditioning, instrumental conditioning, and observational learning. Habituation in effect screens out stimuli that experience has shown to be unimportant. This mechanism allows organisms to respond to more important stimuli, such as those related to survival and propagation.

2. The process of classical conditioning takes place when a neutral conditional stimulus occurs just before an unconditional stimulus that normally elicits a behavior. The response that an organism makes to the unconditional stimulus is already a natural part of its behavior; what the organism learns is to make it in response to new stimuli. The neutral stimulus is linked to the unconditional stimulus (either naturally, because one of them causes the other to occur, or artificially, in an experiment). The organism learns to respond directly to the once-neutral stimulus. When conditional stimuli are presented alone, responses are emitted but are not reinforced, and the conditional response eventually extinguishes (extinction).

3. Classical conditioning of physiological responses can play a role in feelings of emotion. The responses occur when we encounter a person, place, or object that was previously associated with a pleasant or unpleasant situation, and our perception of these responses constitutes an important part of what we call *emotions.* Classical conditioning can also establish various classes of stimuli as objects of fear (phobias) or of sexual attraction (fetishes).

4. Instrumental conditioning involves a change in the likelihood of a response by means of the onset or termination of an appetitive or aversive stimulus. If the response becomes more likely, it is said to have been reinforced; if it becomes less likely, it is said to have been punished. Except in the case of sickness produced by a novel food, the reinforcing or punishing stimulus must follow the behavior almost immediately if it is to be effective.

5. The major difference between classical conditioning and instrumental conditioning is in the nature of the contingencies: classical conditioning involves a contingency between stimuli (CS and US); whereas instrumental conditioning involves a contingency between the organism's behavior and an appetitive or aversive stimulus. The two types of conditioning complement each other. The pairings of neutral stimuli with appetitive and aversive stimuli (classical conditioning) determine which stimuli become conditioned (secondary) reinforcers and punishers. Through the process of instrumental conditioning, the contingencies between an organism's behavior and these stimuli adapt the organism's behavior to its environment.

6. Complex responses, which are unlikely to occur spontaneously, can be reinforced by the method of successive approximations (shaping). For example, teachers use this process to train their students to perform complex behaviors, and something similar occurs when, in the course of learning a new skill, we become satisfied only when we detect signs of improvement.

7. A negatively reinforced response is a form of escape: the response terminates the aversive stimulus. Aversive control can also lead to avoidance, in which the response occurs before the aversive stimulus does, thus preventing it from happening.

8. Intermittent reinforcement produces a

resistance to extinction, probably because it is difficult to tell the difference between intermittent reinforcement and extinction. Two basic kinds of schedules of reinforcement—response-dependent and response-and-time-dependent—have been devised to investigate instrumental conditioning.

9. Generalization is a necessary component of all forms of learning, because no two stimuli, and no two responses, are precisely the same; thus, generalization embodies the ability to apply what is learned from one experience to similar experiences. Discrimination involves the detection of essential differences between stimuli or between situations, so that responding occurs only when appropriate.

10. Social learning theorists tend to emphasize the importance of imitation and the capacity to learn from the experience of others, more than behaviorists do. Bandura's experiments on aggression suggest that a child may learn a response through observation and later, depending on the contingencies of reinforcement, exhibit this behavior or not.

KEY TERMS

appetitive stimulus A stimulus that an organism will attempt to approach; can be used to reinforce a response.

aversive stimulus A stimulus that an organism will attempt to avoid or escape; can be used either to punish or to negatively reinforce a response.

avoidance response The performance of a response that prevents an aversive stimulus from occurring. See also *escape response.*

classical conditioning The process by which a defensive response or appetitive response normally produced automatically by an eliciting stimulus, comes to be produced by a previously neutral stimulus. The previously neutral stimulus is followed shortly by an eliciting stimulus (unconditional stimulus) that normally produces the response (unconditional response), and becomes, after several pairings, a conditional stimulus producing the conditional response.

concept formation Related to generalization, a process in which a person who has learned a strategy that solves a particular problem applies the strategy to similar problems.

conditional response (CR) After classical conditioning, the response that is elicited by the conditional stimulus.

conditional stimulus (CS) After classical conditioning, the stimulus that elicits the conditional response, which resembles the unconditional response.

conditioned aversion The process by which a novel stimulus, such as the taste of a food, followed by an unpleasant reaction, such as illness, results in the organism's avoiding the stimulus.

conditioned punishment A process by which a previously neutral stimulus followed by an aversive stimulus itself becomes capable, through classical conditioning, of punishing a response.

conditioned reinforcement A process by which a previously neutral stimulus followed by an appetitive stimulus itself becomes capable, through classical conditioning, of reinforcing a response.

contingency Occurring only when certain conditions are fulfilled. If an appetitive stimulus is contingent on a particular behavior, the frequency of that behavior will usually increase.

continuous reinforcement schedule (CRF) A schedule whereby every occurrence of a particular response is followed by presentation of the reinforcer.

discrimination The detection of differences between two stimuli or of a change in a stimulus, as shown by changes in an organism's behavior.

discriminative stimulus A stimulus that has been associated with the occurrence or nonoccurrence of an appetitive or aversive stimulus; serves as a basis for instrumental conditioning.

escape response The performance of a response that terminates an aversive stimulus. See also *avoidance response.*

extinction The reduction or elimination of a behavior caused by ceasing the presentation of the reinforcing stimulus.

fetishes Sexual attachments to a class of inanimate objects or situations.

fixed-interval (FI) schedule A schedule of reinforcement in which the first response that is emitted after a fixed interval of time since the previous reinforcement (or the start of the session) is reinforced.

fixed-ratio (FR) schedule A schedule of reinforcement in which reinforcement occurs only after a fixed number of responses have been emitted since the previous reinforcement (or the start of the session).

generalization An organism's tendency, once it has learned to emit a specific behavior when one stimulus is present, to emit that behavior when a similar stimulus is present.

habituation The gradual elimination of an unconditional response (especially an orienting response) by the repeated presentation of the unconditional stimulus. Habituation will not occur to especially noxious stimuli.

instrumental conditioning Operant conditioning; increasing or decreasing the frequency of a response through contingent reinforcement or punishment.

intermittent reinforcement A contingency whereby some, but not all, responses are reinforced. Behaviors that are reinforced intermittently are more resistant to extinction than behaviors that are reinforced on a continuous reinforcement schedule.

long-term habituation Animals of more complex nervous systems are capable of this form of learning in which a response to a stimuli is eliminated forever.

method of successive approximations See *shaping*.

negative reinforcement The removal or reduction of an aversive stimulus that is contingent on a particular response, with an attendant increase in the frequency of that response; the effect of an escape response.

operant chamber An experimental chamber in which animals can be placed for instrumental (or operant) conditioning; contains a device to measure responses and provide reinforcing or punishing stimuli.

operant conditioning See *instrumental conditioning*.

orienting response The response by which an organism orients appropriate sensory organs (such as eyes or ears) toward the source of a novel stimulus.

phobia Excessive, unreasonable fear of a particular class of objects or situations.

postreinforcement pause The tendency of a subject working on a long fixed-ratio schedule to pause after receiving reinforcement before continuing.

preference hierarchy Within the Premack principle, the ranking from high to low of an organism's preferences for certain behaviors.

Premack principle The assertion that the opportunity to engage in a preferred behavior can be used to reinforce the performance of a nonpreferred behavior.

primary punisher A naturally aversive stimulus, such as one that produces pain or nausea, which can be used to punish a response.

primary reinforcer A naturally appetitive stimulus, such as food, water, or warmth, which can be used to reinforce a response.

punishment The suppression of a response by the contingent presentation of an aversive stimulus or the contingent removal of an appetitive stimulus (response cost).

reinforcement The presentation of an appetitive stimulus (positive reinforcement) or the reduction or removal of an aversive stimulus (negative reinforcement) that is contingent on a response; reinforcement increases the frequency of the response.

reinforcing stimulus (reinforcer) A stimulus that, when contingent on a behavior, increases the occurrence of the behavior. See also *reinforcement*.

response-and-time dependent schedule A schedule of reinforcement in which reinforcement is not contingent on the number of responses produced but on the amount of time that has elapsed since the last reinforcer was delivered.

response cost A form of punishment in which a response is followed by the removal of an appetitive stimulus.

response-dependent schedule A schedule of reinforcement in which reinforcement is contingent on response followed by a reinforcer.

schedule of reinforcement The scheme that determines the nature of intermittent reinforcement. See also *fixed-interval (FI) schedule, fixed-ratio (FR) schedule, variable-interval (VI) schedule,* and *variable-ratio (VR) schedule*.

shaping The training of a very low-frequency

response by successively reinforcing responses that are increasingly similar to the desired one; also called the method of successive approximations.

short-term habituation The simplest and most temporary form of habituation.

Skinner box An informal name for an operant chamber.

social punisher A punishing stimulus in the form of the behavior of another person, such as a frown or hostile words.

social reinforcer A reinforcing stimulus in the form of the behavior of another person, such as a smile or kind words.

spontaneous recovery The recurrence of a behavior that was previously extinguished, after a rest period.

target behavior The desired response that is to be conditioned through successive approximations.

unconditional response (UR) The response elicited by the unconditional stimulus in classical conditioning.

unconditional stimulus (US) The unconditional eliciting stimulus in classical conditioning.

variable-interval (VI) schedule A schedule of reinforcement similar to a fixed-interval schedule but characterized by a variable time requirement with a particular mean.

variable-ratio (VR) schedule A schedule of reinforcement similar to a fixed-ratio schedule but characterized by a variable response requirement with a particular mean.

Memory

*T*here is a strong tendency, especially in an age of computers, to think of human memory as something quantitative—as a more or less efficient machine for storing, structuring, and retrieving bits of information. When people ask, "What are some good ways to improve my memory?" they are often thinking in terms of "upgrading the machine" to enlarge their storage capacity. The much-heard question, "Is it wasted effort to cram for an exam?" seems to imply a fear of overload and lost input. But research has shown that our brains are much more complex—and interesting—than even the most advanced computers. True, our memories are sometimes less reliable than those found on silicon chips, but we are much better than computers at quickly recognizing and remembering relations among facts, and we can often reach correct decisions even when the information we receive is vague and incomplete.

Psychologists have learned that human memory does not consist of a filing cabinet into which we place individual items; instead, it consists of multiple stages, each containing different types of information. Studies of people with brain damage indicate that different parts of the brain are somewhat specialized; they participate in learning about different aspects of an experience, but then share their information and permit us to compare these aspects. If the information in our memory is fragmentary, we can often reconstruct what probably happened, based on our knowledge of the world. Is this reconstruction always accurate? Studies of eyewitness reports show how different people, witnessing the same events, can sincerely report different versions. But even though memory can sometimes "fail," the system is still more flexible and creative than any we have been able to construct so far. Indeed, some designers of advanced computers are trying to model them on the human brain.

Experiments have long shown that our memory performs according to what "makes sense" to us from our past experience. A word we have heard before is easier to recall than a random string of letters; a story that "makes sense" is easier to remember than one whose elements do not relate to each other; and details of a chess game are remembered more easily by an expert than by a novice. Clearly, human memory is an ever-changing system whose study remains an intriguing challenge for psychological research.

211

AN OVERVIEW

As we all know, the mere ability to perceive new information is no guarantee that we will be able to remember it later. Thus, it is clear that the learning process is selective; only some experiences become a part of memory.

Research suggests that we possess at least three forms of memory, each with a distinct physiological basis. The first form, called **sensory memory,** lasts for a very brief time—perhaps a second or less—and is difficult to distinguish from the act of perception. The information contained in sensory memory represents the original stimulus fairly accurately. For example, visual sensory memory contains a brief image of a sight we have just seen and auditory sensory memory contains a fleeting echo of a sound we have just heard. Under most circumstances we are not aware of sensory memory; no analysis seems to be performed on the information while it remains in this form. The function of sensory memory appears to be to hold on to information long enough for it to be transferred to the next form, **short-term memory.**

Short-term memory is an immediate memory for stimuli that have just been perceived. We can remember a new item of information (such as a telephone number) as long as we want to by engaging in a particular behavior: rehearsal. However, once we stop rehearsing the information there is no guarantee that we will be able to remember it later. That is, the information may or may not get stored in **long-term memory.**

Short-term memory can hold only a limited amount of information. To demonstrate this fact, read the following numbers to yourself just once, and then close your eyes and recite them back.

1 4 9 2 3 0 7

You probably had no trouble remembering them. Now try the following set of numbers, and go through them *only once* before you close your eyes.

7 2 5 2 3 9 1 6 5 8 4

Very few people can repeat eleven numbers; in fact you may not have even bothered to try, once you saw how many numbers there were. Thus, short-term memory has definite limits. No matter how much you practice, you will probably not be able to recite more than seven to nine *independent* pieces of information that you have seen only once. (As we will see later, there are ways to organize new information so that you can remember more than seven to nine items, but in such cases they can no longer be considered independent.)

If you wanted to, you could recite the numbers again and again until you had memorized them; that is, you could rehearse the information in short-term memory until it was eventually stored in long-term memory. The fact that there are eleven numbers would present no obstacle; long-term memory can accommodate an unlimited number of items of information. The difference in the capacity between short-term and long-term memory indicates that these forms of memory are separate entities.

Some psychologists argue that no real distinction exists between short-term and long-term memory; instead, they are seen as different phases of a continuous process. These psychologists object to the conception of memory as a series of separate units with information flowing from one to the next, as shown in Figure 7.1. And indeed, such a "compartment"

Memories can elicit powerful emotions, as evident with these Vietnam veterans remembering their deceased friends.

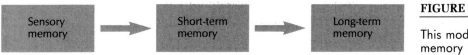

FIGURE 7.1

This model of human memory is too simple.

model is too simple. Short-term memory does not simply contain newly perceived information; it also contains information that has been recalled from long-term memory. As we will see, this fact has led some psychologists to employ the term *working memory* rather than *short-term memory*.

Even if memory is actually a continuous process, with short-term memory simply referring to the early, rapidly changing phase and long-term memory to the late, stable phase, the distinction between these two phases is still useful. For one thing, items in short-term memory are "in our thoughts." A newly perceived stimulus that is in short-term memory is one that we are currently attending to; it is in our consciousness. In contrast, we are actively thinking about very little of the information in long-term memory at any given time. For example, there is probably no item of information that we know better than our own name, but our name is not something we must "think about" all the time. Whenever we need to remember it, it is there.

SENSORY MEMORY

Under most circumstances, we are not aware of sensory memory. Information that we have just perceived remains in sensory memory just long enough to be transferred to short-term memory. In order for us to become aware of sensory memory, information must be presented very briefly, so that we can perceive its aftereffects. For example, a thunderstorm at night provides us with an opportunity to become aware of visual sensory memory. When a bright flash of lightning reveals a scene, we *see* things before we *recognize* them. That is, we see something first, then study the image that is left behind. Although we probably have a sensory memory for each sense modality, research efforts so far have focused on the two most important forms: iconic (visual) and echoic (auditory) memory.

Iconic Memory

Visual sensory memory is referred to as **iconic memory** (*icon* means "image"). To study this form of memory, Sperling (1960) presented visual stimuli to subjects by means of a **tachistoscope** (from *takhistos,* "most swift," and *skopein,* "to see"). Sperling flashed a set of nine letters, such as those shown below, on the screen for 0.05 second.

P   Q   B
C   Z   L
R   K   F

Sperling then asked the subjects to recall as many letters as they could (this is known as the *whole-report* procedure). On the average, they could remember only four or five letters, but they insisted that they could *see* more. However, the image of the letters faded too fast for the subjects to identify them all.

Most times we are unaware of sensory memory. A nighttime thunderstorm makes us aware of visual sensory memory. As the lightning flash reveals the landscape, we see things before we recognize them.

To determine whether the capacity of iconic memory accounted for this limitation, Sperling used a *partial-report* procedure. He asked the subjects to name the letters in only one of the three horizontal rows. Depending on whether a high, middle, or low tone was sounded, they were to report the letters in the top, middle, or bottom line. When people are warned beforehand which line they should pay attention to, they have no difficulty naming all three letters correctly. But Sperling sounded the tone *after* he flashed the letters on the screen. The subjects had to select the line from the *mental image* that they still had; that is, they had to retrieve the information from iconic memory. With brief delays, they recalled the requested line of letters with perfect accuracy. For example, after seeing all nine letters flashed on the screen, they would hear the high tone, direct their attention to the top line of letters in their iconic memory, and "read them off." These results indicated that their iconic memory contained an image of all nine letters.

Sperling also varied the delay between flashing the nine letters on the screen and sounding the high, medium, or low tone. If the delay was longer than one second, the subjects could report only around 50 percent of the letters. This result indicates that the image of the visual stimulus fades quickly from iconic memory. It also explains why subjects who were asked to report *all* the letters failed to report more than four or five. They had to scan their visual sensory memory, identify each letter, and store each letter in short-term memory. This process took time, and during this time the image of the letters in iconic memory was fading. Although their iconic memory originally contained all nine letters, there was time to recognize and report only four or five before the mental image disappeared.

Subsequent studies using Sperling's partial-report procedure have suggested that iconic memory contains only raw, sensory information. For example, Banks and Barber (1977) presented arrays of letters printed in different colors. After the items were flashed on the screen, they presented a tone whose pitch signaled the subjects to say the names of the letters printed in a particular color, just as Sperling had asked for the names of the letters in a particular line. The subjects could accurately do so; thus, iconic memory contains informa-

tion about the color of the items as well as their location. In contrast, iconic memory does not appear to contain information about the *names* of the items. In another experiment, Sperling (1960) presented subjects with an array of numbers and letters. Immediately afterward, he presented a tone whose pitch signified whether the subjects should try to name the numbers or the letters. In this case, partial report did not lead to better performance than whole report. Thus, although location or color can be used to direct people's attention to some items in iconic memory before the image fades, the items cannot be identified as numbers or letters until they have entered short-term memory. And only a few items have time to enter short-term memory before the rest of the image fades.

Echoic Memory

Auditory sensory memory, aptly called **echoic memory,** is necessary for comprehending many sounds, particularly those that constitute speech. When we hear a word pronounced, we hear individual sounds, one at a time. We cannot identify the word until we have heard all the sounds, so acoustical information must be stored temporarily until all the sounds have been received. For example, if someone says "mallet," we may think of a kind of hammer; but if someone says "malice," we will think of something entirely different. The first syllable we hear—*mal*—has no meaning by itself in English, so we do not identify it as a word. However, once the last syllable is uttered, we can put the two syllables together and recognize the word. At this point, the word enters short-term memory. Echoic memory holds a representation of the initial sounds until the entire word has been heard.

Darwin, Turvey, and Crowder (1972) investigated echoic memory with a partial-report procedure similar to the one Sperling employed. On each trial, they presented three different sets of numbers simultaneously, from three different locations (to the left and right of the subject, and straight ahead). The numbers were spoken at a rate of three per second. After presenting the numbers, the experimenters presented a visual stimulus that indicated the location of the sounds the subjects should repeat.

FIGURE 7.2

Revised (but still too simple) model of human memory.

If the cue came soon after the numbers, subjects could accurately repeat what they had just heard from that direction. However, if the delay exceeded four seconds, the subjects did just as poorly as they did using the whole-report procedure. The experimenters concluded that echoic memory lasts less than four seconds.

■ What are the three stages of memory and how do they differ?

■ What do "partial-report" experiments show about the nature of iconic memory and echoic memory?

SHORT-TERM MEMORY

Chunking: Encoding of Information

Our ability to organize information in short-term memory in terms of meaning requires the use of long-term memory. After all, if words have meaning to us, we must have learned this meaning previously. Figure 7.2 contains the diagram that was presented in Figure 7.1, modified to take account of the role that long-term memory plays in organizing information in short-term memory. As we will see later, the diagram is still incomplete.

Information is encoded in short-term memory according to *previously learned rules*. The previously learned rules concern the meaning of words and the ways in which they may be combined to produce sentences. In order for new information to be stored in short-term memory, information must be retrieved from long-term memory, because that is where the previously learned rules are stored. Thus, if we hear the word *tree*, we do not merely store those three sounds (*t* + *r* + *ee*) in short-term memory; we also retrieve the meaning of the sounds from long-term memory and store that meaning as well. We might even form a mental image of a tree.

George Miller (1956) was the first to consider explicitly how information might be encoded in short-term memory. In a series of experiments Miller showed that only about seven *independent* items (numbers, letters, words, or tones with particular pitches) could be stored in short-term memory. However, much longer lists could be retained if the items were related. For example, you would probably have no difficulty retaining the numbers written below in short-term memory, even though there are ten of them.

1   3   5   7   9   2   4   6   8   0

These numbers are easy to retain in short-term memory because we can remember a rule instead of ten independent numbers. In this case, the rule concerns odd and even numbers. **Chunking** is Miller's term for the use of information already present in long-term memory to organize information just received in short-term memory. The actual limit of short-term memory is seven *chunks*, not necessarily seven individual items. Thus, the total amount of information we can store in short-term memory depends on the particular rules we use to organize the information.

We perform some kind of conversion every day, although we are usually unaware of doing so. We perceive an endless stream of sensory information, and we process it by encoding it into chunks, according to rules stored in long-term memory.

A nice example of the power of encoding was given by deGroot (1965), who showed chessboards to expert players. If the positions of the pieces represented an actual game in progress, the experts could glance at the board for a few seconds and then look away and report the position of each piece. However, if the same number of pieces had been placed haphazardly on the board, the experts noticed that their positions made no sense, and they could not remember their positions any better than a nonexpert could. Thus, their short-term memories for the positions of a large number of pieces depended on organizing the pattern of pieces

Listening to song lyrics will make studying verbal material difficult for this student because of intramodal interference.

according to rules, which were stored in long-term memory as a result of years of experience playing chess.

Role of Short-Term Memory in Thinking

It is clear that short-term memory is more than a simple way station between perception and long-term memory. For example, as I write this paragraph I think not only about the words that I have just written (which are stored in short-term memory) but also about *what I want to say next*. Obviously, this planning depends heavily on information stored in long-term memory. Because short-term memory contains information that we are currently thinking about, in-

cluding information that has just been retrieved from long-term memory, some investigators prefer the term **working memory.** The contents of working memory include both new and old information.

The fact that working memory contains both old and new information does not mean that we must discard the distinction between short-term and long-term memory; most psychologists continue to use these terms because, as we will see later, there is evidence for a physiological distinction between them. Even the act of remembering something can itself be a short-term memory. For example, think about the last time you mailed a letter. This information, and your awareness of thinking about it, are presently in your working memory, just as newly presented information would be. If I ask you later, "Do you remember thinking about the last time you mailed a letter?" you will undoubtedly be able to recall the effort you made to remember. Thus, information can reach short-term memory from the act of remembering as well as from the sensory systems. This fact has led to the discovery of an important distinction between two types of long-term memory, episodic memory and semantic memory, which I will discuss later.

Sensory-Specific Representation

Short-term memory can contain a variety of sensory information: visual, auditory, somatosensory, gustatory, and olfactory. It can also contain information about movements that we have just made, and it possibly provides the means by which we rehearse movements that we are thinking about making. As we will see, some aspects of motor short-term memory are very important for remembering and thinking, especially those aspects involved with talking. One of the ways we rehearse verbal information is to say it silently to ourselves.

Evidence for Memory Compartments: Intramodal Interference

Both behavioral and physiological evidence suggests that short-term memory is at least somewhat compartmentalized. That is, the circuits of neurons that contain visual, auditory, somatosensory, gustatory, olfactory, and motor information are somewhat independent and appear to be located in different parts of the brain. First, let us consider some of the behavioral evidence. Many experiments have shown that *intramodal* interference is much more severe than *intermodal* interference. (*Intra* means "within," *inter* means "between," and *modal* refers to a sense modality, such as vision or audition.) These experiments show that when we attempt to retain information in short-term memory, we are more likely to be confused by additional information if it is presented through the same sense modality (intramodal interference) than through a different one (intermodal interference).

In one such experiment, Kroll, Parks, Parkinson, Bieber, and Johnson (1970) presented subjects either visually or acoustically with a single letter (the "memory letter") to be retained in short-term memory. Immediately afterward they had the subjects repeat back a spoken list of unrelated letters. This task forced them to listen to the letters, thus providing auditory interference. Ten or twenty-five seconds after hearing or seeing the memory letter, the subjects were asked to recall it. Figure 7.3 shows the results. When the subjects were asked to recall the letter with no delay (that is, without having to listen to a list of letters), retention

was virtually perfect (around 96 percent). In contrast, ten or twenty-five seconds of auditory interference impaired the subjects' retention of a spoken "memory letter"; retention of a visually presented letter was much better.

The results of this experiment suggest that auditory and visual short-term memory are at least somewhat independent; listening to a series of letters interferes with auditory short-term memory more than with visual short-term memory. Presumably, the subjects could remember the shape of a visual "memory letter" while listening to a list of unrelated letters but found it much more difficult to remember the sound of an auditory "memory letter" while listening to the list.

Memory Compartments and Brain Damage

The behavioral evidence presented in the previous section does not in itself prove that each component of short-term (working) memory involves a different set of neural circuits. To determine whether these memories are anatomically separate, we need physiological evidence.

The best evidence that human short-term memory is divided into sensory-specific components comes from a disorder called **conduction aphasia.** Conduction aphasia, usually caused by damage to a region of the left parietal lobe, appears as a profound deficit in auditory short-term memory. People with conduction aphasia can talk and comprehend what others are saying, but they are very poor at repeating precisely what they hear. When they attempt to repeat words that other people say they often get the meaning correct but use different words. The examples below were attempts of a patient with a mild conduction aphasia to repeat sentences that the examiner read to her. Her responses make it clear that although she cannot repeat the sentences verbatim she comprehends them.

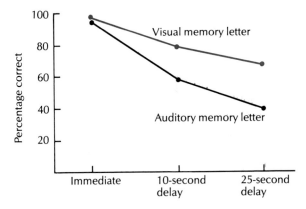

FIGURE 7.3

Memory for a visually or acoustically presented letter immediately after it is presented and after ten or twenty-five seconds of repeating back an acoustically presented list of letters. (Based on data from Kroll, N.E.A., Parks, T., Parkinson, S.R., Bieber, S.L., and Johnson, A.L. *Journal of Experimental Psychology,* 1970, *85,* 220–224.)

Examiner: The auto's leaking gas tank soiled the roadway.

Patient: The car's tank leaked and made a mess on the street.

Examiner: The girl slides first, she swims last.

Patient: She slides before she went swimming.

Warrington and Shallice (1972) compared the ability of a patient with conduction aphasia to retain visual as opposed to acoustic information in short-term memory. They presented one, two, or three letters visually or acoustically and, after a delay, asked the patient to repeat them. As Figure 7.4 shows, acoustically presented information was remembered much more poorly than information that was presented visually. Normally, people remember sequences of letters better when they are presented acoustically.

Most investigators believe that conduction aphasia is caused by brain damage that disrupts the connections between two regions of the cerebral cortex that play important roles in people's language ability: *Wernicke's area*, which is concerned with the perception of speech, and *Broca's area*, which is concerned with the production of speech. (These areas are described in more detail in Chapter 8.) As we will see later in this chapter, behavioral evidence suggests that one of the ways by which we remember information in short-term memory is to "say it to ourselves" silently. Because the brain damage that produces conduction aphasia disconnects regions of the brain involved in speech perception and production, perhaps the damage disrupts acoustical short-term memory by making such subvocal speech difficult or impossible.

Kovner and Stamm (1972) obtained evidence from an experiment with monkeys that also supports the conclusion that short-term mem-ory is compartmentalized. First, they operated on the monkeys, placing wires in various regions of the cerebral cortex. They attached these wires to a connector fastened to the top of each animal's head, so that later they could transmit electrical current through the wires while the animals were performing their task. The electrical current would disrupt the normal functioning of the region of cortex where the wire was located. Next, they trained the monkeys in a *delayed matching-to-sample task*. For a brief period of time, they showed each animal a visual pattern: the sample. After a delay of several seconds with no pattern present, they showed the monkey two patterns, one of which was the same as the sample. If the monkey touched the pattern that matched the sample, it was given a piece of food. If it touched the other pattern, it received nothing. (See Figure 7.5.)

The delayed matching-to-sample task required the monkey to compare its short-term memory of a visual stimulus with an actual stimulus. The experimenters turned on the current for a brief time during the delay interval, while the image of the sample pattern was being retained in visual short-term memory. They stimulated several different areas of the cortex, but only when they stimulated the visual association cortex was the monkey's performance impaired. The current appeared to "erase" the memory. Thus, visual short-term memories appear to be located in the visual association cortex.

FIGURE 7.4

Short-term retention of one-, two-, and three-letter sequences presented acoustically and visually to a patient with conduction aphasia. (From Warrington, E.K., and Shallice, T. *Quarterly Journal of Experimental Psychology,* 1972, 24, 30–40.)

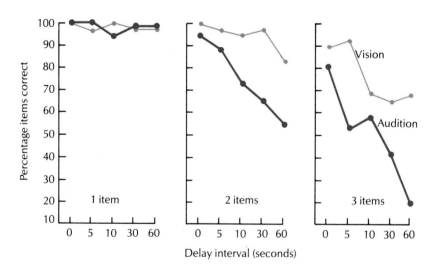

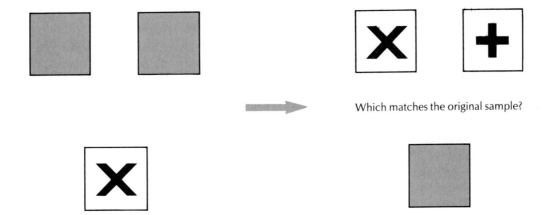

FIGURE 7.5

The delayed matching-to-sample task.

- How do we remember by encoding and chunking?
- What role does short-term memory play in our thinking?
- What does behavioral and physiological evidence show about compartmentalization in short-term memory?

Exchange of Information Within Short-Term Memory

The discussion of short-term memory so far has provided evidence for separate compartments, each containing information derived from a different sensory system. But even though these compartments may be located in different parts of the brain, several of them can each contain particular aspects of an event that just occurred. When we see a written word, we quickly recognize how it sounds and what it means. That is, different kinds of information are retained in different compartments of short-term memory. For example, when we see the word *cat*, we "hear" the sounds we make to say the word, we may imagine what a cat looks like, we may imagine how its fur feels, and so on. The purely visual stimulus gives rise to several different classes of information in short-term memory.

The separate components of short-term memory do not simply work in parallel; they can also communicate with each other and interchange information. For example, look at the series of letters printed below.

phocks

Can you pronounce the "word"? Is it an animal? Does it have a bushy tail? Do people sometimes hunt these animals on horseback? I am sure you answered "yes" to each of my questions. How did you do so?

Although the topic of reading will be discussed in detail in the next chapter, we can consider some of the steps that occurred in this example and what they tell us about the exchange of information between different compartments of short-term memory. Although you probably never saw *phocks* before, you read it to yourself as if it were spelled *fox*. That is, your auditory short-term memory contained the sounds you would make to say this word. Hearing this word inside your head, you could imagine the sight of a fox, picture a fox hunt, and so on. That is, information in visual short-term memory (the letters *p-h-o-c-k-s*) gave rise to information in auditory short-term memory, which in turn gave rise to information in other compartments of short-term memory.

An experiment by Conrad (1964) showed how important intermodal transfer of information can be in short-term memory of verbal material. He briefly showed lists of six letters to his subjects and then asked them to write the letters down. The errors the subjects made were almost always acoustical rather than visual. For instance, people were more likely to write *D* for *T* (these letters sound similar) than they were to write *O* for *Q* (these letters look similar). The results imply that the subjects read the letters, encoded them acoustically ("said them in their minds"), and remembered them by rehearsing the letters as sounds. During this process they might easily mistake a *D* for a *T*.

An experiment by Posner, Boies, Eichelman, and Taylor (1969) measured the time it took for visual information to be translated into verbal information in short-term memory. The investigators flashed a pair of letters on a screen, simultaneously or one after the other. The task of the subjects was to say whether the letters were the same or different. Under one condition, the discrimination was to be made in terms of the letters' shapes. That is, the pair *AA* was to be called "same," but the pair *Aa* was to be called "different." Under the second condition, the discrimination was to be made in terms of the letters' names, not necessarily their shapes. Thus, both *AA* and *Aa* were to be called "same." Posner and his colleagues varied the time between the two stimuli and measured how long it took for the subjects to indicate "same" or "different," which they did by pressing one of two buttons.

Figure 7.6 shows the results. At short delays, subjects could make a shape comparison faster than a name comparison. However, with a delay of one second, the two types of comparisons took approximately the same amount of time. The simplest explanation appears to be that shape comparisons could be made purely in terms of visual information that had just entered short-term memory and thus could be made quickly. In contrast, name comparisons required recognition of the identity of the letter (its name). This comparison could not be accomplished until the visual information was encoded verbally, which took some time. When the letters were presented with a delay interval of one second, the purely visual information about the first letter had apparently faded, so even shape comparisons probably required the subject to use verbally coded information.

Rehearsing and Thinking: Role of Subvocal Speech

When we encounter new information, we often encode some of it verbally. For example, when you saw the letters *p-h-o-c-k-s*, you formed an acoustical image as well as a visual one. But you probably did more than that. In addition to "hearing" the sounds the letters denote, you probably pronounced the word to yourself. We can say things to ourselves, silently, just as we can imagine how something looks, or sounds, or feels. That is, we have an *articulatory* short-term (working) memory, just as we have auditory, visual, and somatosensory short-term memories. In fact, most verbal rehearsal probably entails **subvocal articulation** as well as auditory short-term memory. (*Subvocal articulation* means "unvoiced speech utterance.") For example, read the sentence below and rehearse it a few times, as if you were trying to memorize it. (It is the beginning of the poem "Jabberwocky" from *Through the Looking-Glass* by Lewis Carroll.)

'Twas brillig, and the slithy toves
Did gyre and gimble in the wabe.

If you pay close attention to what you are doing, you will probably find that you not only "hear" the words, but you also say them to

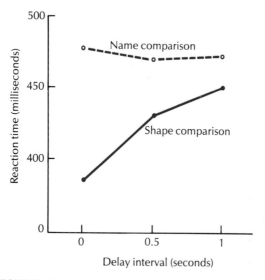

FIGURE 7.6

Reaction time as a function of delay interval in the name-comparison and shape-comparison tasks. (From Posner, M.I., Boies, S.J., Eichelman, W.H., and Taylor, R.L. *Journal of Experimental Psychology*, 1969, 79(1, Pt. 2.)

yourself. In fact, you may even make small movements of your tongue and lips. Studies have shown that actual movements are not necessary for rehearsal; people can learn to keep their tongues and lips absolutely still while retaining verbal information in short-term memory (Garrity, 1977). But even though no actual movement may occur, it is still likely that activity occurs in the neural circuits that normally control speech. When we close our eyes and imagine seeing something, the mental image is undoubtedly caused by the activity of neurons in the visual association cortex. Similarly, when we imagine saying something, the "voice in our head" is probably controlled by activity of neurons in the motor association cortex.

When we rehearse words silently to ourselves, we "hear" them with our auditory association cortex. Thus, the behavior of subvocal articulation probably involves passing information back and forth between neurons in the auditory association cortex and those that control speech movements in the motor association cortex. As we saw earlier, conduction aphasia is a deficit in auditory short-term memory that appears to be caused by a disconnection between regions of the brain involved in the comprehension and production of speech; perhaps the deficit occurs because the disconnection impairs the patient's ability to engage in subvocal articulation.

A phenomenon called the **suffix effect** provides evidence that the representation of verbal material in short-term memory may involve the systems used in subvocal articulation (Horton and Mills, 1984). When subjects hear a list of items that are to be repeated immediately (that is, stored in short-term memory and recalled from it), their performance is poorer when the experimenter signals the end of the list verbally—for example, by saying the word *end*. (The "suffix" is this additional word at the end of the list.) The capacity of short-term memory is limited, and it appears that having to store the word *end* takes up some of the space that is being used to store the list of words. The effect does not occur when a simple tone is used to mark the end of the list, so the interference is caused by information concerning words, not simply by acoustic input.

Studies with nonauditory forms of verbal input such as lip reading and sign language suggest that subvocal articulation plays a role

Verbal rehearsal is a common method actors use to learn their lines.

in the suffix effect. For example, Campbell and Dodd (1980) had subjects watch a videotape recording of an experimenter presenting a list of words (numerical digits from one to nine). The sound track was replaced by noise, so that the subjects had to read the experimenter's lips to perceive the words. In the experimental condition, the experimenter signaled the end of the list by saying *ten*, which the subjects did hear. In the control condition, no suffix was presented. Obviously, because the subjects did not hear the words in the list, there was no direct auditory input into short-term memory. Nevertheless, an auditory suffix (the word *ten*) interfered with their ability to remember the words in the list. Thus, the lip-read words and the word *ten* must have been represented in short-term memory in similar ways. Perhaps the words were all represented at least partially by subvocal speech: the subjects remembered the words they saw the experimenter mouthing by imagining themselves saying the words. When the subjects heard the experimenter say the word *ten*, they also did so themselves, subvocally. This representation took up some of the space available for storing the list of words, so fewer could be recalled.

- What do we know about how information is exchanged between sensory systems in short-term memory?
- What is the role of subvocal speech in verbal short-term memory?

Failure of Short-Term Memory: Decay or Interference?

The essence of short-term memory is its transience (hence its name). At present, good evidence suggests that new information can displace older information that is currently stored in short-term memory, and that previously stored information that has not been displaced can cause confusion. Less compelling evidence suggests that information simply decays from short-term memory if it is not rehearsed.

Decay

In an attempt to determine whether information stored in short-term memory would decay if it were not actively rehearsed, Peterson and Peterson (1959) presented subjects with a set of three consonants, such as h-r-f, and then had them engage in a verbal task that was designed to prevent rehearsal. The task consisted in counting backward by threes. For example, after presenting the three consonants, the experimenter might say "417." The subject would then say, "414, 411, 408, 405," and so on. After a delay, the experimenters stopped the subjects and asked them to recall the letters. Figure 7.7 shows the results: the proportion of letters that were retained fell steadily over the eighteen-second interval. The researchers concluded

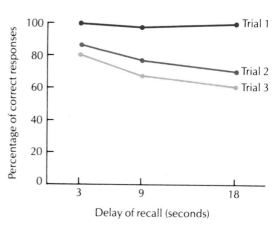

FIGURE 7.8

Percentage of items correctly recalled after the first presentation of the list. (From Keppel, G., and Underwood, B.J. *Journal of Verbal Learning and Verbal Behavior*, 1962, *1*, 153–161.

that short-term memory for the letters simply decayed over time if the material was not rehearsed. However, as we will see, others have disputed this interpretation.

Proactive Inhibition

Previously learned information can affect short-term memory. For example, suppose you are asked to read lists containing the words *muskrat*, *beaver*, *weasel*, *ermine*, *rabbit*, and *opossum*. Soon afterward you are given a list with the words *mink*, *otter*, and *badger* and are then asked to count backward by threes from 578. After thirty seconds you are asked to recall the most recent words. You might mistakenly say one of the words from the earlier lists. This effect is called **proactive inhibition;** previously learned information acts *forward in time* (or *proacts*), causing confusion when we attempt to learn more information later. As we will see, the effect is especially strong when the new information is similar to what we just learned.

Keppel and Underwood (1962) suggested that proactive inhibition was an important factor in the study by Peterson and Peterson, which appeared at first to demonstrate that information in short-term memory simply decayed. Having noted that the Petersons administered two practice trials before their test, Keppel and Underwood followed their procedure but kept track of what happened in the first two trials. As Figure 7.8 shows, the first

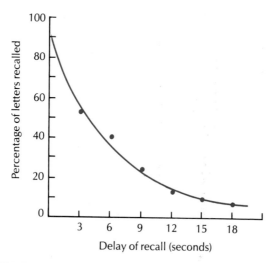

FIGURE 7.7

Percentage of letters recalled after various delays. (From Peterson, L.R., and Peterson, M.J. *Journal of Experimental Psychology*, 1959, *58*, 193–198.)

two trials did have an effect on those that followed: There was no evidence of forgetting on the first trial, some on the second, and even more on the third. Of course, we cannot conclude that decay *never* occurs, but given that performance did not decline until the second trial, the effect of proactive inhibition seems to be more important.

Interference

What causes proactive inhibition? Experiments suggest that the most important cause is interference with the process of *retrieval*. Wickens (1972), like Keppel and Underwood, found that subjects became poorer and poorer at retaining information in short-term memory on successive trials. However, when the category of information was changed, the subjects suddenly performed as well as they had done on the first list. For example, the subjects became poorer and poorer at remembering lists of numbers, but when the experimenter switched to letters of the alphabet, their performance showed a sudden improvement. This phenomenon was called *release from proactive inhibition*. (See Figure 7.9.)

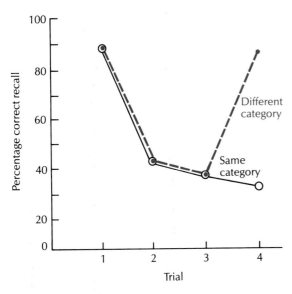

FIGURE 7.9

Release from proactive inhibition. On trial 4, one group of subjects is presented with a list of stimuli from a different category. (From Klatzky, R.L. *Human Memory*, 2nd ed. San Francisco: W.H. Freeman, 1980, after Wickens, 1972.)

Gardner, Craik, and Birtwistle (1972) repeated Wickens's experiment but made a very subtle shift in the nature of the information presented to the subjects. On the first three trials the experimenters presented names of garden flowers such as *rose*, *tulip*, and *carnation*. On the fourth trial they switched to names of wildflowers such as *dandelion* and *daisy*. Control subjects were not told about the switch, nor did they appear to notice it; they showed no release from proactive inhibition. In contrast, subjects who were told about the switch did show release from proactive inhibition, just like Wickens's subjects. The important finding was that release from inhibition occurred whether the subjects were told about the switch beforehand or *after the fourth list had been presented*. This fact means that the major cause of proactive inhibition must be interference with retrieval of information from short-term memory, not with its storage. Telling subjects about a subtle shift in category *after* they have heard the words cannot possibly affect the way the words are stored in short-term memory: they have already been stored. However, it can affect the way the person attempts to retrieve them.

Displacement

Besides proactive inhibition and decay, displacement can also interfere with the retention of information in short-term memory. If we try to cram many pieces of new information in short-term memory, some of the old information gets pushed out. Numerous studies have shown that new information can displace existing information in short-term memory. In fact, we will encounter some of the evidence in the discussion of the serial-position curve, presented in the next section.

Transfer of Information from Short-Term Memory to Long-Term Memory

The Consolidation Hypothesis. An influential theory of memory called *consolidation theory* asserts that short-term memories are retained by short-lived neural activity, whereas long-term memories require structural changes in circuits of neurons. The transfer of information from short-term memory to long-term memory is called **consolidation**, or "making solid." As you will learn later, many variables affect the ease with which we learn new information. Let us consider here some of the classic evidence for the consolidation process.

The Serial-Position Curve

If people are given a list of words to memorize, they tend to remember the first few words and the last few words the best, as Figure 7.10 illustrates. These **serial-position curves** represent the mean percentage of items that subjects remembered from each of the locations in the list. The lists varied in length from ten to forty words. As you can see, the curves are all trough shaped; the subjects were most likely to remember the words from the beginning and end of the lists.

Delay of Reporting and the Recency Effect.

The high probability of recalling the last few words in a list is known as the **recency effect.** Most investigators believe this effect occurs for the following reason: Because short-term memory has a limited capacity, it can store only a few independent items at any one time. Once short-term memory is full, the entry of new information displaces the information that is already there. Therefore, short-term memory contains only the most recently perceived information.

Suppose you were unable to write down the last word or two right away because a delay was imposed after the last word was presented to you. During this delay you would be given a verbal task to prevent you from rehearsing the words. Glanzer and Cunitz (1966) did just this.

They presented a list of fifteen words to two groups of subjects. They asked one group to recall the words right away; the other group was required to wait for thirty seconds before attempting to recall them. During the delay interval the subjects counted aloud.

Figure 7.11 shows the results. The black curve represents the recall of subjects who started without delay. The colored curve represents the performance of subjects who were required to count aloud for thirty seconds before beginning their recall. The recency effect was eliminated; this group did not remember the last few words better than the earlier ones.

These data are consistent with the conclusions that short-term memory can store only a few items, that the most recent items are the easiest to retrieve, and that new information displaces older information.

Opportunity for Rehearsal and the Primacy Effect.

The fact that the first few items of a list are easier to remember than those in the middle is known as the **primacy effect** (*primacy* means "the state of being first"). The explanation is simple, if we assume that rehearsal is necessary to store information in long-term memory. The more time spent rehearsing a particular item, the more likely it becomes that the information will enter (become consolidated into) long-term memory.

It is easy to rehearse the first few words that are presented, but as we hear more and more words, it eventually becomes impossible for us to review them all. Thus, it seems likely that the first few items receive more rehearsal. Rundus and Atkinson (1970) asked subjects to

FIGURE 7.10

A series of serial-position curves. (From Murdock, B.B. *Journal of Experimental Psychology,* 1962, 64, 482–488.)

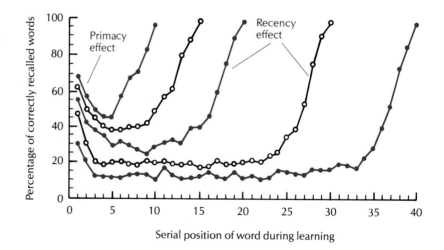

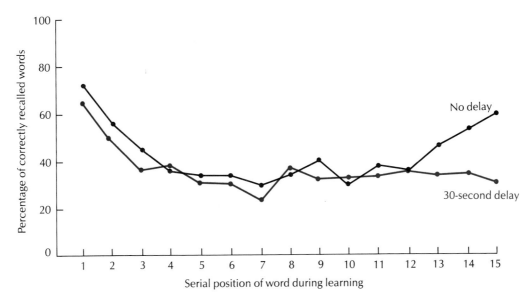

FIGURE 7.11

Serial-position curves obtained after no delay (black curve) and after a delay of thirty seconds (colored curve). Note the lack of the recency effect in the colored curve. (From Glanzer, M., and Cunitz, A.R. *Journal of Verbal Learning and Verbal Behavior,* 1966, 5, 351–360.)

rehearse out loud and made tape recordings of their practice. They found that subjects did indeed rehearse the words at the beginning of the list more often than the later ones.

Amnesia: Head Injury and Consolidation

From the earliest times, people have observed that a blow to the head can affect memory. Let us consider an imaginary case.

Fred, a baseball player, is standing on first base. The pitcher begins his windup, and Fred takes a few steps toward second base. The pitch is wild, and the catcher loses his balance while reaching for it. Taking advantage of the momentary confusion, Fred runs for second base. The catcher sees him running, jumps to his feet, and throws the ball to second base just as Fred arrives there. Fred's foot touches the base in time, but his head comes between the ball, which has been thrown a bit high, and the second baseman's glove. The ball hits Fred just above the ear, and he crumples to the ground. He regains consciousness in the dugout, sees his teammates gathered around him, and sits up slowly. "What happened to me?" he asks. He sits for a while, dazed, then shakes his head tentatively and decides that he will be all right. "I'm OK. I'll go back on base." He leaves the dugout and

heads for first base. "Hey!" one of his teammates yells. "You were on second—you stole second base." Fred looks at him incredulously but notes that the other teammates are nodding. It must be true. He walks to second base, puzzled.

In many similar incidents, people have been hit on the head and have forgotten what happened immediately before the injury. A blow to the head makes the brain bump against the inside of the skull, and this movement apparently disrupts its normal functioning. The blow disrupts short-term memory but not long-term memory. A lack of memory for events that occurred just before an injury is called **retrograde amnesia.** (*Retro-* means *backward:* in this case, backward in time.) Fred, the baseball player, had stood on first base long enough to form a long-term memory for having been there. He saw the wild pitch, ran to second base, and got hit on the head. His memory of the run to second base was in short-term storage and was destroyed when the normal functioning of his brain was temporarily disrupted.

I must note that my example is an uncomplicated one, chosen to illustrate some important principles. Actually, head injury often disrupts people's memories for a period of time afterward, and if the injury is severe enough, the retrograde amnesia can extend back for a period of days or even weeks. Obviously, the loss of memories in such a case involves more than short-term memories. Why recent long-term memories are more vulnerable to injury than older long-term memories is a mystery.

From events such as my simple story we can draw two tentative conclusions. Because only recently perceived information is disrupted by a minor head injury, (1) short-term memory and long-term memory must be physiologically different, and (2) the transfer of information from short-term memory to long-term memory must take time. Information stored in fragile short-term memory is eventually consolidated into more stable long-term memory.

As soon as electroshock treatment came into therapeutic use, hospital personnel noticed that it appeared to produce amnesia for recent events. Zubin and Barrera (1941) confirmed that people who had received electroshock treatments could not remember afterward what had happened just before the electrical current was applied. Electroshock treatment, like head injury, appears to prevent consolidation. Probably, the storm of neural activity disrupts short-term memory and thus prevents the transfer of information to long-term memory. A single electroshock treatment does not damage long-term memory, but repeated treatment can cause permanent harm. Patients who have received hundreds of electroshock treatments have suffered long-term memory loss and become unable to learn anything new.

Because a single electroshock treatment disrupts short-term memory but not long-term memory, we can conclude that the brain stores old and new memories in different ways. The most likely explanation (proposed by Hebb, 1949) is that short-term memories are held by means of neural activity; that is, the information is encoded as a particular pattern of neural firing. Rehearsal is a behavior that permits us to prolong this neural activity. If something disrupts the pattern before consolidation has taken place, the information is lost. An electroshock treatment can produce the disruption by causing neurons to fire wildly, and a mild head injury can temporarily depress the ability of neurons to respond normally.

The physiological evidence suggests that long-term memory involves some physical change in the neural structure of the brain that is not disrupted by electroshock treatment or by mild head injury. That is, there seems to be some sort of "wiring change" that encodes the information. For example, certain synapses between neurons may change in size, or new synaptic connections may develop. The next section discusses the behavioral and physiological characteristics of long-term memory in more detail.

■ What processes have been suggested as reasons for failure of short-term memory?
■ What is the consolidation hypothesis, and how is it supported by the recency effect and the primacy effect?
■ How do head injury and electroshock treatment affect long-term and short-term memory?

LONG-TERM MEMORY

Like short-term memory, long-term memory retains information that is encoded in terms of sensory characteristics, but it also retains information that is encoded in terms of links with information that was learned earlier (that is, *meaning*). As we saw in the section on short-term memory, memory involves intermodal interactions. That is, when we retrieve a memory of an object, we can simultaneously recall what it looks like, sounds like, and feels like. Even though physiological evidence indicates that the memories of these properties are stored in different locations in the brain, they are tied together, undoubtedly by neural connections. Thus, any form of sensory input can cause the retrieval of all modes of storage. The sight of a kitten recalls its furry softness; the sound of a distant whistle evokes an image of a train.

Depth of Processing

One of the most influential models of memory was presented by Craik and Lockhart (1972). They conceived of memory as a by-product of perceptual analysis. A **central processor,** analogous to the central processing unit of a computer, can analyze sensory information on several different levels. Because the central processor has a limited capacity, it cannot deal with all aspects of a stimulus. A person can control the level of analysis by paying attention to different features of the stimulus. If the person focuses on the superficial sensory characteristics of a stimulus, then these features will be stored in memory. If the person focuses on the meaning of a stimulus and the ways in which it relates to other things the person already knows, then these features will be stored in memory. For example, consider this word:

tree

You can see that the word is written in black type, that the letters are lowercase, that the bottom of the stem of the letter *t* curves upward to the right, and so on. Craik and Lockhart referred to these characteristics as surface features, and to their analysis as **shallow processing.** In contrast, consider what the word *tree* means. You can think about how trees differ from other plants, what kinds and varieties of trees you have seen, what kinds of foods and

In some cases, visual images can trigger memories more easily than reading about the same event.

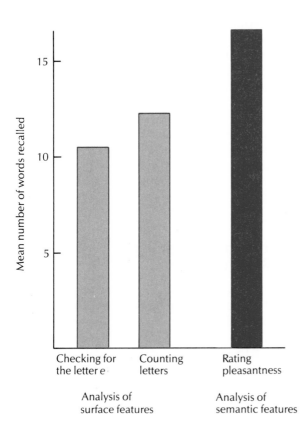

FIGURE 7.12

Mean number of words recalled after performing tasks that required shallow or deep processing. (Based on Craik, F.I.M., and Lockhart, R.S. *Journal of Verbal Learning and Verbal Behavior*, 1972, 11, 671–684.)

what kinds of wood they provide, and so on. These features are called *semantic features,* and their analysis is called **deep processing.** In this context, *semantic* refers to a word's meaning. In general, according to Craik and Lockhart, deep processing leads to better retention than surface processing does.

Among the evidence cited by Craik and Lockhart to support their model were the results from a study by Hyde and Jenkins (1969). These investigators asked subjects to analyze lists of words. Some subjects were asked to analyze surface features—to count the letters in each word or to see whether the word contained the letter *e*. Other subjects were asked to analyze deeper features—to think about the word and decide how pleasant or unpleasant they found it to be. Even though the subjects knew that they would be tested later to see how many words they could recall, those who engaged in a deeper level of processing remembered more words. (See Figure 7.12.)

An interesting experiment by Craik and Tulving (1975) demonstrates the powerful effects of deep processing on learning and remembering. They gave subjects a set of cards, each containing a printed sentence with a missing word, denoted by a blank line, such as "The _____ is torn." After reading the sentence, the subjects

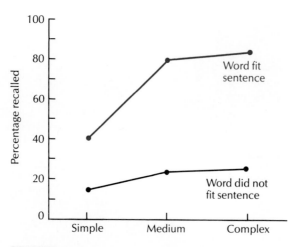

FIGURE 7.13

Percentage of words recalled as a function of the complexity of the sentence in which they were embedded. (From Craik, F.I.M., and Tulving, E. *Journal of Experimental Psychology: General,* 1975, 104, 268–294.)

looked at a word flashed on a screen, then pressed a button as quickly as possible to signify whether the word fit the sentence. In this example, *dress* would fit, but *table* would not.

The sentences varied in complexity. Some were very simple, such as

She cooked the _____.

The _____ is torn.

Others were complex, such as

The great bird swooped down and carried off the struggling _____.

The old man hobbled across the room and picked up the valuable _____.

The sentences were written so that the same word could be used for either a simple or a complex sentence: "She cooked the <u>chicken</u>" or "The great bird swooped down and carried off the struggling <u>chicken</u>." All subjects who participated saw a given word once, in either a simple or a complex sentence.

No mention was made of a memory test, so there was no reason for the subjects to try to remember the words. However, after responding to the sentences, they were presented with them again and were asked to recall the words they had used. Figure 7.13 shows that subjects

were twice as likely to remember a word if it had previously fit into a sentence of medium or high complexity than if it had fit into a simple one. If a word did not fit the sentence at all, it was unlikely to be remembered, and complexity had no effect.

These results suggest that a memory is more effectively established if the item is presented in a rich context—one that is likely to make us think about the item and imagine an action taking place. Consider the different images conjured up by the two sentences that follow (also from Craik and Tulving, 1975).

He dropped the <u>watch</u>.

The old man hobbled across the room and picked up the valuable <u>watch</u>.

The second sentence provides much more information. The word *watch* is remembered in the vivid context of a hobbling old man, and the word *valuable* suggests that the watch is interesting. Perhaps, because the man is old, the watch is too: it might be a large gold pocket watch, attached to a gold chain. The image that is evoked by the more complex sentence provides the material for a more complex memory. This complexity makes the memory more distinctive, and thus helps us pick it out from all the other memories we have. When the incomplete sentence is presented again, it easily evokes a memory of the image of the old man, and of the watch.

Processing of Distinctions or Relationships

Although the concept of depth of processing has been useful in guiding research efforts to understand how we learn and remember, other variables are also important. Einstein and Hunt (1980) have noted that the variables investigated by studies of learning take two general forms: relational processing and item-specific processing. **Relational processing** involves analyzing the ways in which individual items on a list to be learned are related to each other, or to other information that has already been learned. **Item-specific processing** involves analyzing the ways in which individual items are unique, or different from the other items. The

TABLE 7.1

Types of sorting tasks employed by Einstein and Hunt (1980)

Type of Task	Depth of Processing	
	Shallow	Deep
Relational	First letter of word (l, c, b, s, m, or t)	Semantic category (animals, fruits, weather phenomena, occupations, metals, or kitchen utensils)
Individual item	Rating of ease with which word could be rhymed	Rating of pleasantness or unpleasantness of word

results of both of these types of processing can help people learn and remember.

Einstein and Hunt demonstrated that both relational processing and item-specific processing can be carried out on a shallow or deep level. They gave subjects a list of words, each printed on a card, and had them engage in tasks that required shallow or deep processing of either relations or item-specific distinctiveness. The subjects either rated characteristics of the words or placed the cards in piles according to the particular sorting task. (See Table 7.1.)

After reading the cards and performing the tasks, the subjects were asked to recall as many words as they could that they had seen on the cards. (The memory test was a surprise; the subjects had been told only that the experiment was designed to investigate judgments of word characteristics.) In both instances, deep processing led to superior performance; subjects who had made pleasantness ratings performed better than those who had made rhyme ratings, and subjects who had sorted by semantic category performed better than those who had sorted by first letter. The relational and item-specific processing appeared to facilitate remembering by different means; subjects who performed both a deep relational task and a deep item-specific task on the same set of words performed the best of all.

Relational processing can take several forms; categorizing words by their meaning is just one of them. All forms of relational processing rely

on the fact that the learner already knows something about the information that is to be learned: for example, to categorize groups of words, the learner must already know their meanings. The more a person knows about a particular topic, the better he or she will be able to remember information related to that topic. For example, Chiesi, Spilich, and Voss (1979) tested subjects with different levels of knowledge of baseball. They found that experts could remember a brief sequence of events that had occurred in a baseball game much better than nonexperts could, presumably because the experts could perform efficient relational processing of the new information.

A person who is familiar with the strategies used in tennis will be more likely to remember the events that occur during a match.

Another form of relational processing involves sequences of events with cause-and-effect relations. People can remember more information later when the items presented fit together and form a coherent story. Consider the following set of sentences (from deVilliers, 1974):

> A store contained a row of wooden cages. A man bought a dog. A child wanted an animal. A father drove to his house. . . . A boy was delighted with a gift.

DeVilliers presented these sentences to one group of subjects and presented the following set to another group:

> The store contained a row of wooden cages. The man bought a dog. The child wanted the animal. The father drove to his house. . . . The boy was delighted with the gift.

When tested later, the subjects who had read the second set remembered more of the information. The second set of sentences is identical to the first, except that the definite article *(the)* replaces indefinite articles *(a, an)*. Both sets of sentences contain the same amount of information, yet the use of the definite article suggests that the statements are connected. The use of the word *the* implies that the noun to which it refers is familiar; it is something that the reader or listener already knows something about. Therefore, people encountering the second set of sentences tended to perceive them as connected parts of a story and thus remembered them better.

In a related experiment, Stein and Bransford (1979) presented words in sentences that did or did not convey causal relations. For example, they presented the word *fat* in the following two sentences:

> The fat man read the sign.

> The fat man read the sign warning of thin ice.

When subjects encountered the word *fat* in the second sentence, they were more likely to remember it later, especially if the experimenters gave them a clue, such as "Why might the man be doing this?" Presumably, the clue increased the likelihood that the subjects would realize that a person's weight is an important consideration when venturing on thin ice. The vivid image of a fat man reading the sign (presumably while standing on a frozen body of water) was easily recalled later, along with the word *fat*. As you can see, these results are similar to those of Craik and Tulving ("The old man hobbled . . .").

- According to the processing model of memory, how do we use shallow and deep processing?
- In what ways do relational and item-specific processing help us learn?

Episodic and Semantic Long-Term Memory

Long-term memory not only contains sensory information about having perceived particular stimuli; it also transforms information, organizing it in terms of meaning. A study by Sachs (1967) showed that as a memory gets older, sensory information becomes somewhat less important than meaning. She had subjects read a

---

Some photos bring back vivid memories of people and events, which are stored in long-term episodic memory.

passage of prose. At varying intervals after reading a particular sentence in the passage (the *test sentence*), Sachs interrupted the subjects and presented them with another sentence (the *comparison sentence*) and asked them whether it had appeared in the passage. The comparison sentence was sometimes the same as the test sentence and sometimes different. Differences might involve meaning or only word order. For example:

> He sent a letter about it to Galileo, the great Italian scientist.
>
> (test sentence)
>
> Galileo, the great Italian scientist, sent him a letter about it.
>
> (different meaning)
>
> He sent Galileo, the great Italian scientist, a letter about it.
>
> (same meaning, different word order)

The results, shown in Figure 7.14, reveal that the subjects accurately recognized changes when there was no delay between the test sentence and the comparison sentence. However, when a delay was introduced, they had difficulty remembering the specific word order of the original sentence but made very few errors in meaning, even with a 160-syllable delay. Thus, information about the *form* of a sentence disappears faster than information about its *meaning* as the sentence enters long-term memory. (You encountered this distinction between form and meaning in the discussion of conduction aphasia; people with this disorder can paraphrase sentences they hear but cannot repeat the exact words.)

This distinction between information about specific items (such as word order) and more general information about meaning has led to the suggestion that there are two kinds of long-term memory: episodic memory and semantic memory (Tulving, 1972). **Episodic memory** consists of memory about specific things we have done, seen, heard, felt, tasted, and so on. **Semantic memory** consists of conceptual information, such as our knowledge that the sun is a star and that humans are mammals. We can remember when we formed episodic memories. That is their very nature; they are memories of episodes, with information about specific per-

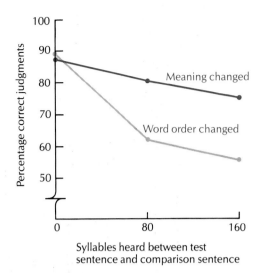

FIGURE 7.14

Percentage of correct judgments as a function of the delay between the test sentence and the comparison sentence. (Based on data of Sachs, J.S. *Perception and Psychophysics*, 1967, 2, 437–442.)

ceptions along with information that places them in a context of time. In contrast, most of us have probably forgotten when we learned that the sun is a star. Although we have developed semantic memories on specific occasions —someone told us that the sun is a star, or we read this fact in a book—we have come across this information so many times that we have forgotten when we first learned it.

When I come to work, I park my car in the lot adjacent to the building. When I leave the building each evening I have to remember where I parked my car that day. Because I always park in the same lot, my semantic memory contains information about which lot to enter. However, because I park in a different space each day, I must use information in episodic memory to find my car again.

Semantic memory can contain more than a blurring together of a series of similar episodic memories; it can also contain products of thinking about what we have already learned. Sometimes we think about things that we already know (we retrieve information from long-term memory and put it in working memory). We realize that some facts are related and come to some conclusions. These conclusions are stored in long-term memory; they are something new that we know. If we remember the occasions when we came to these conclusions,

Most American children have stored the Pledge of Allegiance in long-term memory.

the memory will be episodic. More likely, we will forget these details and develop a new semantic memory. For example, in writing this book I have read articles and books by many other people and have taken notes to help me remember what I read. Later I look at the notes and think about what I have learned. Sometimes I realize that several different experiments are related; I can infer a common principle from them. Forming such a conclusion causes it to be stored in my long-term semantic memory, from which it can later be retrieved when I write about that particular topic.

Physiological Evidence for Episodic and Semantic Memory

Evidence obtained from both humans and laboratory animals suggests that the distinction between episodic and semantic memory is an important one, and that they involve some different brain mechanisms.

Human Memory and Anterograde Amnesia. Damage to particular parts of the brain can permanently impair people's ability to form new long-term memories. The brain damage can be caused by the effects of long-term alcoholism, severe malnutrition, stroke, head trauma, or surgery. When caused by severe malnutrition

or chronic alcoholism, the disorder is called **Korsakoff's syndrome,** after the Russian physician Sergei Korsakoff, who first reported it in the medical literature.

Anterograde amnesia refers to a memory loss for events that occur after a person sustains this type of brain damage. In general, the memory of these people for events that occurred prior to the damage still remains. They can talk about things that happened before the onset of their amnesia, but they cannot remember what happened since. They never learn the names of people they subsequently meet, even if they see them daily for years. On one occasion I met a patient with Korsakoff's syndrome who had been in an institution for eleven years. When I asked how long he had been there, he said, "Oh, about a week."

Investigators have found that people with anterograde amnesia can learn to solve puzzles, perform visual discriminations in a human version of an operant chamber (with pennies as reinforcers), and make skilled movements that require hand-eye coordination. Obviously, their brains are still capable of undergoing the kinds of changes that constitute long-term memory. But in all of these cases, the people do not remember having performed the tasks previously. For example, they may learn the task on one occasion. The next day, the experimenter brings them to the experimental apparatus and asks if they have ever seen it before. The subjects say no, they have not. But then they go on to perform the task well, clearly demonstrating the existence of long-term memory.

Many investigators have suggested that the distinction between what people with anterograde amnesia can and cannot learn is similar to the distinction between semantic and episodic memory. Remembering that you learned to open a particular latch and describing how to open it are examples of episodic memory, because learning the task was an episode in your life. In contrast, *being able to operate the latch* is quite different. This ability is analogous to semantic memory, because it does not require knowledge of a particular occasion during which the knowledge was acquired. Perhaps, then, the brain damage that causes anterograde amnesia disrupts people's ability to form episodic memories, but not their ability to form semantic memories.

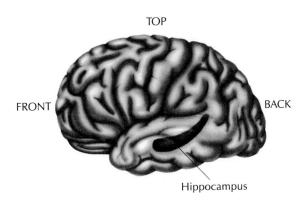

TOP

FRONT   BACK

Hippocampus

FIGURE 7.15

The human hippocampus.

A study by Johnson, Kim, and Risse (1985) supports this suggestion. Often, even normal people grow to like or dislike things—foods, types of music, other people—without being able to say why this is so. For example, a social psychologist (Zajonc, 1968) discovered that simply being exposed to a particular stimulus tends to make us like it, *even when we cannot remember having perceived it before.* Johnson and her colleagues found that when they repeatedly played unfamiliar melodies from Korean songs to amnesic patients, the patients later said that they liked those particular melodies better than others, even though they did not recognize them. The experimenters also presented photographs of two men along with stories of their lives: one man was dishonest, mean, and vicious, and the other was nice enough to invite home to dinner. Twenty days later, the amnesic patients said they liked the picture of the "nice" man better than the "nasty" one, even though they did not remember seeing either of them before.

What parts of the brain are involved in anterograde amnesia? One part seems to be the **hippocampus,** a structure located deep within the temporal lobe, which forms part of the limbic system, long suspected to be involved in emotion. When it is sliced, the hippocampus resembles the curled tail of a sea horse—hence the name *hippocampus,* which means "sea horse." (See Figure 7.15.) Other parts of the brain are involved as well. For example, when severe malnutrition or chronic alcoholism causes Korsakoff's syndrome, the damage does not involve the hippocampus, but instead includes parts of the thalamus and hypothalamus. Investigators dispute whether such damage disrupts a circuit that includes the hippocampus as one of its components, or whether the two types of damage cause anterograde amnesia by disrupting different functions (Squire, 1982). Only further research will resolve this dispute.

Episodic and Semantic Memory in Animals. When researchers study the memory functions of laboratory animals, they usually test what we call semantic memory, because the animals are not required to remember a particular episode. As you would expect, the brain damage that causes anterograde amnesia in humans does not seriously disrupt the animals' performance on such tasks, since this damage does not disrupt semantic memory in humans. However, researchers have devised tasks for animals that involve functions similar to those required for episodic memory. Results of such studies have advanced understanding of the anatomical basis of memory.

Olton and Samuelson (1976) devised a task that requires an animal to remember a recent episode. They constructed a maze consisting of a central octagonal platform with eight arms radiating away from it. They placed a small piece of food at the end of each arm and then put a hungry rat on the central platform. The animals began exploring the arms of the maze, finding and eating the food. As soon as all eight pieces of food were eaten, the experimenters removed the rat and ended the trial. (See Figure 7.16.) After twenty trials, most animals foraged

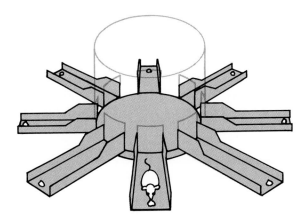

FIGURE 7.16

The eight-arm radial maze used by Olton and his colleagues.

for the food efficiently, entering each arm only once. Even when a series of doors was used to prevent the animals from visiting the arms in a particular order (say, simply working their way clockwise around the maze), the animals avoided retracing their steps (Olton, Collison, and Werz, 1977). Clearly, this performance required them to retain a particular episode in memory—visiting a particular arm of the maze.

Olton and Samuelson found that surgical destruction of the hippocampus impaired the rats' performance. These rats visited the arms in an aimless fashion, often entering arms that they had already visited during the trial. Thus, damage to the hippocampus appears to disrupt the formation of episodic memory in animals, just as it does in humans. (Olton prefers the terms *working memory* and *reference memory*, but his terms are roughly synonymous with those proposed by Tulving.)

In a later experiment, Olton and Papas (1979) demonstrated a clear dissociation in the effects of damage to the hippocampus on episodic as opposed to semantic memory. They trained rats in a seventeen-arm radial maze. Before each trial, they placed food in eight of the arms; the other nine *never* received food. As before, rats with brain damage performed poorly, often entering an arm whose food they had just eaten. However, they soon learned to avoid entering the arms that never held food. Although they could not remember episodes (entering a particular arm on a particular trial), they could learn the general rule that some arms never contained food. The latter form of learning appears to qualify as semantic memory.

The foregoing studies with humans and laboratory animals suggest that the distinction between episodic memory and semantic memory identifies some important characteristics of the process of learning and remembering. The hippocampus and perhaps other parts of the brain are involved in some way in establishing memories for particular episodes.

- How do episodic and semantic long-term memory differ?
- What characteristics of episodic and semantic memory are revealed by subjects with anterograde amnesia?

Reconstruction: Memory as a Creative Process

Much of what we recall from long-term memory is not an accurate representation of what actually happened previously; it is a plausible account of what might have happened, or even of what we think *should* have happened. An experiment by Bartlett (1932) called attention to this fact. He had his subjects read a story or essay or look at a picture, then asked them on several later occasions to retell the prose passage or draw the picture. Each time, the subjects "remembered" the original a little differently. If the original story had contained peculiar and unexpected sequences of events, the subjects tended to retell it in a more coherent and sensible fashion, as if their memories had been revised to make the information accord more closely with their own conceptions of reality. Bartlett concluded that people generally remember only a few striking details of an experience, and that during recall they *reconstruct* the missing portions in accordance with their own expectations. (These expectations would, of course, be contained in semantic memory.)

Many studies have confirmed Bartlett's conclusions and have extended his findings to related phenomena. An experiment by Spiro (1977, 1980) illustrates that people will remember even a rather simple story in different ways, according to their own conceptions of reality. Two groups of subjects read a story about an engaged couple, in which the man was opposed to having children. In one version of the story, the woman was upset to learn this, because she wanted to have children. In the other version, the woman also did not want to have children.

After reading the story, the subjects were asked to fill out some forms. While collecting the forms, the experimenter either said nothing more about the story or "casually mentioned" that the story was a true one and added one of two different endings: The couple got married and have been happy ever since, or the couple broke up and never saw each other again.

Two days, three weeks, or six weeks later, the subjects were asked to recall the story they had read. If at least three weeks had elapsed, the subjects who had heard an ending that contradicted the story tended to "remember" information that resolved the conflict. For example, if they had read that the woman was upset to learn that the man did not want children but were later told that the couple was happily married, the subjects were likely to "recall" something that would have resolved the conflict, such as that the couple had decided to adopt a child rather than have one of their own. If subjects had read that the woman also did not want children but were later told that the couple broke up, then they were likely to "remember" that there was a difficulty with one set of parents. In contrast, the subjects who had heard an ending that was consistent with the story they had read did not remember any extra facts; they did not need them to make sense of the story. For example, if they had heard that the couple disagreed about having a child and later broke up, no new "facts" had to be added.

When asking the subjects to recall details from the story, Spiro also asked them to indicate how confident they were about the accuracy of particular details. He found that the subjects were the most confident about details that had actually not occurred but had been added to make more sense of the story. Thus, a person's confidence in the accuracy of a particular memory is not necessarily a good indication of whether the event actually occurred.

Loftus and her colleagues have investigated the variables that affect the recall of details from episodic memory. The research makes it clear that the kinds of questions used to elicit the information can have a major effect on what the subjects remember. For example, Loftus and Zanni (1975) showed people short films of an accident involving several vehicles. Some subjects were asked, "Did you see a broken headlight?" while others were asked, "Did you see the broken headlight?" The particular question biased the subjects' responses: Although the film did not show a broken headlight, twice as many people who heard the article *the* said they remembered seeing one.

Experiments like these indicate that learning new information and recalling it later are not the passive processes that are implied by the terms *storage* and *retrieval*; we do not simply place an item of information in a filing cabinet and pick it up later. We organize and integrate information in terms of what we already know

about life and have come to expect about particular experiences. Thus, when we recall the memory later, it is likely to contain information that was not part of the original experience. At first, this phenomenon may appear to be maladaptive, because it means that eyewitness testimony cannot be regarded as infallible, even when the witness is trying to be truthful. However, it probably reflects the fact that information about an episode can be more efficiently stored by means of a few unique details. The portions of the episode that are common to other experiences, and hence resemble information already stored in semantic memory, need not be retained. If every detail of an experience had to be encoded uniquely in long-term memory, perhaps we would run out of storage space. Unfortunately, this process sometimes leads to instances of faulty remembering.

Memories can be used in creative, constructive ways to derive information that is not stored in a direct fashion. For example, if I ask you whether you know how many windows your house has, you probably will not know the answer. But you can probably imagine each room, count the number of windows in it, and

Our memories are sometimes more similar to familiar stories than to what actually happened. We reconstruct missing portions in accordance with our own expectations.

keep a running total as you take a mental tour of the house. In cases like this, construction can lead to a useful result.

Aids to Memory: Mnemonic Systems

Some things are exceedingly easy to remember. Suppose you are walking down the street and see someone fall from the roof of a building. You will not have to rehearse this information verbally to remember it; you see it so vividly that the scene remains with you always. Similarly, you can probably remember the missing word in this sentence: "The old man hobbled across the room and picked up the valuable _____." But often we must remember information that does not fit in such a tidy package. When the information is hard to learn, we usually employ a special word to identify the process: *memorization*.

When we can imagine information vividly and concretely, and when it fits into the context of what we already know, it is easy to remember later. People have known this fact for millennia and have devised systems for remembering things in order to take advantage of it. All **mnemonic systems** (from the Greek *mnēme*, meaning "memory") make use of information that is already stored in long-term memory to make memorization an easier task.

Mnemonic systems do not simplify information; in fact, they make it more elaborate. *More information is stored, not less.* However, the additional information makes the material easier to recall. Furthermore, mnemonic systems organize new information into a cohesive whole, so that retrieval of part of the information ensures retrieval of the rest of it. (Do you remember a fat man from an earlier example? What was he doing? Where was he standing?) These facts suggest that the ease or difficulty with which we learn new information depends not on *how much* we must learn, but on *how well it fits with what we already know*. The better it fits, the easier it is to retrieve.

Method of Loci

In Greece before the sixth century B.C., few people knew how to write, and those who did had to use cumbersome clay tablets. Consequently, oratory skills and memory for long epic poems

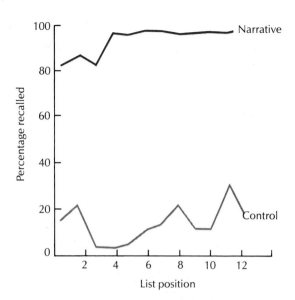

FIGURE 7.17

Percentage of words recalled by control subjects and by subjects who used a narrative strategy. (From Bower, G.H., and Clark, M.C. *Psychonomic Science,* 1969, *13,* 181–182.)

(running for several hours) were highly prized, and some people earned a living by using them. Because people could not carry around several hundred pounds of clay tablets, they had to keep important information in their heads. To do this, the Greeks devised the **method of loci** (*loci* means "places").

To use the method of loci, would-be mnemonists (memory artists) had to memorize the inside of a building. In Greece, they would wander through public buildings, stopping to study and memorize various locations and arranging them in order, usually starting with the door of the building. After memorizing the locations, they could make the tour mentally, just as you could make a mental tour of your house to count the windows. To learn a list of words, they would visualize each word in a particular location in the memorized building and picture the association as vividly as possible. For example, for the word *love* they might imagine an embracing couple leaning against a particular column in a hall of the building. To recall the list, they would imagine each of the locations in sequence, "see" the word, and say it. To store a speech, they would group the words into concepts and place a "note" for each concept at a particular location in the sequence.

Mnemonists could use a single building as a "memory temple" to store many different sequences. Modern psychologists still cannot explain why sequences from different speeches or poems did not become confused with each other.

Narrative Stories

Another useful aid to memory is to organize information into a narrative. Bower and Clark (1969) showed that even inexperienced subjects can use this method. The investigators asked subjects to try to learn twelve lists of ten concrete nouns each. They gave some of the subjects the following advice:

> A good way to learn the list of items is to make up a story relating the items to one another. Specifically, start with the first item and put it in a setting which will allow other items to be added to it. Then, add the other items to the story in the same order as the items appear. Make each story meaningful to yourself. Then, when you are asked to recall the items, you can simply go through your story and pull out the proper items in their correct order.

A typical narrative, described by one of the subjects, was as follows (list words are italicized): "A *lumberjack darted* out of the forest, *skated* around a *hedge* past a *colony* of *ducks*. He tripped on some *furniture*, tearing his *stocking* while hastening to the *pillow* where his *mistress* lay."

Control subjects were merely asked to learn the lists and were given the same amount of time as the "narrative" subjects to study them. Both groups could remember a particular list equally well immediately afterward. However, when all the lists had been learned, recall of all 120 words was far superior in the group that had constructed narrative stories. Figure 7.17 shows the results.

■ What is the role played by reconstruction in recalling information from long-term memory?
■ How do the methods of loci and narrative stories assist us by acting as mnemonic systems?

CHAPTER SUMMARY

1. Memory exists in three forms: sensory, short-term, and long-term. The characteristics of each differ, which suggests that they also differ physiologically.

2. Sensory memory is very brief; it provides temporary storage until the newly perceived information can be stored in short-term memory. Visual sensory memory is referred to as iconic memory; auditory sensory memory is called echoic memory.

3. Short-term memory contains a coded representation of information that has just been perceived, such as the item's name. The capacity for short-term memory is usually seven to nine items of independent information, but by rehearsing the information we can remember it indefinitely (the information becomes part of long-term memory, which has an unlimited number of items of information).

4. Information in short-term memory is encoded (chunked) according to previously learned rules; thus, information in long-term memory determines the nature of the coding.

5. Physiological evidence has shown that each sense modality has its own short-term (working) memory, although the contents are shared by means of interconnections. Complex behaviors such as reading involve intermodal encoding of information.

6. Verbal information especially can be retained indefinitely in short-term memory by means of rehearsal, which probably involves the transfer of information back and forth between auditory short-term memory and brain mechanisms that control speech movements, a phenomenon called subvocal articulation. Conduction aphasia (a disorder that causes a profound deficit in auditory short-term memory) offers evidence that each component of short-term (working) memory involves a different set of neural circuits.

7. Not all information that enters short-term memory subsequently enters long-term memory (is consolidated); some of it is lost by proactive inhibition from previously learned material. Studies suggest that the primary reason is interference with retrieval rather than decay. Other information is displaced by new material before it can be consolidated.

8. Experiments relating to the nature of the serial position curve confirm that short-term memory has a limited capacity and that information there is subject to displacement by new information, whereas long-term memory has unlimited capacity and receives information by means of rehearsal or elaboration of items contained in short-term memory. Data from head injuries and electroshock treatments provide evidence that long-term and short-term memory are physiologically different: short-term memory probably involves neural activity (which can be prolonged by rehearsal) and long-term memory probably involves permanent structural changes in neurons.

9. Long-term memory is a by-product of the perceptual process. The level of processing (performed by a central processor) is controlled by changes in attention. If information is analyzed at a superficial level (shallow processing), then superficial memories will be formed and enter episodic memory. If information is analyzed at a deep level (deep processing), it will enter semantic memory, where it will be connected with other information we already know. Episodic and semantic memory refer to different degrees of specificity in long-term memory. We can remember the time and place we learned an episodic memory but not a semantic memory.

10. The nature of anterograde amnesia also supports the distinction between episodic and semantic memory. People with anterograde amnesia cannot recall events that took place after their brain damage occurred, but they can learn to perform many tasks that do not require verbal rules.

11. The process of reconstruction sometimes introduces new ''facts'' that we perceive as memories and undoubtedly makes more efficient use of the resources we have available for storage of long-term memory. As the effectiveness of mnemonic systems suggests, memory is not limited by complexity. Complex memories are often easier to learn.

KEY TERMS

anterograde amnesia   The inability to learn new information permanently; usually caused by brain damage resulting from chronic alcoholism or head injury. The person typically can remember information that was learned long before the injury and has an adequate short-term memory, but the person cannot form long-term memories.

central processor   A component in the processing model of memory that analyzes sensory information on several different levels.

chunking   The process by which information is simplified by rules and hence can be remembered easily once the rules are learned. For example, the sequence 1 3 5 7 9 11 13 15 is easy to remember if a person knows the rule that describes odd numbers.

conduction aphasia   A disorder, usually caused by damage to the left parietal lobe of the brain, that appears as a profound deficit in auditory short-term memory.

consolidation   The process by which information in short-term memory is stored in long-term memory, presumably in the form of physical changes in neurons in the brain.

deep processing   Level of analysis in memory that focuses on the meaning of two stimuli and the ways in which it relates to other things already known (semantic features); leads to better memory retention.

echoic memory   A form of sensory memory for sounds that have just been perceived.

episodic memory   Memory for specific information, including the time and place in which it was first learned.

hippocampus   A component structure of the limbic system of the brain, located in the temporal lobe; believed to play an important role in learning.

iconic memory   A form of sensory memory that holds a brief visual image of a scene that has just been perceived.

item-specific processing   Thinking about the specific nature of a particular item in a group, as opposed to thinking about relations between the items.

Korsakoff's syndrome An organic brain syndrome that is caused by chronic alcohol abuse or malnutrition and that is characterized by both amnesia for events which have occurred since the brain damage and by inability to learn new information.

long-term memory Relatively permanent memory.

method of loci Mnemonic system that uses various places and locations to organize and retrieve information.

mnemonic system A method by which information can easily be remembered, such as the method of loci.

primacy effect The tendency to remember the early items of a list better than those from the middle of the sequence.

proactive inhibition The tendency for exposure to lists of items to make it difficult to learn subsequent lists of items, especially if the items are related.

recency effect The tendency to remember the later items of a list better than those from the middle sequence.

relational processing Thinking about the relations between items in a group, as opposed to thinking about the specific nature of a particular item.

retrograde amnesia Lack of memory for events that occurred just before a particular trauma, such as chemical or physical injury to the brain.

semantic memory Long-term memory for conceptual information, but not for the time or circumstances of learning it.

sensory memory Very brief memory of a stimulus that has just occurred.

serial position curve Represents the mean percentage of items that subjects remembered from each location on a list; tendency to remember the first and last items from a list.

shallow processing Level of analysis that focuses on superficial sensory characteristics of a stimulus (surface features) in storing a memory.

short-term memory Memory for information that has just been presented; conceptually similar to working memory, which also includes information that has just been retrieved from long-term memory.

subvocal articulation "Talking to oneself" without actually engaging in speech.

suffix effect A phenomenon in short-term memory in which the subject's recall of a list of words is poorer if a verbal end signal is given.

tachistoscope An apparatus (mechanical device) for the brief exposure stimuli, used to study visual recalling iconic memory.

working memory Memory of what has just been perceived and what is currently being thought about; consists of new information and related information that has recently been "retrieved" from long-term memory.

Chapter 8

$$-HC\ell$$

$$C\overset{O}{\underset{}{\parallel}}-O\ CH_2CH_2Br\ +$$

$$Me_3N$$

$$H_2C\overset{O}{\underset{H}{\parallel}}-O\ CH_2CH_2\overset{+}{N}Me_3\quad Br$$

$$RMgX + B$$

$$\overset{O}{\underset{}{\parallel}}$$

$$R-B\diagdown O-B-R$$

$$O-B-R$$

$$-H_2$$

Language

With the exception of sexual behavior (without which our species would not survive), communication is probably the most important of all human social behaviors. Our use of language can be private—we can think to ourselves in words or write diaries that are meant to be seen by no one but ourselves—but language evolved through social contacts among our early ancestors. Verbal behavior, more than any other activity, differentiates our species from that of other animals. Indeed, human civilization could never have developed without language.

The nature of speech production and comprehension has long interested psychologists. The perception of speech requires an extremely rapid, complex analysis of sounds that can vary according to the timbre of a person's voice, and to his or her particular accent. Even the most advanced computer is incapable of such an analysis. How do we comprehend the meaning of speech? As you will see, comprehension involves recognition of the words, analysis of the structure of the sentences, and an understanding of their significance.

Another topic that fascinates psychologists—and anyone else who has watched a child learn to speak—is the nature of language development. How do children manage to learn their first language with such apparent ease, and why does it seem a much harder task for an adult to learn a new language? Does a child's brain possess some special characteristics that are lost later in life, which make it easier for them to learn their native language? Researchers have addressed this question and many others, and although much is yet to be discovered, the past few years have told us much about the acquisition of language abilities.

Although we humans pride ourselves on our unique ability to communicate verbally, research has shown that the ability to communicate is shared with other species. In particular, other primates can be taught to express themselves remarkably well through sign language, and have even been observed teaching the signs to their own infants. Such research will undoubtedly tell us much more about the nature of language, and of the nature of social interactions.

THE FUNCTIONS OF LANGUAGE

Our language provides us with a beautiful medium for thought and expression. We can appreciate fine prose and poetry, enjoy the sound of an actor's voice, converse with a loved one, listen to our children's first words, and think thoughts that could never occur without language. What we know about language so far is a pitifully small part of the entire picture; the quest for an understanding of verbal behavior, the most complex of all our activities, has just begun.

Verbal behavior can take many forms. Here, students at Gallaudet College for the Deaf are saying "I love you" in sign language.

Language As a Set of Rules

Our verbal behavior, both written and oral, is orderly. Linguists would say that our speech follows grammatical rules. For example, English sentences contain noun phrases and verb phrases, and most questions in English are formed by placing the modal auxiliary in front of the verb. But both linguists and psycholinguists acknowledge that people who use language correctly do not consciously learn these rules. (Most people do not know what a modal auxiliary is, even though they can use one properly.) Linguists did not invent the rules of language any more than physicists invented the laws of thermodynamics; they discovered them by studying people's speech and writing. The rules are *descriptions of what people do* when they engage in verbal behavior; they are not *prescriptions for* verbal behavior.

This distinction becomes clearer if we consider another skilled behavior: riding a bicycle. Physicists know how we can balance on a vehicle with two narrow wheels: it involves inertia, the gyroscopic effects of rotating wheels, locating our center of gravity, and other factors, all of which can be incorporated into complicated mathematical equations. But knowing these rules does not really help a person ride a bicycle. A physicist who wants to learn to ride a bicycle must learn the same way that a young child does—by getting on and trying.

Similarly, our verbal behavior must conform to the rules of our language, or we will not be understood by others. However, we do not have to be able to *state* these rules, any more than a bird has to "know" the laws of aerodynamics in order to be able to fly.

Language As a Behavioral Function

Verbal communications accomplish three major functions: they provide information, request information, or request a behavior. Technically, the second and third functions belong to the same category, because a request for information is a request for a particular kind of behavior from the listener; but for our purposes it is worthwhile to maintain a distinction between them, especially because the forms taken by the two kinds of requests are different.

Providing Information

Much of our verbal behavior provides other people with information. If all goes well, the listener learns something and adds new information to memory. But as we saw in Chapter 7, the contents of memory are organized and classified by category; people's classification schemes directly affect the storage and retrieval of information. Therefore, the listener will be able to absorb new information and retrieve it later only if it is stored appropriately. The verbal behavior of the speaker must take account of this fact. For example, a listener will be able to store even complex and detailed new information in short-term memory if the items are organized into a meaningful unit such as a sentence. Compare the difficulty involved in storing the following two sets of fifteen words:

along got the was door crept locked slowly he until passage the he to which

He slowly crept along the passage until he got to the door, which was locked.

By retrieving information that is already contained in long-term memory, the listener recognizes the meaning of the sentence and thus can easily organize the second set of words in short-term memory and subsequently store it in long-term memory.

A speaker who imparts new information helps the listener by placing it in the context of what he or she expects the listener to know already. Suppose Sue says to John:

The man I was telling you about finally died.

From this sentence we can conclude that Sue has previously told John about a particular man ("The man I was telling you about") and that the man's death has been expected ("finally"). The only new information is that the man died. But a simple sentence containing only the new information ("He died.") would not permit John to categorize this information; he would not know where to put it in his memory. "The man I was telling you about" identifies the appropriate category—in this case, a man whom Sue has already mentioned to John.

One of the functions of language is to provide information to other people.

Sometimes a listener fails to identify the category of old information to which the speaker is referring. For example, John may say, "What man?" Sue will then provide more information such as, "You know, the one I was telling you about at the party at Will's house last Saturday."

Because new information must be organized into categories that have already been established in long-term memory, it is essential that the speaker make explicit which is old information and which is new. The communication must be a cooperative endeavor: the speaker uses special behaviors (rules) to specify which information is old and which is new, and the listener must indicate whether he or she recognizes the old information. Clark and Haviland (1977) call the cooperation between speaker and listener the **given-new contract.**

When we say something to another person, unless we are socially inept, we watch for signs that we are being understood—that the listener is identifying old (given) information. Consider the following two exchanges:

> You remember that car I sideswiped? (Listener nods.) Well, it turns out that it belongs to Julie's boss.

> I was telling Charlie that . . . (puzzled look on listener's face) . . . you know, my roommate's brother . . .

Clearly, a speaker must be sensitive to both verbal and nonverbal signs of comprehension and puzzlement. Because writers do not have the benefit of such feedback, they must be particularly careful to identify old information for their readers. If they do not provide adequate cues so that their readers can organize new information in terms of what they already know, the information will not be able to go into the appropriate location in long-term memory.

A speaker uses several methods to identify old (given) and new information for a listener. Two of these methods are use of stress and choice of article.

Use of Stress

Stress, in spoken language, refers to the emphasis placed on a syllable or word. Stress is one of the most important cues that we use to distinguish old from new information. Say the following sentences to yourself, placing stress on the italicized words:

> *Frank* helped the old man.

> Frank helped the *old* man.

> Frank helped the old *man.*

The stress highlights the new information. In terms of the given-new contract, in the first sentence the given (what the listener already knows) is that *someone* helped the old man; the new item is *Frank.* In the second sentence, the given is that Frank helped a man (there were probably several men that the sentence could refer to); the new information is that the man he helped was *old.* In the third sentence, the given is that Frank helped an old person (perhaps an old man and an old woman were present); the new item is *man.*

Choice of Article

Speakers also identify given and old information through the choice of articles: *a, an,* and *the.* Old or given information is usually identified by the definite article *(the),* new information by indefinite articles *(a* or *an).* For example, "I bought *the* car" implies that the listener knows that the speaker was considering buying a particular car. On the other hand, "I bought *a* car" implies that this is a newly mentioned car; thus the listener need not look for a particular car in his or her memory.

Consider the use of indefinite and definite articles in the following passage, as new items of information (a car, an old woman) become old information:

> I just bought *a* car. I am very pleased with it. The salesman told me that *the* car was previously owned by *an* old woman who just drove it to church on Sundays. One thing that puzzled me was that the paint on the steering wheel of *the* car is all worn off even though the odometer says that *the* car was driven only 2000 miles, but the salesman said that *the* old woman had a lot of acid in the sweat from her hands.

Requesting Information

The second major function of speech is to request information; if the verbal behavior is successful, the listener becomes a speaker who provides information.

Wh- Questions

Most requests for information are signaled by a question that begins with a *wh-* word, such as *who, what, when, where, why,* and *which. How* is also considered a *wh-* word, even though it is not spelled that way. A *wh-* question contains an incomplete assertion (a statement of fact), phrased so as to elicit information from the listener. In other words, a *wh-* question is a fill-in-the-blank request to the listener; the *wh-* word represents the blank to be filled. The question "*Where* is the bathroom?" can be rephrased as "The bathroom is *where*?" The listener provides the information that fits the blank.

With a *wh-* question, the speaker tells the listener that he or she knows some old (given) information but needs some new information. The listener must identify the old information, retrieve it from memory, identify what new information is being requested, and supply the missing information. Consider the following questions:

Who carried the box away?

When did the lamp get broken?

How did Ruth manage to convince her?

In the first question, the old information is that *someone* carried the box away; the requested new information is "*Who* is that someone?" and so on.

Yes/No Questions

Often the speaker wants to determine whether a hypothesis is true or false. Suppose you think that Charlotte's birthday is next week, but you are not sure. You ask a friend, "Is Charlotte's birthday next week?" You expect a "Yes" or "No" answer, or perhaps "I don't know."

Most yes/no questions begin with an auxiliary verb: "Does she . . . ," "Will they . . . ," "Has it . . . ," "Are you . . . ," "Should I. . . ." A rise in voice pitch at the end of the sentence provides an additional cue that the sentence is a question. Accordingly, your friend can identify "*Is* Charlotte's birthday next week?" as a yes/no question because of the auxiliary verb *is* at the beginning of the sentence and because you have raised the pitch of your voice at the end of the sentence. He or she responds as if the question were "True or false: Charlotte's birthday is next week." Having determined the assertion that is to be evaluated, your friend must locate the appropriate information, decide whether the assertion matches the information in memory, and say "Yes" or "No."

Requesting a Behavior

Requests for specific behaviors are called **directives.** "Shut the door!" "Take out the garbage," and "Please stop at the store on your way home and buy some milk" all request an action from the listener. So do indirect statements such as "Don't you think it's cold in here?" (meaning

---

We use language to request information from others.

"Close the window"), "Would you mind doing that somewhere else?" (meaning "Go away and do that somewhere else!"), and, "Boy, that looks delicious!" (meaning "Please give me some").

Directives may take a variety of forms, depending largely on who is speaking, who is being spoken to, and the nature of the message. Clearly, requesting a behavior is an important social skill, and knowledge of the appropriate form for the request is essential. If you want to find out what time it is from a well-dressed older stranger, you might say, "Excuse me, could you tell me what time it is?" If you feel timid about approaching the stranger, you might be even more indirect: "I wonder if you'd mind telling me the time." The listener understands these polite forms of address as requests to tell the speaker what time it is, and not as questions about whether he is wearing a watch and is capable of telling time, or whether he would mind consulting his watch. You might approach a casually dressed teenager with a slightly less polite, but also somewhat friendlier and more familiar request, such as "Hi! Do you have the time?" All users of a language understand the protocol for the use of directives. Everyone recognizes that "You have to do this" is an impolite form of address unless the speaker is citing a rule or giving instructions.

Directives take a variety of forms, depending on who is speaking, who is being spoken to, and what behavior is being requested.

- What are the basic functions of spoken and written verbal behavior?
- What are some features that speakers use to distinguish new from old information?
- What are some features of requests for information and behavior?

UNDERSTANDING THE MEANING OF SPEECH

When we speak to someone, we produce a series of sounds in a continuous stream, punctuated by pauses and modulated by stress and changes in pitch. The human auditory system performs a formidably complex task in enabling us to recognize speech sounds. These sounds vary according to the sounds that precede and follow them, the speaker's accent, and the stress placed on the syllables in which they occur. We perceive these units of sound as **phonemes,** which are the elements of speech—the smallest units of sound that contribute to the meaning of a word. For example, the word *pin* consists of three phonemes: /p/ + /i/ + /n/. Thus, the first step in recognizing speech sounds is to identify phonemes. From there we go on to resolve phonemes into larger units of meaning—ultimately as words. These also represent a complex task of recognition.

Although we write sentences as sets of words, with spaces between them, we *say* sentences as a string of sounds, emphasizing some, quickly sliding over others, raising the pitch of our voice on some, lowering it on others. We maintain a regular rhythmic pattern of stress. We pause at appropriate times, but not after each word. Nevertheless, we usually perceive words separately and accurately as basic units of meaning.

Using Language by the Rules

To get a listener to act upon speech, the speaker must follow the "rules" of language, using words with which the listener is familiar and combining them in specific ways. For example, in many languages, word order is an important cue to meaning. "Mary hit John" means something very different from "John hit Mary"; an English speaker combines the words in one way if Mary does the hitting and in another if John does the hitting.

Some people use different rules, in accordance with geographical location or social class. If a person says "I done did it!" we cannot conclude that the speaker is not following the "rules of English grammar," only that he or she is following rules different than the ones that other people may follow. This speaker will never say "I did done it!" or "I do did it!" The rules that he or she follows do not permit these alternatives. One disadvantage in a society in which different groups of people use different linguistic rules is that when communication between these groups is difficult, misunderstandings become more frequent. Another disadvantage is that members of higher socioeconomic groups tend to perceive the speech of people from lower socioeconomic groups as "wrong" and to label the speakers as "inferior."

To understand the meaning of speech, the speaker and listener must follow the same "rules" of language. Some groups of people speak different languages and thus use different linguistic rules.

Syntactical Analysis

We use cues not only from word order but also from suffixes and prefixes (such as *-ing*, *-ed*, *-s*, or *pre-*), modifiers (such as *not*), and auxiliaries (such as *did* or *has*). That is, we respond to the *syntax* of the sentence (*syntax*, like *synthesis*, comes from the Greek *syntassein*, "to put together"). **Syntax** is the science of grammatical construction. The rules that describe how we put words together to form sentences are called **syntactical rules.**

Some commonly used sentences do not require syntactical analysis. For example, we respond to sentences like "Put it down!" "Be quiet!" "What time is it?" or "Wait a minute!" as automatically as to single-word commands like "Stop!" or "Duck!" We have heard these groups of words so often that we pay no attention to the structure of the sentences or to the meaning of the individual words. However, most sentences we encounter each day we have never heard before. For example, most of the sentences in this book are new to you; you have never heard or read them before. But you can understand them. (I hope.) How do we understand the meaning of sentences that we have never encountered before?

Apparently, one of the things we do is analyze the syntactical structure of the sentence; that is, we undo it, or take it apart, and determine what syntactical rules were used to put it together. Once we understand the rules, we can understand the meaning that is intended by the speaker. We are no more conscious of this process than a child is conscious of the laws of physics when he or she learns to ride a bicycle.

Analysis into Constituent Parts. Evidence suggests that listeners analyze sentences piece by piece. Once a constituent part begins, they accumulate the words in short-term memory and hold them there until the constituent ends. Then they analyze the structure of that constituent and encode its meaning more efficiently (perhaps by chunking). **Constituent parts** consist of small groups of words, like phrases, that form grammatical units. Listeners detect the end of one constituent part and the beginning of the next by several means. For example, an adverb or a verb usually marks the end of a noun phrase and the beginning of the verb phrase; when listeners hear "Peter and Ralph *carefully . . . "* they recognize that "Peter and Ralph" constitutes the first phrase, and that "carefully" begins another. They realize that Peter and Ralph did something, and the next constituent will tell them what. Linguists have discovered the rules by which sentences can be analyzed into its constituent parts, and the research of psycholinguists has told us that these parts have psychological reality.

Function Words. Words can be classified according to whether they are function words or content words. **Function words** include determiners, quantifiers, prepositions, and words in similar categories: *a, the, to, in, some, many, and, but, when, since,* and so on. **Content words** include nouns, verbs, and most adjectives and adverbs: *apple, rug, went, caught, heavy, mysterious, thoroughly,* and *sadly.* Content words, therefore, express meaning, and function words express the relations between content words.

Because a function word almost always marks the beginning of a new constituent in a sentence, when we hear a function word we tend to listen for a group of words that will go with it. Consider the following sentence:

She walked *through* the field *that* had been harvested *several* days ago.

The function words *through, that,* and *several* mark the beginnings of constituent phrases.

A study by Fodor and Garrett (1967) provides evidence that we use function words as cues to mark the beginning of a constituent part, indicating that the previous one is over. For example, the following sentences convey the same meaning:

The pen that the author used was new.

The pen the author used was new.

The first sentence uses a function word *(that)* to mark the beginning of a constituent ("that the author used"). A listener can hear the word *that* and assume that a new constituent is beginning. In the second sentence the listener cannot make a decision to mark the beginning of a new constituent until he or she hears the word *used;* it is difficult to predict what the

next word will be. And in fact Fodor and Garrett's subjects more easily understood the sentence containing the word *that.* Thus, besides indicating the relations between words, function words are important cues to the dividing points between the constituent parts of a sentence.

Semantic Analysis

Understanding the meaning of a sentence involves more than analysis; the listener or reader must also decode the meaning of the words in the sentence. **Semantics** (from the Greek *sēma,* meaning "sign") is the study of the meanings represented by words.

Sometimes we can understand what a speaker or writer means even though the syntax of a sentence is ambiguous. Consider the following sentence:

Frank discovered a louse combing his beard.

The *syntax* of this sentence does not tell us whether Frank was combing Frank's beard, the louse was combing the louse's beard, or the louse was combing Frank's beard. But our knowledge of the world and of the usual meaning of words tells us that Frank was doing the combing, because people, not lice, have beards and combs. In other words, we perform a semantic analysis of the sentence.

Just as function words help us determine the syntax of a sentence, content words help us determine its meaning. For example, even with its function words removed, the following sentence still makes pretty good sense:

man placed ladder tree climbed picked apples

You can probably fill in the function words yourself and get "*The* man placed *the* ladder *against the* tree, climbed *it, and* picked *some* apples." We can often guess at function words, which is fortunate, because they are normally unstressed in speech and are therefore the most likely to be poorly pronounced.

We use content words to understand the meaning of ambiguous sentences (for example, we know that a louse does not have a beard) and sentences with complicated syntactical structures. Fillenbaum (1974a, 1974b) showed that we sometimes even ignore syntax when we hear a sentence. Instead, we pay attention to the meaning of the words as they relate to our experience. Thus, semantics can override syntax. Consider the following sentences:

John dressed and had a bath.

Don't print that or I won't sue you.

Over 60 percent of Fillenbaum's subjects failed to notice that these sentences have rather peculiar meanings. The subjects would paraphrase the second sentence as "If you print that, I'll sue you." But that is not what it says. (Read the sentences again —very carefully this time.) When asked to reexamine the original sentences, only about half the subjects noticed their peculiarity, and many who did notice the discrepancy said that they knew what the sentences were really *supposed* to mean, so they rephrased them. Thus the syntax of a sentence partly determines what information enters short-term memory, but our previous nonverbal experiences (such as bathing before dressing) also play an important role.

Relation Between Semantics and Syntax

There is more than one way to say something, and sometimes a particular sentence can mean more than one thing. In Chapter 7 I described an experiment by Sachs that showed that we soon forget the particular form a sentence takes but remember its meaning much longer. I also described the case of a woman with conduction aphasia who had a deficit in verbal short-term memory that made it difficult for her to remember the syntax of a sentence long enough to repeat the words, but she could remember the meaning that the words expressed. Noam Chomsky (1957, 1965), a noted linguist, suggested that sentences are represented in the brain in terms of their meaning, which he called their **deep structure.** The deep structure represents the kernel of what the person intended to say. In order to say the sentence, the deep structure must be transformed into the appropriate **surface structure:** the particular form the sentence takes.

An example of a "slip of the tongue" recorded by Fromkin (1973) gives us some clues about the way in which a sentence's deep structure can be transformed into a particular surface structure.

Rosa always date shranks.

The speaker actually intended to say "Rosa always dated shrinks" (psychiatrists or clinical psychologists). We can speculate that the deep structure of the sentence's verb phrase was something like this: *date* [past tense] + *shrink* [plural]. The words in brackets represent the names of the syntactical rules that are to be used in forming the surface structure of the sentence. Obviously, the past tense of *date* is *dated*, and the plural of *shrink* is *shrinks*. However, something went wrong during the transformation process. Apparently, the past tense rule got applied to the word *shrink*, resulting in *shrank*. The plural rule also got applied, making the nonsense word *shranks*.

Most psychologists agree that the distinction between surface structure and deep structure is an important one. In the previous chapter we saw that conduction aphasia involves difficulty with surface structure more than deep structure, and in a later section of this chapter we will encounter more neuropsychological evidence in favor of the distinction. However, most psycholinguists disagree with Chomsky about the particular nature of the cognitive mechanisms through which deep structure is translated into surface structure.

Martin Luther King Jr. was a master of the art of semantics. Both his ideas (deep structure) and how he presented them (surface structure) were compelling.

■ What is the basic process of syntactical analysis?

■ How do we use the process of semantic analysis?

■ How do syntax and semantics interact in verbal behavior?

DEVELOPMENT OF VERBAL BEHAVIOR IN CHILDREN

How do children learn to communicate verbally with other people? How do they master the many rules needed to transform a thought into a coherent sentence? How do they learn the meanings of thousands of words? And *why* do they do all these things? Do other people shape their babble into words by appropriately

Children are usually eager to learn and practice verbal communication.

reinforcing their behavior, or do innate mechanisms ensure the acquisition of language without reinforcement? This section addresses these and other questions related to children's verbal development.

The Prespeech Period and the First Words

Perception of Speech Sounds

An infant's auditory system is remarkably well developed. Wertheimer (1961) found that newborn infants in the delivery room can turn their head toward the source of a sound. Infants two or three weeks of age can discriminate the sound of a voice from nonspeech sounds. By the age of two months, babies can tell an angry voice from a pleasant one; an angry voice produces crying, whereas a pleasant one causes smiling and cooing.

Psychologists have developed a clever technique to determine what sounds a very young infant can perceive. A special pacifier nipple is placed in the baby's mouth. The nipple is connected by a plastic tube to a pressure-sensitive switch that converts the infant's sucking movements into electrical signals. These signals can be used to turn on auditory stimuli; each time the baby sucks, a particular sound is presented.

If the auditory stimulus is novel, the baby usually begins to suck at a high rate. If the stimulus remains the same, its novelty wears off (habituation occurs), and the rate of sucking goes down. With another new stimulus, the rate of sucking again suddenly increases, unless the baby cannot discriminate the difference; if the stimuli sound the same to the infant, the rate of sucking remains low after the change. Figure 8.1 shows some data collected by this procedure (Trehub, 1976). The rate of sucking per minute increased in response to the sound *zah*, then declined during habituation over a five-minute period. When the auditory stimulus was changed to *rah*, the rate of sucking suddenly increased again, indicating that the infant could discriminate between the two sounds.

Using this technique, Eimas, Siqueland, Jusczyk, and Vigorito (1971) found that one-month-old infants could tell the difference be-

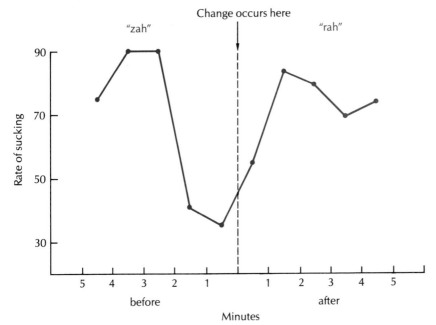

FIGURE 8.1

Data from the auditory perception experiment conducted by Trehub. (From Trehub, S.E., *Child Development*, 1976, 47, 466–472.)

tween the sounds of the consonants *b* and *p.* They presented the sounds *ba* and *pa,* synthesized by a computer. The infants discriminated between speech sounds whose voice-onset time differed by only 0.02 second. Even very early during postnatal development, the human auditory system is ready to make very fine discriminations.

Stages of Infant Speech Sounds

Kaplan and Kaplan (1970) outlined the following four stages of early vocalizations in infants.

Stage 1: Crying. Everyone knows that crying is the first sound that a baby makes. As we saw in Chapter 4, this aversive stimulus is important in obtaining behaviors from the baby's caregivers.

Stage 2: Other Vocalizations and Cooing. At about one month of age, infants start making other sounds, including one that is called *cooing* because of the prevalence of the *oo* sound. Often during this period babies also make a series of sounds that resemble a halfhearted attempt to mimic the sound of crying.

Stage 3: Babbling. At around six months, a baby's sounds begin to resemble those that occur in speech. Some researchers (including Mowrer, 1960) have suggested that speech emerges from babbling. They claim that an infant's babbling contains all the sounds that occur in all languages of the world, and that learning to speak involves a selection process—a narrowing of the range of sounds to those that are actually used in the child's native language. In fact, although babies produce some sounds not heard in English (such as the sound of the French *u*), they do not produce all the sounds that *are* heard in English (Oller, Wieman, Doyle, and Ross, 1976). These sounds come during later stages of language development.

Stage 4: Patterned Speech. At about one year of age, a child begins to produce words. The transition between stages 3 and 4 can occur gradually or abruptly. Sometimes there is a period of silence for several days or weeks during which the child stops babbling altogether, followed by the beginning of patterned speech.

The first sounds that children use to produce speech appear to be the same across all languages and cultures: the first vowel is usually the soft *a* sound of *father,* and the first consonant is a *stop consonant* produced with the lips—*p* or *b.* Thus the first word is often *papa* or *baba.* The next feature to be added is *nasality,* which converts the consonant *p* or *b* into *m.* Thus, the next word is *mama.* Naturally, mothers and fathers all over the world recognize these sounds as their children's attempts to address them.

The development of speech sounds continues for many years. Some sequences are added very late. For example, the *str* of *string* and the *bl* of *blink* are difficult for young children to produce; they usually say *tring* and *link,* omitting the first consonant. Most children recognize sounds in adult speech before they can produce them. Consider this conversation (Dale, 1976):

Adult: Johnny, I'm going to say a word two times and you tell me which time I say it right and which time I say it wrong: *rabbit, wabbit.*
Child: Wabbit is wight and *wabbit* is wong.

Although the child could not pronounce the *r* sound, it is clear that he could recognize it.

The Two-Word Stage

At around eighteen to twenty months of age, children start putting two words together, and their linguistic development takes a leap forward. It is at this stage that linguistic creativity really begins. Consider the creativity in "Allgone outside," said by a child when the door was closed.

Like first sounds, children's two-word utterances are remarkably consistent across all cultures that have been observed. Children use words in the same way, no matter what language their parents speak. Even deaf children who learn sign language from their parents put two words together in the same way as children who can hear (Bellugi and Klima, 1972), and deaf children whose parents do not know sign language invent their own signs and use them in orderly, "rule-governed" ways (Goldin-Meadow and Feldman, 1977). Thus, the grammar of children's language at the two-word stage appears to be universal.

For many years, investigators described the speech of young children in terms of adult grammar, but it is now recognized that their speech simply follows different rules. Young children are incapable of forming complex sentences, partly because their vocabulary is small, partly because their short-term "working" memory is limited (they cannot yet encode a long string of words), and partly because their cognitive development has not yet reached a stage where they can learn complex rules of syntax.

Researchers have used a variety of strategies to uncover young children's regularities of speech and to deduce from these patterns the "rules" that children use. For example, Miller and Ervin-Tripp (1964) recorded two statements by a child: "Christy room." (meaning "This is Christy's room") and "Christy room." (meaning "Christy is in the room"). What grammatical rules enable two different meanings to result in the use of the same two words? Yet it appears that this two-word speech is orderly and that "rules" do govern much of what young children say. Wieman (1974) noted that children often stress one of the words in their two-word sentences; for example, a child may say, "*Christy* room." in one situation and "Christy *room*." in another. If you say these two-word sentences to yourself, stressing the italicized word, you can probably guess which means "Christy is in the room" and which means "This is Christy's room."

Most people have no trouble understanding what the child means in each case, which indicates that the child's use of stress is governed by some rules. Weiman studied children's speech and found that the rules involved the functions that words had in a sentence. The rules allowed her to predict which word would be stressed. For example, when a two-word utterance contains a word indicating a possession and another indicating a noun object, the one indicating possession was stressed. That is, "*Christy* room" means "This is Christy's room."

Wieman's analysis is only one of the many approaches developed to reveal the regularities of children's speech at the two-word stage, and undoubtedly more regularities will become apparent. The importance of Wieman's conclusions is their support for the idea that children's speech is orderly and that the rules that govern stress are complex; they are determined by the relation between the meanings of the two words.

One of the difficulties in determining the rules of children's grammar is that the words by themselves often do not provide enough information for us to infer the meaning of an utterance. Wieman's analysis can be tested only when an observer is present to determine what the child intends to say; the words themselves are ambiguous. If we know nothing about the context of the two sentences, we cannot classify the words. Thus, an adequate description of the regularities of children's speech must take account of the functions that the words perform, and not simply their form. The rules must take account of meaning.

Acquisition of Adult Rules of Grammar

We tend to assume that the simplest rules of grammar are the first to be learned. The trouble with this assumption is that so far there is no accurate way of assessing the complexity of a particular linguistic rule. If we follow children around and record their speech, we can determine the chronological order in which they use grammatical rules. Yet it is possible that children have to master some rules that are relatively complex but very important for communication before they learn simpler rules that are not needed very often. This possibility must govern the following considerations about how children learn adult linguistic rules.

The first words that children use tend to be content words, probably because these words are emphasized in adult speech, and because they refer to objects and actions that children can directly observe (Brown and Fraser, 1964). As children develop past the two-word stage, they begin to learn and use more and more of the grammatical rules that adults use. The first form of sentence lengthening appears to be the expansion of object nouns into noun phrases (Bloom, 1970). For example, "That ball" becomes "That big ball." Next, verbs get used more often, articles are added, prepositional phrases are mastered, and sentences become more complex. These results involve the use of inflections and function words. Function words, you recall, are the little words that help shape the syntax of a sentence. **Inflections** are special suffixes that we add to words to change their syntactical or semantic function. For example, the inflection *-ed* changes most verbs into the past tense (*change* becomes *changed*), *-ing* can make a verb into a noun (*make* be-

comes *making*), and *-'s* indicates possession (*Paul's truck*). Table 8.1 (on the next page) shows the approximate order in which children acquire some of these inflections and function words.

It is more difficult for children to add an inflection or function word to their vocabulary than to add a new content word, because the rules that govern the use of inflections or function words are more complex than those that govern the use of most content words. In addition, content words usually refer to concrete objects or activities. The rules that govern the use of inflections or function words are rarely made explicit; a parent seldom says, "When you want to use the past tense, add *-ed* to the

Researchers believe that the grammar rules used during the two-word stage of language development are consistent across all cultures.

TABLE 8.1

The order in which children acquire some English inflectional suffixes and function words

Item	Example
1. Present progressive: *-ing*	He is sit*ting* down.
2. Preposition: *in*	The mouse is *in* the box.
3. Preposition: *on*	The book is *on* the table.
4. Plural: *-s*	The dog*s* ran away.
5. Past irregular: e.g., *went*	The boy *went* home.
6. Possessive: *-'s*	The girl*'s* dog is big.
7. Uncontractible copula *be*: e.g., *are, was*	*Are* they boys or girls? *Was* that a dog?
8. Articles: *the, a, an*	He has *a* book.
9. Past regular: *-ed*	He jump*ed* the stream.
10. Third person regular: *-s*	She run*s* fast.
11. Third person irregular: e.g., *has, does*	*Does* the dog bark?
12. Uncontractible auxiliary *be*: e.g., *is, were*	*Is* he running? *Were* they at home?
13. Contractible copula *be*: e.g., *'s, -re*	That*'s* a spaniel. They*'re* pretty.
14. Contractible auxiliary *be*: e.g., *-'s, -'re*	He*'s* doing it. They*'re* running slowly.

Adapted from Clark, H.H., and Clark, E.V. *Psychology and Language.* New York: Harcourt Brace Jovanovich, 1977, after Brown (1973).

verb''—nor would a young child understand such a pronouncement. Instead, children must listen to speech and figure out how to express such concepts as the past tense. Studies of children's speech have told us something about the process by which this occurs.

Several investigators have observed that children learn syntactical rules only after they understand the concepts that the rules represent. The acquisition of syntactical rules is not an automatic process: it occurs in response to a perceived need. For example, Slobin (1966) noted that the conditional form ("If . . . then . . .") is very simple syntactically, but children do not learn to use it until their cognitive development has progressed enough for them to understand the concept of conditionality. Cromer (1968) reported that once a child has mastered a concept, the child actively tries to learn ways to express this concept in speech. For example, one child tried to express the past tense with "Uh . . . why did Batman couldn't go fishin?" We can see such attempts as driven by the child's need to be understood.

The most frequently used verbs in most languages are *irregular*; forming the past tense of such verbs in English does *not* involve adding *-ed*. (Examples are *go/went, catch/caught, throw/threw, buy/bought, be/was, see/saw,* and *can/could*.) The past tense of such verbs must be learned individually. Because irregular verbs get more use than regular ones, children learn them first, producing the past tense easily in sentences such as "I came," "I fell down," and "She hit me." Soon afterward, they discover the regular past tense inflection and expand their vocabulary, producing sentences like "He dropped the ball." But they also begin to say "I comed," "I falled down," and "She hitted me." Having learned a rule, they apply it to all verbs, including the irregular ones that they were previously using correctly. In fact, it takes children several years to learn to use the irregular past tense correctly again.

Some English verbs have two acceptable past tense forms, irregular and regular. One familiar example is dive/dived or dive/dove. It has been suggested that many of our verbs that are now regular were previously irregular, and that the tendency of children to overuse the past tense rule caused these verbs to become regular.

Acquisition of Meaning

How do children learn to use and understand words? The simplest explanation is that they hear a word spoken at the same time that they see (or hear, or touch) the object to which the word refers. After several such pairings, they add a word to their vocabulary. Suppose we give a boy a small red plastic ball and say "ball." After a while, the child says "ball" when he sees it.

Yet we cannot conclude from this behavior that the child knows the meaning of *ball*. So far, he has encountered only one referent for the word: a small one made of red plastic. If he says "ball" when he sees an apple or an orange, or even the moon, we must conclude that he does not know the meaning of *ball;* he has made an **overextension**. On the other hand, if he uses the word to refer only to the small red plastic ball, his error would be called an **underextension.** Table 8.2 lists some examples of children's overextensions in learning the meanings of new words.

Both overextensions and underextensions are normal; a single pairing of a word with the object does not provide enough information for accurate generalization. Suppose someone is teaching you a foreign language. She points to a penny and says "pengar." Does *pengar* mean "penny," "money," "coin," or "round"? You cannot decide from this one example. Without further information you may overextend or underextend the meaning of *pengar* if you try to use it. If your teacher then points to a dollar bill and again says "pengar," you will deduce (correctly) that the word means "money."

Many words, including function words, do not have physical referents. For example, prepositions such as *on, in,* and *toward* express relations or directions, and a child needs many examples to learn how to use them appropriately. Pronouns are also difficult; for example, it takes a child some time to grasp the notion that *I* means the speaker: *I* means "me" when I say it, but *I* means "you" when you say it. In fact, parents usually avoid personal pronouns in speaking with their children; instead they use sentences such as "Does baby want another

The words found in books provide children with the opportunity to discover people and experiences they cannot experience directly.

TABLE 8.2

Some overextensions made by children while learning new words

Word	Original Referent	Application
mooi	moon	Cakes, round marks on windows, writing on windows and in books, round shapes in books, round postmarks, letter o
buti	ball	Toy, radish, stone sphere at park entrance
ticktock	watch	All clocks and watches, gas meter, firehose wound on spool, bath scale with round dial
baw	ball	Apples, grapes, eggs, squash, bell clapper, anything round
mem	horse	Cow, calf, pig, moose, all four-legged animals
fly	fly	Specks of dirt, dust, all small insects, child's own toes, crumbs of bread, a toad
wau-wau	dog	All animals, toy dog, soft house slippers, picture of an old man dressed in furs

Adapted from Clark, H.H., and Clark, E.V. *Psychology and Language.* New York: Harcourt Brace Jovanovich, 1977, after E. Clark (1975).

Adults often find it difficult to learn a second language, suggesting that there may be a "critical period" for learning a native language.

Why Children Learn Language

The linguistic accomplishments of young children are remarkable. Even a child who later does poorly in school learns the rules of grammar and the meanings of thousands of words. Some children fail to work hard at school, but no normal child fails to learn to talk. What shapes this learning process, and what motivates it?

There is vigorous controversy about why children learn to speak, and especially to speak grammatically. Noam Chomsky, the noted linguist, observed that the recorded speech of adults is not as correct as the dialogue we read in a novel or hear in a play; often it is ungrammatical, hesitating, and full of unfinished sentences. In fact, Chomsky (1965) characterized everyday adult speech as "defective" and "degenerate." If this is really what children hear when they learn to speak, it is amazing that they manage to acquire the rules of grammar.

Language Acquisition As an Innate Ability

The view that children learn regular rules from apparently haphazard samples of speech has led many linguists to conclude that the ability to learn language is innate; all a child has to do is to be in the company of speakers of a language. McNeill (1970) has proposed that a child's brain contains a "language acquisition device," which embodies rules of "universal grammar"; because each language expresses these rules in slightly different ways, the child must learn the details, but the basics are already there in the brain.

Another reason for the belief that language acquisition is an innate human capacity is the discovery of **language universals:** characteristics that can be found in all languages that linguists have studied. Some of the more important language universals include the existence of noun phrases ("The quick brown fox . . . "), verb phrases (". . . ate the chicken"), grammatical categories of words such as nouns and adjectives, and syntactical rules that permit the expression of subject-verb-object relations ("John hit Andy"), plurality ("two birds"), and possession ("Rachel's pen"). The fact that language universals do exist in languages from all cultures was taken as support for the assertion

one?" (meaning "Do you want another one?") and "Daddy will help you" (meaning "I will help you").

Abstract words such as *apparently, necessity, thorough,* and *method* have no direct referents and must be defined in terms of other words. Therefore, children cannot learn their meanings until after they have learned many other words. Explaining the meaning of *apparently* to a child with a limited vocabulary would be as hopeless a task as my using a Russian dictionary (not a *Russian-English* dictionary) to determine the meaning of a Russian word. Because I do not understand Russian, the definition would be just as meaningless to me as the word being defined.

- What are the four stages of infant vocalization?
- How do we acquire adult rules for grammatical verbal behavior?
- How do words become meaningful to us?

that they were the products of innate brain mechanisms.

Most psychologists disagree with this conclusion. For example, Hebb, Lambert, and Tucker (1973) observe that language universals need not imply the existence of innate grammatical rules; they are more likely caused by the realities of the world. When people deal with each other and with nature, their interactions often take the form of an agent acting on an object. Thus, it is not unreasonable that all languages have ways of expressing these interactions. Similarly, objects come in slightly different shapes, sizes, and colors, so we can expect the need for ways (such as adjectives) to distinguish among them. It is not unreasonable to suppose that the same kinds of linguistic devices have been independently invented at different times and in different places by different cultures. After all, archeologists tell us that similar tools have been invented by different cultures all around the world. People need to cut, hammer, chisel, scrape, and wedge things apart, and different cultures have invented similar devices to perform these tasks. We need not conclude that these inventions are products of a "tool-making device" located in the brain.

Yet another argument that has been advanced in support of the assertion that children do not have to learn the rules of grammar is the claim that children learn language easily, whereas adults learn a new language only with great difficulty. Allegedly, this difference occurs because the development of the human brain includes a "critical period" during which a native language is easily learned. The fact that people who learn a second language after childhood usually speak the second language with the accent of their first language supports this conclusion. However, it is difficult to compare the relative ease with which children and adults learn a language. Most of a child's waking hours are spent in language practice—both in speaking and in listening to the speech of other people. In contrast, unless they are immersed in a new society and have no contact with people who speak their first language, most adults who try to learn a new language spend much less time than children do practicing it. Also, although adults often speak to one another carelessly and ungrammatically, they are less likely to do so when addressing young children. As we will see in the next section, the way people talk to children is very important for their acquisition of language.

How Adults Talk to Children

It has been known for some time that parents use short, simple, well-formed, repetitive sentences and phrases when speaking to their children (Brown and Bellugi, 1964). Their speech does not contain the kinds of faults that supposedly characterize adult speech. In a comprehensive review of the literature, deVilliers and deVilliers (1978) found that adults' speech to children is characterized by clear pronunciation, exaggerated intonations, careful distinctions between similar-sounding phonemes, relatively few abstract words and function words, and a tendency to isolate constituents that

When an adult talks to a child, the speech is simple and repetitive with well-formed, short sentences and exaggerated intonations.

undoubtedly enables young children to recognize them as units of speech. In addition, most speech is in the present tense and refers to tangible objects that the child can see.

Whether they are parents or not, adults tend to act as tutors when talking with children, prompting their answers:

> *Adult:* What do you want?
> *Child:* (no response)
> *Adult:* You want what?

Adults also often expand children's speech by imitating it but putting it into more complex forms (Brown and Bellugi, 1964):

> *Child:* Baby highchair.
> *Adult:* Baby is in the highchair.
>
> *Child:* Eve lunch.
> *Adult:* Eve is having lunch.
>
> *Child:* Throw daddy.
> *Adult:* Throw it to daddy.

Finally, adults tend to provide a running commentary about what is happening:

> Now I'm going to pick up the red ball. See the red ball? Here it is. Oh! Baby dropped it! Baby dropped the red ball. It bumped baby's toe. It's rolled far away.

People also make allowances for the age of the child. Mothers talk differently to two-year-olds than to ten-year-olds (Snow, 1972a); even four-year-old children talk differently to two-year-olds than they do to adults or other four-year-olds (Shatz and Gelman, 1973).

It seems unlikely that these differentiated speech patterns are innately determined. Snow (1972a) compared the speech patterns of a mother talking to a child with her speech patterns when she only pretended to be talking to a child. The woman's speech when the child was absent was simpler than it would have been if addressed to an adult, but when the child was present it was simpler still. Clearly, then, feedback from children is important.

The Role of Feedback from Children

The most important factor controlling adults' speech to children is the child's attentiveness. Both adults and children are very sensitive to whether or not another person is paying attention to them. When a child looks interested, we continue with what we are doing. When we notice signs of inattention, we advance or simplify our level of speech until we regain the child's attention.

An experiment by Snow (1972b) showed that children pay more attention to a tape recording of speech directed to a child than to a recording of speech directed to an adult. Other researchers have found that children respond best to speech that is slightly more complex than their own (Shipley, Smith, and Gleitman, 1969). Interacting with someone who has achieved slightly greater competence appears to be an optimum strategy for most learning; for example, if you want to improve your tennis game, you should play with someone a bit better than you. A poorer player is no challenge, and if you play with someone of professional quality you will hardly get a chance to return the ball. Thus, children modify adults' speech, keeping it at the optimal level of complexity.

The Role of Reinforcement

As we saw in Chapter 6, reinforcement plays an important role in learning: favorable consequences of a particular behavior can make that behavior occur more often. Critics of the notion that reinforcement plays an important role in the acquisition of language stress that parents seldom praise their children for speaking or correct their ungrammatical utterances, yet children manage to learn very complex behaviors. Therefore, they claim, reinforcement cannot be important. The following examples from Brown, Cazden, and Bellugi (1969) illustrate this lack of reinforcement. When Eve said to her mother "He a girl" (meaning "You are a girl"), her mother ignored the inappropriate choice of a pronoun and the lack of a verb and said "That's right." Similarly, Eve's mother accepted the statement "Her curl my hair," because that is what she was doing. However, when Eve's sister Sarah said, "There's the animal farmhouse" (which was grammatically acceptable but factually incorrect), she was corrected; the picture that she was looking at was one of a lighthouse.

Skinner (1957) suggested that the use of language is shaped by contingencies in the child's environment, much as complex behaviors can be shaped in other animals through the reinforcement of behaviors that are successively

Reinforcement plays an important role in learning. The attention adults give to children's earliest babblings is a powerful reinforcer.

closer and closer to the final form. Most linguists and many psychologists have vigorously objected to Skinner's model, on the grounds discussed above. However, a careful analysis shows that much of this criticism misses an essential feature of reinforcement.

The fact that parents do not often reward their children's speech behaviors with praise or tangible reinforcers (such as candy) does not contradict the idea that reinforcement plays an important role in the acquisition of verbal behavior. *Reinforcement* is not synonymous with *reward*; it can occur without the deliberate intervention of another person. It is the *effects* of speech that are reinforcing: a child who says "Milk!" is likely to receive a glass of milk. The adult does not give the child the milk as a reward for correctly saying the word *milk*, but as a response to a request. However, the adult's intention is irrelevant. The glass of milk serves as a reinforcer for the verbal behavior that was instrumental in getting it delivered.

Speech also provides more subtle (and probably more important) reinforcers. We humans are social animals; our behavior is strongly affected by the behavior of others. It is readily apparent to anyone who has observed the behavior of children that the attention of other people is extremely important to them. Children will perform a variety of behaviors that get other people to pay attention to them. They will make faces, play games, even misbehave in

order to attract attention. And, above all, they will talk. Consider yourself in the child's place. Adults or other children are likely to pay attention to you if you start talking to them. If they cannot understand your speech, you are unlikely to maintain their attention.

Thus, reinforcement plays at least two roles in the acquisition of speech. Speech can cause people to provide useful things such as glasses of milk or toys or other amusements, or it can elicit attention and social interaction. Reinforcement can even play a role in the acquisition of the rules of grammar. Simple speech suffices for simple requests. However, more complex requests require more complex speech. If this speech is to be understood, it must be in a form that adults can recognize; that is, it must be grammatical (although the rules do not have to be the full-fledged rules of adult speech—these come slowly and gradually). The acquisition of grammatical speech, then, is reinforced *by the effects of speech that is understood*. For example, a child does not receive explicit reinforcers for learning to use the future tense properly. Instead, reinforcement comes from the effects of using the future tense: the child can get an adult to promise that he or she *will do* something.

Children's mastery of syntactical rules can also be affected by social reinforcement. For example, some linguists have observed that "Milk!" works well for a two-year old child.

Why, then, do children subsequently learn syntactical rules that permit them to say "Mommy, may I please have some milk?" Obviously, they say, this increase in complexity cannot be explained in terms of reinforcement, because either utterance results in the delivery of milk. However, this conclusion ignores the fact that humans tend to model their behavior—including their verbal behavior—on that of other people. In particular, children tend to imitate the behavior of older children and adults. An older child might be understood if he or she spoke "baby talk," but the child would probably be ridiculed by his or her peers. And if an eight-year-old child says "Milk!" his or her parent is likely to say, "You're not getting anything from me until you talk more politely."

It is impossible to prove conclusively that reinforcement is crucial in the acquisition of language. To do so, an experimenter would have to respond to the speech of some children and ignore others or deliberately "misunderstand" them, giving them a toy when they ask for a glass of milk and paying attention to them when they are silent instead of when they speak. Obviously, such an experiment is unconscionable: How satisfactory would the experiment be if the children really failed to learn to speak?

■ What are the arguments for and against language acquisition as an innate ability?
■ How does a child's behavior affect the speech patterns of adults?
■ How are reinforcement processes important in shaping effective verbal behavior?

WHAT WE MAY LEARN FROM LANGUAGE DISORDERS

Studies of the verbal behavior of people with brain damage suggest that mechanisms involved in perceiving and producing speech are located in different areas of the cerebral cortex. These studies have furthered our understanding of the processes of normal verbal behavior and of language disorders.

Speech Comprehension: Evidence from Wernicke's Aphasia

Aphasia (literally, "without utterance") refers to a loss of ability to produce meaningful speech caused by brain damage. As we will see, several different types of aphasia can occur, depending on the location of the brain damage. In the late nineteenth century, a German physician, Karl Wernicke, reported that a particular form of aphasia was caused by damage to a region of auditory association cortex located on the upper part of the temporal lobe of the left side of the brain (Wernicke, 1874). This region of the brain has come to be known as **Wernicke's area,** and the disorder is now called **Wernicke's aphasia.** (See Figure 8.2.)

The most important symptoms of Wernicke's aphasia are very poor speech comprehension and fluent but meaningless speech. That is, people with this disorder fail to comprehend what others say to them, but they themselves talk, in an apparently effortless manner. The problem is, what they say does not make much sense. For example, consider the following dialogue (from Kertesz, 1980):

> *Examiner:* Can you tell me a little bit about why you're here?
> *Patient:* I don't know whata wasa down here for me, I just don't know why I wasn't with up here, at all you, it was neva, had it been walked me today ta died.

The patient who spoke these words acted as if she had said something meaningful. She paused between phrases and dropped her voice at the end of "sentences." We can speculate that because she could not understand other people's speech, she could not realize that her own speech lacked meaning. Typically, the speech of people with Wernicke's aphasia retains some elements of grammar. It contains few content words but is full of function words, especially pronouns, conjunctions, and prepositions.

Most investigators believe that the primary deficit of Wernicke's aphasia is a loss of speech comprehension. Perhaps Wernicke's area contains memories of the sounds of words. These memories are necessary for comprehending other people's speech, and for translating one's own thoughts into words.

Speech Production: Evidence from Broca's Aphasia

As we saw in Chapter 1, Paul Broca, a French physician, discovered that damage to a region of the left frontal cortex caused a severe deficit in speech (Broca, 1861). The deficit is now referred to as **Broca's aphasia,** and the region of cortex is now called **Broca's area.** The symptoms of Broca's aphasia are quite different from those of Wernicke's aphasia. Whereas the speech of a person with Wernicke's aphasia is fluent, meaningless, and at least superficially grammatical, the speech of a person with Broca's aphasia is labored, meaningful, and ungrammatical. Consider the following sample of speech from a man with Broca's aphasia, who was explaining why he had come to the hospital. The dots indicate long pauses, during which the man was trying to find the proper words.

> Ah . . . Monday . . . ah Dad and Paul [patient's name] . . . and Dad . . . hospital. Two . . . ah doctors . . . , and ah . . . thirty minutes . . . and yes . . . ah . . . hospital. And, er Wednesday . . . nine o'clock. And er Thursday, ten o'clock . . . doctors. Two doctors . . . and ah . . . teeth. Yeah, . . . fine. (Goodglass, 1976, p. 278)

Most investigators believe that Broca's area contains memories of the sequences of muscular movements that must be performed to pronounce words. Loss of this area makes it very difficult for people to speak. (See Figure 8.2.)

In addition to its role in the production of words, Broca's area appears to perform some more complex functions. Damage to Broca's area often produces **agrammatism:** loss of the ability to comprehend or produce speech that employs complex syntactical rules. For example, the speech of a person with Broca's aphasia contains many content words but few function words. To test agrammatic subjects for speech comprehension, Schwartz, Saffran, and Marin (1980) showed them a pair of drawings, read a sentence aloud, and then asked them to point to the appropriate picture. The subjects heard forty-eight sentences such as "The clown applauds the dancer" and "The robber is shot by the cop." For the first sample sentence, one pic-

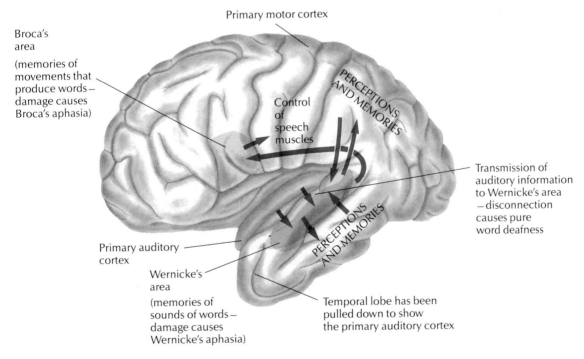

FIGURE 8.2

The functions and interconnections of Broca's area and Wernicke's area.

ture would show a clown applauding a dancer, and the other would show a dancer applauding a clown. On average, the brain-damaged subjects responded correctly to only 62 percent of the pictures (chance would be 50 percent). In contrast, the performance of normal people would be near 100 percent on such a simple task. In another study, Saffran, Schwartz, and Marin (1980) obtained evidence of the subjects' deficits in the use of syntactical rules by showing them simple pictures and asking them to say what was happening. Here are some of the responses:

> *Picture of a girl giving flowers to her teacher:* Girl . . . wants to . . . flowers . . . flowers and wants to. . . . The woman . . . wants to. . . . The girl wants to . . . the flowers and the woman.

> *Picture of a boy being hit in the head by a base-ball:* Boy is hurting to it.

> *Picture of a woman kissing a man:* The kiss . . . the lady kissed . . . the lady is . . . the lady and the man and the lady . . . kissing.

> *Picture of a boy giving a valentine to a girl:* The boy and a valentine and a girl . . . boy . . . the boy put the valentine into this girl.

Given that the frontal lobes govern motor control and, more generally, planning, it is not surprising that damage to Broca's area impairs the production of proper syntax. Syntactical rules involve motor operations in the sense that they entail putting a word into its proper position, adding the correct ending to a verb, and so on. But damage to Broca's area also impairs comprehension. Thus, we cannot say that speech perception is strictly a function of Wernicke's area. It appears that the mechanisms that permit us to translate meaning into syntax (in Chomsky's terms, deep structure into surface structure) are also necessary for us to extract meaning from syntax; encoding and decoding use the same brain mechanisms. This evidence supports the suggestion that in order to comprehend a sentence, listeners do the opposite of what speakers do: They transform a sentence's surface structure back to its deep structure.

If this explanation is true, we can understand why the speech of people with Wernicke's aphasia is full of function words: They have lost the neural circuits necessary for remembering the sounds and meanings of content words, but they retain the mechanisms that control ut-

terances of function words. Their speech is controlled by neural mechanisms in Broca's area that have little meaningful input to guide them, and therefore it consists mostly of function words.

Reading

Apparently, when we read aloud, we use at least two different methods: **phonetic reading** involves seeing individual letters (or small groups of letters) and decoding them into sounds, which we then pronounce, and **whole-word reading** involves seeing a word as a whole and then pronouncing it. Studies of people who have sustained brain damage from strokes or accidental head injury show that damage to one of these processes does not seriously affect the other. Little is known about the location of the brain damage that produces these disorders.

Phonological Dyslexia

Brain-damaged people with **phonological dyslexia** have great difficulty reading phonetically. (*Dyslexia* literally means "faulty speech," but the term is used exclusively to refer to reading.) People with phonological dyslexia can read words that they learned before their stroke or head injury, but they cannot read unfamiliar words. In particular, they cannot read nonwords such as *flape, buflig,* or *strudge,* whereas most normal people can pronounce these sequences of letters by using phonological rules. The fact that these people can continue to read words they already know suggests that they are using a method other than phonetic reading. Presumably, this method involves whole-word recognition.

The exact location of the damage that causes phonological dyslexia is not known, but it usually involves the region near the junction of the parietal, temporal, and occipital lobes.

Surface Dyslexia

In contrast to people with phonological dyslexia, people with **surface dyslexia** can read phonetically, but they have difficulty with whole-word reading. People with this disorder find it easier to read regularly spelled words

Children with dyslexia can sometimes be taught to read by using techniques that rely on other sensory modalities to convey information to the brain.

than irregularly spelled ones. Regularly spelled words are those that conform the the common rules of spelling, such as *church, happy, late,* or *establishment.* Most people can "sound out" these words by using phonetic rules, such as that each letter has a specific sound, the *ch* and *sh* make special sounds, and that an *e* at the end of a word makes an internal vowel long rather than short. Irregularly spelled words do not follow these rules. For example, in *listen* the *t* is silent, in *pint* the *i* is long rather than short, and in *yacht* the *ch* is silent. We must learn these words as specific exceptions, and we therefore have to read them by the whole-word method. Because of difficulty with whole-word reading, a person with surface dyslexia might pronounce *yacht* as "yatchet" but can usually read nonwords that conform to the common rules of spelling.

Some children who are otherwise of normal intelligence have great difficulty learning to read. This form of specific learning disability is called **developmental dyslexia** because it is discovered in the course of development. Although researchers now believe that there are several different forms of developmental dys-

lexia, the disability of most children with this disorder resembles that of adults with surface dyslexia. Preliminary evidence suggests that developmental dyslexia may be caused by abnormal development of the cerebral cortex, especially of speech-related areas in the left hemisphere (Galaburda and Kemper, 1979). More research is needed to determine whether such is actually the case.

The Two Phases of Whole-Word Reading: Recognition and Pronunciation

Whole-word reading entails two phases: *recognition* and *pronunciation.* For most of us, these two phases occur in such rapid sequence that we are unaware that they are separate. However, evidence indicates that recognition of a word is not synonymous with the ability to say it. Two colleagues and I (Margolin, Marcel, and Carlson, 1985) studied a woman who had received a head injury in an automobile accident, resulting in severe damage to the left temporal lobe. Her speech was fluent, but she had severe **anomia;** that is, when speaking she had trouble finding words, especially concrete nouns. (*Anomia* literally means "without name.") For example, when talking about her horse, she might forget the word and say, "You know, an animal . . . I keep it out in the back . . . it's big . . . I take it for rides . . . oh, I know what it is, I just can't say it to you." She had no difficulty pronouncing words once she thought of them or was reminded of them. If we said, "Do you mean *horse?*" she would reply, "Yes, horse!" The patient also had difficulty naming objects shown in pictures, such as a lamp, a boat, a pair of scissors, or a nest. When we tested her ability to read simple words or pronounceable nonwords such as *jess* or *bilt*, she failed utterly.

At first we concluded that the subject had lost the ability to read either phonetically or by the whole-word method. But further testing showed that although the woman could not *pronounce* the words she was shown, she could *recognize* them and understand something about their meaning. When we showed her a printed word along with four pictures, one of which contained the object represented by the word, she chose the correct picture 66 percent of the time (chance would be 25 percent). Similarly, when we showed her one picture along with four printed words, she chose the correct word 85 percent of the time. Thus, in both cases she was able to match words that she could not read with pictures that she could not name. (See Figure 8.3.) Because our subject could not have performed so well unless she could recognize words, we concluded that her whole-word recognition was relatively intact. Chance and additional testing confirmed this view when one day, when she was trying (without success) to read some words that I had typed, she suddenly said, "Hey! You spelled this one wrong." Indeed, I had. But even though she saw that the word was misspelled, she could not say what it was. The next day I gave her a list of eighty pairs of words, one spelled correctly and the other incorrectly. She went through the list quickly and easily, identifying 95 percent of the misspelled words, although she was able to read only five words.

- ■ What do the features of Wernicke's aphasia indicate about speech comprehension?
- ■ What is the difference between phonological and surface dyslexia?
- ■ How would you characterize phonetic and whole-word reading?

COMMUNICATION IN OTHER PRIMATES

The members of most species can communicate with one another. Even insects communicate; a female moth that is ready to mate can release a chemical called a pheromone that will bring male moths from miles away. And a dog can tell its owner that it wants to go for a walk by bringing its leash in its mouth and whining at the door. But until recently, humans were the only species that could use a **language,** a flexible system that uses symbols to express so many meanings.

In the 1960s Beatrix and Allen Gardner, of the University of Nevada, began Project Washoe (Gardner and Gardner, 1969, 1978), a remarkably successful attempt to teach sign language to a female chimpanzee named Washoe. Previous attempts to teach chimps to learn and use human language focused on speech (Hayes, 1952). These attempts failed because chimps

lack the control of tongue, lips, palate, and vocal cords that humans have, and thus they cannot produce the variety of complex sounds that characterize human speech.

Gardner and Gardner realized this limitation and decided to attempt to teach Washoe a **manual language**—one that makes use of hand movements. Chimps' hand and finger dexterity is almost as good as ours, so the only limitations in their ability would be cognitive ones. The manual language the Gardners chose was based on **Ameslan,** the American sign language used by the deaf. Ameslan is a true language: it contains function words and content words and has regular grammatical rules. People can communicate in Ameslan as fast as in spoken languages; they can even make puns based on similarities between signs, just as we make puns based on similarities between sounds.

Washoe was one year old when she began learning Ameslan; by the time she was four, she had a vocabulary of over 130 signs. Like children, she used single signs at first, then began to produce two-word sentences such as "Washoe sorry," "Gimme flower," "More fruit," and "Roger tickle." Sometimes she strung three or more words together, using the concept of agent and object: "You tickle me." She asked and answered questions, apologized, made assertions—in short, did the kinds of things that children would do while learning to talk. She showed overextensions and underextensions, just as human children do. Occasionally she even made correct generalizations by

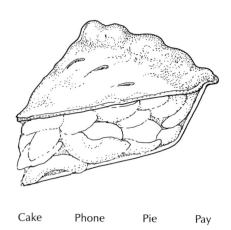

Cake   Phone   Pie   Pay

FIGURE 8.3

One of the stimuli presented to the anomic, dyslexic patient in the study by Margolin, Marcel, and Carlson (1985).

herself. After learning the sign for the verb *open* (as in *open box, open cupboard*), she used it to say "Open faucet," in requesting a drink. She made signs to herself when she was alone and used them to "talk" to cats and dogs, just as children will do. Although it is difficult to compare her progress with that of human children (the fairest comparison would be with that of deaf children learning to sign), it is clear that humans learn language much more readily than Washoe did.

Inspired by Project Washoe's success, a number of other investigators have taught chimpanzees and other primate species to use sign language. For example, Patterson is teaching a gorilla (Patterson and Linden, 1981), and Miles (1983) is teaching an orangutan. Washoe's training started relatively late in her life, and her trainers were not initially fluent in Ameslan. Other chimpanzees, raised from birth by humans who are native speakers of Ameslan, have begun to use signs when they are three months old (Gardner and Gardner, 1975).

Many psychologists and linguists have questioned whether the behavior of these animals can really be classified as verbal behavior. For example, Terrace, Petitto, Sanders, and Bever (1979) argue that the apes simply learned to imitate the gestures made by their trainers, and that sequences of signs such as "please milk please me like drink apple bottle" (produced by a young gorilla) are nothing like the sequences that human children produce. Others have challenged these criticisms (Miles, 1983; Fouts, 1983; Stokoe, 1983), blaming much of the controversy on the method Terrace and his colleagues used to train their chimpanzee.

Certainly, the verbal behavior of apes cannot be the same as that of humans. If apes could learn to communicate verbally as well as children can, then humans would not be the only species to have developed language. The usefulness of these studies rests in what they can teach us about our own language and cognitive abilities. Through them we may discover what abilities animals need in order to communicate the way we do. They may also help us understand the evolution of these capacities.

These studies have already provided some useful information. For example, Premack (1976) has taught chimpanzees to "read" and "write" by arranging plastic tokens into "sentences." Each token represents an object, action, or attribute such as color or shape,

The chimpanzee Washoe was taught sign language. By age four, she knew over 130 signs.

much the way words do. His first trainee, Sarah, whom he acquired when she was one year old, learned to understand complex sentences such as "Sarah insert banana in pail, apple in dish." When she saw the disks arranged in this order, she obeyed the instructions.

Sarah also learned to use word order to denote subject-verb-object, and she applied this syntactical rule to construct new sentences such as "Debby cut banana." She even constructed a syntactical rule of her own; she spontaneously combined "Mary give Sarah apple" with "Mary give Sarah orange," producing "Mary give Sarah apple orange." These linguistic accomplishments are modest in comparison with those of humans. For example, Premack notes that chimpanzees have never been observed to combine "Mary gives me apple" with "I like Mary" to produce "Mary's giving me apple is why I like her." However, it is possible that the linguistic accomplishments of humans and chimpanzees involve similar kinds of cognitive abilities, differing only in degree.

Chimpanzees apparently can use symbols to represent real objects and can manipulate these symbols logically. These abilities are two of the most powerful features of language. For Premack's chimpanzees a blue plastic triangle means "apple." If the chimpanzees are given a blue plastic triangle and asked to choose the appropriate symbols denoting its color and shape, they choose the ones that signify "red" and "round," not "blue" and "triangular." Thus, the blue triangle is not simply a token that the animals can use to obtain apples; it *represents* an apple for them, just as the word *apple* represents it for us.

Other studies have used this "chimpanzee language" to study these animals' cognitive skills. For example, Woodruff, Premack, and Kennel (1978) found that their fourteen-year-old chimpanzee, Sarah, was able to conserve volume. (You may recall from Chapter 4 that Jean Piaget studied the cognitive skill of conservation extensively.) Woodruff and his colleagues showed Sarah two tall cylinders containing equal volumes of water (dyed blue), then poured the contents of one cylinder into a wider container. Naturally, the level of water was lower in this one. Next the trainer gave Sarah a dish containing two plastic tokens, representing "same" and "different," and immediately left the room, so as not to tell Sarah inadvertently which symbol to choose by making unconscious gestures. Sarah had previously learned how to use these tokens: If two objects were the same, she had put "same" between them; if they were different she had put "different" between them. Sarah responded by putting the "same" token between the two containers of water. (See Figure 8.4.)

After giving the sign for "flower," Moja, a chimpanzee produced this drawing.

Sarah also conserved the volume of solids when their shape was transformed; that is, she placed a "same" token between a ball of modeling clay and the same amount of clay rolled into a different shape. However, she was unable to compare the same or different numbers of objects. Having demonstrated no understanding of the concept of number, she could not be tested for conservation of this concept.

One conclusion that has emerged from the studies with primates is that true verbal ability is a social behavior; it builds upon attempts at nonverbal communication in a social situation. The most successful attempts at teaching a language to other primates are those in which the animal and the trainer have established a close relationship in which they can successfully communicate with each other nonverbally, by means of facial expressions, movements, and gestures. Apes and orangutans clearly perceive people as other beings, who can be loved, trusted, feared, or despised. For example, Stokoe (1983) described an encounter with Moja, a young female chimpanzee being trained by the Gardners. Stokoe played a little game with Moja that clearly delighted her:

> After that we were friends, and she invited me to have lunch with her; that is, she pulled me by the hand to her quarters and showed me where to sit, while she played games with [the person] who was trying to get her to cooperate in getting cleaned up for lunch (p. 153).

Nonhuman primates (and humans, for that matter) learn a language best while interacting with others. Such interactions naturally lead to attempts at communication, and if signs (or spoken words) serve to make communication easier and more effective, they will most readily be learned.

One of the most interesting questions asked of researchers in this area is whether animals who learn to communicate by means of signs will teach those signs to their offspring. The answer appears to be yes, they will. Fouts, Hirsch, and Fouts (1983) obtained a ten-month-old infant chimpanzee, Loulis, whom they gave to Washoe to "adopt." Within eight days, the infant began to imitate Washoe's signs. To be certain that Washoe, and not humans, were teaching Loulis the signs he uses, the investigators used only the signs for *who, what, want, which, where, sign,* and *name* in his presence.

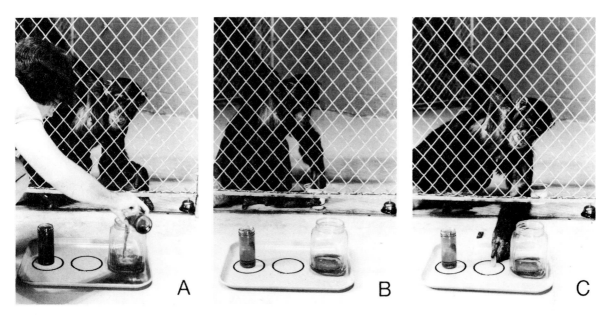

FIGURE 8.4

A chimpanzee demonstrates conservation of liquid. (From Woodruff, G., Premack, D., and Kennel, K. *Science*, 1978, 202, 991–994.)

As Fouts (1983) reported:

[A] sign, *food* [which he now uses], was . . . actively taught by Washoe. On this occasion Washoe was observed to sign *food* repeatedly in an excited fashion when a human was getting her some food. Loulis was sitting next to her watching. Washoe stopped signing and took Loulis' hand in hers, molded it into the *food* sign configuration, and touched it to his mouth several times. . . . [E]vidence has [also] been found indicating very subtle tutorial activity on Washoe's part. For example, when Loulis was first introduced to Washoe, Washoe would sign *come* to Loulis and then physically retrieve him. Later she would sign *come* and approach him but not retrieve him, and finally she would sign *come* while looking and orienting toward him without approaching him. (pp. 71–72)

■ What do we know about the acquisition of verbal behavior by nonhuman primates?

CHAPTER SUMMARY

1. Language is an orderly system of communication and a very important human social behavior. Verbal behavior refers to our use of language through speaking, listening, writing, and reading. Verbal communications accomplish three major functions: they provide information, request information or request a behavior.

2. Meaning is a joint function of syntax (science of grammatical construction) and semantics (study of the meaning of words). We use pauses and function words to make the beginnings of new constituents. Content words refer to objects and actions, and thus express meaning (even in some syntactically ambiguous sentences).

3. Chomsky has suggested that speech production entails the transformation of deep structure into surface structure. Initially, a sentence is represented by a basic kernel of meaning, along with labels indicating which transforming rules should be applied to which words. Just before the sentence is spoken, mechanisms in the brain apply the rules and produce the sentence's surface structure. A listener reverses the process, inferring a sentence's deep structure from its surface structure.

4. The human auditory system is capable of discriminating among speech sounds soon after birth. Human vocalization begins with crying, then develops to cooing and babbling, and finally results in patterned speech. During the two-word stage, children begin to combine words creatively. Their speech is governed by "rules." Children unconsciously adopt the rules, and adults unconsciously understand them. As children grow, and their vocabulary increases, they begin to use adult rules of grammar.

5. Psychologists disagree about what motivates a child to learn language; some believe that innate brain mechanisms contain language universals, universal grammatical rules; others believe that verbal behavior, like other behaviors, is shaped by reinforcement. A careful analysis of the role that language plays in a child's social interactions suggests that the consequences of learning and using language are reinforcing.

6. The effects of brain damage suggest that the memory of the sounds of words is located in Wernicke's area and the memory of the muscular movements needed to produce them is located in Broca's area. Thus, Wernicke's area is necessary for speech perception and Broca's area for speech production. Wernicke's aphasia is characterized by fluent but meaningless speech, scarce in content words but rich in function words. A person with Broca's aphasia has speech that is labored, meaningful, and ungrammatical.

7. A person has two means of recognizing and pronouncing written words: phonetic reading and whole word reading, which seem to be functions of different areas of the brain. A person with phonological dyslexia can only read by the whole word method, whereas a person with surface dyslexia can only read phonologically.

8. Studies of the ability of other primates to learn language enable us to analyze some of the types of experiences that are necessary for acquiring the skills involved in producing and understanding speech. To the extent that apes can be taught at least some of the rudiments of language, their behaviors provide some insights into the ways in which humans acquire language skills.

KEY TERMS

agrammatism A language disturbance; difficulty in the production and comprehension of grammatical features, such as proper use of the function words, word endings, and word order. Often seen in cases of Broca's aphasia.

Ameslan The American sign language used by the deaf.

anomia A language disorder; difficulty in thinking of and saying appropriate words. All forms of aphasia include some form of anomia.

aphasia A language disturbance caused by brain damage that manifests itself in various deficits of speech production or comprehension.

Broca's aphasia Severe difficulty in articulating words, especially function words, caused by damage to Broca's area, a region of the frontal cortex on the left (speech—dominant) side of the brain.

Broca's area See *Broca's aphasia.*

constituent parts Small groups of words, like phrases, that form grammatical units.

content word A noun, verb, adjective, or adverb that conveys meaning.

deep structure The essential meaning of a sentence, without regard to the grammatical features (surface structure) of the sentence that are needed to express it in words.

developmental dyslexia Specific learning disability in reading that is not caused by head injury or disease of the central nervous system; occurs in children, probably as a result of abnormal development of some systems of the brain.

directive Request for specific behavior, such as "shut the door."

function word A preposition, article, or other word that conveys little of the meaning of a sentence but is important in specifying its grammatical structure.

given-new contract The tendency of a speaker (or writer) to use emphasis or grammatical features to inform the listener (or reader) what information expressed in a sentence should be familiar and what information is new.

inflection A change in the form of a word (usually adding a suffix) to denote a grammatical feature such as tense or number.

language   A flexible system that uses symbols to express meaning.

language universals   Characteristics that can be found in all languages that linguists have studied.

manual language   A language that makes use of hand movements.

overextension   The use of a word to denote a larger class of items than is appropriate, for example, referring to the moon as a *ball*; commonly observed in the speech of young children.

phoneme   The minimum unit of sound that conveys meaning in a particular language, such as /P/.

phonetic reading   Reading by decoding the phonetic significance of letter strings, or "sound reading" as opposed to whole-word reading, or "sight reading." Brain injury can abolish one method without affecting the other.

phonological dyslexia   A reading disorder characterized by inability to utilize phonological rules (to "sound out" words by examining their letter sequences).

semantics   The study of the meanings represented by words.

stress   The emphasis placed on a syllable or word in spoken language.

surface dyslexia   A disorder caused by brain damage that results in difficulty in reading by the "whole-word method." People with this disorder have particular difficulty reading irregularly spelled words such as *yacht* or *pint*.

surface structure   The grammatical features of a sentence.

syntactical rules   The rules that describe how we put words together to form sentences.

syntax   The science of grammatical construction.

underextension   The use of a word to denote a smaller class of items than is appropriate, for example, referring only to one particular animal as a dog; commonly observed in the speech of young children.

Wernicke's aphasia   A disorder caused by damage to Wernicke's area, located in the temporal lobe (usually, on the left side), characterized by deficits in the perception of speech and by the production of fluent but rather meaningless speech.

Wernicke's area   See *Wernicke's aphasia*.

whole-word reading   Identification of written words by perception of the words as a whole; contrasts with phonetic reading.

Chapter 9

Intelligence

We acknowledge that some people are more intelligent than others, but just what do we mean by that? We tend to think of people as intelligent if they succeed at tasks that use their heads rather than their hands. Thus, a critic who writes a witty, articulate review of an artist's exhibition of paintings is said to demonstrate his or her intelligence, whereas the painter is said to show his or her *skill*.

At a specific behavioral level, intelligence has been given an operational definition, measurable in terms of consistent performance on verbal and mathematical problems. This kind of problem-solving behavior has been measured in terms of scores on tests, and these tests have proved reliable over time. Consequently, many people think of intelligence as someone's ability to get a score on word and number problems—specifically a score on an I.Q. test. But is intelligence limited to our ability to solve word and number problems?

Are skills in music, art, manual dexterity, and body control also types of intelligence? Recently, cognitive psychologists have begun investigating the types of skills that enable people to survive and flourish, and their research suggests that we should broaden our definition of intelligence to include a wider range of abilities. At a global and functional level, intelligence may be conceived of as any consistent pattern of behavior that results in our success at an endeavor.

One of the most interesting questions in the field of intelligence is also one of the most difficult to answer: Which is more important in determining intelligence—heredity or environment? As you will see, when the question is phrased that way, it cannot be answered. Hereditary and environmental factors interact with each other; the effect of one depends on the nature of the other.

This chapter begins with a discussion of intelligence testing. Next, you will learn about the major approaches psychologists have followed in their ongoing study of the nature of intelligence. The chapter concludes with a discussion of the roles of heredity and the environment in determining intelligence.

APPROACHES TO INTELLIGENCE

Research into the nature of intelligence began with attempts to measure the ways in which people differ. Differences in people's abilities to perform various intellectual tasks presumably reflect individual differences in intelligence. Thus, the **differential approach** to the investigation of intelligence attempts to devise tests that identify and measure such individual differences, so as to discover the underlying factors that constitute intellectual abilities. The differential approach is the basis of the field of

A child working on the object assembly portion of the Wechsler Intelligence Scale for Children, Revised.

psychometrics (the branch of psychology concerned with development of tests of ability and personality) and has dominated research on intelligence for most of this century.

The second major approach to intelligence is the **developmental approach,** which studies the ways in which infants learn to perceive, manipulate, and think about the world. The most influential proponent of this approach was the Swiss psychologist Jean Piaget. Because his work was described in detail in Chapter 4, I will not discuss it further here.

More recently, cognitive psychologists have extended their studies of perception, attention, and memory to the field of intelligence. Their approach, called the **information-processing approach,** emphasizes the components of intellectual processes. For example, they might begin with a particular type of task and analyze the steps people must follow to perform the task. This approach conceives of intellectual abilities as abilities to invoke various sets of cognitive processes to solve different types of problems. Cognitive psychologists are more interested in the nature of the processes than in the ways in which people differ.

Because the study of intelligence began with the development of intelligence tests, I will discuss this topic first.

INTELLIGENCE TESTING

Assessment of intellectual ability, or intelligence testing, is a controversial topic because of its importance in modern society. Unless people have special skills that suit them for a career in sports or entertainment, their economic success depends heavily on formal education, and admission to colleges and eligibility for scholarships are largely determined by the results of tests. In addition, many employers use specialized aptitude tests to help them select among job candidates. Because the scores achieved on these tests have major implications for the quality of people's adult lives, testing has become one of the most important areas of applied psychology. Today there are hundreds of tests of specific abilities, such as manual dexterity, spatial reasoning, vocabulary, mathematical aptitude, musical ability, creativity, and memory. There are also general tests of scholastic aptitude, some of which you have probably taken yourself. These tests vary widely in reliability, validity, and ease of administration.

From Mandarins to Galton

Undoubtedly humans have been aware of individual differences in abilities since our species first evolved. Some people were more efficient hunters, some were more skillful at constructing tools and weapons, and some were more daring and clever warriors. As early as 2200 B.C., Chinese administrators tested civil servants (mandarins) periodically to be sure that their abilities qualified them for their jobs. But in Western cultures differences in social class were far more important than individual differences in ability until the Renaissance, when the concept of individualism came into being.

Although the term *intelligence* is an old one, deriving from the Latin *intellectus* (meaning "perception" or "comprehension"), its use in the English language dates only from the late nineteenth century, when it was revived by the philosopher Herbert Spencer and by the biologist-statistician Sir Francis Galton (1822–1911), the most important early investigator of individual differences in ability. Galton was strongly influenced by his cousin, Charles Darwin, who stressed the importance of inherited differences in the physical and behavioral traits related to a species's survival.

Galton made some important contributions to the study of individual differences. His systematic evaluation of large numbers of people and the methods of population statistics he developed served as models for the statistical tests that are now used in all branches of science. His observation that the distribution of most human traits closely resembles the normal curve developed by the Belgian statistician Lambert Quetelet is the foundation for many modern tests of statistical significance. (See Figure 9.1.)

Galton also outlined the logic of a measure he called **correlation:** the degree to which variability in one measure is related to variability in another. In addition, Galton developed the logic of *twin studies* and *adoptive parent studies* to assess the heritability of a human trait.

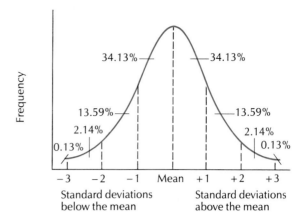

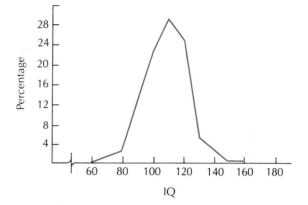

FIGURE 9.1

Top: A mathematically derived normal curve. *Bottom:* A curve showing the distribution of IQ scores of 850 children of 2½ years of age. (From Terman, L.M., and Merrill, M.A. *Stanford-Binet Intelligence Scale.* Boston: Houghton Mifflin, 1960; material cited pertains to the 1960 edition and not to the 4th edition, 1985. Reproduced by permission of The Riverside Publishing Co.)

The Binet-Simon Scale

Alfred Binet, a French psychologist, disagreed with Galton's conception of human intelligence. He and a colleague (Binet and Henri, 1896) suggested that a group of simple sensory tests could not adequately determine a person's intelligence. They recommended measuring a variety of psychological abilities (such as imagery, attention, comprehension, imagination, judgments of visual space, and memory for various stimuli) that appeared to be more representative of the traits that distinguished people of high and low intelligence.

To identify children who were unable to profit from normal classroom instruction and needed special attention, Binet and a colleague, Theodore Simon, assembled a collection of tests, many of which had been developed by other investigators, and published the **Binet-Simon Scale** in 1905. The tests were arranged in order of difficulty, and the researchers obtained **norms** for each test. Norms are data from comparison groups that permit the score of an individual to be assessed relative to his or her peers. In this case, the norms consisted of distributions of scores obtained by children of various ages. Binet and Simon also provided a detailed description of the testing procedure, which was essential for obtaining reliable scores. Without a standardized procedure for administering a test, different testers can obtain different scores from the same child.

Binet revised the 1905 test in order to assess the intellectual abilities of both normal children and those with learning problems. The revised versions provided a procedure for estimating a child's **mental age:** the level of intellectual development that could be expected for an average child of a particular age. For example, if a child of eight scored as well as average ten-year-old children, his or her mental age would be ten years. Binet did not develop the concept of IQ, or *intelligence quotient*. Nor did he believe that mental age derived from the test scores expressed a simple trait called "intelligence"; he conceived of the overall score as the average of several different abilities.

The Stanford-Binet Scale

Lewis Terman, of Stanford University, translated and revised the Binet-Simon Scale in the United States. The revised group of tests, published in 1916, became known as the **Stanford-Binet Scale.** Revisions by Terman and Maud Merrill were published in 1937 and 1960. In 1985 an entirely new version of the Stanford-Binet Scale was published. The scale consists of various tasks grouped according to mental age. Simple tests include identifying parts of the body and remembering which of three small cardboard boxes contains a marble. Intermediate tests include tracing a simple maze with a pencil and repeating five digits orally. Advanced tests include explaining the difference between two abstract words that are close in meaning (such as *fame* and *notoriety*) and completing complex sentences.

The 1916 Stanford-Binet Scale contained a formula for computing the **intelligence quotient (IQ),** a measure devised by Stern (1914). Its rationale is quite simple: If the test scores indicate that a child's mental age is equal to his or her chronological age (that is, calendar age), then the child's intelligence is average; if the child's mental age is above or below the chronological age, then the child is more or less intelligent than average. This relation is expressed as the quotient of mental age (MA) and chronological age (CA). The result is the **ratio IQ:**

$$IQ = \frac{MA}{CA} \times 100$$

The quotient is multiplied by 100 to eliminate fractions. For example, if a child's mental age is ten and the child's chronological age is eight, then his or her IQ is $(10 \div 8) \times 100 = 125$.

The 1960 version of the Stanford-Binet Scale replaced the ratio IQ with the **deviation IQ.** Instead of using the ratio of mental age to chronological age, the new measure compared a child's score with those received by other children of the same chronological age. (The deviation IQ was invented by David Wechsler, whose work is described in the next section.) Suppose a child's score is one standard deviation above the mean for his or her age. (See Chapter 1 for a discussion of standard deviation.) The standard deviation of the ratio IQ scores is 16 points, and the score assigned to average IQ is 100 points; thus, the child's score is 100 + 16 (the standard deviation) = 116. A child who scores one standard deviation below the mean receives a deviation IQ of 84 (100 − 16). (See Figure 9.2.)

As you will recall from Chapter 1, the adequacy of a measure is represented by its reliability and validity. In the case of psychometric testing, reliability is assessed by the correlation between the scores people receive on the same measurement on two different occasions; perfect reliability is 1.0. High reliability is achieved by means of standardized test administration and objective scoring: All test-takers are exposed to the same situation during testing, and all test-givers score responses in the same way. The reliability of the revised 1937 scale for measuring ratio IQ scores was found to be very high, ranging from .98 for people with low IQs to .90 for people with high IQs.

Validity is the correlation between test scores

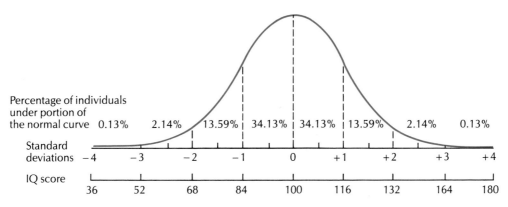

Percentage of individuals under portion of the normal curve   0.13%   2.14%   13.59% | 34.13% | 34.13% | 13.59%   2.14%   0.13%

Standard deviations   −4   −3   −2   −1   0   +1   +2   +3   +4

IQ score   36   52   68   84   100   116   132   164   180

FIGURE 9.2

The rationale for calculating the deviation IQ score.

and another measure of the variable that is being assessed: the **criterion.** For example, suppose you plan to estimate people's wealth by observing how many money-related words they use when describing a picture that illustrates a story. You determine the validity of the test by seeing how accurately it estimated people's actual wealth (the criterion).

Because there is no single definition of intelligence, there is no single criterion measure. However, measures such as success in school correlate rather well with measured IQ (between .40 and .75). Thus, because intellectual ability plays at least some role in academic success, it appears that IQ has some validity.

- What are the three major approaches to intelligence?
- What are the key characteristics of the Binet-Simon and Stanford-Binet scales?
- How are the terms *validity* and *reliability* applied to intelligence tests?

Wechsler's Tests

When David Wechsler was chief psychologist at New York City's Bellevue Psychiatric Hospital, he developed several popular and well-respected tests of intelligence. The Wechsler-Bellevue Scale, published in 1939, was revised in 1942 for use in the armed forces and was superseded in 1955 by the **Wechsler Adult Intelligence Scale (WAIS).** This test was revised again in 1981 (the WAIS-R). The **Wechsler In-**telligence Scale for Children (WISC), first published in 1949 and revised in 1974 (the WISC-R), resembles the WAIS. Wechsler also devised an intelligence test for preschool children, a memory scale, and other measures of ability.

The WAIS-R consists of eleven subtests, divided into two categories: verbal and performance. Table 9.1 (on p. 276) lists the subtests and a typical question or problem for each. The norms obtained for the WAIS-R permit the tester to calculate a deviation IQ score.

The WAIS-R has become the most popular individually administered adult intelligence test. Like the Stanford-Binet Scale, it is very reliable. An important advantage is that it tests verbal and performance abilities separately. Neuropsychologists often use it because people with brain damage tend to score very differently on the performance and verbal tests; thus, comparisons of performance and verbal test scores suggest the presence of undiagnosed brain damage. People with few educational opportunities often do worse on the verbal tests than on the performance tests. The WAIS-R is useful in estimating what their score might have been in a more favorable environment.

The Kaufman Assessment Battery for Children

A recent test of intelligence is the **Kaufman Assessment Battery for Children (K-ABC)** (Kaufman and Kaufman, 1983a, 1983b). This test is based on the distinction between sequential and simultaneous mental processes, which tend to be functions performed by the left and

TABLE 9.1

WAIS-R subtests and typical questions or problems

Subtest	Typical Question or Problem
Verbal	
Information	"What is the capital of France?"
Digit span	"Repeat these numbers back to me: 46239."
Vocabulary	"What does the word 'conventional' mean?"
Arithmetic	"Suppose you bought six postcards for thirteen cents each and gave the clerk a dollar. How much change would you receive?" (Paper and pencil cannot be used.)
Comprehension	"Why are we tried by a jury of our peers?"
Similarities	"How are goldfish and canaries similar to each other?"
Performance	
Picture completion	The tester shows the subject a picture with a missing part (such as a mouse without its whiskers) and says, "Tell me what's missing."
Picture arrangement	The tester shows a series of cartoon pictures (without words) and instructs the subject to arrange them in the proper sequence.
Block design	The tester shows a picture and four or nine blocks divided diagonally into red and white sections, then instructs the subject to arrange the blocks so that they match the design in the picture.
Object assembly	The tester gives the subject pieces of cardboard cut like a jigsaw puzzle and instructs him or her to assemble it. (When properly assembled the pieces form the shape of a common object.)
Digit symbol	The tester presents a set of ten designs paired with the ten numerals and instructs the subject to write the corresponding symbols beneath each of a large series of numerals.

right hemispheres of the brain, respectively. In sequential tasks, time is important, because stimuli presented at different times must be compared and integrated. Examples of sequential tasks include applying rules of grammar, remembering the time sequence of events, and decoding the correspondences between letters and sounds. In simultaneous tasks, all elements are present at the same time and must be compared and integrated in a spatial fashion. Examples of simultaneous tasks include recognizing shapes of letters, interpreting the meaning of maps, and extracting the main ideas from a paragraph. Most complex skills are a mixture of sequential and simultaneous functions; for example, to get from place to place using a map, the interpretation of the map must be translated into a sequence of left and right turns (Kaufman, Kamphaus, and Kaufman, 1985).

The K-ABC has ten subtests, each designed to measure different combinations of skills under the broad categories of sequential and simultaneous processes. These subtests are listed and described in Table 9.2.

The K-ABC provides scores on the following scales: sequential processing, simultaneous processing, achievement, and mental processing. The achievement scale consists of six additional subtests that measure acquired facts and skills, such as arithmetic, reading, and language concepts. This scale presumably reflects the nature of the language spoken in the child's home, along with his or her educational opportunities and motivation. The **mental processing composite (MPC)** is a global estimate of intelligence similar to the IQ, consisting of a combination of both sequential and simultaneous processing scales.

One of the advantages of the K-ABC is that it includes a nonverbal scale, administered in pantomime and responded to by motor gestures, which can be used with language- or hearing-impaired children or with children who do not speak English. According to the authors of the K-ABC, the scores on this battery of tests appear to be less determined by cultural differences than those on the Stanford-Binet Scale or the WISC-R are.

This test battery is a new one; whether it will eventually be used as much as the Stanford-Binet Scale and the WISC-R depends on the perceived value placed on it by counselors and researchers.

TABLE 9.2

Subtests of the Kaufman Assessment Battery for Children

Magic window (Simultaneous)
Measures the child's ability to identify and name an object whose picture is rotated behind a narrow slit so that the picture is only partially exposed at any point in time

Face recognition (Simultaneous)
Measures the child's ability to attend closely to one or two faces in photographs that are exposed briefly, then to select the correct face(s), shown in a group photograph

Hand movements (Sequential)
Measures the child's ability to copy the precise sequence of taps on the table with the fist, palm, or side of the hand as performed by the examiner

Gestalt closure (Simultaneous)
Measures the child's ability to fill in the gaps mentally in a partially completed inkblot drawing, and requires naming or describing that drawing

Number recall (Sequential)
Measures the child's ability to repeat—in sequence—a series of numbers spoken by the examiner

Triangles (Simultaneous)
Measures the child's ability to assemble several identical rubber triangles (blue on one side, yellow on the other) to match a picture of an abstract design

Word order (Sequential)
Measures the child's ability (both with and without an interference task) to point to silhouettes of common objects in the same order as these objects were named by the examiner

Matrix analogies (Simultaneous)
Measures the child's ability to select the picture or design that best completes a 2-inch x 2-inch visual analogy

Spatial memory (Simultaneous)
Measures the child's ability to recall the locations of pictures arranged randomly on a page

Photo series (Simultaneous)
Measures the child's ability to organize a randomly arranged array of photographs illustrating an event and then order them in their proper time sequence

Adapted from Kaufman, A.S., Kamphaus, R.W., and Kaufman, N.L. In *Major Psychological Assessment Instruments*, edited by C.S. Newmark. Boston: Allyn and Bacon, 1985.

The Use and Abuse of Intelligence Tests

Many kinds of institutions use intelligence tests and tests of specific abilities. Schools that group students according to ability usually do so on the basis of test scores. Schools also administer tests to students who appear to be slow learners in order to assess educational needs that may require use of a special program. At selective academic institutions, test scores usually serve as an important criterion for admission. Similarly, many business organizations use ability tests to screen job candidates. Because test scores have such important consequences for people's opportunities, it is essential to know whether intelligence tests are valid and whether they are being used appropriately.

Critics of intelligence testing have argued that intelligence tests do not measure people's abilities at all; rather, they measure what people have learned. Therefore, people's educational opportunities in the home, neighborhood, and school directly influence their performance on intelligence tests. Consider the effects of a person's family background and culture on his or her ability to answer questions such as "Who wrote *Romeo and Juliet?*" "What is a hieroglyphic?" "What is the meaning of *catacomb?*" and "What is the thing to do if another boy (or girl) hits you without meaning

In some cultures, intelligence testing is of great significance. In Japan, intelligence tests are used to determine admission to school at an early age.

to?" (Vernon, 1979, p. 22). Obviously, a child from a middle-class family is much more likely to be able to answer the first three questions than an equally intelligent child from a deprived environment. The answer given to the fourth question is also likely to be culturally determined. Test constructors have responded to this criticism, and modern tests are much less likely to contain questions that are obviously culturally biased.

Unfortunately, the problem of cultural bias has not yet been solved. Even though questions with obvious cultural bias are no longer incorporated into intelligence tests, different experiences can lead to different test-taking strategies in nonobvious ways. For example, Scribner (1977) asked members of the Kpelle tribe in the African country of Liberia to solve the following problem. At first glance, the problem appears to be "culture fair" because it refers to their own tribe and to an occupation they are familiar with.

> All Kpelle men are rice farmers.
> Mr. Smith is not a rice farmer.
> Is he a Kpelle man?

She received answers such as the following:

Subject: I don't know the man in person. I have not laid eyes on the man himself.

Experimenter: Just think about the statement.

Subject: If I knew him in person, I can answer that question, but since I do not know him in person, I cannot answer that question.

Experimenter: Try and answer from your Kpelle sense.

Subject: If you know a person, if a question comes up about him you are able to answer. But if you do not know the person, if a question comes up about him it's hard for you to answer.

We certainly cannot conclude that the Kpelle tribesman in this example is unintelligent. In fact, he probably thought that the experimenter was not demonstrating intelligent behavior by persisting with a stupid question. His explanation in the final two sentences shows that he is in fact using logical deduction based on the premise that it is impossible to talk about people you have not met. The unwillingness to consider a proposition about a person not yet met probably reflects the fact that Kpelle people are not literate; once people read, they learn

to think about people in the abstract as well as people they know in person. Thus, test items like these cannot be used to compare peoples' intellectual ability in different cultures.

Predicting and Measuring Performance

Critics' objections to the more general issue that intelligence tests measure what people have learned, and not what they *can* learn, are also valid. It is clear that two people with identical native abilities can have very different IQ scores. But this possibility does not necessarily prove that intelligence tests are useless. Perhaps what a person has learned is useful in predicting how well he or she will continue to learn in the future.

Intelligence tests have been found to be rather good predictors of a child's scholastic performance. As I mentioned before, the correlation between scores on the 1960 Stanford-Binet Scale and school grades ranges from .40 to .75 (Aiken, 1982). However, critics of these tests question the need for teachers to *predict* children's academic performance. After all, teachers are in a position to observe performance. What information do intelligence tests provide that teachers cannot observe in their classrooms?

Therefore, another potential abuse of intelligence tests is to deprive children who have scored poorly of opportunities to receive an education that will make them competitive later in life.

Ebel (1966) points out additional dangers. First, children who discover they have scored poorly on an intelligence test are likely to suffer feelings of inferiority and may become disinclined to try to learn, believing that they cannot. Second, undue emphasis on testing may affect a school's curriculum and methods of teaching; teachers and administrators may try to teach information and skills that are measured by the tests instead of basing their curriculum on the children's needs. Clearly, schools should use intelligence tests with great caution. If the results are not themselves used intelligently, such tests are actually harmful.

Stability of IQ Scores

It is a common belief that the IQ score measures a permanent and rather stable attribute. But the best evidence on this issue indicates otherwise. In a longitudinal study of sixty-one children born in Berkeley, California, Jones and Bayley (1941) measured the children's IQs repeatedly from the ages of one month to eighteen years. They found that the scores on IQ tests administered early in life have no relation to IQ scores received later, at age eighteen. However, the correlation improves substantially, reaching approximately .90 around age ten or eleven. Furthermore, a child's IQ score does not remain fixed; even after age ten the IQ can change by up to 26 points. Finally, because the sample in this study included only white, English-speaking, middle-class children, the variability seen here is likely to underestimate the variability that would be obtained from a more heterogeneous population.

Identifying Specific Learning Needs

Intelligence testing has other potential benefits when used in accordance with Binet's original purpose: to identify students who require special instruction. Children with severe learning problems are likely to develop a strong sense of inferiority if they are placed in classes with children whose academic progress is much faster than theirs; such children will probably benefit most from special teaching methods. These tests can also identify exceptionally bright students who are performing poorly because they are bored with the pace of instruction or who have been labeled as "troublemakers" by their teachers.

Many otherwise bright children suffer from various specific learning disabilities. Some have trouble learning to read or write, or perform poorly at arithmetic or motor skills. By identifying a specific learning disability in an otherwise bright child, testing helps ensure remedial action and prevents mislabeling.

Identifying Degrees of Mental Retardation

Binet's original use of intelligence tests—to identify children who learn more slowly than most others and who therefore need special training—is still important. Some children are so deficient in intellectual abilities that they require institutional care. Intelligence tests are accepted means of evaluating the extent of a

Some children with Down's Syndrome are moderately retarded, while others score within a normal range on tests of intelligence. Children with Down's syndrome can lead active and demanding lives.

child's disabilities, and thus of the most appropriate remedial program.

The term **mental retardation** was originally applied to children with severe learning problems because they appeared to achieve intellectual skills and competencies at a significantly later age than most children. Their achievements came more slowly; thus, their developmental stages seemed to be retarded. Although most mentally retarded people were formerly relegated to a bleak and hopeless existence in institutions, many successful training programs have been initiated in recent years. The causes of mental retardation are discussed later in this chapter.

Mental retardation is often accompanied by deficits in physical and social skills. The most severe classification, **profound mental retardation,** designates people with a mental age of under three years and with IQ scores under 20. These people usually have severe brain damage, and they almost always also have physical defects. The next category is **severe mental retardation,** with a mental age of three to four years and with IQ scores between 20 and 35. Few of these people learn to read and write unless they are trained by special methods. Both groups need custodial care.

Moderate mental retardation designates people with mental ages ranging from four to seven-and-a-half years and with IQ scores of 36 to 51. Many of these people also require custodial care. **Mild mental retardation** designates people with mental ages of seven-and-a-half to eleven years and with IQ scores of 52 to 67. With adequate training, most mildly mentally retarded people can lead independent lives and perform well at jobs that do not require a great deal of intellectual ability.

- What are some distinguishing features of the Wechsler Adult Intelligence Scale?
- What are key issues in the controversy over the use of intelligence tests to assess and predict children's academic ability?
- What are the standard degrees of mental retardation?

THE NATURE OF INTELLIGENCE: DIFFERENTIAL APPROACHES

Differential (psychometric) approaches to the study of intelligence begin with the assumption that the nature of intelligence can best be investigated by studying the ways in which people differ in their performance on tests of intellectual abilities. There is no doubt that people vary widely in many ways, such as their abilities to learn and use words, to solve arithmetic problems, and to perceive and remember spatial information. The question remains whether intelligence is a global trait or a composite of separate, independent abilities. The fact that psychometricians have devised tests that yield a single IQ score does not in itself mean that intelligence is a single general characteristic. Some investigators have suggested that certain intellectual abilities are completely independent of one another; for example, a person can be excellent at spatial reasoning but poor at solving verbal analogies. Even investigators who believe that intelligence is a global trait acknowledge that people also have specific intellectual abilities and that these abilities are at least somewhat independent. But there is still disagreement between those who believe that the specific abilities are totally independent and those who believe that one general factor influences them all.

Spearman's Two-Factor Theory

Charles Spearman (1927) proposed that a person's performance on a test of intellectual ability is determined by two factors: the **g factor,** which is a general factor, and the **s factor,** which is a factor that is specific to a particular test. Spearman did not call his g factor "intelligence"; he considered the term too vague. He defined the g factor as comprising three "qualitative principles of cognition": apprehension of experience, eduction of relations, and eduction of correlates. A common task on tests of intellectual abilities—solving analogies—requires all three principles (Sternberg, 1985). For example, consider the following analogy:

LAWYER:CLIENT::DOCTOR:_____

This problem should be read as

LAWYER is to CLIENT as DOCTOR is to _____.

Apprehension of experience refers to people's ability to perceive and understand what they experience; thus, reading and understanding each of the words in the analogy requires this principle. *Eduction* (not "education") is the process of drawing or bringing out—that is, of figuring out from given facts. In this case, *eduction of relations* refers to the ability to perceive the relation between LAWYER and CLIENT; namely, that the lawyer works for, and is paid by, the client. *Eduction of correlates* refers to the ability to apply a rule inferred from one case to a similar case. Thus, the person whom a doctor works for and is paid by is obviously a PATIENT. Because analogy problems require all three of Spearman's principles of cognition, he advocated their use in intelligence testing.

Empirical evidence for Spearman's two-factor theory comes from correlations among various tests of particular intellectual abilities. The governing logic is as follows: Suppose we administer ten different tests to a group of people; if each test measures a separate, independent ability, the scores these people make on any one test will be unrelated to their scores on any other and the correlations among the tests will be approximately zero. However, if the tests measure abilities that are simply different manifestations of a single trait, the scores will be perfectly related; the intercorrelations will be close to 1.0. In reality, the intercorrelations among various tests of mental ability usually range from .30 to .70.

If two measures are correlated, then knowing a person's score on one of them allows us to predict, with varying degrees of accuracy, that person's score on the other. If the correlation is equal to 1.0, then we can predict the second score with perfect accuracy. One way of looking at the correlation coefficient is as an estimate of the amount of variability the two measures have in common. The actual amount of common variability is equal to the square of the correlation coefficient: r^2. Thus, if the correlations between pairs of tests of mental ability range from .30 to .70, then we know that from 9 percent to 49 percent of their variance is due to common causes.

Spearman concluded that a general intelligence factor (g) accounted for the common variance shared among different tests of ability. Thus, a person's score on a particular test depended upon two things: the person's specific ability (s) on the particular test (such as spatial reasoning) and his or her level of the g factor, or general reasoning ability. However, even though Spearman's data were consistent with his theory, they do not prove that his theory is correct. The fact that two tests are correlated does not prove that they share a common g factor; they could be sharing a common s factor instead. For example, if we construct and administer two tests, one consisting of fifty multiplication problems and the other of fifty division problems, we will undoubtedly find that people who do well on one test also tend to do well on the other. But this correlation is not necessarily evidence for a common g factor; more likely, the tests share a common s factor, because multiplication and division are similar tasks. Only special methods such as factor analysis can suggest how much of the correlation between two tests can be attributed to an s factor and how much to a g factor.

Evidence from Factor Analysis

Factor analysis is a mathematical procedure developed by Spearman and Pearson that permits investigators to identify common factors or sources of variability among groups of tests. If a group of individual tests tend to correlate with one another but not with other tests, we can conclude that the two groups are measuring different factors. A factor analysis determines which particular tests form groups.

Although factor analysis can give hints about the nature of intelligence, it cannot provide definitive answers. The names given to factors

Spearman believed that intelligence was a global trait. However, he acknowledged that people also have specific abilities such as musical talent.

Fluid intelligence represents a universal ability to learn and solve problems. Crystallized intelligence is defined by tasks that require people to learn information from their culture.

are up to the investigator and are not prescribed by the mathematical analysis. Furthermore, factor analysis can never be more meaningful than the individual tests on which it is performed. To identify the relevant factors in human intelligence, one must include an extensive variety of tests in the factor analysis. For example, experience has shown that the WAIS-R is a useful predictor of scholastic performance and (to a lesser extent) of vocational success. Thus, it appears to measure some important abilities. But a factor analysis of the subtests will never reveal other important abilities that may *not* be measured by the WAIS-R. For example, the WAIS-R does not contain a

test of musical ability. If it did, then a factor analysis would undoubtedly yield an additional factor. Whether musical ability is a component of intelligence depends on how we decide to define intelligence; this question cannot be answered by a factor analysis.

Many investigators have performed factor analyses on tests of intellectual abilities. For example, Louis Thurstone (1938) administered a battery of fifty-six tests to 218 college students, then performed a factor analysis and extracted seven factors, which he labeled *verbal comprehension, verbal fluency, number, spatial visualization, memory, reasoning,* and *perceptual speed.* At first, Thurstone thought that his results contradicted Spearman's hypothesized g factor. However, Eysenck suggested a few years later that a *second* factor analysis could be performed on Thurstone's factors. If the analysis found one common factor, then Spearman's g factor would receive support. In other words, if Thurstone's seven factors had a second-order factor in common, this factor might be conceived of as general intelligence.

Cattell performed a second-order factor analysis and found not one but two major factors. Horn and Cattell (1966) called these factors *fluid intelligence* (g_f) and *crystallized intelligence* (g_c). (You may recall these terms from Chapter 5 in the discussion of the effects of aging on intelligence.) Fluid intelligence is defined by relatively culture-free tasks, whereas crystallized intelligence is defined by tasks that require people to have learned information from their culture—particularly, vocabulary and the kind of information that is learned in schools. Cattell regards g_f as being closely related to a person's native capacity for intellectual performance; in other words, it represents a potential ability to learn and solve problems. In contrast, he regards crystallized intelligence as what a person has accomplished through the use of his or her fluid intelligence—what he or she has learned. Horn differs with Cattell; he cites evidence suggesting that both factors are learned but are also based on heredity. He says that g_f is based on casual learning, while g_c is based on cultural, school-type learning (Horn, 1978).

Figure 9.3 illustrates items from five subtests that load heavily on the g_f (fluid intelligence) factor. Although verbalization can help solve these problems, they are essentially nonverbal

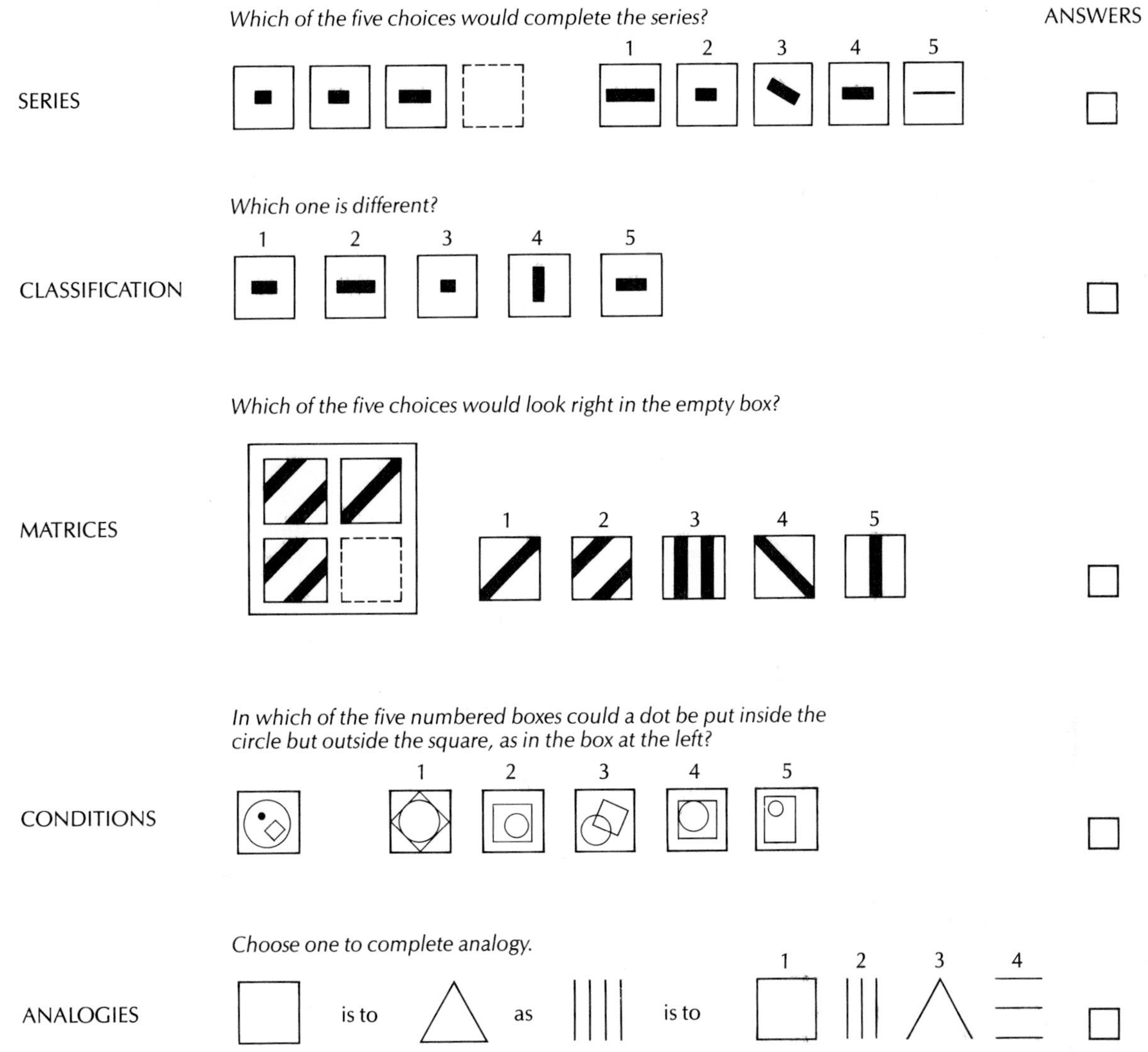

FIGURE 9.3

Five tests that correlate well with Cattell's g_f factor. (From Form B, Scales II and III, IPAT Culture-Fair Test. By permission of the Institute of Personality and Ability Testing, 1602 Coronado Drive, Champaign, Illinois, and the Cattell Scale II, Harrap & Co.)

in form. In addition, the items differ from the types of problems encountered in school, and they do not appear to be closely tied to cultural experience.

Tests that load heavily on the g_c (crystallized intelligence) factor include word analogies and tests of vocabulary, general information, and use of language. According to Cattell, g_c depends on g_f. Fluid intelligence supplies the native ability, whereas experience with language and exposure to books, school, and other learning opportunities develop crystallized intelli-

gence. If two people have the same experiences, the one with the greater fluid intelligence will develop the greater crystallized intelligence. However, a person with a high fluid intelligence exposed to an intellectually impoverished environment will develop a poor or mediocre crystallized intelligence.

No two investigators agree about the nature of intelligence. However, most researchers believe that a small number of common factors account for at least part of a person's performance on intellectual tasks.

■ What are the elements of Spearman's two-factor theory of intelligence?
■ What do factor analytic studies show about the nature of intelligence?

THE NATURE OF INTELLIGENCE: INFORMATION-PROCESSING APPROACHES

As we have seen, differential approaches to the study of intelligence are concerned with how people differ, with the intent of discovering underlying factors. The information-processing approach to the study of intelligence represents an expansion of cognitive psychology into a field formerly dominated by psychometricians. Cognitive psychologists are more interested in the things people do when they solve a task.

The ability to use language is one of the most important aspects of intelligence. Most occupations, even those we do not ordinarily think of as intellectual, require verbal ability.

They hope that by analyzing tasks into the cognitive processes that must be performed to solve them, they will develop a better understanding of the nature of intelligent behavior.

The information-processing approach uses the modern electronic computer as its model for brain functioning. Computers "process information" in ways that are determined by their hardware (electronic circuitry) and software (programs). One interesting approach to understanding the nature of human intelligence is called **artificial intelligence.** Users of this approach attempt to construct computer programs that simulate human abilities, such as the ability to recognize visual patterns or the ability to decode and follow instructions presented in simple English sentences. The hope of investigators working on artificial intelligence is that as we come to understand the steps that computers must follow in order to "perceive" and "think," we will develop insights about how the human brain accomplishes similar tasks.

An Information-Processing Analysis of Verbal Ability

In our culture today, the ability to use words well is one of the most important aspects of intelligence. If we had to predict a person's success in school by using a test of a single ability, then verbal ability would be the best choice; the correlation between tests of verbal ability and school success ranges between .40 and .60 (Matarazzo, 1972). Even in jobs that are not commonly thought of as "intellectual," people must learn many of their vocational skills by reading or being told by others. For example, the relation between success as an Army cook and reading ability is .34; the relation between success as an Army vehicle repairer and listening ability is .38 (Sticht, 1975). Presumably, cooks must read recipes and labels, and vehicle repairers must be able to understand verbal instructions. Thus, study of the nature of verbal ability is an important endeavor.

Both formal tests and informal observations have made it clear that people differ in their verbal ability; thus, psychometricians are probably justified in referring to verbal ability as a "factor" of intelligence. But *how* do people differ in this regard? What are the components of verbal behavior that some people are able to do

Verbal production skills such as writing and speaking have been studied less than other aspects of verbal ability. Shakespeare is a fine example of someone with extraordinary verbal production skills.

well and others do poorly? Simply developing tests to measure individual differences in verbal ability does not explain the nature of these differences. Hunt (1985) has begun an analysis of the operations necessary for one aspect of verbal ability: reading comprehension. Presumably, many of the operations also play a role in comprehending speech. Much less is known about the processes that are necessary for verbal *production* (writing and speaking), partly because we cannot evaluate the quality of people's verbal output independent of the quality of what they have to say. Of course, verbal ability consists of more than reading, but the discussion that follows will serve as an example of

the contribution the information-processing approach can make to our understanding of the nature of intelligence.

Hunt has identified four component processes in reading comprehension—lexical access, comprehension of isolated sentences, comprehension of connected discourse, and allocation of attention in comprehension—and has applied the tools of cognitive psychologists to understanding the elements of each process.

Lexical Access

Lexical access refers to the ability to be able to "get at" a vocabulary item. The term *lexical* refers to words; a *lexicon* is a dictionary. The term *access* is a metaphor, reflecting the similarity between recognizing the meaning of a word and looking it up in a dictionary. When we see a word, perceptual mechanisms of the brain activate the neural circuits that have previously encoded the meaning of the word; in this way, we metaphorically look the word up in the "dictionary" in our head. This activation of neural circuits is referred to as the person's *access* to the information associated with the word. Lexical access has two major components: vocabulary size (number of words in the mental "dictionary") and speed of access. Presumably, people can differ in both of these components.

Vocabulary size is probably the more important of these two components; the correlation between vocabulary size and total verbal ability measured by the WAIS is .85 (Matarazzo, 1972). However, several experiments have shown that speed of access is also an important factor. Speed of lexical access can be measured by several means. A common method is to present the subject with a string of letters on a video screen controlled by a computer. The subject must quickly say "yes" or "no," according to whether or not the letters spell a word. For example, if the letters spell HOUSE, the answer is "yes," but if the letters spell HONSE, the answer is "no." Obviously, the task is an easy one, and hardly anyone makes a large number of mistakes. However, the measure of interest is speed, not accuracy. An electronic circuit attached to a microphone determines how quickly the subject makes the response. The speed of the response is indicative of the speed of lexical access.

Speed of lexical access does appear to measure something that is important in verbal ability. For example, the correlation between speed of lexical access and scores on psychometric tests of verbal ability is approximately .30 (Lansman, Donaldson, Hunt, and Yantis, 1983). College students who rank in the top 25 percent in verbal ability take approximately 65 milliseconds to gain access to a word, whereas students with scores in the bottom 25 percent take approximately 100 milliseconds (Hunt, Lunneborg, and Lewis, 1975). The access time of people with mild mental retardation is approximately 400 milliseconds (Warren and Hunt, 1981).

Comprehension of Isolated Sentences

Hunt's second component in reading comprehension is *comprehension of isolated sentences and expressions*. This process is much more complex than recognition of individual words, because, as we saw in Chapter 8, it depends on recognition of both syntax and semantics. So far, the method that cognitive psychologists have used the most to investigate this component is the *sentence verification task*. The subject first sees a sentence on the video screen—for example:

THE PLUS IS ABOVE THE STAR.

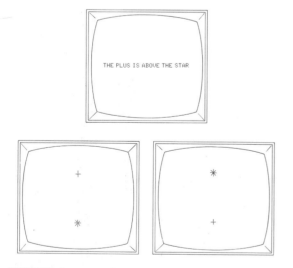

FIGURE 9.4

The sentence verification task. The subject sees the sentence and then one of the displays shown below and must answer "yes" or "no."

Next, the subject sees one of two displays, as shown in Figure 9.4. If the subject sees the display on the left, the correct answer is "yes." If he or she sees the display on the right, the correct answer is "no." Again, literate people do not differ in their accuracy, but they do differ substantially in the speed with which they make their decisions.

In addition, those subjects who perform the fastest on sentence verification tasks tend also to perform well on tests of verbal comprehension; the correlation ranges from .40 to .60 (Baddeley, 1968; Lansman, Donaldson, Hunt, and Yantis, 1983). One possibile explanation for the correlation is that the speed of sentence verification is simply another measure of the speed of lexical access; after all, a person must recognize and understand the words on the screen. However, Palmer, MacLeod, Hunt, and Davidson (1985) have shown that knowing a person's speed of lexical access and speed of sentence verification provides a more accurate estimate of their overall verbal ability than either score by itself; thus, the two tasks measure at least somewhat independent processes.

Carpenter and Just (1975) suggested that the cognitive functions most heavily used in the sentence verification task are holding and manipulating information in working memory (verbal short-term memory). These functions are very important in comprehending sentences. For example, the correlation between overall verbal ability and the ability to repeat back long sequences of letters or digits (a measure of working memory) is between .30 and .40 (Daneman and Carpenter, 1980). An even better predictor of overall verbal ability is a task that requires people to do two things at once: retain information in working memory while analyzing sentence structure in order to comprehend its syntax. Daneman and Carpenter had subjects read lists of sentences and remember the last word in each sentence. For example, they might read the following sentences:

The bear saw the man. My dog barked at a cat.

(The words to be remembered are *man* and *cat*.) People who remembered more words also tended to score higher in verbal comprehension; the correlation between these two measures was .50.

Daneman and Carpenter found that their task correlated even better with a particular skill used in sentence comprehension: the ability to understand the meaning of pronouns that refer back to a noun that occurs early in the sentence. For example, consider this sentence:

> John was older, and presumably wiser, than David, but sometimes he could surprise you with his foolishness.

The pronouns *he* and *his*, introduced in the last clause, clearly refer to *John*. In order to figure this out you must remember how the sentence started while simultaneously analyzing the syntax and meaning of the rest of the sentence. Daneman and Carpenter found that the correlation between their memory task and the ability to understand pronouns like these was .80.

Comprehension of Connected Discourse

The third component in reading comprehension, according to Hunt, is *comprehension of connected discourse*. Of course, comprehending connected discourse requires the first two components, lexical access and comprehension of isolated sentences, but it adds some new demands. For example, consider the following sentences (Hunt, 1985):

> I learned a lot about the bars in town yesterday. Do you have an aspirin?

To understand what the writer (or speaker) means, you must do more than simply understand the words and analyze the sentence structure. You must know something about bars: that they serve alcoholic beverages and that "learning about them" probably involves some drinking. You must also realize that drinking alcohol can lead to a headache and that aspirin is a remedy for headaches.

Hunt notes that most often, when we describe an event to someone else, we do not spell out all the details. Consider this story:

> Tony was hungry. He went to the restaurant and ordered a pizza. When he was finished, he found he had forgotten to take his wallet with him. He was embarrassed.

To understand this story, you must know that after eating in a restaurant you are expected to pay, and because Tony had forgotten his wallet he had no money with him. Schank and Abelson (1977) suggested that knowledge about events and interactions in real life is organized into *scripts*. Once the speaker or writer establishes which script is being referred to, the listener or reader can fill in the details.

Cognitive psychologists studying reading comprehension have found that individuals with strong verbal abilities allocate their attention to passages they believe are important.

Hunt suggests that important components in the comprehension of connected discourse are the knowledge of scripts and the ability to recognize which script the speaker or writer is referring to. So far, research has not revealed much about the nature of these components.

Allocation of Attention

Hunt's fourth component in reading comprehension is the *allocation of attention*. Presumably, a person with high verbal ability can recognize which aspects of connected discourse require close attention and analysis, and which aspects require only cursory examination. Wagner and Sternberg (1983) demonstrated the relation between verbal ability and this skill. They had subjects read prose passages, telling them that they would later be tested on the details of some passages and only the barest outlines of others. Readers who scored well on a standard test of reading ability allocated their time accordingly; they took relatively more

According to Sternberg, people who are intelligent will be more effective when encountering a novel situation, such as when these older adults confront a computer for the first time.

time reading the passages that they expected to have to remember in detail. In contrast, poor readers spent the same amount of time with each passage.

As you can see, cognitive psychologists know more about the elementary processes than the complex ones; lexical access is understood better than the allocation of attention. However, even though the task of analyzing verbal abilities is still in its early stages, the information-processing approach to this important aspect of intelligence is yielding promising and interesting results.

An Information-Processing Theory of Intelligence

Sternberg (1985) has devised a theory of intelligence that derives from the information-processing approach. Sternberg's theory is in three parts; he calls it a *triarchic* ("ruled by three") theory. The three parts of the theory deal with three aspects of intelligence: compo-

nential intelligence, experiential intelligence, and contextual intelligence.

Componential intelligence consists of the mental mechanisms that people use to plan and execute tasks. The components revealed by the analyses of verbal ability that I just described come under this heading. Sternberg suggests that the components of intelligence serve three functions. **Metacomponents** ("transcending" components) are the processes by which people decide the nature of an intellectual problem, select a strategy for solving it, and allocate their resources. For example, we saw earlier that good readers vary the amount of time they spend on a passage according to how much information they need to extract from it. This decision is controlled by a metacomponent of intelligence. **Performance components** are the processes actually used to perform the task—for example, lexical access and working memory. **Knowledge-acquisition components** are those the person uses to gain new knowledge by sifting out relevant information and integrating it with what he or she already knows.

The second part of Sternberg's theory deals with **experiential intelligence.** An intelligent person, according to the theory, is able to deal more effectively with novel situations than an unintelligent person. He or she is better able to analyze the situation and bring mental resources to bear on the problem, even if one like it has never been encountered before. After encountering a particular type of problem several times, the intelligent person is also able to "automate" the procedure so that similar problems can be solved without much thought, freeing mental resources for other work. A person who has to reason out the solution to a problem every time it occurs will be left behind by people who can give the answer quickly and automatically. Sternberg suggests that this distinction is closely related to Horn and Cattell's conception of fluid and crystallized intelligence. According to Sternberg, tasks that utilize fluid intelligence are those that demand novel approaches, whereas tasks that utilize crystallized intelligence are those that demand mental processes that have become automatic.

The third part of Sternberg's theory deals with **contextual intelligence.** This form of intelligence perhaps reflects the behaviors that were subject to selective pressure in our evolutionary history. Contextual intelligence takes three forms. The first form, **adaptation,** consists in fitting oneself into one's environment by developing useful skills and behaviors. In different cultures adaptation will take different forms. For example, knowing how to distinguish between poisonous and edible plants is an important skill for a member of a hunter-gatherer tribe, and knowing how to present oneself in a job interview is an important skill for a member of an industrialized society.

The second form of contextual intelligence, **selection,** refers to the ability to find one's own niche in the environment. For example, Feldman (1982) studied some of the child prodigies who appeared on the "Quiz Kid" radio and television shows in the United States during the 1940s and 1950s. These children were selected for the ability to answer factual knowledge questions quickly and had very high IQ scores. Feldman's follow-up study indicated that the ones with the most distinguished careers were those who had found something that interested them and had stuck to it. Those who failed to do so accomplished very little, despite their high IQs. According to Sternberg, the difference was a reflection of the selective aspect of contextual intelligence.

The third form of contextual intelligence is **shaping.** Sometimes it is not possible or profitable to adapt to one's environment or to select a new one. In such a case, intelligent behavior consists in shaping the environment itself. For example, a person whose talents are not appreciated by his or her employer may decide to start his or her own business.

The importance of Sternberg's emphasis on practical intelligence is supported by observations of people with damage to their frontal lobes. Even after sustaining massive damage to the frontal lobes (for example, after an automobile or motorcycle accident), people often continue to score well on standard tests of intelligence; thus we are tempted to conclude that their intelligence is unimpaired. But such people lose the ability to plan their lives or even their daily activities. I became familiar with the case of a formerly successful physician who received a head injury that severely damaged his frontal lobes. Even though he still had a high IQ as measured by intelligence tests, he could no longer carry out his practice. He became a delivery truck driver for his brother, who owned a business. He was able to carry out

this job only because his brother did all the planning for him, carefully laying out his route and instructing him to call him if he encountered any trouble. The man's behavior lost its flexibility and insightfulness. For example, if he found the front door locked at a business to which he was supposed to deliver an order, it would not occur to him to go around to the back; his brother would have to suggest that by telephone. Clearly, the man's behavior lacked a very crucial component of intelligence. The fact that this component is not measured by most intelligence tests indicates that they are missing something important.

One aspect of contextual intelligence is discovering something that one enjoys and does well, such as finding a satisfying occupation. This man has found his niche as a stonecutter working on great cathedrals.

Marcel Marceau is a good example of someone who excels in bodily-kinesthetic intelligence.

Because so many categories and subcategories have been introduced in this section, I have collected the terms described here in Table 9.3.

TABLE 9.3

An outline of Sternberg's triarchic theory of intelligence

Componential intelligence
    Metacomponents (e.g., planning)
    Performance components (e.g., lexical access)
    Knowledge-acquisition components (e.g., ability to acquire vocabulary words)
Experiential intelligence
    Novel tasks
    Automated tasks
Contextual intelligence
    Adaptation (adapting to the environment)
    Selection (finding a suitable environment)
    Shaping (changing the environment)

A Neuropsychological Theory of Intelligence

As we saw in the example I just presented, neuropsychological observations have provided us with some important insights about the nature of intelligence. Gardner (1983) has suggested a theory of intelligence based on a neuropsychological analysis of human abilities. As you have seen in previous chapters, localized brain damage can impair specific types of abilities. For example, damage to various parts of the left hemisphere can impair verbal abilities, and damage to various parts of the right hemisphere can impair the ability to orient well in space or to produce and recognize facial expressions of emotion. Gardner concludes that intelligence falls into six categories: *linguistic intelligence, musical intelligence, logical-mathematical intelligence, spatial intelligence, bodily-kinesthetic intelligence,* and *personal intelligence.* Bodily-kinesthetic intelligence includes the types of skills that athletes, typists, dancers, or mime artists exhibit. Personal intelligence includes awareness of one's own feelings and also includes the ability to notice and make distinctions among other individuals—in other words, to be socially aware.

Three of Gardner's types of intelligence—verbal intelligence, logical-mathematical intelligence, and spatial intelligence—are not unusual, having been identified previously by many other researchers. But why include the others? According to Gardner, all six abilities are well represented in the brain, in that specific brain damage can selectively impair them. For example, people with damage to the left parietal lobe can sustain an **apraxia,** an inability to perform sequences of voluntary skilled movements. In contrast, people with damage to the right parietal lobe "lose touch with themselves." For one thing, they are likely to ignore the left side of their bodies, failing to shave or apply makeup to the left side of their faces or to put on the left sleeve of their shirts or coats. In addition, they tend to become unaware of their physical condition; for instance, although they may have a paralyzed arm and leg, they do not take the disability into account when they make plans for the future. In another example of a neuropsychological relation, people with damage to the frontal or temporal lobes—

especially of the right hemisphere—may have difficulty evaluating the significance of social situations. These examples illustrate bodily-kinesthetic intelligence and personal intelligence.

Psychometric tests of intelligence have emphasized the kinds of skills that can easily be tested at a desk or table, with paper and pencil or small puzzles. In general, we have tended not to consider skill at moving one's body as a measure of intelligence, although this talent was undoubtedly selected during the evolution of our species. Individuals who could more skillfully prepare tools, hunt animals, climb trees, scale cliffs, and perform other tasks requiring physical skills were more likely to survive and reproduce. Psychometricians have indeed developed mechanical aptitude tasks, primarily to help employers select skilled prospective employees, but such skills have generally been regarded as representing something less than intelligence. If a person has good verbal skills, most people in Western cultures will not regard the person as less intelligent if he or she is also clumsy; similarly, they will not credit a person who has poor verbal skills with a measure of intelligence just because the person is physically skilled.

Gardner's theory has the advantage of being based on neuropsychological realities; it also accommodates the views of intelligence held by some non-Western cultures. For example, Gardner would recognize the ability of a member of the Puluwat culture of the Caroline Islands to navigate across the sea by using the stars as a demonstrated example of intelligence (Gladwin, 1970).

- How does the information-processing approach to intelligence account for the relation of reading ability to verbal ability in general?
- What are the four major component processes that make up reading ability?
- What are the key features of Sternberg's triarchic theory of intelligence?
- What are the key features of Gardner's neuropsychological theory of intelligence?
- What are the advantages, if any, of Gardner's theory?

THE ROLES OF HEREDITY AND ENVIRONMENT

Abilities of various kinds—intellectual, athletic, musical, and artistic—appear to run in families. Why is this so? Are the similarities due to common heredity, or are they solely the result of a common environment, with similar educational opportunities and exposure to people with similar kinds of interests? As we will see, the evidence suggests that both hereditary and environmental factors play a role.

Ideally, the investigation of the role of hereditary and environmental factors in intellectual ability should resemble any other scientific enterprise: Evidence should be obtained; hypotheses should be formulated and tested; and the subsequent discussion, analysis, and

A stimulating home environment can greatly facilitate a child's intellectual development.

constructive debate should lead to additional hypotheses and data gathering. However, discussion of this issue has been characterized by animosity, personal attacks, emotional outbursts, and defensive posturing.

One group of scientists reason that if heredity has a role in intellectual ability, then some people may conclude that certain racial groups are intrinsically "inferior" to others. Such a conclusion would give legitimacy to differential treatment of people on the basis of race. To avoid such an outcome, these scientists have attempted to discredit the work of others whose evidence suggests that hereditary factors do play a role in intelligence. For example, Jensen (1969) presented evidence that he said indicated that most of the observed difference between the IQ scores of American blacks and whites is genetically caused. His paper produced an uproar that has only partly subsided. A recent publication on the subject (Jensen, 1985) was followed by critiques by thirty-two experts, which were in turn followed by a rebuttal by Jensen. Although most of the participants in the debate still hold their opinions firmly, they are now beginning to exchange arguments based on the scientific merits of the issue.

Among other things, this section attempts to analyze and dispose of many misconceptions that cloud the issue of heredity versus environment. If we understand how genetic and environmental influences manifest themselves and interact with each other, we will be less likely to draw unjustified conclusions.

The Meaning of Heritability

When we ask how much influence heredity has on a given trait, we are usually asking what the **heritability** of the trait is. Heritability is a statistical measure that expresses the extent to which the observed variability in a trait is a direct result of genetic variability. The value of this measure can vary from zero (no correlation) to 1.0 (perfect correlation). The heritability of many physical traits in most cultures is very high; for example, eye color is affected almost entirely by hereditary factors and little, if at all, by the environment. Thus, the heritability of eye color is close to 1.0.

Heritability is a concept that many people

misunderstand. It does not describe the extent to which the inherited genes are responsible for producing a particular trait; it measures the relative contributions of differences in genes and differences in environmental factors to the overall observed variability of the trait in a particular population. An example may make this distinction clear. Consider the heritability of hair color in the Eskimo culture. Almost all young Eskimos have black hair, whereas older Eskimos have gray or white hair. Because all the members of this population possess the same versions of the genes that determine hair color, the genetic variability with respect to those genes is essentially zero. All the observed variability in hair color in this population is explained by an environmental factor: age. Therefore, the heritability of hair color in the Eskimo culture is zero.

As with hair color, we are forced to infer the heritability of a person's intelligence from his or her observed performance. Thus, looking at a person's IQ score is equivalent to looking at the color of a person's hair. By measuring the correlation between IQ score and various genetic and environmental factors, we can arrive at an estimate of heritability. Clearly, even if hereditary factors do influence intelligence, the heritability of this trait must be considerably less than 1.0 because, as we have seen, so many environmental factors (such as the mother's prenatal health and nutrition, the child's nutrition, the educational level of the child's parents, and the quality of the child's school) can influence it.

Interaction Between Heredity and Environment

Interaction refers to events whose effects influence each other. For example, suppose that because of genetic differences some children are calm and others are excitable. Suppose that the excitable children will profit most from a classroom in which distractions are kept to a minimum and teachers are themselves calm and soothing. Further suppose that the calm students will profit most from an exciting classroom that motivates them to work their hardest. If this were true, then the actual performance of the students would be based on an interaction between heredity and environment. If all the students were taught in a calm classroom, the excitable children would perform best and hence learn more and obtain better IQ scores. If all students were taught in an exciting classroom, the calm children would do better and obtain the higher scores.

The effects of genetic variation and environmental variation on the observed variation of a trait can be expressed in a simple formula:

observed variance = genetic variance
$\qquad\qquad$ + environmental variance

or:

$$OV = GV + EV$$

However, this formula cannot apply to our example of the calm or excitable children. In this example, higher IQ scores cannot be explained by a genetic difference in the children or by an environmental difference in the classroom or even by both factors added together. A third factor must be added to express the interaction of genetic and environmental factors. Thus:

$$OV = GV + EV + \text{interaction}$$

Certain abilities tend to run in families. The Wyeth family has been painting for three generations. Below on the left is *The Giant (1923)* by N. C. Wyeth. On the right is a painting by his son, Andrew Wyeth, *Braids (1978)*. Andrew's son Jamie is also a well-known painter.

As you will see in the following section, evidence for an interaction effect in human intelligence is circumstantial, not direct. However, Cooper and Zubek (1958) gathered evidence in the laboratory that illustrates the interaction between heredity and environment. By selectively interbreeding rats who learn a maze very quickly or very slowly, Tryon (1940) successfully bred two strains of rats: "maze-bright" rats and "maze-dull" rats. Cooper and Zubek raised groups of both strains of rats in three different environments: a standard environment, an impoverished environment, and an enriched environment containing many objects with which the rats could interact. Presumably the rats, like people, would be affected by their environment: A more stimulating environment would favor "intellectual" development, whereas an impoverished environment would suppress it. The investigators then tested the six groups of rats on their ability to learn a maze.

The results, shown in Figure 9.5, reveal a very strong interaction between heredity and environment. All rats raised in the impoverished environment performed poorly; they made many errors while learning the maze. Rats that were raised in the enriched environment all performed well; when they had been raised in a more favorable environment, even the maze-dull rats did rather well. Only under the standard conditions did the two strains of rats perform differently.

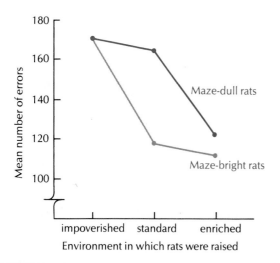

FIGURE 9.5

Mean number of errors of maze-dull and maze-bright rats raised in various environments. (Based on data from Cooper, R.M., and Zubek, J.P. *Canadian Journal of Psychology*, 1958, 12, 159–164.)

From these results we can conclude that (1) heredity has a strong effect on a rat's ability to learn a maze; (2) a rat's early environment has a strong effect on its ability to learn a maze; and (3) the effect of a rat's heredity depends on the environment in which it is raised—the two factors interact. Although we have no comparable experimental data from humans, the graph in Figure 9.5 suggests that it is important to provide people with an optimum environment, whatever their heredity may be.

Prenatal and Postnatal Factors

Both biological and environmental factors occurring before or after birth can affect intellectual abilities. Newborn infants cannot be said to possess any substantial intellectual abilities; rather, they are more or less capable of *developing* these abilities during their life. Therefore, prenatal influences can be said to affect a child's *potential* intelligence by affecting the development of the brain. Factors that impair brain development will necessarily also impair the child's potential intelligence.

Prenatal influences may be either genetic or nongenetic (environmental); and genetic factors may be either hereditary or nonhereditary.

For example, the best-known genetic causes of mental retardation are Down's syndrome and phenylketonuria, discussed in Chapter 4. Down's syndrome is caused by abnormal genetic material—the presence of an extra twenty-first chromosome; it is not a heritable disorder. Hereditary genetic influences include (among others) inherited metabolic disorders such as phenylketonuria that interfere with normal brain development. Phenylketonuria results in brain damage and mental retardation unless it is recognized early in life so that a special diet can be administered. It is conceivable that as-yet unknown hereditary differences in brain chemistry and structure affect an individual's potential intelligence, as well.

Harmful prenatal environmental factors include physical trauma (perhaps through injury to the mother in an automobile accident) and toxic effects. A developing fetus can be exposed to toxins by a variety of ways: from diseases contracted by the mother during pregnancy (such as German measles), from smoking, or from the ingestion of alcohol or poisons (such as mercury or lead). Any of these factors can result in mental retardation. Positive prenatal environmental factors include an excellent diet and good medical care for the mother.

From birth onward, a child's brain continues to develop. Environmental factors can either promote or impede that development. Postnatal factors such as birth trauma, diseases that affect the brain, or toxic chemicals can prevent optimum development and thereby affect the child's potential intelligence. For example, encephalitis (inflammation of the brain), when contracted during childhood, can result in mental retardation. So can the ingestion of poisons such as mercury or lead.

Educational influences in the environment, including (but not limited to) schooling, enable a child to attain his or her potential intelligence. By contrast, a less-than-optimum environment prevents the fullest possible realization of potential intelligence. Experience with mentally retarded people demonstrates this point. Known causes account for only approximately 25 percent of observed cases of mental retardation. In addition, people whose mental retardation has no obvious physical cause are likely to have close relatives who are also mentally retarded. These findings strongly suggest that many of the remaining 75 percent of cases are hereditary. However, environmental causes (such as poor nutrition or the presence of environmental toxins) can produce brain damage in members of the same family; thus, not all cases of *familial* mental retardation are necessarily *hereditary*.

Clearly, the interactive effects of environmental and genetic factors are complex. The effects of hereditary factors on adult intellectual ability are necessarily indirect, and many environmental factors exert their effects throughout a person's life. Given that an adult's intellectual abilities are the product of a long chain of events, it is impossible to isolate the effects of the earliest factors. The types of genetic and environmental factors influencing potential intelligence at each stage of development can be summarized as follows:

Conception: A person's genetic endowment sets limits on his or her brain anatomy and thus on his or her potential intelligence.

Prenatal development: Good nutrition and a normal pregnancy result in optimum brain development and optimum potential intelligence. Drugs, toxic substances, poor nutrition, and physical accidents can impair brain development, thus lowering potential intelligence. Genetic disorders such as phenylketonuria and Down's syndrome can impair brain development, thus lowering potential intelligence.

Birth: Anoxia (lack of oxygen) or head trauma can cause brain damage, thus lowering potential intelligence.

Infancy: The brain continues to develop and grow. Good nutrition continues to be important. Sensory stimulation and interaction with a responsive environment are important for cognitive development. An infant's environment and brain structure jointly determine his or her intelligence.

Later life: A person's intelligence continues to be jointly determined by environmental factors and brain structure and chemistry. Brain damage from strokes is more likely to affect specific abilities, whereas metabolic disturbances or infections of the brain can adversely affect brain structure and chemistry, thus decreasing general intelligence. Later in life, dementing diseases such as Alzheimer's disease

can severely impair brain structure and chemistry, thus reducing intelligence. As we saw in Chapter 5, normal aging usually causes a decline in fluid intelligence but leaves crystallized intelligence relatively intact.

■ In terms of intelligence, what is the meaning of heritability?
■ How can the interaction between heredity and environment affect intelligence?
■ What are the prenatal and postnatal factors that can affect intelligence?

Family Studies of Intelligence

By now it is clear that no single definition of intelligence is adequate. Intelligence tests give some indication of a person's ability to perform well academically and in some occupations, and research indicates that there is some meaning to the concept of a general factor in intellectual ability. Although a single number such as an IQ score cannot express the complexity of a person's pattern of performance on a variety of tasks, the heritability of IQ continues to be a topic of interest to researchers. Their reasoning on the subject of heritability of IQ usually takes into account the crucial factors of genetic and environmental variability, discussed earlier in this section, and is generally based on three major considerations:

1. Heritability of a trait depends on the amount of variability of genetic factors in a given population. Because the ancestors of people living in developed Western nations came from all over the world, genetic variability is likely to be much higher there than in an isolated tribe of people in a remote part of the world. Therefore, if a person's IQ score is at all affected by genetic factors, the measured heritability of IQ will be higher in, say, North American culture than in an isolated tribe.

2. The relative importance of environmental factors in intelligence depends on the amount of environmental variance (EV) that occurs in the population. In a society with a low variability in the environmental factors relevant to intellectual development—one in which all children are raised in the same way by equally skilled and conscientious caregivers, all schools are equally good, all teachers have equally effective personalities and teaching skills, and no one is discriminated against—the effects of EV would be small and those of GV (genetic variance) would be large. In contrast, in a society in which only a few privileged people receive a good education, environmental factors would be responsible for much of the variability in intelligence: the effects of EV would be large relative to those of GV.

3. Heritability is affected by the degree to which genetic inheritance and environment interact. For example, we saw that people who are inherently calm or excitable might profit from different types of instructional methods and attain different levels of intellectual development depending on their environment.

Twin Studies

Because monozygotic (identical) twins share identical sets of chromosomes, they are genetically identical. They have also shared virtually the same environment in the uterus. For all practical purposes, they are two examples of the same person. Some researchers have tried

---

By studying monozygotic twins separated at birth and raised in different families, researchers attempt to assess the heritability of intelligence.

to estimate the heritability of IQ in a given culture by studying many sets of monozygotic twins who were separated at birth and raised in different families.

There are problems inherent in such studies. First, some of these studies have failed to take sufficient account of the similarity of the environments in which the isolated twins were raised. If the home and school environments of isolated twins are similar, environmental variability will be low, so estimates of heritability will necessarily be high in comparison. However, if some individuals had been raised in wealthy homes, some in poor ones, some in loving homes, some in homes in which they were regularly abused, some in societies with compulsory educations, and some in cultures where schools are unknown, the correlation undoubtedly would have been lower.

Second, adoption agencies often attempt to place brighter and healthier children in families with better education and higher socioeconomic status. This tendency introduces a spurious correlation between child and adoptive parent that increases the estimate of environmental effects and lowers the estimate of hereditary effects.

Finally, adoptive parents usually adopt a child only after discovering that they cannot have one of their own, and they often have to wait to adopt a child; therefore, they tend to be older than biological parents. If parental age affects a child's intellectual development, it will reduce the validity of comparisons between adopted and biological children.

Other estimates of heritability have compared monozygotic twins with dizygotic (fraternal) twins, both reared together. Whereas monozygotic twins have idental genetic material, dizygotic twins are no more closely related than any two siblings who were born at different times. On the average, 50 percent of the chromosomes of dizygotic twins are identical (compared with 100 percent for monozygotic twins). Because twins who are reared together share approximately the same environment, researchers have estimated heritability by observing the difference in correlation between the two types of twins.

Many studies have used these two methods—adopted twins and comparisons between monozygotic and dizygotic twins—to estimate the heritability of IQ scores. Most of these studies calculated that hereditary factors accounted for

TABLE 9.4

Correlations in intelligence between pairs of people with varying kinships and estimates of relative contributions of genetic and environmental factors

Relationship	Rearing	Percentage of Genetic Similarity	Correlation	Number of Pairs
Same individual	—	100%	.87	456
Monozygotic twins	together	100	.86	1417
Dizygotic twins	together	50	.62	1329
Siblings	together	50	.41	5350
Siblings	apart	50	.24	203
Parent–child	together	50	.35	3973
Parent–child	apart	50	.31	345
Adoptive parent–child	together	?	.16	1594
Unrelated children	together	?	.25	601
Spouses	apart	?	.29	5318

	Estimates of contributions of genetics and environment to variability in intelligence	
Comparison	Genetics	Environment
Monozygotic twins together versus dizygotic twins together	.58	.28
Parent–offspring together versus parent–offspring apart	.50	.04
Siblings together versus siblings apart	.25	.25

Adapted from Henderson, N.D. *Annual Review of Psychology*, 1982, *33*, 403–440.

approximately 80 percent of the observed variance, while environmental factors accounted for approximately 20 percent.

More recent studies, using methods that yield more accurate estimates, indicate that the heritability of intelligence, as measured by IQ tests, is lower than was previously supposed. The most sophisticated method, the **family-of-twins design,** involves the study of adult monozygotic twins, their spouses, and their offspring (Henderson, 1982). Thus, such studies embrace several relationships: the monozygotic twins themselves, siblings (the twins' children), half-siblings (the children of one twin are, genetically speaking, half-siblings of the children of the other twin), and the twins with their offspring. Geneticists have devised formulas to calculate the heritability of a trait from the values of the correlations between various family members. Using these formulas, Rose, Harris, Christian, and Nance (1979) obtained estimates of heritability of IQ ranging from .40 based on the half-sibling relationship to .56 based on the offspring-parent relationship.

Table 9.4 presents correlations in intelligence between people of varying kinships, and

estimates based on these data of the relative contributions of genetic and environmental factors. The data used in the table were obtained from a summary of several recent studies by Henderson (1982). The top portion of the table shows that the correlation between two people is indeed related to their genetic similarity. (See Table 9.4, top.) The bottom portion shows that estimates of the importance of common genetic and environmental factors vary considerably, depending on the type of comparison made. Estimates of genetic influence range from 25 to 58 percent, and estimates of environmental influence range from 4 to 28 percent. The rest of the variability is due to the interaction between heredity and environment and to errors in measurement. (See Table 9.4, bottom.)

It is important not to misinterpret the meaning of estimates of environmental and genetic influences. For example, if the contribution of environmental influence is estimated at 28 percent, we cannot conclude that changes in a person's environment can produce only a 28-percent change in his or her IQ score. An esimate of environmental influence never indicates how much effect environmental factors *can* have on a trait; it indicates only how much of the *variability* of that trait in that population appears to be related to the environmental variation that is actually present. Suppose we were to raise some babies in stimulating, responsive environments, others in mediocre environments, and still others in environments so impoverished that words were never spoken. The babies in the impoverished environments would never even learn to talk, and their IQs would be very low. We would find that environmental factors accounted for nearly 100 percent of the observed variance in this population, with genetic factors being almost negligible.

The Issue of Race and Intelligence

Efforts to relate intelligence to race are still controversial. First, people who pursue the issue usually define race in a meaningless and illogical way. Second, because the environments of people of different racial groups differ, it is impossible to assess the relative effects of heredity and environment.

Defining Racial Groups

A biologist uses the term *race* to identify a population of plants or animals that has some degree of reproductive isolation from other members of the species, with which it is perfectly capable of interbreeding. Groups of humans whose ancestors mated only with other people in a restricted geographical region tend to differ from other groups on a variety of hereditary traits, including stature, hair color, skin pigmentation, and blood type. However, subsequent migrations and conquests caused the interbreeding of many different groups of people. As a result, human racial groups are much more similar than, say, races of dogs, so that classifying people on the basis of race is a difficult and somewhat arbitrary matter.

Many researchers have used the trait of skin pigmentation to classify people by race. Evidence suggests that the selective value of differing amounts of skin pigmentation is related to its ability to protect against the effects of sunlight (Loomis, 1967). Such protection was important near the equator, where the sun is intense all year, but was less important in

temperate zones. And because vitamin D is synthesized primarily through the action of sunlight on deep layers of the skin, *lack* of pigmentation was advantageous to people who lived in areas with long winters. The selective advantage of differences in skin pigmentation is obvious, but there is no plausible reason to expect these differences to be correlated either with other physical measures or with measures of intellectual ability. Both the tallest (the Masai) and the shortest (Pygmy) people in the world have black skin. Nor are shape of nose and forehead, hair texture, blood groups, and many other physical features well correlated with skin pigmentation. We would never classify varieties of dogs by color, assigning golden retrievers and Chihuahuas to one group and black Labrador retrievers and Scotties to another. Why, then, should we do so with humans? People who ask: "Are there racial differences in intelligence?" almost always mean: "Are blacks inherently less intelligent than whites?"

Thus, the issue of race and intelligence as presently conceived does not appear to be meaningfully defined and is not likely to produce significant research findings.

Environmental Differences

A large number of studies have established that Americans who are identified as "black" score an average of 85 on IQ tests, whereas Americans who are identified as "white" score an average of 100 (Jensen, 1982). Thus, although some blacks score better than some whites, on the average whites do better on these tests.

We still do not know why these differences exist, but it is likely that environmental factors play an important role. In the United States, as in many other countries, racial membership is a cultural phenomenon, not a biological one. Black people and white people are treated differently: The average black family is poorer than the average white one; blacks usually attend schools of lesser academic quality than whites; pregnant black women typically receive poorer medical care than their white counterparts, and their diet tends to be not as well balanced; and so on. In these circumstances, it would not be surprising if people's IQ scores differed in accordance with whether they had been raised as blacks or as whites.

Some investigators have attempted to use statistical means to "remove" the effects of environmental variables, such as socioeconomic status, that account for differences in performance between blacks and whites. These efforts are subject to criticism on several grounds. On the other hand, a study by Scarr and Weinberg (1976) provides unambiguous evidence that environmental factors can substantially increase the measured IQ of a black child. Scarr and Weinberg studied ninety-nine black children who were adopted while they were young into white families of higher-than-average educational and socioeconomic status. The expected average IQ of black children in the same area who were raised in black families was approximately 90. The average IQ of the adopted group was observed to be 105.

Some authors have flatly stated that there are no racial differences in biologically determined intellectual capacity. But this claim, like the one asserting that blacks are inherently less intelligent than whites, lacks scientific support. Although we know that blacks and whites have different environments, and that a black child raised in an environment similar to that of a white child will receive a higher IQ score, the question of whether or not any racial hereditary differences exist has not been answered. However, given that there is at least as much variability in intelligence between two people selected at random as there is between the average black and the average white, knowing a person's race tells us very little about how intelligent he or she may be.

The interesting and more valid racial questions are those that will be addressed by social psychologists and anthropologists. These questions concern issues such as the prevalence of prejudice, ethnic identification and cohesiveness, fear of strangers, and the tendency to judge something (or someone) that is different as inferior.

- What are the three major considerations that researchers must take into account in evaluating the relative importance of genetic or environmental factors on intelligence?
- What are some of the results and limitations of the twin studies and family-of-twin studies of intelligence?
- How does the role of environmental differences affect the relation of race to intelligence?

CHAPTER SUMMARY

1. Research into the nature of intelligence has developed in three ways: the differential approach (deals with testing to identify and measure individual differences), the developmental approach (studies the ways infants learn to perceive, manipulate, and think about the world), and the information-processing approach (emphasizes the components of intellectual processes).

2. Binet developed a test to assess students' intellectual abilities in order to identify children with special educational needs. The Stanford-Binet Scale now calculates IQ. Wechsler's two tests for adults (WAIS-R) and for children (WISC-R) are widely used today. Information provided by the verbal and performance scores of Wechsler's tests helps neuropsychologists diagnose brain damage and can provide a rough estimate of the innate ability of poorly educated people. The Kaufman Assessment Battery for Children (K-ABC) distinguishes between sequential and simultaneous mental processes; it includes a nonverbal scale and appears to be less culturally differentiated than the Stanford-Binet Scale or WISC-R. Because no single criterion measure of intelligence exists, intelligence tests are validated by comparing the scores with measures of achievement, such as scholastic success.

3. Although intelligence is often represented by a single score (the IQ), modern investigators do not deny the existence of specific abilities. Whether a general factor also exists is still uncertain. Spearman's theory of a g (general intelligence) factor and an s (specific) factor was disputed by Thurstone's findings of seven specific factors. Further analysis by Eysenck and Cattell found two major factors within the seven specific factors: fluid intelligence (potential or native ability) and crystallized intelligence (actual learned ability).

4. The information-processing approach to intelligence is based on tasks developed by cognitive psychologists in their laboratories. Understanding of the components of intelligence is limited to those components tested by the types of tasks developed. Analysis of verbal ability suggests that reading comprehension depends on four processes: lexical access (consisting of vocabulary size and speed of access), comprehension of isolated sentences (primarily consisting of working memory span), comprehension of connected discourse (primarily consisting of knowledge of "scripts" and rapid and accurate access to them), and allocation of attention. Analysis of deductive reasoning suggests that the most important strategy in solving syllogisms is the ability to construct models and manipulate them, which involves spatial abilities and working memory span.

5. Variability in all physical traits is determined by a certain amount of genetic variance, environmental variance, and an interaction between genetic and environmental factors. Heritability refers to the degree in which genetic variance is responsible for the observed variability of a particular trait in a particular population.

6. Intellectual development is affected by many factors. A person's heredity determines his or her potential intelligence, which may be reduced during prenatal or postnatal development by injury, toxic chemicals, poor nutrition, or disease. In order to achieve full potential, a person must have an environment that will foster the learning of facts and skills needed to function well in society.

KEY TERMS

adaptation　Fitting oneself into one's environment by developing useful skills and behaviors.

apraxia　An inability to perform sequences of voluntary skilled movements.

artificial intelligence　A field of study in which computer programs are designed to stimulate human perception, learning, or problem-solving, with the expectation that the details of such programs will help the investigator understand the nature of the relevant human brain mechanisms.

Binet-Simon Scale　A collection of tests published in 1905 to identify children who were unable to profit from normal classroom instruction and needed special attention.

componential intelligence　Mental mechanisms that people use to plan and execute tasks.

contextual intelligence　Form of intelligence perhaps reflecting behaviors subject to selective pressure in our evolutionary history, including adapting, selection, and shaping.

correlation　Degree to which variability in one measure is related to variability in another.

criterion　A standard used to validify something being measured.

developmental approach　Studies the ways in which infants learn to perceive, manipulate, and think about the world.

deviation IQ　A measure that compares a chilld's score on the Stanford-Binet Scale with those received by other children of the same chronological age.

differential approach　In the investigation of intelligence, attempts to devise tests that identify and measure individual differences.

experiential intelligence　Mental resources that allow a person to analyze a situation and automate a correct response.

factor analysis　Mathematical procedure developed by Spearman and Pearson to identify common factors or sources of variables among groups of tests.

family-of-twins design　A method involving the study of adult monozygotic twins, their spouses, and their offspring in determining heritability.

g factor　General intelligence or general reasoning ability factor.

heritability　The degree to which the variability of a particular trait in a particular population of organisms is a result of genetic differences among those organisms.

information-processing approach　Emphasizes the components of intelligence.

intelligence quotient (IQ)　A simplified single measure of general intelligence; by definition, the ratio of a person's mental age to his or her chronological age, multiplied by 100; often derived by other formulas.

interaction Events whose effects influence each other.

Kaufman Assessment Battery for Children (K-ABC) An intelligence test based on the distinction between sequential and simultaneous mental processes, which tend to be functions performed by the left and right hemispheres of the brain, respectively.

knowledge acquisition components Process of learning new knowledge by sifting out and integrating relevant information.

lexical access The ability to be able to "get at" a vocabulary item.

mental age The measure of a person's intellectual development. A child with a mental age of eight performs as well on intelligence tests as the average child of that age.

mental processing composite (MPC) Global estimate of intelligence used on the K-ABC that is similar to IQ and consists of a combination of sequential and simultaneous processing scales.

mental retardation Mental development that is substantially below normal; often caused by some form of brain damage or abnormal brain development.

metacomponents Processes by which one decides the nature of an intellectual problem, selects a strategy for solving it, and allocates needed resources.

mild mental retardation Designates people with mental ages from seven-and-a-half to eleven years and IQ scores of 52 to 67.

moderate mental retardation Designates people with mental ages from four to seven-and-a-half years and IQ scores of 36 to 51.

norms Data from comparison groups that permit the score of an individual to be assessed relative to his or her peers.

performance components Processes used to perform a task.

profound mental retardation Designates people with a mental age under three years and IQ scores below 20.

ratio IQ The quotient of mental age divided by chronological age.

selection The ability to find one's niche in the environment.

severe mental retardation Designates a person with a mental age of three to four years and an IQ score between 20–35.

s factor A factor that is specific to a particular test.

shaping Shaping or restructuring one's environment.

Spearman's two-factor theory Theory that a person's performance on a test of intellectual ability is determined by two factors: the g (general) factor and the s (specific) factor.

Stanford-Binet Scale A test of intelligence for children; provides the standard measure of the IQ.

Wechsler Adult Intelligence Scale (WAIS) Intelligence test divided into verbal and performance categories.

Wechsler Intelligence Scale for Children (WISC) Intelligence test for children similar to WAIS.

MOTIVATION, EMOTION, AND CONSCIOUSNESS

Students and experts alike are fascinated by the subjects we are about to explore. Indeed, the mysteries of human consciousness, motivation, and emotions are often what triggers one's first interest in psychology. Part C brings together what we have learned about the interaction among physical, psychological, and cognitive processes over the lifespan to focus on the chief interest of psychologists: human behavior.

The study of human behavior is often the study of motivation. Any attempt to discover why people behave as they do requires us to ask questions about motives: we want to know why we seek out certain situations or avoid others.

The tendencies to approach pleasant situations and avoid unpleasant ones have been the basis of much motivation research, especially in the area of achievement, or goal-directed behavior. Beginning in the late 1940s, David McClelland and other researchers have theorized that a person's achievement motivation results from the combination of at least two variables—the desire to succeed (pleasant) and the desire to avoid failure (unpleasant). Depending on a person's expectations of success or failure in attaining a given goal, and on how important that goal is, the person's motivation to achieve is either strengthened or weakened.

That is, the tendency to approach success *minus* the tendency to avoid failure gives a measure of one's willingness to select difficult tasks, one's ability to perform well on them, and one's persistence in doing them despite failure. If a situation sparks the desire for success more than the fear of failure, the person will be strongly motivated to achieve; but if the situation raises fears of failure that override the desire for success, the person will be less strongly motivated.

To this equation of achievement motivation Matina Horner added a second negative incentive, which she termed "fear of success." Like fear of failure, this additional fear—

women who scored high in fear of success did better when working alone on the tasks, whereas those with low scores did much better when the tasks were competitive. Horner concluded that the achievement motivation of significant numbers of women may be lessened by fear of success in a competitive, male-dominated society which may judge them to be "unfeminine" and, perhaps, socially unattractive.

Several researchers have followed up—and sometimes questioned—Horner's conclusions, which were based on data gathered in the mid-1960s, when sexual stereotypes were more prevalent in American society. There also was a methodological weakness in the study, in that females responded only to Anne's success, and males responded only to John's. In the 1970s, Feather and Raphelson gathered new data in America and Australia (where sex roles are generally more traditional), and they asked both males and females to respond to both Anne's and John's success. Australian and American men created more fear-of-success stories for Anne than for John, and so did Australian women; but American women *did not*. Perhaps the less traditional roles and increased awareness of sexual stereotyping that have resulted from the feminist movement have reduced the tendency of American women to fear success. Another possibility—more significant for our understanding of motivation—is that the fear of success evidenced in these studies may not be comparable to the fear of failure in its influence on achievement motivation. Rather than altering the equation between the desire to succeed and the fear of failure, the data about fear of success may simply document prevailing cultural stereotypes at particular times in particular places.

Approaching . . . or Avoiding Intimacy

Similar issues concerning sex differences and the methodologies of projective techniques like the TAT have arisen in studies of affiliation. Like achievement motivation, the basic human need to affiliate with others—to be "social animals"—combines two antagonistic tendencies: desire for intimacy and fear of rejection. Again, desire or fear may dominate in a given situation, and a person either seeks or avoids affiliation depending on the importance of the contact and the expectation that it will be pleasurable or

however illogical it first seems—may oppose the desire for success and thereby may lower achievement motivation.

Do females "fear success"? Do males "fear intimacy"? Horner identified fear of success when she investigated why female and male subjects often respond differently to the ambiguous cues on the Thematic Apperception Test (TAT), which is used to explore people's fantasies, thereby revealing their underlying motives.

Subjects view a series of pictures that show people in ambiguous situations; the task is to make up a story about what is happening in each picture. Because the pictures are so open-ended, the subject has to "fill in the blanks" by fantasizing, and the particular fantasy chosen provides insights into what that person seeks and avoids. The *themes* expressed in a person's fantasies give clues to that person's motives.

In Horner's study, subjects of both sexes were asked to create a story when prompted by a sentence saying either that Anne (for female subjects) or that John (for male subjects) had achieved top standing in medical school. Responding to that cue, 62 percent of females but only 10 percent of males wrote stories that showed high fear of success. In companion studies subjects performed verbal tasks in both competitive and noncompetitive settings;

not. And just as fear of success has been proposed as a component of females' achievement motivation, so has "fear of intimacy"—another seemingly illogical concept—been proposed as an aspect of males' affiliation patterns.

". . . men perceived danger in affiliation and connection, while women saw it in competition and isolation."

In examining stories written by college students, Susan Pollak and Carol Gilligan of Harvard University noted differences in how males and females responded to a TAT picture showing a couple sitting on a bench near a river. Of eighty-eight males in the study, 21 percent projected violent outcomes in response to this picture; not one of the fifty females did so. The researchers then coded all the stories for violence and the context in which it occurred, finding that 51 percent of males responded with violence to at least one of the four pictures considered, as compared with only 22 percent of the females. More significantly, when the TAT pictures were grouped according to whether they primarily showed achievement situations (man alone at desk in office building; two women working in a laboratory) or affiliation situations (the couple sitting on the bench; a male trapeze artist grasping the wrists of his female partner), 25 percent of males but only 6 percent of females responded with violence to the pictures of affiliation, compared with 7 percent and 16 percent, respectively, to pictures showing achievement. Next, the content of the stories was analyzed to discover how the subjects themselves perceived each situation, rather than accepting the presumed motivational categories of the pictures. With this approach 26 percent of males but no females projected violence in affiliation situations, compared with 1 percent of males and 12 percent of females who saw violence in achievement situations. Pollak and Gilligan concluded that the men perceived danger in affiliation and connection, while the women saw it in competition and isolation.

A strong reaction to this study came from Cynthia Benton and associates at the University of California, Los Angeles, who attempted to

replicate the research and clarify its methodology. Expressing concern about ambiguities in the classification of the TAT pictures, and arguing that the researchers' instructions had been unusual, the California team set up experimental conditions that repeated and also altered the original ones. Using such means the researchers disputed the methods and conclusions of the Harvard study and pointed to the pitfalls of classification systems used in projective techniques like the TAT.

Pollak and Gilligan objected to this critique of their study, arguing that the variable conditions did not truly replicate their work and that the California team had ignored their efforts to avoid the pitfalls of classification by performing a content analysis of the subjects' stories. A second reaction came from the group at UCLA, defending the replication approach used by Benton and pointing to "fundamental errors" in the statistical inferences of Pollak and Gilligan. Finally, the Harvard researchers repeated their objections to the UCLA work and defended their statistical inferences. They ended by questioning the purpose of the critiques: "Was [the] aim to explore the nature and distribution of violent fantasies or to attack the messenger who bears unwelcome news of sex differences?" Until human behavior and our abilities to assess it are less ambiguous, the study and application of motivation will remain complex and controversial; in part because we can never know for sure what another person's motives are, and in part because methodology is such a central issue.

MODESTO JR. COLLEGE

Chapter 10

Consciousness

Consciousness of our own existence has long played an important role in thinking about the nature of reality. According to Réné Descartes, the seventeenth century philosopher and scientist, "I think; therefore I exist." But a dilemma underlies this famous statement, which has never really been resolved by any theory of consciousness. Descartes experienced his own consciousness, but no one else did. Our experience of self-awareness is absolutely private; there is no way that another person's consciousness can be directly observed. Thus, as with other problems that psychologists investigate, the study of consciousness must involve observable behaviors, such as words, gestures, or facial expressions. As you will learn, a good case can be made that consciousness is a social phenomenon, related to our ability to communicate with other members of our species.

This chapter explores the nature of human self-awareness: knowledge of our own existence, behavior, perceptions, and thoughts. What factors affect human consciousness? How do we direct our attention from one event to another, becoming aware of some things but ignoring others? In sleep we have our most basic altered form of consciousness, and again, our everyday knowledge of it has been through the spoken retelling of dreams, and the observation of people while they sleep. From these observations come questions that psychologists have tried to answer—Why do we remember some dreams better than others? What is the function of sleep-walking? Is it the acting out of a dream? As researchers have measured the physical effects of sleep, still more questions are raised—What causes sleepwalking? If we "lose" it, do we need to "make it up"? Do we work out anxieties during sleep? Do we have "unexpressed desires" that only emerge through dreams? Such questions can only be answered by measuring or observing an external behavior that may point to an explanation of a private event in our consciousness.

One of the most intriguing puzzles in the study of consciousness has been centered on the phenomenon of hypnosis. Can a person control another's mind and behavior? As we shall see, the explanations have centered around a form of communication, either a split consciousness which forms a "hidden observer" of our own behavior, or a desire to conform socially to another person's expectations. As with the study of other aspects of consciousness, even the most private of experiences still requires an objective explanation.

CONSCIOUSNESS AS A SOCIAL BEHAVIOR

Why are we aware of ourselves? What purpose is served by our ability to "know" that we exist, that events occur, that we are doing things, and that we have memories? If we view consciousness as an adaptive trait of the human species, the most likely explanation lies in its relation to communication. Because of our ability to communicate, we are aware of ourselves. Thus, because language is a social phenomenon, so is consciousness.

Consciousness is a private experience: Each person can directly experience only his or her own consciousness. However, we all realize that other people are conscious, too, because they can *tell* us they are. Most people say that their consciousness consists of an "inner voice" that they use to talk to themselves about what they are perceiving, or remembering, or thinking about. If we are aware of something, we can talk about it. If we are *not* aware of something, we cannot. Suppose we ask someone whether they can close their eyes and imagine what the steering wheel of their car looks like. If they say "yes," we conclude that their consciousness contains this image. If they say "no," we conclude it does not. Thus, we make inferences about other people's consciousness from their verbal behavior.

This chapter will view consciousness as a phenomenon produced by verbal processes. Its physiological basis is the activity of language mechanisms of the brain. To understand this phenomenon better, let us examine the nature of verbal communication. The use of language is important to our species because it provides a means for one person to influence the behavior of another person. Everyone who has the ability to communicate verbally knows how to send and how to receive: how to express his or her thoughts in words and how to respond to the words uttered by others. And because we can both send and receive verbal messages, we can send and receive them to ourselves. We can talk to ourselves, aloud or silently. When we think in words, we are undoubtedly using the same brain mechanisms that control speech, without actually moving our muscles.

This view of human self-awareness is not the only one. However, it seems to be the most useful one, because, as you will see, it helps explain a variety of phenomena that are related to consciousness.

CONSCIOUSNESS AND THE BRAIN

If human consciousness is related to speech, then it seems likely that it is related to the brain mechanisms that control the comprehension and production of speech. This conclusion has an interesting implication: It suggests that for us to be aware of a piece of information, the information must be transmitted to neural circuits in the brain that are responsible for our communicative behavior. Several reports of cases of human brain damage support this suggestion.

As we have already seen, brain damage can alter human consciousness. For example, in Chapter 7, I described the phenomenon of anterograde amnesia, primarily caused by brain damage from malnutrition or chronic alcoholism (Korsakoff's syndrome) or by removal of parts of the temporal lobes, including the hippocampus. You will recall that people with these disabilities cannot form new verbal memories, but they can learn some kinds of tasks. However, they remain unaware that they have learned something, even when their behavior indicates that they have. Thus, the brain damage does not prevent all kinds of learning, but it does prevent conscious awareness of what has been learned.

Global Unawareness: A Case of Isolation Aphasia

Geschwind, Quadfasel, and Segarra (1968) described the case of a woman who had suffered severe brain damage from inhaling gas from an unlit water heater. The damage spared the primary auditory cortex, Wernicke's area, Broca's area, and the connections between these areas. (You will recall from Chapter 8 that Wernicke's area is involved in speech perception, and Broca's area is involved in speech production.) However, the damage destroyed large parts of the visual association cortex and isolated the speech mechanisms from other parts of the brain. In fact, the syndrome they reported is referred to as **isolation aphasia.** Thus, although the brain's speech mechanisms could receive auditory input and could control the muscles used for speech, they received no information from the other senses or from the neural circuits that contain memories concerning past experiences and the meanings of words.

The woman remained in the hospital for nine years, until she died. During this time she made few voluntary movements except with her eyes, which were able to follow moving objects. She gave no evidence of recognizing objects or people in her environment. She did not spontaneously say anything, answer questions, or give any signs that she understood what other people said to her. By all available criteria, she was not conscious of anything that was going on. However, the woman could *repeat* words that were spoken to her. And if someone started a poem she knew, she would finish it. For example, if someone said, "Roses are red, violets are blue," she would respond with "Sugar is sweet, and so are you." She even learned new poems and songs. Her case suggests that consciousness is not simply activity of the brain's speech mechanisms; it is activity prompted by information received from other parts of the brain concerning memories or events presently occurring in the environment.

Lack of Verbal Access to Visual Perceptions: A Case of Visual Agnosia

The case I just described was that of a woman who appeared to have completely lost her awareness of herself and her environment. In other instances, people have become unaware of particular kinds of information. Recently, two colleagues and I studied a young man whose brain had been damaged by an inflammation of the blood vessels and who consequently suffered from visual agnosia (Margolin, Friedrich, and Carlson, 1985). The man had great difficulty identifying common objects by sight. For example, he could not say what a hammer was by looking at it, but he quickly identified it when he was permitted to pick it up and feel it. He was not blind; he could walk around without bumping into things, and he had no trouble making visually guided movements to pick up an object that he wanted to identify. The simplest conclusion would be

that his disease had damaged the neural circuits responsible for visual perception.

However, the simplest conclusion was not the correct one. Although the patient had great difficulty in visually identifying objects or pictures of objects, he often made hand movements that appeared to be related to the object he could not identify. For example, when we showed him a picture of a pistol he stared at it with a puzzled look, then shook his head and said that he couldn't tell what it was. While continuing to study the picture, he clenched his right hand into a fist and began making movements with his index finger. When we asked him what he was doing, he looked at his hand, made a few tentative movements with his finger, then raised his hand in the air and moved it forward each time he moved his finger. He was unmistakably miming the way a person holds and fires a pistol. "Oh!" he said. "It's a gun. No, a pistol." Clearly, he was not aware what the gun was until he paid attention to what his hand was doing. Similarly, once he looked at a picture of a belt and said it was a pair of pants. We asked him to show us where the legs and other parts were. When he tried to do so, he became quite puzzled. His hands went to the place where his belt buckle would be (he was wearing hospital pajamas) and moved as if he were feeling one. "No," he said. "It's not a pair of pants—it's a belt!"

The patient's visual system was not normal, yet it functioned better than we could infer from only his verbal behavior. That is, his perceptions were much more accurate than his words indicated. The fact that he could mime the use of a pistol or feel an imaginary belt buckle with his hands indicated that his visual system worked well enough to initiate appropriate nonverbal behaviors, though not the appropriate words. Once he felt what he was doing, he could name the object. The process might involve steps such as those shown in Figure 10.1 on the next page.

Although the patient had lost his ability to read, speech therapists were able to teach him to use finger spelling to read. He could not say what a particular letter was, but he could learn to make a particular hand movement when he saw it. After he had learned the finger-spelling alphabet used by deaf people, he could read slowly and laboriously by making hand movements for each letter and feeling the words that his hand was spelling out.

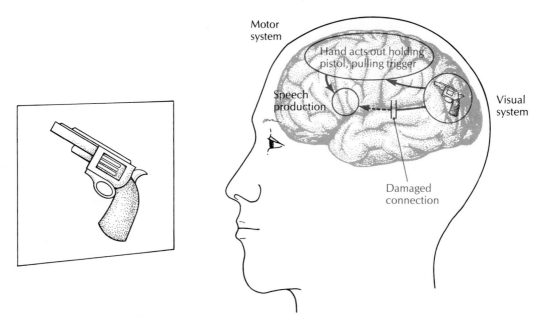

FIGURE 10.1

Hypothetical exchanges of information within the brain of the patient with visual agnosia.

This case supports the conclusion that consciousness is synonymous with a person's ability to talk about his or her perceptions or memories. In this particular situation, disruption of the normal interchange between the visual perceptual system and verbal system prevented the patient from being directly aware of his own visual perceptions. It was as if his hands talked to him, telling him what he had just seen.

The Split-Brain Syndrome

One surgical procedure demonstrates dramatically how various brain functions can be disconnected from each other and from verbal mechanisms. It is used for people who have very severe epilepsy that cannot be controlled by drugs. In these people, violent storms of neural activity begin in one hemisphere and are transmitted to the other by the **corpus callosum,** a large bundle of axons that connect corresponding parts of the cortex on one side of the brain with those on the other. Both sides of the brain then engage in wild neural firing, and stimulate each other, causing a generalized epi-

leptic seizure. These seizures can occur many times each day, preventing the patient from leading a normal life. Neurosurgeons discovered that cutting the corpus callosum (the **split-brain operation**) greatly reduced the frequency of the epileptic seizures. Figure 10.2 illustrates this procedure.

Sperry (1966) and Gazzaniga and his associates (Gazzaniga, 1970; Gazzaniga and LeDoux, 1978) have studied these patients extensively. After the two hemispheres are disconnected, they operate independently; their sensory mechanisms, memories, and motor systems can no longer exchange information. The effects of these disconnections are not obvious to the casual observer, for the simple reason that only one hemisphere—in most people, the left—controls speech. The right hemisphere of an epileptic person with a split brain can understand speech reasonably well, but it is poor at reading and spelling, and because Broca's speech area is located in the left hemisphere, it is totally incapable of producing speech.

Because only one side of the brain can talk about what it is experiencing, most observers do not detect the independent operations of the right side of a split brain. Even the patient's left brain has to learn about the independent existence of the right brain. One of the first things that these patients say they notice after the operation is that their left hand seems to have a "mind of its own." For example, patients may find themselves putting down a book held in the left hand, even if they are reading it with great interest. At other times, they surprise themselves by making obscene gestures (with the left hand) at inappropriate times. Each side of the brain is connected to the opposite side of the body, controlling its movements and receiving sensations from it. Thus, the right hemisphere controls the movements of the left hand, and these unexpected movements puzzle the left hemisphere, the side of the brain that controls speech.

One exception to the crossed representation of sensory information is the olfactory system. When a person sniffs a flower through the left nostril, only the left brain receives a sensation of the odor. Thus, if the right nostril of a patient with a split brain is plugged up, leaving the left nostril open, the patient will accurately identify odors verbally. If the odor enters the right nostril, the patient will say that he or she smells nothing. But in fact the right brain has perceived the odor and can identify it. This ability is demonstrated by an experiment in which the patient is told to reach for some objects that are hidden from view by a partition. If asked to use the left hand, with the left nostril plugged up, he or she will select the object that corresponds to the odor—a plastic flower for a floral odor, a toy fish for a fishy odor, a model tree for the odor of pine, and so forth. But if the left nostril is plugged up, the right hand fails this test, since it is connected to the left hemisphere, which did not smell the odor. (See Figure 10.3 on page 312.)

Sometimes the hands conflict, with one hand trying to put a book down, while the other is trying to pick it up. (Can you guess which hand is which?) It was even reported that a man with a split brain attempted to beat his wife with one hand and protect her with the other. Did he *really* want to hurt her? Yes and no, I guess.

As we saw in Chapter 2, the left hemisphere, besides giving us the ability to read, write, and speak, is good at other tasks that require verbal abilities, such as mathematics and logic, whereas the right hemisphere excels at tasks of perception and has a much greater artistic abil-

ity. If a patient with a split brain tries to use his or her right hand to arrange blocks to duplicate a geometrical design provided by the experimenter, the hand will hopelessly fumble around with the blocks. Often, the left hand (controlled by the right hemisphere) will brush the right hand aside and easily complete the task. It is as if the right hemisphere gets impatient with the clumsy ineptitude of the hand controlled by the left hemisphere.

The effects of cutting the corpus callosum reinforce the conclusion that consciousness depends on the ability of speech mechanisms in the left hemisphere to receive information from other regions of the brain. If such communication is interrupted, then some kinds of information can never reach consciousness.

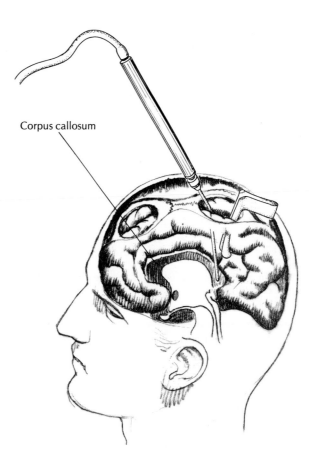

Corpus callosum

FIGURE 10.2

The split-brain operation. (From Gazzaniga, M.S. *Fundamentals of Psychology.* New York: Academic Press, 1973.)

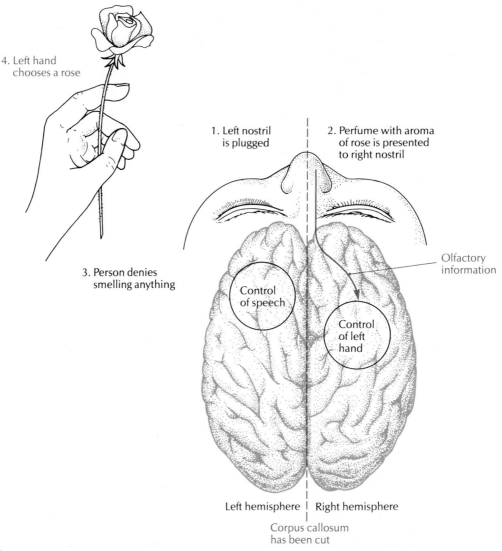

4. Left hand chooses a rose

1. Left nostril is plugged

2. Perfume with aroma of rose is presented to right nostril

3. Person denies smelling anything

Olfactory information

Control of speech

Control of left hand

Left hemisphere | Right hemisphere

Corpus callosum has been cut

FIGURE 10.3

Identification of an object in response to an olfactory stimulus by a person with a split brain.

■ What do we learn about consciousness from the symptoms of isolation aphasia, a particular case of visual agnosia?

■ What does the split-brain syndrome add to our understanding of consciousness?

SLEEP

Sleep is certainly a state of altered consciousness; during sleep we have dreams that can be just as vivid as waking experiences, and yet we forget most of them as soon as they are over. In fact there are two distinct kinds of sleep, thus two states of altered consciousness. We spend approximately one third of our lives sleeping—or trying to. Many people are preoccupied with sleep or with the lack of it. Collectively, they consume tons of drugs each year in an attempt to get to sleep. Advertisements for nonprescription sleep medications imply that a night without a full eight hours of sleep is a physiological and psychological disaster. Does missing a few hours—or even a full night—of sleep actually harm us? What does sleep do for us?

The Stages of Sleep

Sleep is not a uniform state. We can sleep lightly or deeply; we can be restless or still; we can have vivid dreams or our consciousness can be relatively blank. Researchers who have studied sleep have found that its stages usually follow an orderly, predictable sequence.

Most sleep research takes place in a sleep laboratory. (See Figure 10.4.) Because a person's sleep is affected by his or her surroundings, a sleep laboratory contains one or more small bedrooms, furnished and decorated to be as homelike and comfortable as possible. Sleep during the first night or two is likely to be somewhat different from usual, because of the new environment. However, by the third night sleep is essentially normal, and from this point on, observations can be considered useful.

The most important apparatus of the sleep laboratory is the **polygraph,** which is located in a separate room. This machine records on paper the output of various devices that can be attached to the subject. For example, the polygraph can record the electrical activity of the brain (an **EEG,** or **electroencephalogram**) through small metal disks pasted to the scalp; it can record electrical signals from muscles (an **EMG,** or **electromyogram**) or from the heart (an **EKG,** or **electrocardiogram**); or it can record eye movements (an **EOG,** or **electro-oculogram**) through small metal disks attached to the skin around the eyes. Other special transducers can detect respiration, sweating, skin or body temperature, and other physiological states.

Let us look at a typical night's sleep of a male college student on his third night. The EEG electrodes are attached to his scalp, EMG electrodes to his chin, EKG electrodes to his chest, and EOG electrodes to the skin around his eyes. Wires connected to these electrodes are plugged into the amplifiers of the polygraph. The output of each amplifier causes a pen on the polygraph to move up and down while a continuous sheet of paper moves by.

The EEG record distinguishes between alert and relaxed wakefulness. When a person is alert, the tracing looks rather irregular, and the pens do not move very far up or down; the EEG shows high-frequency (15–30 Hz), low-amplitude electrical activity called **beta activity.** When a person is relaxed and perhaps somewhat drowsy, the record shows **alpha activity,**

a medium-amplitude, medium-frequency (8–12 Hz) rhythm. (See Figure 10.5 on p. 314.)

The technician leaves the room, the lights are turned off, and the subject closes his eyes. As he grows drowsy, his EEG changes from beta activity to alpha activity. The first stage of sleep (stage 1) still contains some alpha activity, marked by the colored bracket in Figure 10.6A on p. 315. The EMG shows that his muscles are still active, and his EOG indicates slow, gentle, rolling eye movements. As sleep progresses, it gets deeper and deeper, moving through stages 2, 3, and 4. The EEG gets progressively slower in frequency and higher in amplitude. (See Fig-

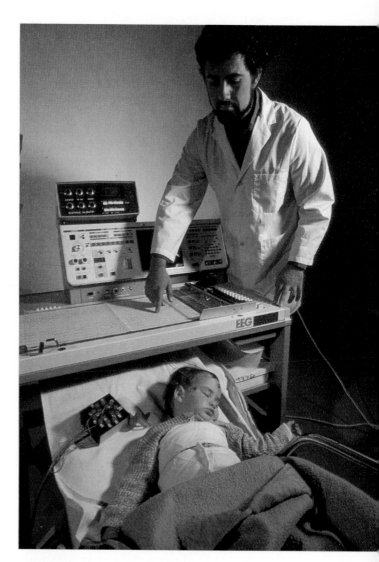

FIGURE 10.4

The polygraph machine records physiological changes that occur during sleep.

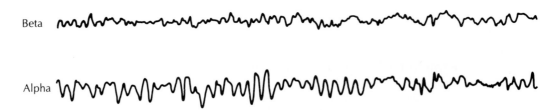

Beta

Alpha

FIGURE 10.5

Top. Beta activity, characteristic of alert wakefulness. *Bottom.* Alpha activity, characteristic of relaxed, drowsy wakefulness or light sleep.

ure 10.6, B, C, and D.) Stage 4 consists mainly of **delta activity,** characterized by relatively high-amplitude waves occurring at 3–5 Hz. Our subject becomes less responsive to the environment, and it is more difficult to awaken him. Environmental stimuli that caused him to stir during stage 1 produce no reaction during stage 4. The sleep of stages 3 and 4 is called **slow-wave sleep.**

Stage 4 sleep is reached in less than an hour and continues for about a half hour. Then, suddenly, the EEG begins to indicate lighter levels of sleep, back through stages 3 and 2 to the activity characteristic of stage 1. The subject's heart begins to beat more rapidly and his respiration alternates between shallow breaths and sudden gasps. The EOG shows that the subject's eyes are darting rapidly back and forth, up and down. The EEG record looks like that of a person who is awake and active. Yet the subject is fast asleep. Although his EMG is generally quiet, indicating muscular relaxation, his hands and feet twitch occasionally. (See Figure 10.6, E.)

At this point the subject is dreaming. He has entered another stage of sleep that has several names: paradoxical sleep, active sleep, rapid eye movement (REM) sleep, and desynchronized sleep. The most popular name is **rapid eye movement (REM) sleep.** The REM sleep lasts about twenty to thirty minutes, followed by approximately one hour of slow-wave sleep. A typical night's sleep consists of four or five of these ninety-minute cycles. Figure 10.7 on page 316 shows a record of a person's stages of sleep; the colored shading indicates REM sleep.

A person in REM sleep exhibits an EEG with irregular waves of low voltage, rapid eye movements, brief twitches of the hands and feet, and rapid, irregular heart rate and breathing. The EMG shows that the facial muscles are still. In fact, physiological studies have shown that, aside from occasional twitching, a person actually becomes paralyzed during REM sleep. Males are observed to have partial or full erections, which are usually not associated with sexual arousal, although both males and females sometimes have dreams of a sexual nature, occasionally ending with orgasm. Studies have found that women's vaginal secretions increase during REM sleep.

People who do not get enough sleep at night may find it difficult to remain alert during the day.

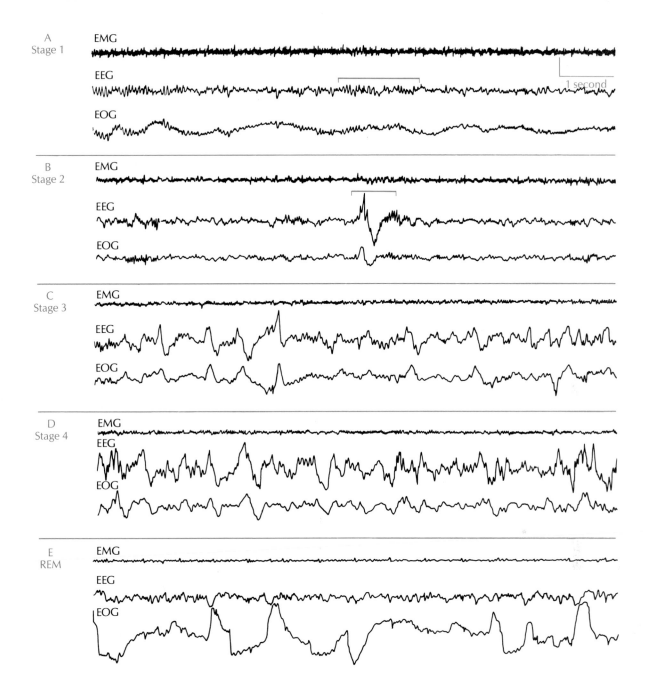

FIGURE 10.6

A polygraph recording of the various stages of sleep. *A.* Stage 1. The
bracket indicates alpha activity. *B.* Stage 2. The bracket indicates a
waveform called a *K-complex* often seen during this stage. *C.* Stage 3.
D. Stage 4. Note the predominance of delta activity, the high-amplitude,
low-frequency EEG waves. *E.* Stage REM sleep. Note the low-amplitude,
high-frequency EEG waves, the relative lack of activity in the EMG, and
the prominent eye movements on the EOG. (From Cohen, D.B. *Sleep &
Dreaming: Origins, Nature and Functions.* New York: Pergamon Press,
1979. Copyright 1979, Pergamon Press, Ltd.)

FIGURE 10.7

Typical progression of stages during a night's sleep. (From Hartmann, E., *The Biology of Dreaming.* Springfield, Ill.: C.C. Thomas, 1967.)

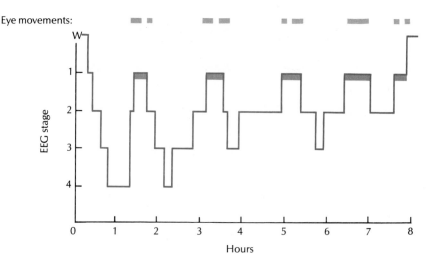

Dreaming

States of Consciousness During Sleep

A person who is awakened during REM sleep and asked whether anything was happening will almost always report a dream. The typical REM-sleep dream resembles a play or movie— it has a narrative form. Conversely, reports of narrative, storylike dreams are rare among people awakened from slow-wave sleep. In general, mental activity during slow-wave sleep is more nearly static; it involves situations rather than stories and generally unpleasant ones. For example, a person awakened from slow-wave sleep might report a sensation of being crushed or suffocated. The painting shown in Figure 10.8 was inspired by a dream typical of slow-wave sleep.

Unless the sleep is heavily drugged, almost everyone has four or five bouts of REM sleep each night, with accompanying dreams. Yet if the dreamer does not happen to awaken while the dream is in progress, it is lost forever. Some people who claimed not to have had a dream for many years slept in a sleep laboratory and found that in fact they did dream. They were able to remember their dreams because the investigator awakened them during REM sleep.

Because we recall dreams only if we awaken during their progress, light sleepers tend to remember more dreams than heavy sleepers; we are also most likely to recall dreams that occur toward morning, just before awakening, when our sleep is lightest. Many people in psy-

chotherapy learn to remember their dreams so that they can discuss them with their therapists. Apparently, they are somehow able to awaken themselves during REM sleep.

The reports of people awakened from REM and slow-wave sleep make it clear that people are conscious during sleep, even though they may not remember any of their experiences then. Lack of memory for an event does not mean that it never happened; it only means that there is no permanent record accessible to conscious thought during wakefulness. Thus, we are able to say that slow-wave sleep and REM sleep reflect two different states of consciousness.

Symbolism in Dreams

For as long as humans have used language to communicate, dreams have played a special role in society. Some people have acted as interpreters of dreams. Battles have been averted or begun because of a general's dream. People have decided on their careers, marriage partners, and places of residence on the basis of what their dreams told them. Today, many books are available to tell us what our dreams really mean. Do dreams in fact have some special, hidden meaning that we can extract from them?

Investigators who have carefully studied REM-sleep dreams report that most dreams are extremely prosaic (Hall, 1966). The overwhelming majority of them occur in ordinary settings, in which not much happens. And even if the situation seems to demand strong emotion, the dreamer often reports that he or she did not feel very excited or upset; almost everything is taken for granted in a dream. In contrast, people often do appear to be upset when they are awakened from the kinds of dreams that occur in slow-wave sleep.

If most dreams are so prosaic, why do we remember such bizarre ones? The explanation appears to lie in the sheer number of dreams. Each of us probably has over 100,000 dreams during a lifetime, and even if we remember only a small percentage of them, that is still a large number of dreams. We are most likely to dwell upon, and tell others about, only the most interesting and unusual dreams. The dull, commonplace ones are quickly forgotten.

Nowadays not many people believe that dreams can predict the future, but many do believe that the proper interpretation of a dream could give them some insight into their own psyches. Sigmund Freud attributed much to dreams and started a tradition of a particular form of dream analysis. He believed that dreams had a **latent** ("hidden") **content,** consisting of wishes that came out of unfulfilled sexual desires, especially those resulting from sexual conflicts during infancy that had never been resolved. Although the latent content was what the dream was really about, Freud argued that social taboos prevented the dreamer from confronting the topic of the dream directly. Instead, the latent content was disguised in a way that could safely be tolerated. The latent content was transformed into the dream's **manifest content:** the actual, simple description of the dream's plot. Dreams were assumed to be full of symbols and hidden meanings. For example, any elongated object—a pencil, a tree, a stick, or a chimney, to name but a few—represented a penis. Vaginas were symbolized by any sort of container, even an automobile or a boat. Riding a horse, shooting a gun, or even climbing a flight of stairs was taken to represent sexual intercourse.

Most of Freud's followers today would expand the scope of a dream's latent content to include more than sexual matters; they agree that people are motivated by other kinds of urges, as well. But is the basic notion of hidden symbols correct? There is no doubt that some objects or occurrences are symbolized, but is

the meaning of all these symbols hidden from the dreamer? And is it not possible that sometimes the symbol is not a symbol at all but is really what it seems to be? Does a dream about paddling a canoe through some rapids invariably symbolize unexpressed sexual desires? Does the canoe necessarily represent a woman's sexual organs? Or is it possible that it is just a canoe, and the dream represents a not-so-subtle desire to go canoeing?

Hall (1966), who admits to the validity of symbolism in dreams, does not believe that the symbols are usually hidden. For example, a person may plainly engage in sexual intercourse in one dream and have another dream that involves shooting a gun. Surely the "real" meaning of shooting the gun need not be hidden from a dreamer who has undisguised dreams of sexual intercourse at other times or who has an uninhibited sex life during waking. Why should this person disguise sexual desires while dreaming? As Hall says, people use their own symbols, and not those of anyone else. They represent what the dreamer thinks, and

FIGURE 10.8

The Nightmare (1781), by Johann Heinrich Fuseli, Swiss, 1741–1825. (Oil on canvas, 40" X 50". Gift of Mr. and Mrs. Bert L. Smokler and Mr. and Mrs. Lawrence A. Fleischman, Acq. no. 55.05. Courtesy of the Detroit Institute of Arts.)

therefore their meaning is usually not hidden from the dreamer.

The view that symbols in dreams are the private property of the dreamer is supported by the results of experiments that have attempted to insert material into dreams by presenting subjects with stimuli or situations before or during sleep. According to a summary of studies on dreaming, "Subjects most often select something other than [what the experimenter intends]. . . . If they do dream of [what the experimenter intends] . . . , it is most often represented in some personal associative way rather than directly, making identification difficult. . . ." (Webb and Cartwright, 1978, p. 243). In other words, the symbols that the subject uses may disguise the material from the experimenter, but not necessarily from the dreamer.

Sometimes people dream about things that they avoid thinking about while awake, and these dreams may be filled with symbols whose significance they cannot recognize. In such cases, a good psychotherapist may be able to use information from the dreams to understand what problems are bothering the client, in order to help the client with his or her difficulties. However, we cannot infer from these relatively rare situations that all dreams of all people are filled with symbols whose meanings can be understood only by a person with special training.

Functions of Sleep

We do not yet know definitely what functions sleep performs. One hypothesis is that sleep provides our bodies (including our brains) with a chance to repair themselves. Another hypothesis views sleep simply as a behavioral response.

Sleep As Repair

Perhaps our bodies just get worn out by performing waking activities for sixteen hours or so. There is a definite relationship between the number of hours we stay awake and how sleepy we feel. Perhaps waking activities use up some vital substances that can be regenerated only when we sleep. Or perhaps wakefulness produces some toxic chemicals that are broken down during sleep. However, there is no compelling evidence to support either of these possibilities. The amount of physical activity people engage in has a rather small effect on the amount of sleep they need.

Shapiro, Bortz, Mitchell, Bartel, and Jooste (1982) found that people who had participated in a very long (ninety-two kilometer) running race slept longer than normal the following two nights. Slow-wave sleep increased about 45 percent, while REM sleep decreased. The data suggest that slow-wave sleep plays a role in helping people recuperate from the effects of muscular exertion. However, *lack of exercise* does not substantially reduce sleep; Ryback and Lewis (1971) had healthy subjects spend six weeks resting in bed and observed no changes in either REM or slow-wave sleep. Thus, it is unlikely that the sole function of sleep is recuperation from the effects of exercise the previous day.

Researchers have found that some other physiological events appear to be tied to sleep. For example, the rate of protein synthesis in the brains of cats greatly increases during REM sleep (Drucker-Colin and Spanis, 1976). However, we cannot conclude that we sleep *in order to* produce brain proteins; the increased neural activity that accompanies REM sleep may cause the increase in protein synthesis. Researchers have not yet found any toxic chemicals that are produced during wakefulness that must be disposed of during sleep, or any vital substances that are used up during wakefulness that must be manufactured during sleep. Thus, if sleep serves a repair function, investigators have not yet found out what must be repaired. For now we must conclude that the evidence for sleep as repair is not very strong.

The Effects of Total Sleep Deprivation. The effects of starvation are easy to detect: The person loses weight, becomes fatigued, and will eventually die if he or she does not eat again. By analogy, it should be easy to discover why we sleep by seeing what happens to a person who goes without sleep. The intense discomfort that we experience when we are deprived of sleep makes us feel that sleep is more than an adaptive response; we consider it necessary for our well-being. Yet research shows that sleep deprivation does little more than make one feel very sleepy.

Several dozen people have been kept awake for upward of 200 hours, without any remarkable effects (Dement, 1974; Webb, 1975). People who are kept awake for so long get very sleepy, of course. Their eyelids itch and droop, and they have trouble doing dull, routine tasks. However, when they are properly motivated, they can perform almost as well as they did before the sleep deprivation began. A famous case was reported in which a disk jockey stayed awake for several days to gain publicity for a charity and became "psychotic" as a result of his sleep deprivation. But his case appears to be unique; other people who have stayed up just as long remained perfectly stable. Therefore, the disk jockey's psychosis cannot be blamed directly upon the lack of sleep. His abnormal behaviors appear to have been the result of stress (which sleep deprivation certainly causes) in a susceptible individual. Most people get a bit grouchy if they are kept awake for several days, but they do not become crazy.

Feelings of sleepiness do not continue to increase indefinitely as the period of sleep deprivation goes on. Sleepiness follows the day-night cycle, reaching its maximum around 4:00 A.M. During the day, subjects find it fairly easy to ward off sleep. And when they finally go to sleep again, they do not make up all the sleep they missed. Most of them sleep approximately fifteen hours and feel fine after that.

These results certainly do not support the hypothesis that sleep serves a vital physiological function. When we miss sleep, we get very sleepy; but there is no evidence that our bodies suffer any measurable harm.

The Effects of REM-Sleep Deprivation. There is considerable evidence that although total sleep deprivation does little more than make a person very sleepy, *selective* deprivation of REM sleep has demonstrable effects. People who are sleeping in a laboratory can be selectively deprived of REM sleep; an investigator awakens them whenever the polygraph record indicates that they have entered REM sleep. The investigator must also awaken control subjects just as often at random intervals to eliminate any effects produced by being awakened several times.

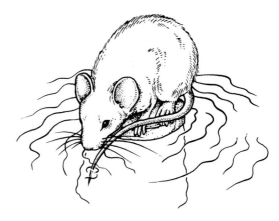

FIGURE 10.9

The flowerpot technique. (From Carlson, N.R. *Physiology of Behavior*, 3rd ed. Boston: Allyn and Bacon, 1986.)

Experimenters can selectively deprive laboratory animals of REM sleep by housing them in cages that contain a small island surrounded by water. The island often consists of an upturned flowerpot; hence the term **flowerpot technique.** (See Figure 10.9.) When the subject (usually a mouse) enters REM sleep, its muscles become paralyzed, its head slumps, and its face splashes into the water, causing the animal to awaken. Soon the animal learns not to enter REM sleep while it is on the platform.

If an animal or person is deprived of REM sleep for several nights and is then allowed to sleep without interruption, the onset of REM sleep becomes more frequent. It is as if a need for REM sleep builds up, forcing the organism into this state more often. When the subject is no longer awakened during REM sleep, a rebound phenomenon is seen: the subject engages in many more bouts of REM sleep than normal during the next night or two, as if the organism were "catching up" on something important that it missed.

Many studies with laboratory animals have shown that deprivation of REM sleep affects retention of new tasks learned during the previous day. For example, Rideout (1979) gave hungry mice one opportunity to run through a maze each day and find food at the end. After each day's trial he deprived some of them of REM sleep by putting them on a small platform in a cage filled with water. The mice who were deprived of REM sleep learned their way around the maze more slowly than the mice who were not deprived of REM sleep.

Deprivation of REM sleep in humans appears to have a greater effect on the assimilation of events that produce strong emotions than it does on simple learning. The saying "Things will look better in the morning" appears to be true. For example, Greenberg, Pillard, and Pearlman (1972) had subjects view a film of a very bloody and gruesome circumcision rite performed by a primitive tribe. This film produces anxiety when it is watched the first time, but if it is watched again on a later date the effect is much smaller. Greenberg and his col-

Researchers studying the functions of sleep have found little support for the idea that sleep provides the body with a chance to repair itself.

leagues showed the film twice, on two separate days, to two groups of subjects. One group was permitted to sleep normally; the other group was deprived of REM sleep. The sleep-deprived subjects showed much less reduction in anxiety at the second viewing than the subjects who were permitted to obtain REM sleep. The results suggest that REM sleep may perform a role in reducing anxiety produced by events that occurred during the day; perhaps we really do "work things out" during REM sleep.

We cannot be sure what REM sleep accomplishes, but there appears to be a definite relation between this state and the learning and assimilation of emotional experiences. The sleep of a newborn infant is mostly REM sleep. Does this fact have any relation to the tremendous amount of learning that occurs early in life, or is it somehow related to the growth and development of the brain? Perhaps both factors are important.

Sleep As a Response

Another view, championed by Webb (1975), is that sleep is an instinctual behavioral response, like sexual intercourse. That is, there is no physiological need for sleep or sexual intercourse as there is for food and water. Rather, sleep serves a useful purpose for the survival of the individual and the species—or at least it did when the brain mechanisms of sleep were evolving.

There is no doubt that sleep is an active function of the brain. Sleep is definitely a response, not simply a state that we enter by default when we are not awake. The brain does not just "run down" at the end of the day. An ingenious experiment by Magni, Moruzzi, Rossi, and Zanchetti (1959) proved that an animal sleeps because parts of the brain (we could call them "sleep circuits") become active and put the rest of the brain to sleep.

The investigators tied off some branches of the blood vessels leading to a cat's brain, isolating the blood supply of the brain stem from that of the front part (including the cerebral hemispheres). They permitted the cat to fall asleep and then injected an anesthetic into the brain stem. This treatment caused the animal to awaken. Thus, anesthesia of the brain stem brings a period of sleep to an end. Magni and

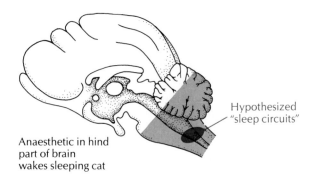

Anaesthetic in hind
part of brain
wakes sleeping cat

FIGURE 10.10

The experiment by Magni, Moruzzi, Rossi, and Zanchetti (1959).

his colleagues concluded that some portion of the brain stem contains circuits that produce sleep. If these circuits are suppressed by an anesthetic, the cat cannot sleep. (See Figure 10.10.)

Now let us consider Webb's suggestion that sleep is a response that is useful for the survival of a species. As Allison and Chichetti (1976) have shown, different animals sleep for very different amounts of time, and the amount of time seems to be related both to the animal's way of obtaining food and to its exposure to predators. In general, animals that have a safe place to stay will sleep for relatively long periods, unless they have high metabolic rates that require a lot of food gathering. The short-tailed shrew has a safe burrow but sleeps very little; it must eat around the clock or die. The ground squirrel also has a safe burrow, but because this animal is larger and consequently has a lower metabolic rate, it does not need to eat so often. It sleeps fourteen hours a day. So does a gorilla, which obviously does not need to sleep in a burrow to protect itself. Cattle, sheep, deer, zebras, and other animals that can be preyed upon sleep very little: about two hours per day, and only in brief naps.

These sleeping patterns make sense in terms of the ecological niche of each species. For example, most primates are well adapted to daytime activity. They are agile, have good vision, and are usually adept at climbing trees. Their sense of smell is not very useful in detecting animals that are dangerous to them; they rely for the most part on vision, although audition is also important. Some primates are principally vegetarians and obtain their foods from bushes and trees. These nutrients are readily available during the day, so there is no advantage to gathering them at night. Primate species ancestral to our own were omnivorous, eating plants and other animals. Their main method of killing other animals was to use a weapon. This activity is visually guided, thus requiring daylight.

Primates, then, are best adapted to the daylight world. Food is harder to obtain at night, and exposure to predators is greater because it is harder to see other animals; it makes good sense to find a safe place to stay during the night and to remain inactive there rather than moving around and wasting energy. Thus, it is plausible to view sleep as an adaptive instinctual behavior—one that keeps the animal quiet and out of harm's way.

The logic of this hypothesis is persuasive, and this account may well be correct. However, it does not necessarily follow that the *only* functions accomplished by sleep are safety and energy conservation. It is possible that the neural mechanisms for sleep originally evolved for these purposes but subsequently took on additional functions, such as synthesis of protein in the brain, facilitation of memory storage, and emotional assimilation.

- What are the stages of sleep and what are the methods used to measure these stages?
- What types of dreams occur during slow-wave sleep and REM sleep?
- What are the functions of sleep that are best supported by research evidence?

Sleep Disorders

Sleep does not always go smoothly, and some of the brain mechanisms that are responsible for sleep can malfunction, causing medical problems that manifest themselves while a person is awake. Fortunately, some of the things that sleep researchers have learned can help people with sleep-associated disorders.

Insomnia

Almost everyone has probably suffered from insomnia at least once. A few people have difficulty sleeping most nights; some of them take sleep medications for their ailment. Yet according to most sleep researchers, sleep medications are the major *cause* of insomnia. Thus, insomnia is today's most prevalent **iatrogenic** ("physician-produced") **disorder,** because physicians succumb to pressure from their patients to give them sleeping pills.

So far as anyone knows, insomnia is not a disease. It is a symptom of a variety of conditions, including depression, anxiety, and chronic pain, and can even be produced by the anticipation of a happy event; a child may well lose sleep the night before a birthday party. There is no evidence that some people's brains contain a faulty sleep mechanism that can be fixed with a drug.

Sleep medications provide only symptomatic relief; the sleep produced by them is not normal, and relief is temporary. People need ever-increasing doses and soon become dependent on the drug. Sleep medications initially suppress REM sleep, but even with escalating doses of the drug, a more normal amount of REM sleep soon begins to occur, as if a compensatory mechanism allows it to break through the effects of the medication. Discontinuation of the drug produces a rebound effect: the brain's REM-sleep mechanism recovers, and restlessness, unpleasant dreams, and frequent awakenings predominate throughout the night. One or two such experiences are usually enough to convince most people that they "need" the sleeping pills to which they have become addicted. As people increase the number of sleeping pills taken each night, they reach a point where they are still drugged when they awaken. When it becomes difficult to function normally in the morning, they resort to stimulants to counteract the effects of the depressant drugs. Finally, they become addicted to alternating doses of depressants and stimulants in order to sleep and wake.

Not everyone becomes caught in such a cycle. Many people use sleep medications only rarely, or in low doses. But it is worth considering whether sleeping pills are *ever* necessary. A sedative or tranquilizer may be appropriate for some situations, such as counteracting shock when a loved one has died. But in the absence of such circumstances, it is important to realize that a sleepless night—or even two or three in a row—does not appear to cause any physiological harm. People who tend toward neuroticism

and hypochondria generally feel that they *need* sleep and that they will somehow be harmed if they do not get enough of it. Because worrying about insomnia is a common cause of insomnia, just knowing that a sleepless night is harmless will often solve the problem. Other people use real or imagined insomnia as an excuse for their lack of success in life, telling themselves that they would do much better if only they could get enough sleep. For these people, insomnia may serve as a defense against the painful reality of their lives.

Many people who believe themselves to be insomniacs actually are not. We are often very poor at estimating how much sleep we get. Some people have reported lying awake all night, yet the record obtained in a sleep laboratory shows that they actually fell asleep in approximately thirty minutes and got seven or eight hours of sleep. Many of these people feel better as soon as they find out just how much sleep they are getting.

In addition to people who do not sleep as much as they believe they should and those who imagine that they do not sleep at all, there are a few people who have recurring dreams of lying in bed, trying to fall asleep. The next day, they often feel as bad as if they had really stayed awake.

A common cause of insomnia in older people and infants is **sleep apnea.** (*Apnea* means "without breathing.") People with sleep apnea cannot sleep and breathe at the same time. When they fall asleep, they stop breathing, the content of carbon dioxide in their blood builds up, and they awaken, gasping for air. After breathing deeply for a while, they go back to sleep and resume the cycle. Some people who suffer from sleep apnea are blessed with a lack of memory for this periodic sleeping and awakening; others are aware of it and dread each night's sleep. Fortunately, some types of sleep apnea in adults can be corrected by throat surgery. Many investigators have suggested that sleep apnea accounts for the **sudden infant death syndrome** ("crib death"), which mysteriously kills babies in their sleep. They believe that a mild infection, combined with an underdeveloped respiratory center (located in the medulla), is responsible for the children's failure to awaken when they stop breathing.

Insomnia can neither kill nor disable you. If a more basic problem, such as depression, seems to be causing your insomnia, get professional help. If there are no obvious causes and the insomnia is not severe, try doing your worrying, or whatever else it is that might interfere with sleep, *before* going to bed. Make bed a place where you sleep, not where you worry. Establish and follow a regular routine when you get ready for bed. If you do not fall asleep in a reasonable amount of time, do not lie there fretting. Get up and do something else, and do not go back to bed until you feel drowsy. Even if you are up most of the night, stay up until you feel sleepy enough to doze off as soon as you get into bed. Remember that you will survive even if you miss a night's sleep. Make yourself get up at a regular time; if you make yourself get up in the morning, you will probably find it easier to fall asleep the next night.

Disorders Associated with REM Sleep

Two important characteristics of REM sleep are dreaming and paralysis. It is likely that the paralysis results from a mechanism that prevents us from acting out our dreams. In fact, damage to certain areas of a cat's brain will produce just that result: the cat, obviously asleep, acts as if it were participating in a dream (Jouvet, 1972). It walks around stalking imaginary prey and responding defensively to imaginary predators.

Dreams and muscular paralysis are fine when a person is lying in bed. But sometimes a person is struck down by paralysis while actively going about his or her business. The person falls to the ground and lies there, paralyzed but fully conscious. These attacks of **cataplexy** (*kata-*, "down"; *plessein*, "to strike") generally last less than a minute. The attacks are usually triggered by strong emotional states, such as anger, laughter, or even lovemaking. People who have cataplectic attacks tend also to enter REM sleep as soon as they fall asleep, in contrast to the normal ninety-minute interval.

People who suffer from cataplexy also tend to have vivid **hypnagogic hallucinations** just before they fall asleep, during which they are paralyzed. The hallucinations, which are almost certainly premature dreams, are often continuations of events that have actually occurred. For example, a patient in a sleep laboratory experienced a hypnagogic hallucination in which the experimenter, who had just attached the electrodes, was attempting to cut off his ear

Most of us have suffered from insomnia at one time or another. However, people who work unusual shifts often suffer sleep disorders.

with a scalpel (Dement, 1974). Thus, the disorder appears to involve overactive REM-sleep mechanisms; the cataplexy is probably caused by inappropriate activity of the brain mechanism that keeps a person paralyzed during dreaming.

Cataplexy appears to be a biological disorder, probably involving inherited abnormalities in the brain. In fact, researchers have even developed breeds of dogs that are subject to attacks of cataplexy. Cataplexy can be treated by drugs that increase the activity of neurons that use a particular transmitter substance (serotonin) to communicate with other neurons. In contrast, LSD and mescaline, drugs that produce visual hallucinations, *inhibit* the activity of serotonin-secreting neurons. These findings suggest that there may be a relation between dreams and the hallucinations caused by LSD: serotonin-stimulating drugs are likely to reduce them, whereas serotonin-inhibiting drugs make them more likely to occur.

Cataplexy and hypnagogic hallucinations are symptoms of a more general disorder called **narcolepsy** (literally, "numbness seizure"). Another common symptom of narcolepsy is a **sleep attack,** a sudden wave of irresistible sleepiness. Unlike attacks of cataplexy, sleep attacks can be warded off temporarily, until the person can get to a safe place. After a brief period of normal sleep, the person wakes up feeling refreshed. Sleep attacks can usually be controlled with amphetamine.

Disorders Associated with Slow-Wave Sleep

Several phenomena occur during the deepest phase (stage 4) of slow-wave sleep. These events include sleepwalking, sleeptalking, night terrors, and enuresis.

Sleepwalking can be as simple as getting out of bed and right back in again, or as complicated as walking out of a house and climbing into a car. (Fortunately, sleepwalkers apparently do not try to drive.) We know that sleepwalking is not the acting out of a dream, because it occurs during stage 4 of slow-wave sleep, when the EEG shows high-amplitude slow waves and the person's mental state generally involves a static situation, not a narrative. Sleepwalkers are difficult to awaken, and once awakened they are often confused and disoriented. However, contrary to popular belief, it is perfectly safe to wake them up.

Sleepwalking is *not* a manifestation of some deep-seated emotional problem. Most sleepwalkers are children, who almost invariably outgrow this behavior. The worst thing to do, according to sleep researchers, is to try to get them treated for it. Of course, a house inhabited by a sleepwalker should be made as safe as possible, and the doors should be kept locked at night. For some reason, sleepwalking runs in families; Dement (1974) tells of a family whose grown members were reunited for a holiday celebration. In the middle of the night they woke to find that they had all gathered in the living room—during their sleep.

Sleeptalking sometimes occurs as part of a REM sleep dream, but it more usually occurs during other stages of sleep. Often it is possible to carry on a conversation with the sleeptalker;

this capability indicates that the person is very near the boundary between sleep and waking. During this state sleeptalkers are very suggestible. So-called truth serums are used in an attempt to duplicate this condition, so that the person being questioned is not on guard against giving away secrets and is not functioning well enough to tell elaborate lies. Unfortunately for the interrogators (and fortunately for the rest of the population), there are no foolproof, reliable truth serums.

Night terrors, like sleepwalking, occur most often in children. In this disorder, the child wakes, screaming with terror. When questioned, the child does not report a dream, and often seems confused. Usually the child falls asleep quickly without showing any aftereffects and seldom remembers the event the next day. Night terrors are not the same as nightmares, which are simply frightening dreams from which one happens to awaken. It appears that night terrors are caused by sudden awakenings from the depths of stage 4 sleep. The sudden, dramatic change in consciousness is a frightening experience for the child.

The final disorder of slow-wave sleep, **enuresis,** or "bedwetting," is fairly common in young children. Most children outgrow it, just as they outgrow sleepwalking or night terrors. Emotional problems can trigger enuresis, but bedwetting does not itself indicate that a child is psychologically unwell. The problem with enuresis is that, unlike the other stage 4 phenomena, there are aftereffects that must be cleaned up. Parents dislike having their sleep disturbed and get tired of frequently changing and laundering sheets. The resulting tension in family relationships can make the child feel anxious and guilty and can thus unnecessarily prolong the disorder.

Fortunately, a simple training method often cures enuresis. A moisture-sensitive device is placed under the bed sheet; when it gets wet it causes a bell to ring. Because a child releases a few drops of urine before the bladder begins to empty in earnest, the bell wakes the child in time to run to the bathroom. In about a week, most children learn to prevent their bladders from emptying and manage to wait until morning. Perhaps what they really learn is not to enter such a deep level of stage 4 sleep, in which the mechanism that keeps the bladder from emptying seems to break down.

- How are the various types of insomnia treated?
- What kind of treatment is used for sleep disorders associated with REM sleep?
- What kind of treatment is used for sleep disorders associated with slow-wave sleep?

HYPNOSIS

Hypnosis is a specific and unusual phenomenon in which one person apparently controls another person's behavior, thoughts, and perceptions. Under hypnosis, a person can be induced to bark like a dog, act like a baby, or tolerate being pierced with needles. Although these examples are interesting and amusing,

Franz Anton Mesmer (1734–1815) discovered hypnosis. Here he is seen hypnotizing a criminal to force a confession of guilt.

hypnosis is important to psychology because it provides insights about the nature of consciousness and has applications in the fields of medicine and psychotherapy.

Hypnosis, or **mesmerism** was discovered by Franz Anton Mesmer (1734–1815), an Austrian physician. He found that when he passed magnets back and forth over people's bodies (in an attempt to restore their "magnetic fluxes" and cure them of disease), they would often have convulsions and enter a trancelike state, during which almost miraculous cures could be achieved. As Mesmer discovered later, the patients were not affected directly by the magnetism of the iron rods; they were responding to his undoubtedly persuasive and compelling personality. We now know that convulsions and trancelike states do not necessarily accompany hypnosis, and we also know that hypnosis does not cure physical illnesses. Mesmer's patients obviously had psychologically produced symptoms that were alleviated by suggestions made while they were hypnotized.

The Induction of Hypnosis

A person undergoing hypnosis can be alert, relaxed, tense, lying quietly, or exercising vigorously. There is no need to move an object in front of someone's face or to say "You are getting sleepy"; an enormous variety of techniques can be used to induce hypnosis in a susceptible person. The only essential feature seems to be the subject's understanding that he or she is to be hypnotized. Moss (1965) reported having sometimes simply said to a well-practiced subject, in a normal tone of voice, "Please sit in that chair and go into hypnosis," and the subject complied in a few seconds. Sometimes this approach worked even on volunteers who had never been hypnotized before. (Of course, these people had some expectations about what the word *hypnosis* means; their behavior conformed to their expectations.)

Obviously, soothing, friendly words are more persuasive than hostile ones, but most investigators agree that no special tricks are necessary to induce hypnosis. This is not to say that the words the hypnotist uses have no effect; if he or she emphasizes the word *sleep*, the subjects are more likely to enter a drowsy trance than a relatively alert one.

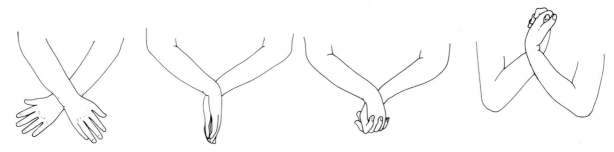

FIGURE 10.11

The procedure used by Pattie (1937).

Characteristics of Hypnosis

Hypnotized people are very suggestible; they will do things in conformity with what the hypnotist says, even to the extent of appearing to misperceive reality. Under hypnosis, people can be instructed to do things that they would not be expected to do under normal conditions, such as acting out imaginary scenes or pretending to be an animal. Hypnotized people can be convinced that an arm cannot move or is insensitive to pain, and they then act as if that is the case; hypnosis can thus be used to induce paralysis or anesthesia. They can also be made to see things that are not there **(positive hallucinations)** or can be persuaded that objects that are actually present are gone from view **(negative hallucinations).**

One of the most dramatic phenomena of hypnosis is that of **posthypnotic suggestibility,** in which a person is given instructions under hypnosis and follows those instructions after returning to a nonhypnotized state. For example, the hypnotist might tell a subject that he will become unbearably thirsty when he sees the hypnotist wind her watch. Usually the hypnotist also admonishes the subject not to remember anything upon leaving the hypnotic state, so that **posthypnotic amnesia** is also achieved. After leaving the hypnotic state, the subject acts normally and professes ignorance of what he perceived and did during hypnosis, perhaps even apologizing for not having succumbed to hypnosis. The hypnotist later winds her watch, and the subject suddenly leaves the room to get a drink of water.

Studies indicate that when changes in perception are induced in hypnotized subjects, the changes occur not in the subject's actual perceptions but in their verbal reports about their perceptions. For example, an experiment by Pattie (1937) indicates that local anesthesia induced by hypnotic suggestion is not the same as anesthesia produced by drugs. Pattie suggested to hypnotized subjects that they could feel nothing with one hand. He then had them cross their wrists so that their forearms formed an **X**, turn their palms together, interlace their fingers, and twist their hands toward their bodies until their thumbs pointed upward. (See Figure 10.11.) In such a position, it is very difficult for someone to tell which hand is being touched by another person. (Try it yourself; fold your hands as Figure 10.11 shows, have someone touch three or four fingers in rapid succession, and try to say to which hand the touched fingers belong.) Pattie touched several fingers on both of the subjects' hands and asked them to count the number of times they were touched. If in fact they could not feel sensations from the "anesthetized" hand, they should not have counted the touches made to this hand, but they included many of these touches in the total count. It therefore appears that the hypnotized subjects were not anesthetized; they simply acted as if they were.

Many studies have also shown that hypnotically induced blindness or deafness does not take the same form that it would if the sensory information was no longer being analyzed by the brain. For example, Miller, Hennessy, and Leibowitz (1973) used the *Ponzo illusion* to test the effects of hypnotically induced blindness. Although the two parallel horizontal lines in the left portion of Figure 10.12 are the same length, the top one looks longer than the bottom one. This effect is produced by the presence of the slanted lines to the left and right of the horizontal ones; if these lines are not present, the horizontal lines appear to be the same length. Through hypnotic suggestion, the experimenters made the slanted lines "disappear," but even though the subjects reported that they could not see the slanted lines (a negative hallucination), they still perceived the upper line as being longer than the lower one. This result indicates that the visual system continues to process sensory information during hypnotically induced blindness; otherwise, the subjects would have perceived the lines as being equal in length. The reported blindness appears to occur not because of altered activity in the visual system but because of altered activity in the verbal system (and in consciousness).

Antisocial Behavior Under Hypnosis

It has been theorized that people can be induced to commit antisocial acts—even crimes—while under hypnosis, but most professionals assert that people cannot simply be told to perform an act that grossly violates their moral code, such as picking up a gun and killing someone on command. Some people have also proposed that hypnotized subjects can be made to misperceive a situation and thus inadvertently violate their code of conduct. For example, a subject might be given a gun and told to "shoot at that paper target," when the target is actually another person. However, after reviewing attempts to trick people or directly induce them to commit antisocial acts under hypnosis, Barber (1969) concluded that hypnosis does not lower people's inhibitions against committing criminal acts, nor does it appear that people can be tricked into committing them.

Explanations of Hypnosis

Hypnosis has been called a special case of learning, a transference of the superego, a goal-directed behavior shaped by the hypnotist, a role-playing situation, and a restructuring of perceptual-cognitive functioning. In other words, no one yet knows exactly what it is. Hypnosis has been described as a state of enhanced suggestibility, but that is simply a description, not an explanation. Many people have advanced theories of hypnosis; a book by Sheehan and Perry (1976) describes six of them. I will discuss two theories that have been most influential.

Hilgard's Neodissociation Theory

Hilgard (1977, 1979) proposes that hypnosis represents a dissociation (division) of consciousness into separate channels of mental

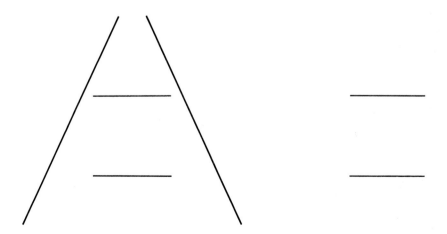

FIGURE 10.12

The Ponzo illusion. The short horizontal lines are actually the same length.

Ernest Hilgard believes that hypnosis represents a division of consciousness into different channels of mental activity.

activity. He refers to his theory as **neodissociation** (neo- means "new") to distinguish it from earlier theories dating back to the turn of the century. To give some examples of the types of dissociation described by Hilgard, hypnotically induced blindness involves a division between visual perception and consciousness, and hypnotically induced paralysis involves a division between consciousness and muscular control of particular parts of the body. Judging from the cases of brain damage I described earlier, the role of dissociation in hypnosis seems plausible. Perhaps hypnotic suggestion can induce neural inhibition that prevents transmission of some of the messages between the verbal system ("consciousness") and the perceptual and motor systems of the brain.

Hilgard (1973) discovered a hypnotic phenomenon that has become particularly important to his theory. He called this phenomenon the **hidden observer.** Hilgard defined the hidden observer as a part of a hypnotized person's consciousness that has become dissociated from the rest.

To bring forth the hidden observer, Hilgard told his subjects that although they would be hypnotized, when he placed his hand on their shoulder he would be in direct communication with a hidden part of them that would be able to hear him and talk with him, unknown to the other part of their consciousness.

Hilgard hypnotized subjects and had them plunge their arms in a bucket of ice water. (This procedure eventually produces intense pain without causing physical harm.) Through hypnotic suggestion, he made the pain diminish. Then, when he used the special instructions to bring forth the "hidden observer," the subjects began reporting much more intense pain. The results indicated that during hypnosis, part of the subjects' consciousness was dissociated from feelings of pain, but another part (the "hidden observer") remained completely aware of the pain.

Many experiments have confirmed that the phenomenon of the "hidden observer" exists. However, as we will see in the next section, some investigators dispute its significance.

Barber's Social Role Theory

All the behavioral and perceptual phenomena discussed so far in this book have obvious survival value for the organism; that is, functional analysis of a behavioral phenomenon usually points to a plausible reason for the occurrence of the behavior. Therefore, if hypnotic phenomena occurred only when a person was hypnotized, it would be difficult to understand why the brain happened to evolve in such a way that people can be hypnotized. A theory of hypnosis by Barber (1979) indicates that at least some aspects of hypnosis are related to events that can happen every day.

Barber argues that hypnosis should not be viewed as a special state of consciousness, in the way that sleep is a state of consciousness that differs from waking; rather, the hypnotized person is acting out a social role. Thus, the phenomena of hypnosis are social behaviors, not manifestations of a special state of consciousness. Hypnotized subjects willingly join with the hypnotist in enacting a role that is expected of them. Some of the rules governing this role are supplied by the direct instructions of the hypnotist, others are indirectly implied by what the hypnotist says and does, and still others consist of expectations that the subjects already have about what hypnotized people do.

If hypnosis can be described as role playing, then why are so many people willing to play this role? Barber (1975) submits that the suspension of self-control that occurs during hypnosis is very similar to our "participation" in the story of a movie or novel. When we go to a movie or read a book, we generally do so with the intent of becoming "swept up" in the story. We willingly let the filmmaker or author lead us through a fantasy.

Many hypnotic phenomena are striking and would seem impossible to achieve without hypnosis. However, researchers have successfully demonstrated all of them without hypnosis. If subjects are given carefully worded instructions that strongly motivate them to cooperate with the experimenter, they can learn to ignore painful stimuli, act as if they were a child, imagine themselves seeing nonexistent objects, fail to remember a list of words they have just read, and so on. The essential difference is that they realize that they are pretending, whereas hypnotized subjects generally believe that their behavior is involuntary. As Spanos, Gwynn, and Stam (1983) put it, "subjects must maintain control of their responding but, nonetheless, come to interpret and describe their goal-directed enactments as being involuntary 'happenings'" (p. 486).

As we saw earlier, the "hidden observer" appears to provide strong support for Hilgard's neodissociation theory. However, some experiments indicate that even this phenomenon is actually a role played according to a script supplied by the hypnotist. For example, Spanos, Gwynn, and Stam (1983) hypnotized people and had them place one of their arms in a bucket of ice water. They gave instructions that the subjects would not feel the pain, and indeed the subjects reported that their arms felt numb. Then they gave two different sets of instructions designed to elicit the "hidden observer." One set was similar to the instructions used by Hilgard, suggesting that the subject had a hidden part that "continued to remain aware of everything going on around it, and everything going on in [the subject's] body." Another set suggested that the hidden part was "*less aware* of everything going on around it, and everything going on in [the subject's] body" (italics mine). The experimenters then elicited ratings of pain from the subjects and from the subjects' "hidden observers."

The results showed that depending on the type of instructions the subjects were given, the "hidden observer" reported either more or less pain than the "rest" of the hypnotized person. (See Figure 10.13.) As we saw, Hilgard explained the "hidden observer" in terms of a division of consciousness. Spanos and his colleagues proposed that the subject actually was playing two roles. In the condition used by Hilgard, the subject ignored the pain according to

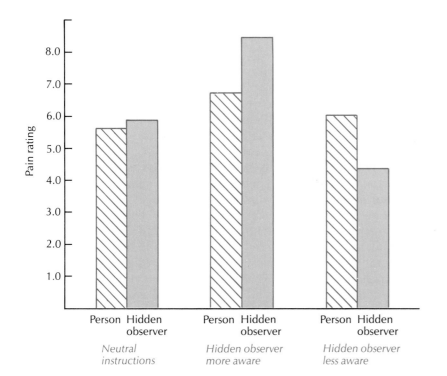

FIGURE 10.13

Pain ratings of the "person" and the "hidden observer" as a function of the experimenter's instructions regarding the nature of the hidden observer. (Based on data from Spanos, N.P., Gwynn, M.I., and Stam, H.J. *Journal of Abnormal Psychology*, 1983, 92, 479–488.)

the instructions that pain would not be felt and then paid attention to it when the hypnotist asked the "hidden observer" to come forth. According to this view then, the "hidden observer" does not seem to be a part of a person's consciousness that remains aware of reality; instead, it, like the other aspects of a hypnotized person's consciousness, follows the instructions of the hypnotist.

Susceptibility to Hypnosis

Not everyone can be hypnotized. In fact, the ability to be hypnotized appears to be a stable trait; if a person can be hypnotized on one occasion, he or she probably can be hypnotized on another. However, attempts to relate personality to hypnotic susceptibility have yielded few definitive results. Susceptibility does not appear to be related strongly to any particular personality type (Hilgard, 1979). What does appear to be related to susceptibility to hypnosis is the ability to produce vivid mental images, a high capacity for becoming involved in imaginative activities, and a rich, vivid imagination (Kihlstrom, 1985). You can readily see that such people would be likely to participate vicariously in a story.

As we saw in Chapter 2, the left hemisphere is more involved in sequential tasks, including verbal tasks, and the right hemisphere is more involved in simultaneous tasks, including picture perception and perception of space. In addition, several studies have indicated that the right hemisphere is more involved in social interactions (Kolb and Whishaw, 1985). There are some hints that hypnosis may be related to the functions of the right hemisphere. For example, Sackheim, Paulus, and Weiman (1979) found that people who are easily hypnotized tend to sit on the right side of the classroom. In this position, they see most of the front of the room with their right hemispheres, so perhaps their choice represents a preference for right-hemisphere involvement in perceptual tasks. This preference may represent a generally increased sensitivity to social roles, including those involved in hypnosis. I hasten to add that this hypothesis is speculative and may very well be wrong, but at least it points the way to some hypotheses that can be tested experimentally.

Uses of Hypnosis

Hypnosis can play a useful role in medicine, dentistry, and psychotherapy. The analgesia (insensitivity to pain) produced by hypnosis is more effective than that produced by morphine, tranquilizers such as Valium, or acupuncture (Stern, Brown, Ulett, and Sletten, 1977). Thus, it can be used to suppress the pain of childbirth or of having one's teeth drilled or to prevent gagging when a dentist is working in a patient's mouth. However, because not all people can be hypnotized, and because the induction of hypnosis takes some time, few physicians or dentists use hypnosis to reduce pain—drugs are easier to administer. Hypnosis can also be used to help people break a bad habit such as smoking or overeating. As we have seen, hypnosis is a useful tool for research into human consciousness. Finally, hypnosis is often used in psychotherapy to help the patient discuss painful memories whose inaccessibility is impeding progress.

One use of hypnosis that has been severely criticized lately is as an aid in criminal investigations. Some police departments employ officers who are trained in hypnosis. If victims of crime or witnesses to crimes cannot supply the investigators with sufficient details to identify the criminal, they are occasionally hypnotized to "help refresh their memory." One technique that is sometimes used is the *television technique*. Witnesses are told that they can "zoom in" on details that they have forgotten (such as the criminal's face or the license plates of the car involved in an accident) or "freeze the frame" to examine fleeting details at their leisure (Reiser and Nielsen, 1980).

The problem with this use of hypnosis is that through their eagerness to provide helpful information and their belief in the expertise of the hypnotist, witnesses come to "see" details that were never present at the scene of the crime. In one case, after being hypnotized, a witness to a murder identified a person as the murderer. However, testimony later showed that the witness was 270 feet away. Under the lighting conditions present at the time, this witness could not possibly have seen the murderer's face beyond 25 feet away (*People* v. *Kempinski*, 1980).

Laurence and Perry (1983) demonstrated that through suggestion, hypnosis can induce false memories, in which the subjects sincerely come to believe. They hypnotized subjects and asked whether they had been awakened by some loud noises on a particular night. (They first ascertained that in fact the subjects had not been awakened then.) Most of the subjects reported that yes, they had heard some loud noises. When the subjects were interviewed by another experimenter later, in a nonhypnotized condition, 48 percent said that they had heard some loud noises on the night in question. Even after the experimenter told these subjects that the hypnotist had suggested that the noises had occurred, almost half of them still insisted that the noises had occurred. One said, "I'm pretty certain I heard them. As a matter of fact, I'm pretty damned certain. I'm positive I heard these noises" (p. 524). The results strongly suggest that the testimony of people who have been hypnotized by an investigator to "help refresh their memory" is not necessarily trustworthy.

■ What is Hilgard's neodissociation theory of hypnosis and how does Barber's social role theory of hypnosis explain Hilgard's "hidden observer"?

■ What are the characteristics of people who are susceptible to hypnosis, and how do these relate to theories of hypnosis?

■ What are the uses and the limitations of hypnosis?

CHAPTER SUMMARY

1. Consciousness can be viewed as being synonymous with verbal processes. Its physiological basis is the activity of language mechanisms of the brain. The private use of language ("thinking to oneself") is clearly conscious. Private nonverbal processes are conscious if we can describe them—that is, if their activities are available to the neural mechanisms of language. In the same way, we are conscious of *external* events only if we can think (and verbalize) about them. Thinking to ourselves and being aware of our own existence derive from our ability to talk about our existence and experiences to others.

2. The suggestion that consciousness is a function of our ability to communicate with each other receives support from some cases of human brain damage. People with isolation aphasia can perceive speech and talk without apparent awareness and patients with visual agnosia can identify objects seen nonverbally, although they are not aware of what they are seeing. Thus, brain damage within the cerebral hemispheres can disrupt a person's verbal access to (awareness of) perceptual mechanisms without destroying these mechanisms. And although a person whose corpus callosum has been severed can make perceptual judgments with the right hemisphere, he or she cannot talk about them and appears to be unaware of them.

3. Sleep consists of several stages of slow-wave sleep, characterized by increasing amounts of delta activity in the EEG, and REM sleep, characterized by beta activity in the EEG, rapid eye movements, general paralysis, and dreaming. Sleep is a behavior; it is an active process triggered by neural mechanisms situated in the brain stem. Sleep has been explained both as a state during which the body restores itself and as an adaptive response. REM sleep appears to be important for integrating memories of events that happened during the preceding day; it also plays some role in sorting out emotionally significant memories.

4. Some sleep disorders appear to be caused by malfunctions of the brain's sleep mechanisms. Cataplectic attacks are caused by activation, at inappropriate times, of the mechanism that causes paralysis during REM sleep. Hypnagogic hallucinations are premature dreams. The REM-sleep mechanisms appear to be under the control of neurons that secrete serotonin as a transmitter substance; drugs that stimulate this type of neuron are useful in treating cataplexy and hypnagogic hallucinations. Insomnia appears to be a symptom of a variety of physical (sleep apnea) and emotional (depression) disorders, and not a disease entity. The disorders of slow-wave sleep include sleep-walking, sleeptalking, and night terrors.

5. Hypnosis is a form of verbal control over a person's consciousness in which the hypnotist's suggestions affect some of the subject's perceptions and behaviors. Although some people have viewed hypnosis as a mysterious, trance-like state, investigations have shown its phenomena to be similar to many phenomena of normal consciousness.

6. Hilgard regards hypnosis as a form of dissociation, in which some streams of consciousness are divided from others. In this way, perceptions can be separated from consciousness, and consciousness can be separated from motor control. The "hidden observer" supports this conclusion. In contrast, Barber asserts that being hypnotized is similar to participating vicariously in a narrative, which is something we do whenever we become engrossed in a novel, movie, or drama, experiencing genuine feelings of emotion, even though the situation is not "real." Studies by proponents of the hypothesis that hypnosis is the enactment of a social role have shown that the characteristics of the "hidden observer" can be affected by suggestion.

7. Whatever its causes, hypnosis has been shown to be useful in reducing pain, eliminating bad habits, and helping people talk about painful thoughts and memories. However, because hypnotic suggestion can easily implant false memories that the subjects come sincerely to believe in, most investigators distrust hypnosis as a tool of criminal investigation.

KEY TERMS

alpha activity   Rhythmical activity of the electroence phalogram with a frequency between 8 and 12 cycle per second, usually indicating a state of quiet relaxation.

beta activity   Irregular, high-frequency activity of the electroencephalogram, usually indicating a state of alertness or arousal.

cataplexy   A form of narcolepsy in which the person collapses, becoming temporarily paralyzed but not unconscious; usually triggered by anger or excitement; apparently re-lated to the paralysis that normally accompanies REM sleep.

corpus callosum   A large bundle of axons ("white matter") that connects the cortex of the two cerebral hemispheres.

delta activity   Rhythmical activity of the electroencephalogram, a recording of the brain's activity, with a frequency between 3 and 5 cycles per second, indicating deep (slow-wave) sleep.

electrocardiogram (EKG)   The measurement and graphical presentation of the electrical activity of the heart, recorded by means of electrodes attached to the skin.

electroencephalogram (EEG)   The measurement and graphical presentation of the electrical activity of the brain, recorded by means of electrodes attached to the scalp.

electromyogram (EMG)   The measurement and graphical presentation of the electrical activity of muscles, recorded by means of electrodes attached to the skin above them.

electro-oculogram (EOG)   The measurement and graphical presentation of the electrical activity caused by movements of the eye, recorded by means of electrodes attached to the skin adjacent to the eye.

enuresis   Bedwetting.

flowerpot technique   Used in sleep deprivation experiments; placing a subject (usually a mouse) on an island (often an upturned flowerpot) in water so that when the animal's head slumps, the water wakes it up.

hidden observer   Hypnotic phenomenon, discovered by Hilgard, referring to the dissociation of part of the person's subconscious.

hypnagogic hallucination   The perception of nonexistent objects and events just before sleep; a symptom of narcolepsy, presumably a premature dream.

hypnotic suggestibility   The tendency of a person to follow the suggestions of a hypnotist.

iatrogenic disorder   A mental or physical disorder caused by attempts to treat another disorder.

isolation aphasia   A language disturbance that includes inability to comprehend speech or produce meaningful speech, along with the ability to repeat speech and learn new sequences of words; caused by brain damage that isolates the brain's speech mechanisms from other parts of the brain.

latent content   According to Freud, the hidden

meaning of a dream—usually an unfulfilled desire—as opposed to the obvious plot, or manifest content.

manifest content According to Freud, the plot or description of the content of a dream, as opposed to its hidden meaning, or latent content.

mesmerism Hypnosis, named after Anton Mesmer who discovered hypnotic induction, believing it to be related to animal magnetism.

narcolepsy A neurological disorder in which a person suffers from irresistible sleep attacks and often cataplexy and hypnagogic hallucinations.

negative hallucination The perception that a stimulus that is present is actually absent; can be induced by hypnotic suggestion.

neodissociation Theory of Hilgard's that hypnosis represents a division of consciousness into separate channels of mental activity.

polygraph Apparatus used in sleep laboratories to record on paper the output of various devices (such as the EEG, EMG, EKG, and EOG) attached to the subject.

positive hallucination The perception of an object that is not actually present; can be induced by hypnotic suggestion; a frequent symptom of psychosis.

posthypnotic amnesia Failure to remember what occurred during hypnosis; induced by suggestions made during hypnosis.

posthypnotic suggestibility The tendency of a person to perform a behavior suggested by the hypnotist some time after the person has left the hypnotic state.

rapid eye movement (REM) sleep Stage of sleep that exhibits beta activity in the EEG, rapid eye movements, general paralysis, and dreaming.

sleep apnea A disorder characterized by inability to breathe while asleep.

sleep attack A symptom of narcolepsy; a sudden wave of irresistible sleepiness.

slow wave sleep The deeper sleep of stages 3 and 4 when delta activity predominates.

split-brain operation A surgical procedure that severs the corpus callosum, thus abolishing the direct connections between the cortex of the two cerebral hemispheres.

sudden infant death syndrome Crib death; responsible for death of babies in their sleep, possibly due to sleep apnea, failure to breathe when asleep.

Motivation

If psychology seeks to discover causes of behavior, perhaps its most basic question is "Why did you do that?" or "What motivated you?" We use the term "motivate" to designate any way that we are "moved" to act or want something. The "why" of our actions involves approaching or avoiding basic things that people need—such as food, water, sex, social support and recognition, and abstract objectives such as personal achievement or fulfillment.

Early attempts to explain motivation assumed that a measurable physical "need" or "drive" existed for reinforcers such as food or sex. But such theories could not explain certain activities and behaviors: Why would someone spend two years sailing around the world alone? Why would someone risk his or her life to jump out of an airplane at 10,000 feet? In these instances, no process in the body can be measured to confirm that a need or drive is really operating. Although the idea of a need does not explain the motivating cause for many behaviors, it is a useful term when describing how a behavior persists among people or within individuals.

Some of the most interesting and productive work in motivation explores factors that affect how people continue to persist or persevere in a behavior. Why do some people work hard and others quickly give up when they encounter difficulty? Have people who give up easily learned somewhere that trying to accomplish goals is useless? What encourages people to continue eating far beyond their body's need for food? How do previously learned patterns affect our desire to do something in the present? Do people work harder at activities they have chosen for themselves, or do they work equally as hard at something chosen for them? As you will see, research that explores repeated patterns of behavior helps explain the conditions affecting what activities we are most likely to choose.

Psychologists also study the influence of physiological processes on motivation. Some behaviors, such as eating and aggression, have a strong biological component. The processes by which we stop and start eating are at least partially governed by biological processes. Aggressive behavior seems at least in part to be produced by innate brain mechanisms.

In this chapter, you will read about different theories psychologists have proposed to explain motivation, as well as attempts by researchers to provide an answer to the question of why people act the way they do.

MECHANISMS OF MOTIVATION

In common usage, motivation refers to a driving force that moves us to a particular action; for example, certain behaviors are likely to help us attain success, recognition, and financial well-being, while other, more prosaic ones provide the next meal or drink of water. **Motivation** (derived from a Latin word meaning "to move") can affect the *nature* of an organism's behavior, the *strength* of its behavior, and the

Theories of motivation attempt to explain why people strive to overcome great odds.

persistence of its behavior. It is impossible to separate motivation from reinforcement; we are motivated to perform a behavior to gain (or avoid losing) a reinforcer, or to avoid (or escape from) a punisher. Some reinforcers and punishers are obvious, such as food or pain; others are subtle, such as smiles or frowns.

Motivation is evident in two types of phenomena: reactions to discriminative stimuli and reactions to deprivation. Discriminative stimuli that were previously associated with reinforcement or punishment will elicit approach or avoidance behaviors. For example, we will approach people with whom we have had pleasant interactions, and avoid those who have annoyed us. Being deprived of particular items or situations often motivates seeking behaviors. For example, being deprived of water will motivate behaviors that obtain a drink, and working on a dull, routine task for a long time will motivate behaviors that produce a change of scene.

Drive and Drive-Reduction Theory

The earliest attempt to explain the nature of motivation and reinforcement stated that biological needs, caused by deprivation of the necessities of life, are unpleasant. According to this theory, the physiological changes associated with, say, going without food for several hours, produce an unpleasant state called *hunger*. Hunger serves as a **drive**, energizing an organism's behavior. The organism then engages in behaviors that in the past have obtained food. The act of eating reduces hunger. This reduction of drive is reinforcing. Thus we have the drive hypothesis of motivation and the **drive-reduction hypothesis** of reinforcement. (See Figure 11.1.)

Not all drives are based on biological needs like the ones for food and water. The most obvious example is the drive associated with sexual behavior. An organism can survive without sexual behavior, but sex drive is certainly motivating, and sexual contact is certainly reinforcing. Similarly, most organisms placed in a featureless environment will soon become motivated to seek something new; they will work at a task that gives them a view of the world outside.

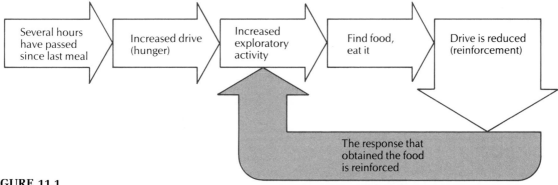

FIGURE 11.1

The drive-reduction theory of motivation and reinforcement.

Any theory of motivation and reinforcement that depends on the concept of drive confronts a serious problem: how to detect and measure a particular drive. Theoretically, at least, physiological need can be measured, so it is possible to determine when it is present. For instance, if physiological measurements show that a person is dehydrated, we know that he or she is thirsty and thus is likely to perform behaviors that were previously reinforced by the opportunity to drink. However, we have no way of measuring drives that are not based on physiological need. Suppose you obtain great pleasure from watching a set of color slides taken by a friend while on vacation. According to the drive-reduction hypothesis, your "exploratory drive" or "curiosity drive" is high, and looking at vacation slides reduces it, providing reinforcement. But there is no way to measure this drive and thus confirm that it actually exists.

The most important logical problem with drive theories of motivation is that a great many events can serve as reinforcers. If each of these events is reinforcing because it reduces a particular drive, then we are forced to postulate a large number of drives, almost none of which can be measured. Consider a woman who very much enjoys listening to music. What drive induces her to turn on her stereo system? What drive is reduced by this activity?

Is Drive Reduction Reinforcing?

There is reason to believe that reinforcement is caused by events that *increase* drive, not reduce it. At first this assertion might seem absurd—after all, we eat to make hunger go away,

don't we? However, the answer seems to be that we do not. Eating certainly makes hunger go away, but we need not assume that the disappearance of hunger explains why we eat. In fact, the *immediate* effect of eating is to increase drive; tasting and swallowing food makes us become more hungry, not less. (That is why we refer to small amounts of tasty food before the main meal as "appetizers.") Only later, after swallowing many mouthfuls of food, do we experience satiety.

In what has become a classic experiment, Sheffield, Wulff, and Backer (1951) permitted male rats to run down a runway to a goal box containing a sexually receptive female rat. The male was allowed to engage in preliminary sexual activity, but as soon as he mounted the female the experimenter removed him from the goal box. The males were not permitted to ejaculate; thus, the behavior of running toward the goal box was followed by increases in drive. Instead of finding this treatment aversive, the males ran toward the females faster and faster; their approach was reinforced by sexual behavior that was never completed. The drive-reduction hypothesis clearly cannot explain this effect.

Another phenomenon provides further support for the conclusion that reinforcement does not consist of drive reduction. In 1954, James Olds and Peter Milner discovered quite by accident that electrical stimulation of parts of the brain can reinforce an animal's behavior. The investigators were trying to determine whether electrical stimulation of the reticular formation (located in the back part of the brain stem) would help rats learn to run through a maze faster. They operated on a group of rats, inserting a small wire in their brains. Because this surgical procedure had only recently been developed and was not very accurate, one of the wires wound up about half a brain's length away from its target. This accident was a lucky one for the investigators, because they discovered a phenomenon they would not have seen if the wire had been located where they intended it to be.

Olds and Milner had heard that electrical stimulation of some parts of the brain could be aversive, so that animals would work to avoid having the current turned on. They decided to make sure that this was not the case for their rats, because aversive stimulation might interfere with the animals' performance in the maze. Here is Olds's report of what happened to the rat with the misplaced wire:

> I applied a brief train of 60-cycle sine-wave electrical current whenever the animal entered one corner of the enclosure. The animal did not stay away from that corner, but rather came back quickly after a brief sortie which followed the first stimulation and came back even more quickly after a

The drive-reduction theory states that the act of eating is reinforcing because it reduces hunger, which is an aversive drive.

briefer sortie which followed the second stimulation. By the time the third electrical stimulus had been applied the animal seemed indubitably to be "coming back for more." (Olds, 1973, p. 81)

Realizing that they had witnessed something important, Olds and Milner put more wires in rats' brains, and allowed the rats to press a switch that controlled the current to the brain. The rats quickly learned to press the switch at a rate of over 700 times per hour. Subsequent studies obtained response rates of several thousand presses per hour.

Why does electrical stimulation of certain areas of the brain reinforce an animal's behavior? Does the stimulation reduce drive? The answer appears to be quite the opposite. If an animal that has learned to press a lever in order to receive electrical brain stimulation receives such stimulation, the animal is likely to engage in a "motivated" behavior, such as eating, drinking, mating, fighting, escape, or object carrying. (The behavior depends on the area stimulated and the opportunities available.) The stimulation appears to produce what we would label as drive. For example, if the lateral hypothalamus is stimulated, a rat will seek out food and will even work for its delivery. Even an animal satiated by a large meal will still press a lever for the delivery of food. Thus, the stimulation seems to make the animal hungry. If hunger is a drive, then the brain stimulation appears to increase the level of that drive.

The drive-reduction hypothesis of reinforcement states that drives like hunger are unpleasant. Accordingly, electrical brain stimulation that makes an animal hungry should be aversive. Yet the facts are just the opposite; this stimulation is actually reinforcing. The same is true for stimulation that elicits the other behaviors—drinking, mating, attack, and so on. Results such as these have led some investigators to suggest that reinforcement is provided by engaging in behaviors of this type (Glickman and Schiff, 1967).

The Concept of Optimal Arousal

If we examine our own behavior, we will find that most events that we experience as reinforcing are also exciting, or drive increasing. The reason a roller coaster ride is fun is certainly not because it *reduces* drive. The same is true for skiing, surfing, or viewing a horror film. Likewise, an interesting, reinforcing conversation is one that is exciting, not one that puts you to sleep. And people who engage in prolonged foreplay and sexual intercourse do not view these activities as unpleasant because they are accompanied by such a high level of drive. The experiences we really want to repeat (that is, the ones we find reinforcing) are those that increase, rather than decrease, our level of arousal.

However, there are times when a person wants nothing more than some peace and quiet; in this case, avoidance of exciting stimuli would be reinforcing. Negative reinforcement is also accomplished by the removal of aversive stimuli: taking off a shoe that pinches reduces an unpleasant sensation and makes us feel much better. In an attempt to find a common explanation for both positive and negative reinforcement, some psychologists have proposed the **optimum level hypothesis** of reinforcement and punishment: when the arousal level is too high, less stimulation is reinforcing; when it is too low, more stimulation is desired (Hebb, 1955; Berlyne, 1966).

The hypothesis that organisms seek an optimal level of arousal is certainly plausible. Any kind of activity—even the most interesting and exciting one—eventually produces satiety; something that was once reinforcing becomes bothersome. (Even the most avid video game player eventually moves on to something else.) Presumably, participation in an exciting behavior gradually raises an organism's arousal above its optimum level. However, the logical problem that plagues the drive-reduction hypothesis also applies to the optimum level hypothesis. Because we cannot measure an organism's drive or arousal, we cannot say what its optimum level should be.

Expectancy Theory

As we saw, the concept of *incentive* refers to the energizing effects of an anticipated goal. In Spence's theory, incentive is related to drive; without drive, the animal does not make anticipatory responses toward the goal, and hence incentive does not occur. Other theorists have used the concept of incentive in other ways.

The drive-reduction theory has difficulty explaining many behaviors. Some experiences are reinforcing because they are stimulating and exciting, and actually increase the level of drive.

Expectancy theories of motivation deal with people's expectations about what might happen if they engage in particular behaviors.

Motivation for Success or Against Failure

The theory of **achievement motivation,** devised by McClelland and his colleagues in the late 1940s, is based on a person's evaluation of a goal (McClelland, Atkinson, Clark, and Lowell, 1953). The theory assumes that the source of human motivation is the *need to achieve,* first described by Murray (1938) as the tendency for people to strive to do something difficult as well and as quickly as possible.

According to the theory of achievement motivation, the motivation to perform a particular task is a function of three variables. First, let us consider two of them: the person's expectation of succeeding at the task and the perceived value of the goal. It seems reasonable that motivation cannot be solely determined by the perceived value of a goal. For example, I would very much value winning a Nobel Prize, but I realize that the probability of my doing so is about as high as the likelihood of my getting hit by a meteorite. Therefore, the hope of winning a Nobel Prize cannot be said to motivate my behavior. The third factor that determines a person's level of motivation is the need to achieve, which McClelland and his colleagues referred to as **success motivation.** This need is considered to be an intrinsic, stable personality trait.

Not all stimuli cause approach behavior; some stimuli elicit negative feelings, which express themselves in a tendency to withdraw from the situation. One of the reasons that people may tend to withdraw from a task is the **motivation to avoid failure.** The theory of achievement motivation regards this need as a basic personality trait, like the need to achieve. McClelland and his colleagues assumed that the aversiveness of failing a particular task is related to the probability of success at that task. That is, failing a very difficult task is to be expected, so that doing so is not very aversive. However, failing an *easy* task is very aversive, because it implies that the person is really incompetent.

The relation among the variables—the expectation of success, the perceived value of success, motivation to achieve success, and motivation to avoid failure—is stated in a formula that permits the experimenter to predict a person's **resultant motivation,** which consists of the tendency to achieve success minus the tendency to avoid failure on a particular task.

The need to achieve refers to the tendency for people to strive to perform a difficult task as well as possible.

Measuring Expectancy

The test used to measure a person's success motivation was devised by Murray (1936). The test, called the **Thematic Apperception Test (TAT)** consists of a set of cards containing drawings of ambiguous situations. The person being tested is asked to examine each card and tell a story about what is going on. From the details of these stories, the examiner determines how motivated the person is to achieve success. (The TAT will be described more fully in Chapter 15.) A person's motivation to avoid failure is usually measured with the **Test Anxiety Questionnaire (TAQ),** devised by Sarason and Mandler (1952). Presumably, people's anxiety about taking tests is caused by their motivation to avoid failure.

The theory of achievement motivation has been tested by varying the probability of success and seeing how people approach the task. The theory predicts that people who possess a reasonable amount of success motivation will tend to choose tasks of moderate difficulty; very easy tasks have a high probability of success but the incentive value of succeeding at them is low. Similarly, very difficult tasks have a high incentive value but a low probability of success. In other words, people with good success motivation prefer to work at tasks that present a reasonable challenge.

In contrast, consider the effects of task difficulty on the behavior of people with a high motivation to avoid failure. For them, the tendency to avoid failure is highest for tasks of intermediate difficulty and lowest for very easy or very hard tasks. Failing a very easy task is very aversive, but because the task is so easy, such an outcome is unlikely. And although difficult tasks are unlikely to lead to success, failing them is not very aversive because *everyone* fails them.

You can see that according to the theory of achievement motivation, people with high success motivation will tend to maximize pleasant feelings by choosing tasks of intermediate difficulty, whereas those with high motivation to avoid failure will tend to minimize unpleasant feelings by choosing very difficult or very easy tasks.

Isaacson (1964) tested predictions of the theory of achievement motivation by comparing

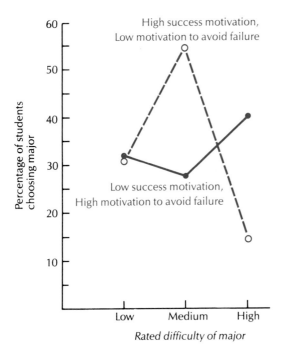

FIGURE 11.2

Percentage of students choosing majors of varying difficulty as a function of success motivation and motivation to avoid failure. (Redrawn from data of Isaacson, R.L. *Journal of Abnormal and Social Psychology,* 1964, 68, 447–452.)

two groups of male college students, one group with high success motivation and the other with high motivation to avoid failure (as measured by the TAT and TAQ, respectively). He found that students who scored high in success motivation tended to choose majors of intermediate difficulty, whereas students with a high motivation to avoid failure tended to choose the most difficult or the easiest majors. (See Figure 11.2.) This pattern of results is what would be predicted by the theory of achievement motivation.

The theory of achievement motivation has received attention from psychologists because it focuses on a category of human behaviors that are not easily explained in terms of biological need. In addition, it makes specific predictions that can be tested experimentally. It is not a comprehensive theory of behavior because it deals only with need for achievement and fear of failure. Thus, the theory does not explain such behaviors as obtaining food and water, keeping warm, or visiting new and interesting places.

■ What are the main features of the drive reduction theory?
■ What are the problems with drive-reduction theory and the alternative optimum arousal hypothesis?
■ What features of expectancy theory may help to explain human motivation?

Perseverance

Some people work hard even though the rewards for their work seem to occur very seldom. We refer to these people as "well motivated": they **persevere,** or continue to perform, even though their work is not regularly reinforced. Others give up easily or perhaps never try. Understanding the effects of reinforcement helps us explain why some people persevere while others do not.

Effects of Intermittent Reinforcement

We saw in Chapter 6 that when an organism's behavior is no longer reinforced, the behavior eventually ceases, or extinguishes. If the behavior was previously reinforced every time it occurred, extinction is very rapid. However, if it was previously reinforced only intermittently, the behavior persists for a long time. Intermittent reinforcement leads to perseverance, even when reinforcers are no longer received.

Many human behaviors are reinforced on intermittent schedules that require the performance of long sequences of behaviors over long intervals of time. It seems likely that a person's previous experience with various schedules of reinforcement affects how long and how hard the person will work between occasions of reinforcement. If all attempts at a particular endeavor are reinforced (or if none are) the person is unlikely to pursue a long and difficult project that includes the endeavor. If we knew more about a person's previous history with various schedules of reinforcement, we would probably know more about his or her ability to persevere when the going gets difficult (that is, when reinforcements become scanty).

The effects of intermittent reinforcement on perseverance occur even in very young animals. For example, Chen and Amsel (1980a)

The ability to obtain satisfaction when working on a long, laborious task depends on intermittent reinforcement of subgoals.

obtained these effects in rats as young as eleven days of age. And under some conditions, the effects of intermittent reinforcement on perseverance are long lived (Chen and Amsel, 1980b). These observations support the suggestion that perseverance as an individual behavioral trait is at least partially determined by early experience.

The Role of Conditioned Reinforcement

Another phenomenon that affects the tendency to persevere is conditioned reinforcement. When stimuli are associated with reinforcers, they eventually acquire reinforcing properties of their own. For example, the sound of the food dispenser reinforces the behavior of a rat that is being trained to press a lever.

Motivation is not merely a matter of wanting to do well and to work hard. It also involves the ability to be reinforced by the immediate products of the work being done. If a person has regularly been exposed to particular stimuli in association with reinforcers, that person's behavior can be reinforced by those stimuli. In addition, if the person has learned how to recognize self-produced stimuli as conditioned reinforcers, the performance of the behaviors that produce them will be "self-reinforcing." For example, you will recall the little schoolgirl I mentioned in Chapter 6 who tirelessly practiced writing the letters of the alphabet. She did so because she had learned to recognize the letters and had previously been praised by her teacher (and perhaps by her parents, as well) for producing letters that looked the way they should. Thus, the production of properly formed letters provided a conditioned reinforcer, which kept her working. As you know, the usual name for this process is *satisfaction*.

Intrinsic Motivation

Because most examples of reinforcement involve something that happens after an organism performs a task, people often tend to conceive of reinforcement as something separate from the task. However, as we saw in the previous section, performance of a task can be its own reward. This phenomenon is often referred to as **intrinsic motivation** because the reinforcement is an intrinsic part of the task itself. Some intrinsic reinforcers, such as the satisfaction the little girl derived from writing the letters properly, are conditioned reinforcers. Other intrinsic reinforcers are probably effective for other reasons, such as their novelty or the control they permit the organism to exert on its environment. (As we'll see, "making things happen" seems to be intrinsically reinforcing.)

Undermining of Intrinsic Motivation. Researchers have found that *extrinsic reinforcers*—

those delivered to the subject after performing a task—can often make the task become less intrinsically reinforcing. That is, extrinsic reinforcement can often undermine intrinsic motivation.

One of the most famous experiments demonstrating the **undermining of intrinsic motivation** was performed by Lepper, Greene, and Nisbett (1973). These investigators visited a nursery school and provided children with paper and a set of colored felt-tipped pens, which were not normally available. The children were tested individually. The experimenter gave the paper and pens to a child and watched the child draw for six minutes. Then some children were given an extrinsic reinforcer: a three-by-five-inch card with "Good Player Award" inscribed on it and containing a large gold star with a red ribbon. The experimenter wrote the child's name and school on the card, and let the child place the card on a bulletin board for all the rest of the class to see. The children's behavior made it clear that the "Good Player Award" pleased them very much.

Some children received the extrinsic reinforcer as a surprise; they had no idea it would be presented. Other children were led to expect it; before they began to draw pictures with the felt-tipped pens they were told someone had "brought along a few of these Good Player Awards to give to boys and girls who will help him out by drawing some pictures for him. See? It's got a big gold star and a bright red ribbon, and there's a place here for your name and your school."

The experiment thus consisted of three groups: children who were "bribed" to draw pictures, and two groups of children who drew pictures on their own accord, presumably because doing so was intrinsically reinforcing. One of these two groups received an unexpected reward, and the other did not. Several days later the experimenters returned and unobtrusively watched the children to see whether they chose to play with the felt-tipped pens, which the teacher, under the experimenters' direction, placed on a table. The experimenters recorded the amount of time each child spent playing with the pens. The results are shown in Figure 11.3.

You can see that an unexpected award slightly increased the time the children spent

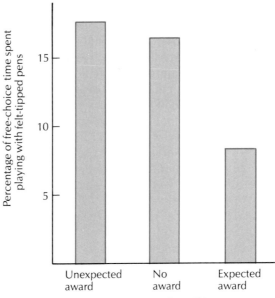

FIGURE 11.3

Percentage of time spent playing with felt-tipped pens as a function of expected or unexpected awards. (Based on data of Lepper, M.R., Greene, D., and Nisbett, R.E. *Journal of Personality and Social Psychology*, 1973, 28, 129–137.

Intrinsic motivation refers to reinforcement provided by a task. For Hulda Crooks, climbing Mt. Fuji at the age of 90 was its own reward.

drawing the pictures in the follow-up session. However, the children who were "bribed" to draw appeared to have become much less interested in drawing; that is, the extrinsic reinforcement undermined intrinsic motivation. The children who made drawings because they were being "bribed" to do so may have concluded (perhaps not consciously) that they did not much like drawing pictures with felt-tipped pens. After all, their previous experience told them that things you do for bribes are generally things you do not want to do. (This explanation is derived from *attribution theory*, which is described in more detail in Chapter 13.)

Because reinforcers are used to train children, pay workers, and change the behavior of people with behavior problems, the fact that extrinsic reinforcement can sometimes undermine intrinsic motivation has led to serious concern among researchers in the fields of education, management, and behavior therapy. Some investigators have even suggested that extrinsic reinforcement should be avoided, because it will make people work less hard. However, everyday observations reveal that reinforcement can *increase* intrinsic motivation as well as decrease it. For example, if a person with a flair for telling jokes regularly gets laughs when he does so, the reinforcers (laughs) will certainly increase rather than decrease his interest in telling jokes. Subsequent research has confirmed such observations.

The most important characteristic of an extrinsic reinforcer is that it be *based on the person's performance.* That is, if reinforcers are given when the person's performance improves, the task will tend to become more intrinsically motivating. However, if the reinforcers are given merely for doing the task—regardless of whether the task is done poorly or well—then intrinsic motivation will be undermined. Deci (1975) suggested that reinforcement can imply that the subject is being controlled by the experimenter, which most people perceive as aversive because people in general do not like to be controlled by others. However, when the reinforcement implies that a person is performing competently, it can increase intrinsic motivation. Deci (1971) found that verbal reinforcement ("that's very good; it's much better than average for this [puzzle]") led to large increases in the time people spent working on the puzzles during their free time.

It is important to realize that *most* reinforcement is contingent on people's performance. If we tell a story well, we are rewarded by signs of interest by other people. When making something, the quality of the product is determined by how skillfully and diligently we work. And those things we do well we tend to enjoy. The undermining of intrinsic motivation appears to occur only when events imply that we are doing something because someone else is making us do it.

Preference for Free Choice. Even though scientists must assume that the world is a cause-and-effect system that is controlled by stable laws, most people (even scientists) feel as if they are able to choose what they do and resist feeling that they are being coerced. Suppose that we visit a restaurant and read the menu. We consider the alternatives and then decide what to order. We feel as if we are free to choose; and even after we place our order, we believe that *we could have chosen something different.* Scientific determinism says otherwise: our choice was determined by the state of our nervous system at the time we placed our order, which reflects everything about our genetic makeup and our past history, including our knowledge of foods we like and dislike, foods we have eaten recently, and so on.

Given that people feel as if they are free to choose, it is up to the scientist to investigate the nature and possible causes of that feeling. Many studies have shown that we tend to value activities that we choose more than those that are chosen for us. Even the *illusion* of choice increases the value of an activity. For example, Swann and Pittman (1977) brought elementary school children into a room containing several interesting toys and games. Some children were simply instructed to begin playing a drawing game with felt-tipped pens; others were told that they could choose but were in fact subtly persuaded to play the drawing game. Later, when the children were permitted to play with whatever toy or game they chose, those in the "free choice" group played with the felt-tipped pens more than those who had simply been instructed to do so. Having "chosen" to play with the pens, the children preferred this task when they actually were free to choose.

There are many potential explanations for people's preference for free choice. Most of these explanations are predicated on the fact that humans are rational, thinking creatures, for whom cognitive processes control important categories of behavior. However, experiments have shown that we humans are not the only species that prefers "free choice." Catania and Sagvolden (1980) gave hungry pigeons the chance to choose one of two conditions: to peck at a particular plastic disk (chosen by the experimenters) and receive food, or to peck at either one of two plastic disks and receive food. The pigeons preferred the situation in which they could choose the disk, although they did not receive any more food this way. This finding suggests that preference for choice is an intrinsic property of animals and does not depend on cognitive processes unique to humans. But it does not tell us whether preference for free choice is determined innately or whether something in the animal's history reinforced the tendency for such a preference; only further study will answer this question.

■ What are the motivating roles of intermittent and conditioned reinforcers?
■ How can reinforcement affect intrinsic motivation?
■ How is intrinsic motivation related to preference for free-choice situations?

Failure to Persist: Learned Helplessness

A large body of evidence suggests that organisms can learn that they are powerless to affect their own destinies. Maier and Seligman (1976) reported a series of experiments demonstrating that animals can learn that their own behavior *has no effect* on an environmental event. This result is exactly the opposite of what has been assumed to be the basis of learning. All the examples of learning and conditioning cited so far have been instances in which one event predicts the occurrence of another. **Learned helplessness** involves learning that an aversive event *cannot* be avoided or escaped.

Overmeier and Seligman (1967) conducted the basic experiment. They placed a dog in a cloth sling, with its legs protruding through four holes in the cloth. They then administered a series of inescapable, unpredictable shocks through metal plates taped to the bottoms of the dog's hind feet. (See Figure 11.4.) Next, they placed the dog in a large box equipped with a floor composed of metal rods. (See Figure 11.5 on page 346.) They presented a warning stimulus and a few seconds later they passed electrical current through the floor, giving the dog a shock. If the dog jumped over a small barrier after the warning stimulus was presented, it

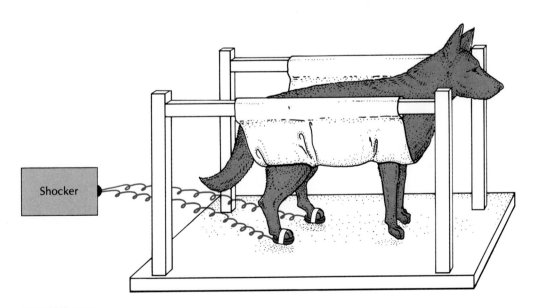

FIGURE 11.4

Learned helplessness: the method used to administer inescapable shocks in the study by Overmeier and Seligman (1967).

could avoid the shock. Normal dogs learned to jump over the barrier and avoid the shock, but dogs that had previously received inescapable shocks in the sling failed to learn. They just squatted in the corner and took the shock, as if they had learned it made no difference what they did. They had learned helplessness.

Seligman (1975) has suggested that the phenomenon of learned helplessness has important implications for behavior. When people have experiences that lead to learned helplessness, they become depressed and their motivational level decreases. The change in motivation occurs because the helplessness training lowers their expectation that trying to perform a task will bring success. As we saw, expectancy theories of motivation state that incentive is determined by the value of a particular goal and the expectation of succeeding at it; thus, a decrease in expectancy leads to a decrease in the incentive to perform. Seligman suggested also that learned helplessness has the characteristics of a personality trait; that is, people who have had major experiences with insoluble tasks will not try hard to succeed in other types of tasks, including ones they could have otherwise solved.

Seligman's theory of learned helplessness has been challenged by other investigators, who have explained the phenomenon in other ways. For example, McReynolds (1980) observed that when people experience a situation in which reinforcements are not contingent on their responding, their responding extinguishes. If the situation then changes to one in which responding will be reinforced, the people will continue not to respond unless they perceive that the schedule of reinforcement has changed. The more similar the second situation is to the first, the more likely it becomes that the person will act "helpless." This explanation describes the phenomenon of learned helplessness as a failure to discriminate between the condition under which responding is reinforced and the condition under which it is not. Further research will have to determine whether learned helplessness is, as Seligman asserts, a stable personality trait, or whether it can be explained by the principles of instrumental conditioning.

Physiology of Reinforcement

As we saw earlier, electrical stimulation of parts of the brain can be reinforcing. Perhaps this effect occurs because the stimulation artificially turns on neural circuits in the brain that

FIGURE 11.5

Learned helplessness: the apparatus used to train an avoidance response in the experiment by Overmeier and Seligman (1967).

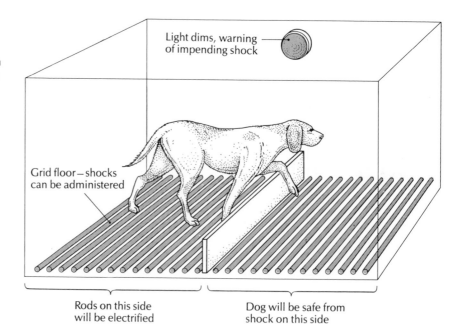

Light dims, warning of impending shock

Grid floor—shocks can be administered

Rods on this side will be electrified

Dog will be safe from shock on this side

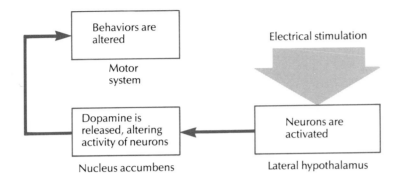

FIGURE 11.6

The neural circuits responsible for the reinforcing effects of electrical stimulation of the lateral hypothalamus.

are responsible for increasing the strength of a response under conditions of natural reinforcement. Since the discovery of reinforcing brain stimulation in 1954, hundreds of experiments have been devoted to determining whether this possibility is true, and if so, what the nature of the brain's reinforcement mechanism is.

Although the story is far from being complete, we can make some conclusions about the physiology of reinforcement. Because what gets reinforced are *behaviors,* neural mechanisms of reinforcement must be connected with motor systems of the brain. In particular, electrical stimulation of the lateral hypothalamus is reinforcing, and it also elicits species-typical behaviors such as eating, drinking, object carrying, or sexual activity. Thus, neurons stimulated by the electricity must somehow be connected to neural circuits that control these behaviors. In fact, it appears that electrical stimulation of the lateral hypothalamus activates neurons whose terminal buttons release a transmitter substance called dopamine in a particular region of the forebrain. This region, the **nucleus accumbens,** contains neurons that send their axons to another part of the forebrain that plays an important role in movement. If drugs prevent the release of dopamine by these neurons or block the effects of dopamine release, then electrical stimulation of the lateral hypothalamus is no longer reinforcing. (See Figure 11.6.)

Of course, neurons in the lateral hypothalamus are normally activated by something other than pulses of electricity from an electrode that has been placed there. A series of experiments with monkeys by Rolls and his colleagues (Rolls, 1982) have traced one neural pathway related to the reinforcing effects of food. Rolls and his colleagues found that visual stimuli of various kinds, including both the sight of food and neutral stimuli, would activate neurons in a portion of the visual association cortex located on the temporal lobe. These neurons send axons to a variety of places, including the **amygdala** (Latin for "almond"), located within the temporal lobe. The investigators found that some of the neurons in a particular region of the amygdala were activated only by the sight of food and food-related stimuli. These neurons responded whether the animal was hungry or not.

The neurons in the amygdala send axons to several regions of the brain, including the lateral hypothalamus and other parts of the forebrain. Rolls and his colleagues found some neurons in the lateral hypothalamus that responded only to stimuli related to the reinforcing effects of food. One class of neurons responded only when the animal was shown stimuli that had previously been associated with food. For example, these neurons might respond when a monkey was shown a blue syringe that the experimenters had used to inject food into its mouth, but not when the monkey was shown a red one that had not been used to deliver food. If the experimenters then switched the syringes, using the red one but not the blue one to deliver food, the neurons began responding to the red syringe instead of the blue one. Significantly, these neurons responded only when the animal was hungry; thus, their activity was controlled by the animal's motivational state as well as by the relevance of the stimulus. Presumably, when a hungry monkey's behavior is reinforced by food-related stimuli, activation of these neurons causes the release of dopamine in the nucleus accumbens, which then causes changes in behavior. (See Figure 11.7 on page 348.)

FIGURE 11.7

The neural circuits that may be responsible for the behavioral effects of discriminative stimuli that have been associated with food.

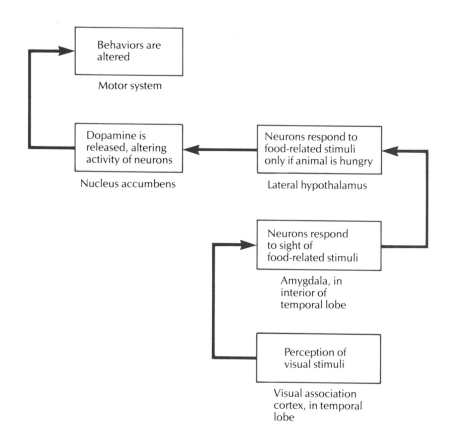

Reinforcing Effects of Drugs

Humans find the ingestion of a variety of chemicals reinforcing: the sap of the opium poppy, the juice of the coca leaf, the resin of the hemp plant, and any number of synthetically produced compounds. The behavior of people who take these drugs is strongly motivated toward acquiring them. We cannot explain the reinforcing effects of all of these substances, but we are making some progress in understanding why some people enjoy taking stimulants, such as amphetamine and cocaine, and the opiates, such as morphine and heroin.

Stimulant Drugs. Amphetamine, cocaine, and various other drugs act as stimulants, but even more important, their physiological effects are very reinforcing. People, rats, monkeys, dogs, and many other animals will work hard in order to receive these drugs. Why?

As you learned in Chapter 2, stimulants such as amphetamine and cocaine appear to produce their reinforcing effect by slowing the re-uptake of dopamine. Because the dopamine is taken back into the terminal button more slowly, it is in contact with the postsynaptic neuron for a longer time and thus exerts a more profound effect. As we just saw, reinforcement appears to depend on the release of dopamine. Thus, drugs such as amphetamine and cocaine may be such effective reinforcers because they mimic the pharmacological effect of natural reinforcers. And besides being reinforcing in their own right, small amounts of amphetamine or cocaine increase the effectiveness of a variety of other reinforcers, including electrical stimulation of the brain (Stein and Ray, 1960).

Opiates. You learned in Chapter 2 that opiates such as morphine and heroin affect behavior because they mimic the effects of the brain's own opiates (the endorphins), which are released in times of stress or arousal. Opiates activate circuits of neurons in the brain by stimulating receptors located on neurons in many parts of the brain. One of the effects of such stimulation is analgesia: a decrease in sensitivity to stimuli that cause pain.

Another effect of opiates, more important to the topic of this chapter, is reinforcement. When an organism is aroused (for example, during fighting or sexual behavior), some cells in its brain secrete endorphins. These chemicals circulate throughout the brain and stimulate the appropriate receptors, activating neural systems that decrease pain. In addition, the endorphins also activate neural circuits that increase the organism's attention to what is happening and keep the organism doing whatever it was doing. In other words, the endorphins reinforce the organism's behavior. The survival value of this system is obvious: it is important that a fighting or mating organism continue what it is doing and not be easily inhibited by pain. A fighting organism that suddenly stops because of pain may be killed; a mating one will not reproduce.

When a person takes an opiate, the drug artificially stimulates the endorphin receptors in his or her brain and thus activates mechanisms of arousal, analgesia, and reinforcement. The analgesia is probably irrelevant in this case, but the activating and reinforcing effects are certainly not.

- What is learned helplessness and what are the conditions that lead to it?
- What are the three basic stages in the physiological mechanisms of reinforcement?

EATING

Physiological needs can be very potent motivators: starving people have killed others for food. And you can undoubtedly imagine how hard you would struggle to breathe if something obstructed your windpipe. To survive, we all need air, food, water, various vitamins and minerals, and protection from extremes in temperature. Complex organisms possess physiological mechanisms that detect deficits or imbalances associated with these needs and mechanisms that permit them to engage in behaviors that can bring conditions back to normal, known as **regulatory behaviors.** This process of detection and correction is called homeostasis ("stable state"). Deficits or imbalances can be said to motivate an organism because they cause it to perform the appropriate regulatory behaviors, such as eating. As you

may have surmised, the optimum-level hypothesis of reinforcement is based on the concept of homeostasis.

Simply put, motivation to eat is aroused when there is a deficit in the body's supply of stored nutrients, and it is satisfied by a meal that replenishes this supply. A person who exercises vigorously uses up the stored nutrients more rapidly and consequently must eat more food. Thus, the amount of food a person normally eats is regulated by need. But what, exactly, causes a person to start eating, and what brings the meal to an end? These are simple questions, yet the answers are complex. There is no single physiological measure that can tell us reliably whether a person should be hungry. Hunger is determined by a variety of conditions, so instead of asking what the *cause* of hunger is, we must ask what the *causes* are.

What Starts a Meal?

Although hunger and satiety appear to be two sides of the same coin, investigations have shown that the factors that cause a meal to begin are different from the ones that end it. Therefore, I will consider these two sets of factors separately.

Cultural and Social Factors

Most of us in Western society eat three times a day. When the time for a meal comes, we get hungry and eat, consuming a relatively constant amount of food. The regular pattern of food intake is not determined solely by biological need; it is at least partially determined by habit. If you have ever had to miss a meal, you may have noticed that your hunger did not continue to grow indefinitely. Instead, it subsided some time after the meal would normally have been eaten, only to grow again just before the scheduled time of the next one. Hunger, then, can wax and wane according to a learned schedule.

Besides learning *when* to eat, we learn *what* to eat. Most of us would refuse to eat fresh clotted seal blood, but many Eskimos consider it a delicacy. What we accept as food depends on our culture. Our tastes are also shaped by habits acquired early in life. A child whose family eats nothing but simple "meat-and-potato"

Cultural and social factors influence what and when we eat. We are likely to eat more when we are with others who are doing the same thing.

dishes will probably not become a venturesome gastronome.

Our immediate environment also affects our hunger. We are much more likely to feel hungry, and to consume more food, in the presence of companions who are doing the same. Even a chicken that has finished its meal will start eating again if it is placed among other chickens who are busily eating. Similarly, you may sometimes join some friends at their table just after you have eaten. You say, no, you don't want to eat . . . well, perhaps just a bite to keep them company—and you eat almost as much as they do.

Physiological Factors

Cultural and social factors assuredly influence when and how much we eat. But everyone would also agree that the "real" reason for eating must be related to the fact that the body needs nourishment: If all other factors were eliminated, eating would be determined by some internal physiological state. What are the internal factors that cause us to eat?

Many years ago, Cannon and Washburn (1912) suggested that hunger resulted from an empty stomach. The walls of an empty stomach rubbed against each other, producing what we commonly identify as hunger pangs. (Cannon also suggested that thirst was produced by a dry mouth, because a loss of body fluid resulted in a decreased flow of saliva. Some skeptics called Cannon's explanation of hunger and thirst the "spit and rumble theory.") However, removal of the stomach does not abolish hunger pangs. Inglefinger (1944) interviewed patients whose stomach had been removed because of cancer or large ulcers; their esophagi had been attached directly to their small intestines. Because they had no stomachs to catch and hold food, they had to eat small, frequent meals. Despite their lack of a stomach, these people reported the same feelings of hunger and satiety that they had had before undergoing the operation.

A more likely cause of hunger is depletion of the body's store of nutrients. One of the most important fuels for the body is glucose, a simple sugar. The body can convert any foodstuff into glucose, so a person does not need to eat sugar in order to keep glucose in the blood. Normally, the body stores the nutrients received from a meal in the form of animal starch **(glycogen)** and fat. Later, when the digestive system is empty, the body lives on its stored nutrients. The animal starch is broken down into glucose, and the fats are broken down into fatty acids. Both of these substances serve as fuels; the brain primarily lives on glucose, and the rest of the body lives on fatty acids. (See Figure 11.8.)

For a long time, investigators assumed that the detectors that signaled hunger were located in the brain, but they had difficulty locating them. A chance observation led to a solution. In the late 1960s, Mauricio Russek noticed that an injection of glucose into the abdominal cavity of a hungry dog reduced the animal's hunger, whereas an injection of the same amount of glucose into the dog's bloodstream had little effect on the amount of food it subsequently ate. If the glucose detectors were located in the brain, the injection of glucose into the bloodstream should have been more effective, because a substance reaches the brain much faster when it is injected directly into the bloodstream. Russek (1971) therefore reasoned that the receptors might be somewhere in the abdomen instead of in the brain.

Pathways used when digestive system contains food

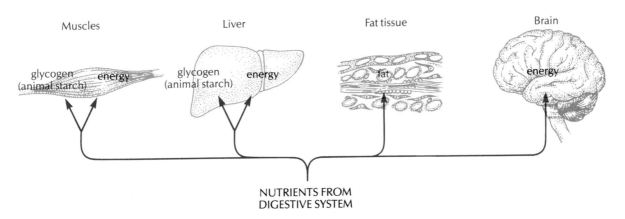

Pathways used when digestive system is empty

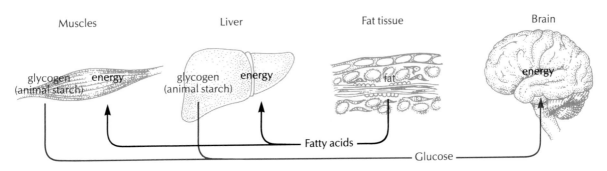

FIGURE 11.8

The metabolic pathways used when the digestive system contains food, and when it is empty.

Where in the abdomen might the detectors be? Russek noted that all water-soluble nutrients that are absorbed from the intestines are carried by the bloodstream directly to the liver. Some of these nutrients get no farther; the liver stores them as animal starch. (See Figure 11.9.) The liver is thus the first organ to "know" when the digestive system is empty and nutrients are no longer being absorbed from the intestines. The liver also serves as a major storage site for animal starch, so it "knows" when this starch has all been converted to glucose, and it is time to eat. Therefore, the liver appeared to be a good candidate in Russek's search for the detectors for hunger.

Russek operated on a dog and installed a small plastic tube in the blood vessel that transports nutrients from intestine to liver. He deprived the animal of food for a while so that it would be hungry. Just before allowing the dog

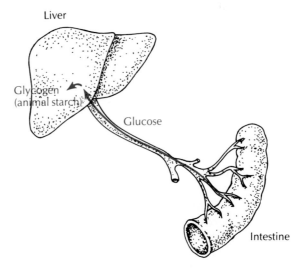

FIGURE 11.9

Glucose received from the intestine is converted into glycogen (animal starch) in the liver.

Physiological factors are not the only reasons for eating. Habit also plays an important role.

to eat, he injected a small amount of glucose through the tube into the blood vessel leading to the liver. The injection produced a sudden loss of hunger; the dog ate very little. Control injections of nonnutritive solutions had no effect. The results indicate that the detectors for hunger are located in the liver; an injection of glucose into the blood vessel that serves the liver deceives these detectors just as holding a candle under a thermostat will cause the furnace to be turned off.

Subsequent studies have confirmed the existence of hunger detectors in the liver. Investigators have identified cells that respond to glucose and convey information through a nerve that connects the liver with the brain. The precise nature of these detectors is not yet known, and it is debatable whether they respond specifically to the availability of glucose or to the availability of other nutrients, as well. However, we can conclude that the internal stimulus for hunger is a decreased availability of nutrients (principally glucose). The detectors in the liver signal the brain and stimulate hunger.

What Stops a Meal?

It appears that receptors in the liver detect the fact that the body's supplies of stored energy are getting low by measuring glucose or some other nutrient in the blood. Through their connection with the brain, these receptors are able to stimulate hunger. But what ends hunger? What brings a meal to its finish? Consider what happens when you eat. Your stomach fills with food, and the digestive process begins. However, for a good part of an hour no appreciable amounts of nutrients are absorbed from the intestines into the bloodstream. Therefore, the body's supply of fuel is not replenished until a rather long time after the meal begins; thus, the liver does not receive information about the meal until many minutes have elapsed. If you were to continue to eat until your body's need for nutrients was satisfied, your stomach would burst. Detectors somewhere other than the liver must stop the meal.

Physiological Factors

Although evidence suggests that the primary cause of hunger is not an empty stomach, the primary cause of satiety (that is, the cessation of hunger, caused by eating) seems to be a *full* stomach. Many studies have shown that satiety is caused by entry of a sufficient quantity of nourishing food into the stomach. Therefore, the stomach must contain receptors that detect the presence of food. It has been known for a long time that hunger can be abolished by injecting food into an animal's stomach by means of a flexible tube. Even though the animal does not get to taste and smell the food, it will not subsequently eat. More recently, Davis and Campbell (1973) showed how precisely the stomach can measure its contents. The investigators allowed rats to eat their fill and then removed some food from their stomachs. When they let the rats eat again, they ate almost exactly as much as had been taken out.

The stomach appears to contain receptors that inform the brain about the chemical nature of its contents, as well as the quantity. The ability to detect the chemical nature of food that has entered the stomach is important, because eating should stop relatively soon if the food is very nutritious but should continue for a longer time if it is not. Deutsch, Young, and Kalogeris

(1978) injected either milk or a dilute salt solution into hungry rats' stomachs, and thirty minutes later allowed them to eat. The rats that received injections of milk ate less than the ones that received the salt solution. Because the rats could not taste what was put in their stomachs, the effect had to come from receptors there. The nature of these receptors is not known, but they must respond to some chemicals present in food. You can try an experiment of your own: Drink two glasses of water when you are very hungry and see if this satisfies your appetite.

The Role of Learning

Omnivores such as humans eat many different kinds of foods in their lifetimes. Because food can differ widely in its nutritional value, we must eat different quantities of different foods if we are to regulate our body weight. Booth and his colleagues have performed several studies that show that humans can learn to control their intake of food according to its caloric content. For example, Booth, Mather, and Fuller (1982) fed people a three-course meal for lunch on several consecutive days. The meal consisted of a fixed amount of hot soup followed by a large plate of small sandwiches, from which the people could take all they wanted. A fixed amount of gelatin dessert was served at the end of the meal. The experimenters could increase the nutritional value of the soup by adding starch, which itself could not be tasted. They provided two flavors of soup, one associated with the low-calorie soup and one associated with the high-calorie soup. Booth and his colleagues counted the number of sandwiches people ate after having taken in few calories or many calories in the soup.

On the first day, the nutritional value of the soup had no effect; people ate the same number of sandwiches whether they had just eaten the high-calorie soup or the low-calorie soup. However, on the *second* day, the type of soup did have an effect. People who ate the high-calorie soup on two successive days ate fewer sandwiches on the second day, and those who ate the low-calorie soup ate more of them. (See Figure 11.10.) Presumably, people who ate the high-calorie soup felt overfull later, and those who ate the low-calorie soup felt hungry soon after. These sensations altered their subsequent behavior.

Obesity

The mechanisms that control eating generally do a good job. When people eat especially nutritious food, they soon learn to eat less. When they begin to exercise more, and hence burn up their store of nutrients faster, they soon start eating more. However, some people do *not* control their eating habits and become too fat or too thin. Does what we have learned about the normal regulation of food intake help us understand these disorders?

There is no single, all-inclusive explanation for obesity, but there are many partial ones. Four hypotheses are as follows.

Habit. Habit plays an important role in the control of food intake. Early in life, when we are most active, we form our ideas about how much food constitutes a meal. Later in life we become less active, but we do not always reduce our food intake accordingly. We fill our plates according to what we think is a proper-sized meal (or perhaps the plate is filled for us), and we eat everything, ignoring the satiety signals that might tell us to stop before the plate is empty.

Metabolism. Some people appear to be destined for obesity; they become fat even though they eat less food than most thin people do.

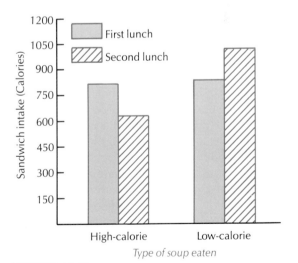

FIGURE 11.10

Sandwich intake after eating high-calorie or low-calorie soup. (Based on data from Booth, D.A., Mather, P., and Fuller, J. *Appetite*, 1982, 3, 163–184.)

Society's obsession with thinness leads many people to become preoccupied with dieting.

Rose and Williams (1961) studied pairs of people who were matched for weight, height, age, and activity. Some of these pairs differed by a factor of two in their intake of food (that is, one ate twice as much as the other). These results make it clear that some people convert their food into body tissue (principally fat) very efficiently but others do not. People with an efficient metabolism have difficulty keeping thin, while people with an inefficient metabolism can eat large meals without getting fat. In fact, some people must live on a "semistarvation" diet to maintain their weight at normal levels. In a society that produces an abundance of food but admires thinness, inefficiency in producing fat is a definite advantage.

Nonobese people respond to overeating very differently from obese people. For example, Sims and Horton (1968) fed volunteer subjects

of normal weight up to 8000 calories a day, which is much more than most obese people normally consume. Their weight gain was rather modest, ranging between 15 and 25 percent. Furthermore, when the subjects were permitted to select their own diet, they quickly returned to their normal weights. By contrast, quick and relatively painless weight loss is clearly not the experience of most obese people who attempt to lose weight.

Differences in metabolism appear to have a hereditary basis. Griffiths and Payne (1976) have reported that the children of obese parents ate *less* than the children of nonobese parents but nevertheless weighed more. Obviously, their metabolisms were more efficient. James and Trayhurn (1981) suggested that under some environmental conditions, metabolic efficiency is advantageous. That is, in places where food is only intermittently available in sufficient quantities, being able to stay alive on small amounts of food and to store up extra nutrients in the form of fat when food becomes available for a while is a highly adaptive trait. Therefore, the variability in people's metabolisms may reflect the nature of the environment experienced by their ancestors. For example, physically active lactating women in Gambia manage to maintain their weight on only 1500 calories per day (Whitehead et al., 1978). This efficiency, which allows people to survive in environments in which food is scarce, can be a disadvantage when food is readily available, because it promotes obesity.

Developmental Factors. Events that occur early in life can predispose a person toward obesity. Whatever its cause, obesity during childhood is a very strong predictor of obesity during adulthood (Stunkard and Burt, 1967). It has been suggested that juvenile obesity predisposes a person toward adult obesity through an increase in the number of fat cells. Obese people have, on the average, five times as many fat cells as nonobese people (Hirsch and Knittle, 1970). In addition, it has been shown that rats who are fed a fattening diet early in life will grow an increased number of fat cells. In contrast, if they are fattened up during adulthood, their fat cells will grow in size but not increase in number (Knittle and Hirsch, 1968). Perhaps juvenile obesity causes an increase in the number of fat cells, which makes it difficult to lose weight later in life.

Another event that has been shown to predispose people toward obesity is early prenatal malnutrition. During the winter of 1944–1945 people in the Netherlands suffered a severe shortage of food. Even pregnant women received an extremely meager diet. A follow-up study of draftees in the Dutch armed forces showed that men whose mothers had been malnourished during the first two trimesters of pregnancy were twice as likely to become obese later in life (Ravelli, Stein, and Susser, 1976). These findings were later confirmed by a laboratory experiment using rats (Jones and Friedman, 1982). This phenomenon may help explain why obesity is seen more often in people of lower socioeconomic status (Goldblatt, Moore, and Stunkard, 1968); perhaps mothers in this group are more likely to receive inadequate nutrition during pregnancy.

Activity. Obviously, people who eat a constant number of calories each day will gain weight if they exercise less, and lose weight if they exercise more. A study reported by Mayer (1955b) confirms that activity has a strong effect on eating and body weight. Mayer and his colleagues studied a group of men in a racially homogeneous community in India. They measured food intake and body weight and estimated the amount of energy the men expended in their jobs. People who expended at least moderate amounts of energy (such as clerks, mechanics, drivers, and carriers) all weighed about the same, although the carriers, who worked the hardest, ate more food than the clerks, who expended the least physical energy. These people matched their food intake to their expenditure of energy.

However, the relation between food intake and physical activity broke down in the case of people with sedentary occupations: head clerks, supervisors, and shop owners. These people expended very little energy but ate almost as much as the carriers, who worked the hardest. Their weight was correspondingly higher: The shop owners weighed approximately 45 percent more than the carriers.

The results suggest that relative inactivity leads to obesity. Of course, we must recognize that the most sedentary people also had the highest incomes, which could influence their diet; an observational study like this one does not permit us to determine causes unequivocally.

- What are the physiological mechanisms and learning processes that initiate eating?
- What physiological mechanisms and learning processes bring a meal to its end?
- What factors may produce obesity?

AGGRESSIVE BEHAVIOR

Aggression is a serious problem in almost all human societies; thus, it has attracted the attention of many behavioral scientists. Investigators have conducted research into the biological and social aspects of aggressive behavior. One issue they have examined is whether human aggression is closely related to the species-typical behaviors seen in other species, which appear to be genetically determined. Zoologists and physiological psychologists have investigated aggression in wild animals and in laboratory animals, while sociologists, political scientists, social psychologists, and psychologists interested in the role of classical and instrumental conditioning have studied human aggression. You already learned about a famous study on the socially learned aspects of aggression in Chapter 6, and you will learn more about the social aspects of aggression in Chapter 14. This section examines the role of biological and social aspects of motivation in acts of aggression.

Ethological Studies of Aggression

Social Relevance of Intraspecific Aggression

The utility of species-typical behaviors such as sexual activity, parental behavior, food gathering, and nest construction is obvious; it is easy to understand their value to survival. But violence and aggression are also seen in many species, including humans. If aggression is harmful, one would not expect it to be so prevalent in nature. Ethologists—zoologists who study the behavior of animals in their natural environments—have analyzed the causes of aggression and have shown that it, too, often has value for the survival of a species.

Intraspecific aggression involves an attack made by one animal upon another member of its species. Ethologists have shown that intra-specific aggression has several biological advantages. First, it tends to disperse a population of animals, forcing some into new territories, where necessary environmental adaptations may increase the flexibility of the species. Second, when accompanied by rivalry among males for mating opportunities, intra-specific aggression tends to perpetuate the genes of the healthier, more vigorous animals.

Human cultures, however, are very different even from those of other species of primates. Perhaps intraspecific aggression has outlived its usefulness for humans and we would benefit from its elimination. In any case, we must understand causes of human aggression to eliminate it or direct it to more useful purposes.

Threat and Appeasement

Ethologists have discovered a related set of behaviors in many species: ritualized threat gestures and appeasement gestures. **Threat gestures** enable an animal to communicate aggressive intent to another before engaging in actual violence. For example, if one dog intrudes on another's territory, the defender will growl and bare its teeth, raise the fur on its back (presumably making it look larger to its opponent), and stare at the intruder. Almost always, the dog defending its territory will drive the intruder away. Threat gestures are particularly important in species whose members are able to kill each other (Lorenz, 1966; Eibl-Eibesfeld, 1980). For example, wolves often threaten each other with growls and bared teeth but rarely bite each other. Because an all-out battle between two of these animals would probably end in the death of one and the serious wounding of the other, the tendency to perform ritualized displays rather than engage in overt aggression has an obvious advantage to survival of the species.

To forestall an impending attack, one of the animals must show that it does not want to fight—that it admits defeat. The submissive animal makes an **appeasement gesture.** If a pair of wolves get into a fight, one usually submits to the other by lying down and exposing its throat. The sight of a helpless and vulnerable opponent presumably terminates the victor's hostility, and the fight ceases. The aggression of the dominant animal is *appeased.*

Appeasement gestures are even a part of human behavior. Suppose you are a male of average size standing at a bar next to a muscular, 280-pound male wearing a jacket with a skull and crossbones stenciled on the back. Would you stare directly at his face? And if he happened to stare at you, would you stand up tall and meet his gaze or slouch down a bit, displaying a diffident look on your face?

Biology of Aggression

Brain Mechanisms

Experiments by physiological psychologists have confirmed that aggressive behaviors are species-typical responses; they have found that electrical stimulation of various parts of the brain—in particular, the hypothalamus and structures in the limbic system—can either trigger or inhibit an attack of one animal upon another. In addition, destruction of some brain structures can increase or decrease the likelihood of aggressive attacks. These studies indicate that the limbic system and hypothalamus exert a modulating effect on neural circuits located in the brain stem that contain the actual programs for muscular movements that constitute attack behaviors. As we will see in Chapter 12, the limbic system is involved in producing feelings of emotion that accompany species-typical behaviors such as attack.

Some neurosurgeons, aware of the results of these experiments with animals, have attempted to control instances of human violence by means of brain surgery. Certain people exhibit periods of extreme rage in which they attempt to kill anyone in their presence. Often they "black out" during these episodes, remembering nothing that happened or recalling a fit of violence that they deeply regret.

In some cases, removal of tumors or damaged areas of the brain have eliminated people's outbursts of violent behavior; presumably, the behavior was triggered when the tumors or damaged areas stimulated neural circuits involved in aggression. Because these operations removed abnormal brain tissue, no one has criticized them. However, another procedure is very controversial. **Psychosurgery** involves the removal of brain tissue to alter a person's behavior, without direct evidence that the tissue was abnormal. Reviews by Valenstein (1973, 1980) concluded that the usefulness of psychosurgery in controlling violent behavior in humans has not been demonstrated. In general, preoperative and postoperative evaluations of psychosurgery have been performed carelessly. The main criterion for success has often been whether the procedure makes it easier for the supervisory personnel in an institution to handle the patient. As a result of the generally low quality of observations, it is impossible to evaluate the usefulness of psychosurgery in the alleviation of violence. Most investigators believe it is *not* warranted. We do not yet know enough about the neural mechanisms of aggressive behavior to justify removing parts of the human brain unless these parts are definitely shown to be diseased or damaged. However, some forms of psychosurgery, designed to alleviate suicidal depression or compulsive behaviors, *do* show promise. These approaches are discussed in Chapter 17.

Hormones and Aggression

In birds and most mammals, androgens appear to exert a strong effect on aggressiveness. You will recall from Chapter 5 that testosterone has an organizational effect on the development of sex organs and the brain and an activational effect during adulthood. Testosterone also appears to exert the same effects on some forms of aggressive behavior. If a male mouse is raised in isolation, it will fiercely attack other male mice. But if a male mouse is castrated early in life, before its brain has matured, it will not attack another male when it grows up, even if it is given injections of testosterone (Conner and Levine, 1969).

Given that men are generally more aggressive than women (Maccoby and Jacklin, 1974) and that male sexual behavior in humans depends on the presence of testosterone, perhaps this hormone also influences men's aggressive behavior. In fact, a few reports suggest that drugs that counteract the effects of androgens seem to suppress aggressive behavior in men with records of criminal violence (Moyer, 1976). However, there is not yet enough evidence to permit any definite conclusions.

Social Variables That Affect Human Aggression

Aggressive behavior clearly has a large social component. It is frequently carried out against other people or in a setting where social influence is likely to be a major factor. Thus it has been investigated intensively by social psychologists; and as we will see in Chapter 14, they have approached the issue either in terms of a reaction to frustration or as an imitation of observed aggression. The process of observational learning as described in Chapter 6 has already been shown to be a major influence on aggressive behavior.

Imitation of Aggression

Consider the significance of a conversation like this one:

> *Parent:* I don't know what to do with Johnny. His teacher says he is simply impossible. He just can't keep from hitting and kicking other children.
> *Friend:* Perhaps he needs more discipline.
> *Parent:* But I spank him all the time!

Why does Johnny persist in being aggressive, even though this behavior is regularly punished? Some psychologists would suggest that instead of suppressing his violent behavior, frequent spankings have *taught* him to be aggressive. When his parents become upset with his

In some instances, society legitimizes the expression of aggression.

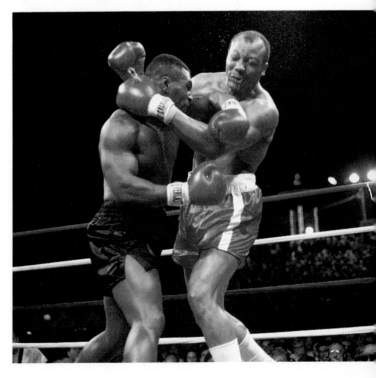

behavior, they resort to physical violence. And Johnny learns to imitate them. As we saw in Chapter 6, laboratory research by Albert Bandura has shown that children readily learn to imitate adults' aggressive behavior.

A large percentage of nonviolent people may have been spanked at least once when they were children, with no obvious harm. But it is clear that when parents habitually resort to aggression, their children are likely to do the same. In the extreme case of child abuse, parents who beat their children usually turn out to have been victims of child abuse themselves; this unfortunate trait seems to be passed along like an unwanted family heirloom (Parke and Collmer, 1975).

■ What is the adaptive significance of aggression, and the nature and value of ritualized aggression?
■ What evidence is there for the role of brain mechanisms and hormones in aggression?

CHAPTER SUMMARY

1. Motivation, a driving force that moves us to a particular action, more specifically is a tendency to perform a class of behaviors that brings an organism in contact with an appetitive stimulus (reinforcer) or moves it away from an aversive stimulus (punisher).

2. The hypothesis that reinforcement involves increases and not decreases in drive has been modified to suggest that organisms strive to attain optimum levels of arousal. This might explain reinforcement and punishment as two sides of the same coin, but optimum level can be determined only by observing the organism's behavior (it cannot therefore explain the behavior).

3. Expectancy theory has emphasized that potential reinforcers are effective to the degree that an organism expects them to occur. The theory of achievement motivation suggests that the tendency to perform a task is a function of this expectancy, along with the perceived value of the goal and the personality traits of success motivation and motivation to avoid failure.

4. Perseverance, an important characteristic of motivation, is controlled by the organism's previous history with intermittent reinforcement and its opportunity to develop behaviors that produce conditioned reinforcers, such as satisfaction.

5. Most organisms prefer behaviors that they are free to choose. If people receive reinforcers according to their level of accomplishment, such reinforcers will increase, not decrease, intrinsic motivation.

6. The phenomenon of learned helplessness may well be a factor in psychological disorders such as depression.

7. Studies of the physiological and behavioral effects of drugs and electrical stimulation of the brain have increased our understanding of the neural mechanisms of reinforcement and motivation. Studies have suggested that the release of dopamine in the brain is an essential component of reinforcement (blocking dopamine receptors diminishes the effectiveness of reinforcers).

8. Physiologically, a person eats because lowered supplies of stored nutrients are detected by receptors in the liver. A person stops eating because other detectors, located in the walls of the stomach, are able to monitor both the quality and quantity of good eating.

9. Obesity has many causes, both genetic and environmental. A person's metabolism may be too efficient; prenatal malnutrition or eating habits learned in infancy may lead to obesity.

10. Aggression serves useful purposes in the majority of species, yet most human societies attempt to suppress it in order to protect its victims. Studies of other species reveal the presence of mechanisms to avert violence: threat gestures warn of an impending attack, while appeasement gestures propitiate the potential aggressor.

11. Studies by physiological psychologists confirm that the brain contains neural mechanisms that control aggressive behaviors and that androgens influence the development and activation of these circuits. No clear demonstration has been shown that psychosurgery, the removal of brain tissue to alter a person's behavior, has been effective in the alleviation of violence.

KEY TERMS

achievement motivation An expectancy theory of motivation based on the need to achieve—a need to attempt and successfully complete a task—and the motivation to avoid failure.

amygdala A part of the limbic system of the brain located deep in the temporal lobe. Damage causes changes in emotional and aggressive behavior.

appeasement gesture A stereotype gesture made by a submissive animal in response to a threat gesture by a dominant animal; tends to inhibit an attack.

drive A motivating physiological condition of an organism.

drive-reduction hypothesis The hypothesis that a drive (resulting from physiological need or deprivation) produces an unpleasant state that causes an organism to engage in motivated behaviors. Reduction of drive is assumed to be reinforcing.

expectancy theories Theories to explain motivation, which deal with expectations about what might happen if people engage in particular behaviors.

glycogen An insoluble carbohydrate that can be synthesized from glucose or converted to it; used to store nutrients.

intraspecific aggression An attack by one organism on a member of the same species.

intrinsic motivation The ability of a particular activity to produce reinforcing effects; examples include games, puzzles, and hobbies.

learned helplessness A response to exposure to an inescapable aversive stimulus, characterized by reduced ability to learn a solvable avoidance task; thought to play a role in the development of some psychological disturbances.

motivation Driving force that moves us to a particular action, or, more specifically, a tendency to perform a class of behaviors that bring an organism in contact with an appetitive stimulus or move it away from an aversive stimulus.

motivation to avoid failure Within the theory of achievement motivation, a basic personality trait like the need to achieve. Aversiveness of failing a task is related to the probability of success at that task.

nucleus accumbens Region of the force brain containing neurons activated by dopamine.

optimum level hypothesis Explanation for both positive and negative reinforcement; when arousal level is too high, less stimulation is reinforcing; when it is too low, more stimulation is desired.

persevere To persist in a task despite lack of regular reinforcement.

psychosurgery The destruction of brain tissue in an attempt to eliminate maladaptive behavior or otherwise treat a mental disorder.

regulatory behavior Physiological mechanism that, once deficits or imbalances of basic needs are detected, behaves to bring conditions back to normal.

resultant motivation Tendency to achieve success minus tendency to avoid failure.

success motivation Need to achieve; factor in determining a person's level of motivation.

Test Anxiety Questionnaire (TAQ) Test used to measure a person's level of motivation.

Thematic Apperception Test (TAT) Test used to measure a person's success motivation.

threat gesture A stereotyped gesture that signifies that one animal is likely to attack another member of the species.

undermining of intrinsic motivation Condition in which extrinsic reinforcers can undermine intrinsic motivation if they are unrelated to a person's performance.

Emotion

In a real sense, emotions are what life is all about. Life without emotions would be bland and empty. When important things happen to us, they change our feelings. What have we learned about emotions? They are evoked by particular kinds of situations, they occur in association with approach or avoidance behaviors, and they are accompanied by expressions such as smiles and frowns that show others what we are feeling. Most psychologists who study emotions focus on one or more of these questions: What kind of situations produce emotions? What kinds of feelings do people report experiencing? What type of emotional behaviors do they engage in? What physiological changes do people undergo as they experience emotions?

Experimental research on human emotions is a difficult endeavor, primarily because ethical and practical considerations make it almost impossible to evoke strong emotions in subjects who volunteer to participate in experiments. Nevertheless, psychologists have learned much about the nature of emotional expression and recognition. Experiments with members of different cultural groups, with blind children, and with animals have shown that although many emotions are expressed innately, we have to learn to recognize the expression of most emotions in others.

This chapter discusses research and theories on the nature of emotions, including the type of stimuli that elicit them and the nature of the feelings that accompany them. As you will see, the major conclusion that will be drawn is that emotions, like consciousness and language, are social phenomena. That is, we display our feelings to others because it is usually advantageous to do so.

This chapter also examines the role of the body's stress reactions, which occur when the primitive "flight-or-fight" responses are evoked. Can emotions interfere with people's performance and lead to physical illness? Research on topics such as this demonstrates how psychologists try to uncover the relations between environmental events and the behaviors, thoughts, and feelings they bring forth.

361

THE NATURE OF EMOTION

Although no general theory of emotion is available to give us a consistent definition, the term **emotion** is generally used by psychologists for a display of feelings that are evoked when important things happen to us. Emotions are relatively brief and occur in response to events in the environment (or their mental re-creation, as when we remember something embarrassing we did in the past and experience the feelings of embarrassment again). In contrast, **moods** are considered to be longer-lived and generally weaker than emotions. Behaviorally, moods consist of tendencies to react more strongly to situations that would be likely to evoke only mild emotional reactions in others. For example, if one day a person reacts with anger to situations that most people would ignore, we label the person's mood as *grouchiness* or *irritability*. Much less is known about mood states than about emotions, because the conditions that control them are less distinct. Chapter 16 discusses mental disorders that consist of abnormal alterations in mood. **Temperament** is similar to mood but is even longer-lived. Temperament refers to a person's general disposition, or typical pattern of affective reaction to various situations. (In this context, the noun *affect*, pronounced "AFF ekt," refers to a feeling that accompanies an emotion.) Some people are especially sensitive to criticism and easily become angry or depressed. Others are generally cheerful and tend to see the bright side of situations. Temperament is thus an aspect of personality, the topic of Chapter 15.

The Mythology of Emotion: Emotions As Causes of Behavior

Even though the word *emotion* comes from the Latin *emovere*, meaning "to move out," we almost always describe an emotion as something that *happens to us* and makes us do something. Until recently, the word *passion* (which comes from the same root as *passive*) was commonly used to describe feelings of emotion. Through constant use, these metaphors have come to sound perfectly natural. When we experience an emotion, we tend to perceive ourselves as passive and helpless.

The belief that we are not responsible for our emotions or for our behavior when we are gripped by them permits us to indulge in unbecoming behavior and later to absolve ourselves of blame, at least partially. We can get away with hurting others or acting foolishly so long as we can point to an overpowering emotion that "made us do it." It appears that society as a whole suffers as a result. If people have an excuse for bad behavior, they are more likely to engage in it.

In contrast, we do not attempt to absolve ourselves of responsibility for *good* acts. Imagine someone saying, "I just couldn't help myself. I saw her drowning and before I knew it, I was struck by an altruistic frenzy. When I regained control of myself, I found that I had dragged her onto the shore." We attribute such acts to our intellect, so that we can take credit for them, while blaming bad behaviors on our uncontrollable emotions.

Practical Problems of Research

No single, comprehensive theory of emotion has been proved correct. Theories based on experimental data are restricted in scope, and those that take into account the range and subtlety of human emotion involve a great deal of unsupported speculation.

One of the major difficulties in objectively studying human emotions is *producing* them in subjects. Researchers can ask a subject to make a facial expression that corresponds to a particular emotion, but they cannot expect the subject actually to experience strong fear, ecstasy, or grief. (The facial expressions will cause their feelings to change, as we will see, but feelings produced in this way are less intense than the ones that occur naturally.) Only motivationally relevant situations can reliably produce strong emotions, and such situations are difficult to create in the laboratory.

Furthermore, the methods that would produce strong emotions are unethical. Fear is probably the easiest emotion to evoke, and earlier investigators used clever stratagems to frighten their subjects. One investigator attached difficult-to-remove electrodes to a subject's fingers. The electrodes soon began to produce "accidental" shocks, the "old, unreliable" equipment began to smoke, and the experimenter showed fright himself, trying to fix the apparatus before the subject was electrocuted. The deceit succeeded in making the subject frightened, but concern with the ethical treatment of subjects rules out such procedures today. Studies that propose to treat subjects in this way would be turned down by research review committees, and scientific journals would refuse to publish them.

EXPRESSION AND RECOGNITION OF EMOTIONS

This section reviews theories and research on the expression and recognition of emotions. To most people, the primary characteristics of emotions are the feelings they produce. However, feelings are private and cannot be shared directly with others. To psychologists, then, the most important aspect of an emotion is what might appear to be the most superficial one: its expression in facial gestures and other visible bodily reactions.

As we will see, the available evidence indicates that emotional responses consist of particular patterns of movements, controlled by brain mechanisms that an organism inherits from its ancestors. If this is true, then emotions have been important enough to survival to affect the inheritance of these brain mechanisms. But natural selection cannot possibly operate on *feelings*—it must operate on some traits of the organism that affect its ability to survive and reproduce. In the case of emotions, the traits consist of behaviors that are important to survival and reproductive success because they communicate vital messages to other members of the species.

Darwin's Contributions

Charles Darwin (1872/1965) suggested that human expressions of emotion have evolved from similar expressions in other animals. He said that emotional expressions are innate, unlearned responses consisting of a complex set of movements, principally of the facial muscles. The selective value of emotional expressions is that they permit animals to send and

Popular movies often portray emotions as the cause of behavior. In *Fatal Attraction*, a woman's passionate obsession with a married man results in a murder.

receive messages concerning their emotional state. For example, a young chimpanzee finds it useful to detect annoyance in a full-grown male while there is still time to get away from him. Thus, a man's sneer and a wolf's snarl are biologically determined response patterns, both controlled by innate brain mechanisms, just as coughing and sneezing are. (Of course, men can sneer and wolves can snarl for quite different reasons.)

Other investigators subsequently challenged Darwin's conclusions on the grounds that his data were biased. Many investigators concluded not only that Darwin's methods were flawed but also that his conclusions were incorrect. For example, Williams (1930) described a festive ceremony held in Melanesia, in the southwest Pacific:

> The guests, arriving in their several parties, come riding single file into the village, each party headed by its man of first importance, befeathered club on shoulder. No smile adorns his face, but rather an expression of fierceness, which however unsuited it may seem to the hospitable occasion, is nevertheless [considered to be] good form. (p. 29)

Another investigator (Klineberg, 1938) noted that expressions of emotion are not consistent even in Western society. Eventually, however, Ekman and Friesen (1971) demonstrated that,

  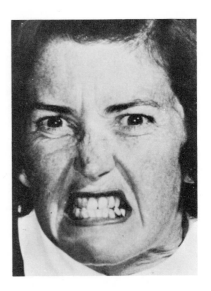

FIGURE 12.1

In a study by Ekman and Friesen, subjects were asked to match each story
with the appropriate photograph. (From Ekman, P. *The Face of Man:
Expressions of Universal Emotions in a New Guinea Village.* New York:
Garland STPM Press, 1980.)

even though Darwin's data were not gathered
under carefully controlled conditions, and
even though the observations of Williams and
Klineberg were accurate, Darwin's conclusions,
and not those of his critics, were correct.

Cross-Cultural Studies: Are Expressions Universal?

In 1967 and 1968 Ekman and Friesen carried
out some observations that validated those of
Darwin (Ekman, 1980). They visited an isolated
tribe in a remote area of New Guinea—the
South Fore tribe. This group of 319 adults and
children had never been exposed to Western
culture. They had never seen a movie, lived in
a Western town, or worked for someone from
outside their culture. Therefore, if they were
able to identify accurately the emotional expressions of Westerners as well as they could
identify those of members of their own tribe,
and if their own facial expressions were the
same as those of Westerners, it would seem that
these expressions were not culturally determined.

Because translations of single words from
one language to another are not always accu-

rate, Ekman and Friesen told little stories to
describe an emotion instead of presenting a single word. They told the story to a subject, presented three photographs of Westerners depict-
ing three different emotions, and asked the
subject to choose the appropriate one. Here are
three examples of the stories:

> *Fear*—She is sitting in her house all alone and
> there is no one else in the village; and there is no
> knife, ax, or bow and arrow in the house. A wild
> pig is standing in the door of the house and the
> woman is looking at the pig and is very afraid of it.
> The pig has been standing in the doorway for a few
> minutes and the person is looking at it very afraid
> and the pig won't move away from the door and
> she is afraid the pig will bite her.
> *Happy*—Her friends have come and she is happy.
> *Anger*—She is angry and is about to fight. (Ekman,
> 1980, p. 130)

Now look at Figure 12.1 to see whether you
would have any trouble matching each of these
stories with one of the photographs shown
there.

Table 12.1 shows that the people in the South
Fore tribe accurately identified all the expressions except for surprise and fear, which they
tended to confuse, perhaps because for the peo-

ple of this tribe surprising events are often also dangerous ones.

In a second study, Ekman and Friesen asked their subjects to make the kind of face they thought people would make if they were experiencing the events recounted in the little stories. The researchers videotaped these efforts, made photographs of the appropriate frames, and showed the photographs to American college students, who accurately identified all the emotions portrayed except for surprise and fear. (Note that this outcome is consistent with the judgments of Western expressions by the South Fore people.) Four photographs of the expressions of the South Fore people are shown in Figure 12.2 on the next page. The caption beneath each photograph describes the story used to elicit the expression.

The results of this careful cross-cultural study (and of others that have produced similar data) suggest strongly that situations that would be expected to have motivational relevance—to provide appetitive or aversive stimuli—produce consistent patterns of contraction in the facial muscles, whatever the person's culture. This conclusion suggests that the patterns of movement are inherited—wired into the brain, so to speak. The consistency of facial movements suggests an underlying consistency of emotion throughout our species.

TABLE 12.1

Judgments of emotion by people in the South Fore tribe of New Guinea

Emotion Described	Percentage Whose Judgments Agreed With Those Made by Members of Literate Cultures
Happiness	92
Sadness	79
Anger	84
Disgust	81
Surprise	68
Fear resulting from anger, disgust, or sadness	80
Fear resulting from surprise	43

Adapted from Ekman, P., and Friesen, W.V. Constants across cultures in the face and emotion. *Journal of Personality and Social Psychology*, 1971, *17*, 124–129.

■ What problems confront researchers attempting to study emotions?
■ How did Darwin contribute to the study of emotions, and what criticisms were raised against him?
■ How did cross-cultural studies of expression and recognition of emotions support Darwin's conclusions?

The Social Nature of Emotional Expressions in Humans

A good case can be made that emotions exist because expressions of emotion communicate important information to other members of the species. An interesting study by Kraut and Johnson (1979) showed that people are more likely to express signs of happiness in the presence of other people than when they are alone. The investigators unobtrusively observed whether people smiled in three situations: while bowling and making a strike or missing one, while watching a hockey game and seeing the home team score or be scored against, and while walking down a street on a beautiful day or a hot and humid one. They found that the happy situations (making a strike, seeing the home team score, or experiencing a beautiful day) produced only small signs of happiness when the people being observed were alone. However, when the people were interacting socially with other people, they were much more likely to smile. For example, bowlers who made a strike usually did not smile when the ball hit the pins. However, when the bowlers turned around to face their companions, they often smiled.

Of course, under some conditions, we suppress expressions of emotion according to display rules, as we will see in the next section. But when we do express emotions, they tend to be displayed toward other people.

When people see someone expressing an emotion, they tend to imitate the expression. This tendency to imitate appears to be innate. Field, Woodson, Greenberg, and Cohen (1982) had adults make facial expressions in front of infants. The infants' own facial expressions were videotaped and were subsequently rated by people who did not know what expressions

"Your friend has come and you are happy."

"Your child has died."

"You are angry and about to fight."

"You see a dead pig that has been lying there a long time."

FIGURE 12.2

In a study by Ekman and Friesen, subjects were asked to make faces (shown in the photographs) when they were told the stories. (From Ekman, P. *The Face of Man: Expressions of Universal Emotions in a New Guinea Village.* New York: Garland STPM Press, 1980.)

were being displayed by the adults. Field and her colleagues found that even newborn babies (with an average age of thirty-six hours) tended to imitate the expressions they saw. Clearly, the effect cannot be a result of learning. Figure 12.3 shows three photographs of the adult expressions and the expressions they elicited in a baby. Can you look at them yourself without changing your own expression, at least a little?

Perhaps imitation provides one of the chan-nels by which organisms communicate their emotions. For example, if we see someone looking sad, we tend to assume a sad expression ourselves. The feedback from our own expression helps put us in the other person's place and makes us more likely to respond with solace or assistance. And perhaps one of the reasons we derive pleasure from making some-one else smile is that their smile makes us smile and feel happy.

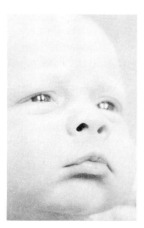

FIGURE 12.3

Photographs of happy, sad, and surprised faces posed by an adult, and the responses made by the infant. (From Field, T. In *Development of Nonverbal Behavior in Children*, edited by R.S. Feldman. New York: Springer Verlag, 1982.)

Control of Emotional Expression: Display Rules

We all realize that our expressions of emotions can be read by other people. In recognition of this fact, we sometimes try to hide our true feelings, attempting to appear impassive or even to display an emotion different from what we feel. At other times, we may exaggerate our emotional response to make sure that others see how we feel. For example, if a friend tells us about a devastating experience, we make sure that our facial expression conveys sadness and sympathy.

Researchers have studied all these phenomena. Attempting to hide an emotion is called **masking.** Attempting to exaggerate or minimize the expression of an emotion is called **modulation.** And attempting to express an emotion we do not actually feel is called **simulation.** Ekman and Friesen (1975) refer to these phenomena as **display rules.** Although the patterns of muscular movements that accompany particular feelings are biologically determined, these movements can, to some extent, be controlled by display rules. (See Figure 12.4 on the next page.)

Most display rules are culturally determined. For example, in Western society it is impolite for a winner to show too much pleasure and for

The expression of emotions is one way we communicate information to other people. Studies indicate that we are more likely to express emotions when others are present.

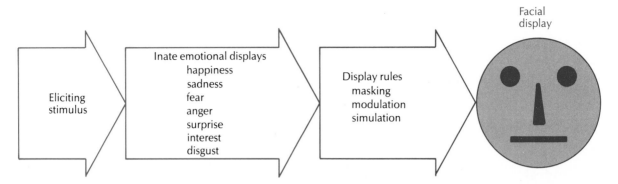

FIGURE 12.4

Innate emotional displays can be modified by display rules. (Adapted from
Ekman, P., and Friesen, W. *Semiotica*, 1969, 1, 49–98.)

a loser to show too much disappointment. The expression of these emotions is supposed to be modulated downward. Also, in many societies it is "unmanly" to cry or show fear and "unfeminine" to show anger.

Several studies have found that North American boys and girls differ in their facial expressions of emotion as they get older, presumably because they learn about their society's sex-stereotyped display rules. Very young infants show no sex differences in facial expression (Field, 1982). However, by the time they are in nursery school, boys and girls begin to differ. Buck (1975, 1977) showed various types of color slides to nursery school children and unobtrusively videotaped their faces as they watched. Some slides were pleasant, some puzzling, and some unpleasant. He showed the videotapes of the children to adults (university students) and asked them to try to guess the nature of the children's emotional expressions. Buck assumed that the accuracy of the ratings would indicate the degree of emotional expression. Indeed, the adults could guess the girls' emotions more accurately than the boys'.

Ekman and his colleagues (Ekman, Friesen, and Ellsworth, 1972; Friesen, 1972) attempted to assess a different kind of culturally determined display rule. They showed a distressing film to Japanese and American college students, singly and in the presence of a visitor, who was described to the subjects as a scientist. Because the Japanese culture discourages public display of emotion, the researchers expected that the Japanese students would show fewer facial expressions of emotion when in public than when alone.

The researchers recorded the facial expressions of their subjects with hidden cameras while the subjects viewed a film showing a gruesome and bloody coming-of-age rite in a primitive tribe. The results were as predicted. When the subjects were alone, American and Japanese subjects showed the same facial expressions. When they were with another person, the Japanese students were less likely to express negative emotions and more likely to mask these expressions with polite smiles. Thus, people from both societies used the same facial expressions of emotion but were subject to different social display rules.

When people attempt to mask the expression of a strongly felt emotion, they usually are not completely able to do so. That is, there is some **leakage,** or subtle sign of the emotion (Ekman and Friesen, 1969). Ekman and Friesen (1974) investigated this phenomenon. They showed an unpleasant film of burns and amputations to female nursing students. After watching the film, the subjects were interviewed by an experimenter, who asked them about the film. Some of the subjects were asked to pretend to the interviewer that they had seen a pleasant film. The experimenters videotaped the subjects during the interviews and showed these tapes to a separate group of raters, asking them to try to determine whether the people they were watching were being honest or deceptive. The raters were shown videotapes of the subjects' faces or bodies. The results indicated that the raters could detect the deception better when they saw the subjects' bodies than when they saw their faces; apparently, people are better at masking signs of emotion shown by their facial muscles than those shown by muscles in other parts of their body. Presumably, people recognize the attention that is paid to the face and learn to control their facial expressions better than the movements of the rest of the body.

Theories Based on a Functional Analysis of Emotional Behavior

Darwin suggested that emotional expressions had evolved because of the survival value of the ability to communicate emotional reactions. His suggestion is generally accepted by twentieth-century theorists. For example, Tomkins (1962, 1963, 1982) asserts that there are nine innate emotions, based on the types of movements and expressions that people exhibit. The three positive affects are *interest* (or *excitement*), expressed by a fixed or tracking stare (in the case of a moving object) with the eyebrows down; *enjoyment* (or *joy*), expressed by a smile; and *surprise* (or *startle*), expressed with raised eyebrows and an eyeblink. The six negative affects are *distress* (or *anguish*), expressed by crying; *fear* (or *terror*), expressed by withdrawal, wide open eyes, trembling, and pale, cold, and sweating skin; *shame* (or *humiliation*), expressed by a lowering of the head and eyes; *contempt*, expressed by raising the upper lip in a sneer; *disgust*, expressed by protrusion and lowering of the lower lip; and *anger* (or *rage*), expressed by a frown, clenched jaw, and reddening of the face. Tomkins's classifications were adopted as a starting point by other theorists. For example, the categories used by Ekman and Friesen in their cross-cultural study were based on Tomkins's work.

Facial expressions of emotion communicate useful information to other members of the species. For instance, signs of surprise or fear alert other animals that something important or dangerous may be near; signs of disgust suggest that something—perhaps a food that previously made the animal ill—is to be avoided; signs of anger warn the recipient to retreat or be ready to fight; signs of sadness (distress) invite sympathy and consolation; and signs of interest directed toward another animal suggest a willingness to engage in social interaction, perhaps including sexual activity. Some signs are used to reinforce or punish another animal's behavior: A smile (a sign of enjoyment) serves as a

reinforcer, and an expression of contempt serves as a punisher. A sign of shame probably prevents other animals from attacking a transgressor that acknowledges its wrongdoing.

Another theorist (Plutchik, 1962, 1980) has devised a classification scheme based on the adaptive significance of various classes of species-typical behaviors. The functions of these behaviors include the following: *protection* involves avoidance of danger or harm; *destruction* involves attacking another animal or an inanimate source of danger; *reproduction* involves courting, mating, and possessing another; *reintegration* involves calling for assistance or sympathy because of a loss of something important; *incorporation* (or *affiliation*) involves forming bonds with other members of the species; *rejection* involves expelling harmful substances such as poisons; *exploration* involves mapping the environment; and *orientation* involves turning toward a novel object or situation and paying attention to it. Table 12.2 on the next page shows the relation of these categories of functions to some representative species-typical behaviors that accomplish the functions; it gives some typical causes of the behaviors and also lists the emotions that accompany them.

The display of emotion is culturally determined. At the memorial service for victims of the space shuttle disaster, females openly expressed emotions while males tended to suppress them.

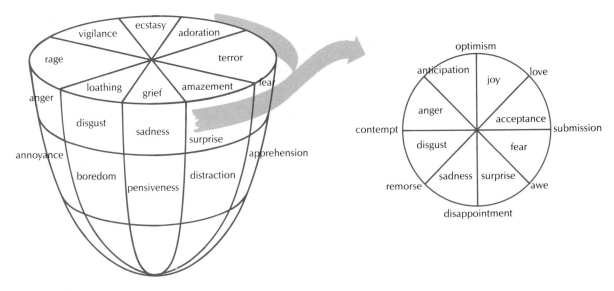

FIGURE 12.5

Plutchik's model of emotion. (Adapted from Plutchik, R., in *Approaches to Emotion*, edited by K.R. Scherer and P. Ekman. Hillsdale, N.J.: Lawrence Erlbaum Associates, 1984.)

Plutchik suggested that his eight categories actually represent polar opposites; for example, protection is the opposite of reproduction, because they involve avoidance and approach behaviors, respectively. In addition, the strength of the behavioral tendencies associated with each of these categories can vary from weak to strong, and thus the feelings associated with them can similarly vary. He suggested a theoretical model of emotion based on these two dimensions: the feelings that accompany the four opposing behavioral functions and the strength of those feelings. Figure 12.5 illustrates his model. The circle at the top of the diagram includes the four pairs of feelings in their most intense forms: rage/terror, loathing/adoration, grief/ecstasy, and amazement/vigilance. The next lower level includes the corresponding terms you already saw in Table 12.2. A slice through this level, shown at the right, indicates composite emotions that consist of combinations of two adjacent primary emotions. For example, love is a combination of joy and acceptance. Below this level are still weaker forms of the emotions, and at the bottom is a quiet state lacking in excitement. The model is shaped like a cone because Plutchik concluded that weaker emotions are much more similar to each other than stronger ones.

Plutchik's model is both interesting and plausible, yet, like other theories of emotion, it is difficult to test experimentally. However, by focusing on the functional significance of various classes of behaviors, it may help guide research on the evolution of emotions.

TABLE 12.2

Plutchik's categories of species-typical behaviors, functions, and emotional labels

Species-Typical Behaviors	Functions	Emotional Labels
Withdrawing, escaping	Protection	Fear
Attacking, biting	Destruction	Anger
Mating, courting	Reproduction	Joy
Crying for help	Reintegration	Sadness
Pair bonding, grooming	Affiliation	Acceptance
Vomiting, spitting out	Rejection	Disgust
Examining, mapping	Exploration	Expectancy
Stopping, freezing	Orientation	Surprise

Adapted from Plutchik, R., *Emotions: A general psychoevolutionary theory.* In Scherer and Ekman (1984).

- What evidence indicates that emotional expression in humans is a social behavior?
- What processes are used by people to control their emotional expressions?
- What are the main features of the two theories that are based on a functional analysis of emotional behavior?

FEELINGS OF EMOTION

As with other aspects of emotion, there is no comprehensive theory that fully explains why our emotional feelings arise as they do or what causes them. Yet from very early times, people have associated emotions with physiological responses. It is easy to understand why this is the case. Strong emotions can cause increased heart rate, irregular breathing, queasy feelings in the internal organs, trembling, sweating, reddening of the face, or even fainting. The question is, do these physiological changes *constitute* emotions, or are they merely symptoms of some other underlying process? Do we feel frightened because we tremble, or do we tremble because we are frightened?

The James-Lange Theory

William James (1842–1910), an American psychologist, and Carl Lange (1834–1900), a Danish physiologist, independently suggested similar explanations for emotion, which most people refer to collectively as the **James-Lange theory** (James, 1884; Lange, 1887). Basically, the theory states that emotion-producing situations elicit an appropriate set of physiological responses, such as trembling, sweating, and increased heart rate. The situations also elicit behaviors, such as clenching of the fists or fighting. The brain receives sensory feedback from the organs that produce these responses, and the feedback constitutes emotion. As James put it:

The bodily changes follow directly the perception of the exciting fact, and . . . our feelings of the same changes as they occur is the emotion. Common sense says we lose our fortune, are sorry, and weep; we meet a bear, are frightened, and run; we are insulted by a rival, are angry, and strike. The

Tomkins believes that there are nine innate emotions, one of which is joy.

hypothesis here to be defended says that this order of sequence is incorrect, that the one mental state is not immediately induced by the other and that the bodily manifestations must first be interposed between. The more rational statement is that we feel sorry because we cry, angry because we strike, afraid because we tremble, and not that we cry, strike, or tremble because we are sorry, angry or fearful, as the case may be.

. . . If we fancy some strong emotion, and then try to abstract from our consciousness of it all the feelings of its bodily symptoms, we find we have nothing left behind, no "mind stuff" out of which the emotion can be constituted, and that a cold and neutral state of intellectual perception is all that remains. (James, 1890, pp. 449–451)

To James, the theory that emotions are no more than perceptions of our physiological and behavioral responses suggested some practical consequences. We can "conquer undesirable emotional tendencies . . . by assiduously, and in the first instance cold-bloodedly, go[ing] through . . . the *outward movements* of those contrary dispositions which we prefer to cultivate" (p. 462). in other words, if we practice smiling at someone who makes us angry, our anger will eventually disappear.

James's description of the process of emotion might strike you as being at odds with your

own experience. Most of us feel that we experience emotions directly, internally. The outward manifestations of our emotions seem to us to be secondary events. But have you ever found yourself in an unpleasant confrontation with someone else and discovered that you were trembling, even though you did not think that you were so bothered by the encounter? Or did you ever find yourself blushing in response to some public remark that was made about you? Or did you ever find tears coming to your eyes while watching a film that you did not think was affecting you? What would you conclude about your emotional states in situations like these? Would you ignore the evidence from your own physiological reactions?

Chapter 13 describes a topic of research called *attribution*, by which process we make conclusions about the causes of other people's behavior. James's approach is closely related to the process of attribution; he suggests that our own emotional feelings are based on what we find ourselves doing and on the sensory feedback we receive from the activity of our internal organs. Thus, when we find ourselves trembling and feel queasy, we experience these responses as fear. Where feelings of emotions are concerned, we are self-observers.

For many years there was little experimental support for the James-Lange theory. Nevertheless, the theory continued to receive attention. James was a brilliant thinker and a persuasive writer, and the influence of his appeals to introspection and common sense is still strong. In addition, his theory was never disproved, although many arguments were directed against it. As we will see, we now have some evidence in favor of it, although not enough to be able to conclude that it is correct. But first let us examine the principal criticisms, offered by Walter Cannon (1871–1945), a prominent physiologist who developed a theory of emotion of his own (Cannon, 1927).

1. "The viscera [internal organs] are relatively insensitive structures." Thus, feedback would be poor, and we could not possibly discriminate the many emotions we can experience merely from our internal organs.

2. "The same visceral changes occur in very different emotional states."

The James-Lange theory suggests that emotional reactions occur in response to stimulating situations.

3. "Artificial induction of the visceral changes typical of strong emotions does not produce them." Thus, injection of a hormone that increases heart rate does not cause the subject to experience an emotional change.

4. "Visceral changes are too slow to be a source of feeling." After all, emotional changes can be abrupt.

5. "Total separation of the viscera from the central nervous system does not alter emotional behavior."

More recent evidence suggests that Cannon's criticisms are not relevant. For example, although the viscera are not sensitive to cutting and burning, they provide much better feedback than Cannon suspected. Moreover, people are sensitive to a wide variety of patterns of activity in the viscera, and many changes in the viscera can occur rapidly enough so that they *could* be the causes of feelings of emotion.

Cannon cited the fact that cutting the sensory nerves between the internal organs and the central nervous system does not abolish emotional behavior in animals. However, this does not prove that *feelings* of emotion survive this surgical disruption. We do not know how the animal feels; we know only that it will snarl and attempt to bite if it is threatened. In any case, James did not attribute all feelings of emotion to the internal organs; he also said that feedback from muscles was important. The threat might make the animal snarl and bite, and the feedback from the facial and neck muscles might constitute a "feeling" of anger, even if feedback from the internal organs was cut off.

Hohman (1966) collected data from humans that established the importance of feedback from physiological responses in feelings of emotion. He questioned people who had suffered damage to the spinal cord about how intense their emotional feelings were. If feedback is important, one would expect that emotional feelings would be less intense if the injury were high (that is, close to the brain) than if it were low, because a high spinal cord injury would cut off more of the body from the brain. In fact, this is precisely what Hohman found: the higher the injury, the less intense the feeling.

The comments of patients with high spinal cord injuries suggest that the severely dimin-ished feedback does change their feelings but not necessarily their behavior.

> I sit around and build things up in my mind, and I worry a lot, but it's not much but the power of thought. I was at home alone in bed one day and dropped a cigarette where I couldn't reach it. I finally managed to scrounge around and put it out. I could have burned up right there, but the funny thing is, I didn't get all shook up about it. I just didn't feel afraid at all, like you would suppose.
>
> Now, I don't get a feeling of physical animation, it's sort of cold anger. Sometimes I act angry when I see some injustice. I yell and cuss and raise hell, because if you don't do it sometimes, I've learned people will take advantage of you, but it doesn't have the heat to it that it used to. It's a mental kind of anger. (Hohman, 1966, pp. 150–151)

These comments suggest that we do not necessarily engage in emotional behavior *because of* our feelings; lacking these feelings, people still engage in the same behaviors for "rational" reasons. Perhaps these reasons are also the real causes of the emotional behavior of people with intact spinal cords.

Feedback from Simulated Emotions

An interesting experiment by Ekman, Levenson, and Friesen (1983) revealed that feedback from simulated emotional expressions can affect the activity of the autonomic nervous system. This finding gives some degree of support to James's and Lange's assertions that feedback from physiological and behavioral responses provides the feelings of emotions.

Ekman and his colleagues asked subjects to move particular facial muscles to simulate the emotional expressions of fear, anger, surprise, disgust, sadness, and happiness. They did not tell the subjects what emotion they were trying to produce, but only what movements they should make. For example, to simulate fear, they asked the subjects to "Raise your brows. While holding them raised, pull your brows together. Now raise your upper eyelids and tighten the lower eyelids. Now stretch your lips horizontally." (You can see this expression if you look back at the left photograph in Figure 12.1 on p. 364.) While the subjects made the expressions, the investigators monitored several physiological responses controlled by the autonomic nervous system.

When we see emotion expressed, such as in this ticker-tape parade in
honor of returning hostages, we often find ourselves imitating it.

The simulated expressions did alter the activity of the autonomic nervous system. In fact, different facial expressions produced somewhat different patterns of activity. For example, anger increased heart rate and skin temperature, fear increased heart rate but decreased skin temperature, and happiness decreased heart rate without affecting skin temperature. Not all the patterns were unique to a particular facial expression; for example, fear and sadness produced one type of pattern, while happiness, disgust, and surprise produced another. However, it is possible that monitoring of more physiological responses would distinguish more patterns; for example, the patterns produced by fear and sadness undoubtedly differ in some ways.

Why should a particular pattern of movements of the facial muscles cause changes in the activity of the autonomic nervous system? Perhaps the connection is a result of experience; in other words, perhaps the occurrence of particular facial movements along with changes in the autonomic nervous system leads to classical conditioning, so that feedback from the facial movements becomes a conditional stimulus that can elicit the autonomic response. Or perhaps the connection is innate. As we saw earlier, the adaptive value of emotional expressions is that they permit animals to communicate their feelings and intentions. One of the ways in which this occurs may be through imitation; as we saw, even infants imitate expressions they see. The internal feedback we receive when we make a facial expression in response to another person's expression may be one of the factors that evokes feelings of empathy.

The Role of Cognition in Feelings of Emotion

One of the current controversies among psychologists interested in emotion is the relative importance of automatic processes (such as classical conditioning) and cognitive processes (especially those involving conscious thought). The person most responsible for directing researchers' attention to the possible interaction between cognition and activation of the autonomic nervous system is Stanley Schachter. Schachter (1964) proposed that emotions are determined *jointly* by perception of physiological responses and by cognitive assessment of a specific situation. He described three conditions that elicit emotion:

> Given a state of physiological arousal for which an individual has no immediate explanation, he will "label" this state and describe his feelings in terms of the cognitions available to him. To the extent that cognitive factors are potent determiners of emotional states, . . . precisely the same state of physiological arousal could be labelled "joy" or "fury" or any of a great diversity of emotional labels. . . .
>
> . . . given a state of physiological arousal for which an individual has a completely appropriate explanation (e.g., "I feel this way because I have just received an injection of adrenalin"), no evaluative needs will arise, and the individual is unlikely to label his feelings in terms of the alternative cognitions available. . . .
>
> . . . given the same cognitive circumstances, the individual will react emotionally or describe his feelings as emotions only to the extent that he experiences a state of physiological arousal. (p. 53)

Thus, to him, emotion is cognition plus perception of physiological arousal. Both are necessary.

To test this hypothesis, Schachter and Singer (1962) arranged to induce physiological arousal in groups of subjects placed in various situations. All subjects were told that they were part of an investigation on the effects of a vitamin called "suproxin" on visual perception. No such vitamin exists. The investigators gave some subjects injections of adrenaline, a hormone that stimulates a variety of autonomic nervous system effects associated with arousal, such as increased heart rate and blood pressure, irregular breathing, warming of the face, and mild trembling. Other subjects received a control injection of a salt solution, which has no physiological effects.

Next the researchers placed some subjects in an anger-provoking situation, in which they were treated rudely and subjected to obnoxious test questions such as the following: "How many men, besides your father, has your mother slept with? (a) one, (b) two, (c) three, (d) four or more." Others were treated politely and saw the antics of another "subject" (a confederate who was hired by the experimenters), who acted silly and euphoric. The experimenters hoped that these two situations, together with the physiological reactions produced by the injections of adrenaline, would promote either negative or positive emotional states.

Finally, some subjects were correctly informed that the injections they received would produce side effects such as trembling and a pounding heart. Others were told to expect irrelevant side effects or none at all. Schachter and Singer predicted that the subjects who knew what side effects to expect would correctly attribute their physiological reactions to the drug and would not experience a change in emotion. Those who were misinformed would note their physiological arousal and conclude that they were feeling especially angry or happy, as the circumstance dictated. The subjects reported their emotional states in a questionnaire.

Can our thoughts influence our feelings? Psychologists disagree about the role cognition plays in eliciting emotions.

The results were not as clear-cut as the experimenters had hoped. The adrenaline did not increase the intensity of the subjects' emotional states. However, subjects who expected to experience physiological arousal as a result of the injection reported much less of a change in their emotional state than those who did not expect it, *regardless of whether they had received the adrenaline or the placebo*; in other words, no matter what their physiological state was, they felt less angry or happy after having been exposed to one of the emotional situations. This suggests that we *interpret* the significance of our physiological reactions, rather than simply experiencing them as emotions.

Nisbett and Schachter (1966) provided further evidence that subjects can be fooled into attributing their own naturally occurring physiological responses to a drug, and thus into feeling less "emotional." First, they gave all subjects a placebo pill (one with no physiological effects). Half the subjects were told that the pill would make their hearts pound, their breathing increase, and their hands tremble; the other half (the control subjects) were told nothing about possible side effects. Then the researchers strapped on electrodes and gave the subjects electrical shocks. All subjects presumably experienced pain and fear, and consequently their heart rate and breathing increased, they trembled, and so on. Yet the subjects who perceived their reactions as drug-induced were able to tolerate stronger shocks than the control subjects and they reported less pain and fear. Thus, cognition can affect people's judgments about their own emotional states, and even their tolerance of pain.

The precise nature of the interaction between cognition and physiological arousal has not been determined. For example, in the Nisbett and Schachter experiment, although the verbal instructions about effects of the placebo did affect the subjects' reaction to pain, it did not seem to do so through a logical, reasoned process. In fact, Nisbett and Wilson (1977) later reported that subjects did *not* consciously attribute their increased tolerance of pain to the effects of the pill.

Some psychologists, such as Lazarus (1984), believe that emotions are produced only by cognitive processes. Others, such as Zajonc (1984), go to the other extreme, saying that cognitive appraisal is not necessary and that emotions are automatic, species-typical responses that are heavily influenced by classical conditioning. Although the two sides of the debate appear to have been drawn sharply, it seems clear that both automatic processes and conscious deliberation play a role in the expression and feelings of emotion. A person can become angry after realizing that someone's "kind words" actually contained a subtle insult; obviously, this anger is a result of cognition. On the other hand, we also saw that through the process of classical conditioning, stimuli can evoke emotional reactions before we have time to realize what is happening. In some cases, we may be acting hostile and angry without realizing what we are doing; if cognitive processes are responsible for our anger, they are certainly not conscious, deliberate ones.

Schachter's major contribution to the study of emotion was to make other psychologists consider the complex interactions between the automatic and conscious processes that are responsible for producing and perceiving emotional responses. Because in many ways emotions are what life itself is all about, we should not be surprised that emotions are influenced by—and in turn have an influence on—so many different types of variables.

■ How does the James-Lange theory explain emotion, and what are Cannon's criticisms of this theory?

■ What are the physiological effects of feedback from simulated emotion expression?

■ What is the role of cognition in Schachter's theory of emotion?

Physiological Mechanisms of Emotion

The Cannon Theory of Emotion

Besides criticizing the James-Lange theory, Cannon proposed one of his own. He suggested that emotional feelings are produced by activity of the thalamus, which receives information from all regions of the cerebral cortex, where emotion-producing stimuli are perceived. The visceral changes that accompany emotions are produced by activity of the hypothalamus, which controls the autonomic nervous system. You will recall from Chapter 2 that the autonomic nervous system regulates the activity of the blood vessels, sweat glands, and the internal organs. (See Figure 12.6.)

As a result of continuing research on brain functions, more recent investigators have suggested that emotional responses involve activity of the **limbic system** as well as the hypothalamus. The limbic system comprises a series of brain structures that include a portion of the hypothalamus and a portion of the thalamus. Electrical stimulation of parts of the limbic system can elicit a variety of physiological responses controlled by the autonomic nervous system, such as changes in heart rate, respiration, or sweating, and can also elicit a variety of behavioral responses such as defensive reactions or excited exploratory activity. In humans, such stimulation can result in feelings of pleasure, anger, fear, or rage (Sem-Jacobsen, 1968). Because the artificial stimulation cannot produce the same patterns of neural activity that are evoked by natural stimuli, the feelings it produces are not identical to normal emotions. However, the similarity does implicate these neural systems in emotion.

As we will see, studies with people whose brains have been damaged by injury or disease suggest that the limbic system is at least partly under the control of neural circuits in the cerebral cortex. Perceptions of emotion-producing situations take place in the cortical association areas, which then stimulate circuits in the hypothalamus and limbic system that lead to changes in the autonomic nervous system and to some species-typical emotional behaviors. In addition, perception (that is, conscious awareness) of one's own emotional state probably also takes place in the cerebral cortex. (See Figure 12.7 on the next page.)

The Role of the Cortex

The emotional behavior of people who have suffered brain damage has provided some insights into the role of the cerebral cortex in emotions. In general, the right hemisphere appears to play a more important role in both feelings and expressions of emotion and in the perception of emotions in other people. Within the cerebral hemispheres, the temporal and parietal lobes appear to play an important role in the perception of emotions, and the frontal lobe plays an important role in emotional expression.

Emotional Expression and Brain Damage

For a long time clinicians have noted differences in the emotional behavior of patients with damage to the right or left hemisphere. People who have sustained damage to the left hemisphere often suffer a **catastrophic reaction,** an episode of severe anxiety and depression, presumably in response to their awareness of their neurological deficits. In contrast,

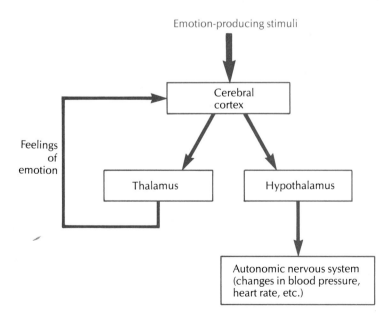

Emotion-producing stimuli

Cerebral cortex

Feelings of emotion

Thalamus

Hypothalamus

Autonomic nervous system (changes in blood pressure, heart rate, etc.)

FIGURE 12.6

Cannon's physiological theory of emotion.

FIGURE 12.7

A more modern model of
the brain mechanisms of
emotion.

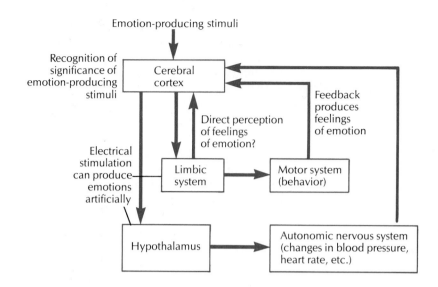

people with right-hemisphere damage often
show an **indifference reaction,** acting noncha-
lant about their disorder. People with damage
to either hemisphere often have a paralyzed
arm and leg, but those with damage to the right
hemisphere, even when they acknowledge that
they cannot walk, often continue to make plans
that do not take account of their impairments
and show no concern about their deficits. One
man I met had suffered a stroke that had produced severe damage to his right hemisphere.
His left arm and leg were totally paralyzed;
thus, he was confined to a wheelchair because
he could not walk. However, on several occasions he cheerfully wheeled to the door of the
rehabilitation center so that he could "go for a
walk outside." This man was very intelligent,
receiving superior scores on verbal subtests of
the WAIS-R even after his stroke. However,
some aspects of his judgment were obviously
impaired.

Presumably, the right hemisphere is specialized to some extent for recognizing emotionally
relevant situations and for organizing the pattern of emotional responses. Thus, people with
damaged left hemispheres become anxious and
depressed because their intact right hemispheres recognize the devastating nature of the
neurological impairments and assign emotional significance to this assessment. But
when the right hemisphere is damaged, although the left hemisphere can perform an objective inventory of these impairments, the person attaches no emotional significance to the
results of the inventory and often fails to makes
use of the information in making plans. The
patient acts cheerful and indifferent; the left
hemisphere *knows,* but just does not seem to
care.

Just as the left posterior regions of the cerebral cortex are important for the perception of
speech and the left frontal regions are important for the production of speech, it appears
that similar regional specialization exists in the
right hemisphere for the recognition and production of emotional expressions. Ross (1981)
reported case studies of patients who had received damage to the right posterior frontal cortex, to the right parietal/temporal cortex, and to
both regions. Frontal damage impaired the patients' use of facial gestures and tone of voice to
express emotion, but not their comprehension
of other people's emotional expressions. In
contrast, patients with posterior damage could
produce emotional expressions but could not
recognize those of other people. Large lesions
involving the two areas impaired both production and recognition. (See Figure 12.8.)

The results of Ross's study are particularly
interesting because they seem to be analogous
to disturbances in language production and
comprehension that follow damage to the corresponding areas of the left hemisphere. You
will recall from Chapter 8 that left temporal lesions lead to Wernicke's aphasia, a disorder of
speech perception, and that left frontal lesions
lead to Broca's aphasia, a disorder of speech
production. However, Ross's conclusions are
based on the data from only a few patients, and
the results must be confirmed by other investigators before we can confidently accept them as
fact.

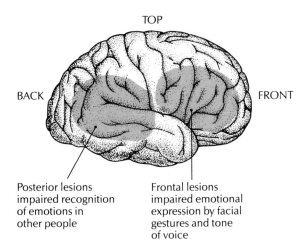

TOP

BACK | FRONT

Posterior lesions impaired recognition of emotions in other people

Frontal lesions impaired emotional expression by facial gestures and tone of voice

FIGURE 12.8

According to Ross (1981), damage to the frontal lobe or temporal and parietal lobes of the right hemisphere can impair expression or recognition of emotions.

■ What are the roles that the hypothalamus, limbic system, and cerebral cortex appear to play in emotions?

■ How do different areas of the brain appear to affect emotional expression, based on brain-damage evidence?

EMOTION AND HEALTH

The fact that we have more words for negative emotions than for positive ones may reflect our tendency to use emotions as excuses for bad behavior, but it undoubtedly also stems from the fact that many events producing strong feelings are unpleasant or harmful. Such changes in the environment trigger a variety of physiological responses in our bodies that help preserve our physical and mental health. Unfortunately, there are some conditions to which it is difficult to adapt.

The Stress Response

Walter Cannon remarked that we have inherited physiological mechanisms designed to protect us from physical dangers. For example, when threatened by a wild animal, our ancestors had to flee, defend themselves, or perish.

The **flight-or-fight reaction** consisted of hormonal secretions and changes in the autonomic nervous system that prepared the body for vigorous physical activity, such as running, climbing a tree, or fighting for one's life (Cannon, 1929). These responses included increases in heart rate, blood pressure, blood flow to the muscles, rate of breathing, and utilization of glucose. They ended when the person escaped from the animal or conquered it.

Another physiologist, Hans Selye, studied the response pattern of the endocrine system and autonomic nervous system to a variety of dangerous or harmful stimuli, which he called the **stress response** (Selye, 1956). His research concentrated on the role of the adrenal glands. When an organism is stressed, its pituitary gland secretes **adrenocorticotropic hormone (ACTH),** which stimulates the adrenal glands to secrete a hormone known as **corticosterone.** This hormone produces some of the physiological changes that occur during the stress response, many of which Cannon had previously described. The hormone is vital; if an animal's adrenal glands are removed, it will die when it is subjected to mild stress that would have no effect on the health of a normal animal.

The stress response is useful in the short run, but it can have aftereffects that are deleterious to one's health. For example, although corticosterone helps the body ready itself for intense physical activity, it also suppresses the body's immune system and impairs the body's ability to heal itself when it is injured. In earlier times, our ancestors were presumably exposed to intermittent dangers, so the deleterious effects of the stress response did not manifest themselves. However, many investigators have noted that conditions in modern society are such that some people are stressed continuously, and thus are subjected to the harmful long-term effects of the flight-or-fight response.

Stress in Modern Society

Our society contains many opportunities for people to fulfill themselves with interesting jobs and diverting recreation, but it also contains many opportunities for people to encounter stressful situations. And people's responses to these situations have both direct and indirect effects on their health. Some situations can, by eliciting the stress response, increase people's susceptibility to gastrointestinal diseases, heart

TYPE **Z** BEHAVIOR
Drawing by D. Reilly; © 1987
The New Yorker Magazine, Inc.

attacks, strokes, diabetes, tuberculosis, influenza, pneumonia, and perhaps even cancer (Miller, 1983). Stressful situations can also impair health *indirectly,* by eliciting responses such as smoking, drinking, overeating, or drug abuse, all of which have harmful effects. In our society, the most common conditions that produce stress are excessive workloads, dissatisfaction with one's job or one's employer, competition in the workplace, or conflicts produced by trying to work while raising one's children (Krantz, Grunberg, and Baum, 1985). In these situations, neither flight nor fight is possible, so the body sustains a chronic stress reaction, which leads to impaired health.

Evidence gathered by epidemiologists strongly supports the conclusion that conditions present in our society can evoke stress reactions. For example, one of the most important risk factors in heart disease and stroke is hypertension (high blood pressure). In modern industrialized societies, most people's blood pressure rises as they grow older. In stable and relatively primitive societies, blood pressure is generally lower and does *not* increase with age. However, if people migrate from these societies into an industrialized one, their blood pressure takes on the pattern of their "civilized" counterparts (Cassel, 1973).

Coping with Stress

So what can be done? Two major variables affect the stress response: differences in the environment and differences between individuals. With respect to the environment, psychologists obviously have little control over the economy, the state of international tension, or the weather; but they can try to discover the environmental conditions that minimize the stressful impact of unpleasant circumstances. With respect to individual differences, it is important to note that events that cause a severe stress response in one person may have no effect on another. Some of these individual differences are learned, whereas others are undoubtedly affected by a person's genetic history.

First, let us consider the role of environmental factors. Many variables affect the degree to which a particular situation causes a stress response. For example, *knowing when the unpleasant event will occur* and *being able to make a response* greatly reduces the stressful effects of unpleasant experiences. If, without warning, an animal receives a painful shock to its feet from time to time, it will exhibit a stress response, and its health will consequently suffer. However, Weiss (1968, 1970, 1971) found that if the animals received signals that told them when shocks would occur and when they were safe, they showed fewer signs of stress. He also found that if they could turn the shocks off for a while by making the simple response of turning a wheel, they withstood the ordeal better. In all the experiments, the control animals received the same number of shocks as the experimental animals, so the differences in the health of the subjects could be attributed directly to the warning signal or to the ability of make a coping response. Weiss also exposed the rats to a conflict situation: The animals could make a response that would turn off the shock for a period of time, but making the response caused a single shock to be delivered. These animals suffered the worst stress of all groups. Thus, having control of a situation is not always an unmixed blessing.

Another environmental variable that affects the stress reaction is the degree of social support a person receives. When people have close ties to others and are part of a closely knit group, they tend to live longer and show fewer health-related signs of stress (Berkman and Syme, 1979). This fact points out the importance of social organizations in providing such support for people who have become isolated by the death or migration of family members.

Individual differences result from environmental and genetic factors. Obviously, genetic factors themselves cannot be changed, but if more is known about personality variables that affect the stress response, perhaps therapists can find ways to help people cope more effectively with their environment. It is clear that an understanding of the role of individual differences will require study of the ways that different kinds of variables interact with each other. For example, studies have shown that recovery from a heart attack is affected by stressful situations and by a person's ability to cope with them. Cromwell, Butterfield, Brayfield, and Curry (1977) studied three variables that affect recovery, and discovered some interesting interactions. *Participation, information,* and *anxiety* were all important factors. If people participated actively in recovery, then receiving information about their illness increased their chances of recovery. However, if they did not participate actively, then receiving the information *reduced* their chances of recovery, perhaps by making them feel more helpless. In addition, information helped people who initially were anxious, but harmed people who were not. Clearly, no simple set of rules will tell a physician or psychologist how to help people cope with their illness. Instead, different people need to be treated in different ways.

One of the most important attempts to relate personality to the ability to cope with stress was made by Friedman and Rosenman (1959), who identified a behavior pattern that appeared to predict susceptibility to cardiovascular disease. They characterized the disease-prone **Type A pattern** as one of excessive competitive drive, impatience, hostility, fast movements, and rapid speech. People with the **Type B pattern** were less competitive, more patient, more easygoing and tolerant, and moved and talked more slowly; they were also less likely to suffer from cardiovascular disease. Friedman and Rosenman developed a questionnaire that distinguished these two types of people. And indeed, several studies found that Type A people were more likely than Type B people to have heart attacks (Review Panel, 1981). However, more recent studies suggest that although the classification scheme captures some personality variables that predict susceptibility to cardiovascular disease, it also captures some that are not (Matthews, 1984). It remains for future research to distinguish better between the two categories.

If some personality characteristics cause a

Stressful situations in which neither flight nor fight is possible can have serious health consequences, such as cardiovascular disease.

person to cope poorly with stressful situations, then perhaps it is possible to change these characteristics, so that people will be less likely to suffer from stress-related health problems. Indeed, attempts have been made to change people's personality from Type A to Type B (Suinn, 1982; Thoresen, Friedman, Gill, and Ulmer, 1982). Although some success has been reported, further study will be needed to determine whether behavioral intervention aimed at changing the Type A characteristics will provide enough of a change in a person's risk of heart disease to justify the time and expense that the effort requires. Studies indicate that behavior patterns such as smoking, overeating, and abuse of alcohol account for approximately 50 percent of the mortality from the ten leading causes of death in the United States (Center for Disease Control, 1980). Thus, finding out how to alter these behaviors may be the most important task of psychologists interested in improving people's health.

■ What are the elements of the stress response, and what are its results?
■ What are some conditions that contribute to stress reactions, and some conditions that may modify it?

CHAPTER SUMMARY

1. Emotions are the feelings produced by motivationally relevant situations. Psychologists have studied the situations that produce emotions, the behaviors associated with them, and the physiological changes that accompany them.

2. The effect of emotions on social behavior is seen in the facial gestures that we make to express our feelings to each other. Darwin believed that the expressions of emotion by facial gestures was innate and that muscular movements were inherited behavioral patterns. Recent evidence supports this: emotional expressions are innate behavior patterns.

3. Emotional expression is a social behavior. The fact that infants imitate people's facial expressions suggests that imitation is an innate tendency. Perhaps the function of imitation is to evoke similar emotions in the receiver so that the receiver will engage in an appropriate behavior.

4. Expressions of emotion may be masked, modulated, or simulated according to culturally determined display rules. But even when a person attempts to mask his or her expression of emotion, some leakage occurs, particularly in movements of the body.

5. Several theories of emotion have been based on a functional analysis of the biological significance of emotional displays. Tomkins suggests that there are nine primary emotions, based on innate patterns of body movement and facial expression. These expressions communicate useful information to other members of the species. Plutchik's classification of species-typical behaviors presents a model in which emotions can differ in their intensity and some emotions can combine, forming composites.

6. The James-Lange theory is a physiological explanation of emotion that states that emotion-producing situations elicit an appropriate set of physiological responses (trembling, sweating, increased heart rate, etc.). The situations elicit behaviors. The brain receives sensory feedback from the organs that produce these responses, and the feedback constitutes emotion. In other words, emotional states are not the causes of these reactions but the results.

7. Cannon's criticism of the James-Lange theory, one point of which was that visceral changes (of the internal organs) are too slow to be a source of feeling, has been disputed by recent evidence. In Hohman's study, people with spinal cord damage showed a lack of emotional intensity because they had lost feedback from their senses. However, behavior was not necessarily affected, so emotional feelings and behaviors may be at least somewhat independent.

8. Emotions are undoubtedly not the products of automatic processes or conscious deliberations but involve both factors. Experiments involving placebos rather than a drug showed that subjects could tolerate greater pain (and control an emotional state), showing that cognitive assessment is an important factor.

9. Recent investigations have suggested that emotional responses involve the activity of the limbic system and the hypothalamus. Electrical stimulation of part of the limbic system can elicit a variety of physiological responses. In humans, such stimulation can result in feelings of pleasure, anger, fear, or rage.

10. Stress response is a physiological mechanism that activates the endocrine system and the autonomic nervous system when harmful or dangerous stimuli are present. The pituitary gland secretes adrenocorticotropic hormone (ACTH), which stimulates the adrenal glands to secrete the hormone corticosterone. This produces physiological changes, such as increases in heart rate, blood pressure, blood flow to the muscles, rate of breathing, etc.

11. Modern society has many long-term stressful situations. The stress response can have harmful after effects, increasing people's susceptibility to gastrointestinal diseases, heart attacks, strokes, and other illnesses. An important attempt to relate personality to the ability to cope with stress is the identification of Type A pattern (a person with excessive competitive drive, impatience, hostility, fast movements, and rapid speech) and Type B pattern (a person who is less competitive, more patient, easygoing and tolerant, and moves and talks more slowly). Type A pattern seems to be more susceptible to cardiovascular disease.

KEY TERMS

adrenocorticotropic hormone (ACTH) A hormone secreted by the pituitary gland, which stimulates the adrenal gland.

catastrophic reaction Severe and overwhelming depression in a person who has sustained brain damage, usually in the left hemisphere.

corticosterone A hormone secreted by the adrenal gland which produces some of the physiological changes that occur during the stress reponse.

display rules Culturally determined rules that modify the expression of emotion in a particular situation.

emotion A display of feelings that is evoked when important things happen to people.

flight-or-fight reaction Hormonal secretions and changes in the autonomic nervous system that prepare the body for vigorous physical activity.

indifference reaction A disorder produced by damage to the right hemisphere of the brain, characterized by a person's indifference to his or her neurological disorders.

James-Lange theory A theory of emotion that suggests that behaviors and physiological responses are directly elicited by situations, and that feelings of emotion are produced by feedback from these behaviors and responses.

leakage A subtle sign of emotion that is evident when people try to mask the expression of a strongly felt emotion.

limbic system A set of interconnected structures of the brain, important in emotional and species-typical behavior. Includes the amygdala, hippocampus, and part of the hypothalamus.

masking An attempt a person makes to hide an emotion.

modulation An attempt a person makes to exaggerate or minimize the expression of an emotion.

moods A person's tendency to react more strongly to situations that would be likely to evoke only mild emotional reactions in others.

simulation An attempt a person makes to express an emotion he or she does not actually feel.

stress response The response of the endocrine system and the autonomic nervous system to a variety of dangerous or harmful stimuli.

temperament A person's general disposition or pattern of affective reaction to various situations. Similar to mood but longer-lived.

Type A pattern A disease-prone lifestyle characterized by excessive competitive drive, impatience, hostility, fast movements, and rapid speech.

Type B pattern A lifestyle characterized by a lack of competitiveness, patience, an easygoing and tolerant attitude, and somewhat slow movements and speech. Type B individuals are less disease-prone than Type A individuals.

SOCIAL PROCESSES

All fundamental aspects of human behavior—from an infant's earliest attachment through to the development of sexuality, aggression, motivation, and cognition—are initiated and shaped by interactions with others. Even self-awareness, seemingly so private, is primarily a social phenomenon, for it requires language to be meaningful. In fact, most of what you think of as "you" is the product of interactions with others. Your personality, memories, desires—even your secrets—reflect your responses to your environment. Although stimuli from the physical environment keep you alive (by making you seek air, water, food, and physical security), it is the behavior of others that provides desirable or undesirable social stimuli and thus shapes your development as a person. In Part D we continue the investigation of human behavior, but our vantage point now is located outside the individual in an effort to understand our social relations.

Naturally enough, a central issue regarding human behavior is the degree to which we can influence or control it, for better or worse. The question, then, is: What is the *greatest* influence on human behavior? If we knew the answer to that, we might improve our lives by shaping the environment to derive the greatest benefit from that influence. We might turn people away from antisocial, abnormal behaviors that endanger themselves or others; we might steer people toward behaviors that enhance their potential for growth and happiness.

As scientists have sought valid theories and supporting evidence to explain the variety of human behavior, many ideas have been discarded along the way, including the belief that we are shaped solely by either genetics or the environment. Rather, our physical inheritance and social environment appear to interact throughout our lives to make us who we are. Some physical traits, like eye color, do result

solely from genetics; but height, weight, and left- or righthandedness can be influenced in part by a person's environment. Similarly, some behaviors and mental conditions (certain kinds of schizophrenia, Alzheimer's disease) are genetic in origin, whereas others are shaped primarily by one's social experiences.

"You know almost nothing about a kid from knowing if he is the oldest or the youngest. . . ."

When it comes to personality traits, ongoing research, such as that at the University of Minnesota, has studied identical twins who were separated at birth and reared apart. This research reveals that heritability accounts for 30 to 60 percent of a given trait. Until recently, it was generally assumed that the environment provided the remaining influence, from 40 to 70 percent, depending on the trait. It was also thought that the strongest environmental influence came from the family, with peers, teachers, and neighbors as secondary socializing agents. New research now indicates that the family's influence on personality traits is less uniform than has been assumed; in fact, "the family" itself is not the same for different children raised within it.

Several studies at the University of Texas compared the personalities, intelligence, and emotional adjustment of adopted children who, from infancy on, were raised by the same family. The researcher, John Loehlin, found a near-zero correlation among the children for traits of personality, and only slightly higher correlations for intelligence. Thus, there seems to be little evidence that a common family environment provides a common influence on these traits. In other studies of identical twins and fraternal twins reared by the same family, Loehlin determined that differences in personality between twins resulted from their different experiences—from environment—whereas their similarities in personality almost always could be traced to their common genetic inheritance. Ten other twin studies have reached similar conclusions, including one that compared twelve thousand adult twins in Sweden.

If the family does not exert a common influence on each child's personality, it does tend to shape children's attitudes similarly. Siblings are more likely to share religious and political affiliations than they are to exhibit similar personality traits. The important point here is that what children *do not share* within the common environment of the family is what shapes their development into unique persons. The family itself and the generally similar environment it provides to all its children have only slight effects on personality trait development. Far more important are the different experiences and perceptions that the children have; *these* are the environmental influences that truly shape personality.

Unique Experiences, Unique Personalities

What are the different experiences and perceptions that influence children within the same family, and why should they be so different? Is it simply birth order that makes each child's family experiences unique? Do parents give more attention to first-born children and have higher expectations of them than of younger brothers and sisters? Although some research (and popular wisdom) supports this idea, most research does not. "You know almost nothing about a kid from knowing if he is the oldest or the youngest," says psychologist Denise Daniels, of Stanford University. Instead, she and others are investigating "life events that make the major difference in how children turn out." To do so, Daniels has developed a scale by which siblings compare their feelings and experiences concerning their parents' love and attention, their jealousy of brothers and sisters, and their popularity with other children. Among the results so far are the findings that the child who feels closest to the father is most likely to expect and achieve more in a career; that the shyest children have the fewest problems with their siblings; and that the most sociable children feel closest to their sisters and brothers. We saw earlier that members of the same family often have different memories of events because they perceive and process the events differently. Patients in psychotherapy often complain that they were treated worse than their siblings, and no doubt they believe they were. Such beliefs are what make the family environment unique for each child, and they often lead to friction in the family. Psychologist Gene Brody, of the University of Georgia, has found that children perceive subtle differences in how parents respond to them and their siblings. They note and tally every compliment and complaint, every smile and frown, and they keep track of their own standing. The more differently a child is treated, the more hostile he or she is likely to be later.

Stella Chess, a psychiatrist at New York University Medical Center, notes that children themselves elicit variable responses from their parents and thus influence how they are treated compared with their sisters and brothers. If one child is moody and slow to adapt while another is easily approached and open to change, the parents are more likely to show the latter child signs of pleasure and approval. Many parents treat boys and girls differently, expecting all their sons to enjoy "roughhousing" and all their daughters to behave "like a lady." A sickly child or an especially gifted one may, to siblings, seem to get all the attention. There are many reasons to treat children differently, and many of the reasons are valid. In fact, parents who attempt to treat all their children identically run the risk of *mistreating* some of them. By failing to adjust to each child's tempera-

ment, strengths, and weaknesses, parents can unwittingly make a child feel inadequate.

The new research undercuts many of our assumptions about family life. Most notably, the family's influence as a socializing force seems to be less pervasive and seems to operate differently than has been supposed. On the one hand, genetics—not the family environment—accounts for many of the similarities among siblings; on the other hand, differences in personality traits are related to each child's experiences and perceptions within the family. The idea that siblings share a genetic basis for similar traits but develop differently in response to unique personal environments enriches our understanding of how nature and nurture interact. The idea is new, however, and not all psychologists would agree. Many behavioral scientists remain skeptical, maintaining that, in a uniform environment, children are affected almost identically by their families. Others wait to see whether this new view of family life will be supported when researchers look beyond the middle-class American families represented in these studies.

Whether this line of research is upheld or turns in other directions, for now it offers some intriguing explanations for why each child in a family develops uniquely. Indeed, for all the similarities among the billions of people alive right now, we cannot be subdivided into twelve astrological signs, or into four humors, or into seven days of the week. Rather, psychologists are finding evidence that we subdivide into billions—unique billions.

Social Psychology: Attitudes and Attribution

In certain ways, we are all practicing social psychologists. Each of us uses principles of social psychology to construct theories about why people behave the way they do. Within the field of social psychology, the process by which people explain the causes of events and behavior is called *attribution*.

Although the scientific investigation of attribution is a recent phenomenon, it has contributed to an increased understanding of a number of traditional research topics in social psychology, such as attitudes and self-perception. For example, we now know that our attitudes are influenced by the attributions we make about other people who hold similar or dissimilar attitudes. We also know that we observe our own behavior in ways that resemble our observations of others and make similar attributions about its causes.

One interesting question that has received a great deal of attention from social psychologists is whether attitudes affect behavior, or whether behavior affects attitudes. We usually think that our attitudes cause us to behave in certain ways, but research has demonstrated that sometimes we change our attitudes to correspond with our behavior. How do we explain differences between what we say (our attitudes) and how we act (our behavior)? In this chapter you will learn how psychologists have tried to provide answers to these and other interesting questions about attitudes: How do people develop strong attitudes? Why are some attitudes more resistant to change than others? What is the most effective way of changing someone's attitude?

The task of the research social psychologist is complex and sometimes controversial. When studying social phenomena, closely controlled laboratory studies are not always possible. Often researchers must stage realistic laboratory situations using confederates who act as if they are fellow subjects. Is this practice deceptive? Are the results of these experimental situations valid? Can they be generalized to real-world situations? As you read the evidence, you will discover how researchers have tried to overcome these challenges.

389

ATTRIBUTION

Our behavior is affected by stimuli in our environment, and aside from the necessities of life, such as food, water, and air, the behavior of other people provides our most important reinforcing and punishing stimuli. Our social environment is at least as important as our physical one. Thus, learning what kind of behavior to expect from particular people in particular sit-

Social psychologists attempt to explain why people behave the way they do. Explaining behavior often requires the study of attitudes.

uations is a crucial ability. Knowing why people act as they do may help us predict what they will do in a particular situation, so that we may be able to promote pleasant interactions and to avoid unpleasant ones. This knowledge will probably also cause us to be less susceptible to other people's attempts to manipulate us. We may even be able to use our skills in analyzing social interactions to understand our own behavior.

The process by which people infer the causes of other people's behavior is called **attribution.** The study of attribution has had a profound impact on social psychology, contributing to increased understanding of persuasion, interpersonal attraction, group behavior, self-evaluation, and attitudes and opinions.

The Implicit Psychologist

As we saw in Chapter 8, everyone who is able to use a language knows a large set of complex rules of grammar, but few people know how to describe those rules. Similarly, although we all attribute causes to events every day, often without giving the matter much thought, the reasons for the choices we make are not always obvious to us. Our knowledge of human behavior is based on attributions. From them we construct theories of social behavior. These theories allow us to organize our observations and to predict the probable outcomes of our own behavior. If our theories are correct, we can affect the behavior of other people in ways that benefit us.

Implicit psychology involves both attribution and the formation of private theories of reality. Unlike the theories of psychologists, in which the methods, assumptions, and data are explicitly stated, implicit psychological theories are private and often cannot be explained by their owner. Indeed, people do not regard their implicit theories as theories at all, but as facts. Consequently, they tend not to revise the theories when provided with contradictory data. Many prejudices and superstitions can best be understood as products of faulty implicit theories of human nature.

Kelley (1967, 1971) has suggested that we reach most of our conclusions about the causes of events by the **covariance method.** *Covariance* refers to a phenomenon in which two events are observed to vary together or simply to occur together, like thunder and lightning. According to Kelley's definition of the covariance method, "The effect is attributed to that condition which is present when the effect is present and which is absent when the effect is absent" (1967, p. 194). For example, if John blushes, stammers, and becomes inarticulate whenever Susan is in the room but acts and speaks normally when she is not, we will decide that her presence flusters him.

Scientists use the covariance method to determine the causes of natural phenomena when they perform an experiment. Occasionally, we, too, perform "experiments" to test our hypotheses: *I wonder if she's interested in me. I'll look directly at her and see if she smiles back.* More often, however, we observe other people's behavior and form conclusions based on our past experience. In normal social situations, most attributions involve only the gathering of data and the formation of hypotheses.

Disposition Versus Situation

The primary classification that we make concerning the causes of a person's behavior is the relative importance of **situational factors** versus **dispositional factors** (Heider, 1958). As we will see in Chapter 15, there is great debate among personality theorists over whether behavior is determined more by enduring traits or by situational factors. One of the tasks of socialization is to learn what behaviors are expected in various kinds of situations. In this way we learn both what to expect from others and how to behave so as not to elicit disapproval. Once we learn that in certain situations most people act in a specific way, we expect others to act similarly in those situations. For example, when people are introduced, they are expected to look at each other, smile, say something like "How do you do?" or "It's nice to meet you," and perhaps offer to shake the other person's hand. If people act in conventional ways in given situations, we are not surprised. Their behavior appears to be dictated by social custom—by the characteristics of the situation —and we therefore learn very little about them as individuals.

As we get to know other people, we also learn what to expect from them as individuals.

This man parachuted into a stadium during a baseball game. According to attribution theory, we would attribute his unusual behavior to dispositional factors.

We learn about their *dispositions*—the kinds of behaviors that they tend to engage in. We learn to characterize people as friendly, generous, suspicious, pessimistic, or greedy by observing their behavior in a variety of situations. Sometimes we even make inferences from a single observation. If someone's behavior is seriously at variance with the **situational demands,** we attribute his or her behavior to internal, or dispositional, causes (Jones and Davis, 1965). For example, if we see a person refuse to hold a door open for someone in a wheelchair, we assign some negative personality characteristics to him or her. Similarly, if a young boy receives some candy and shares it with his little sister, we attribute a generous nature to the child, because we assume that young children are typically selfish.

In contrast, if we observe that a person conforms to situational demands, we tend to give his or her behavior very little significance and do not use it to make dispositional attributions.

This phenomenon is called **discounting.** For example, if someone asks an acquaintance for the loan of a coin to make a telephone call, we do not conclude that the person is especially kind and generous if he or she complies. The request is reasonable and costs little; the situational demand is to lend the money. However, if the person has some change but refuses to lend it, we readily attribute dispositional factors such as stinginess or meanness to that person.

Sources of Information

Kelley (1967, 1971, 1973) has also suggested that we attribute the behavior of other people to external (situational) or internal (dispositional) causes on the basis of *consensus, consistency,* and *distinctiveness.*

If a behavior is **consensual**—that is, if it is shared by a large number of people—we tend to attribute the behavior to external causes. The behavior is assumed to be demanded by the situation. For example, if the weather is hot and you see a group of people splashing in the water of a fountain, you will probably conclude that they are trying to get some relief from the oppressive heat. You attribute their behavior to external causes. However, if you see only one person cavorting in the water while others watch, you will probably conclude that he or she is showing off. If only one person does something, he or she must be doing it for personal, or internal, reasons.

We also base our attributions on **consistency**— that is, on whether a person's behavior occurs reliably over time. For example, if you meet someone for the first time and notice that she speaks slowly and without much expression, stands in a slouching posture, and sighs occasionally, you will probably conclude that she has a sad and listless disposition. Now suppose that after she has left, you mention to a friend that the young woman seems very passive and depressed. Your friend says, "No, I know her pretty well, and she's usually very cheerful and friendly." With this new evidence about her behavior, you will reassess your conclusion and perhaps wonder what happened to make her act so sad. If a person's pattern of behavior is consistent, we attribute the behavior to internal causes; inconsistent behaviors lead us to seek external causes.

Distinctiveness is closely related to consistency. If a person behaves in the same way under different circumstances, we attribute the behavior to personality characteristics—to his or her disposition. However, if the person's behavior varies according to circumstances, we tend to attribute the behavior to external causes—the situation. For example, suppose a mother observes that her little boy is generally polite and well behaved, but that whenever he plays with the child across the street, he comes home with his clothes dirty and acts sassy toward her until she has rebuked him a few times. She does not conclude that her boy is rude or messy; she will probably conclude that the child across the street has a bad influence on him. Because her child's rude and messy behavior occurs only under a distinctive circumstance (the presence of the child across the street), she attributes it to external causes.

- What is attribution? Why is it important to the social psychologist?
- What is the difference between disposition and situation as explanations for behavior?
- What sources of explanation do people use to make attributions?

Attributional Biases

When we make attributions, we do not function as impartial, dispassionate observers; our biases affect our conclusions about the actor (the person performing the behavior). This section describes the more important biases and some research into their causes.

The Fundamental Attributional Error

When attributing the behavior of an actor to possible causes, an observer tends to overestimate the significance of dispositional factors and underestimate the significance of situational factors. If we see a driver turn in front of an oncoming car, we are more likely to say "She is a terrible driver" than "She was distracted by her children yelling in the back

TABLE 13.1

Ratings of general knowledge of self and opponent in a mock quiz game

Condition	Measure	
	Rating of Self	Rating of Opponent
Subjects devised questions		
Subject as questioner	53.5[a]	50.6[b]
Subject as contestant	41.3[a,c]	66.8[b,c]
Experimenter prepared questions		
Subject as questioner	54.1	52.5
Subject as contestant	47.0	50.3

Note: Scores with the same superscripts differed significantly from each other.
Adapted from Ross, L.D., Amabile, T.M., and Steinmetz, J.L. Journal of Personality and Social Psychology, 1977, 35, 485–494.

seat." Ross (1977) calls this bias the **fundamental attributional error.** Many of the other attributional biases can be explained as consequences of this one.

The fundamental attributional error is remarkably potent. Even when evidence indicates otherwise, people seem to prefer dispositional explanations to situational ones. A study by Ross, Amabile, and Steinmetz (1977) demonstrates this tendency. Pairs of students played a contrived "quiz game" in which the questioner was permitted to ask any question he or she wanted to, no matter how obscure or esoteric. In this situation a person can easily stump someone else by choosing some topic that he or she knows more about than the average person. After the game the subjects were asked to rate both their own level of general knowledge and that of their opponent. Table 13.1 lists the ratings. Subjects who played the role of contestant tended to rate the questioner as much more knowledgeable than themselves. (See top row, Table 13.1.) Apparently they attributed the difficult questions to factors internal to their opponents rather than to the situation. When the subjects served as questioners, they did not make an internal attribution; they rated themselves as only slightly more knowledgeable than the person they questioned. (See bottom row, Table 13.1.) Thus, a person is less likely to make the fundamental attributional error when he or she is the actor (the person who is performing the behavior—in this case, the questioner).

Why do we make the fundamental attributional error when we observe the behavior of others but not when we explain the causes of our own behavior? Jones and Nisbett (1971) suggested two possible reasons. First, we have a different focus of attention when we view ourselves. When we ourselves are doing something, we see the world around us more clearly than we see our own behavior. However, when we observe someone else doing something, we focus our attention on what is most salient and relevant: that person's behavior, and not the situation in which he or she is placed.

A second possible reason for these differences in attribution is that different types of information are available to us about our own behavior and that of other people. We have more information about our own consistency (we are more likely to remember how we acted under the same circumstances at different times), and we also have a better notion of which stimuli we are attending to.

False Consensus

The second attributional error is the tendency of an observer to perceive his or her own response as representative of a general consensus. Thus, if someone disagrees with the observer or behaves in a way that the observer would not, the actor is seen as deviant. This error has been called **false consensus.**

Ross, Greene, and House (1977) asked college students to walk around campus for thirty minutes while wearing a large sandwich-board sign that read "EAT AT JOE'S" as part of a study on communication techniques. After deciding whether they would wear the sign, the students were asked to estimate how many of their peers would volunteer. Both those who agreed to wear the sign and those who refused estimated that approximately two-thirds of their peers would do likewise. The results indicate that people's estimates of what other people will do are influenced by their own inclinations.

One explanation accounts for false consensus in terms of defense of ego or self-esteem. Presumably, people do not like to think of themselves as being too different from other people, so they prefer to think that most other people will act in the way that they do.

Another possible explanation is that people tend to place themselves in the company of others who are similar to themselves (Ross, 1977). As we will see in the next chapter, an important variable in interpersonal attraction is similarity in behavior and attitudes. Thus, when people conclude that other people are more similar to themselves than they actually are, the error may be a result of a sampling bias rather than of a need to minimize damage to their egos.

We tend to attribute our own success to internal causes.

Motivational Biases

Both of the attributional biases discussed so far are logical, or intellectual. Others appear to be related to motivation—that is, to processes with personal significance for the observer.

Credit for Success, Blame for Failure. People tend to attribute successful outcomes of their own behavior to internal causes, while they attribute their failures to external causes. For example, a person is likely to perceive a high score on a test as a reflection of his or her intelligence and motivation but to attribute a low score to an unfair examination, boring and trivial subject matter, or lack of opportunity to study properly. Similarly, football players and coaches tend to credit their wins to internal causes such as determination and skill but blame their losses on external causes such as luck or injuries (Lau and Russell, 1980).

Johnson, Feigenbaum, and Weiby (1964) enlisted students in an educational psychology course in a trial program of teaching mathematics to fourth-grade boys. The experimenters arranged the tests so that the performance of some boys would appear to improve during the teaching sessions, while the performance of others would stay the same or get worse. The "teachers" who had worked with boys whose test performance improved later cited their own teaching skills as the cause. Those who had worked with boys who did not improve blamed the poor performance on the low motivation or intelligence of the learner.

The perception of outside observers is quite different from the perception of a person who has personal involvement with the success or failure of an enterprise. Beckman (1970) performed an experiment similar to the one I just described but obtained attributional judgments both from the teachers and from observers. Unlike the teachers, the observers blamed the teachers for the students' poor performance but attributed good performance to the students' intelligence and motivation.

A review of the literature has shown that people are not inevitably self-serving in their attributions (Arkin, Cooper, and Kolditz, 1980). For example, Ross, Bierbrauer, and Polly (1974) devised an extremely realistic teacher-student situation in which the teachers were able to make detailed observations of their students' performance. With more information available, they were less likely to blame the students for their failure while taking credit for success. Thus, although we give ourselves the benefit of the doubt when the causes of success or failure are not clear, we will make attributions that are not favorable to ourselves when our observations demand them.

The Illusion of Personal Causation. Independent of the tendency to take credit for our successes and to avoid blame for our failures, we appear to have a tendency to assume that when we do something, our action will have an effect on subsequent events, even when logically these events cannot be related to our behavior. We have a fallacious belief in **personal causation.** In an experiment illustrating this phenomenon, Langer (1975) allowed some subjects to select a fifty-cent lottery ticket and simply handed one to others. When asked later how much money they would accept to sell their ticket, the subjects who had been given a ticket were willing to sell it for approximately two dollars, whereas those who had selected their ticket wanted nearly nine dollars. The element of choice led to an illusion of personal causation; the chosen ticket was perceived as more likely to be a winner.

The illusion of personal causation may be an innate tendency. More likely, however, it is simply a generalization from our previous experience with reality. When we intend our behavior to have an effect on the environment, it often does. We push something and it moves. We say something and other people react. Thus, we come to regard our own efforts as causal. (Be careful to read the word as *cau-sal*, not *cas-u-al*.) Because some people are more successful than others at making things happen, different people will have differing degrees of belief in the potency of their efforts. This important personality variable is discussed in Chapter 15.

■ What is the fundamental attribution error? How does research help to explain why it occurs?
■ What is the error of false consensus?
■ What are the two most important motivational biases in attribution? What are the research findings on these biases?

ATTITUDES AND THEIR FORMATION

Another example of the discrepancy between what a person believes and what he or she actually does is demonstrated in the study of attitudes. The investigation of attitudes and factors that influence their change formerly constituted the bulk of research in social psychology (Eagly and Himmelfarb, 1978). During the 1960s, interest in the topic sharply declined, principally because many studies found a low correlation between people's expressed attitudes and their actual observed behavior. However, in the past few years experiments have shown that under certain conditions people's attitudes and behavior are rather closely associated. Once psychologists were able to demonstrate that attitudes really could predict behavior, interest in the field revived.

Formation of Attitudes

The ways in which we form our attitudes are somewhat similar to the ways in which we are persuaded to change them. However, the process of attitude formation is usually more subtle than that of attitude change. Attitudes have both an *affective* and a *cognitive* component. The affective component consists of the kinds of feelings that a particular topic arouses. The cognitive component consists of a set of beliefs about that topic.

Affective Components of Attitudes

Affective components of attitudes can be very strong and pervasive. The bigot feels uneasy in the presence of people from a certain religious, racial, or ethnic group; the nature lover feels exhilaration from a pleasant walk through the woods. These feelings were probably established principally through direct or vicarious classical conditioning.

Direct classical conditioning is straightforward. Suppose you meet someone who seems to take delight in embarrassing you. She makes clever, sarcastic remarks that disparage your intelligence, looks, and personality. Unfortunately, her remarks are so clever that your attempts to defend yourself make you appear

Affective components of attitudes are slow to change. Although many Americans express attitudes of equality between the sexes, it was not until 1984 that a woman was nominated to a vice-presidential ticket by a major party.

even more foolish. After a few encounters with this person, it is likely that the sight of her or the sound of her voice will immediately evoke feelings of dislike and fear in you. Your attitude toward her will be negative.

Vicarious classical conditioning undoubtedly plays a major role in transmitting parents' attitudes to their children. People are skilled at detecting even subtle signs of fear, hatred, and other negative emotional states in other people,

especially when they know them well. Thus, children perceive their parents' prejudices and fears even if these feelings are unspoken. Children who see their parents recoil in disgust at the sight of members of some ethnic group are likely to learn to react in the same way. Humans have a strong tendency to acquire classically conditioned responses themselves by observing them to be elicited in other people by the conditional stimulus (Berger, 1962).

The affective component of attitudes tends to be rather resistant to change; it persists for some time even after a person has altered his or her opinion on a particular subject. For example, a person may successfully overcome a childhood racial prejudice and be completely fair and impartial in dealing with people of other races. This person, however, may experience unpleasant emotional arousal at the sight of a racially mixed couple. This discrepancy between belief and feelings often makes people feel guilty.

Cognitive Components of Attitudes

We acquire most beliefs about a particular topic quite directly: We hear or read a fact or opinion, or other people reinforce our statements expressing a particular attitude. Someone may say to a child: "Blacks are lazy" or "You can't trust whites" or "We Czechs are better than those Slovaks." A group of racially prejudiced people will probably ostracize a person who makes positive statements about the group or groups they are prejudiced against. Conversely, conscientious parents may applaud their child's positive statements about other ethnic groups or about social issues such as environmental conservation.

Children, in particular, form attitudes through imitating, or **modeling,** the behavior of people who play an important role in their lives. Children usually repeat opinions expressed by their parents. In the United States, many children label themselves as Democrats or Republicans long before they know what these political parties stand for. Often they ask their parents, "What are we, Republicans or Democrats?" without considering whether they might have any choice in the matter. The tendency to identify with the family unit (and later, with peer groups) provides a strong incentive to adopt the group's attitudes.

ATTITUDES AND BEHAVIOR

Do Attitudes Predict Behavior?

People do not always behave as their expressed attitudes and beliefs would lead us to expect. In a classic example, LaPiere (1934) drove through the United States with a Chinese couple. They stopped at over 250 restaurants and lodging places and were refused service only once. Several months after their trip, LaPiere wrote to the owners of the places they had visited and asked whether they would serve Chinese people. The response was overwhelmingly negative; 92 percent of those who responded said that they would not. Clearly, their behavior gave less evidence of racial bias than their expressed attitudes did.

As I mentioned earlier, many studies in the 1960s (such as Wicker, 1969) observed a poor relationship between attitudes and behavior, and Abelson (1972) even suggested that the concept of attitudes be dispensed with altogether. However, subsequent studies have shown that attitudes and behavior are related, although several factors can affect the relation.

Degree of Specificity

One important variable that affects the correspondence between a person's attitude and behavior is the degree of specificity. If you measure a person's general attitude toward a topic, you will be less likely to be able to predict his or her behavior; behaviors, unlike attitudes, are specific events. As the attitude being measured becomes more specific, the person's behavior becomes more predictable. For example, Weigel, Vernon, and Tognacci (1974) measured people's attitudes toward a series of topics that increased in specificity from "a pure environment" to "the Sierra Club" (an American organization that supports environmental causes). They used the subjects' attitudes to predict whether they would volunteer for various activities to benefit the Sierra Club.

Children form attitudes by modeling the attitudes of their parents: "It's not whether you win or lose, but how you play the game."

TABLE 13.2

Correlation between willingness to join or work for the Sierra Club and various measures of related attitudes

Attitude Scale	Correlation
Importance of a pure environment	.06
Pollution	.32
Conservation	.24
Attitude toward the Sierra Club	.68

Based on Wiegel, R. H., Vernon, D.T.A., and Tognacci, L.N. *Journal of Personality and Social Psychology*, 1974, 30, 724–728.

Table 13.2 shows the results. A person's attitude toward environmentalism was a poor predictor of whether he or she would volunteer, but his or her attitude toward the Sierra Club itself was a much better predictor. For example, a person might favor a pure environment but also dislike organized clubs or have little time to spare for meetings. This person would express a positive attitude toward a pure environment but would not join the club or volunteer for any activities to support it.

Self-Attribution

Another variable that affects the relation between attitude and subsequent behavior is the way in which the person has formed his or her attitude. If a person has developed an attitude that is based on the opinions or persuasive arguments of other people, the attitude will usually be a poor predictor of behavior. In contrast, an attitude formed through **self-attribution** is likely to be an excellent predictor of behavior.

Self-attribution occurs because we are all self-observers. We see how we behave in various situations and make attributions about our own dispositions, just as we make them about other people's. If we observe that someone else habitually avoids talking with fat people, we can conclude that the person has a negative attitude toward them. If we find ourselves avoiding fat people, we can make a similar self-attribution.

A number of studies have found that when a person has had the opportunity to perform relevant behaviors, he or she is more likely to express attitudes that are consistent with subsequent behaviors. For example, Regan and Fazio

(1977) had some subjects spend time playing with five puzzles; others merely heard descriptions of the puzzles. All subjects were asked to rate their interest in each puzzle.

Later, the subjects were given some "free time" during which they could play with the puzzles if they chose. The correlation between ratings and later activity with the puzzles was .54 for subjects who had actually played with the puzzles, but only .20 for those who had merely heard them described. Therefore, it appears that attitudes that are based on people's previous behavior are better predictors of their future behavior.

- How do affective and cognitive components contribute to the formation of attitudes?
- What are two factors that can affect the correspondence between a person's attitudes and behavior?

Does Behavior Affect Attitudes?

Cognitive Dissonance Theory

Although we usually regard our attitudes as causes of our behavior, our behavior also affects our attitudes. Two major theories attempt to explain the effects of behavior on attitude formation: cognitive dissonance and self-perception. The oldest theory, developed by Leon Festinger (1957), is that of **cognitive dissonance.** According to Festinger, when we perceive a discrepancy between our attitudes and behavior, between our behavior and self-image, or between one attitude and another, an unpleasant state of dissonance results. In the earlier example, a person feels guilty if she believes herself to be racially unprejudiced but finds that she avoids the company of racially mixed couples. The woman experiences a conflict between her belief in her own lack of prejudice and the evidence of prejudice from her behavior. This conflict produces dissonance, which is aversive.

In Festinger's view, an important source of human motivation is **dissonance reduction;** the aversive state of dissonance motivates a person to reduce it. (Because dissonance reduction involves the removal of an aversive stimulus it serves as a reinforcer.) A person can achieve dissonance reduction by (1) reducing the importance of one of the dissonant elements, (2) adding consonant elements, or (3) changing one of the dissonant elements.

Suppose a student believes that he is very intelligent, but he invariably receives bad grades in his courses. Because the obvious prediction is that intelligent people get good grades, the discrepancy causes the student to experience dissonance. To reduce this dissonance, he may decide that grades are not important, and that intelligence is not very closely related to grades. He is using strategy 1, by reducing the importance of one of the dissonant elements—the fact that he received bad grades in his courses. Or the student can dwell on the belief that his professors were unfair or that his job leaves him little time to study. In this case, he is using strategy 2 to reduce dissonance by adding consonant elements—other factors can account for his poor grades and hence explain the discrepancy between his perceived intelligence and grades. Finally, the student can use strategy 3 to change one of the dissonant elements: he can either start getting good grades or revise his opinion of his own intelligence. Other factors (how hard he is willing to work, how important it is for him to feel that he is intelligent) will determine which of these changes he makes in his opinions.

Induced Compliance. Most people believe that although it is possible to induce someone to do something, it is much harder to get someone to change his or her opinion. However, Festinger's theory of cognitive dissonance and supporting experimental evidence indicate otherwise. Under the right conditions, when people are coerced into doing something or are paid to do so, the act of compliance causes a change in their attitudes.

Dissonance theory predicts that dissonance occurs when a person's behavior has outcomes that are harmful to self-esteem; there is a conflict between the person's belief in his or her own worth and the fact that he or she has done something that damages this belief. The person will then seek to justify the behavior. For example, suppose you are having a picnic at a park. While idly throwing stones, you happen to break a beer bottle that someone carelessly discarded. You think vaguely about retrieving the broken pieces of glass, but somehow you do not get around to doing it. Later you hear the cries of a little girl who has been playing nearby and has cut her feet badly on the broken glass. You will feel ashamed of yourself for not having picked up the pieces of broken glass, but you will probably try to lighten your share of the blame by saying to yourself, "The slob who left the bottle there is really responsible" or "Why weren't that girl's parents watching her more closely?"

Similarly, a poorly paid vacuum-cleaner sales representative is likely to convince himself that the shoddy merchandise he sells is actually good. Otherwise, he must question why he works for such a company that pays him poorly and requires him to lie to prospective customers about the quality of the product in order to make a sale.

Festinger and Carlsmith (1959) verified this observation by having subjects perform very boring tasks such as putting a number of spools on a tray, dumping them out, putting them on the tray again, dumping them out again, and so on. After this exercise, the experimenter asked each subject whether he or she would help out in the study by trying to convince the next subject that the task was very interesting. Some subjects received one dollar for doing so, others received twenty dollars. Control subjects were paid nothing; their assistance was presumably an expression of willingness to help the experimenter. It was predicted that the subjects who were paid only one dollar would perceive the task as being relatively interesting. They had been induced to lie to a "fellow student" (actually, a confederate of the experimenters) for a paltry sum. Like the vacuum-cleaner sales representative, they should convince themselves of the worth of the experiment so as to maintain their self-esteem. Figure 13.1 on the following page shows that the poorly paid subjects did in fact rate the task better than control subjects or those who were well paid. Clearly, our actions *do* have an effect on our attitudes; when faced with inconsistency between our behavior and our attitudes, we often change our attitudes to suit our behavior.

Steele and Liu (1981) obtained evidence that supports the suggestion that self-esteem plays a role in attitude changes motivated by cognitive dissonance. They induced subjects to write essays containing arguments against providing

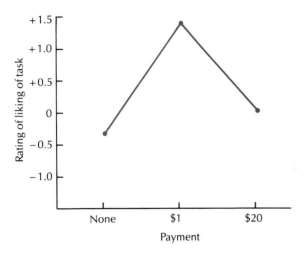

FIGURE 13.1

Ratings of liking of task by people who received no payment or payment of one dollar or twenty dollars. (Based on data from Festinger, L., and Carlsmith, J.M. *Journal of Abnormal and Social Psychology*, 1959, *58*, 203–210.)

further state funding for facilities for the handicapped. We might reasonably expect that doing so would have negative effects on the subjects' self-esteem. The experimenters told some of the subjects that after they wrote the essay they would be asked to help blind students by recording midterm and final exams onto cassettes. Presumably, this chance to help handicapped people would counteract any harm to self-esteem that would be produced by writing an essay contrary to the interests of handicapped people. Indeed, Steele and Liu found that an opinion shift occurred only in those subjects who had not been told that they would be asked to help blind students.

Evidence for Arousal. Croyle and Cooper (1983) have obtained physiological evidence that induced compliance produces arousal, indicating the likely presence of the aversive drive that Festinger originally hypothesized. The experimenters chose as their subjects Princeton University students who disagreed with the assertion "Alcohol use should be totally banned from the Princeton campus and eating clubs." The subjects were induced to write an essay containing strong and forceful arguments in favor of the assertion or in opposition to it. While the subjects were writing the essay, the experimenters measured the electri-

cal conductance of their skin, which is known to be a good indicator of the physiological arousal that accompanies stress. Some subjects were simply told to write the essay. Other subjects were told that their participation was completely voluntary and that they were free to leave at any time; they even signed a form emphasizing the voluntary nature of the task. Of course, all subjects felt social pressure to continue the study, and all of them did. However, those who were simply told to write the essay should feel less personal responsibility for what they wrote and would therefore be expected to experience less cognitive dissonance than those who believed that they had exercised free choice in deciding to participate.

The results were as the experimenters had predicted; subjects in the "free choice" condition who had written an essay that contradicted their original opinion showed both a change in opinion and evidence of physiological arousal. Those subjects who were simply told to write the essay or who wrote arguments that they had originally agreed with showed little sign of arousal or attitude change. (See Figure 13.2.)

Other evidence suggests that the physiological arousal that accompanies conflict is necessary for attitude changes. For example, Cooper, Zanna, and Taves (1978) found that sedatives reduced attitude changes and that amphetamine increased attitude changes in an induced-compliance experiment similar to the one I just described. Presumably, the drugs reduced or increased the unpleasant arousal caused by the conflict. In another study on induced compliance, Steele, Southwick, and Critchlow (1981) found that a small drink of an alcoholic beverage reduced attitude changes. The authors suggested that one of the causes of excessive alcohol consumption might be the ability of alcohol to remove unpleasant arousal caused by dissonance.

Conflict Resolution. The theory of cognitive dissonance predicts that our decision-making behavior should have an effect on our attitudes. The effect should be strongest when we make a difficult decision based on conflicting tendencies. For example, suppose a young lawyer is offered two jobs. One is at a prestigious firm that pays well and offers good chances for advancement but expects only top-notch work from its employees; the firm has a reputation for firing even veteran employees if their performance lags. The other offer is from a less prestigious firm; if she takes this job, she will never fulfill her ambitions for recognition. However, the working conditions are pleasant, and the firm is very loyal to its employees; few employees are ever fired. Thus, the lawyer would be assured of lifelong employment.

Suppose the young lawyer is initially torn between these two choices but finally decides to accept one of the job offers. Once the choice is made, her attitudes will probably undergo a change. If she chooses the high-powered firm, she is likely to perceive the practice of rewarding an employee's loyalty, as opposed to his or her ability, as a weak and contemptible practice, because this belief will reduce any residual doubts about the wisdom of her choice. Conversely, if she chooses the other firm, she will probably tell herself that loyalty is an important virtue and that she is glad she did not commit herself to work in such an inhumane place. Besides, the fact that she will not have to

worry about losing her job means that she can concentrate on the task at hand and will actually become a better lawyer.

Attitudes and Expenditures. Festinger's theory of cognitive dissonance accounts for yet another relation between behavior and attitudes: our tendency to value an item more if it costs us something. For example, some people buy extremely expensive brands of cosmetics even though the same ingredients are used in much cheaper brands. Presumably they believe that if an item costs more it must work better. Following the same rationale, most animal shelters sell their stray animals to prospective pet owners, not only to help defray their operating costs but also because they assume that a pet that has been purchased will probably be treated better than one that was free.

Aronson and Mills (1959) verified this phenomenon. The experimenters subjected female college students to varying degrees of embarrassment as a prerequisite for joining what was

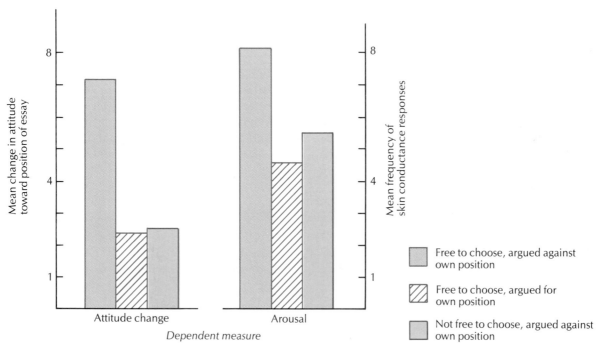

FIGURE 13.2

Mean change in attitude toward the position advocated by the essay and mean frequency of skin conductance responses (a physiological index of arousal) in subjects who argued for or against their own position. (Based on data of Croyle, R.T., and Cooper, J. *Journal of Personality and Social Psychology*, 1983, *45*, 782–791.)

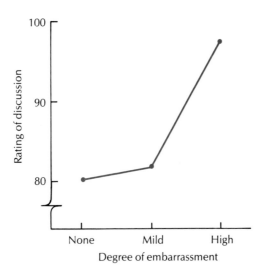

FIGURE 13.3

Ratings of a discussion by people who sustained varying amounts of embarrassment. (Based on data from Aronson, E., and Mills, J. *Journal of Abnormal and Social Psychology*, 1959, *67*, 31–36.)

promised to be an interesting discussion about sexual behavior. To produce slight embarrassment, they had the subjects read five sex-related words (such as *prostitute, virgin,* and *petting*) to the experimenter, who was male. To produce more severe embarrassment, they had the women read aloud twelve obscene four-letter words and two sexually explicit passages of prose. The control group read nothing at all. The "interesting group discussion" turned out to be a tape recording of a very dull conversation. (When psychologists put their minds to it, they can produce excruciatingly boring material. Sometimes this happens inadvertently.)

Festinger's theory predicts that the women who had to go through an embarrassing ordeal in order to join the group would experience some cognitive dissonance. They gave up something—some pride or self-esteem—to obtain a goal that they initially perceived to be worthwhile: the privilege of participating in an interesting discussion. This investment should make them view the "discussion" more favorably, so that their effort would not be perceived as having been completely without value. The results were as predicted: The subjects who had been embarrassed the most rated the discussion higher than did the control subjects or the subjects who had experienced very slight embarrassment. Clearly, we value things at

least partly by how much they cost us. (See the graph in Figure 13.3.)

The effect of cognitive dissonance on attitude change does not always appear to depend on conscious deliberation; in this context, *cognitive* does not necessarily mean *conscious.* Aronson (1975) reported that the subjects apparently did not "decide" to like the discussion because of the embarrassment they had gone through. As he notes:

> We occasionally asked our subjects why they had responded as they did. The results were very disappointing. For example, in the [Aronson and Mills study] . . . , subjects did a lot of denying when asked if the [embarrassment] had affected their attitudes toward the group or had entered into their thinking at all. When I explained the theory [of cognitive dissonance] to the subjects, they typically said it was very plausible and that many subjects had probably reasoned just the way I said, but not they themselves.

It is possible, of course, that the subjects were lying or had forgotten their thought processes, but the conclusion that the influence occurred unconsciously is certainly a reasonable one.

- What is cognitive dissonance? How does this theory explain the effects of behavior on attitudes?
- What effect do induced compliance and self-esteem have on a person's attitudes?
- What are the effects of conflict resolution and expenditures on attitude change?

Self-Perception Theory

Daryl Bem (1972) has proposed an alternative to the theory of cognitive dissonance. He defined **self-perception theory** in the following way:

> Individuals come to "know" their own attitudes, emotions, and other internal states partially by inferring them from observations of their own overt behavior and/or the circumstances in which this behavior occurs. Thus, to the extent that internal cues are weak, ambiguous, or uninterpretable, the individual is functionally in the same position as an outside observer, an observer who must necessarily rely upon those same external cues to infer the individual's inner states. (p. 2)

Bem noted that an observer who attempts to make judgments about someone's attitudes, emotions, or other internal states must examine the person's behavior for clues. He suggested that people analyze their own internal states in a similar way, making attributions about the causes of their own behavior.

Bem's theory derives from an analysis of behavior in terms of reinforcement, punishment, and discriminative stimuli that signal the particular contingencies in a particular situation. In other words, the theory uses the principles of instrumental conditioning to explain a person's behavior and attitudes.

Bem provided the following example to illustrate his claim. Suppose you see a friend running into the room, holding a broom over his head. Many psychologists assert that in order to understand this behavior, you would have to know what his intentions were—what his goal was in performing the behavior. But Bem noted that the goal can be deduced from the stimuli that are present. If a mouse has run into the room just beforehand, you will probably assume that your friend is chasing the mouse with the intent of killing it or driving it outside again. If the mouse has run into the room just afterward, you will probably assume that the mouse is chasing your friend; his intent is to escape from it. Finally, if there is no mouse at all, you may wonder whether your friend is angry at you and is planning to attack you with the upraised broom. Your attributions are based on your observations of environmental stimuli, namely, the presence or absence of a mouse and its relation to your friend's entering the room. You have no way of looking inside your friend's head to see whether he is determined to kill the mouse or is afraid of it. (We will assume that you cannot see the expression on his face.) Therefore, you cannot understand his behavior by discovering his intent. Instead, you *analyze the situation.* You perceive that the mouse is the stimulus controlling your friend's behavior and thus attribute his behavior to it. You may conclude that your friend is determined or afraid, but only *after* you have decided what accounts for his behavior.

When we make conclusions about our own internal states, such as attitudes or intents, our reasons are often very clear; the situation provides such obvious clues that there is no doubt about why we have behaved in a given way. If

Just as we observe others and make judgments about the causes of their behavior, we also analyze our own intentions.

we see a mouse and start chasing it with a broom, we know exactly why we are running with a broom in our hands. In more complex situations, an analysis of the situation does not provide such clear-cut reasons. If we cannot determine the causes from the situation, we must turn to our own behavior for clues.

You will recall the experiment by Festinger and Carlsmith (1959) in which students who were paid only one dollar later rated a boring task as more interesting than did those who were paid twenty dollars. How does self-perception theory explain these results?

Suppose an observer watches a subject who has been paid one dollar to deliver a convincing speech to another student about how interesting a task was. Because being paid such a small sum is not a sufficient reason for calling a dull task interesting, the observer will probably conclude that the student actually enjoyed the task. Lacking good evidence for external causes, the observer will attribute the behavior to a dispositional factor: interest in the task. Bem argued that the subject makes the same inference about himself or herself. Because the subject was not paid enough to tell a lie, he or she must have enjoyed the task. The principal advantage of self-perception theory is that it makes fewer assumptions than does dissonance theory; it does not postulate a motivating aversive-drive state. But as Croyle and Cooper's experiment showed, some conflict situations *do* produce arousal. Perhaps self-perception and cognitive dissonance occur under different situations, producing attitude changes for different reasons. Further evidence will be needed to determine whether the theories are competing or complementary.

Impression Management

So far we have assumed that reports of attitudes are trustworthy—that subjects rate their attitudes truthfully. But research indicates that this is not always the case. In some situations a person's expressed attitude appears to be affected by his or her desire to look good to others. This phenomenon has been called **impression management**: we manage people's impression of ourselves so that we are seen in a favorable light.

When a person appears to change his or her attitude, an observer does not simply note this fact in a neutral manner. Instead, the observer often forms positive or negative opinions about the actor. Consider this story, reported in a newspaper:

> The Very Republican Lady from Columbus, Ohio, looked sternly at former Texas Gov. John Connally and asked: "What are your views on the ERA?" "I'm for it," Connally shot back. "I've been for it since 1962." The Very Republican Lady, obviously no fan of the Equal Rights Amendment, glared. After a short, pained silence, Connally began to revise and extend his remarks. "Actually, I have mixed feelings," he said. "If the amendment would weaken or destroy family life, I'd have to take another look. . . . I wouldn't have voted to extend the time for ratification. That was wrong.

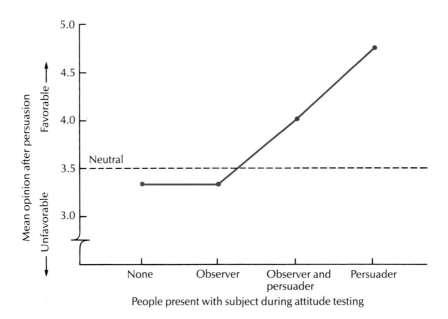

FIGURE 13.4

Subjects' agreement with a persuasive argument in the presence or absence of an observer and/or persuader. Numbers higher than 3.5 indicate agreement; those below 3.5 indicate disagreement. (Based on data from Braver, S.L., Linder, D.E., Corwin, T.T., and Cialdini, R.B. *Journal of Experimental Social Psychology*, 1977, 13, 565–576.)

. . . So for all practical purposes I guess you could say I'm against it today." (*Des Moines Register*, 1980)

Governor Connally seemed to change his attitude in a rather short time. The apparent reason for his change is disapproval of a potential voter and, by implication, of other voters who shared her point of view. Does this change of attitude affect your opinion of Governor Connally?

In general, when a person is persuaded to change his or her opinion, an observer will rate the person as being somewhat less attractive and intelligent, whereas the persuader will rate the person positively (Cialdini, Braver, and Lewis, 1974; Cialdini and Mirels, 1976). If people are aware of this phenomenon, then perhaps they will admit to different amounts of attitude change, depending on whether or not there are witnesses present.

Braver, Linder, Corwin, and Cialdini (1977) asked subjects the following question: "How favorable would you be toward shortening the number of years of medical training for doctors, thus permitting the training of more doctors and the lengthening of each doctor's active practice?" After giving their answers they joined two other people who were supposedly other subjects. One of them (the persuader) gave a persuasive speech in favor of shortening the duration of medical training.

The subjects were then exposed to one of four experimental conditions: (1) the observer left, leaving the subject in the presence of only the persuader; (2) the persuader left, leaving the subject in the presence of only the observer; (3) neither of them left; and (4) both of them left. The subjects were then asked again to give their opinion about the length of medical training. Figure 13.4 shows the results. If only the persuader was present, subjects expressed a relatively favorable response to the suggested decrease in length of training. If both persuader and observer were present, subjects expressed a slightly less favorable opinion. If subjects were alone or if only an observer was present, they expressed somewhat unfavorable opinions.

All subjects heard exactly the same persuasive arguments; the only difference was in the situation in which their attitudes were measured the second time. It seems reasonable to attribute their expressed opinions to something

The persuasiveness of a message depends upon characteristics of the listener as well as characteristics of the communicator.

other than genuine attitude change; they appeared (consciously or not) to express an opinion that would make the best impression on their audience.

■ What is self-perception theory? How does it compare to Festinger's theory of cognitive dissonance?
■ What is the role of impression management in self-reports of attitudes and attitude change?

ATTITUDE CHANGE AND PERSUASION

Persuasion is the process by which people induce others to change their attitudes. Many variables affect this process—who the persuader is, what he or she has to say, how it is said, and how receptive the person is to the argument.

Characteristics of the Communicator

Attitude change often depends a great deal on who presents the message. Some people are more persuasive than others. The three most important factors in the communicator's ability to change other people's opinions appear to be expertise, motives, and attractiveness.

Expertise

Expertise refers to the amount of knowledge that the communicator appears to have about the topic of the message. For example, people are likely to accept a surgeon's assertion that a particular operation is dangerous, because he or she is considered an expert on the topic of surgery. Producers of television commercials also try to make their actors look like experts. The man who recommends cough medicine to you sits at a large desk, in front of a bookcase full of weighty-looking books. He dresses in dignified, "doctorlike" clothes and tries to convey the impression that he really knows what he is talking about.

Aronson, Turner, and Carlsmith (1963) demonstrated the importance of the communicator's expertise in persuasion. They asked college students to evaluate two passages of poetry, then showed them evaluations that were supposedly written either by a famous poet (T.S. Eliot) or by a student at a small college. (In fact, the experimenters wrote the evaluations.) The students read evaluations that were very similar to their own, somewhat different from them, or very different from them. Later the subjects were asked to evaluate the poems again, and the experimenters measured the amount of shift in their opinions. Figure 13.5 shows the results. The messages supposedly written by the communicator with a high level of expertise (T.S. Eliot) were much more effective in altering the subjects' opinions than were those supposedly written by another student. In fact, if the students believed the message to have been written by a source with little expertise, they appeared to be better able to resist the persuasive effects of the message. Apparently, to change someone's mind, the communicator must do so in small steps, unless he or she is an expert on the subject (or knows how to act like one).

Motives

Suppose a woman who sells Tornado vacuum cleaners tells you that they are better than Cyclone vacuum cleaners. Probably you will not find this message persuasive. You will attribute her assertion to the fact that she stands to make money from the sale, rather than to a genuine belief. In contrast, if an automobile salesman tells you not to buy the more expensive model because the only difference between it and the cheaper one is some fancy trim, you will probably believe him, because he stands to make less money from the sale of the cheaper model.

Attribution theory explains these reactions. You will recall from our discussion earlier in the chapter that we attribute causal relations to events that occur together. We know that a sale results in a commission for the salesperson, which is a reinforcing event; so when the person tries to make a sale, we attribute his or her efforts to a desire to make money. But if a salesperson urges a potential customer to buy a product that results in a smaller commission—an event that would produce less reinforcement—we perceive this behavior as distinctive, hence internally caused. Because we have ruled out greed, we conclude that the person is honest and trustworthy.

Another important motivational factor is our perception of whether or not the communicator *wants* to persuade us. If we think that the com-

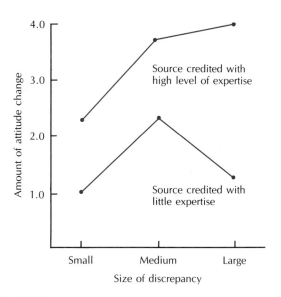

FIGURE 13.5

Amount of attitude change caused by high- and low-credibility sources as a function of discrepancy between the subject's and the persuader's expressed attitude. (From Baron, R.A., and Byrne, D. *Social Psychology: Understanding Human Interaction*, 2nd ed. Boston: Allyn and Bacon, 1977; after Aronson, Turner, and Carlsmith (1963).)

municator does not really care about convincing us, the message is more persuasive. Advertisers capitalize on this fact by producing commercials in which an actor portraying an average man or woman, supposedly filmed by a hidden camera, compares two brands of toilet paper, scouring powder, or some other product and concludes that the sponsor's brand is better. We are meant to believe that the person has no stake in the outcome, and thus is not trying to persuade the television viewer. Attribution theory can also explain this phenomenon. If we cannot attribute the "average person's" behavior to motivational variables like greed, we conclude that he or she believes that the product is actually better.

Attractiveness

People find a message from an attractive person more persuasive than one from an unattractive person. The two most important characteristics of attractiveness are physical good looks and similarity to the viewer. Mills and Harvey (1972) have suggested that these characteristics affect persuasiveness because they present a good model for the recipient, who sees the communicator's attractiveness and wants to be more like him or her. In an attempt to become more similar to the model, the recipient adopts his or her attitudes. If the persuader is too different from the recipient, the gap will be too large to bridge, and the recipient will not try to change.

When Does It Matter?

The effectiveness of a persuasive message is related to characteristics of the communicator only when the recipient does not consider the topic to be important (Petty and Cacioppo, 1981). For example, Chaiken (1980) exposed subjects to persuasive messages from likeable or dislikable communicators. Some messages contained several arguments; others contained a few. Some subjects expected to be interviewed later about the topic; others did not. Subjects who did not expect to be interviewed later were affected by the likability of the persuader and not by the number of arguments. Those who expected to be interviewed later were not affected by the likability of the persuader; instead, their attitude change was affected by the number of arguments.

Apparently, when an issue is made to be important to the recipient, people pay more attention to the nature of a persuasive message, and less attention to its source. (Perhaps this finding suggests why so many political candidates seem to prefer to avoid real issues during their campaigns for office.)

Characteristics of the Message

Although persuasion depends on the characteristics of the communicator, most people are persuaded by the content of a message and not merely by who presents it.

Argumentation

People who hope to persuade others to their own point of view often wonder whether it is more effective to present specific arguments that support a particular opinion or merely express an opinion; to present arguments only in favor of their own position or arguments for both sides of the issue. The answer is: It depends.

If the communicator is attractive, then argumentation is less important, perhaps because the recipients model the persuader's behavior instead of concentrating on the logic of the message. However, if the communicator is an authority on the subject, arguments do count; the appeal to the recipients is apparently more logical (Norman, 1976).

If people initially favor the communicator's viewpoint to some degree, it is more effective to present only one-sided arguments; the recipient may find arguments for the other side to be persuasive. However, if the recipients initially favor the opposing point of view, it is easier to persuade them by first presenting arguments for their side, then subsequently discrediting them with arguments for the opposite position (Baron and Byrne, 1981). Apparently, the two-sided presentation seems less biased and thus more persuasive.

Repetition

The more often we encounter something, the more we tend to like it, or at least we tend not to object to it.

The effect of exposure applies, for example, to people's preferences for words. Zajonc

Don't Die
of
Embarrassment.

Don't be too embarrassed to talk about condoms.
Condoms can help prevent AIDS. Insist on the use
of a condom if you have sex with a person
whose health and drug history is unknown.

DON'T DIE OF EMBARRASSMENT.

New York State Health Department
AIDS HOTLINE 1-800-541-AIDS

That fear can be a powerful persuasive force is
demonstrated by this ad warning of the dangers
of the disease AIDS.

Shaver, Travis, and Kreveld, 1972). (Sponsors
of television commercials should learn about
this finding.)

Fear

Fear can be used not only to compel obedience
("Do this or I'll shoot you!") but also to change
people's attitudes. Most messages that attempt
to persuade you to stop smoking, to fasten your
seatbelt, or to lose excess weight are based on
fear: if you don't do this, the results will be
lung cancer, a mangled body, or a heart attack.

Experiments have attested the effectiveness
of fear-producing methods of persuasion. Pictures of rotten teeth and diseased gums persuade people of the importance of oral hygiene
more effectively than pictures of plastic teeth
(Evans, Rozelle, Lasater, Dembroski, and Allen,
1970). If the fear-inducing message also contains a specific recommendation of action, it is
even more persuasive (Rogers, 1975). Rogers
cites three factors that make fear-inducing
messages effective in changing attitudes:
(1) noxiousness of the event being depicted,
(2) the perceived likelihood that the event may
occur, and (3) the perceived effectiveness of the
recommended response in avoiding the event.

(1968) found that when subjects chose the
word they preferred from pairs of antonyms
(fast-slow, hot-cold, and so on), 82 percent of
the time they chose the word that was in more
frequent everyday use. When he presented
nonwords such as *afworbu*, *civadra*, and
zabulon, he found that the more times these
novel stimuli were presented, the better the
subjects liked them.

Many other studies have demonstrated the
positive effect of exposure on preference, with
stimuli ranging from geometric figures to musical compositions. But two other factors interact
with frequency of exposure. First, only relatively complex stimuli profit from repeated
observation; apparently people get tired of simple stimuli (Smith and Dorfman, 1975). Second, repetition of even complex stimuli loses
its effect when carried on indefinitely (Zajonc,

Characteristics of the Recipient

Not everyone is equally susceptible to persuasion. When the topic of a persuasive message is
unrelated to the recipient's field of expertise,
the recipient's personality characteristics play
an important role. The most important of these
appears to be *self-esteem*. A person whose self-
esteem is low tends to be receptive to a persuasive message. People with high self-esteem are
much more resistant; they have confidence in
their own opinions and less need to conform
and be accepted by the communicator.

Self-esteem is also related to intelligence; intelligent people are likely to have confidence in
their own abilities, whereas less intelligent
people are likely to be aware of their shortcomings.

Less enduring characteristics of the recipient
are also important. Salespeople have known for
a long time that a recipient's mood plays a role

in his or her persuadability. For example, Janis, Kaye, and Kirschner (1965) found that subjects who received a snack were more likely to be persuaded than those who did not.

Development of Resistance to Persuasion

Social psychologists have studied the ways of helping people resist persuasion. Just as the best way to inoculate people against many diseases is to expose them to a mild form of the illness in order to organize their defenses against it, the best defense against persuasion is previous exposure to the arguments. McGuire and Papageorgis (1961) presented two kinds of arguments to subjects on various issues with which they were likely to agree. Some subjects heard a **supportive defense,** consisting of arguments in favor of the issue; others heard a **refutational defense**—a presentation of several arguments on the other side of the issue, followed by counterarguments refuting them. A few days later, the experimenters presented the subjects with persuasive messages opposing their previous point of view. Subjects who had heard the refutational defense were much more likely to maintain their original opinion; a taste of the opposition's arguments strengthened them against the effects of persuasion.

Some studies have confirmed the effectiveness of refutational defense, whereas others have found that it is no more effective than supportive defense (Cialdini, Petty, and Cacioppo, 1981). The distinguishing variable appears to be the nature of the topic. If the topic is an assertion that our culture takes for granted as being true, then refutational defense is especially effective. Presumably, most people are unfamiliar with arguments against cultural truisms; thus, inoculation against them is especially effective.

- What are the major variables that affect whether people are persuaded to change their attitudes?
- What characteristics of the communicator facilitate or inhibit attitude change?
- What effect does the content of the message have on persuasion?
- What makes one person more receptive to persuasion than another?

CHAPTER SUMMARY

1. We are all students of social behavior, because we are all members of society. The ability to understand the causes of other people's behavior and predict what they are likely to do is an important skill and affects our own attitudes and behavior. The process by which people infer the causes of other people's behavior is called attribution.

2. Implicit psychology involves both attribution and the formation of our own private theories of reality. We do not regard our implicit theories as theories at all, but as facts. Many prejudices and superstitions can best be understood as products of faulty implicit theories of human nature.

3. Like scientists, people use the covariance method to determine cause and effect: Events that occur together are assumed to be causally related. We attribute particular instances of behavior to two types of causes: situational and dispositional. If a behavior is consensual (many people are acting in the same way), we attribute it to situational factors. If a behavior is consistent (a person acts the same way in a variety of situations), we attribute it to dispositional factors. If a behavior is distinctive (occurring only under certain circumstances), we attribute it to situational factors.

4. Ross identified the fundamental attributional error: overreliance on dispositional factors; underreliance on situational factors. We are most likely to make the fundamental attributional error when trying to understand the causes of other people's behavior, because we are more aware of the environmental factors that affect our own behavior.

5. False consensus refers to the tendency to believe that others act and believe much as we do. We also tend to take credit for success and shun blame for failure, and many of us have an exaggerated belief in the efficacy of our own behaviors (personal causation).

6. The principal reasons for poor correspondence between attitudes and behavior involve differences in degree of specificity of the attitude and behavior, the opportunity a person has had to observe his or her own attitude-related behavior, and external constraints that prevent a person's acting on his or her attitudes.

7. Attitudes have affective components, primarily formed through direct or vicarious classical conditioning, and cognitive components, formed through direct instruction or through instrumental conditioning or modeling.

8. Festinger's theory of cognitive dissonance suggests reasons for interactions between attitudes and behavior. It proposes that discrepancies between attitudes and behavior, between behavior and self-image, or between one attitude and another lead to the unpleasant state of cognitive dissonance. Reduction of this dissonance by changing the importance of dissonant elements, adding consonant ones, or changing one of the dissonant elements, provides negative reinforcement. This theory explains why we value more highly things that cost us something; it also predicts that behaviors—even induced compliance—can lead to attitude changes.

9. Bem's alternative to cognitive dissonance—self-perception theory—suggests that many of our attitudes are based on self-observation. When our motives are unclear, we look to the situation for the stimuli and probable reinforcers and punishers that cause us to act as we do. For example, subjects who are paid one dollar to persuade fellow students to perform a boring task have a more favorable attitude toward it because genuine interest is a more likely explanation for their own behavior than the receipt of such a small sum.

10. Another important variable is impression management: We sometimes profess attitudes in order to please a persuader or to show other people that we have enough self-confidence not the be manipulated easily.

11. Persuasion is the process by which people induce others to change their attitudes. Attitude change depends on the communicator of the message and his or her expertise, motives, and attractiveness. It also depends on the importance of the topic to the recipient; the more important the topic is, the more the persuasive argument becomes more important than its source. Repetition and fear are both used to persuade. The susceptibility of the recipient to persuasion can depend on his or her knowledge of the topic. The recipient's personality and intelligence influence his or her acceptance or resistance to a message. A refutational defense is more effective than a supportive defense in preparing people to resist persuasion.

KEY TERMS

attribution Assigning cause to an event, including a person's behavior, or assigning a personality characteristic to a person. Attributions can apply to others or to oneself.

cognitive dissonance An unpleasant state of tension caused when a disparity exists between a person's beliefs or attitudes and behavior, especially beliefs or attitudes that are related to one's self-esteem.

consensus General agreement within a group. In attribution theory, consensus refers to a behavior that is also being performed by other people; a high level of consensus suggests that the behaviors are caused by external events.

consistency The tendency to act in similar ways to a particular situation on different occasions.

covariance method According to attribution theory, the strategy by which people infer causation; if events occur together we infer that one of them caused the other to happen.

discounting The tendency to reject dispositional factors as causes of a behavior when the behavior is apparently one that most people would perform under existing circumstances.

dispositional factor A cause of behavior that is related to one's personality characteristics and preferences. See also *situational factor*.

dissonance reduction Resolution of a state of

cognitive dissonance, accomplished through adding consonant elements that explain away the conflict, reducing the importance of one of the dissonant elements, or changing one of the dissonant elements.

distinctiveness The tendency to act in different ways in different situations. In attribution theory, high distinctiveness suggests that the behaviors are caused by external events.

false consensus Tendency of the observer to see his or her own response as representative of a general consensus.

fundamental attributional error The tendency to overestimate the importance of personality traits and underestimate the importance of situational variables as causes of other people's behavior.

implicit psychology A set of inferences (attributions) that people make in everyday life about the causes of people's behavior, including predictions of what they are likely to do.

impression management Performance of behavior that is calculated to give other people a particular impression of one's personal characteristics.

modeling Changing a person's behavior by providing an example of desirable behavior and (usually) overtly or covertly reinforcing that behavior.

personal causation The belief that one's behavior has important effects on one's environment.

refutational defense A presentation of several arguments against the issue, followed by counterarguments refuting them.

self-attribution Attribution about our own disposition based on self-knowledge of our behavior in various situations.

self-perception theory Bem's alternative to the theory of cognitive dissonance, based on principles of instrumental conditioning, that a person's own inner state is understood by observation of his or her own behavior, as though the person were an outsider.

situational demand The effects of a particular situation on the behavior of people exposed to it; if most people act in a certain conventional way, the situational demands are said to be strong.

situational factor A cause of behavior that is related to the situation rather than to the actor's personality traits. See also *dispositional factor*.

supportive defense Arguments in favor of the issue, as related to studies in persuasion.

Chapter 14

Social Psychology: Influence and Attraction

Social psychologists use scientific methods to study the effects of people on each other. People's interactions affect all aspects of behavior: thoughts, emotions, perceptions, and personalities. The behavior—or even the mere presence—of other people exerts a powerful influence on our own thoughts and behaviors. We are aware of some of these influences; for example, people's persuasive arguments make us think about whether to engage in a particular behavior. The thoughts lead us to decide whether we will change our opinions or perform the behavior. Yet we are usually unaware of most social influences. When these influences are pointed out to us later, we often find it difficult to believe that they could have affected our opinions or behavior.

Psychological studies have long demonstrated the power of social influence. Why do people conform? Why do they obey authority? These questions have been addressed by prominent researchers such as Solomon Asch and Stanley Milgram. Their work provides us with fascinating examples of what we can learn by applying scientific methods to the study of human interaction. Other researchers have examined such questions as: What is the effect of "peer pressure" on our behavior? If some one does us a favor, why do we feel impelled to return it? Why is it hard for people to go back on their commitments? Does violence on television contribute to the incidence of violence in real life? Why do we find some people more attractive than others?

As you can see, social influence affects almost every aspect of our lives, from why we behave the way we do to who we choose as friends and lovers. You may wonder why we need scientific studies to answer these questions. The answer is that many times we are not sure what influenced us to act the way we did. By conducting scientific investigations of social influence, psychologists can establish patterns and try to predict behavior. Many times the findings surprise us; what we think influenced us really had little effect at all, while a factor of which we were not aware turned out to be the most influential one. Thus, to discover the precise factors that determine the effects of social influences, today's psychologists must be good detectives as well as careful scientists.

SOCIAL INFLUENCES

Imitation: Do As Others Do

Probably the most powerful social influence on our behavior and attitudes is the behavior of other people. If we see people act in a particular way, we tend to act in that way, too. Sometimes, we observe that people are *not* performing a particular behavior; if so, we too tend not to perform that behavior.

The tendency to conform exerts a powerful influence on human behavior.

Conformity

Most of us cherish our independence and like to think that we do what we do because *we* want to do it, not because others decree that we should. But none of us is immune to social influences, and most instances of conformity benefit us all. If we see someone whose face has been disfigured by an accident or disease, we do not stare at the person or comment about his or her appearance. If someone drops a valuable item, we do not try to pick it up and keep it for ourselves. If we lose a tennis match, we do not cry and pout; instead, we smile and congratulate the victor. If we have a cold, we try not to sneeze in someone else's face. Each society has developed norms that define the ways in which we should behave in various situations, and following these norms generally makes us feel more comfortable and also helps the group function smoothly.

Solomon Asch (1951) demonstrated just how powerful the tendency to conform can be, even on simple perceptual judgments. He asked several groups of seven to nine students to estimate lengths of lines that were presented on a screen. A sample line was shown at the left, and the subjects were to choose which of the three lines to the right matched it. (See Figure 14.1.) The subjects gave their answers orally.

In fact there was only one subject in each group; all the others were confederates of the experimenter. The seating was arranged so that the subject answered last. Under some conditions, the confederates made incorrect responses. When they made incorrect responses on six of the twelve trials in an experiment, 76 percent of the subjects went along with the group on at least one trial. Under control conditions, when the confederates responded accurately, only 5 percent of the subjects made an error.

Group pressure did not affect the subjects' perceptions; it affected their behavior. That is, the subjects went along with the group decision even though the choice still looked wrong to them. When they were questioned later, they said that they had started doubting their own eyesight or had thought that perhaps they had misunderstood the instructions. The subjects who did not conform felt uncomfortable about disagreeing with the other members of the group.

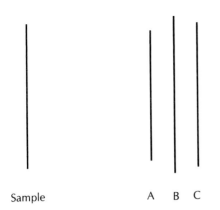

FIGURE 14.1

An example of the stimuli used by Asch (1951).

The Asch effect shows how strong the tendency to conform can be. Faced with a simple, unambiguous task in a group of strangers who showed no signs of disapproval when the subject disagreed with them, a large majority of subjects nevertheless ignored their own judgments and agreed with the obviously incorrect choice made by the other people.

People's tendency to imitate the behavior of others is a tool used by many people who are in the business of influencing others. Sometimes the people setting the example are fictitious. For instance, bartenders and coatroom attendants often put some folding money in the container they set out to solicit tips; presumably they hope that customers will follow the example they themselves have established. Psychologists, too, have demonstrated the effectiveness of such a ploy. When Schofield (1975) merely asked twenty female college students to read and review some pamphlets, only seven agreed to do so. When she also said, to another group of twenty, that "she was pleased that most women in the previous groups" had complied with her requests, seventeen subjects agreed to help.

Sometimes accomplices are enlisted to serve as examples, with the expectation that their behavior will influence that of others. For instance, Fuller and Sheehy-Skeffington (1974) showed that the canned laughter that accompanies almost all comedy shows on television induces people to laugh more themselves and to rate the material as funnier, especially if it is not very funny to begin with (as seems to be the case for the overwhelming majority of the shows). This phenomenon occurs *despite* the fact that most people say that they detest canned laughter.

Bystander Intervention

In 1964 in New York City, a woman named Kitty Genovese was chased and repeatedly stabbed by an assailant, who took thirty-five minutes to kill her. The woman's screams went unheeded by at least thirty-eight people who watched from their windows. No one tried to stop the attacker; no one even made a quick, anonymous telephone call to the police. When the bystanders were questioned later, they could not explain their inaction. "I just don't know," they said.

As you can imagine, people were appalled and shocked by the bystanders' response to the Kitty Genovese murder. Commentators said that the apparent indifference of the bystanders attested to the fact that American society, especially in urban areas, had become cold and apathetic. The reporter who first publicized the story agreed.

> It can be assumed . . . that their apathy was indeed one of the big-city variety. It is almost a matter of psychological survival, if one is surrounded and pressed by millions of people, to prevent them from constantly impinging on you, and the only way to do this is to ignore them as often as possible. Indifference to one's neighbor and his troubles is a conditioned reflex in life in New York as it is in other big cities. (Rosenthal, 1964)

Experiments performed by social psychologists suggest that this explanation is wrong—people in cities are not generally indifferent to the needs of other people. The fact that Kitty Genovese's attack was not reported is not remarkable because thirty-eight people were present; it is precisely because so many people were present that the attack was *not* reported.

Latané and Darley have extensively studied the phenomenon of **bystander intervention.** Their experiments have shown that when a person may be in need of assistance, the presence of other people who are doing nothing *inhibits* people from giving aid. For example, Darley and Latané (1968) staged an "emergency" during a psychology experiment. Each subject participated in a discussion about personal problems associated with college life with one, two, or five other people by means of

Bystander apathy reflects our tendency to imitate the inaction of others more than our indifference to other people. Groups such as New York's Guardian Angels work to counteract bystander apathy.

an intercom. The experimenter explained that the participants would sit in individual rooms so that they would be anonymous and hence would be more likely to speak frankly. The experimenter would not listen in but would get their reactions later in a questionnaire. Actually, only one subject was present; the other voices were simply tape recordings.

During the discussion one of the people, who had previously said that he sometimes had seizures, apparently had one. His speech became incoherent, and he stammered out a request for help.

> I-er-I-uh-I've got a-a one of the-er-sei- - - - - er-er -things coming on and-and-and I could really-er-use some help so if somebody would-er-give me a little h-help-uh-er-er-er-er-er c-could somebody-er-er-help-er-uh-uh-uh (choking sounds). . . . I'm gonna die-er-er-I'm . . . gonna die-er-help-er-er-seizure-er-[chokes, then quiet]. (Darley and Latané, 1968, p. 379)

As Figure 14.2 shows, almost all subjects left the room to help the victim when they were the only witness to the seizure. However, when there appeared to be other witnesses, the subjects were much less likely to try to help. In addition, those who did try to help reacted more slowly if other people appeared to be present.

Darley and Latané reported that the subjects who did not respond were not indifferent to the plight of their fellow student. Indeed, when the experimenter entered the room, they usually appeared nervous and emotionally aroused, and asked whether the victim was being taken care of. The experimenters did not receive the impression that the subjects had decided not to act; rather, they were still in conflict, trying to decide whether they should do something. "On the one hand, subjects worried about the guilt and shame they would feel if they did not help the person in distress. On the other hand, they were concerned not to make fools of themselves by overreacting, not to ruin the ongoing experiment by leaving their intercom, and not to destroy the anonymous nature of the situation which the experimenter had earlier stressed as important" (Darley and Latané, 1968, p. 382).

These results have been replicated in other experimental settings, including incidents staged outside the laboratory. When a person is faced with a situation that *may* call for assistance, the person will tend to take his or her cue from other people; if they are doing nothing,

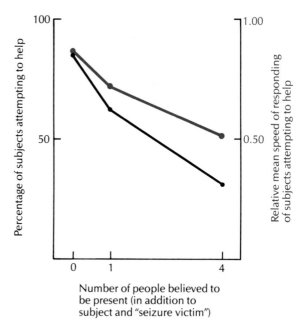

FIGURE 14.2

Percentage of subjects attempting to help as a function of the number of other people that the subject believed to be present. (Based on data from Darley, J.M., and Latané, B. *Journal of Personality and Social Psychology*, 1968, 8, 377—383.)

then he or she, too, will tend not to do anything. People tend to imitate the inaction of other bystanders. Presumably, people's thoughts go like this: "Well, no one else is doing anything, so I'd better not stick my neck out. I guess I don't understand what's going on." As Cialdini (1984) points out, conditions that discourage bystander intervention are more often met in cities than in small towns or rural areas, and these conditions lead to the impression that city dwellers are apathetic and uncaring. Because more is happening in cities, people cannot always be sure that a particular situation actually represents an emergency. In addition, because cities have higher population densities, an emergency is more likely to be attended by a large group of bystanders.

If an emergency *clearly* requires bystander intervention, people are much more likely to render assistance, even if other bystanders are present. Clark and Word (1972, 1974) staged realistic "accidents" in a room adjacent to one in which individual subjects, or subjects in groups of two to five, were answering a questionnaire. The accidents involved a maintenance man who apparently fell from a ladder or a technician who apparently received a severe electrical shock. All of the groups of subjects came to the man's assistance.

Social Facilitation: When Someone Is Watching

As we just saw, the behavior of other people has a powerful effect on our own. But studies have shown that even the *mere presence* of other people can affect a person's behavior. Triplett (1897) published the first experimental study on **social facilitation.** He had people perform a number of simple tasks, such as turning the crank of a fishing reel. He found that his subjects turned the crank faster and for a longer time if other people were present. Although many other studies found the same effect, some investigators reported just the opposite phenomenon: If the task was difficult and complex, the presence of an audience *impaired* the subjects' performance. You yourself have probably noticed that you have difficulty performing certain tasks if someone is watching you.

Robert Zajonc (1965) has suggested an explanation for the phenomenon of social facilitation. He claims that the presence of people who are watching a performer (or whom the performer *perceives* as watching) raises that person's arousal level. Presumably, the increase in arousal has the effect of increasing the probability of performing *dominant responses:* responses that are most likely to occur in a particular situation. When the task is simple, the dominant response is generally the correct one, so an audience improves performance. When the task is complex, a person can perform a number of different responses and must decide which one is appropriate. The presence of the audience makes the selection of the appropriate behavior more difficult, because the increased arousal tends to cause the person to perform the dominant response, which may not be the correct one. Suppose you are trying to assemble an intricate piece of machinery. A part is sticking. You want to bang on it, but you know that doing so will not help. You must gently manipulate it into place. Just then, a curious bystander approaches and stands close to you, asking if he or she can watch. You say yes and turn back to the task. The part seems to be giving you even more trouble than before, and you suddenly start banging on it.

Subsequent experiments have supported Zajonc's explanation. Martens (1969) tested the prediction that the presence of a group increases a person's level of arousal. While subjects performed a complex motor task alone or in the presence of ten people, the experimenter

The presence of an audience usually improves performance of simple tasks but may impair performance of complex tasks.

determined physiological arousal by measuring the sweat present on the subjects' palms. The presence of an audience produced a clear-cut effect: the subjects who performed in front of other people had sweatier palms.

An experiment by Zajonc and Sales (1966) showed that the presence of an audience can raise the probability of dominant responses. The experimenters read aloud a list of fictitious Turkish words and had subjects pronounce each of them from one to sixteen times. Then they asked the subjects to watch a screen, on which the words would be flashed too rapidly to be seen clearly, and to guess which word had been presented. In fact the experimenters flashed a meaningless jumble of shapes on the screen. Subjects who performed this part of the task alone guessed that they saw many of the words that they had heard. They were more likely to say the words that they had rehearsed more often, but they also chose a good number of the least-practiced ones. Other subjects performed in the presence of two people who had supposedly asked the experimenter whether they could watch the procedure. With this audience present, the subjects tended to stick with the words that they had practiced the most; it was as if their increased arousal caused them to make only dominant responses. Perhaps they found it harder to think of words they had not rehearsed as often. (See Figure 14.3.)

Why does the presence of a group increase a person's arousal? One important factor seems to be whether the subjects perceive the group as observing (and thus evaluating) their performance. Cottrell, Wack, Sekerak, and Rittle (1968) had their subjects perform a task like the one used by Zajonc and Sales. During the word-guessing phase, some subjects were tested alone; others were tested in the presence of two blindfolded or unblindfolded people. Only the subjects who were actually watched by other people showed the expected increase in dominant responses.

■ What does research say about the nature of conformity?

■ What are the conditions that facilitate or inhibit bystander intervention?

■ What effects can an audience have on a person's performance? How have psychologists attempted to explain these effects?

Social Loafing: Share the Load

As we just saw, people usually try harder when other people are watching them. However, when the other people are co-workers rather than observers, the presence of a group sometimes results in a *decrease* in effort, or **social loafing**. Thus, the whole is often less than the sum of its individual parts. Many years ago Ringelmann (cited by Dashiell, 1935) measured the effort that people made when pulling a rope in a mock tug-of-war contest against a device that measured the exerted force. Presumably, the force exerted by eight people pulling together in a simple task would be at least the sum of their individual efforts, or even somewhat greater than the sum, because of the phenomenon of social facilitation. However, Ringelmann found total force exerted was about half what would be predicted by the simple combination of individual efforts. The subjects exerted less force when they worked in a group.

More recent studies have confirmed these results and have extended them to other behaviors. For example, Latané, Williams, and Harkins (1979) asked subjects alone, in pairs, or in groups of six to shout as loudly as they could. The subjects wore blindfolds and headphones that played a loud noise. Thus they could not

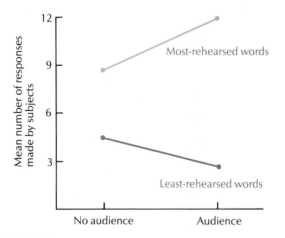

FIGURE 14.3

Number of responses of most-rehearsed and least-rehearsed words made by subjects in the presence or absence of an audience. (Based on data from Zajonc, R.B., and Sales, S.M. *Journal of Experimental Social Psychology*, 1966, 2, 160–168.)

hear the shouting of the other subjects nor could they see or be seen by the other people in their group. When subjects shouted alone they made more noise than when they shouted in groups; their group effort was only 82 percent of their individual effort.

Several variables determine whether the presence of a group will produce social facilitation or social loafing. One of the most important of them is *identifiability*. Williams, Harkins, and Latané (1981) asked subjects to shout as loud as they could individually or in groups. Subjects who were told that the equipment could measure only the total group effort shouted less loudly than those who were told that the equipment could measure individual efforts. The latter shouted just as loudly in groups as they did alone. These results suggest that a person's efforts in a group activity are affected by whether or not other people can observe his or her individual efforts. If they can, social facilitation is likely to occur; if they cannot, then social loafing is likely to occur.

We can analyze the effect of identifiability on effort in terms of reinforcement. When a person's efforts can be measured by other people, that person can potentially receive social reinforcers such as approval or acknowledgment of a job well done. The person can also receive disapproval for failing to work hard enough. In other words, *contingencies of reinforcement* (cause-and-effect relations) are present. When a person's efforts are submerged in those of the group, these contingencies cannot apply, and the quality of individual effort declines.

Another variable that determines whether social facilitation or social loafing occurs is *responsibility*. If a person's efforts are duplicated by those of another person (and if his or her individual efforts are not identifiable), the person is likely to exert less than maximum effort. Harkins and Petty (1982) had subjects work in groups of four on a task that required them to report whenever a dot appeared in a particular quadrant of a video screen. In one condition, each subject watched an individual quadrant and was solely responsible for detecting dots that appeared there. In the other condition all four subjects watched the same quadrant; thus, the responsibility for detecting dots was shared. Subjects did not loaf when they were responsible for their own quadrant; under this condition they worked as hard as subjects working alone.

If the effort of each person in a group activity cannot be measured, individual effort may decrease. This phenomenon is known as social loafing.

As Latané and his colleagues point out, social loafing has implications for group efforts outside the laboratory. They note that social loafing is observed in tasks that require intellectual effort as well as physical work. For example, Petty, Harkins, and Williams (1980) found that subjects who participated in a group effort to evaluate a persuasive message worked less hard at the task than did subjects who had to perform their own evaluations. Consequently, the subjects who worked alone were more persuaded by good arguments and less persuaded by poor arguments than people who worked in a group. (See Figure 14.4 on p. 420.) These results suggest that a person who wants to influence the attitudes of other people should meet with groups of people if he or she does not have good arguments. (Perhaps this phenomenon explains why politicians like to address mass rallies.)

Latané and his colleagues also point out the relevance of their studies to an observation made by Turner (1978). Apparently, it is difficult to achieve good quality control on the production line at pickle factories. Dill pickle halves must be stuffed into jars by hand, and only pickles of certain sizes will do; long ones will not fit, and short ones will float around in the jar, looking "cheap and crummy." Because the conveyor belt moves inexorably, workers

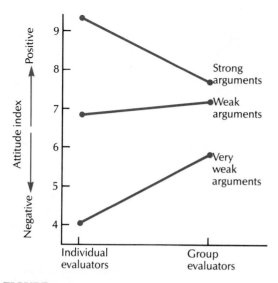

FIGURE 14.4

Social loafing in cognitive effort. Attitude changes of subjects evaluating arguments individually or as members of a group after hearing strong, weak, or very weak arguments. (From Petty, R.E., Harkins, S.G., and Williams, K.D. *Journal of Personality and Social Psychology*, 1980, *38*, 81–92.)

tend to fill the jars with whatever pickles are at hand; if they stop to look for pickles of the proper size, the jars pile up. Jars that are filled with pickles of the wrong size must be culled by inspectors, and this activity adds considerably to the cost of production. However, because there is no way to tell which worker has filled which jar, there is little incentive for a worker to choose the pickles carefully.

Reciprocity: Do unto Others

Another very strong social influence is **reciprocity,** the tendency to pay back favors others have done for us. When someone does something for us, we feel uncomfortable until the debt is discharged. For example, if people invite us to their house for dinner, we feel obliged to return the favor in the near future. And owing a social debt to someone we do not like is especially distasteful. Often people will suffer in silence rather than ask for help from someone they dislike.

The strong human tendency to pay back favors is almost certainly the basis for trade; we can give goods and services to other people with the assurance that we will receive some-

thing in return. In some primitive cultures, people do not explicitly trade goods but make "gifts" to each other. For example, a person who obtains some food on a hunting trip will share it with other members of the tribe. Another person who is particularly skilled at making tools provides them for others. Even though the goods and services do not have prices and are not explicitly traded, people who receive them from others feel obliged to do what they can in return.

Returning Favors and Atoning for Causing Harm

Experiments by social psychologists have confirmed the strength of reciprocity in human interactions. For example, Regan (1971) enlisted the participation of college students in an experiment that supposedly involved art appreciation. During a break, some subjects were treated to a soft drink by the experimenter or by another "subject" (a confederate); others received nothing. After the experiment, the confederate asked the subject to purchase some raffle tickets that he was selling. Compliance with the request was measured by the number of tickets that each subject bought. Figure 14.5 shows the results. The subjects whom the confederate treated to a soft drink purchased the most raffle tickets. Getting a free drink from the experimenter also had an effect. Perhaps the subjects responded to the example of doing a favor for someone else; they probably thought well of the experimenter and, with this example fresh in mind, complied with the confederate's request so that they, too, would be thought well of.

People trying to sell something often try to capitalize on the reciprocity rule by giving the potential customer a free sample. Once the person has accepted the "gift," the sales representative tries to get him or her to return the favor by making a purchase. If you have ever accepted a piece of food from a person handing out samples in a supermarket, you realize it is awkward to walk away without purchasing.

Besides feeling obligated to pay back favors, we also feel obligations to make amends when our behavior causes someone harm or discomfort. For example, Carlsmith and Gross (1969) had subjects participate in a "learning task." The subject served as "teacher," and another student (actually, a confederate) served as "learner." Following the experimenter's instructions, the subject informed the learner when he was wrong by operating a switch that (1) purportedly delivered an electrical shock to the learner or (2) sounded a buzzer. (In the first condition, the "learner" did not actually receive a shock.)

After the experiment appeared to be over, the learner asked the teacher whether he or she would be willing to circulate a petition to help stop the construction of a freeway through a redwood forest in California. Seventy-five percent of the subjects who believed they had shocked the learner complied with the request, compared with 25 percent of the subjects who had simply sounded a buzzer. Presumably, the subjects did a favor for the victim in compensation for the pain they had caused.

Reciprocal Concessions

In most cases, reciprocity is not the result of a deliberate, reasoned process; usually, we act automatically, without thinking about the cause of our behavior. This characteristic of reciprocity is illustrated in the way we respond when another person makes a demand while

The exchange of gifts is an example of the power of social influence. We often feel uncomfortable if someone gives us a gift and we do not reciprocate.

giving the appearance of having done us a favor.

One of the best ways to get someone to do something for you is to make a very large request and when that is declined, make a "concession" and ask for a much smaller one. This strategy is often used by people who are negotiating the terms of a contract, such as a union contract specifying wages and working conditions. Both sides make demands that they are sure will not be met and then grudgingly retreat from them, acting as if they are doing the other side a favor. Of course, in such situations, the strategy has become so well understood that it probably has little effect. But if people have not had practice with such negotiating tactics, the effect of making an apparent concession can be very strong. And people who comply with the second, smaller request usually feel satisfied.

Cialdini and Ascani (1976) demonstrated this strategy in an experiment. They approached college students and asked them whether they would be willing to donate a pint of blood; 32 percent of them agreed to do so. (This group of subjects is called the *low only* group, because only the lesser request was made of them.) They asked another group of

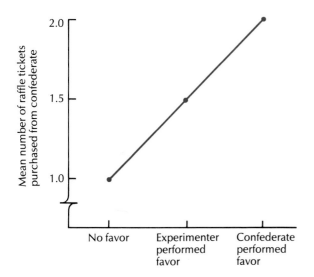

FIGURE 14.5

Mean number of raffle tickets purchased from a confederate when subjects received a favor or no favor from the experimenter or confederate. (Based on data from Regan, D.T. *Journal of Experimental Social Psychology*, 1971, 7, 627–639.)

students (the *high-low* group) whether they would give a pint of blood every six weeks for a minimum of three years; not surprisingly, none of them agreed. The experimenters then retreated from their original request and asked whether the students would be willing to donate a single pint of blood. This time 49 percent said yes—17 percent more than in the *low only* group. The subjects acted as if the experimenters had done them a favor by retreating from their large, unreasonable request to a much more modest one. Apparently, the students found it difficult to refuse the second request. And the agreement had a lasting effect; when the subjects arrived at the blood center to donate blood, 84 percent of the *high-low* group agreed to give blood again later, whereas only 43 percent of *low only* group agreed to do so.

Making a Commitment: It's Hard to Say No Once You've Said Yes

Once people commit themselves by making a decision and acting on it, they are reluctant to renounce their commitment. For example, have you ever joined one side of an argument on an issue that you do not really care about, only to find yourself vehemently defending a position that just a few minutes ago meant almost nothing to you? I know that I certainly have. This phenomenon was demonstrated by a clever experiment by Knox and Inkster (1968). The experimenters asked people at the betting windows of a racetrack how confident they were that their horse would win. They questioned half of the people just before they had made their bets, the other half just afterward. The

Studies suggest that once people make a commitment, they are reluctant to go back on it. While terminating a marriage may not be as difficult as it once was, most people are hesitant to renounce their commitment.

people who had already made their bets were more confident than those who had not yet paid. Their commitment increased the perceived value of their decision.

An experiment by Freedman and Fraser (1966) showed that commitment has a long-lasting effect on people's tendency to comply with requests. They sent a person posing as a volunteer worker to call on home owners in a residential California neighborhood, asking them to perform a small task: to accept a three-inch-square sign saying "Keep California Beautiful" or "Be a safe driver," or to sign a petition supporting legislation favoring one of these goals. Almost everyone agreed. Two weeks later, the experimenters sent another person to ask these people whether they would be willing to have a public service billboard erected in front of their house. To give them an idea of precisely what was being requested, the "volunteer worker" showed the home owners a photograph of a house almost completely hidden by a huge, ugly, poorly lettered sign saying "DRIVE CAREFULLY." Over 55 percent of the people agreed to this obnoxious request! In contrast, fewer than 20 percent of householders who had not been contacted previously agreed to have such a billboard placed on their property. For obvious reasons, Freedman and Fraser referred to their procedure as the *foot-in-the-door technique*.

Needless to say, people trying to influence our purchasing behavior also use the foot-in-the-door technique. Many jurisdictions in the United States have passed "cooling off" laws that permit people to back out of contracts they have signed to purchase goods while under the influence of high-pressure tactics. These laws have had the desired effect: many people have had second thoughts about whether they really needed the items they had been coerced into buying and have cancelled their orders in a day or two. However, as Cialdini (1984) notes, many sellers have begun enlisting the power of commitment to make it difficult for people to reverse their decisions: they now have people fill out the sales contract themselves, not simply sign it. Cialdini quotes a training program for sales representatives at one firm as saying that the procedure is "a very important psychological aid in preventing customers from backing out of their contracts" (p. 86). Obviously,

the "aid" in this case is perceived from the vantage point of the seller, not the buyer.

Commitment increases people's compliance even when the reason for the original commitment is removed. For example, some unscrupulous car salespeople offer to sell a car for an unusually low price. The surprised buyer agrees, thinking that he or she had gotten an especially good deal. Then, after doing some preliminary paperwork—which succeeds in getting the customer to make a commitment—the salesperson disappears for a while, only to return with the sad news that the sales manager will not permit such a low price. However, the salesperson can still offer a good price, even if it is not nearly as good as the first. All too often, the customer agrees to the higher price, even though it is not one that he or she would have agreed to in the first place. This technique is called *low-balling*.

Commitment probably increases compliance for several reasons. First, the act of complying with a request in a particular category may change a person's self-image. Through the process of attribution, people who sign a petition to support a beautiful environment may come to regard themselves as "public-spirited" individuals. Thus, when they hear the billboard request, they find it difficult to refuse. After all, they are public spirited, so how can they say no? Saying no would imply that they did not have the courage of their convictions—that they were unwilling to put their money where their mouth was. Thus, this reason has at its root a person's self-esteem; to maintain good self-esteem, the person must say yes to the large request.

Commitment may also increase compliance because the first, smaller request changes people's perception of compliance in general. Evidence supporting this suggestion was provided by Rittle (1981). While sitting in a waiting room before participating in an experiment, some adult subjects were approached by an eight-year-old child who was having trouble operating a vending machine. Later, while answering a series of questions designed to disguise the true nature of the experiment, they were asked to rate their perception of how unpleasant it might be to provide help for other people. After the subjects had answered all the questions and the study was apparently over, the interviewer

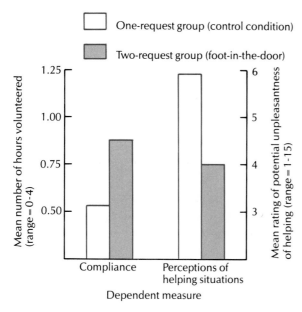

FIGURE 14.6

Mean number of hours volunteered and mean rating of potential unpleasantness of volunteering of control subjects and subjects who first helped a child. (Based on data from Rittle, R.H. *Personality and Social Psychology Bulletin*, 1981, 7, 431–437.)

then asked them whether they would volunteer between thirty minutes and four hours of their time to participate in a research project. The results showed that subjects who had helped the child rated helping as less unpleasant and were more willing to participate in the research project than people who had not helped the child. (See Figure 14.6.)

The results suggest that when a person helps someone else, he or she finds that doing so is not at all unpleasant; in fact, helping a young child probably increases one's self-esteem and hence reinforces helping behavior. Thus, the person's attitudes toward helping behavior in general probably becomes more positive, and this changed attitude translates itself into behavior.

■ What is social loafing? What variables determine whether social facilitation or social loafing are likely to occur?

■ What are the research findings on the principle of reciprocity?

■ What are the research findings on the effects of making a commitment?

Reactance: You Say "Do This," I Do That

As we saw in Chapter 11, most people like to perceive themselves as being in control; they prefer to believe that they have free choice in their behavior. Even pigeons prefer to choose which plastic disk to peck in order to receive food; thus preference for free choice is probably a biological characteristic of complex organisms. When people perceive that their freedom of choice is being constrained by the actions of others, they often react in a way that affirms their ability to choose. For example, if people perceive that someone is trying to manipulate their choice, they often choose to do the *opposite* of what the manipulator is trying to get them to do. This phenomenon is called **psychological reactance** (Brehm and Brehm, 1981).

An interesting example of psychological reactance occurred when Dade County, Florida (the location of the city of Miami), passed an antipollution ordinance that prohibited the possession and use of laundry detergents containing phosphates. Mazis and his colleagues (Mazis, Settle, and Leslie, 1973; Mazis, 1975) studied the attitudes and behavior of women in Miami and in Tampa, another Florida city where phosphates had not been banned. They found that many women in Miami laid in an enormous supply of detergents containing phosphates before the ban went into effect. Others organized carpools to neighboring counties to purchase detergents containing phosphates. As a result of the ban, the perceived value of the prohibited products was increased; compared with women in Tampa, who were free to choose whatever detergent they liked, the women in Miami rated phosphate detergents as gentler, easier to pour, better whiteners and stain removers, and more effective in cold water.

Some studies suggest that reactance, like the preference for freedom of choice, may be a biological tendency. At the very least, it can be said that reactance occurs at an early age. Brehm and Weintraub (1977) studied the behavior of two-year-old children tested individually in a playroom that contained two equally attractive toys. One toy was placed on each side of a transparent plastic barrier. In one condition, the barrier was low enough so that the children could easily reach over it and pick up the toy behind it. In another condition, the barrier was too tall for the children to surmount; in order to reach the toy behind it, the children had to go around the barrier. The experimenters recorded how quickly the children touched each toy; as Figure 14.7 shows, the tall barrier apparently made the toy behind it look more attractive, because it was touched much faster than the easily available toy. The low barrier had no effect.

The data in Figure 14.7 were obtained from the boys in the experiment. Brehm and Weintraub found that girls did not show reactance in this situation; no matter what the size of the barrier was, they touched the closer toy more quickly. Other experiments have suggested that females are less likely than males to show psychological reactance to physical restrictions of their freedom; instead, they tend to react against *socially imposed* restrictions (Brehm and Brehm, 1981).

Psychological reactance, like several other social influences, may be related to self-esteem. In general, we perceive effective and powerful people as having more freedom of choice than ineffective and weak people, and most of us prefer to think of ourselves as belonging in the

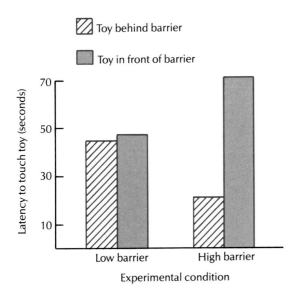

FIGURE 14.7

Reactance. Latency (time it takes) to touch a toy in front of a barrier or behind it. (Based on data from Brehm, S.S., and Weintraub, M. *Journal of Personality and Social Psychology*, 1977, 35, 830–836.)

former category. (Indeed, as we will see in Chapter 15, belief in one's freedom of choice and ability to control one's environment are important features of personality. In addition, as we will see in Chapter 17, several forms of psychotherapy attempt to help people with their psychological problems by increasing these beliefs.) However, despite the possible role of self-esteem, we must remember the example of the pigeons who prefer free choice. Unless we are willing to believe that pigeons have self-images, we must conclude that at least some instances of psychological reactance are automatic reactions that are not produced by deliberate consideration.

Rational or Irrational Control

As you have seen in this section, many social variables influence our behavior automatically. Perhaps, in reading about them, you engaged in a bit of covert psychological reactance, saying to yourself, "Canned laughter doesn't make *me* laugh" or "I'd help the man having the seizure even if other people were around" or "I am influenced by a person's ideas, not by what he or she looks like" or "I'd never give a shock to someone else even if the experimenter said I had to." After all, being vulnerable to the effects of social influence means your choices are constrained by your automatic reactions.

At first glance, instances of social influence may appear to be bad; perhaps we would be better off if all of our behavior was under rational, conscious control. But as Cialdini (1984) points out, such a conclusion is not warranted. Most of the time, our species profits from our tendencies to be fair in our interactions with others, to take our cues for acting from each other, and to honor our commitments. If in every situation we encountered in our lives we had to expend time and effort consciously deciding what to do, we would be exhausted at the end of the day and get hardly anything done. For most normal people in most situations, the automatic, unconscious reaction is the best and most efficient one. We should save our cognitive efforts for the times when they count the most. However, no general rule works all the time; exceptions can occur that have bad effects. For example, an authority figure can order us to do things that hurt ourselves or others, and advertisers and sales representatives who know the rules can induce us to purchase items we do not need. In cases like these, the best protection is awareness of the rules; if you know them (and now you do), you are more likely to detect when someone is trying to manipulate you, so that you can then engage in a carefully thought-out reaction instead of an automatic one.

Petty and Cacioppo (1981) have studied some of the variables that determine whether people act automatically in response to social influences or whether they consciously and rationally debate the alternatives with themselves and then decide what they should do. These researchers found, in general, that people consciously reflect about issues that are important to themselves because they are experts on the matter or because the issues will affect their lives. For example, Petty, Cacioppo, and Goldman (1981) asked student subjects to rate the "broadcast quality" (sound quality) of recorded statements presenting arguments in favor of requiring seniors at the university to pass a comprehensive examination in order to graduate. The students were led to believe that the university chancellor was seriously considering such a proposal. Some students were told that the change would take place next year and thus would affect them. Others were told that the change would take place in ten years.

The experimenters manipulated a variable that is known to influence people's attitudes under certain conditions: authority. Some subjects were told that the message they heard was prepared by students in a class at a local high school. Others were told that it was prepared by the Carnegie Commission of Higher Education, chaired by a professor of education at Princeton University. Actually, the experimenters prepared the messages themselves. Two different messages were recorded. One message had strong arguments, such as "average starting salaries are higher for graduates of schools with the exam" and "graduate and professional schools show a preference for undergraduates who have passed a comprehensive exam." The other message had very weak arguments, such as "most of my friends support the proposal" and "the risk of failing the exam was a challenge most students would welcome." As you can see, a person who listened to the tapes carefully would be more likely to be persuaded by the strong arguments than by the weak ones; the quality of the arguments appealed to people's ability to think rationally.

Petty and his colleagues found that students who believed that the proposal would affect them apparently paid attention to the quality of the arguments, because their attitudes toward the proposal were swayed by the strong arguments but not by the weak ones. For these subjects, it did not matter whether the message was attributed to the high school class or to the distinguished commission. However, students who believed that the change was ten years away were affected more by the source of the message than by its contents; they tended to agree with the voice of authority.

Attractive People: It's Hard to Refuse Them

People tend to be most influenced by requests or persuasive messages from attractive people. As we will see in a later section, physical good looks are one of the most important factors in determining whether we find a particular person likable.

People generally find it difficult to say no to an attractive person, even though they usually deny being influenced by such a "superficial" characteristic as looks. For example, Efran and Patterson (1976) had subjects rate the attractiveness of the candidates in the 1974 Canadian federal election. They found that the most attractive candidates received two and one-half times as many votes as the least attractive ones. However, when they surveyed Canadian voters, they found that the overwhelming majority of them denied that their vote had been affected in the least by the candidates' looks. People are either not conscious of the influence of this phenomenon or unwilling to admit to it.

Kulka and Kessler (1978) demonstrated the effect of good looks on people's behavior in a controlled experiment. They staged a mock trial of a negligence suit in which someone was suing another person for damages. The subjects served as jury members and decided how much money the plaintiff should be awarded. Physically attractive plaintiffs received an average of $10,051, but physically unattractive plaintiffs received only $5,623. Who says justice is blind?

Why is attractiveness such a potent influence on people's behavior? The most likely explanation involves classical conditioning and—again—self-esteem. The phenomenon of classical conditioning says that when people have positive or negative reactions to some stimuli, they begin to have positive or negative reactions to other stimuli that are also present. Thus, as Cialdini (1984) notes, some people irrationally blame the weather forecaster for bad weather. Similarly, in ancient times, a messenger bringing news about a battle to the ruler of Persia was treated to a banquet if the news was good and beheaded if it was bad.

Advertisers regularly pay tribute to the effectiveness of association when they have attractive models and celebrities appear with their products. For example, Smith and Engel (1968) showed two versions of an advertisement for a new car. One version included an attractive young woman and the other did not. When the subjects subsequently rated the car, those who saw the advertisement with the attractive young woman rated the car as faster, more appealing, more expensive looking, and better designed.

Besides making products or opinions more attractive by being associated with them, attractive people are better able to get others to comply with their requests. This phenomenon, like so many others, probably has self-esteem at its root. One of the reasons why people tend to comply with the requests of attractive people is that they want to be liked by attractive people; in their minds, being liked by attractive people makes them more desirable, too. Clearly, people tend to emphasize their associations with attractive and important people; we have all encountered name droppers who want us to think that they are part of a privileged circle of friends. This phenomenon is even demonstrated by fans of sports teams. Cialdini, Borden, Thorne, Walker, Freeman, and Sloan (1976) found that university students were more likely to wear sweatshirts featuring the university name on Mondays after the football team had won a game than after the team had lost. They also found in telephone interviews with students that the pronouns "we" and "our" (as in "our victory") were prominent after wins, but that the pronouns "they" and "their" (as in "their defeat") were prominent after losses.

Authority: We're Loyal Followers

People tend to comply with the requests of people in authority and to be swayed by their persuasive arguments, and such obedience is generally approved by society. For example, the Bible describes God's test of Abraham, who is ordered to sacrifice his beloved son Isaac. Just as he is about to plunge the knife, an angel tells him to stop; he has proved his obedience. Cohen and Davis (1981) cite a more recent, if less dramatic, example of unthinking obedience. A physician prescribed ear drops for a

As justification for covert acts running counter to the United States government's policy, Lt. Col. Oliver North claimed that he was obeying authority.

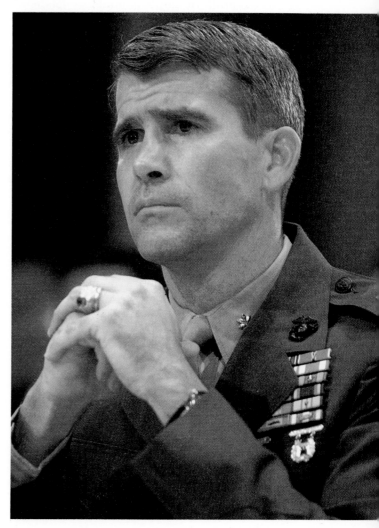

hospitalized patient with an ear infection. His order read "place in R ear." Unfortunately, he apparently did not put enough space between the abbreviation for *right (R)* and the word *ear,* because the nurse delivered the ear drops rectally. Neither she nor the patient thought to question such treatment for an earache.

An interesting study showed that we tend to perceive authority figures as larger than life (literally). Wilson (1968) introduced a man to his classes in an Australian college as a visitor from Cambridge University. In different classes, he introduced the man as a student, a demonstrator, a lecturer, a senior lecturer, or a professor. Later, he asked the students in his classes to estimate the visitor's height. The average estimates are shown in Figure 14.8; as you can see, the "professor" was perceived as being over three and one-half inches taller than the "student."

A disturbing example of mindless obedience was obtained in a series of experiments performed by Milgram (1963), who advertised for subjects in local newspapers in order to obtain as representative a sample as possible. The subjects served as "teachers" in what they were told was a learning experiment. A confederate (a middle-aged accountant) serving as the "learner" was strapped into a chair "to prevent excessive movements when he was shocked," and electrodes were attached to his wrist. The subjects were told that "although the shocks can be extremely painful, they cause no permanent tissue damage."

The subject was then brought to a separate room, where there was an apparatus containing dials, buttons, and a series of switches that supposedly delivered shocks ranging from 15 to 450 volts in intensity. The subject was instructed to use this apparatus to deliver shocks to the learner in the other room. Beneath the switches were descriptive labels ranging from "slight shock" to "danger: severe shock."

The learner gave his answers by pressing the appropriate lever on the table in front of him. Each time he made an incorrect response, the experimenter told the subject to throw another switch and give a larger shock. At the 300-volt level, the learner pounded on the wall and then stopped responding to the questions. The experimenter told the subject to consider no answer as an incorrect answer. At the 315-volt level, the learner pounded on the wall again. If the subject hesitated in delivering a shock, the experimenter said, "Please go on." If this admonition was not enough, the experimenter said, "The experiment requires that you continue," then "It is absolutely essential that you continue," and, finally, "You have no other choice; you *must* go on." The factor of interest was how long the subjects would continue to administer shocks to the hapless victim.

A majority of subjects gave the learner what they believed to be the 450-volt shock, despite

FIGURE 14.8

Mean perceived height of a person as a function of his status. (Based on data from Wilson, P.R. *Journal of Social Psychology,* 1968, 74, 97–102.)

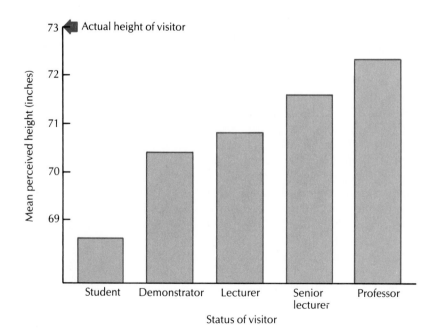

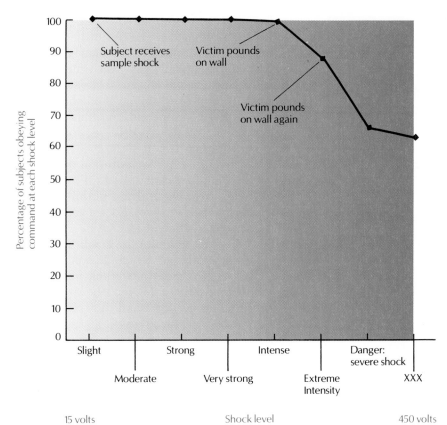

FIGURE 14.9

Data from one of Milgram's studies of obedience. (From Baron, R.A., and Byrne, D. *Social Psychology: Understanding Human Interaction*, 2nd ed. Boston: Allyn and Bacon, 1977; after Milgram, 1963.)

the fact that he pounded on the wall twice and then stopped responding altogether. (See Figure 14.9.)

In a later experiment, when the confederate was placed in the same room as the subject and his struggling and apparent pain could be observed, 37.5 percent of the participants—over one-third —obeyed the order to administer further shocks (Milgram, 1974). Thirty percent were even willing to hold his hand against a metal plate to force him to receive the shock.

Milgram's experiments indicate that a significant percentage of people will blindly follow the orders of authority figures, no matter what the effects are on other people. Milgram had originally designed his experimental procedure to understand why ordinary people in Germany had participated in the murders of millions of innocent people during World War II. He had planned to perfect the technique in the United States and then travel to Germany to continue his studies. The results he obtained made it clear that he did not have to leave home.

Most people find the results of Milgram's studies surprising; it seems impossible that for such a large proportion of people the social pressure to conform to the experimenter's orders is stronger than the subject's own desire not to hurt someone else. As Ross (1977) points out, this misperception is an example of the fundamental attributional error. People tend to underestimate the effectiveness of situational factors and to overestimate the effectiveness of dispositional ones. Clearly, the tendency to obey an authority figure is amazingly strong. Perhaps we should emphasize to our children the importance of doing no harm to others as least as much as we emphasize obeying an authority figure.

- ■ What does the research say about reactance and its relation to self-esteem?
- ■ What are the conditions under which people's behavior is affected by rational or irrational social influences?
- ■ Why is it difficult for people to refuse the requests of attractive people?
- ■ What are the research findings concerning the effects of authority on compliance?

AGGRESSION AND SOCIAL INFLUENCE

Milgram's research on obedience provides disturbing evidence of the powerful nature of social influence. This section of the chapter examines the relationship between social influence and another topic of interest to social psychologists: aggression. In Chapter 11, we saw that biological factors can play a role in triggering aggressive behavior. Our concern here is with identifying the social factors that help explain when and why aggressive behavior occurs. As you will see, early attempts to explain aggression looked for explanations within the individual. More recently, researchers have focused on environmental factors which lead to aggressive behavior.

Frustration and Aggression

An influential hypothesis proposed by Dollard, Doob, Miller, Mowrer, and Sears (1939) stated that frustration causes aggression. In general

While frustration does not always lead to aggression, the overcrowded conditions on the highway may have contributed to the shootings that occurred on the Los Angeles Freeways during the summer of 1987.

usage, the term *frustration* refers to an unpleasant feeling produced by an unfulfilled desire. However, Dollard and his colleagues defined **frustration** specifically as "an interference with the occurrence of an instigated goal-response at its proper time in the behavior sequence"—that is, as a condition that prevents the occurrence of an expected reinforcer. Expectation (implied by the term *goal-response*) plays a crucial role in the definition of frustration. For example, I cannot be said to be frustrated by not winning millions of dollars from my state's lottery. However, if I am very thirsty and put my last piece of change in a vending machine to get something to drink, my goal-response of drinking—which I expect to be able to do—is frustrated if the machine keeps my money but fails to deliver a beverage.

According to Dollard and his colleagues, frustration invariably increases an organism's tendency to engage in aggressive behavior and accounts for *all* instances of aggression. Their rationale was that frustration produces a drive that motivates the aggressive behavior; if this drive finds an outlet in the form of aggressive behavior, it will be reduced and the organism will no longer behave aggressively.

Berkowitz's Modification

An analysis by Berkowitz (1978) disposes of the hypothesis that all aggressive acts are caused by frustration. Aggressive behaviors, like any other, can be reinforced. A dog can be trained to attack. An assassin can be hired to kill a person. Frustration does not play a causal role in either of these cases. Pain is also an effective agent in producing aggressive behavior. If two animals are placed in a small cage and receive electrical shocks to their feet, they are likely to fight.

On the other hand, although some forms of aggression do not involve frustration, perhaps frustration invariably increases an organism's tendency to behave aggressively. To investigate this possibility, Berkowitz (1978) had subjects sit on a stationary bicycle and attempt to adjust their rate of pedaling to match that of a person in another room; if they succeeded, they would receive a reward. Near the end of the run, frustration was introduced in some subjects, who suddenly received signals indicating that they were failing to match their partners' speed. Some subjects were told that a malfunction of the equipment had caused the failure; others were told that their partners were at fault. Subjects in both experimental groups reported that they were angry; subjects in a control group were not. Thus, frustration caused anger even when it was produced by factors apparently outside of anyone's control.

The next phase of the experiment tested actual aggression, by giving the subject an opportunity to punish the fictitious partner's behavior by pressing a button that allegedly delivered a loud, noxious noise. The perceived source of frustration did have an effect on aggressive behavior: subjects who believed that the partner was to blame pressed the button more often and longer than did those who blamed the apparatus or control subjects who had not expected to receive a reward.

From the results of these and other experiments, Berkowitz has suggested modifying the frustration-aggression hypothesis to account for the effects of other aversive stimuli, including pain. In our evolution, pain became a potent elicitor for aggressive behavior; if an animal was in pain and another animal was present, the latter was likely to be the source of the pain. Thus, animals who attacked when in pain were more likely to survive than those who failed to respond.

Berkowitz and Frodi (1977) found that pain does elicit aggressive behavior in humans. They induced pain in volunteer subjects by having them place their hand in a tank of ice water. (The effect is painful but does not cause physical harm.) Control subjects placed their hand in cool water. After seven minutes, the subjects were permitted to reward or punish the behavior of a (fictitious) person in the next room. Subjects who were experiencing pain administered more shocks than did control subjects. They also reported feeling annoyance, irritation, and anger, as well as pain and discomfort.

In conclusion, at least some forms of aggression appear to be produced by aversive stimuli, frustration being just one example.

Aggression and Catharsis

Dollard and his colleagues have accepted Freud's suggestion that aggression consists of response tendencies that are energized by a drive, and this hypothesis has been incorporated into many ethological theories. Various physiological and environmental influences increase the level of this drive. Once aroused, the aggressive drive must eventually find an outlet in actual aggressive behavior or in some symbolic substitute. The Freudian and ethological models of aggression emphasize the importance of **catharsis** (*katharsis* is Greek for "purge").

Experimental evidence suggests that acting out aggression tends to lead to even *more* aggression. Geen, Stonner, and Shope (1975) made some subjects angry by having a confederate unfairly give them an excessive number of electrical shocks while they were attempting to solve a problem. Afterward some subjects were given the opportunity to punish their tormenter by supposedly delivering a shock whenever he made an error in a learning task. During a second learning task, all subjects were given the same opportunity. However, this time they could turn a dial to determine how intense the shock would be. The subjects' blood pressure was taken several times during the experiment. According to the catharsis model, the subjects who were able to punish the confederate twice should have shown less anger during the second learning task, because their anger should have been released during the first task, whereas those who did not punish their tormenter during the first learning task should still have been angry, therefore causing them to set the shock intensity higher.

The blood-pressure readings were in accord with the catharsis hypothesis: After each opportunity to punish the confederate, the subjects' blood pressure fell, presumably reflecting a decrease in anger. However, the *behavioral* effects were just the opposite: Subjects who had shocked the confederate during the first learning task shocked him even more during the second, and their responses on a questionnaire indicated they felt more hostile toward him. Although aggression appeared to purge anger, it seemed to increase aggressive tendencies.

The apparent reason for the increase is that the reduction of unpleasant feelings creates the conditions for *negative reinforcement*, which is achieved through the termination of an aversive stimulus. Thus, when a person gives vent to feelings of hostility and feels better afterward, the experience tends to increase the likelihood that aggressive behavior will recur.

Can aggressive behavior be learned through imitation? Research suggest that viewing television violence may make people more aggressive.

Imitation of Aggression

Social learning theory provides a different explanation of the origin of aggressive behavior. It suggests that aggression is a learned behavior. As we saw in Chapter 6, learning can take place through observation and imitation. You may recall the famous study by Albert Bandura which demonstrated that children readily learn to imitate aggressive behavior. Learning by imitation is of great concern to social psychologists, in part because of the possible link between television violence and aggression.

Most people would agree that it would be unfortunate if real people were as violent as the ones we see on television. Does the continued observation of violence in the mass media lead children to choose aggressive means to solve their problems, or are the representatives for the television networks correct when they argue that children have no trouble separating fact from fancy, and that the networks only give us what we want anyway?

Field studies suggest, but do not prove, that long-term viewing of violence on television causes children to be more violent. For example, Lefkowitz, Eron, Walder, and Huesmann (1977) observed a correlation of .31 between boys' viewing of violence and their later behavior. They reported that the greater the boys' preference was for violent television at age eight, the greater their aggressiveness was both

at that age and ten years later, at age eighteen. (Girls were found to be much less aggressive, and no relation was observed between television viewing and violence.)

Feshbach and Singer (1971) carried out a bold and interesting field study in an attempt to manipulate directly the amount of violence seen by boys on television, and thus to determine whether the viewing would affect their later aggressiveness. With the cooperation of directors of various private boarding schools and homes for neglected children, half of the teenage boys were permitted to watch only violent television programs, the other half only nonviolent ones. Six months later, no effect was seen on the behavior of the boys in the private schools. The boys in the homes for neglected children who had watched violent programs tended to be slightly *less* aggressive than those who had watched the nonviolent ones.

Two factors prevent us from concluding that violent television programs promote pacifism or at least have no effect. First, by the time people reach their teens, they may be too old to be affected by six months of television viewing; the critical period may come earlier. Second, some of the boys resented not being allowed to watch their favorite (in this case, violent) television programs, and this resentment may have made them more aggressive.

As with many other complex social issues, we lack definitive evidence that television violence makes members of our society more aggressive. However, the stakes in this particular issue are high enough that we should tolerate some uncertainty and choose what is clearly the lesser of two evils. Given both the possibility that violence on television has a harmful effect and the fact that no harm can come from reducing the amount of aggression on the airwaves, we should make every effort to provide a more peaceful and constructive model of human behavior to our children.

■ What is the relationship between frustration and aggression?
■ What is the experimental evidence concerning the role of catharsis in suppressing aggression?
■ What are the research findings concerning the relationship between television violence and aggression?

INTERPERSONAL ATTRACTION

Humans are very social animals. We make friends, eat and drink together in groups, join clubs, and form close associations with our mates and children. The behavior of other people serves as our most important source of reinforcing and aversive stimuli. Why do we enjoy the company of some people and not others?

A number of factors determine *interpersonal attraction*—that is, people's tendency to approach each other and evaluate each other positively. Some of these factors are characteristics of the individuals themselves; others are determined by the environment.

The simplest and most parsimonious explanation for interpersonal attraction is that people who serve as sources of reinforcing stimuli for each other tend to remain in each other's company. As you will recall from Chapter 6, stimuli that are regularly associated with reinforcing stimuli will themselves become reinforcing stimuli, through the process of classical conditioning. Thus, we learn to prefer the company of people who regularly provide us with social reinforcement.

The nature of social reinforcement is quite varied. Acknowledgment of our abilities and accomplishments and appreciation of our intelligence and wit are certainly desirable characteristics in a close friend. Other characteristics, such as talent and physical attractiveness, also endear others to us; having an attractive and accomplished friend suggests to ourselves and to others that we, too, are worthy of respect.

Positive Evaluation

Humans have a real need to be evaluated positively—to be held in high regard by other people. This need is expressed in interpersonal attraction. Byrne and Rhamey (1965) studied the effects of positive personal evaluations on attraction. First, they asked subjects to express their attitudes toward twelve issues. Then they described a fictitious stranger, explaining what his attitudes were on the twelve issues. The subjects were told that the stranger had read their attitude survey and had accordingly evaluated them positively or negatively. Finally, the experimenters asked the subjects to rate the

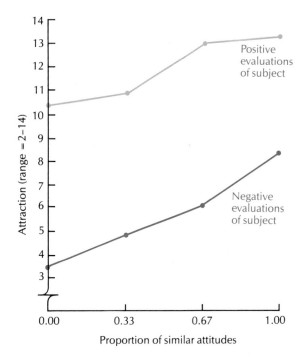

FIGURE 14.10

Ratings of the description of a stranger who was said to have evaluated the subject positively or negatively, as a function of similarity in attitudes between stranger and subject. (From Baron, R.A., and Byrne, D. *Social Psychology: Understanding Human Interaction,* 2nd ed. Boston: Allyn and Bacon, 1977; after Byrne and Rhamey, 1965.)

amount of attraction they felt toward the stranger. As Figure 14.10 shows, subjects reported being more attracted if the stranger's attitudes were similar to theirs. The most important factor was whether the stranger approved of them; subjects who were evaluated positively reported being much more attracted to the stranger than did those who were rated negatively.

In situations involving real people, the effects of evaluation are even more pronounced. Geller, Goodstein, Silver, and Sternberg (1974) had female college students individually join group discussions with two other women, confederates of the experimenter. During the discussion, the confederates either treated the subject normally or ignored her, showing a lack of interest in what she said and changing the subject whenever she spoke. The subjects who were ignored found the conversations distressing; they felt very unhappy and even gave *themselves* poor ratings. Being ignored is a form of negative evaluation by other people, and it exerts a powerful effect.

Shared Opinions

A second factor that influences interpersonal attraction is the degree to which people hold similar opinions. This factor, too, can be explained in terms of social reinforcement. Presumably, a person who shares our opinions is likely to approve of us when we express them. Also, having friends who have similar opinions guarantees that our opinions are likely to find a consensus; we will not often find ourselves in the unpleasant position of saying something that brings disapproval from other people.

Byrne and Nelson (1971) measured various attitudes of their subjects and then had them read descriptions of the attitudes of a stranger. After learning about this person's attitudes, the subjects rated how much they liked or disliked the stranger. The scatter plot shown in Figure 14.11 presents the results. The points, which represent individuals, cluster along an imaginary diagonal line; there was an excellent relation between shared attitudes and attraction. The more similar the stranger's attitudes were to those of the subject, the better the stranger was liked.

In the real world, similarity of attitudes is not the only factor determining the strength of interpersonal attraction. Other kinds of similarities are also important, such as age, occupational status, and ethnic background. Friends tend to have similar backgrounds as well as similar attitudes.

Physical Appearance

We do judge people by the characteristic that is supposed to be only skin deep; men prefer beautiful women, and women prefer handsome men. Again, social reinforcement provides a likely explanation for this phenomenon. Although aesthetics (such as our attraction to a beautiful painting) may account in part for our attraction to good-looking people, self-esteem probably plays a more important role. Someone who is seen in the company of an attractive person and is obviously favored by this person is likely to be well regarded by other people ("If she's so good looking and she likes him, then he must really have something going for him").

Walster, Aronson, Abrahams, and Rottman (1966) studied the effects of physical appearance at a dance at which college students were paired by a computer. Midway through the evening, the experimenters asked the subjects to rate the attraction they felt toward their partners and to say whether they thought they would like to see them in the future. For both sexes, the only characteristic that correlated with attraction was physical appearance. Intelligence, grade-point average, and personality variables seemed to have no significant effect. Berscheid, Dion, Walster, and Walster (1971) found that although physical appearance may be the most important variable in determining attraction between people who are randomly paired by a computer, when people choose

FIGURE 14.11

Ratings of attraction toward a stranger as a function of similarity in attitudes between stranger and subject. (From Byrne, D., and Nelson, D. *Journal of Personality and Social Psychology*, 1971, 1, 659–663.)

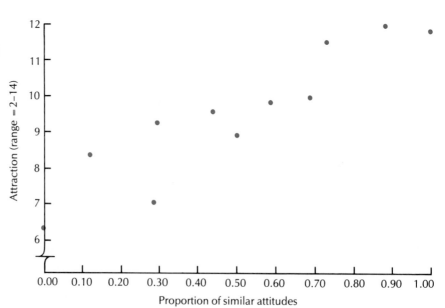

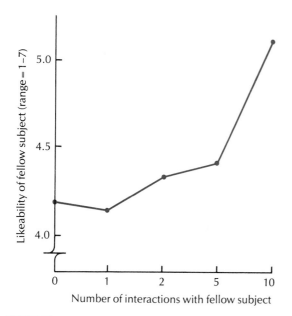

FIGURE 14.12

The rated likability of a fellow subject as a function of number of interactions. (Based on data from Saegert, S.C., Swap, W., and Zajonc, R.B. *Journal of Personality and Social Psychology,* 1973, 25, 234–242.)

their own partners they tend to pick someone who is about as physically attractive as they are.

When people first meet someone with a good physical appearance, they rate the person as probably holding attitudes similar to their own (Schoedel, Frederickson, and Knight, 1975) and tend to assume that they have good personalities, successful marriages, and high occupational status (Dion, Berscheid, and Walster, 1972; Adams and Huston, 1975). In fact, physically attractive people usually do possess many of these characteristics, probably because they receive favorable treatment from society.

Familiarity

Fortunately for the majority of us who are not especially beautiful or handsome, the variable of exposure influences people's attitudes toward others; the more frequent the exposure, the more positive the attitude.

Even in the brief time it takes to participate in an experiment, familiarity affects interpersonal attraction. Saegert, Swap, and Zajonc (1973) had college women participate in an experiment supposedly involving the sense of taste. Groups of two students (all were subjects—no confederates this time) entered booths, where they tasted and rated various liquids. The movements of the subjects from booth to booth were choreographed so that pairs of women were together from zero to ten times. Afterward, the subjects rated their attraction to each of the other people in the experiment. The amount of attraction the subjects felt toward a given person was related to the number of interactions they had had. (See Figure 14.12.)

Many factors determine how we choose our companions; similarity and familiarity are two important aspects of interpersonal attraction.

Liking and Loving:
Differences in Nature or Degree?

The simplest explanation for the intense interpersonal relationship we call "love" is that it is merely a strong form of liking. According to this explanation, the feeling we have for the person whom we love is qualitatively no different from the attraction that we feel for other people, except for the added feelings derived from sexual intimacy, if that occurs. However, some studies have suggested that love is qualitatively different from liking, because the phenomenon of reinforcement cannot explain some of the factors that affect this special kind of interpersonal attraction that people can feel. As Walster and Berscheid (1971) have put it, "Passion sometimes develops in conditions that would seem more likely to provoke aggression and hatred" (p. 47).

Dutton and Aron (1974) had an attractive young woman interview male college students as they walked across a suspension bridge spanning a gorge 280 feet deep. The bridge was 5 feet wide and 450 feet long and had "a tendency to tilt, sway, and wobble, creating the impression that one is about to fall over the side" (p. 511). The same woman interviewed control subjects on a more conventional, sturdy bridge spanning a 10-foot drop.

The men who were interviewed on the suspension bridge appeared to find the woman more attractive than did those who were interviewed on the ordinary one. They were more likely to make sexually related responses to a brief personality test. Perhaps more significantly, they were much more likely to telephone the woman later. The interviewer gave her telephone number to all subjects with the suggestion that they call her if they wanted to discuss the experiment further.

The results suggest that the anxiety evoked by standing on a precarious suspension bridge increased the men's sexual attraction toward

Social psychologists study even such personal topics as romantic love.

the woman. At first, this finding appears to be incompatible with the suggestion that interpersonal attraction stems from reinforcement. The subjects met the woman in the context of aversive stimuli, not reinforcing ones; therefore, she should subsequently have become an aversive stimulus herself and elicited avoidance behaviors, not telephone calls.

Dutton and Aron explained their results in terms of attribution theory: a man experiences increased arousal in the presence of a woman; he attributes it to the obvious stimulus—the woman—and concludes he is attracted to her. Later he acts on this by telephoning her.

Several researchers have acknowledged that adversity and unpleasant arousal seem to increase interpersonal attraction between men and women. Rubin (1973) noted that couples of mixed religious background reported stronger degrees of romantic love. Presumably, the conflict that followed their choice of each other (especially among other family members) provided arousal that strengthened their mutual attraction. Similarly, an ancient Roman expert advised men to take their women to the Colosseum to see the gladiators fight, because the experience would increase their amorousness.

But Kenrick and Cialdini (1977) suggested that misattributed arousal was not the best explanation for this phenomenon. To begin with, it is unlikely that a person who is standing on a swaying suspension bridge cannot identify the source of his or her arousal; most people have more insight than that into the source of their emotions. If the subjects had correctly attributed their arousal to the bridge, they would not have needed to attribute it to the woman standing on it. Furthermore, a person who is present in an aversive situation does not necessarily become an aversive stimulus by association; instead, he or she can become a conditioned reinforcer. Consider what happened to the subjects. They started walking across a narrow, swaying bridge suspended above a deep gorge and met a calm, attractive young woman who stopped them and asked them to participate in an experiment. They spent several minutes talking with her, then continued on their way. Probably this encounter reduced rather than increased their fear. The woman seemed calm and reassuring and accustomed to standing on the bridge; therefore, she served as an example to the students. Her presence may also have distracted them from the view of the rocks far

below. Because the reduction of an aversive stimulus is a negative reinforcer, the men's increased attraction toward the woman can be accounted for in terms of reinforcement, not misattribution. The woman's presence became a conditioned reinforcer because it was associated with reduction of fear.

This conclusion is consistent with the results of many studies performed with other animals. For example, you will remember from Chapter 4 that infant monkeys cling to their mothers when they are frightened by novel stimuli. In addition, ethologists have noted that the presence of predators causes animals to congregate together. Undoubtedly this tendency exists in humans too: when we are faced with danger or adversity, we seek the company of others.

A further study by Dutton and Aron (1974) demonstrated that the presence of another person can reduce aversive arousal. They led a group of male subjects to expect to receive a weak electrical shock, a strong and painful electrical shock, or no shock. During a delay period, some subjects waited alone; others waited with a young woman. Presumably, the subjects who anticipated receiving a strong shock were unpleasantly aroused. As in the bridge experiment, subjects who were expecting a shock reported more attraction than did those who were not expecting a shock. Dutton and Aron also asked the subjects to rate their level of anxiety. Those who had waited with the young woman reported less anxiety than did control subjects who had waited alone. Although the investigators explained the increased attraction in terms of attribution theory, the fact that the woman's presence decreased the subjects' arousal provides important support for the negative reinforcement hypothesis.

The negative reinforcement hypothesis can also explain Rubin's (1973) findings on couples of mixed religious background. The aversive feelings produced by family conflicts are decreased when the couples are together. Thus, the presence of the partner is reinforcing.

■ What are the effects of positive evaluation, shared opinions, physical appearance, and familiarity on interpersonal attraction?

■ What is the role of reinforcement in romantic attraction?

CHAPTER SUMMARY

1. One of the most important influences on our behavior is provided by other humans. We tend to imitate the behavior of other people, conforming to social norms and preferring not to disagree with attitudes and judgments expressed by others. This tendency undoubtedly serves us well most of the time, but the fact that people are less likely to assist someone if other bystanders are present shows that imitation can also have unfortunate effects.

2. When other people watch us work, their presence tends to raise our level of arousal, thus facilitating simple tasks and interfering with difficult ones (*social facilitation*). If we work with others on a joint task and if our individual contribution cannot be measured, we tend to exert less effort than if we were working alone. However, this phenomenon, called *social loafing*, will not occur if each member of the group has responsibility for a specific portion of the task.

3. When someone does us a favor, we tend to reciprocate, doing something for them when we have the opportunity. This tendency probably serves as the historical basis for trade, but the individual can sometimes be tricked into returning a small favor with a big one. When we commit ourselves to a course of action, we tend to honor these commitments. We even act consistently with prior commitments when we are not conscious of having made them.

4. We do cherish our freedom, or at least the illusion of freedom. When people are forbidden from doing something, they tend to value the prohibited act even more than they did previously. As parents will testify, this phenomenon, called reactance, is especially strong in young children.

5. Not everyone is treated equally by other people. Attractive people and people who are perceived as authority figures tend to get what they want from others; we find it difficult to say no to them. The social pressure to obey authority can override a basic desire not to harm others, thus demonstrating the fundamental attributional error. People underestimate situational factors and overestimate dispositional factors.

6. What relationship does social influence have on aggression? Although biological factors can trigger aggressive behavior, environmental factors are probably more often responsible. The frustration-aggression hypothesis suggests that thwarting an organism's opportunity to obtain a reinforcer is the sole cause of aggression. However, some forms of aggression are not caused by frustration; for example, violence can be explicitly reinforced. Berkowitz suggested that unpleasant stimuli such as pain and the effects of frustration increase an organism's tendency to behave aggressively.

7. The catharsis hypothesis has received mixed support. Although the opportunity to engage in aggression may indeed relieve a person's *feelings* of anger, it is likely to increase further violence.

8. Although some simple human aggressive behaviors may be innate, most are learned. Field studies on the effects of televised violence are not conclusive; observational studies have revealed a modest relation between preference for violent television shows and boys' aggressiveness, but we cannot be sure that the relation is causal. An attempt to manipulate aggression by forcing children to watch violent or nonviolent shows was inconclusive because many children resented their loss of choice.

9. Although the factors that influence interpersonal attraction are complex and not yet fully understood, they all appear to involve social reinforcement (and, in the case of lovers, physical reinforcement). In turn, people learn to act in ways that reinforce friends and lovers, to maintain and strengthen their ties with them. Attraction is increased by positive evaluation of oneself by the other person, by shared opinions, by physical good looks, and by familiarity.

10. Attribution undoubtedly plays an important role in interpersonal attraction; for example, our beliefs about why other people act as they do certainly affect how much we like them. Yet a careful analysis suggests that the reason why romantic bonds can be strengthened by adversity lies in the phenomenon of negative reinforcement. The presence of another person makes an unpleasant situation more tolerable, and this reduction in strength of an aversive stimulus confers on the other person the status of a conditioned reinforcer.

KEY TERMS

bystander intervention Phenomenon associated with the presence of other people inhibiting the action of any one person.

catharsis According to Freud, the release, through relatively harmless means such as symbolic aggression or vigorous sports, of energy from a drive that might otherwise result in undesirable behavior.

frustration The prevention of an expected appetitive stimulus; said to result in aggression.

psychological reactance A tendency, found especially in children, to resist perceived attempts by others to control the person's behavior.

reciprocity Tendency to pay back favors others have done for us.

social facilitation The facilitating effect of the presence of a group of people on the behavior of one or more of its members.

social loafing The tendency for people working in groups in which their contributions are not identifiable to expend less effort than they would working alone.

Personality

Psychologists who study human personality, like the rest of us, are interested in predicting behavior. They attempt to determine what characteristics people possess and to assess the value of these characteristics in predicting people's behavior in various situations. But there is another issue that interests psychologists who study personality: How and why do people differ from one another? As you will see, a number of very different personality theories have been proposed to explain individual differences.

When studying personality, we must be careful to avoid the nominal fallacy; describing a personality characteristic is not the same as explaining it. However, identification is the first step in understanding the nature of human personality. What types of research efforts are necessary to study personality? Some psychol-

ogists devote their efforts to the development of tests that can reliably measure differences in personality. Others try to determine the events—biological and environmental—that cause people to behave as they do.

Psychologists disagree about many aspects of personality, including the best way to classify individual differences, whether personality characteristics are relatively stable or change in response to particular kinds of situations, and whether biological or environmental factors are more important in determining personality. In this chapter, you will learn how psychologists have attempted to answer these questions, and you will be introduced to the major theories of personality: trait theories, behavioral/cognitive theories, psychodynamic theories, and humanistic theories.

441

TRAIT THEORIES OF PERSONALITY

Types and Traits

It has long been apparent that people differ in temperament, or personality characteristics. The earliest known explanation for these individual differences is the *humoral theory*, proposed by the Greek physician Galen in the sec-

William Sheldon suggested that body types are associated with different personalities. According to his theory, a person who is plump (endomorph) is relaxed, sociable, and even-tempered. His research was subsequently found to be too simplistic.

ond century and based on then common medical beliefs that had originated with the ancient Greeks. The body was thought to contain four humors, or fluids. People were classified according to the disposition supposedly produced by the predominance of one of these humors in their system.

Although later biological investigations discredited this theory, the notion that people could be divided into different **personality types** persisted long afterward. Theories of personality type attempt to assign people to different categories, which vary in accordance with the theory. For example, Freud's theory, which maintains that people go through several stages of psychosexual development, predicts the existence of different types of people who have problems associated with each of these stages.

Personality types are very useful in formulating hypotheses, because when a theorist is thinking about personality variables it is easiest to think of extreme cases—prototypes, so to speak. However, most modern investigators reject the notion that individuals can be assigned to discrete categories; instead, they generally conceive of individual differences as quantitative, not qualitative. Rather than classify people by categories, or types, most investigators prefer to measure the degree to which an individual expresses a particular **personality trait.**

A simple example illustrates the difference between types and traits. We could classify people into two different *types*: tall people and short people. Indeed, we use these terms in everyday speech. But we all recognize that height is best conceived of as a *trait*—a dimension on which people can differ along a wide range of values. We can easily observe that people differ in height in a *continuous* rather than a *dichotomous* manner. If we measure the height of a large sample of people, we will find instances all along the distribution, from very short to very tall. (See Figure 15.1.)

Identification of Personality Traits

For centuries, people have assessed other people's personality characteristics on a rather casual, informal basis. We assume that people tend to behave in particular ways in particular situations. Trait theories of personality fit this common-sense view.

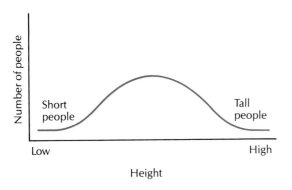

Number of people

Short
people

Tall
people

Low   High

Height

FIGURE 15.1

The distribution of height is continuous, not dichotomous.

Allport: Cardinal and Central Traits

The psychologist who is most closely associated with the early development of trait theories of personality is Gordon Allport (1897–1967). Allport suggested that personality is structured in a hierarchical fashion. **Cardinal traits** are powerful, all-encompassing personality characteristics that can be used to predict the behavior of some people in almost all situations. For example, a person whose life is dedicated to social climbing exhibits this cardinal trait constantly: his or her every move in social situations is related to status. However, most people are not so unidimensional. Instead, their behavior is controlled by a variety of **central traits** such as assertiveness, submissiveness, honesty, or kindness. These traits determine which behaviors will occur in a particular situation. According to Allport, personality traits describe the range of potential behaviors that a person can engage in; for example, a submissive person will find it very difficult to take charge and tell other people what to do. Given the constraining effects of personality traits, the particular behaviors that a person performs will be determined by the situations he or she encounters.

Allport stimulated research into the nature of personality traits, but he himself did not conduct much research into their particular nature. Most of the data on specific personality traits were collected by two researchers, Raymond Cattell and Hans Eysenck. These psychologists used the method of factor analysis to determine reliable patterns in people's behavior.

Cattell: Factor Analysis

You will recall from Chapter 9 that factor analysis seeks out test items that tend to be correlated with each other. This method entails making a wide variety of observations of the behavior of a large number of people. Usually the observations are limited to responses to a number of questions on a paper-and-pencil test, but occasionally the investigator observes people's behavior in seminatural situations. Mathematical procedures then permit the investigator to determine which particular items tend to be answered in the same way by a given person, so as to infer the existence of common factors. For example, a shy person would tend to say "no" to statements such as "I attend parties as frequently as I can" and "When I enter a room full of people, I like to be noticed." In contrast, nonshy people would tend to say "yes" to these statements. However, the trait of shyness would probably not determine whether people would say "yes" or "no" to statements such as "I worry about my health a lot" or "I often get an upset stomach." The response to these statements would be related to the trait of hypochondriasis (excessive concern with one's health).

According to Eysenck, extraverted people tend to seek out interactions with others. They also crave excitement and enjoy social events such as parties.

TABLE 15.1

Cattell's sixteen personality factors, obtained by factor analysis

Factor	Description of High Score	Description of Low Score
A	Outgoing, participating	Reserved, detached
B	Intelligent, abstract thinking	Less intelligent, concrete thinking
C	Emotionally stable, calm	Emotionally less stable, easily upset
E	Assertive, stubborn	Humble, conforming
F	Sober, serious	Happy-go-lucky, enthusiastic
G	Conscientious, rule-bound	Evades rules, feels few obligations
H	Venturesome, uninhibited	Shy, restrained, timid
I	Tender-minded, sensitive	Tough-minded, realistic
L	Suspicious, hard to fool	Trusting, free of jealousy
M	Imaginative, careless of practical matters	Practical, regulated by external realities
N	Shrewd, calculating	Forthright, natural
O	Apprehensive, troubled	Self-assured, confident
Q_2	Experimenting, liberal, free-thinking	Conservative, respecting established ideas
Q_2	Self-sufficient, resourceful	Group-dependent, "joiner"
Q_3	Controlled, follows self-image	Undisciplined self-conflict, follows own urges
Q_4	Tense, frustrated, driven	Relaxed, tranquil, unfrustrated

Based on Cattell, R.B., and Stice, G.F. *Handbook for the Sixteen Personality Factor Questionnaire,* Champaign, Ill.: Institute for Personality and Ability Testing, 1962.

In practice, psychologists ask people hundreds of questions and mathematically identify the factors that the different questions assess, such as shyness or hypochondriasis. To the degree that people possess orderly personality traits, they tend to answer certain clusters of questions in a particular way. Cattell (1946) began with hypotheses he formulated by observing people's actual behavior. Based on analyses of these observations, he devised thousands of questions, which he presented to subjects in the form of questionnaires. He performed factor analyses on the data and constructed new, improved tests. Eventually he identified sixteen personality factors. Table 15.1 lists them in order of importance.

Eysenck: Introversion-Extraversion

Eysenck also used the factor analytical method to devise his theory of personality. His research suggested that personality is controlled by two important dimensions: **introversion-extraversion** and **neuroticism.** Here are Eysenck's definitions of introversion and extraversion, which are seen as opposite ends of a single scale:

The typical introvert is a quiet, retiring sort of person, introspective, fond of books rather than people; he is reserved and distant except to intimate friends. He tends to plan ahead, "looks before he leaps," and mistrusts the impulse of the moment. He does not like excitement, takes matters of everyday life with proper seriousness, and likes a well-ordered mode of life. He keeps his feelings under close control, seldom behaves in an aggressive manner, and does not lose his temper easily. He is reliable, somewhat pessimistic, and places great value on ethical standards.

The typical extravert is sociable, likes parties, has many friends, needs to have people to talk to, and does not like reading or studying by himself. He craves excitement, takes chances, often sticks his neck out, acts on the spur of the moment, and is generally an impulsive individual. He is fond of practical jokes, always has a ready answer, and generally likes change; he is carefree, easygoing, optimistic, and "likes to laugh and be merry." He prefers to keep moving and doing things, tends to be aggressive and loses his temper quickly; altogether his feelings are not kept under tight control, and he is not always a reliable person. (Eysenck and Rachman, 1965, p. 19)

Eysenck's second dimension, neuroticism, is a measure of a person's stability. For example, a neurotic person would tend to say "yes" to the following questions: "Do ideas run through your head so that you cannot sleep?" "Are you inclined to be moody?" and "Do you often make up your mind too late?" The combination of this dimension with the dimension of introversion-extraversion results in a variety of personality characteristics. Figure 15.2 illustrates the combinations of these dimensions and relates them to the four temperaments described by Galen.

Eysenck (1982) believes that a person's degree of introversion-extraversion depends on the ease with which he or she can be aroused; easily aroused people tend to learn social prohibitions and to become more restrained and inhibited. These people become introverts. His research has shown that introverts are more sensitive to pain, more easily fatigued, and more easily bored, that they work more slowly and carefully on tasks, and that their performance gets worse when they are excited. Neurotic people are emotionally unstable; they worry, often have complaints such as headaches, dizziness, upset stomachs, and changes in heart rhythms. Eysenck believes that the biological cause of this behavior pattern is a rapid, intense physiological response to stress that declines slowly after the stressful situation ends.

Eysenck's theory has received considerable support, especially from his own laboratory, which has been especially productive. However, a recent study suggests that one of his dimensions, introversion-extraversion, actually reflects two related but different personality traits. Most researchers, including Eysenck, have identified as introverts people who tend to be reserved during social contacts with strangers (thus expressing shyness) and those who prefer their own company or feel uncomfortable with others (thus expressing unsociability). Cheek and Buss (1981) hypothesized that people could be shy and sociable, preferring to be with other people but feeling anxious when they were, or they could be nonshy and unsociable, feeling comfortable with other people but preferring their own company. They compiled a set of statements they believed would be related to one or the other of these traits and presented them to a group of subjects. Some results are shown in Table 15.2 on page 446.

The investigators performed a factor analysis of the results and found, as they had predicted, that two factors did exist. The factors of shyness and sociability were related, but some shy people were sociable, and some nonshy people were unsociable. In a second study they used their new tests to measure people's degree of

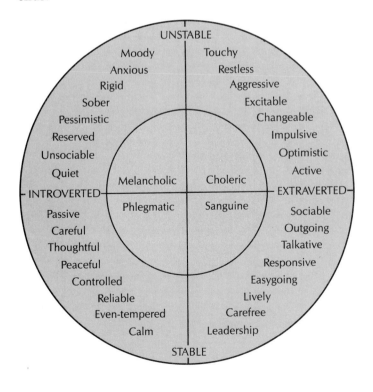

FIGURE 15.2

According to Eysenck, the two dimensions of neuroticism (stable versus unstable) and introversion-extraversion combine to form a variety of personality characteristics. The four personality types based on the Greek theory of humors are shown in the center. (From Eysenck, H.J. *The Inequality of Man.* San Diego, Calif.: Edits Publishers, 1975.)

TABLE 15.2

Some items loading heavily on the factors of shyness and sociability

Shyness

I feel tense when I'm with people I don't know well.

I feel inhibited in social situations.

When conversing, I worry about saying something dumb.

I am often uncomfortable at parties and other social functions.

Sociability

I like to be with people.

I welcome the opportunity to mix socially with people.

I prefer working with others rather than alone.

I find people more stimulating than anything else.

Adapted from Cheek, J.M., and Buss, A.H. *Journal of Personality and Social Psychology*, 1981, *41*, 330–339.

shyness and sociability and had the people (who were strangers to each other) meet in pairs and converse with each other for five minutes. Not surprisingly, they found the unshy people, whether they were sociable or not, tended to talk more than shy people. Observers' ratings showed that *shy and sociable* people appeared to be the most tense and inhibited; in contrast, *shy and unsociable* people were less tense. Presumably, the people who were shy and sociable had a desire to associate with others but were afraid that they would fail; thus, the social situation put their longing and their fear in conflict, making them tense. However, people who were shy and unsociable had no desire to associate with others, so the situation provided nothing to worry about. (See Figure 15.3.) The experiment indicates that the two traits—shyness and sociability—are partly independent, and both must be taken into account in describing personality.

Heritability of Personality Traits

Several trait theorists, such as Allport, Cattell, and Eysenck, asserted that at least some aspects of personality are determined by a person's genetic history. In a large study of 800 sets of adolescent twins, Loehlin and Nichols (1976) used tests to measure a variety of personality characteristics and estimated their heritability

FIGURE 15.3

Time spent talking by people of high and low sociability and shyness, along with observers' ratings of degree of tenseness and inhibition. (Based on data from Cheek, J.M., and Buss, A.H. *Journal of Personality and Social Psychology*, 1981, *41*, 330–339.)

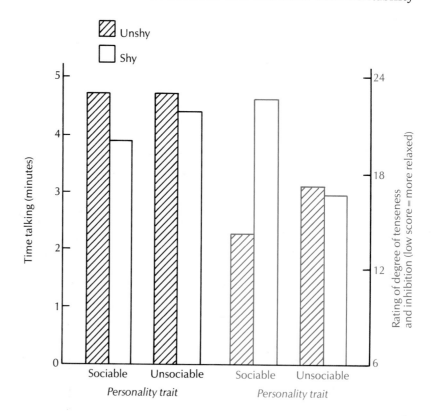

by comparing dizygotic and monozygotic twins. They found a substantial contribution from heredity, in that monozygotic twins were generally more similar in measures of these traits than dizygotic twins. Because monozygotic twins are more genetically similar than dizygotic twins, this finding suggests that differences in temperament are related to genetic factors. In contrast, environmental family influences were not statistically significant.

Two longitudinal studies on pairs of twins have shown that some genetically influenced behavioral traits seen in infancy show a reasonable amount of stability over the years. Goldsmith and Gottesman (1981) found that *activity level* was the first stable, genetically influenced trait to emerge, followed by *task persistence* and *irritability* at four years, and *active adjustment* and *fearfulness* at seven years. Matheny, Wilson, Dolan, and Krantz (1981) interviewed mothers about their twins' behavioral characteristics during the children's first six years. They found that various measures of emotionality and sociability—particularly *temper, activity level, attention* (or *task persistence*), *irritability,* and *social responsiveness*—were especially stable during development. The monozygotic twins were more similar than the dizygotic twins, suggesting that the traits have a genetic component.

Daniels and Plomin (1985) used another technique to assess the heritability of the traits of shyness and sociability. They compared the personality traits of adopted children with their biological mothers, who had not raised them, and their adoptive mothers, who had. They found that the biological mothers' degree of introversion-extraversion was significantly related to the sociability and shyness of their offspring; in contrast, they observed no relation between the scores of the adoptive mothers and their adopted children. Because the biological mothers did not raise the children, their behavior could not have affected them; thus, the relation must have resulted from genetic factors.

Daniels and Plomin also found evidence suggesting that family environment may have influenced the children's behavior. Children in families that "perceive themselves to be involved in cultural events, like to learn about new and different things, often have friends over to visit, are active in sports and recreation,

express their feelings and thoughts openly, and give family members the freedom to do as they wish" tended not to be shy (p. 120).

- How would you distinguish between personality types and personality traits? Give examples of each.
- According to Allport, how do cardinal and central traits differ?
- What contributions were made by Cattell and Eysenck to the identification of personality traits?
- What are the implications of the twin and adoption studies on the heritability of personality traits?

BEHAVIORAL/COGNITIVE THEORIES OF PERSONALITY

Some psychologists, such as Cattell and Eysenck, are interested in the ways in which people differ with respect to their personality traits. Other psychologists are more interested in the ways in which people's behavioral characteristics are determined by what they encounter in their environment. This section considers the behaviorist and social-learning approaches to personality.

Behaviorism

The most famous and influential behaviorist is B.F. Skinner, whose writings are either beautifully insightful and persuasive or infuriatingly wrong, according to the reader's point of view. Perhaps it is unfair to Skinner to call his view of human personality a "theory," because he dislikes the term, at least as most psychologists use it. Skinner does not believe that most concepts dear to the hearts of personality theorists—those that deal with internal states and dispositions—are of any use in understanding human behavior. Instead, he believes that we must simply study an individual's behavior in response to his or her environment. According to Skinner, what we need to determine are the re-

TABLE 15.3

Nature and effects of process and content social rewards

Process Social Rewards (Reinforcing Only at Moderate Levels)			
Reward	**Deficiency**	**Excess**	**Associated Trait**
Mere presence of others	Isolation	Crowding	Loneliness
Attention from others	Shunning	Conspicuousness	Exhibitionism vs. shyness
Responsivity of others	Boredom	Overarousal	Sociability
Initiation of others	No interaction	Intrusiveness	Sociability and shyness

Content Social Rewards (Reinforcing at High Levels)		
Reward	**Its Opposite**	**Associated Trait**
Deference from others	Insolence, disrespect	Formality
Praise from others	Criticism	Self-esteem
Sympathy from others	Disdain	Emotionality
Affection from others	Hostility, rejection	Self-esteem

Adapted from Buss, A.H. *Journal of Personality and Social Psychology,* 1983, 44, 553–563.

lations between stimuli and responses; nothing is gained by assuming the existence of personality structures within the individual. Here is how Skinner puts it:

It is often said that a science of behavior studies the human organism but neglects the person or self. What it neglects is a vestige of animism, a doctrine which in its crudest form held that the body was moved by one or more indwelling spirits. When the resulting behavior was disruptive, the spirit was probably a devil; when it was creative, it was a guiding genius or muse. Traces of the doctrine survive when we speak of a *personality,* of an ego in ego psychology, or an *I* who says he knows what he is going to do and uses his body to do it, or of the role a person plays as a persona in a drama, wearing his body as a costume. (1974, p. 184)

Skinner believes that human behavior is ultimately explainable in terms of the principles of instrumental conditioning. This approach is called **radical behaviorism.** *Radical* derives from the Latin word *radix,* meaning "root." Hence, radical behaviorism is behaviorism that is pure to the root.

In Skinner's view, personality traits are best conceived of as behavioral tendencies produced by a person's history of reinforcement. For example, if a child's performance is reinforced on a variable-interval or variable-ratio schedule, he or she is likely to become industrious, because intermittent reinforcement leads to steady work and resistance to extinction. Conversely, if a child is given frequent, noncontingent reinforcers independent of his or her performance, the child will probably learn to be lazy. A child who is frequently punished will probably become timid and fearful or especially aggressive, depending on the schedule of punishment.

Skinner does not make a serious attempt to study enduring personality traits that might be a result of a person's heredity. Although he does not rule out hereditary factors in temperament, he views a person's conditioning history as more important and interesting. His goal is to be able to predict and control behavior, and nonmodifiable behaviors do not hold much interest for him.

Social Learning Theory

Social learning theory is derived from the behavioral approach to personality, but it differs from Skinner's radical behaviorism in its use of cognitive concepts, which are not directly observable. Social learning theorists believe that learning is the most important factor in personality development, and that interactions with other people provide the most important experiences. Buss (1983), in discussing the types of reinforcing stimuli that can be provided by other people, describes two major types of social rewards. **Process rewards** involve social stimulation; they are pleasant in moderate amounts, but too much or too little is aversive. **Content rewards** involve relationships between individuals; they consist of bipolar dimensions, with one end being reinforcing and the other end being aversive. These two types of rewards (or punishers) have effects on personality traits; process rewards are related to sociability, whereas content rewards are related to formality (politeness), self-esteem, and emotionality. (See Table 15.3.)

Social learning theorists emphasize the effects of the person on the environment as well as the effects of the environment on the person. These theorists attempt to understand covert behaviors such as planning and thinking, which cannot entirely be understood by examining the immediate environment, because they depend so much on the person's genetic makeup and earlier experiences. According to Mischel (1973), the most important personality characteristics are those that determine how people perceive and categorize various situations and how much value they place on particular social reinforcers and punishers. These characteristics lead them to perceive situations in certain ways and to form expectations about what might happen. These cognitions determine their goals or plans and select which behaviors will take place in a particular situation.

Social learning theorists make much use of the term *self*. For example, they discuss people's self-concepts, their tendency to engage in self-praise or self-criticism, and their ability to exercise self-control. A **self-concept** is a person's perception of his or her own personality and ability. **Self-praise** and **self-criticism** are responses people make after perceiving their own behavior and its consequences; obviously, these responses are learned by observing the behavior of others. For example, in Chapter 6, I described the example of a little girl learning how to write. When she succeeded in printing a letter that looked like the one her teacher made, she "praised herself" as her teacher had done in the past and experienced a feeling of satisfaction. As we saw, this process is an example of conditioned reinforcement. **Self-control** refers to people's ability to withhold a response that is normally elicited by a particular situation. For example, a child exercises a form of

self-control called **delay of gratification** when he or she waits patiently for a larger reward rather than immediately taking a smaller one. Children differ considerably in their ability to delay gratification; thus, the ability serves as an important personality trait (Bandura and Mischel, 1965; Mischel, 1977).

Bandura: Self-Efficacy

Bandura (1977) has developed a concept he calls *self-efficacy*, which consists of people's belief in their ability to succeed in the tasks they set out to accomplish. Thus, self-efficacy combines two issues important to social learning theorists: self-concept and self-control. Because Bandura has applied the concept of self-efficacy to psychotherapy, it will be described in more detail in Chapter 17.

Social learning theorists believe that social rewards are an important determinant of personality. Social stimulation is reinforcing only in moderation; too much stimulation can be aversive.

Studies demonstrate that we are emotionally and psychologically healthier if we attribute our successes to our own efforts (internal control) rather than external factors.

Social learning theorists differ from behaviorists in the role they assign to the process of reinforcement. According to behaviorists, learning does not occur without reinforcement. Social learning theorists agree that reinforcement is very important, but they assert that some learning can take place without it. Bandura (1977) says that much social learning takes place through observation; people see what other people do and what happens as a result, and they learn new responses by watching this process take place. They do not have to engage in overt behaviors or to experience reinforcement or punishment directly.

Locus of Control

Although behavioral and social learning theorists tend to focus on the situational factors that are responsible for behavior, most of us believe that our personality traits and intentions are at least partly responsible for what we do. But this belief is not uniform; people differ in the degree of control they attribute to themselves. Some people believe that fate, or a deity, or people in authority determine what happens to them; they attribute their behavior to external control. They have what psychologist Julian Rotter (1966) calls an **external locus of control.** Others believe that their destiny is up to them; they accept credit for their successes, and responsibility for their failures. These people have what Rotter calls an **internal locus of control.** The two groups of people are called *externals* and *internals,* respectively.

At first glance, it might appear that attribution to internal control would always be more desirable, but this is not true for all situations. A slave who believes that he is responsible for his own situation is obviously going to be unhappier than one who realizes that external forces have shaped his fate. In some environments, belief in external control is both logical and desirable. For example, Lao (1970) has shown that black people in the southern United States are most likely to be mentally and emotionally healthy if they attribute their social status to external forces and their personal accomplishments to internal forces (that is, to their own efforts). These attributions are obviously realistic: A black person's social status receives its definition from a predominantly white society, and, given this situation, the person will not accomplish much unless he or she exerts considerable effort.

Many studies have shown that the internal-external trait is an important personality variable. It seems probable that this trait is a function of experience. Whatever the cause may be, internals and externals act very differently in most situations.

In many psychological experiments, internals appear to go their own way. If they think they have figured out what the experimenter wants them to do, they behave contrary to the external control. Strickland (1970) tried to reinforce subjects' choice of the verb from among four words written on cards. She would nod and say "um-hm" each time a verb was chosen. Internals who perceived the strategy apparently did not like being manipulated; they tended to avoid choosing verbs until the experimenter stopped nodding and saying "um-hm." These subjects appeared willing to demonstrate that they knew the correct answer, so long as doing so did not make them look as if they were being manipulated.

Internals are not simply more stubborn than externals. Ritchie and Phares (1969) found that internals and externals were equally susceptible to changes in their opinions if they were given well-reasoned arguments. However, externals were more swayed by poorly reasoned statements attributed to authority figures (such as the Secretary of the United States Treasury) than by those attributed to their own peers (such as a college sophomore). Internals were not affected by the source of the statement.

Internals and externals also differ in their reactions to tasks that appear to be controlled by chance as opposed to skill. Karabenick and Srull (1978) ascertained whether subjects were internals or externals. They then had the subjects perform a task. Half the subjects were told that their performance would depend on their skill; the other half were told that their success would depend on chance. In fact, the subjects' success was controlled by the experimenters. After performing the task, the subjects were asked to report their scores to the experimenter. Internals tended to exaggerate their scores in the skill-determined task, and externals tended to exaggerate their scores in the luck-determined task. The subjects appeared to exaggerate the scores on the kinds of tasks that were most important to their own self concept: Internals believed themselves to be skillful; externals believed themselves to be lucky.

■ What is Skinner's radical behaviorism? How does it relate to the study of personality?

■ What is social learning theory? How does it compare to the radical behavioristic approach to personality?

■ How do people with an internal locus of control differ from people with an external locus of control?

The Trait Versus Situation Controversy

Both behaviorists and social learning theorists stress the influence of the environment on behavior. They tend to place less emphasis on the role of deep-seated personality traits. In contrast, trait theorists assume that people's dispositions are relatively stable, permitting others to predict how particular people will behave in various situations. Mischel (1968, 1976) has criticized the concept of stable personality traits. He has suggested that situations, and not traits, best predict behavior. Consider two situations: a party to celebrate someone's winning a large sum of money in a lottery and a funeral. Certainly people will be much more talkative, cheerful, and outgoing at the party than at the funeral. But suppose you know a person's score on a test of introversion-extraversion. How much will this knowledge enable you to predict whether he or she will be talkative and outgoing? In this case, it would seem that knowing the situation has much more predictive value than knowing the test score.

Cross-Situational Reliability

Several studies have shown that people tend to behave inconsistently (Mischel, 1968; Bem, 1972). For example, various personal characteristics, such as attitude toward authority and moral behavior have typically showed a **cross-situational reliability** of less than .30. That is, the correlation between people's attitudes or behavior in two different situations was less than .30. A correlation of .30 means that less than 10 percent of the variability in people's behavior is a result of differences in personality traits. If personality traits account for less than 10 percent of the variability in human behavior, then perhaps the assessment of personality traits is not very useful.

Other psychologists responded to these criticisms. For example, Epstein (1977) noted that traits are more stable than some of these measures had suggested. He made two general points. First, assessments of cross-situational reliability usually involve testing a group of people on two occasions and correlating their behavior in one situation with their behavior in the other. Epstein showed that repeated measurements across several days yielded much higher correlations; reliability measures approached .80.

Second, the question "Which is more important in determining a person's behavior, the situation or his or her personality traits?" is similar to the question "Which is more important in determining a person's intelligence, heredity or environment?" and the answer to both questions is "It depends." As we saw in Chapter 9, heritability depends on the particular population that is being considered. For example, heritability of hair color is zero in a population that is homogeneous for this trait, such as Eskimos, but is high in heterogeneous populations. Similarly, the degree to which personality traits can be used to predict behavior depends on the variability of that trait within the population and on the variability of the situations.

Epstein suggested a useful analogy. Suppose we want to predict how long it takes a person to finish a race. We test a very heterogeneous group of people—young, old, fat, thin, athletic, and sedentary—in a 100-meter and a 200-meter

race. Obviously, we would predict that people will take longer to finish the 200-meter race. However, the range of finishing times will be very great. In fact, it will undoubtedly take less time for the faster runners to finish the 200-meter race than it will take the slower runners to finish the 100-meter race. Knowing which race a person runs, then, does not tell us much. In contrast, knowing a person's running ability tells us much more. In this case, the trait of running ability is more informative than the length of the race.

Now suppose all the contestants are male Olympic-class runners. It is likely that all of them will finish the race within a few seconds of each other. If we want to predict how long it will take for each runner to finish, the more useful information will be the race in which the contestant is running, not his running ability. The situation is now much more predictive than the personal characteristics of the runners.

More recently, Mischel (1977, 1979) has acknowledged that personality traits are also often important. The importance depends on a number of factors, including the variability of situations and the homogeneity of the population that is being observed. Mischel (1977) also pointed out that some situations, by their very nature, severely constrain a person's behavior, whereas others permit a wide variety of responses. He noted that some situations are "powerful," in that they largely determine people's responses, with little variability present. For example, red lights cause almost all motorists to stop their cars. In this case, knowing the particular situation (the color of the traffic light) predicts behavior better than knowing something about the personality characteristics of the drivers. Conversely, some situations are "weak" and have little control over people's behavior. For example, a card on the TAT (discussed later in this chapter) with the instructions to tell a story will lead to very different behaviors from different people; in this case, knowing something about the people's personality traits has high predictive value.

Just as situations can be classified as strong or weak, we can probably classify personality variables as strong or weak in their predictive value. Consider a person who is so terribly depressed that she will not talk to anyone, but hangs her head, weeping quietly. She does so whether she is along in her room or among a

Some situations exert strong control over people's behavior. In this crowded subway, even someone who is usually calm and easygoing would probably become angry at the pushing and the overcrowded conditions.

group of people at a party. Or consider a violent psychopath who attacks anyone who comes near him. He has to be restrained to be prevented from hurting others. The behavior of these people is much less dependent on situations than the behavior of most people. Although these are extreme cases, it seems likely that some personality variables predict behavior better than others in a variety of situations.

Personality and situations are usually conceived of as independent variables, but this is not always true. In laboratory settings, experimenters assign people to various situations; here, situation and personality are truly independent. However, as Bem and Allen (1974) pointed out, people in real life are more able to choose the situations they enter. Thus, even though a party is a moderately powerful situation and tends to produce extraverted behaviors, introverted people may stay away from parties to avoid situations that encourage behaviors with which they are not comfortable. Similarly, extraverts may avoid situations in which they are alone. The fact that people choose their own situations means that personality traits *interact* with situations.

In acknowledgment of this interaction, psychologists appear to have reached a consensus in the situation-trait controversy. The original question, "Which is more important in determining a person's behavior, the situation or his or her personality traits?" has proved to simplistic. Some types of personality traits will prevail in most situations, some situations will dictate the behavior of most of the participants, and there are also interactions between situation and personality that require the analysis of both variables.

Predicting People's Behavior: The Template Method

The fact that people's personality traits can interact with situations in determining how people behave makes it difficult to predict how a particular person will behave in a particular situation. Bem and Funder (1978) have proposed a method for predicting the results of these interactions. They suggest that **templates** ("patterns") can be constructed for various situations and personality traits that can be used to categorize person-by-situation interactions. For example, suppose a person is considering

whether to attend a particular college. Should he or she do so? Knowing how well he or she would do at the "average" college or knowing how well the "average" student does at that college is not especially useful. What the student wants to know is how he or she, in particular, will do at that college.

Bem and Funder suggested that this information can be supplied through templates that describe various types of students who have attended the college. For example, "students who are hard working but somewhat shy tend to get good grades [at this college] but do not have much interaction with the faculty; students who are bright and assertive often get involved in faculty research projects but as a consequence have little social life and get lower grades than they should . . . ," and so forth (Bem and Funder, 1978, p. 486). All that students need to do is find the template that matches their own personal characteristics and decide whether they would be satisfied with the outcome. If it is unsatisfactory, then they should try to find better outcomes from the templates supplied by other colleges.

Bem and Funder tested their hypothesis by using templates to assess the ability of children to delay gratification. They found that the patterns of personality traits (rated by the children's parents) were quite different in two different tests of the ability: (1) a choice between waiting and receiving the snack the children liked most or immediately eating the one they liked less and (2) measurement of how long they would work on a puzzle and refrain from opening a gaily wrapped gift that was set in front of them. The most important characteristics in experiment 1 were having high standards of performance, having a low intellectual capacity, being emotionally nonexpressive, having poor verbal fluency, and not being curious and eager too learn. The most important characteristics in experiment 2 were not attempting to transfer blame to others and making plans and thinking ahead. As Bem and Funder noted, the types of children portrayed by these two templates are quite different. Thus, even though both studies are concerned with delay of gratification, a different type of child performs best in each situation. Their method promises to provide a useful way in which to characterize the interactions between people and situations.

- What is the controversy over the relative importance of traits and situations as predictors of behavior?
- What does the research on this controversy suggest is more important in predicting behavior, traits or situations?

THE PSYCHODYNAMIC APPROACH TO PERSONALITY

The work of Sigmund Freud has had a profound and lasting effect on twentieth-century society. Terms such as *ego, id, libido, repression, rationalization, Oedipus complex,* and *fixation* became as familiar to most Western laypeople as to clinicians. Before Freud formulated his theory, people believed that most behavior was determined by rational, conscious processes, although strong emotions might drive some to do irrational things. Freud was the first to claim that what we do is *often* irrational, and that the reasons for our behavior are seldom available to our conscious mental processes. The mind, to Freud, was a battleground for the warring factions of instinct, reason, and conscience. The term **psychodynamic** refers to this struggle among the various aspects of personality.

Sigmund Freud (1856–1939) was a Viennese physician who acquired his early training in neurology in the laboratory of Ernst Wilhelm von Brücke, an eminent physiologist and neuroanatomist. Freud's work in the laboratory consisted mostly of careful anatomical observation rather than experimentation. This approach also characterized his later work with human behavior; he made detailed observations of individual patients and attempted to draw inferences about the structure of the human psyche from these cases. (*Psyche,* from the Greek *psukhē,* meaning "breath" or "soul," refers to the mind.) Freud did not try to carry out any psychological experiments. His disciples have continued in his tradition of observing and analyzing the verbal reports of patients.

Freud hoped to obtain a position at a university and continue his research, but the fact that he was Jewish made it impossible for him to obtain such a post. He therefore decided to set up a private medical practice of his own. Before doing so, he studied in Paris with Jean Martin Charcot, who was investigating the usefulness of hypnosis as a treatment for hysteria. Patients with hysteria often experience paralysis of some part of the body, or loss of one of the senses, without any detectable physiological cause. The fact that hypnosis could be used either to produce or to alleviate these symptoms suggested that they were of psychological origin. Charcot proposed that hysterical symptoms were caused by some kind of psychological trauma. Freud was greatly impressed by Charcot's work and became even more interested in problems of the mind.

Freud returned to Vienna and opened his medical practice. He began an association with Josef Breuer, a prominent physician who helped him get his practice established. Freud and Breuer together published a book called *Studies on Hysteria,* and one of the cases cited in it, that of Anna O., provided the evidence that led to some of the most important tenets of Freud's theory.

Anna O. was treated by Breuer twelve years before he and Freud published their book. She suffered from an incredible number of hysterical symptoms, including loss of speech, disturbances in vision, headaches, and paralysis and loss of feeling in her right arm. Under hypnosis, Anna was asked to go back to the times when her symptoms had started. Each of her symptoms appeared to have begun just when she was unable to express a strongly felt emotion. While under hypnosis, she experienced these emotions again and the experience gave her relief from her hysterical symptoms. It was as if the emotions had been bottled up, and reliving the original experiences uncorked them. This release of energy (which Breuer and Freud called *catharsis*) presumably eliminated the hysterical symptoms.

The case of Anna O. is one of the most-reported cases in the annals of psychotherapy. However, Breuer's original description appears to be inaccurate in some of its most important respects (Ellenberger, 1972). Apparently the woman was not at all cured by Breuer's hypnosis and psychotherapy. Ellenberger discovered the existence of hospital records indicating that Anna O. (actually, Bertha Pappenheim) continued to take morphine for the distress caused by the disorders that Breuer had allegedly cured.

Freud appears to have learned later that the cure was a fabrication, but this fact did not become generally known until recently. However, Breuer's failure to help Anna O. with her problems does not mean that we must reject psychoanalysis. Although Breuer's apparent success inspired Freud to examine the unconscious, Freud's theory of personality must stand or fall on its own merits, evaluated by more modern evidence.

The case of Anna O., along with evidence obtained from his own clinical practice, led Freud to reason that human behavior is motivated by instinctual drives, which when activated, supply psychic energy. This energy is aversive, because the nervous system seeks a state of quiet equilibrium. According to Freud, if something prevents the psychic energy caused by activation of a drive from being discharged, psychological disturbances will result. (As we saw in Chapter 11, not all psychologists agree that organisms invariably seek a state of reduced drive.)

Structures of the Mind: The Id, Ego, and Superego

Freud was struck by the fact that psychological disturbances could stem from events that a person apparently could no longer consciously recall, although they could be revealed during hypnosis. This phenomenon led him to conclude that the mind consists of both unconscious and conscious elements.

Freud divided the mind into three structures: the id, the ego, and the superego. The operations of the **id** are completely unconscious. Its forces provide the energy for all psychic processes. The id contains the **libido,** which is the primary source of motivation; this force is insistent and is unresponsive to the demands of reality.

The **ego** is the self. It controls and integrates behavior. It acts as a mediator, negotiating a compromise among the pressures of the id, the counterpressures of the superego, and the demands of reality. The ego's functions of perception, cognition, and memory perform this mediation. The ego is driven by the **reality principle,** or the ability to delay gratification of a drive until an appropriate goal is located. To ward off the demands of the id when these demands cannot be gratified, the ego used **defense mechanisms** (described later.) Some of the functions of the ego are unconscious.

The **superego** is subdivided into the conscience and the ego-ideal. The **conscience** is the internalization of the rules and restrictions of society. It determines which behaviors are permissible and punished wrongdoing with feelings of guilt. The **ego-ideal** is the internalization of what the person would like to be—his or her goals. The superego like the id, is unconscious and is subject to irrational thought. For example, guilt feelings are not always rational.

Freud proposed that the mind is made up of the id, the ego, and the superego. Police work can be seen as performing the duties of the superego, such as enforcing the rules and regulations of society.

Freud found the mind to be full of conflicts. A conflict might begin when one of the two primary drives, the **sexual instinctual drive** or the **aggressive instinctual drive,** is aroused. These drives demand gratification but are often held in check by **internalized prohibitions** against the behaviors he drives end to produce. Internalized prohibitions are characteristics of the superego. They are rules of behavior learned in childhood that protect the person from the guilt that he or she would feel if the instinctual drives were allowed to express themselves. The result of the conflict is **compromise formation,** in which a compromise is reached between the demands of the instinctual drive and the suppressive effects of internalized prohibitions. According to Freud, phenomena such as dreams, artistic creations, and slips of the tongue (we now call them *Freudian slips*) are examples of compromise formation.

Freud believed that the *manifest content* of a dream—its actual story line—is only a disguised version of its *latent content* (its hidden message), which is produced by the unconscious. The latent content might be an unexpressed wish related to the sexual or aggressive instinctual drive. For example, a small boy might want to kill his father and sleep with his mother (thus satisfying both instinctual drives). However, if he acted out this scenario in a dream, he would experience very painful guilt and anxiety. Therefore, the **preconscious** (an intermediate system between the conscious and the unconscious) transforms the nasty wishes of the unconscious into a more palatable form; the manifest content of the dream might be that his father became ill, and that the boy helped his mother around the house, assuming some of his father's chores. These chores would substitute for the sexual activity that his unconscious was really interested in. The manifest content of this dream manages to express, at least partly, the latent content supplied by the unconscious.

Defense Mechanisms

According to Freud, the ego contains defense mechanisms that become active whenever unconscious instinctual drives of the id come into conflict with internalized prohibitions of the superego. The signal for the ego to utilize one of its defenses is the state of **anxiety** produced by

Can the behavior of members of the Women's Christian Temperance Union who crusaded in favor of prohibition be explained by Freud's concept of reaction formation?

an intrapsychic conflict. This unpleasant condition motivates the ego to apply a defense mechanism, and thus reduce the anxiety. Six of the most important defense mechanisms are described below.

Repression is a means of preventing an idea, feeling, or memory from reaching consciousness. For example, Freud theorized that Anna O. had repressed the memories causing the conflicts underlying her hysterical symptoms. Repression is the one phenomenon described by Freud that has received experimental attention.

Reaction formation involves replacing a threatening idea with its opposite. An often-cited example of a reaction formation is that of a person who is aroused and fascinated by pornographic material but whose superego will not permit this enjoyment. In consequence, he or she becomes a militant crusader against pornography. Reaction formation can be a very useful defense mechanism in this situation, permitting sexually acceptable interaction with the forbidden object. The crusader against pornography often studies the salacious material to see just how vile it is, so that he or she can better educate others about its harmful nature. Thus, enjoyment becomes possible without feelings of guilt.

Projection involves denial of one's own unacceptable desires and the discovery of evidence of these desires in the behavior of other people. For example, a man who is experiencing a great deal of repressed hostility may perceive the world as being full of people who are hostile to him. In this way, he can blame someone else for any conflicts in which he engages.

Sublimation is the diversion of psychic energy from an unacceptable drive to an acceptable one. For example, a person may feel strong sexual desire but find its outlet unacceptable because of internalized prohibitions. Despite repression of the drive, is energy remains and finds an outlet in another drive, such as artistic or other creative activities. Freud considered sublimation to be an important factor in artistic and intellectual creativity. He believed that people have a fixed amount of drive available for motivating all activities; therefore, surplus sexual instinctual drive that is not expended in its normal way can be used to increase a person's potential for creative achievement.

Rationalization is the process of inventing an acceptable reason for a behavior that is really being performed for another, less acceptable reason. For example, a man who feels guilty about his real reasons for purchasing a magazine containing pictures of naked men or women may say, "I don't buy the magazine for the pictures. I buy it to read the interesting and enlightening articles it contains."

Conversion is the provision of an outlet for intrapsychic conflict in the form of a physical symptom. The conflict is transformed into blindness, deafness, paralysis, or numbness. (This phenomenon has also been called *hysteria*, which should not be confused with the common use of the term to mean "running around and shouting and generally acting out of control.") For example, a person might develop blindness so that he or she will no longer be able to see a situation that arouses a strong, painful intrapsychic conflict. In Chapter 16 we will examine the case of a man who became hysterically blind, apparently because he became jealous watching his wife nurse their child. Anna O.'s problem would also be described as a conversion reaction.

Freud's Psychosexual Theory of Personality Development

Freud believed that the prime mover in personality development was the sexual instinctual drive, which is present in everyone from earliest childhood. In the healthy person, this drive is expressed in certain specific ways at each level of physical development.

Because newborn babies can do little more than suck and drink, their sexual instinctual drive finds an outlet in these activities. Even as babies become able to engage in more complex behaviors, they continue to receive most of their sexual gratification orally. The early period of the **oral stage** of personality development is characterized by sucking and is passive in character. Later, as babies become more aggressive, they derive their pleasure from biting and chewing.

The **anal stage** of personality development begins during the second year of life. Now babies begin to enjoy emptying their bowels (*anal* is derived from *anus*, the opening of the large intestine). During the early part of this stage, called the **expressive period,** babies enjoy expelling their feces. Later, in the **retentive period,** they derive pleasure from storing them up.

At around age three, children discover that it is fun to play with their penis or clitoris and they enter the **phallic stage.** (*Phallus* means "penis," but Freud used the term bisexually in

According to Freud's psychosexual theory of development, people fixated at the aggressive phase of the oral stage overindulge in habits like eating and smoking.

this context.) Children also begin to discover the sex roles of their parents, and they attach themselves to the parent of the other sex. A boy's attachment to his mother is called the **Oedipus complex,** after the Greek king of mythology who unknowingly married his mother after killing his father. A girl's attachment to her father is called the **Electra complex.** In Greek mythology, Electra (along with her brother) killed her mother and her mother's lover to avenge her father's death. Although Freud initially accepted the concept of the Electra complex, devised by one of his followers, Carl Jung, both Freud and Jung later rejected it.

In boys, the Oedipus complex normally becomes repressed by age five, although the conflicts that occur during the phallic stage continue to affect their personalities throughout life. A boy's wish to take his father's place is suppressed by his fear that his father will castrate him as punishment. (In fact, Freud believed that young boys regarded females as castrated males.) The conflict is finally resolved when the boy begins to model his behavior on that of his father, so that he achieves **identification** with the father.

Girls supposedly experience fewer conflicts than boys do during the phallic stage. According to Freud, the chief reason for their transfer of love from their mother (who provided primary gratification during early life) to their father is **penis envy.** A girl discovers that she and her mother lack this organ, so she becomes attached to her father, who has one. This attachment persists longer than the Oedipus complex, because the girl does not have to fear castration as revenge for usurping her mother's role. Freud believed that penis envy eventually becomes transformed into a need to bear children. The missing penis is replaced by a baby.

After the phallic stage, there is a **latency period** of several years, during which the child's sexual instinctual drive is mostly submerged. At the onset of puberty, the person begins to form adult sexual attachments to age-mates of the other sex. Because the sexual instinctual drive now finds its outlet in heterosexual genital contact, this stage is known as the **genital stage.**

Freud's psychosexual theory of personality development has been extremely influential because of its ability to explain personality disorders in terms of whole or partial **fixation,** or

"holding in place," at an early stage of development. For example, fixation at the oral stage might result from early (or delayed) weaning from breast to bottle to cup. Someone whose personality is fixed at the early oral stage might be excessively passive. "Biting" sarcasm or compulsive talking would represent fixation at the later, aggressive phase of the oral stage. Other oral-stage activities include habits like smoking and excessive eating.

Improper toilet training can result in fixation at the anal stage. People fixated at the anal-expressive period are characterized as destructive and cruel, while anal-retentives are seen as stingy and miserly. Finally, people who do not successfully pass through the phallic stage may experience a variety of emotional problems. Freud believed that homosexuality stems from unresolved problems during this stage.

■ What are the structures of the mind according to Freud? How would you describe each of these structures?
■ What is the purpose of a defense mechanism? What are the most important defense mechanisms?
■ What are the five stages of personality development that Freud proposed? How would you characterize each stage?

Theoretical Outgrowths of Freud's Theory: The Neo-Freudians

Freud had a number of disciples, known as neo-Freudians, who were strongly influenced by his theoretical formulations. They accepted many of his ideas, such as the central role of the unconscious in personality development, but had difficulty with the strong emphasis Freud placed on biological factors. They placed greater emphasis on social influences, such as people's interpersonal relationships. Among the most influential of the neo-Freudians are Carl Gustav Jung, Alfred Adler, Karen Horney, Erich Fromm, and Erik Erikson.

Jung

Carl Gustav Jung (1875–1961) believed strongly in the power of the unconscious but disagreed with Freud over the nature of the

Jung's notion of the collective unconscious includes an archetype for the all-knowing father-figure. This archetype could be represented in eastern cultures by Buddha and in western cultures by Lincoln.

unconscious. Jung distinguished between what he termed the personal unconscious and the collective unconscious. The **personal unconscious** is similar to Freud's idea of the unconscious. In contrast, the **collective unconscious** is a universal storehouse of humankind's ancestral past (Jung, 1916). It is present at birth and contains myths, dreams, and symbols shared by all of humankind. The collective unconscious is also the source of all creativity.

Jung also believed there were two basic personality orientations: introversion and extraversion. Introversion describes a person who is inwardly focused, and who tends to be quiet and reserved. Extraversion describes a person who is focused on the external world and who tends to be outgoing and active.

Adler

In his theory of personality, Alfred Adler (1870–1937) emphasized the social determinants of human behavior. He believed that people consciously strive for perfection in order to overcome feelings of inferiority, which originate in childhood. According to Adler, once children become aware that they cannot do all the things that adults can do, they experience feelings of inferiority. Consequently, they **strive for superiority**, which propels them to develop and grow. In addition, Adler believed that people have an innate social interest. This motivates people to strive to achieve goals that will contribute to a better society and improve the quality of life.

Horney

Another psychoanalyst to emphasize social influences was Karen Horney (1885–1952). Horney focused on the important role of social relationships in personality development. According to her theory, children discover they are totally dependent on adults for their basic needs. If the parents are loving and dependable, the child develops normally. However, if the parents are indifferent or inconsistent, the child will develop feelings of insecurity. As a result, the child experiences basic anxiety. **Basic anxiety** occurs when the child feels isolated, helpless, and hopeless. These feelings may be accompanied by **basic hostility,** which is the child's anger over the parent's indifference. To cope with these feelings, children develop unhealthy ways of dealing with the world (Horney, 1937).

Fromm

Erich Fromm (1900–1980) strongly believed that personality development is influenced by social factors. He identified five personality orientations that describe ways individuals interact in society: receptive, exploitative, hoarding, marketing, and productive (Fromm, 1941). No one orientation would be adequate to describe someone; people are a blend of two or more orientations. Fromm also believed in the goodness of people. He felt people consciously strive for love, truth, and freedom.

Erikson

Erik Erikson (1902–   ) also emphasized social aspects of personality development rather than biological factors. He also differed with Freud in regard to when personality development takes place. For Freud, the most important development occurs during early childhood; Erikson emphasized the ongoing process of development throughout the lifespan. Erikson's developmental stages were discussed in Chapter 5.

Modern Research on Psychodynamic Constructs

Although Freud's psychodynamic theory has had a profound effect on psychological theory, psychotherapy, and literature, his theory has received little experimental support, mainly because he referred to concepts that are poorly defined and that cannot be observed directly. How is one to study the ego, the superego, or the id? How can one prove (or disprove) that an artist's creativity is the result of a displaced aggressive or sexual instinctual drive?

Repression

The one Freudian phenomenon that has undergone experimental testing is repression. This phenomenon is very important to Freud's theory, because it is one of the primary ego defenses and because it operates by pushing memories (or newly perceived stimuli) into the unconscious. Thus, experimental verification of repression would lend some support to Freud's notions of intrapsychic conflict and the existence of the unconscious.

However, the results have not been conclusive. Typically, the researchers in repression experiments ask subjects to learn some material associated with an unpleasant, ego-threatening situation, then compare their memory for the information with that of subjects who learned the material under nonthreatening conditions. If repression occurs, the threatened subjects should remember less of the material than the nonthreatened subjects. Some studies have reported positive results, but later experiments have shown that other, non-Freudian phenomena could explain them more easily. Perhaps the most important point here is that none of the experiments can really be said to have threatened the subjects' egos, producing the level of anxiety that would lead to the activation of a defense mechanism. Any experimental procedure that did so would probably be unethical.

One representative experiment on repression used a threat to the ego that has a certain amount of plausibility. D'Zurilla (1965) showed subjects ten pictures of inkblots, with two words beneath each inkblot, and asked the subjects to select the word that best described each inkblot. After making their ten choices, subjects in the experimental group were told that the task they had just performed was a test of latent homosexuality (homosexual tendencies that have not yet been fully expressed) and that they had chosen nine out of ten responses indicating this tendency. Control subjects were told that they were helping the experimenter in developing a new psychological test. Five minutes later, both groups were tested to see how many of the twenty words they could remember. The experimental subjects remembered fewer of the words than the control subjects did, perhaps because they were repressing painful memories. The experimenter then told the experimental subjects that they had been deceived, and that the test had nothing at all to do with homosexuality. In a subsequent memory test, the experimental subjects did as well as control subjects. Perhaps the repression had been lifted; because the memories were no longer painful and ego threatening, the conscious was given free access to them.

But there is a simple explanation. D'Zurilla asked the subjects what they had thought about during the five-minute period right after the first test. Most of the experimental subjects reported that they had been thinking about the test and brooding about the inkblots, their alleged homosexual tendencies, and related subjects. This response is quite the opposite of what Freud would have predicted; the subjects should have *avoided* these thoughts if they were painful. Perhaps the poor performance in the first recall test of the twenty words simply stemmed from interference; the subjects were preoccupied with thinking about what they had just been told about themselves. They were probably more interested in worrying about their scores on the test than in trying to remember the twenty words for the experimenter.

This experiment suggests the difficulty involved in testing even the most specific prediction of Freud's theory. It is very hard (perhaps impossible) to prove that a person's behavior is a result of unconscious conflicts.

Self-Deception

Another important feature of Freud's theory is the assertion that people often defend their egos by deceiving themselves. Many psychologists and philosophers have addressed the question of whether **self-deception** is possible. Gur and Sackheim (1979) have analyzed the process and reviewed experimental evidence on the subject. They conclude that self-deception requires that three conditions be met: (1) the person must simultaneously hold two contradictory beliefs, (2) the person must be unaware of one of these beliefs, and (3) motivational factors must be responsible for

determining which belief is conscious, and which is not. If a person is conscious of having two contradictory beliefs, we can conclude that the person is indecisive but not that he or she is engaging in self-deception; thus, the person must not be conscious of one of these beliefs. And just as lying to another person is a motivated behavior, so is lying to oneself.

An experiment by Quattrone and Tversky (1984) demonstrated that people do, indeed, deceive themselves if conditions provide the proper motivation. The experimenters arranged a test of people's physiological reactions, on which it was easy to "cheat." If the subjects believed that a particular type of response indicated that they had a healthy heart, they tended to make that response. Obviously, cheating on the test could not change the health of their heart, any more than putting an ice cube in a person's mouth before taking his or her temperature makes a fever go away. Afterwards, when the experimenters explained the experiment, most of the subjects denied that they had "cheated." Clearly, people's behavior can be affected by beliefs that they do not admit to themselves.

■ In what major ways did the neo-Freudians differ from Freud?
■ Does modern research on repression and self-deception support Freud's concept of defense mechanisms? Why or why not?

HUMANISTIC THEORIES OF PERSONALITY

Humanistic theories of personality are known as the "third force" because they developed in reaction to both psychoanalytic and behavioral theories. They opposed the determinism and pessimism inherent in psychoanalytic theory; they also opposed the mechanistic view of humankind put forth by the behaviorists. Humanistic theories offer an optimistic view, emphasizing a person's natural striving for positive growth and self-determination. Two major theorists in the humanistic tradition are Abraham Maslow (1908–1970) and Carl Rogers (1902–1987).

Maslow and Self-Actualization

Abraham Maslow studied a group of people he believed had reached their full potential. He called these people **self-actualizers** (Maslow, 1954). Among those he studied were historical subjects such as Lincoln and Beethoven, as well as contemporaries such as Eleanor Roosevelt. Maslow wanted to discover what made self-actualizers different from ordinary people. He came up with a list of sixteen distinguishing characteristics (see Table 15.4).

In addition to his work with self-actualizers, Maslow developed a theory of motivation based on human needs. As Figure 15.4 shows, he proposed that human needs are organized in hierarchical fashion, with the most basic physiological needs at the bottom and needs for self-actualization at the very top. Maslow believed that people must satisfy lower level needs before concerning themselves with higher level needs.

Rogers and the Self

Like Maslow, Carl Rogers shared the humanistic assumption that people are basically good;

FIGURE 15.4

Maslow's hierarchy of needs.

left to their own devices, people will naturally strive toward positive growth and self-actualization. Two concepts are central to Rogers' theory of personality: the organism and the self. The **organism** is the totality of a person's experience. The **self** is the private "I" or "me" that is known only to the person. To the extent that the organism and the self are similar, a person is said to be well-adjusted. To describe a person whose experience of the organism and experience of the self are congruent, Rogers used the term **fully-functioning.** Fully-functioning individuals are characterized by openness to experience, positive social relations, unconditional self-regard, and an absence of defensiveness (Rogers, 1961). According to Rogers concepts, to the degree that the organism and the self are not congruent, one's psychological health suffers. Rogers developed his own form of psychotherapy, which you will read about in Chapter 17.

- What is the humanistic approach to personality and how does it differ from the psychodynamic and behavioristic approaches?
- What is self-actualization?
- How does Rogers define a fully-functioning person?

TABLE 15.4

Characteristics of Self-Actualized Individuals

Identify with mankind.

Realistically oriented.

Resist conformity to the culture.

Do not confuse means with ends.

Accept themselves and others.

Spontaneous.

Autonomous and independent.

Sense of humor is philosophical rather than hostile.

Creative.

Problem-centered rather than self-centered.

Detached and need privacy.

Had mystical or spiritual experiences.

Transcend the environment rather than cope with it.

Relationships are deeply emotional.

Democratic values and attitudes.

Fresh appreciation of people and things.

From Maslow, A., *Motivation and Personality.* New York: Harper & Row, 1954

ASSESSMENT OF PERSONALITY TRAITS

You have just learned about the many different theories that have been proposed to explain personality. Similarly, there are many different ways of measuring personality. The final section of the chapter explains how personality tests are constructed and describes some of the more useful and popular personality tests.

Test Construction

The Rational Strategy

The **rational strategy** of measurement requires prior definition of a trait, based on a theory of personality or on clinical observations. From this definition the investigators make predictions about the behavior of people who differ with respect to the trait. For example, to develop a test of "decisiveness" the investigators would list a number of ways in which the behavior of people at the extremes of the dimension would be expected to differ; they would then write items that are relevant to these differences. For instance, decisive people would be expected to answer "yes" to "I make up my mind quickly and have few regrets later" but "no" to "I usually rely on other people's advice when making important decisions." The test would consist of a number of items like these. A person's score would be the total number of "decisive" responses.

The success of this strategy depends on two important factors. First, the theory must be correct, at least with respect to the trait that is being assessed. Second, there must be good correspondence between a person's response and his or her behavior in the situation depicted in a particular question. If a person affirms that he or she relies on other people's advice but in fact never does so, then the question is not measuring what the test constructors think it is.

The Empirical Strategy

The second way to devise a test that measures a personality trait is the **empirical strategy.** Investigators who use this method do not care whether a person's answer bears any relation to

reality. For example, it would not matter whether a person actually relies on other people's advice; it would matter only that a person tends to *answer this question in a particular way,* and that the answer correlates with other measures of the trait in question. To device a test of "decisiveness" by empirical means, a psychologist would write a large number of questions, much as the investigator using the factor analytical method would. After administering the test to a group containing a large number of decisive and indecisive people (the **criterion group**), the investigator would perform a statistical analysis of their answers, retaining those questions that were answered differently by the two groups of people and discarding all the others. The investigator would then devise a new test, using only the good questions, and administer it to a new group of decisive and indecisive people. The decision to retain a particular item would be completely empirical. For example, if decisive people answered "yes" to the item "I prefer oak trees to maples," the question would be used again. It would not matter that there was no apparent logical relation between the item and the trait being assessed. Once the best questions were selected and the worst ones weeded out, the investigator would publish the final form of the test.

The empirical method can be used only when the investigator *already knows* how to identify the traits to be measured. There must be some way to measure the criterion (in this case, decisiveness). Investigators generally use the empirical strategy of test construction when the usual way to measure a personality trait is difficult and expensive—for example, if the measurement requires hours of individual testing by a specially trained person. If a simple paper-and-pencil test can be devised that classifies people in the same way as the expensive method, an obvious savings will result.

Objective Tests of Personality

Many kinds of tests have been devised to measure personality traits. The two major types are objective tests and projective tests. The responses that subjects can make on **objective tests** are severely constrained by the test design; the questions asked are unambiguous, and explicit rules for scoring the subjects' responses can be specified in advance. Responses are usually restricted to agreement or disagreement with a statement (yes/no or true/false) or to selection from a set of alternatives (multiple choice).

One of the oldest and most widely used objective tests of personality is the **Minnesota Multiphasic Personality Inventory (MMPI)**, devised by Hathaway and McKinley in 1939. Their original purpose in developing the test was to produce an objective, reliable method for identifying various personality traits that were related to a person's mental health. The developers believed that this test would be valuable in assessing people for a variety of purposes. For instance, it would provide a specific means of determining how effective psychotherapy was; improvement in people's scores over the course of treatment would indicate that the treatment was successful.

Hathaway and McKinley used the empirical strategy to devise their test. They wrote 504 true/false items and administered the test to several groups of people in mental institutions in Minnesota who had been diagnosed as having certain specific disorders. These diagnoses had been arrived at through psychiatric interviews with the patients. Such interviews are expensive, so a simple paper-and-pencil test that accomplished the same result would be quite valuable. The control group consisted of relatives and friends of the patients, who were tested when they came to visit them. (It is questionable whether these people constituted the best possible group of normal subjects.) The responses were analyzed empirically, and the questions that correlated with various diagnostic labels were included in various scales. For example, if people who had been diagnosed as paranoid tended to say "true" to "I believe I am being plotted against," this question would become part of the paranoia scale.

The current revised version of the MMPI includes over 500 questions, grouped into ten clinical scales and four validity scales. (See Table 15.5.) A particular item can be used on more than one scale. For example, people who are depressed and people who are hypochondriacal (excessively concerned with their health) tend to agree that they have gastrointestinal problems. The clinical scales include many diagnostic terms traditionally used, such as *hypochondriasis, depression,* or *paranoia.*

The validity scales were devised to provide the tester with some assurance that the subjects are answering questions reliably and accurately, and that they can read the questions and pay attention to them. The **? scale** (cannot say) is simply the number of questions not answered. A high score on this scale indicates either that the person finds some questions irrelevant or is evading painful issues.

The **L scale** (lie) contains items such as "I do not read every editorial in the newspaper every day" and "My table manners are not quite as good at home as when I am out in company." A person who disagrees with questions like these is almost certainly not telling the truth. A high score on the L scale suggests the need for caution in interpreting other scales and also reveals something about the subject's personality. In particular, people who score high on this scale tend to be rather naive; more sophisticated people realize that no one is perfect and do not try to make themselves appear to be so.

The **F scale** (frequency) consists of items that are answered one way by at least 90 percent of the normal population. A high score indicates carelessness, poor reading ability, or very unusual personality traits. Usual responses are "false" to items such as "I can easily make other people afraid of me, and sometimes do for the fun of it" and "true" to items such as "I am liked by most people who know me."

The **K scale** (defensiveness) was devised to identify people who are trying to cover up their feelings to guard against internal conflicts that might cause them emotional distress. A person receives a high value on the K scale by answering "false" to statements such as "Criticism or scolding hurts me terribly" and "At periods my mind seems to work more slowly than usual." People who score very *low* on this scale tend to be in need of help or to be unusually immune to criticism and social influences.

Because the MMPI was devised by empirical means, the scales that are based on diagnostic categories can be only as valid as the original classification of the patients. Despite this potential drawback, the MMPI has proved to be very useful in clinical diagnosis. As well as being used in clinical assessment, the MMPI has also been extensively in personality research, and a number of other tests, including the *California Psychological Inventory* and the *Taylor Manifest Anxiety Scale,* are based on it.

TABLE 15.5

Scales of the MMPI

Scales	Criteria
Validity scales	
? (Cannot say)	Number of items left unanswered
L (Lie)	15 items of overly good self-report, such as "I smile at everyone I meet" (answered true)
F (Frequency)	64 items answered in the scored direction by 10 percent or less of normals, such as "There is an international plot against me" (answered true)
K (Correction, or defensiveness)	30 items reflecting defensiveness in admitting to problems, such as "I feel bad when others criticize me" (answered false)
Clinical scales	
Hs (Hypochondriasis)	33 items derived from patients showing abnormal concern with bodily functions, such as "I have chest pains several times a week" (answered true)
D (Depression)	60 items derived from patients showing extreme pessimism, feelings of hopelessness, and slowing of thought and action, such as "I usually feel that life is interesting and worthwhile" (answered false)
Hy (Conversion hysteria)	60 items from neurotic patients using physical or mental symptoms as a way of unconsciously avoiding difficult conflicts and responsibilities, such as "My heart frequently pounds so hard I can feel it" (answered true)
Pd (Psychopathic deviate)	50 items from patients showing a repeated and flagrant disregard for social customs, emotional shallowness, and inability to learn from punishing experiences, such as "My activities and interests are often criticized by others" (answered true)
Mf (Masculinity-femininity)	60 items from patients showing homoeroticism and items differentiating between men and women, such as "I like to arrange flowers" (answered true, scored for femininity)
Pa (Paranoia)	40 items from patients showing abnormal suspiciousness and delusions of grandeur or persecution, such as "There are evil people trying to influence my mind" (answered true)
Pt (Psychasthenia)	48 items from neurotic patients showing obsessions, compulsions, abnormal fears, and guilt and indecisiveness, such as "I save nearly everything I buy, even after I have no use for it" (answered true)
Sc (Schizophrenia)	78 items from patients showing bizarre or unusual thoughts or behavior, frequent withdrawals, and delusions and hallucinations, such as "Things around me do not seem real" (answered true) and "It makes me uncomfortable to have people close to me" (answered true)
Ma (Hypomania)	46 items from patients showing emotional excitement, overactivity, and flight of ideas, such as "At times I feel very 'high' or very 'low' for no apparent reason" (answered true)
Si (Social introversion)	70 items from persons showing shyness, little interest in people, and insecurity, such as "I have the time of my life at parties" (answered false)

Projective Tests of Personality

Projective tests of personality are quite different in form from objective ones. They are designed to be ambiguous, so that the person's answers will reveal more about him or her than agreement or disagreement with statements provided by the test constructor would show. The assumption is that the subject will "project" his or her personality into the ambiguous situation and thus make responses that give clues to this personality. In addition, the ambiguity of the test makes it unlikely that subjects will have preconceived notions about which answers are socially desirable. Thus it will be difficult for a subject to give biased answers in an attempt to look better (or worse) than he or she actually is.

The Rorschach Inkblot Test

One of the oldest projective tests of personality is the **Rorschach Inkblot Test,** published in 1921 by Hermann Rorschach, a Swiss psychiatrist. The test consists of ten pictures of inkblots, originally made by spilling ink on a piece of paper that was subsequently folded in half, producing an image that is symmetrical in relation to the line of the fold. Five of the inkblots are black and white, and five are in color. (See Figure 15.5.) The subject is shown

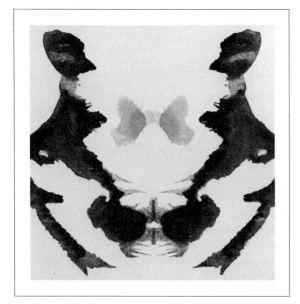

FIGURE 15.5

An item from the Rorschach Inkblot Test.

each card and asked to describe what it looks like. Then the cards are shown again, and the subject is asked to point out the features that he or she used to determine what was seen. The responses, and the nature of the features that the subject uses to make them, are scored on a number of dimensions.

In the following example described by Pervin (1975), a person's response to the inkblot shown in Figure 15.5 might be "Two bears with their paws touching one another playing pattycake or could be they are fighting and the red is the blood from the fighting."

The classification of this response, also described by Pervin, would be as follows: *large detail* of the blot was used, *good form* was used, *movement* was noted, *color* was used in the response about blood, an *animal* was seen, and a *popular response* (two bears) was made.

A possible interpretation of the response might be as follows:

> Subject starts off with popular response and animals expressing playful, "childish" behavior. Response is then given in terms of hostile act with accompanying inquiry. Pure color response and blood content suggest he may have difficulty controlling his response to the environment. Is a playful, childlike exterior used by him to disguise hostile, destructive feelings that threaten to break out in his dealings with the environment? (Pervin, 1975, p. 37)

Although traditionally the interpretation of people's responses to the Rorschach Inkblot Test was based on psychoanalytical theory, many investigators have used it in an empirical fashion. That is, a variety of different scoring methods have been devised, and the scores obtained by these methods have been correlated with clinical diagnoses, just as investigators have done with people's scores on the MMPI. When this test is used empirically, the style and content of the responses are not interpreted in terms of a theory (as Rorschach interpreted them) but are simply correlated with other measures of personality.

The Thematic Apperception Test

Another popular projective technique, the Thematic Apperception Test (TAT), was developed by the American psychologists Henry Murray and C.D. Morgan to measure various psychological *needs*. People are shown a picture of a

FIGURE 15.6

An item from the Thematic Apperception Test. (From Murray, H.A. *Thematic Apperception Test.* Cambridge, Mass.: Harvard University Press. Copyright 1943 by the President and Fellows of Harvard College, copyright 1971 by H.A. Murray.)

very ambiguous situation, such as the one in Figure 15.6, and are asked to tell a complete story about what is happening in the picture, explaining the situation, what led up to it, what the characters are thinking and saying, and what the final outcome will be. Presumably, the subjects will "project" themselves into the scene, and their story will reflect their own needs. As you might imagine, scoring is difficult and requires a great deal of practice and skill. The tester attempts to infer the psychological needs expressed in the stories.

Phares (1979) has presented the responses of one woman to six TAT cards with a clinician's interpretation of her responses. Questions asked by the examiner are in parentheses.

Card 3BM. Looks like a little boy crying for something he can't have. (Why is he crying?) Probably because he can't go somewhere. (How will it turn out?) Probably sit there and sob himself to sleep.

Card 3GF. Looks like her boyfriend might have let her down. She hurt his feelings. He's closed the door on her. (What did he say?) I don't know.

Card 9GF. Girl looks like somebody's run off and left her. She's ready for a dance. Maid's watching to see where she goes. (Why run off?) Probably because she wasn't ready in time.

Card 10. Looks like there's sorrow here. Grieving about something. (About what?) Looks like maybe one of the children's passed away.

Card 13MF. Looks like his wife might have passed away; he feels there's nothing more to do.

Card 20. Looks like a man that's ready to rob something. Hiding behind a high fence of some kind. Has his hand in his pocket with a gun ready to shoot if anybody comes out.

(Interpretation) The TAT produced responses that were uniformly indicative of unhappiness, threat, misfortune, a lack of control over environmental forces. None of the test responses were indicative of satisfaction, happy endings, etc. . . . In summary, the test results point to an individual who is anxious and, at the same time, depressed. Feelings of insecurity, inadequacy, and lack of control over environmental forces are apparent, as are unhappiness and apprehension. These factors result in a constriction of performance that is largely oriented toward avoiding threat and that hampers sufficient mobilization of energy to perform at an optimal level. (Phares, 1979, p. 273)

The pattern of responses in this case is quite consistent; few people would disagree with the conclusion that the woman is sad and depressed. However, not all people provide such clear-cut responses. It is much more difficult to interpret differences in the stories of people who are relatively well adjusted. As a result, it is hard to distinguish among people with different but normal personality traits.

Just at the Rorschach Inkblot Test has provided raw material for empirically determined scales, the TAT has been used to provide responses for a variety of personality tests. For example, as we saw in Chapter 11, the developers of the theory of achievement motivation have devised a special scoring system for the TAT to measure people's need to achieve.

■ What are the two primary strategies of test construction?
■ How was the Minnesota Multiphasic Personality Inventory constructed? What are its primary uses?
■ How do objective and projective tests differ?

CHAPTER SUMMARY

1. Personality characteristics can be conceived of as types or traits. Today many psychologists conceive of personality differences as being represented by quantitative traits. A theory must identify possible traits and make some predictions about how they will affect people's behavior. For example, Allport suggested that personality was structured hierarchically, with cardinal traits exerting all-encompassing control over people's behavior, and central traits controlling which behaviors occur in a particular situation.

2. Traits can also be derived through factor analysis, as Cattell and Eysenck did. Cattell's factor analyses indicated the existence of sixteen personality factors. In contrast, Eysenck's research suggested that personality is determined by two dimensions: introversion-extraversion and neuroticism. Research by Cheek and Buss suggested that introversion-extraversion is not a unitary factor but includes two partly independent factors: shyness and sociability.

3. Twin studies have shown that monozygotic twins are temperamentally much more similar than dizygotic twins; thus, a person's genetic history seems to have a pronounced effect on his or her personality. The most heritable personality traits appear to be related to activity level and irritability, to motivational characteristics such as task persistence, and to social characteristics such as fearfulness, shyness, and sociability.

4. Skinner's approach to understanding the causes of behavior is based on the principles of reinforcement and punishment. His analysis consists in examining the reinforcement and punishment contingencies present in a person's environment, along with the discriminative stimuli that signal that these contingencies are operating. He attributes the different patterns of behavior of different individuals (their personality traits) to their previous experience with different kinds of contingencies

5. Behaviorism is also the parent of social learning theory. This theory applies the principles of reinforcement to human motivation and social interactions. Social learning theory embraces concepts such as expectancy and emphasizes phenomena such as observational learning. Many investigators agree with Skinner about the importance of reinforcement but disagree with his insistence that intervening variables be abandoned. For example, Bandura developed the concept of self-efficacy, which he has applied to a particular form of psychotherapy.

6. One important personality trait concerns a person's perceived locus of control; externals believe that their fate is governed by outside forces, whereas internals believe that their fate is determined by their own efforts.

7. In the past, psychologists have disagreed about the relative importance of situations and personality traits in determining a person's behavior. It now appears that personality traits are correlated with behavior, especially when multiple observations are made. In addition, some situations (such as a funeral or a stoplight) are more "powerful" than others, exerting more control on people's behavior. Also, traits and situations interact: some people are affected more than others by a particular situation and people tend to choose the types of situations in which they find themselves. The template method permits an investigator to determine which pattern of personality traits is most likely to lead people to behave in a particular way in a particular situation.

8. Freud believed that the mind is full of conflicts between the primitive urges of the libido and the internalized prohibitions of the superego. According to Freud, these conflicts tend to be resolved through compromise formation and through ego defenses such as repression, sublimation, and reaction formation. His theory of psychosexual development, a progression through the oral, anal, phallic, latent, and genital stages, provided the basis for a theory of personality and personality disorders. Although Freud was a brilliant and insightful thinker his theory has not been experimentally verified, primarily because most of his concepts are unobservable, and therefore untestable. Freud's important contribution to psychology was his realization that not all the causes of our behavior are available to consciousness; many are unknown to us.

9. Freud's disciples, called neo-Freudians, placed greater emphasis on social factors. Jung distinguished between a personal unconscious, similar to Freud's idea of the unconscious, and a collective unconscious, a universal storehouse of humankind's ancestral past. Jung also defined two basic personality orientations: introversion and extraversion. Adler believed that people have an innate social interest and a striving for superiority. Horney focused on the important role of social relationships, especially parent-child, in personality development. Fromm identified five personality orientations: receptive, exploitive, hoarding, marketing, and productive. Erikson presented personality development as continuing throughout a person's life, beyond childhood (which Freud limited it to).

10. Research on a factor common to all of Freud's proposed defense mechanisms—self-deception—shows that people do indeed deceive themselves. Self-deception implies the simultaneous holding of contradictory beliefs while not being aware of one of them for motivational reasons.

11. Humanistic theories of personality developed in reaction to both psychoanalytic and behavioral theories. Maslow, a humanistic theorist, defined people who had reached their full potential as self-actualizers and listed sixteen characteristics of such people. Rogers, like Maslow, believed that people strive towards self-actualization and are then fully-functioning.

12. In order to evaluate his or her theory the investigator must next devise tests to measure traits and then assess the validity of these tests. Tests of personality can be constructed by rational or empirical means. The rational strategy requires a detailed theory that can predict the behavior of people with various personality traits; the test is constructed in accordance with these predictions. The empirical strategy requires that the investigator first identify (perhaps by an expensive and time-consuming method) people who do or do not possess a particular personality trait. The investigator then assembles a criterion group consisting of a mixture of such people and gives them a test that comprises a large number of items. Only those items that are answered differently by people with and without the trait are retained in the final form of the test.

13. Objective tests contain items that can be answered and scored objectively, such as true/false or multiple-choice questions. One of the most important objective personality tests is the Minnesota Multiphasic Personality Inventory, which was empirically devised to discriminate among people who had been assigned various psychiatric diagnoses; it has since been used widely in research on personality. Projective tests, such as the Rorschach Inkblot Test and the Thematic Apperception Test, contain ambiguous items that presumably elicit answers that reveal aspects of the subjects' personalities. Because answers can vary widely, test administrators receive special training to interpret them.

KEY TERMS

aggressive instinctual drive According to Freud, an innate drive that must eventually express itself in some form of aggression, either actual or symbolic.

anal stage According to Freud, the second stage of psychosexual development, during which the infant obtains gratification by passing or retaining feces.

anxiety Vague, uneasy, fearfulness.

basic anxiety In Horney's theory of personality development, a child's feelings of isolation, helplessness, and hopelessness.

basic hostility A child's anger over parents' indifference, according to Horney.

cardinal traits In Allport's theory, powerful, all-encompassing personality characteristics that can be used to predict the behavior of some people in almost all situations.

central traits For Allport, traits that determine which behavior will occur in a particular situation.

collective unconscious According to Jung, a universal storehouse of humankind's ancestral past, including myths, dreams, and symbols.

compromise formation Result of conflict between demands of instinctual drive and internalized prohibitions.

conscience Part of the superego in Freud's mind structure that internalizes the rules and restrictions of society.

content reward Socially reinforcing stimuli involving bipolar relationships between individuals, one reinforcing, the other aversive; related to formality, self-esteem, and emotionality.

conversion A defense mechanism, according to Freud: the provision of an outlet for intrapsychic conflict in the form of a physical symptom, such as blindness.

criterion group A group of subjects whose behavior is used to validate a psychological test. For example, if people diagnosed by other means as extraverted tend to receive higher scores than randomly selected people on a test of extraversion, the test receives support as being valid.

cross-situational reliability The likelihood that a person will act in similar ways in different situations; a measure of the degree to which knowledge of a person's personality traits enables one to predict his or her behavior.

defense mechanism According to Freud, one of several methods by which the ego protects itself from conflicts between the conscience and instinctual drives.

delay of gratification The ability to forego a reinforcer in order to receive an even more desirable one later.

ego According to Freud, the structure of the mind that possesses memory and mediates the drives of the id and the internalized prohibitions of the superego.

ego-ideal Part of the superego in Freud's mind structure that internalizes what the person would like to be.

Electra complex In psychodynamic theory, the desire of a girl to replace her mother as object of her father's affections.

empirical strategy The development of psychological tests by presenting a variety of more or less randomly assembled items to a criterion group. Items that are regularly answered in one way by members of the criterion group are retained; the others are discarded.

expressive period In Freud's theory of personality development, the early part of the anal stage in which babies enjoy expelling their feces.

external locus of control According to Rotter, the belief that fate, or a deity, or people in authority determine a person's life.

extraversion A personality trait; the tendency to seek the company of other people and to engage in conversation and other social behaviors with them.

fixation Failure to develop beyond an early stage of development, according to Freud.

F scale One of the validity scales of the Minnesota Multiphasic Personality Inventory (MMPI) concerned with frequency.

fully-functioning According to Rogers, a person whose experience of the organism and of the self are congruent.

genital stage According to Freud, the final stage of psychosexual development, during which a person receives gratification through genital sexual contact with a person of the opposite sex.

id One of Freud's three divisions of the mind; contains the instinctual drives.

identification According to Freud, the modeling of a child on the same-sex parent.

internal locus of control The belief that one's own destiny is up to the individual, according to Rotter.

internalized prohibition In Freud's theory, the check on behaviors aroused by the sexual instinctual drive or the aggressive instinctual drive.

introversion A personality trait; the tendency to avoid the company of other people, especially large groups of people; shyness.

K scale In the MMPI, a validity scale devised to detect defensiveness.

latency period According to Freud, one of the stages of psychosexual development during which the child experiences little sexual instinctual drive; follows the phallic stage and precedes the genital stage.

libido According to Freud, the psychic energy associated with instinctual drives.

L scale A validity scale in the MMPI concerned with telling lies.

Minnesota Multiphasic Personality Inventory (MMPI) One of the most widely used objective tests of personality.

neuroticism According to Eysenck, an important dimension of personality which indicates a person's stability.

objective test A psychological test that can be scored objectively, such as a multiple-choice or true/false test.

Oedipus complex According to Freud, the desire of a boy to replace his father and have sexual relations with his mother.

oral stage According to Freud, the first stage of psychosexual development, during which an infant receives primary gratification by sucking.

organism According to Rogers, the totality of a person's experience.

penis envy In Freud's explanation, the reason for a girl's transfer of love from her mother to her father.

personality trait A relatively stable pattern of behavior that is at least somewhat predictable in a variety of situations.

personality type Classification of people by their temperament and disposition.

personal unconscious According to Jung, mental processes that govern behavior with the individual's awareness.

phallic stage According to Freud, the third stage of psychosexual development, during which a person receives primary gratification from touching his or her genitals.

preconscious According to Freud, an intermediate system between the conscious and the unconscious.

process reward A social reward involving social stimulation.

projection According to Freud, an ego defense mechanism in which a prohibited drive is attributed to another person.

projective test A psychological test that attempts to determine a person's attitudes, personality, or motivation through his or her responses to ambiguous stimuli.

psychodynamics The struggle of various conflicting forces within the personality.

? scale In the MMPI, a validity scale for all questions not answered.

radical behaviorism Skinner's approach to human behavior in terms of the principles of instrumental conditioning.

rationalization According to Freud, an ego defense mechanism in which a person gives an acceptable reason for a behavior that is actually motivated by a prohibited drive.

rational strategy The development of a psychological test by means of including items that appear to be related to the trait in question; contrasts with the empirical strategy.

reaction formation According to Freud, an ego defense mechanism in which a person experiences feelings opposite to a prohibited drive, such as disgust toward sexual material that the person actually finds interesting.

reality principle According to Freud, the ability to delay gratification of a drive until an appropriate goal is located.

repression According to Freud, an ego defense mechanism that prevents threatening material from reaching consciousness.

retentive period According to Freud, the latter part of the anal stage wherein babies enjoy storing up their feces.

Rorschach Inkblot Test A projective test of personality in which subjects respond to a series of symmetrical inkblots.

self According to Rogers, the private "I" that is known only to the individual.

self-actualizers According to Maslow, people who have reached their full-potential.

self-concept A person's perception of his or her own personality and ability.

self-control A person's ability to withhold a response normally elicited by a situation.

self-criticism Negative response of a person after perceiving his or her own behavior and its consequences.

self-deception The tendency to hold contradictory beliefs with importance to the believer, some of which are unconscious.

self-praise Positive response of a person after perceiving his or her own behavior and its consequences.

sexual instinctual drive According to Freud, an innate drive that must eventually express itself and produce some form of sexual gratification.

strive for superiority A person's conscious strive for perfection to overcome feelings of inferiority that originate in childhood, according to Adler.

sublimation According to Freud, an ego defense mechanism in which a person finds an outlet for a prohibited drive in other behaviors, especially creative or artistic activity.

superego According to Freud, the part of the mind that incorporates prohibitions that a person has learned from society; includes the conscience and the ego-ideal.

template A method for predicting the results of the interaction of a person's personality traits with a situation.

PSYCHOLOGICAL DISORDERS AND THEIR TREATMENT

Our study of psychology has demonstrated how complex we human beings are. Every aspect of our lives blends innumerable biological and psychological factors so seamlessly that their interaction went unnoticed for most of human history. Our forebears accounted for illness and death much as they accounted for evil and bad fortune—through superstition and supernatural explanations. Today we have glimpsed the complexity of our lives and have had some success in sorting it out. We have learned to isolate and label variables and, through controlled experiments, to develop theories about their causes and effects. This scientific method has revealed much about complex systems, including the fact that they tend to break down.

Part E investigates the causes and treatment of psychological "breakdowns"—of mental disorders. It should be no surprise that maladaptive behaviors are at least as complex as adaptive ones, in that they also often result from an interaction between biological and environmental factors. But the study of mental disorders is complicated beyond complexity because, by nature, the variables under scrutiny are abnormal. It thus is more difficult to assemble a population of experimental and control subjects who are "matched" in terms of symptoms and other variables, and it is far more difficult to conduct an ethical experiment when subjects suffer from disorders in the first place.

Perhaps the difficulties of experimentation account in part for the numerous, diverse approaches that are undertaken to help people eliminate maladaptive behaviors and replace them with adaptive ones. After all, until the cause of a disorder is identified, treatment can only be tentative. And since there are many theoretical explanations for mental disorders, there are many kinds of psychotherapy to alleviate them. In recent years this situation has been compounded by

advances in medical technology, biochemistry, and neurology, among other fields, from which we learn that some mental disorders may reflect biology more than environment.

Consider clinical depression, a mood disturbance that is currently divided into three subcategories in the Diagnostic and Statistical Manual of Mental Disorders. Ranging from chronic unhappiness to such severe symptoms as the inability to feel pleasure, sleeplessness, and loss of appetite, depression is far more disruptive than what we commonly call "the blues." It can persist for months at a time and often recurs in episodes over many years. It has been linked to 60 percent of suicides, and even victims who survive that impulse sacrifice much of their lives to depression, losing their spouses, jobs, friends, and health. Depression is not a problem restricted to a few troubled people. Up to 40 million Americans will suffer from it at least once in their lives; over a third of them, more than once. According to one alarming estimate, only 20 to 30 percent of victims seek treatment. Others either misunderstand or refuse to acknowledge their plight, expecting that "things will get better, soon." If they go untreated, however, they may increase the chances that their depression will become a chronic fact of life. Finally, the evidence is that depression is increasing, particularly among young adults in their midtwenties to midforties.

Among mental disorders, then, depression is unusually common; it can be chronic or catastrophic (or both); and it is caused by—what? Do the various forms of depression have similar origins and similar treatments? Are they caused and cured by common means, with the severity of the problem determining how aggressive treatment will be? How tentative are the theories about causes? How controversial are the treatments?

During the last century and most of this one, depression was viewed as an abnormal mental state brought on by real or imagined environmental factors. For some reason, a depressed person "just couldn't get over" whatever the problem was. Given this view, the best cure was thought to be time (which "heals all wounds") because, in time, the environment changes. Meanwhile, a period of rest, fresh air, sunshine, and good nutrition was the best remedy, followed by new activities to help the person "get on with life." For those genuinely depressed, however, rest is not restful, the sun does not shine, the air is not fresh, and getting on with life is of no interest. Thus, while time may pass, not all wounds heal, and so various forms of psychotherapy were enlisted to help patients come to terms with events that triggered depression.

New Theories, New Treatments

Although successes could be claimed with these approaches, it was puzzling that not all patients could be helped. Another puzzle was why, if depression is triggered by the environment, not everyone falls victim to it; after all, most of us experience sad, even tragic events at some point in life. Why should some people become depressed, while others do not? And why should some respond to treatment, some not, and still others have recurring bouts of depression? Questions like these led to new theories about causes and, of course, to new treatments. Electroconvulsive therapy, it was found, could literally "jolt" some patients out of depression by passing a controlled electrical current through electrodes attached to the head. Unfortunately, this more radical approach sometimes expunged not only depression but also portions of the patient's memory. Better results were achieved, at least with manic-depressive patients, when it was discovered that the drug lithium could bring a pa-

... most practitioners today believe that the causes of depression are both biological and psychological ... victims inherit a genetic predisposition to the disorder. ...

tient's wild mood changes into balance. Other psychotherapeutic drugs were developed as well, on the theory that depression may be caused by a chemical imbalance in the brain.

By the 1950s, health professionals debated both environmental and physiological theories about the causes of depression, since patients responded to both kinds of treatment. But still the basic questions persisted: If depression is an abnormal response to the environment, why should electricity or drugs relieve it? And if the cause is physiological, why should psychotherapy help? Both treatment approaches have been somewhat successful, and today they often are used in tandem—some form of psychotherapy is combined with some form of drug or electroshock therapy. Because so many different treatments alleviate depression, most practitioners today believe that the causes are both biological and psychological. There is evidence that victims of depression may inherit a genetic predisposition to the disorder, which then is triggered in response to life's events or even by the body's chemistry.

Researchers have known for some time that depression often hits more than one member of a family, and often more than one generation. In fact, studies of depressed patients indicate that two-thirds of their relatives have also been depressed. Now it appears that a genetic link may have been established. Eighty-one members of an Amish family were studied by Janice Egeland and others at the University of Miami School of Medicine. Blood samples revealed that almost 80 percent of the subjects who had a common genetic pattern on one of their chromosomes also suffered from manic depression. The assumption is that this marker signals a gene by which family members can inherit a predisposition to manic depression, and perhaps to schizophrenia. The fact that young children can be diagnosed and treated for depression also adds weight to the biological argument. Research suggests that a child whose mother has suffered from depression has a 30 percent chance of developing the problem by age six or seven.

Despite this evidence of genetic and physiological factors, no one who treats depression is ready to discount the psychological explanations—or treatments. Besides the more traditional forms of psychotherapy, including analysis, several newer approaches focus more on relationships "here and now." In addition, psychotherapy is often combined with electroshock or drug therapy.

While there are many approaches to treating depression, none seems reliable enough, by itself, to be recommended above the others in all cases. Sometimes drug therapy dramatically alters the condition; however, drugs have undesirable side effects, and they may address the symptoms more than the underlying disorder. To assess the relative effectiveness of drugs versus psychotherapy, the National Institute of Mental Health recently studied three groups of patients and found that, while the group treated with drugs made faster progress over a sixteen-week period, the two groups in psychotherapy caught up during the latter weeks of the study, and severely depressed patients were helped more by psychotherapy than by drugs. In another study, 95 percent of patients who were not helped by either drugs or psychotherapy did benefit from electroshock treatment within six weeks. Thus, each theory and each treatment has merit, but none can promise to eradicate depression or keep it under control throughout a patient's life. However, people are benefiting from these various treatments, and our research continues.

Psychological Disorders

Life is complex, and things do not always go smoothly. We are all beset by major and minor tragedies. Why are some people, but not others, able to cope with life's problems? What is abnormal behavior?

Most of us would have a difficult time precisely specifying the differences between normal and abnormal behavior. Some psychologists have argued that abnormal behavior is culturally defined, and that behavior that is considered evidence of a mental disorder in one culture would be considered normal in another. There is some truth in this assertion, but severe disorders such as schizophrenia occur in people of all cultures, regardless of their particular lifestyles.

The difficulties that psychologists have in attempting to define abnormal behavior and to categorize disorders are similar to the ones faced by physicians in trying to categorize diseases. But the attempt to define and categorize is not an end in itself; it is just the first step toward identifying the causes of a disorder and developing ways to prevent it or treat it.

Many times the precise causes of psychological disorders cannot be specified. Often researchers are faced with trying to unravel a mystery as they attempt to parcel out the relative influence of biochemical, genetic, and environmental factors. Despite such obstacles, researchers are much closer than ever before to identifying the causes of certain disorders. For example, some severe disorders now appear to be caused by physiological abnormalities, such as inherited differences in the biochemical properties of various systems of the brain. Undoubtedly, a person's chances of developing such a disorder depends on interactions between physiological and environmental factors. As you will see as you read this chapter, there are still many discoveries waiting to be made about the role of genetics, physiology, and the environment in the development of psychological disorders.

477

CLASSIFICATION AND DIAGNOSIS

The Value of Classification

There are dangers in classifying a person's mental disorder. No classification scheme is perfect, and no two people with the same diagnosis will behave in exactly the same way. Yet once people are labeled, they are likely to be perceived as having all the characteristics that are assumed to accompany that label; their behavior will probably be perceived selectively and interpreted in terms of the diagnosis. Mental health professionals, like other humans, tend to simplify things by pigeonholing people.

Some kinds of mental disorders are relatively easy to explain; although the person's behavior is clearly inappropriate and maladaptive, it can be seen as an exaggeration of a reaction that a "normal" person might have. These disorders have traditionally been called **neuroses.** In contrast, **psychoses** reflect severe disruptions in thought processes. Psychotic behavior is illogical and qualitatively different from the behavior of either normal people or people with neuroses. Psychotic people appear to be crazy; they are not simply overreacting to stress. Although investigators and therapists often try to explain specific psychotic behaviors as strategies for coping with life problems, in most cases the explanations are not nearly so satisfactory as

The distinction between normal and abnormal behavior is not always clear. Many behaviors that are unusual or abnormal are not necessarily indicators of a serious psychological disorder.

they are for other kinds of mental disorders. Some people believe that whereas most neuroses are learned disorders of behavior, psychoses result from biological defects (although they may be triggered by environmental events).

A study by Rosenhan (1973) demonstrated the strength of the tendency to pigeonhole through methods that created a stir among clinical psychologists and psychiatrists. After testing volunteers to be sure that they were in no way psychotic, he arranged for them to seek admission as patients in various psychiatric hospitals. To gain admission, they complained of only one symptom—that they heard voices saying "empty," "hollow," and "thud." (Hallucinations are symptoms indicative of schizophrenia.) All other statements were as true and accurate as they could make them, and they did not behave abnormally. Furthermore, after they were admitted, they did not complain of the voices any more.

Most of the volunteers were diagnosed as psychotic. Once they were in the hospitals, Rosenhan said, the staff explained their behavior as symptomatic of their mental illness. None of the mental health professionals realized that the pseudopatients were normal, although some of their fellow patients did, apparently from the fact that they openly took notes. One patient said, "You're not crazy. You're a journalist or a professor. You're checking up on the hospital" (Rosenhan, 1973, p. 252). When the pseudopatients were released, the diagnosis in almost every case was "schizophrenia, in remission." (*Remission* means "a lessening in extent or degree.")

When these results were published, some people concluded that psychiatric diagnosis was a useless endeavor if it could not distinguish between normal people and schizophrenics. However, a closer examination of the facts shows that the data do not warrant this conclusion. The clinicians were not required to distinguish between *normal* people and people with a mental disorder; they were required to detect that some people were *pretending* to have symptoms of schizophrenia. In fact Spitzer (1975) has shown that on the basis of the data that the clinicians had, no other diagnosis would have been justified. He noted that the pseudopatients insisted on admission to the hospitals, which itself is an important symptom of mental or emotional disturbance. Moreover, their behavior after admission was not in fact normal; a normal person would go to the nursing station and say, "I'm really not crazy— I just pretended to be. Now I want to be released." The pseudopatients remained passive.

Rosenhan's study and Spitzer's criticism have stimulated much public discussion about an important issue. They also reinforce the value of following the scientific method (discussed in Chapter 1). We should certainly criticize any tendency of mental health professionals to view patients' behavior only in terms of an initial psychiatric diagnosis. However, we should not blame them for making a reasonable diagnosis when a patient lies about symptoms that are almost never found in people who are not psychotic.

Because labeling can have bad effects, perhaps we should abandon all attempts to classify and diagnose mental disorders. However, proper classification does have advantages for a patient.

With few exceptions, the recognition of a specific diagnostic category precedes the development of a successful treatment for that disorder. Treatments for diseases such as diabetes, syphilis, tetanus, and malaria were found only after the disorders could be reliably diagnosed. A patient may have a multitude of symptoms, and before the cause of the disorder (and hence its treatment) can be discovered, the primary symptoms must be identified. For example, a mental disorder called **Graves' disease** is characterized by irritability, restlessness, confused and rapid thought processes, and, occasionally, delusions and hallucinations. Little was known about the endocrine system during the nineteenth century, when Robert Graves identified the disease, but we now know that this syndrome results from oversecretion of thyroxine, a hormone produced by the thyroid glands. Treatment involves prescription of antithyroid drugs or surgical removal of the thyroid glands, followed by administration of appropriate doses of thyroxine. Graves's classification scheme for the symptoms was devised many years before the physiological basis of the disease could be understood, but once enough was known about the effects of thyroxine, physicians were able to strike Graves' disease off the roll of mental disorders.

On a less spectacular scale, different kinds of neuroses respond to different behavioral treatments, and different psychoses respond to different drugs. If future research is to reveal more about the causes and treatments of these disorders, we must be able to classify specific mental disorders reliably and accurately.

Another important reason for properly classifying mental disorders is that some disorders have a good prognosis, in that the patient is likely to improve soon and is unlikely to have a recurrence of the problem. Other disorders have progressive courses, so that the patient is less likely to recover from these disorders. In the first case, the patient can obtain reassurance about his or her future; in the second case, the patient's family can obtain assistance in making realistic plans.

The DSM-III-R Classification Scheme

Mental disorders can be classified in a number of ways, but the system most commonly used in North America today is the one presented in the American Psychiatric Association's **Diagnostic and Statistical Manual III-R (DSM-III-R).** Table 16.1 lists these classifications, with several subclassifications omitted for the sake of simplicity. The ones described in this chapter are preceded by a colored dot. (See Table 16.1.)

The DSM-III classification scheme was devised in an attempt to provide a reliable, universal set of diagnostic categories, with diagnostic criteria specified as explicitly as possible. In the area of the major diagnostic categories, the DSM-III has proved itself more reliable than its predecessors (Grove, Andreasen, McDonald-Scott, Keller, and Shapiro, 1981). The DSM-III-R is a refinement of the DSM-III. Some parts of the DSM-III classification scheme have been criticized as having been chosen with an eye to third-party reimbursement. Critics have suggested that problems such as "tobacco withdrawal" and "developmental arithmetic disorder" have been officially labeled as mental disorders so that clinicians can receive compensation for their services from insurance companies and public welfare organizations.

■ What are neuroses? What are psychoses?

■ What are the advantages and disadvantages of classifying mental disorders?

■ What is the DSM-III-R?

TABLE 16.1

The DSM-III-R classification of disorders

Axis I: Clinical syndromes

Disorders usually first evident in infancy, childhood, or adolescence
  Disruptive behavior disorders
  Anxiety disorders of childhood or adolescence
  Eating disorders
  Gender identity disorders
  Tic disorders
  Elimination disorders
  Speech disorders not elsewhere classified
  Other disorders of infancy, childhood, or adolescence

Organic mental disorders
  Dementias arising in the senium and presenium
  Psychoactive substance-induced organic mental disorders
  Organic brain syndrome whose etiology is unknown

Psychoactive substance use disorders

Schizophrenia
  • Disorganized
  • Catatonic
  • Paranoid
  • Undifferentiated
  Residual

Mood disorders
  • Bipolar disorders
    Mixed bipolar disorder
    Manic bipolar disorder
    Depressed bipolar disorder
    • Cyclothymia
  Depressive disorders
    • Major depression
    • Dysthymia (or depressive neurosis)

Anxiety disorders
  • Panic disorder
    • With agoraphobia
    • Without agoraphobia
  Agoraphobia without history of panic disorder
  • Social phobia
  • Simple phobia
  • Obsessive-compulsive disorder
  Post-traumatic stress disorder
  Generalized anxiety disorder

Somatoform disorders
  Body dysmorphic disorder
  • Conversion disorder
  • Hypochondriasis
  • Somatization disorder
  Somatoform pain disorder
  Undifferentiated somatoform disorder
Dissociative disorders
  • Multiple personality disorder
  • Psychogenic fugue
  • Psychogenic amnesia
  Depersonalization disorder
Sexual disorders
  Paraphilias
  Sexual dysfunctions
  Other sexual disorders
Sleep Disorders
  Dyssomnias
  Parasomnias
Factitious disorders
Impulse control disorders not elsewhere classified
Adjustment disorder
Psychological factors affecting physical condition
Conditions not attributable to a mental disorder that are a focus of attention or treatment

Axis II: Specific developmental disorders and personality disorders

Developmental disorders
  Mental retardation
  Pervasive developmental disorders
  Specific developmental disorders
    Academic skills disorders
    Language and speech disorders
    Motor skills disorders
  Other developmental disorders
Personality disorders
  • Antisocial personality disorder
  Paranoid personality disorder
  Schizoid personality disorder
  Schizotypical personality disorder
  Borderline personality disorder
  Histrionic personality disorder
  Narcissistic personality disorder
  Avoidant personality disorder
  Dependent personality disorder
  Obsessive-compulsive personality disorder
  Passive-aggressive personality disorder

NONPSYCHOTIC MENTAL DISORDERS

Nonpsychotic mental disorders used to be called *neuroses,* and often still are. Most neuroses are strategies of perception and behavior that have gotten out of hand; they are characterized by pathological increases in anxiety and/or by defense mechanisms that are applied too rigidly, so that they have become maladaptive. Neurotic people are anxious, fearful, depressed, and generally unhappy. However, unlike people who are afflicted with psychoses, they do not suffer from delusions or severely disordered thought processes. Furthermore, they almost universally realize that they have a problem; most neurotics are only too aware that their strategies for coping with the world are not working.

Neurotic behavior is usually characterized by avoidance rather than confrontation of problems. People with neuroses turn to imaginary illnesses, oversleeping, or convenient forgetfulness to avoid having to confront stressful situations. Even normal people sometimes use these strategies. Any teacher can attest that a disproportionate number of students seem to be struck by illness and other emergencies just before examination time. But a neurotic person adopts avoidance as a way of life.

Neurotic people tend to limit their functioning severely through overdependence on their maladaptive strategies, and the increasing hopelessness of their situation makes them cling even more tenaciously to self-defeating patterns of behavior. These defenses are all they know. Their imagined problems inevitably produce real ones, and eventually they may turn to someone for help in their despair.

Anxiety Disorders

Several important types of mental disorders are classified as anxiety disorders, with fear and anxiety as the salient symptoms. Some categories of anxiety disorders are panic disorder, generalized anxiety disorder, and obsessive-compulsive disorder. Because generalized anxiety differs from panic disorder primarily in its severity, I will not discuss it specifically. People suffering from panic disorder have no adequate defense against their fears, whereas those suffering from obsessive-compulsive disorder use stereotyped rituals to reduce their anxiety. *Phobias,* another category of anxiety disorders, are characterized by excessive fears of particular objects or situations.

Panic Disorder

Description. People with **panic disorder** suffer from episodic attacks of acute anxiety—periods of acute and unremitting terror that grip them for variable lengths of time, from a few seconds to a few hours. The estimated incidence of panic disorder is between 1 and 2 percent of the population (Robbins, Helzer, Weissman, Orvaschel, Gruenberg, Burke, and Regier,

Panic attacks are characterized by intense fear and anxiety. Researchers believe biological factors may be at least partially responsible for the development of panic disorders.

1984). Women are approximately twice as likely as men to suffer from panic disorder. The disorder usually has its onset in young adulthood; it rarely begins after age thirty-five (Woodruff, Guze, and Clayton, 1972).

Panic attacks include many physical symptoms, such as shortness of breath, clammy sweat, irregularities in heartbeat, dizziness, faintness, and feelings of unreality. The victim of a panic attack often feels that he or she is going to die. Leon (1977) described a thirty-eight-year-old man who suffered from frequent panic attacks.

> During the times when he was experiencing intense anxiety, it often seemed as if he were having a heart seizure. He experienced chest pains and heart palpitations, numbness, shortness of breath, and he felt a strong need to breathe in air. He reported that in the midst of the anxiety attack, he developed a feeling of tightness over his eyes and he could only see objects directly in front of him (tunnel vision). He further stated that he feared that he would not be able to swallow.
>
> . . . The intensity of the anxiety symptoms was very frightening to him and on two occasions his wife had rushed him to a local hospital because he was in a state of panic, sure that his heart was going to stop beating and he would die. His symptoms were relieved after he was given an injection of tranquilizer medication. . . . He began to note the location of doctor's offices and hospitals in whatever vicinity he happened to be . . . and he became extremely anxious if medical help were not close by. (Leon, 1977, pp. 112, 117)

Between panic attacks, people with panic disorder tend to suffer from **anticipatory anxiety.** Because attacks can occur without apparent cause, these people anxiously worry about when the next one might strike them. Sometimes a panic attack that occurs in a particular situation can cause the person to fear that situation; that is, a panic attack can cause a phobia, presumably through classical conditioning. Anxiety is a normal reaction to many stresses of life, and none of us is completely free from it. In fact, anxiety is undoubtedly useful in causing us to be more alert and to take important things seriously. However, the anxiety we all feel from time to time is obviously different from the intense fear and terror experienced by a person gripped by a panic attack.

Possible Causes. Of all the nonpsychotic disorders discussed in this chapter, panic disorder is the least adaptive, and this fact makes it diffi-

cult to explain. Parental influence may be an important factor in the development of panic disorder. Jenkins (1969) observed that people with this disorder tend to come from families with neurotic mothers and in which the parents hold up a high standard of accomplishment while simultaneously failing to recognize actual achievements of their children.

Because the physical symptoms of panic attacks are so overwhelming, many patients reject the suggestion that they have a mental disorder, insisting that their problem is medical. In fact, some evidence suggests that panic disorder may have biological origins. First, the disorder tends to run in families; approximately 20 percent of the **first-degree relatives** of a person with panic disorder also have panic disorder (Crowe, Pauls, Slymen, and Noyes, 1980). (First-degree relatives are a person's parents, children, and siblings.) Of course, the relation could be the result of either hereditary or environmental factors. However, one study observed a higher concordance rate in monozygotic twins than in dizygotic twins, which suggests that hereditary factors may be important (Slater and Shields, 1969).

Panic disorder is accompanied by an elevated blood level of lactic acid, which is a by-product of muscular activity. In fact, an injection of lactic acid can trigger a panic attack in susceptible people (Klein and Rabkin, 1981). In addition, up to half of the people with panic disorder have an abnormality of a major valve in the heart (Hafeiz, 1980). Finally, drug therapy has proved itself very effective in preventing panic attacks. (Drug treatment will be described in Chapter 17.) These findings, along with the evidence that panic disorder may be somewhat heritable, suggest that biological factors may play a role in this disorder.

Phobias

Description. Phobias, named after the Greek god *Phobos*, who frightened one's enemies, are irrational fears of objects or situations. Because phobias are so specific, clinicians have coined a variety of inventive names. (See Table 16.2.)

Almost all of us have one or more irrational fears of specific objects or situations, and it is difficult to draw a line between these fears and **phobias.** If someone is afraid of spiders but manages to lead a normal life by avoiding them, it would seem inappropriate to say that person has a mental disorder. Similarly, many otherwise normal people are afraid of speaking in public. The term *phobia* should be reserved for people whose fear makes their life difficult. One of the diagnostic criteria of the DSM-III-R is "significant distress because of the disturbance."

The DSM-III-R recognizes three types of phobias: agoraphobia, social phobia, and simple phobia. **Agoraphobia** (*agora* means "open space") is a fear of "being alone [away from home] or in public places from which escape might be difficult or help not available in cases of sudden incapacitation, e.g., crowds, tunnels, bridges, public transportation." Agoraphobia can be severely disabling; some people with this disorder have stayed inside their houses or apartments for years, being afraid to venture outside. Many people with agoraphobia also suffer from panic attacks; in fact, fear of having a panic attack when away from home may actually be the cause of the phobia. **Social phobia** is an exaggerated "fear of, and compelling desire to avoid, a situation in which the individual is exposed to possible scrutiny by others and fears that he or she may act in a way that will be

The most severe of all phobias is agoraphobia. People suffering from agoraphobia fear being alone or away from home. They may also fear being in public places where a clear escape route is not apparent.

humiliating or embarrassing." Most people with social phobia are only mildly impaired. **Simple phobia** includes all other phobias, such as fear of snakes, darkness, or heights. They are often caused by a specific traumatic experience. Simple phobias are the easiest of all types of phobias to treat.

The incidence of agoraphobia is approximately 5 percent and that of simple phobia is approximately 10 percent (Robbins, Helzer, Weissman, Orvaschel, Gruenberg, Burke, and Regier, 1984), but approximately one-third the population sometimes exhibit phobic symptoms (Goodwin and Guze, 1984). Both males and females are equally likely to exhibit social phobia, but females are more likely to develop agoraphobia or simple phobias. Phobias that begin to develop in childhood or early adolescence (primarily simple phobias) are likely to disappear, whereas those that begin to develop after adolescence are likely to endure. Social phobia tends to begin during the teenage years, whereas agoraphobia tends to begin during a person's middle or late twenties. These disorders rarely have their first appearance after age 30.

TABLE 16.2

Names and descriptions of some phobias

Name	Object or Situation Feared
Acrophobia	Heights
Agoraphobia	Open spaces
Ailurophobia	Cats
Algophobia	Pain
Astraphobia	Storms, thunder, lightning
Belonophobia	Needles
Claustrophobia	Enclosed spaces
Hematophobia	Blood
Monophobia	Being alone
Mysophobia	Contamination or germs
Nyctophobia	Darkness
Ochlophobia	Crowds
Pathophobia	Disease
Pyrophobia	Fire
Siderophobia	Railways
Syphilophobia	Syphilis
Taphophobia	Being buried alive
Triskaidekaphobia	Thirteen
Zoophobia	Animals, or a specific animal

Possible Causes. Psychoanalytical theory attributes phobias to distress caused by intolerable unconscious impulses, such as an unresolved Oedipus or Electra complex. Whether or not this is true, almost all psychoanalysts and behaviorists believe that phobias are learned by means of classical conditioning, as Chapter 6 discussed. The following example, reported by Hofling (1963) illustrates this process:

> Miss E.M., a woman . . . 22 years of age, was referred to a psychiatrist . . . for treatment of a set of severe phobias. . . . After a number of interviews the precipitating conflict could be elucidated.
>
> At the time of onset, Miss M. had been doing secretarial work. . . . Although intellectually competent and physically very attractive, the patient had always been extremely shy in any personal situation involving a man. She led a restricted social life and very seldom went out on dates. . . . While working for the firm, Miss M. secretly developed a romantic interest in one of the young executives, an interest that she scarcely acknowledged even to herself. She . . . learned, in casual office conversation, that he was married.
>
> . . . One morning, arriving at work an unaccustomed few minutes late, Miss M. found herself alone in an elevator with the young executive. The man made a complimentary but slightly suggestive remark about the patient's dress. Miss M. blushed and became highly embarrassed, tense, and anxious. By dint of considerable effort, she managed to get through the day's work. The next morning, as she was about to enter the elevator, she experienced an attack of anxiety so severe as to verge upon panic. She left the building, walked about for nearly an hour, and then was able to return. This time she climbed six flights of stairs to the office.
>
> During succeeding days the patient made several efforts to use the elevator, but she invariably found herself becoming too anxious to do so. . . . Eventually, the use of the stairs became as disturbing as that of the elevator. At this point, the patient was compelled to ask for a leave of absence. . . . At no point did the patient consciously associate her attacks of anxiety with the young executive. . . . She considered the nature of her illness to be inexplicable. (pp. 325–326)

The patient suffered a severe anxiety attack after her encounter with the man in the elevator. Although clinicians would disagree about the reasons for her shyness and avoidance of sexual desires, all would agree that the aversive experience created the conditions for the phobia. The woman learned to avoid the elevator, where the experience had occurred. Unfortunately, the learning generalized to other stimuli, including the stairway, and as a result it became impossible for her to continue working in the building.

To say that phobias are learned through classical conditioning does not explain this disorder completely. Many people have traumatic experiences, but few of them go on to develop phobic disorders. Lacey and Lacey (1962) suggested that some people's autonomic nervous systems are particularly reactive to unpleasant environmental stimuli, and that this reactivity predisposes them to developing phobias. It is possible that a susceptibility to agoraphobia is inherited. Harris, Noyes, Crowe, and Chaudhry (1983) looked at the incidence of mental disorders in the first-degree relatives of people with and without agoraphobia. They found that the incidence of agoraphobia or anxiety disorders was twice as high in the relatives of people with agoraphobia. In contrast, simple or social phobias do not appear to run in families (Goodwin, 1983). The predisposing factor for developing these phobic disorders may be environmental; people who develop them tend to be from stable families with overprotective mothers (Goodwin and Guze, 1984).

As we will see in Chapter 17, the same classes of drugs that are useful in treating panic attacks also reduce the symptoms of agoraphobia. However, the most long-lasting results are obtained from behavior therapy.

Obsessive Compulsive Disorder

Description. As the name implies, people with an **obsessive compulsive disorder** suffer from **obsessions**—thoughts that will not leave them—and **compulsions**—behaviors that they cannot keep from performing. Unlike people with panic disorder, obsessive compulsives have a defense against anxiety—namely, their compulsive behavior. Unfortunately, the need to perform this behavior often becomes more and more demanding on their time, until it interferes with their careers and daily lives.

The incidence of obsessive compulsive disorder is approximately 2 percent. Females are slightly more likely to have this diagnosis. Like panic disorder, obsessive compulsive disorder most commonly begins in young adulthood (Robbins, Helzer, Weissman, Orvaschel, Gruenberg, Burke, and Regier, 1984).

There are two principal kinds of obsessions: obsessive doubt or uncertainty, and obsessive fear of doing something that is prohibited. We all experience doubts about future activities (such as whether to look for a new job, eat at one restaurant or another, or wear a raincoat or take an umbrella) and about past activities (such as whether one has turned off the coffeepot and whether one should have worn dressier clothes), but these uncertainties, both trivial and important, preoccupy some obsessive compulsives almost completely. Others are plagued with the fear that they will do something terrible—swear aloud in church, urinate in someone's living room, kill themselves or a loved one, or jump off a bridge—although they seldom actually do anything antisocial. And even though they are often obsessed with thoughts of killing themselves, fewer than 1 percent of them actually attempt suicide. Kraines (1948) described the case of a young woman who

> complained of having "terrible thoughts." When she thought of her boy-friend she wished he were dead; when her mother went down the stairs, she "wished she'd fall and break her neck"; when her sister spoke of going to the beach with her infant daughter, the patient "hoped that they would both drown." These thoughts "make me hysterical. I love them; why should I wish such terrible things to happen? It drives me wild, makes me feel I'm crazy and don't belong to society; maybe it's best for me to end it all than to go on thinking such terrible things about those I love." (p. 183)

Unlike obsessive fears, compulsions are actual behaviors. Klein and Howard (1972) described the following case:

> He felt a compulsive, irrational need to look into a mirror and stare into his eyes, feeling that they were "stiff.". . . Striving to cease staring at his eyes, he painted over all the mirrors in his house. But then he began to look for dirt in the indentations of his hands. When he no longer could tolerate this, he wore gloves, but became obsessed with the thought of the dirt that might be in the glove stitching. Then he had to stare at his trousers and shoes, check his socks and shoelaces, count the holes in his belt, straighten his underwear, and determine if his eyebrows were straight. The time spent performing these rituals increased from minutes to hours a day. He constantly thought about committing suicide. (p. 209)

Most compulsions fall into one of four categories: counting, checking, cleaning, and avoidance. Davison and Neale (1974) reported the case of a woman who washed her hands more than five hundred times a day because she feared being contaminated by germs. The hand washing persisted even when her hands became covered with painful sores.

Most of us have been obsessed by persistent thoughts and have been afflicted by compulsions from time to time. For example, sometimes a tune (often an irritating commercial jingle) just will not go away. And if we are under stress, we often find ourselves making repetitive movements, such as drumming our fingers

"I've lost the will to obsess."

Drawing by Lorenz; © 1987
The New Yorker Magazine, Inc.

An artist's depiction of
women exhibiting signs of
hysteria, now known as
somatization disorder.

on the table or chewing on a pen or pencil. Perhaps obsessive compulsive disorder can be viewed as normal thought and behavior patterns carried to the extreme.

Possible Causes. There are several possible causes for an obsessive compulsive disorder. Unlike simple anxiety states, this disorder can be understood in terms of defense mechanisms. Some investigators have suggested that obsessions serve as devices to occupy the mind and displace painful thoughts. This strategy is seen in normal behavior; a person who "psychs himself up" before a competitive event by telling himself about his skill and stamina is also keeping out self-defeating doubts and fears. Like Scarlett O'Hara in *Gone with the Wind*, with her "I'll think about it tomorrow," we all sometimes say, "Oh, I'll think about something else" when our thoughts become painful.

If painful, anxiety-producing thoughts become frequent, and if turning to alternative patterns of thought reduces anxiety, then the principle of reinforcement predicts that the person will turn to these patterns more frequently. Just as an animal learns to jump a hurdle to escape a painful foot shock, a person can learn to think about a "safe topic" to avoid painful thoughts. If the habit becomes firmly established, the obsessive thoughts may persist after the original reason for turning to them—the situation that produced the anxiety-arousing thoughts—no longer exists. A habit can outlast its causes.

■ What are the symptoms, incidence, and possible causes of panic disorder?
■ What are the symptoms, incidence, and possible causes of the three types of phobias?
■ What are the symptoms, incidence, and possible causes of obsessive compulsive disorder?

Somatoform Disorders

The primary symptoms of **somatoform disorder** are physical (*soma* means "body"). The two most important somatoform disorders are somatization disorder and conversion disorder.

Somatization Disorder

Somatization disorder used to be called *hysteria*. The older term derives from the Greek *hystera*, meaning "uterus," because of the ancient belief that various emotional and physical ailments in women could be caused by the uterus, which wandered around inside the body, searching for a baby. (As a remedy, Hippocrates recommended marriage.) It is true that somatization disorder is almost exclusively seen in women; however, the modern use of the term *hysteria* does not imply any gynecological problems. Robbins, Helzer, Weissman, Orvaschel, Gruenberg, Burke, and Regier (1984) found that the incidence of somatization disorder was less than 1 percent of the female population and found no cases in males. In fact, almost all males who have been diagnosed as having somatization disorders have been involved in legal disputes about compensation for injuries or disability; thus, their symptoms may have been prompted by financial gain (Rounsaville, Harding, and Weissman, 1979). Somatization disorder is often chronic, lasting for decades.

Description. Somatization disorder is characterized by complaints of symptoms for which no physiological cause can be found. Obviously, a proper diagnosis can be made only after medical examination and laboratory tests indicate the lack of disease. The DSM-III-R requires that the person have a history of complaining of physical symptoms for several years. The complaints must include at least thirteen symptoms from a list of thirty-five, which fall into the following categories: conversion or psychoneurologic symptoms, gastrointestinal symptoms, female reproductive symptoms, psychosexual symptoms, pain, and cardiopulmonary symptoms. These symptoms must also have led the person to take medication, see a physician, or substantially alter his or her life. Almost every woman who receives the diagnosis of somatization disorder reports that she does not experience pleasure from sexual intercourse. Obviously, everyone has one or more physical symptoms from time to time that cannot be explained through a medical examination, but few people chronically complain of at least thirteen of them. Although people with somatization disorder often make suicide attempts, they rarely succeed in killing themselves.

Somatization disorder resembles another somatoform disorder, **hypochondriasis.** *Hypochondria* means "under the cartilage." Greek physicians thought that the disorder occurred when black bile collected under the breastbone, which is made of cartilage. Unlike people with somatization disorder, who complain of specific physical symptoms, hypochondriacs demonstrate an excessive fear of illness. They interpret minor physical sensations as indications that they may have a serious disease.

The following quotations from Purtell, Robins, and Cohen (1951) illustrate the range of symptoms reported by people with somatization disorder.

I can't eat pastries. Always pay for it. I can't eat steak now. I throw up whole milk. I always throw up the skins of tomatoes. Pudding made with canned milk makes me sick. I have to use fresh milk.

I am sore all over. I can't explain it. I have been sick all my life. Now I am alone since my husband died, and the doctor said I must come for help. It has taken $10,000 to keep me alive. This is my 76th hospitalization.

It is important to note that the complaints of a person with somatization disorder consist of *symptoms*, not *signs*. **Symptoms** are reports of feelings or perceptions that people make to their physicians—for example, reports of pains, of dizziness, or of discomfort during intercourse. In contrast, **signs** are objective, consisting of observable evidence for physical malfunctioning, such as an elevated temperature, a rash, or an inflammation. People with somatization disorder spend a lot of time in physicians' offices and in hospitals. Figure 16.1 shows the incidence of major operations performed on people with somatization disorder, medically ill control subjects, and healthy control subjects. As you can see, people with somatization disorder underwent an impressive number of operations, beginning after adolescence. (See Figure 16.1.)

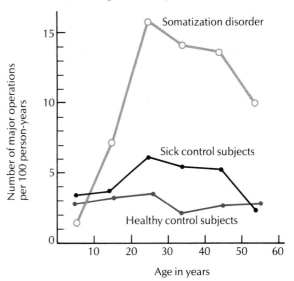

FIGURE 16.1

Major operations for healthy control subjects, sick control subjects, and people with somatization disorder. (From Cohen, M.E., Robins, E., Purtell, J.J., Altmann, M.W., and Reid, D.E. *Journal of the American Medical Association*, 1953, *151*, 977–986.)

Possible Causes. Somatization disorder is most common in poorly educated women of low socioeconomic status (Guze, Woodruff, and Clayton, 1971). The disorder also runs in families; Coryell (1980) found that approximately 20 percent of the first-degree female relatives of people with somatization disorder also had the disorder. In addition, many studies have shown that somatization disorder is closely associated with antisocial personality disorder (which will be described in a later section). First-degree male relatives of women with somatization disorder have an increased incidence of alcoholism or antisocial behavior, and the first-degree female relatives of convicted male criminals have an increased incidence of somatization disorder (Woerner and Guze, 1968; Guze, Wolfgram, McKinney, and Cantwell, 1967). These results suggest that a particular environmental or genetic history leads to different pathological manifestations in men and women. Hereditary factors appear to play at least a partial role; Cadoret (1978) observed a relation between somatization disorder and antisocial behavior in first-degree relatives who were raised in different households.

Conversion Disorder

Description. Formerly called *hysterical neurosis, conversion type*, **conversion disorder** is characterized by physical complaints that resemble neurological disorders but have no underlying organic pathological basis. The symptoms include blindness, deafness, loss of feeling, and paralysis. Some investigators refer to these conditions as *pseudoneurological* disorders. According to the DSM-III-R, in order to be classified as a conversion disorder there must be some apparent psychological reason for the symptoms; they must occur in response to an environmental stimulus that produces a psychological conflict, or they must permit the person to avoid an unpleasant activity or to receive support and sympathy. Unlike somatization disorder, conversion disorder can afflict both men and women.

The term *conversion*, when applied to a mental disorder, derives from psychoanalytical theory, which states that the energy of an unresolved psychic conflict is converted into a physical symptom. Hofling (1963) described one such case as follows.

The patient had taken the day off from work to be at home with his wife and [newborn] baby. During the afternoon, he had felt somewhat nervous and tense, but had passed off these feelings as normal for a new father. . . .

. . . The baby awoke and cried. Mrs. L. said that she would nurse him. . . . As she put the baby to her breast, the patient became aware of a smarting sensation in his eyes. He had been smoking heavily and attributed the irritation to the room's being filled with smoke. He got up and opened a window. When the smarting sensation became worse he went to the washstand and applied a cold cloth to his eyes. On removing the cloth, he found that he was completely blind.

. . . Psychotherapy was instituted. . . . The visual symptoms disappeared rather promptly, with only very mild and fleeting exacerbations during the next several months. . . .

. . . He had been jealous of the baby—this was a difficult admission to make—and jealous on two distinct counts. One feeling was, in essence, a sexual jealousy, accentuated by his own sexual deprivation during the last weeks of the pregnancy. The other was . . . a jealousy of the maternal solicitude shown the infant by its mother. (1963, pp. 315–316)

Although the sensory deficits or paralyses of people with conversion disorders do not result from damage to the nervous system, these people are not faking their illnesses. People who deliberately pretend that they are sick in order to gain some advantage are said to be **malingering.** Malingering is not defined as a mental disorder by the DSM-III-R. Although it is not always easy to distinguish malingering from a conversion disorder, two criteria are useful. First, people with a conversion disorder are usually delighted to talk about their symptoms in great detail, whereas malingerers are reluctant to do so, for fear of having their deception discovered. Second, people with a conversion disorder usually describe the symptoms with great drama and flair but do not appear to be upset about them. This blasé attitude is so striking that it has been called *la belle indifférence* ("fine unconcern").

Conversion disorders must also be distinguished from somatization disorder and psychosomatic disorders. As we just saw, somatization disorder consists of complaints of medical problems, but the examining physician is unable to see any signs that would indicate physical illness. In contrast, a patient with conversion disorder gives the appearance of

Drawing by Gross; © 1986

having a neurological disorder such as blindness or paralysis. **Psychosomatic disorders** are not fictitious or imaginary symptoms; they are real organic illnesses that are caused or made worse by psychological factors. For example, stress can cause gastric ulcers, asthma, or other physical symptoms. Ulcers caused by stress are real, not imaginary. Successful therapy would thus require reduction of the person's level of stress as well as surgical or medical treatment of the lesions in the stomach.

Because conversion disorders can affect any part of the body, it is very important that clinicians distinguish between organic illness and conversion disorders. An organic illness can be mistaken for a conversion disorder, and there is nothing to prevent a person with a conversion disorder from also having an organic illness. Whitlock (1967) examined the subsequent medical history of patients diagnosed as having conversion disorders and found that more than 60 percent of them later were found to have organic diseases, in contrast to 5 percent of people with other types of mental disorders. The ailments of the people with "conversion disorders" included head injury (received before diagnosis), stroke, encephalitis, and brain tumors.

Possible Causes. Psychoanalytical theory suggests that the psychic energy of unresolved conflicts (especially those involving sexual desires that the patient is unwilling or unable to admit to having) becomes displaced into physical symptoms. In other words, psychoanalysts regard conversion disorders as primarily sexual in origin.

Behaviorists have suggested that conversion disorders can be learned for a variety of reasons. This assertion gains support from the finding that people with these disorders usually suffer from physical symptoms of diseases with which they are already familiar (Ullman and Krasner, 1969). A patient often mimics the symptoms of a friend. Furthermore, the patient must receive some kind of reinforcement for having the disability; he or she must derive some benefit from it.

Ullman and Krasner cited a case that was originally reported by Brady and Lind (1961). A soldier developed an eye problem that led to his discharge, along with a small disability pension. He worked at a series of menial jobs, returning periodically to the hospital for treatment of his eye condition. He applied for a larger disability pension several times but was turned down because his vision had not become worse. After twelve years, the man, who was currently being forced by his wife and mother-in-law to spend his spare evenings and weekends doing chores around the house, suddenly became "blind." Because of his total disability, he was given special training for the blind and received a larger pension. He also received a family allowance from the community and no longer had to work around the house. In this case, both criteria described by Ullman and Krasner were met: the patient was familiar with the disorder (he had a real eye disorder), and his symptoms were reinforced.

Dissociative Disorders

Description. Like *conversion disorder,* the term **dissociative disorder** comes from Freud. The original name of the disorder was *hysterical neurosis, dissociative type.* According to psychoanalytical theory, a person develops a dissociative disorder when a massive repression fails to keep a strong sexual desire from consciousness. As a result, the person resorts to dissociating one part of his or her mind from the rest.

The most common dissociative disorder is **psychogenic amnesia,** in which a person "forgets" all his or her past life, along with the conflicts that were present, and begins a new one. The term *psychogenic* means "produced by the mind." Because amnesia can also be produced by physical means—such as epilepsy, drug or alcohol intoxication, or brain damage—clinicians must be careful to distinguish between amnesias of organic and psychogenic origin. Any person with amnesia must undergo a complete neurological examination and appropriate laboratory tests.

A **fugue** (pronounced *fyoog*) is a special form of amnesia in which the person leaves and starts a new life elsewhere. (*Fugue* means "flight.") Henderson and Gillespie (1950) re-

ported the following case of psychogenic amnesia compounded by fugue:

> A clergyman, the Rev. Ansell Bourne, disappeared from a town in Rhode Island. Eight weeks later a man calling himself A.J. Brown, who had rented a small shop six weeks previously in a town in Pennsylvania and had stocked it with confectionery, etc., woke up in a fright and asked who he was. He said he was a clergyman, that his name was Bourne, and that he knew nothing of the shop or of Brown. He was subsequently identified as the Rev. Ansell Bourne by his relatives, and remained terrified by the incident and unable to explain it. (p. 192)

Multiple personality is a very rare, but very striking, dissociative disorder. The DSM-III-R defines this condition as "the existence within the person of two or more distinct personalities or personal states, each of which is dominant at a particular time." According to the DSM-III-R, "in classic cases, the personality and personal state each have unique memories, behavior patterns, and social relationships." Only about a hundred cases of multiple personality have been documented, and some investigators believe that many, if not most of them, are simulations, not actual mental disorders. In one well-publicized case (the "Hillside strangler"), the person was shown to be faking a multiple personality disorder in an attempt to escape punishment for having committed several brutal murders. In fact, the murderer had an antisocial personality disorder (described in the next section of this chapter). Multiple personality disorder has received much attention; people find it fascinating to contemplate several different personalities, most of whom are unaware of each other, existing within the same person. Lipton (1943) gave an account of the case of Sara and Maud K.:

> In general demeanor, Maud was quite different from Sara. She walked with a swinging, bouncing gait contrasted to Sara's sedate one. While Sara was depressed, Maud was ebullient and happy. . . . In so far as she could Maud dressed differently from Sara. Sara had two pairs of slippers. One was a worn pair of plain gray mules; the other, gaudy, striped, high-heeled, open-toed sandals. Sara always wore the mules. Maud would throw them aside in disgust and don the sandals. Sara used no make-up. Maud used a lot of rouge and lip stick, painted her fingernails and toenails deep red, and put a red ribbon in her hair. She liked red and was quickly attracted by anything of that color. Sara's favorite color was blue.

One possible explanation for the occurrence of multiple personalities is that the disorder permits people to freely engage in behaviors that otherwise would cause tremendous feelings of guilt.

People with antisocial personality disorder can be both charming and dangerous. Theodore Bundy, who was convicted of the brutal murder of two women, maintained an inappropriate, jovial attitude throughout the trial.

Sara was a mature, intelligent individual. Her . . . I.Q. [was] 128. [Maud's I.Q. was 43.] Sara's vocabulary was larger than Maud's, and she took an intelligent interest in words new to her. When Maud heard a new word, she would laugh and mispronounce it or say, "That was a twenty-five cent one." In sharp contrast to Sara, Maud's grammar was atrocious. A typical statement was, "I didn't do nuttin'." Sara's handwriting was more mature than Maud's.

Sara did not smoke and was very awkward when she attempted it. Maud had a compulsion to smoke. At times she insisted she "had to" and would become agitated and even violent if cigarettes were denied her. She would smoke chain fashion as many cigarettes as were permitted. . . .

Maud had no conscience, no sense of right and wrong. She saw no reason for not always doing as she pleased. She felt no guilt over her incestuous and promiscuous sexual relationships. Sara on the other hand had marked guilt feelings over her previous immoral sexual behavior.

It seemed that Sara changed to Maud at the point when Sara's feeling of guilt was greatest. (pp. 41–44)

Possible Causes. Dissociative disorders are usually explained as responses to severe conflicts resulting from intolerable impulses or responses to guilt stemming from an actual misdeed. Partly because they are rare, dissociative disorders are among the least understood of the mental disorders. In general, the dissociation is advantageous to the person. Amnesia enables the person to forget about a painful or unpleasant life. A person with fugue not only forgets but also leaves the area to start a new existence. And multiple personalities allow a person to do things that he or she would really like to do but cannot, because of the strong guilt feelings that would ensue. The alternate personality can be one with a very weak conscience.

ANTISOCIAL PERSONALITY DISORDER

The DSM-III-R includes twelve personality disorders, which are abnormalities in behavior that impair social or occupational functioning. Examples include paranoid personality disorder, narcissistic personality disorder, obsessive compulsive personality disorder, and passive-aggressive personality disorder. Personality disorders are not classified as actual mental disorders.

The only personality disorder I will specifically discuss here is the one that has the most major effect on society: antisocial personality disorder.

Characteristic Symptoms

People have used many different terms to label what we now call **antisocial personality disorder.** Prichard (1835) used the term *moral insanity* to describe people whose intellect was normal but in whom the "moral and active principles of the mind are strongly perverted and depraved . . . and the individual is found to be incapable . . . of conducting himself with decency and propriety." Koch (1889) introduced the term *psychopathic inferiority*, which soon became simply *psychopathy* (pronounced *sy KOP a thee*); a person who displayed the disorder was called a *psychopath*. The first version of the DSM (the DSM-I) used the term *sociopathic personality disturbance,* which was subsequently replaced by the present term, *antisocial personality disorder.* Today, most clinicians still refer to such people as *psychopaths* or *sociopaths,* and I will, too, in this section.

People with antisocial personality disorder cause a considerable amount of distress in society. Many criminals can be diagnosed as psychopaths, and most psychopaths have a record of criminal behavior. The diagnostic criteria of the DSM-III-R include evidence of at least three types of antisocial behavior before age fifteen and at least four after eighteen. The adult forms of antisocial behavior include such things as inability to sustain consistent work behavior; lack of ability to function as a responsible parent; repeated criminal activity, such as theft, pimping, or prostitution; inability to maintain enduring attachment to a sexual partner; irritability and aggressiveness including fights or assault; failure to honor financial obligations; impulsivity and failure to plan ahead; habitual lying or use of aliases; and consistently reckless or drunken driving. Clearly, people with symptoms of antisocial personality disorder are people most of us would not want to become overly friendly with or to get close to.

The incidence of antisocial personality disorder has been estimated at 4 percent among men and less than 1 percent among women (Robbins, Helzer, Weissman, Orvaschel, Gruenberg, Burke, and Regier, 1984). However, we cannot be sure that this figure is accurate, because psychopaths do not voluntarily visit mental health professionals for help with their "problem." Indeed, most of them feel no need to change their ways and may even resist or refuse help if it is offered. Psychopaths who are indicted for serious crimes will often be seen by psychiatrists in order to determine whether they are "sane," and some will feign mental illness so that they will be committed to a mental institution rather than to a prison. Once they reach the institution, however, it is often the case that they will quickly "recover" so that they can be released.

Cleckley (1976), one of the most prominent experts on psychopathy, has listed sixteen characteristic features of antisocial personality

TABLE 16.3

Cleckley's primary characteristics of antisocial personality disorder

1. Superficial charm and good "intelligence"
2. Absence of delusions and other signs of irrational thinking
3. Absence of "nervousness" or [neurosis]
4. Unreliability
5. Untruthfulness and insincerity
6. Lack of remorse or shame
7. Inadequately motivated antisocial behavior
8. Poor judgment and failure to learn by experience
9. Pathologic egocentricity and incapacity for love
10. General poverty in major affective reactions
11. Specific loss of insight
12. Unresponsiveness in general interpersonal relations
13. Fantastic and uninviting behavior . . .
14. Suicide rarely carried out
15. Sex life impersonal, trivial, and poorly integrated
16. Failure to follow any life plan

(From Cleckley, H., *The Mask of Sanity,* 5th edition. St. Louis, Mo.: C.V. Mosby Company, 1976, pp. 337–338.)

disorder. (See Table 16.3.) Cleckley's list of features provides a good picture of what most psychopaths are like.

Psychopathic Behavior Patterns

Most investigators believe that the primary defects in people with antisocial personality disorder are their failure to learn to avoid aversive stimuli, their inability to form close social attachments, and their emotional unexcitability. Normal people learn not to perform behaviors that bring punishment, and if they do something that has been punished in the past, they will feel anxious and perhaps guilty. Psychopaths neither avoid these behaviors nor feel guilty about them. They are not indifferent to punishment; they simply do not change their behavior in order to avoid it. And although most psychopaths do not show signs of genuine guilt, they can make a show of remorse if they think that doing so will prevent them from being punished for their misdeeds. Normal people become attached to others and empathize with them, sharing their moods. Although some psychopaths know how to act friendly, they do not appear to empathize with others and do not share happiness or grief.

Cleckley (1976) suggested that the psychopath's defect "consists of an unawareness and a persistent lack of ability to become aware of what the most important experiences of life mean to others. . . . The major emotional accompaniments are absent or so attenuated as to count for little" (p. 371). Some investigators have hypothesized that this lack of involvement is caused by an unresponsive autonomic nervous system. If a person feels no anticipatory fear of punishment, then he or she is perhaps more likely to commit acts that normal people would be afraid to do. Similarly, if such a person feels little or no emotional response to other people and to their joys and sorrows, he or she is unlikely to establish close relationships with them. Some investigators (Quay, 1965) have even suggested that criminal behavior by psychopaths is also a result of their unresponsiveness; they seek thrills from crime because these acts provide enough stimulation to make them feel something.

Many experiments have found that psychopaths do show less reactivity in situations involving punishment. For example, Hare

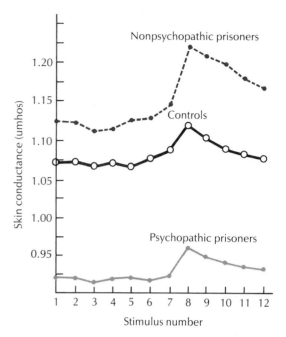

FIGURE 16.3

Changes in skin conductance in anticipation of a painful electric shock (at the number 8) of psychopathic prisoners, nonpsychopathic prisoners, and nonpsychopathic control subjects. (From Hare, R.D. *Journal of Abnormal Psychology,* 1965, *70,* 442–445.)

(1965a) paired a tone (conditional stimulus) with a painful electrical shock (unconditional stimulus) and measured changes in the electrical conductance of people's skin, which is controlled by the autonomic nervous system. Stimuli that produce pain or anxiety normally increase this conductance, presumably by causing changes in the rate of blood flow and sweating. As Figure 16.2 shows, psychopaths exhibited fewer conditional responses than nonpsychopathic control subjects.

In another experiment, Hare (1965b) demonstrated that psychopaths show fewer signs of anticipatory fear. All subjects watched the numbers 1 through 12 appear in sequential order in the window of a device used to present visual stimuli. They were told that they would receive a very painful shock when the number 8 appeared. As Figure 16.3 shows, psychopathic subjects showed much less anticipatory responsiveness than did normal control subjects or nonpsychopathic criminals.

We do not yet know what causes the deficits in emotion and empathy that are displayed by

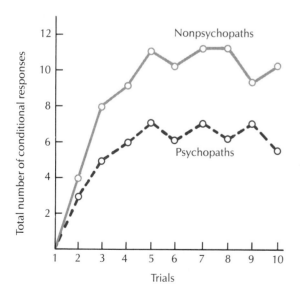

FIGURE 16.2

Aversive classical conditioning of psychopathic and nonpsychopathic subjects. (From Hare, R.D. *Journal of Psychology,* 1965, *59,* 367–370.)

psychopaths. These people often (but not always) come from grossly disturbed families that contain alcoholics and other psychopaths. As we saw earlier, the women in families with psychopathic men have an unusually high incidence of somatization disorder. Guze, Wolfgram, McKinney, and Cantwell (1967) found that approximaetly 20 percent of the first-degree relatives of men convicted of felonies were psychopaths and one-third were alcoholics. Cloninger and Guze (1973) found that one-third of the male first-degree relatives of women convicted of felonies were psychopaths and one-half were alcoholics. In addition, twin studies suggest that the relation may be at least partly a result of heredity; Christiansen (1970) found that the concordance rate for psychopathy was 36 percent for monozygotic twins and only 12 percent for dizygotic twins.

This painting was done by an 18-year-old male who suffered from schizophrenia. Today, he is working as a stockbroker. The painting depicts a ghost, the "other self" that he was always talking to.

- What are the symptoms, incidence, and sex-linked features of somatization disorder?
- What are the symptoms, incidence, and possible causes of conversion disorder?
- What are the symptoms, incidence, and possible causes of three dissociative disorders?
- What are the symptoms and incidence of antisocial personality disorder?

SCHIZOPHRENIA

Schizophrenia, the most common psychosis, includes several types, each with a distinctive set of symptoms. For many years there has been a controversy about whether schizophrenia is one disorder with various subtypes, or whether each subtype constitutes a distinct disease. Because the prognosis differs for the various subtypes of schizophrenia, they appear to differ at least in severity. However, a particular individual may, at different times, meet the criteria for different subtypes. As we will see later, recent biological evidence suggests that there are two basic types of schizophrenia, which do not correspond to the DSM-III-R classifications.

The term *schizophrenia* (pronounced *skit so FREE nee a*) comes from the Greek words *schizein*, "to split," and *phrēn*, "mind." But the term does *not* imply a split or multiple personality. *Schizophrenia* is probably the most misused psychological term in existence. People often say that they "feel schizophrenic" about an issue when they really mean that they have mixed feelings about it. A person who sometimes wants to build a cabin in Alaska and live off the land and at other times wants to take over the family insurance business may be undecided, but he or she is not schizophrenic.

Eugen Bleuler (1911–1950), who coined the term *schizophrenia*, believed this disorder resulted from splitting, or disorganization, of various functions of the mind, so that thoughts and feelings no longer worked together normally.

Characteristic Symptoms

This section describes the symptoms that are seen in all types of schizophrenia, although they may not all be present in any one person diagnosed as schizophrenic. Later sections will describe symptoms that are usually associated with each particular type of schizophrenia.

Thought Disorders

Disordered thought is probably the most important symptom of schizophrenia. Schizophrenics have great difficulty arranging their thoughts logically. In conversation, they jump from one topic to another, as new associations come up. Often they utter **neologisms** (new and meaningless words) or choose words for their rhyme rather than for their meaning. As a schizophrenic patient noted (in a period of relative lucidity):

> My thoughts get all jumbled up. I start thinking or talking about something but I never get there. Instead, I wander off in the wrong direction and get caught up with all sorts of different things that may be connected with things I want to say but in a way I can't explain. People listening to me get more lost than I do. . . .
>
> My trouble is that I've got too many thoughts. You might think about something, let's say that ashtray and just think, ah, yes, that's for putting my cigarette in, but I would think of it and then would think of a dozen different things connected with it at the same time. (McGhie and Chapman, 1961, p. 108)

Delusions

A **delusion** is a belief that is obviously contrary to fact, and many schizophrenics hold such beliefs. People with *delusions of persecution* believe that others are plotting against them. *Delusions of grandeur* entail false beliefs in one's power and importance, such as a conviction that one is really a messiah, or a famous scientist, or the possessor of powers that could destroy the world. *Delusions of control* are related to delusions of persecution; the person believes that he or she is being controlled by others by such means as radar or tiny radio receivers implanted in his or her brain.

Hallucinations

Hallucinations are perceptions of stimuli that are not actually present. The most common schizophrenic hallucinations are auditory, but they can also involve any of the other senses. The typical schizophrenic hallucination consists of voices talking to the person. Sometimes

Schizophrenics may experience visual hallucinations. However, the most common schizophrenic hallucinations are auditory.

they order the person to do something; sometimes they scold the person for his or her unworthiness; sometimes they just utter meaningless phrases. Olfactory hallucinations are also fairly common; often these contribute to the delusion that others are trying to kill the person with poison gas. Boisen (1960) reported the following experience of hallucinations:

> There was music everywhere and rhythm and beauty. . . . I heard what seemed to be a choir of angels. I thought it the most beautiful music I had ever heard. Two of the airs I kept repeating over and over until the delirium ended. . . . This choir of angels kept hovering around the hospital and shortly afterward I heard something about a little lamb being born up-stairs in the room just above mine. This excited me greatly and next morning I made some inquiries about that little lamb. . . .
>
> The next night I was visited, not by angels, but by a lot of witches. . . . I could hear a constant

tap-tapping along the walls, all done according to some system. This was due, it seemed, to the detectives in the employ of the evil powers who were out to locate the exact place where I was. Then the room was filled with the odor of [sulfur]. I was told that witches were around and from the ventilator shaft I picked up paper black cats and broomsticks and poke bonnets. I was greatly exercised, and I stuffed my blanket into the ventilator shaft. I finally not only worked out a way of checking the invasion of the black cats, but I found some sort of process of regeneration which could be used to save other people. I had, it seemed, broken an opening in the wall which separated medicine and religion. I was told to feel on the back of my neck and I would find there a sign of my new mission. I thereupon examined and found a shuttle-like affair about three-fourths of an inch long. (pp. 119–120)

This potpourri of symptoms included auditory, then olfactory, then visual hallucinations, which were then followed by delusions of persecution and grandeur, and, finally, a somatosensory hallucination.

Anxiety

Patients with schizophrenia often become frightened by their lack of control over their own thoughts and feelings, especially in the early part of a schizophrenic episode. Their world seems to be crumbling as they feel themselves descend into madness. As one patient put it:

> Everything seemed different and strange. It was like I had entered an alien world where nothing was the same as I had known it. I no longer knew who I was, or even where the environment left off and I began. I didn't even seem to exist anymore as a distinct person—just parts of me "floating around" here and there in space. (Coleman, 1976, p. 294)

Emotional Withdrawal

Schizophrenics often lose interest in the real world and withdraw into themselves. They may show indifference to events that would be expected to affect them deeply, such as the death of a close relative. Often they resist efforts to bring them back to reality and become hostile when a therapist attempts to do so. It is possible that the withdrawal is a defense against the panic and anxiety that occur early in episodes of schizophrenia.

Types of Schizophrenia

Most cases of schizophrenia do not fit neatly into one of the categories described below. Many are diagnosed as **undifferentiated schizophrenia;** that is, the patients have delusions, hallucinations, and disorganized behavior but do not meet the criteria for catatonic, paranoid, or disorganized schizophrenia. In addition, some patients' symptoms change after an initial diagnosis, and their classification changes accordingly.

Catatonic Schizophrenia

Catatonic schizophrenia (from the Greek *kateinein,* meaning "to stretch or draw tight") is characterized by various motor disturbances, including **catatonic postures**—bizarre, stationary poses maintained for many hours—and *waxy flexibility,* in which the person's limbs can be molded into new positions, which are then maintained. Contrary to popular assumptions, catatonic schizophrenics are often aware of all that goes on about them and will talk about what happened after the episode of catatonia subsides.

Immobility is not the only motor symptom of catatonic schizophrenia. People with the disorder often engage in bouts of wild, excited movement, becoming dangerous and unpredictable. Before modern medication eliminated almost all need to use straitjackets, it was the catatonic schizophrenic who was most likely to wear this device. (The word is *strait,* by the way, and not *straight.* To *straiten* means to "limit or restrict.")

Paranoid Schizophrenia

The preeminent symptoms of **paranoid schizophrenia** are delusions of persecution, grandeur, or control, although delusions can also occur in other forms of schizophrenia. A case reported by Davison and Neale (1982) illustrates how bizarre the delusions of a paranoid schizophrenic can be. Roger felt that he was a "born soldier" and in fact wore an Army jacket and kept his hair cut short, even though the army had rejected him for psychiatric reasons. After being treated on an outpatient basis for several weeks, he had to be committed to a hospital.

> He had threatened to blow up an Army recruiting post, claiming that aliens from another planet had

taken over. He now believed that he was one of the last "true" earthmen. The aliens had already infiltrated the bodies of most human beings, beginning first with those of army men and then moving into the bodies of the rest of the human race as well. (p. 406)

The word *paranoid* has become so widely used in ordinary language that it has come to mean "suspicious." However, not all paranoid schizophrenics believe that they are being persecuted. Some believe that they hold special powers that can save the world, or that they are Christ, or Napoleon, or the President of the United States.

Given that paranoid schizophrenics are among the most intelligent of psychotic patients, it is not surprising that they often build up delusional structures incorporating an immense wealth of detail. Even the most trivial event is interpreted in terms of a grand scheme, whether it is a delusion of persecution or a delusion of grandeur. The way a person walks, a particular facial expression or movement, or even the shapes of clouds can acquire special significance.

Disorganized Schizophrenia

Disorganized schizophrenia once had a relatively innocuous-sounding name, **hebephrenic schizophrenia.** (Hebe, the Greek goddess of youth and spring, was usually portrayed as being rather silly. Thus, *hebephrenia* denotes a "silly mind.") However, disorganized schizophrenia is a serious disorder. Usually it is progressive and irreversible. People with disorganized schizophrenia often display signs of emotion, especially silly laughter, that are inappropriate to the circumstances. Also, their speech tends to be a jumble of words: "I came to the hospital to play, gay, way, lay, day, bray, donkey, monkey" (Snyder, 1974, p. 132). The speech of a seriously deteriorated hebephrenic is often called **word salad.**

Schizophreniform Disorder

Although the DSM-III-R assigns **schizophreniform disorder** (formerly called an **acute schizophrenic episode**) to the category of "psychotic disorders not elsewhere classified," this disorder differs from schizophrenia only in its shorter duration. Because episodes tend to

begin and end rapidly, patients are likely to be overwhelmed by the sudden changes in their thought processes and are therefore also likely to feel panic and anxiety. Acute schizophrenic episodes also tend to be *undifferentiated;* that is, they involve a wide variety of symptoms. Schizophreniform disorder has the best prognosis of all types of schizophrenia.

■ What are the characteristic symptoms of schizophrenia?
■ What are the symptoms of the major types of schizophrenic disorders?

Possible Origins of Schizophrenia

Eugen Bleuler (1911–1950), one of the pioneers in the diagnosis and study of schizophrenia, divided the disorder into **process** and **reactive** forms. Patients with a general history of good mental health were designated as having reactive schizophrenia, on the assumption that their disorder was a *reaction* to stressful life situations. Typically, these patients soon recovered, and few experienced another episode. Today these people would be diagnosed as having schizophreniform disorder or, if a plausible source of stress could be identified, a brief reactive psychosis. Patients with indications of mental illness early in life were designated as process schizophrenics and were considered to have a chronic disorder. Process schizophrenia would include all the other types of schizophrenia described in the previous section.

Evidence from modern research supports the distinction between process and reactive schizophrenia. Clinicians have observed that the symptoms displayed by patients at the time of diagnosis can be used to predict the likelihood of eventual recovery. Astrup and Noreik (1966) followed patients over a thirty-year period and compared their clinical symptoms with the outcome of their disorder. Predictors of eventual recovery were delusions, thought disturbances, hallucinations, and change of personality at the onset of the schizophrenic episode. Presumably, these symptoms are characteristic of the fast onset of a reactive form of schizophrenia. (Of course, they also occur in severe paranoid schizophrenia, which has an unfavorable prognosis.) Unfavorable signs were long duration of illness, emotional blunting, and inadequate motor reflexes. As we will see, these results are consistent with the distinctions between *positive* and *negative* symptoms that have recently been made as a result of biological studies.

If process schizophrenia does have its roots in early life, then it is important to determine what the early signs are. The ability to identify people with a high risk of schizophrenia while they are still young might make it possible to institute some form of therapy before the disorder becomes advanced. The early signs might

Unlike the cooperative behavior shown in this classroom setting, abrasive and antisocial traits in boys and withdrawn or passive behavior in girls were determined to be characteristics of preschizophrenics (Watt and Lubansky, 1976).

also indicate whether the causes of schizophrenia are biological, environmental, or both.

Watt and Lubansky (1976) attempted to relate childhood behavior patterns to schizophrenia in adulthood. First, they obtained a list of all patients from ages fifteen to thirty-four in mental institutions in Massachusetts. They also obtained a list of students who had attended the public high school in a large Boston suburb and identified among them fifty-four who later became schizophrenic patients. They selected a group of control subjects who had not developed schizophrenia, matching them with the patients on the basis of age, sex, race, and social class of the parents. Then the researchers examined the comments of the subjects' teachers in their school records and attempted to relate the kinds of comments made with the probability of a subsequent onset of schizophrenia.

There were sharp sex differences in the results. Boys who had become schizophrenic were rated as less conscientious and as more abrasive and antisocial than the control subjects. Teachers found them disagreeable and described them as emotionally unstable. In contrast, the girls who had become schizophrenic were generally described as withdrawn or introverted, insecure, and passive. The control girls tended to be rated as more nervous, restless, and emotional. No strong differences were seen in intelligence or academic achievement. Preschizophrenics had somewhat lower IQ scores and scholastic performance, but the difference was not great, and childhood intelligence was not related to the amount of time spent in a mental hospital later.

The results support the hypothesis that schizophrenia is a disorder that strikes people who are different from others even in childhood. However, the study revealed nothing about whether these differences resulted from physiological disorders or from the behavior of other family members during the schizophrenics' infancy and early childhood.

Heritability

The heritability of schizophrenia has now been firmly established. In one of the best studies, Kety, Rosenthal, Wender, and Schulsinger (1968) examined Denmark's *folkeregister*, which contains a lifelong record of Danish citizens. From it, they compiled two lists: one of

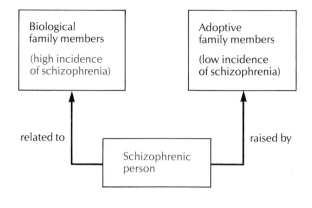

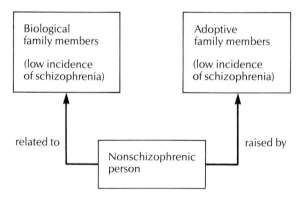

FIGURE 16.4

The results and conclusions of the adoption study by Kety, Rosenthal, Wender, and Schulsinger (1968).

children who had been adopted and who later became schizophrenic, and one of adopted children who did not. They found that the incidence of schizophrenia in the adoptive families of people who were schizophrenic was as low as in the adoptive families of control subjects who were not schizophrenic, but that the incidence of schizophrenia in the children's *biological* families was much higher than normal. Because the children were raised by their adoptive families, and not by their biological families, there are no grounds for concluding that learning played a role in the transmission of the disorder; rather, the transmission would appear to have been hereditary. (See Figure 16.4.) The same study found that only chronic (process) schizophrenia was related to schizophrenia in the biological family. Acute (reactive) schizophrenia was *not* related to a family history of mental disturbances. This finding fur-

ther supports the conclusion that the process and reactive forms of schizophrenia are indeed different disorders, with different causes.

Although heredity studies have shown that the likelihood of developing schizophrenia increases significantly if a person has schizophrenic relatives, this disorder is not a simple trait that is inherited like eye color. Most people with schizophrenic relatives do *not* develop schizophrenia. Studies estimate that even if both parents are schizophrenic, the probability that their child will develop schizophrenia is 30 percent or less.

Most investigators believe that a person inherits a *predisposition* to become schizophrenic; in their view, most environments will foster normal development, whereas certain other environments will trigger various disorders, including schizophrenia. Until recently, researchers thought that the important factors were social in nature, and that schizophrenia was a reaction to stress in a susceptible individual. Although social factors cannot be ruled out, evidence now suggests that at least some cases of schizophrenia may be a result of disease. This evidence will be reviewed in a later section.

Biochemical Factors

The Dopamine Hypothesis. Two classes of drugs have been found to affect the symptoms of schizophrenia. Cocaine and amphetamine *cause* these symptoms, both in schizophrenics and in nonschizophrenics, while antipsychotic drugs *reduce* them. Because both types of drugs affect neural communication in which dopamine serves as a transmitter substance, investigators have hypothesized that abnormal activity of these neurons is the primary cause of schizophrenia.

Earlier in this century, when cocaine was cheap and freely available, there was an epidemic of cocaine psychosis, caused by injections of large amounts of the substance. Heavy users of cocaine developed a syndrome that closely resembled paranoid schizophrenia, and in fact many were diagnosed as having this disorder. The addicts became suspicious and believed that others were plotting against them, heard voices talking to them, and often had tactile hallucinations, such as the feeling that small insects had burrowed under their skin.

Clinicians have also observed that abuse of amphetamine (whose pharmacological effects are similar to those of cocaine) causes a temporary psychosis that resembles schizophrenia. Griffith, Cavanaugh, Held, and Oates (1972) used seven subjects who were users of amphetamine but who had no previous history of psychotic behavior. The experimenters administered a very heavy dose of the drug—10 milligrams of dextroamphetamine every hour. All seven of the subjects became psychotic within two to five days. At first the subjects lost their appetite and could not sleep. About eight hours before overt signs of psychosis occurred, they became withdrawn and would not discuss their thoughts and feelings. Later, the subjects admitted that during this time they began to have paranoid thoughts, but they felt that these thoughts were drug induced and fought to keep control over them. When the psychosis finally emerged, the subjects began to talk about their thoughts and feelings. They all developed paranoid delusions, including one of being controlled by a "giant oscillator." Their symptoms disappeared a few hours after discontinuing the drug.

Amphetamine and related substances also make all kinds of naturally occurring schizophrenia worse: paranoids become more suspicious, disorganized schizophrenics become sillier, and catatonics become more rigid or hyperactive. Davis (1974) injected an amphetaminelike drug into schizophrenic patients whose symptoms had abated. Within one minute, each patient's condition changed "from a mild schizophrenia into a wild and very florid schizophrenia." One of them began to make a clacking noise, then pounded a pad of paper with a pencil until he shredded it. He said he had been "sending and receiving messages from the ancient Egyptians."

People with a diagnosis of schizophrenia constitute the largest proportion of patients in mental hospitals. Until around 1955, the number of patients in mental hospitals grew steadily every year; then the number of patients began to decline. Several factors led to this decrease, including a growing tendency to treat patients in community-based facilities. But one of the important factors was the introduction of **chlorpromazine** (trade name: Thorazine).

Chlorpromazine and other antipsychotic drugs are remarkably effective in alleviating the symptoms of schizophrenia. Hallucinations diminish or disappear, delusions become less striking or cease altogether, and the patients' thought processes become more coherent. These drugs are not merely tranquilizers; for example, they cause a patient with catatonic immobility to begin moving again, as well as causing an excited patient to quiet down. In contrast, true tranquilizers such as Librium or Valium only make a schizophrenic patient slow-moving and groggy.

Amphetamine, cocaine, and the antipsychotic drugs act on synapses (the junctions between nerve cells) in the brain. As you may recall from Chapter 2, one neuron passes on excitatory or inhibitory messages to another by liberating a small amount of transmitter substance from its terminal button into the synaptic cleft. The chemical activates receptors on the surface of the receiving neuron, and the activated receptors either excite or inhibit the receiving neuron. Drugs such as amphetamine and cocaine cause the *stimulation* of receptors for dopamine, a transmitter substance. In contrast, antipsychotic drugs block dopamine receptors and *prevent* them from becoming stimulated. These findings have led investigators to hypothesize that schizophrenia may be caused by excessive activity of dopamine in the brain. (See Figure 16.5.)

Schizophrenia as a Neurological Disorder

Modifications in the Dopamine Hypothesis. Although the dopamine hypothesis has for several years been the dominant biological explanation for schizophrenia, recent evidence suggests that it can offer only a partial explanation. From the early days of treating schizophrenia with antipsychotic drugs, clinicians recognized that some patients' symptoms were not improved by medication. Crow and his colleagues (Crow, 1980; Crow, Cross, Johnstone, and Owen, 1982) suggested that the reason for this failure to improve is that there are two types of schizophrenic symptoms: positive and negative. *Positive symptoms* include the hallmarks of schizophrenia: delusions, hallucinations, and thought disorders. *Negative symptoms* include loss of emotional response, decreased speech, lack of drive, and diminished social

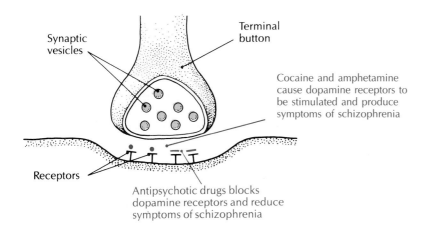

Synaptic vesicles

Terminal button

Cocaine and amphetamine cause dopamine receptors to be stimulated and produce symptoms of schizophrenia

Receptors

Antipsychotic drugs blocks dopamine receptors and reduce symptoms of schizophrenia

FIGURE 16.5

By blocking dopamine receptors on the postsynaptic membrane, antipsychotic drugs interfere with the neuron's response to this transmitter substance.

interaction. Because antipsychotic drugs alleviate positive, but not negative, symptoms of schizophrenia (Angrist, Rotrosen, and Gershon, 1980), perhaps those patients who do not get better with medication have primarily negative symptoms.

Once investigators began paying more attention to negative symptoms, they discovered evidence for brain damage in patients exhibiting these symptoms. For example, Stevens (1982a) noted that many patients with chronic schizophrenia demonstrate symptoms that clearly indicate neurological disease, especially with regard to eye movements. These symptoms include decreased rate of eye blink; staring; lack of blink reflex in response to a tap on the forehead; turning of the eyes to the side, accompanied by an arrest in speech; poor visual pursuit movements; poor pupillary reactions to light; and elevation of the eyebrows. In addition, catatonia is seen in nonpsychotic patients with a variety of neurological disorders. When Stevens (1982b) examined slices of brains of deceased schizophrenic patients, she found clear evidence for brain damage that suggested either a disease process that had occurred earlier in life and had partly healed or one that was slowly progressing at the time of the patient's death. Other investigators examined CAT scans of patients with schizophrenia. For example, Weinberger and Wyatt (1982) compared CAT scans of the brains of fifty-eight schizophrenics and fifty-six controls matched by age. They found that the ventricles of the schizophrenic patients were, on average, twice as large as those of the normal subjects. Enlargement of the hollow ventricles of the brain

indicates the loss of brain tissue elsewhere; thus, the evidence implied the existence of some kind of neurological disease.

Loss of brain tissue, as assessed by CAT scans, appears to be related to negative symptoms of schizophrenia, but not to positive ones (Johnstone, Crow, Frith, Stevens, Kreel, and Husband, 1978). In addition, patients with loss of brain tissue respond poorly to antipsychotic drugs (Weinberger, Bigelow, Kleinman, Klein, Rosenblatt, and Wyatt, 1980). These studies suggest that positive and negative symptoms of schizophrenia have different causes: positive symptoms are a result of overactivity of dopamine synapses, whereas negative symptoms are produced by actual loss of brain tissue.

Several studies have indicated that the cause of brain damage in schizophrenia may be a viral infection. Torrey, Torrey, and Peterson (1977) noted that people who were born in late winter are significantly more likely to develop schizophrenia than those who were born during other times of the year. Similar seasonal variation is seen in diseases that are known to be caused by viruses, such as chickenpox and measles.

Stevens (1982a) suggested that schizophrenia from viral sources is produced by a combination of hereditary and environmental factors. Perhaps the virus causes no brain damage in people with nonschizophrenic heredity but damages the brains of people with an inherited susceptibility to the disease.

Much more research will be necessary before investigators can determine whether in fact overactivity of dopamine synapses does indeed produce positive symptoms of schizophrenia

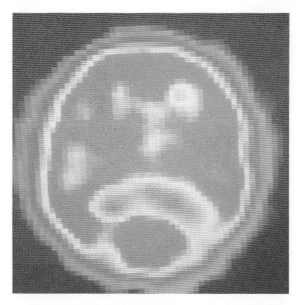

A PET scan of a normal brain.

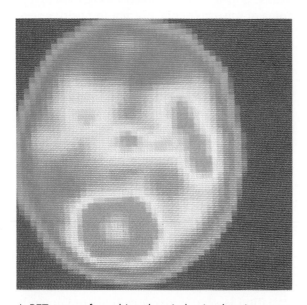

A PET scan of a schizophrenic brain showing activity (red) in the visual cortex, even though the eyes are closed. The schizophrenic is "seeing" a world that is not there.

and whether a viral infection produces the brain damage that results in negative symptoms. But such biological explanations for schizophrenia will not lessen the usefulness of psychotherapy (discussed in the next chapter) in the treatment of this disorder. Experience has shown that it is not enough merely to medicate a schizophrenic patient with chlorpromazine. It is also important to teach the person

how to structure a new life and how to cope with the many problems that he or she will encounter in reentering society. Psychotherapy is at present the only hope for those patients with predominantly negative symptoms, who are not helped by antipsychotic drugs.

- What are the differences between process and reactive schizophrenia?
- What are the principal findings of the studies on the heritability of schizophrenia?
- What drugs reduce the symptoms of schizophrenia?
- What evidence suggests that schizophrenia is a neurological disorder? What evidence suggests it may be the result of a viral infection?

MOOD DISORDERS

In contrast to schizophrenia, whose principal symptom is thought disorders, **mood disorders** (also known as *affective disorders*) are primarily disorders of emotion. The most severe affective disorders are **bipolar disorder** and **major depression.** Bipolar disorder is characterized by alternating periods of mania (wild excitement) and depression; major depression is unrelieved by bouts of mania. The incidence of major depression is approximately 5 percent, and that of bipolar disorder is approximately 1 percent (Robbins, Helzer, Weissman, Orvaschel, Gruenberg, Burke, and Regier, 1984). Although both sexes are equally likely to develop a bipolar disorder, females are at least twice as likely as males to suffer from major depression. Bipolar disorder tends to begin during the late twenties, and major depression tends to begin around age forty.

A less severe mood disorder is called **dysthymia** (pronounced *dis THIGH me a*). The term comes from the Greek *dus*, "bad," and *thymos*, "spirit." Dysthymia used to be called *depressive neurosis.* The primary difference between this disorder and major depression is its lack of delusions and hallucinations and its relatively low severity. Similarly, **cyclothymia** resembles bipolar disorder but does not include delusions and hallucinations. Cyclothymia also tends to be less severe than dysthymia.

Mania

Mania (the Greek word for "madness") is characterized by wild, exuberant, unrealistic activity. During manic episodes, people are usually elated and self-confident; however, contradiction or interference tends to make them very angry. Their speech and, presumably, their thought processes, become very rapid. They tend to flit from topic to topic and are full of grandiose plans, but their thoughts are less disorganized than those of a schizophrenic. Manic patients also tend to be restless and hyperactive, often pacing around ceaselessly. They often have delusions and hallucinations—typically of a nature that fits their exuberant mood. Davison and Neale (1982) recorded a typical interaction:

> THERAPIST: Well, you seem pretty happy today. CLIENT: Happy! Happy! You certainly are a master of understatement, you rogue! (Shouting, literally jumping out of seat.) Why I'm ecstatic. I'm leaving for the West coast today, on my daughter's bicycle. Only 3100 miles. That's nothing, you know. I could probably walk, but I want to get there by next week. And along the way I plan to contact a lot of people about investing in my fishing equipment. I'll get to know more people that way—you know, Doc, "know" in the biblical sense (leering at therapist seductively). Oh, God, how good it feels. It's almost like a nonstop orgasm. (p. 232)

The usual response that manic speech and behavior evokes in another person is one of sympathetic amusement; in fact, when an experienced clinician finds himself or herself becoming amused by a patient, the clinician begins to suspect the presence of mania. Because very few patients exhibit only mania, the DSM-III-R classifies all cases in which mania occurs as bipolar disorder. Patients with bipolar disorder usually experience alternate periods of mania and depression. Each of these periods lasts from a few days to a few weeks, usually with several days of relatively normal behavior in between. Many therapists have observed that there is often something brittle and unnatural about the happiness during the manic phase, as though the patient is making himself or herself be happy to ward off an attack of depression. Indeed, some manic patients are simply hyperactive and irritable rather than euphoric.

One type of antidepressant drug, **lithium carbonate,** is effective in treating bipolar disorder, though as yet no one knows why. Lithium carbonate is a simple inorganic compound. Its active ingredient is the element lithium, a metal that is closely related to sodium, which is found in ordinary table salt. (In fact lithium chloride was used as a sodium-free salt substitute until it was found to be toxic in large doses.) Lithium carbonate has been called the "wonder drug" of psychiatry; it is effective in most cases of bipolar disorder and it has few side effects as long as the dosage is carefully controlled. Many people who are being treated with lithium carbonate are leading perfectly normal lives.

Depression

Depressed psychotics are extremely sad and are usually full of self-directed guilt. Beck (1967) identified five cardinal symptoms of depression: (1) a sad and apathetic mood, (2) feelings of worthlessness and hopelessness, (3) a desire to withdraw from other people, (4) sleeplessness and loss of appetite and sexual desire, and (5) change in activity level, to either lethargy or agitation. Most people who are labeled "depressed" have a dysthymia; a minority of them have a major affective disorder. Major depression must be distinguished from grief caused by death of a loved one. People who are griev-

Wild, exuberant activity is a characteristic of people suffering from the manic phase of a bipolar disorder.

ing feel sad and depressed but do not fear losing their minds or have thoughts of self-harm. Because many people who do suffer from major depression or the depressed phase of bipolar disorder commit suicide, these disorders are potentially fatal. The fatality rate by suicide for major depression is estimated at 15 percent (Guze and Robins, 1970).

Victims of major depression usually report that time seems to pass very slowly, but laboratory studies have shown that their estimates of elapsed time are as good as those of normal people (Mézey and Cohen, 1961). Such patients also believe that their intelligence is impaired, but studies have shown that depressed psychotics score as high as normal people on tests of intelligence (Granick, 1963). In general, depressed patients magnify and exaggerate evaluations of themselves. If they succeed at a task, they feel much better than normal people, and if they fail, they feel much worse (Loeb, Beck, Diggory, and Tuthill, 1966).

Severe depression can make life seem so negative that the victims become despondent and some even have thoughts of self-harm.

Roots of Mood Disorders

Psychoanalytical Theory

Freud believed that the roots of depression are established when a child becomes fixated at the oral phase of psychosexual development. This particular fixation produces an excessively dependent personality. Later in life, if a loved one dies, the person **introjects,** or "incorporates," the dead person. Unconscious hostility toward the dead person, along with anger at being deprived of his or her company, becomes directed inward. The self-directed hostility eventually creates the feelings of guilt and unworthiness that characterize depression. For people whose depression occurs without any apparent environmental stress, Freud hypothesized a *symbolic* loss of a loved one. For example, a person might interpret a short-tempered response as a sign that a loved one no longer returns his or her affection.

There are serious problems with the psychoanalytical explanation of depression. First, many investigators dispute the reality of Freud's stages of psychosexual development and deny that people can become fixated in the oral stage. Certainly there is no solid evidence that such a fixation occurs. Second, Freud's

theory does not explain why people direct hatred at themselves instead of turning inward the *love* they feel toward the dead person. Finally, the concept of symbolic loss is a useless intervening variable: it cannot be observed—and thus it can never be proved or disproved.

Cognitive Theory

Beck (1967) suggested that the changes in affect seen in depressive psychoses are not primary but instead are secondary to changes in cognition. That is, the primary disturbance is a distortion in the person's view of reality. For example, a depressed person may see a scratch on the surface of his or her car and conclude that the car is ruined. Or a person whose recipe fails may see the unappetizing dish as proof of his or her unworthiness. Or a nasty dunning letter from a creditor is seen as a serious and personal condemnation.

In contrast with psychoanalytical theory, which emphasizes the role of the unconscious in the emergence of mental disorder, Beck's theory emphasizes the role of a person's judgment in contributing to his or her own emotional state. Though not yet proved correct, this theory has served a useful function in alerting therapists to the importance of considering the thought processes, as well as the feelings, of a patient with an affective psychosis.

Heritability

Like schizophrenia, the affective disorders appear to have a genetic component. People who have first-degree relatives with a major affective disorder are ten times more likely to develop these disorders than are people without afflicted relatives (Rosenthal, 1970). Furthermore, the concordance rate for bipolar disorder is 72 percent for monozygotic twins, compared with 14 percent for dizygotic twins. For major depression, the figures are 40 percent and 11 percent, respectively (Allen, 1976). Thus, bipolar disorder appears to be more heritable than major depression. The apparent existence of a genetic component suggests that people may inherit certain physiological traits that increase their vulnerability to the affective psychoses.

Biochemical Factors

Two forms of medical treatment that have proved successful in alleviating the symptoms of affective disorders are **electroconvulsive therapy (ECT)** and **antidepressant drugs.** Their success indicates that physiological disorders may underlie these conditions. Because no one knows how electroconvulsive therapy works, it cannot yet provide information about the biochemical factors in affective disorders; discussion of this treatment is therefore deferred until Chapter 17. More is known about the biochemical effects of the antidepressant drugs, and this knowledge has led investigators to speculate that the affective disorders may have physiological causes.

Currently, two types of antidepressant drugs are in widespread use. The use of lithium carbonate in relieving bipolar disorder was discussed earlier. The other class includes the **tricyclic antidepressant drugs,** such as imipramine. (*Tricyclic* refers to their molecular structure.) Experiments with laboratory animals have shown that these drugs have stimulating effects on synapses that utilize two transmitter substances, norepinephrine and serotonin.

Other drugs, including **reserpine,** which is used to treat high blood pressure, can *cause* episodes of depression. Reserpine lowers blood pressure by blocking the release of norepinephrine muscles in the walls of blood vessels, thus causing the muscles to relax. However, because the drug also blocks the release of norepinephrine and serotonin in the brain, a common side effect is depression. This side effect strengthens the argument that biochemical factors in the brain play an important role in depression.

Several studies have found evidence for biochemical abnormalities in the brains of people with affective disorders. It is not possible to take samples of transmitter substances directly from the living brain. But when transmitter substances are released, a small amount gets broken down by enzymes in the brain, and some of the breakdown products accumulate in the cerebrospinal fluid or pass into the bloodstream and collect in the urine. Investigators have analyzed cerebrospinal fluid and urine for these substances.

For example, Träskman, Åsberg, Bertilsson, and Sjöstrand (1981) measured the level of **5-HIAA** (a compound that is produced when serotonin is broken down) in the cerebrospinal fluid of depressed people who had attempted suicide. The level of 5-HIAA was significantly lower than that of control subjects; this finding implies that there was less activity of serotonin-secreting neurons in the brains of the depressed subjects. In fact, 20 percent of the subjects with levels below the median subsequently killed themselves, whereas none of the subjects with levels above the median committed suicide. Taube, Kirstein, Sweeney, Heninger, and Maas (1978) obtained evidence for decreased activity of neurons that secrete norepinephrine; they found low levels of **MHPG** (produced when this transmitter substance is broken down) in the urine of patients with affective disorders. Thus, decreased activity of serotonin- and norepinephrine-secreting neurons appears to be related to depression. Presumably, the tricyclic antidepressant drugs alleviate the symptoms of depression by increasing the activity of these neurons.

Although the brain biochemistry of patients with affective disorders appears to be abnormal, we cannot be certain that a biochemical imbalance is the first event in a sequence that leads to depression. It is possible that environmental stimuli cause the depression, which then leads to biochemical changes in the brain. For example, the brain levels of norepinephrine are lower in dogs who have been presented with an inescapable electric shock and have developed learned helplessness (Miller, Rosellini, and Seligman, 1977). The dogs certainly did not inherit the low norepinephrine levels;

they acquired them as a result of their experience. The findings so far suggest that a tendency to develop affective psychoses is heritable, and that low levels of norepinephrine and serotonin are associated with these disorders. However, the cause-and-effect relations have yet to be worked out.

Relation to Sleep Cycles

A characteristic symptom of the affective disorders is sleep disturbances. Usually, people with a major affective disorder have little difficulty falling asleep, but they awaken early and are unable to get back to sleep again. (In contrast, people with dysthymic disorder are more likely to have trouble falling asleep and getting out of bed the next day.) Kupfer (1976) reported that depressed patients tend to enter REM sleep sooner than normal people and spend an increased time in this state during the last half of sleep. Noting this fact, Vogel, Vogel, McAbee, and Thurmond (1980) deprived depressed patients of REM sleep by awakening them whenever the EEG showed signs that they were entering this stage. Remarkably, the deprivation decreased their depression. These findings are supported by the observation that treatments that alleviate depression, such as electroconvulsive therapy and the tricyclic antide-

presant drugs, profoundly reduce REM sleep in cats (Scherschlicht, Polc, Schneeberger, Steiner, and Haefely, 1982).

Goodwin, Wirz-Justice, and Wehr (1982) suggested that the affective disorders are caused by a disturbance in the brain mechanisms that control sleep/waking cycles. They reviewed a large number of studies that they and other investigators had performed and found that many physiological and biochemical rhythms were disrupted in depressed people. In fact, they could sometimes predict when a person with bipolar disorder would switch from mania to depression by observing changes in their daily rhythm of fluctuations in body temperature. These interesting findings and speculations will have to be confirmed by future research.

■ What are the symptoms and incidence of the major mood disorders?
■ How would you describe manic and bipolar disorders? What drug is used to treat bipolar disorders?
■ What are the views of psychoanalytic theorists and cognitive theorists regarding major depression?
■ What evidence suggests that heredity, biochemical factors, and sleep cycles may be related to the major mood disorders?

CHAPTER SUMMARY

1. The value of classification and diagnosis lies in the potential identification of disorders with common causes. Once disorders are classified, research can be carried out with the goal of finding useful therapies. The principal classification scheme in North America for mental disorders is the DSM-III-R.

2. People with nonpsychotic mental disorders, previously called *neuroses*, have adopted strategies that have a certain amount of immediate payoff but in the long run are maladaptive. In contrast, *psychoses* involve obviously maladaptive features—delusions, hallucinations, disordered thought processes, and inappropriate emotional states.

3. Anxiety disorders include anxiety states and phobias. Anxiety states include panic disorder and obsessive compulsive disorder. Panic disorder is the least adaptive of all neurotic disorders; the person has no defense against his or her discomfort. In contrast, obsessive compulsive disorder provides thoughts or behaviors that prevent the person from thinking about painful subjects or to ward off feelings of guilt and anxiety.

Simple phobias can probably be explained by classical conditioning; some experience (usually early in life) causes a particular object or situation to become a conditioned aversive stimulus. The fear associated with this stimulus leads to escape behaviors, which are reinforced because they reduce the person's fear. Agoraphobia is a much more serious disorder, and it is apparently not caused by a specific traumatic experience. Social phobia is a fear of being observed or judged by others.

4. Somatoform disorders include somatization disorder, hypochondriasis, and conversion disorder. Somatization disorder comprises complaints of symptoms of illness without underlying physiological causes. Almost all people with this disorder are women, and most are indifferent to sexual intercourse. Conversion disorder includes specific neurological symptoms, such as paralysis or sensory disturbance, that are not produced by a physiological disorder.

5. Dissociative disorders are rare but interesting. Psychogenic amnesia (with or without fugue) appears to be a withdrawal from a painful situation or from intolerable guilt. Because amnesia is a common symptom of brain injury or neurological disease, physical factors must be ruled out before accepting a diagnosis of psychogenic amnesia. Multiple personalities are even more rare, and presumably occur because they permit a person to engage in behaviors that are contrary to his or her code of conduct.

6. The hallmarks of antisocial personality disorder, also called *psychopathy* or *sociopathy*, are an apparent indifference to the effects of one's behavior on other people, impulsiveness, failure to learn from experience, sexual promiscuity and lack of commitment to a partner, and habitual lying. A large number of criminals are psychopaths, and many psychopaths become criminals.

Psychopathy tends to run in families, and there is evidence from twin studies that heredity, as well as a poor environment, may contribute to its development. Unfortunately, the disorder is difficult to treat, because psychopaths do not perceive themselves as being in need of improvement.

7. The principal positive symptoms of schizophrenia include thought disorders; delusions of persecution, grandeur, and control; and hallucinations. The principal negative symptoms include withdrawal, apathy, and poverty of speech. The DSM-III-R classifies schizophrenia into several subtypes, including undifferentiated, catatonic, paranoid, and disorganized, but it appears that the distinctions between process and reactive schizophrenia, and between positive and negative symptoms, are more important.

8. People who develop chronic, process schizophrenia appear to be different from other people even as children, which suggests that the disorder has its roots very early in life. Indeed, heritability studies have shown a strong genetic component in schizophrenia, although they do not rule out the possibility of interaction with adverse environmental situations as a causal factor.

9. Positive symptoms of schizophrenia can be produced in normal people, or made worse in schizophrenics, by drugs that stimulate dopamine synapses (cocaine and amphetamine) and can be reduced or eliminated by those that block dopamine receptors (the antipsychotic drugs). These findings have led to the dopamine hypothesis, which states that schizophrenia is caused by an inherited biochemical defect that causes dopamine neurons to be overactive, producing disorders in attentional mechanisms.

More recent studies indicate that schizophrenia can best be conceived of as two different disorders. The positive symptoms are produced by overactivity of dopamine neurons and can be treated with the antipsychotic drugs, but the negative ones, which do not respond to these drugs, are caused by brain damage.

10. The major affective disorders are primarily disorders of emotion, although delusions are also characteristically present. Bipolar disorder consists of alternating periods of mania and depression, whereas major depression consists of depression alone. The mood states are not precipitated by environmental events; there is no external reason for these people to feel sad or elated.

11. Heritability studies strongly suggest a biological component to the mood disorders. This possibility receives support from the finding that biological treatments effectively reduce the symptoms of these disorders, whereas reserpine can cause depression. These facts, along with evidence from biochemical analysis of the breakdown products of norepinephrine and serotonin in depressed patients, suggest that depression results from underactivity of neurons that secrete norepinephrine or serotonin. However, the finding that stress can reduce the amount of norepinephrine produced in an animal's brain warns us to be careful

about making inferences about cause and effect.

Recent evidence suggests that the primary physiological disorder in the affective psychoses may manifest itself in terms of abnormalities in sleep/waking rhythms. Studies have shown that REM-sleep deprivation alleviates the symptoms of depression, and all known biological treatments for depression themselves reduce REM sleep.

KEY TERMS

acute schizophrenic episode See schizophreniform disorder.

agoraphobia A mental disorder; fear of and avoidance of being alone in public places. Often accompanied by panic attacks.

anticipatory anxiety Fear of having a panic attack; may lead to the development of agoraphobia.

antidepressant drugs Drugs that are used to treat psychotic depression, one of the affective disorders.

antisocial personality disorder A personality disorder characterized by a consistent pattern of such behaviors as truancy, delinquency, lying, promiscuity, drunkenness or substance abuse, theft, vandalism, and fighting.

bipolar disorder A serious affective disorder characterized by alternating periods of mania and depression; a form of psychosis.

catatonic posture Motor disturbance of catatonic schizophrenia in which bizarre, stationary poses are maintained for hours.

catatonic schizophrenia A form of schizophrenia in which a person remains immobile, often in bizarre postures, or exhibits wild hyperactivity.

chlorpromazine Antipsychotic drug effective in alleviating symptoms of schizophrenia.

compulsion The feeling that one is obliged to perform a behavior, even if one prefers not to do so.

conversion disorder A psychological disorder in which a person experiences physical symptoms such as anesthesia, paralysis, or illness without organic cause; a type of somatoform disorder.

cyclothymia A mental disorder similar to bipolar disorder but less severe.

delusion A belief that is held even though evidence or logic shows it to be false. Delusions are important symptoms of psychoses. A delusion of control is a false belief that one's thoughts and behaviors are being controlled by other people or other forces; a delusion of grandeur, that one is famous, powerful, or important; and a delusion of persecution, that others conspire to harm or thwart one.

Diagnostic and Statistical Manual III-R (DSM-III-R) The system and manual developed by the American Psychiatric Association that provide specific criteria for the diagnosis of mental disorders.

disorganized schizophrenia A serious form of schizophrenia characterized by incoherent speech and inappropriate affect.

dissociative disorder A category of mental disorders that includes such disturbances as amnesia not caused by brain dysfunction, fugue, and multiple personality.

dysthymia Depression that is not severe or prolonged enough to be classified as a psychotic mood disorder.

electroconvulsive therapy (ECT) Induction of a seizure by passing a brief surge of electricity through a person's head; used to treat severe psychotic depression. Also called *electroshock treatment*.

first-degree relative A person's parents, children, and siblings.

5-HIAA Compound produced when serotonin is broken down.

fugue A pathological behavior in which a person develops amnesia and leaves to start a new life elsewhere.

Graves' disease Disease characterized by irritability, restlessness, confused and rapid thought processes, and, occasionally, delusions and hallucinations.

hebephrenic schizophrenia The obsolete term for disorganized schizophrenia.

hypochondriasis A psychological disorder characterized by excessive concern and preoccupation with one's health, along with frequent fears of suffering from serious illness.

introjection The incorporation of a dead loved one into one's own psyche, eventually leading to self-directed hostility and feelings of guilt according to Freud.

lithium carbonate A simple salt that is used to treat bipolar disorder.

major depression Psychotic depression characterized by extreme sadness, feelings of guilt and unworthiness, and delusions.

malingering Deliberate simulation of the symptoms of a real disease, generally to avoid work or unpleasant situations or to receive compensation.

mania Extreme exuberance, characterized by rapid thoughts, restlessness, sleeplessness, and grandiose plans; seen in bipolar disorder.

MHPG Breakdown product of norepinephrine.

mood disorder A serious psychological disorder (psychosis) in which a person is excessively, unrealistically sad (depression) or elated (mania).

multiple personality A psychological disorder in which a person displays very different behaviors at different times, giving the impression of having distinct and different personalities.

neologisms New and meaningless words, sometimes uttered by schizophrenics.

neurologist A physician who treats disorders of the nervous system.

neurosis A mental disorder of less severity than a psychosis. The term is not used in the new Diagnostic and Statistical Manual III-R of the American Psychiatric Association.

obsessions Recurrent, persistent thoughts and ideas.

obsessive compulsive disorder A neurotic disorder characterized by obsessions and compulsions.

panic disorder A psychological disorder characterized by frequent panic attacks, during which a person experiences great fear and symptoms such as shortness of breath, heart palpitations, sensations of choking, dizziness, sweating, faintness, and fear of dying.

paranoid schizophrenia A type of schizophrenia characterized by delusions of persecution, grandeur, or control.

phobia A mental disorder characterized by excessive and irrational fear of an object or situation.

process schizophrenia Designation of the chronic (rather than reactive) form of schizophrenia.

psychogenic amnesia Amnesia caused by psychological conflicts and unpleasant situations, and not by brain injury.

psychosis A serious mental disorder, such as schizophrenia.

psychosomatic disorder A real physical illness that is caused or made worse by psychological factors, especially emotional stress.

reactive schizophrenia Form of schizophrenia that is a reaction to stressful life situations, with high recovery rate.

reserpine Drug used to treat high blood pressure that can cause depression as a side effect.

schizophrenia A serious mental disorder (psychosis) characterized by disordered thoughts, delusions, hallucinations, and often bizarre behaviors.

schizophreniform disorder Formally called *acute schizophrenic episode*; has the best prognosis of all types of schizophrenia.

sign Observable evidence of physical malfunctioning, such as high temperature, rash, or inflammation.

simple phobia All phobias (irrational fears) other than agoraphobia and social phobia.

social phobia A mental disorder characterized by excessive and irrational fear of situations in which the person is observed by others.

somatization disorder A mental disorder characterized by numerous vague symptoms of physical disorders in the absence of obvious physical diseases; a type of somatoform disorder.

somatoform disorder A category of mental disorders characterized by symptoms of physical disorders, including conversion disorder, somatization disorder, and hypochondriasis.

symptom Report of a feeling or perception that a person makes to his or her own physician.

tricyclic antidepressant drug A drug (for example, imipramine) used to treat major depression; named for the shape of the molecule.

undifferentiated schizophrenia Diagnosis other than catatonic, paranoid, or disorganized schizophrenia.

word salad The jumble of words indicative of the deteriorated speech of a disorganized schizophrenic.

Approaches to Treatment

In the past, research on the treatment of psychological disorders has attempted to answer a single question: Is psychotherapy effective? The apparent simplicity of the question is deceptive, as psychologists have found when they tried to answer it. Research suggests that the answer is a qualified "yes." Meanwhile, millions of people are flocking to the psychotherapist's office. According to a recent source, one in three Americans has already visited a psychotherapist, and in one year another 15 million will make approximately 120 million visits to psychotherapists (*The New York Times Magazine*, August 30, 1987, p. 28).

Recently, researchers have attempted to specify optimal conditions for therapeutic change. They have examined questions such as how people change and what therapist and client variables facilitate change. Researchers concerned with measuring the outcome of psychotherapy have also set aside the global question of whether or not psychotherapy is effective in favor of a more specific question: What type of therapy is most effective with what problems, for what people, and under what conditions? Although the question is undoubtedly more complex, the answers may prove more valuable. For example, researchers have found that cognitive therapy seems to be superior to drug therapy in treating some forms of depression, and certain anxiety disorders seem best treated by a behavior therapy that exposes the person to the feared situation.

So rather than searching for the elusive treatment that works for all people all the time, psychologists are now directing their efforts at identifying therapies that are successful in treating specific disorders. Perhaps one day people can receive therapy specifically tailored for their particular disorder.

HISTORICAL BACKGROUND

Early Treatment of Mental Illness

Mental disorders have been with us since human existence began. For most of that time, people afflicted with these disorders have been regarded, variously, with awe or fear. Sometimes, the delusions of people whom we would now probably classify as paranoid schizophrenics were regarded as prophetic; these people were seen as instruments through whom gods or spirits were speaking. More often, they were considered to be occupied by devils or evil spirits and were made to suffer accordingly.

Many painful and degrading practices were directed at people's presumed possession by evil spirits. Those who were thought to be unwilling hosts for evil spirits were subjected to curses or insults designed to persuade the demons to leave; if this approach had no effect, exorcism was tried, to make the person's body an unpleasant place for devils to reside, through beatings, starving, near-drowning, and the drinking of foul-tasting concoctions. Many people who were perceived as having accepted their condition voluntarily—as being in league with the devil—actively participated in their own prosecution and conviction. The delusional schemes of psychotics often include beliefs of personal guilt and unworthiness, and

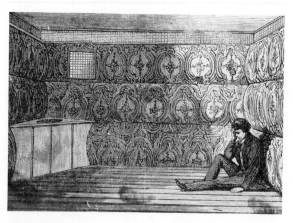

FIGURE 17.1

A patient restrained in a padded isolation chamber. Such devices were used to treat people with mental disorders in the nineteenth century.

FIGURE 17.2

In many instances, mentally ill individuals placed in asylums were subjected to worse treatments than if they had remained in the mainstream of society.

in a society that accepted the notion that there were witches and devils, these people were ready to imagine themselves as being evil and degraded. They "confessed" to unspeakable acts of sorcery and welcomed their own persecution and punishment. Until the eighteenth century, many Europeans accepted the idea that devils and spirits were responsible for peculiar behavior in some people. A few believed that these disorders reflected diseases, and that they should be treated medically and with compassion.

As belief in witchcraft and demonology waned, the clergy, the medical authorities, and the general public began to regard people with mental disorders as ill, and torture and persecution eventually ceased. However, the lives of these people were not necessarily better as a result. Undoubtedly, many people with mental disorders were regarded as strange but harmless and managed to maintain a marginal existence in society. Others were sheltered by their families. The unfortunate ones were those who were consigned to the various "asylums" that were established for the care of the mentally ill. Most mental institutions were hideously inhumane. Patients were often kept in chains and sometimes wallowed in their own excreta. Those who displayed bizarre catatonic postures or who had fanciful delusions were exhibited to the public, for a fee. Many of the treatments designed to cure mental patients were little better than the tortures that had previously been used to drive out evil spirits. Patients were tied up, doused in cold water, bled, made to vomit, spun violently in a rotating chair, and otherwise assaulted by the fruits of "modern science." (See Figures 17.1–17.3.)

The mistreatment of the mentally ill did not go unnoticed by humanitarians. A famous and effective early reformer was Philippe Pinel (1745–1826), a French physician. In 1793, Pinel was appointed director of La Bicêtre, a mental hospital in Paris. Pinel believed that most mental patients would respond well to kind treatment. As an experiment, he removed the chains from some of the inmates, took them out of dungeons, and allowed them to walk about the hospital grounds. The experiment was a remarkable success; an atmosphere of peace and quiet replaced the previous noise, stench, and general aura of despair. Many patients were eventually discharged. Pinel's success at La Bicêtre was repeated when he was given charge of Salpêtrière Hospital. (See Figure 17.4 on page 514.) From what we now know about psychoses, many patients eventually recover—or at least get much better—without any treatment at all. But if a person was put in one of the mental institutions that existed at that time, he or she never had a

chance to show improvement; from our present perspective, the conditions would seem to have been designed to *prevent* recovery.

Pinel's success encouraged similar reforms elsewhere. In the United States, the campaign for humane treatment of mental patients was led by Dorothea Dix (1802–1887), who raised millions of dollars for the construction of mental hospitals and spurred the reform of many mental health facilities. The process took a long time; until very recently, some large mental hospitals were little more than warehouses for severely affected patients, who received little or no treatment but were merely provided with the necessities of life. Today there is much greater emphasis on treatment in community-based facilities, and the discovery of the anti-psychotic drugs has freed many patients who would otherwise have spent their lives in mental institutions.

The Development of Psychotherapy

The modern history of specific treatments for mental disorders probably began with Franz Anton Mesmer (1734–1815), an Austrian physician who practiced in Paris in the late eighteenth and early nineteenth centuries. As we saw in Chapter 10, he devised a theory of "magnetic fluxes" in which he attempted to effect cures by manipulating iron rods and bottles of chemicals. What he actually did was hypnotize his patients, thereby alleviating some of their symptoms, especially those of psychological origin. Accordingly, hypnosis was first known as *mesmerism*.

A French neurologist, Jean Martin Charcot (1825–1893), began his investigations of the therapeutic uses of hypnosis when one of his

FIGURE 17.3

A crib used to restrain violent patients in a New York asylum in 1882. Many people with mental illnesses were subjected to inhumane treatments.

FIGURE 17.4

Philippe Pinel releasing the shackles from the insane at La Bicêtre.

students hypnotized a woman and induced her to display the symptoms of a conversion reaction (formerly called *hysteria*). Charcot examined her and concluded that she was a hysterical patient. The student then woke the woman, and her symptoms vanished. Charcot had previously believed that hysteria had an organic basis, but this experience changed his opinion, and he began investigating its psychological causes.

Just before Sigmund Freud began private practice, he studied with Charcot in Paris and observed the effects of hypnosis on hysteria. Freud's association with Charcot, and later with Breuer, started him on his life's study of the determinants of personality and the origins of mental illness. As we saw in Chapter 15, Freud formulated a psychodynamic theory of personality, which has proved to be one of the most influential attempts to explain human behavior. He also founded the practice of psychoanalysis, which many psychiatrists, and some psychologists, use today to treat patients with psychological problems.

The rest of this chapter describes five approaches to the treatment of mental disorders: insight psychotherapies, behavior therapies, cognitive behavior therapies, group therapies, and biological treatments.

In practice, most clinical psychologists are not unalterably wedded to a particular system of therapy. Although each therapist discovers that he or she deals best with particular kinds of problems, most practitioners adopt a variety of techniques to achieve therapeutic results

with their clients, as we will see in the section on eclectic treatment. The final section of the chapter considers research evaluating the usefulness of the various forms of therapy.

INSIGHT PSYCHOTHERAPIES

The case of Anna O., who was supposedly cured of hysteria by talking about various conflicts while under hypnosis (Chapter 15), probably marks the beginning of **insight psychotherapy.** Insight psychotherapy is based on the assumption that people are essentially normal, but that they learn maladaptive thought patterns and behaviors. Once a patient understands the causes of his or her problems, they will cease; insight will lead to a cure.

Most forms of psychotherapy (those that are not based on biological treatment or on modification of the client's behavior) rely upon insight for behavioral change. Some therapies, such as psychoanalysis, emphasize causes in the patient's past. Others, such as client-centered therapy, emphasize the present; they attempt to get the patient to see the effects of his or her patterns of behavior and to find more adaptive ways of living.

Psychoanalysis

Description

Freud's psychodynamic theory of personality serves as the basis for **psychoanalysis,** the first formal psychotherapeutic procedure devised. Psychoanalysis means just what its name implies: A person's psyche, or mind, is analyzed. Freud asserted that psychopathology was caused by unconscious fears and motives. By bringing unconscious conflicts to consciousness, the client comes to understand the reasons for his or her behavior and realizes that the childhood conditions under which the causes developed no longer exist. Once this realization occurs, the conflicts can be resolved.

The first step, bringing the unconscious to light, involves relaxing or tricking the ego's

Drawing by Gross; © 1986

Psychoanalysis emphasizes causes of behavior which are rooted in a person's childhood, especially in the child's relationship with the mother.

defense mechanisms, which suppress unconscious thoughts. One technique used to accomplish this goal is **free association,** in which the client is encouraged to talk about anything and everything that he or she thinks of. Before beginning free association, the psychotherapist says something like this:

> In ordinary conversation, you usually try to keep a connecting thread running through your remarks excluding any intrusive ideas or side issues so as not to wander too far from the point, and rightly so. But in this case you must talk differently. As you talk various thoughts will occur to you which you like to ignore because of certain criticisms and objections. You will be tempted to think, "that is

irrelevant or unimportant, or nonsensical," and to avoid saying it. Do not give in to such criticism. Report such thoughts in spite of your wish not to do so. Later, the reason for this injunction, the only one you have to follow, will become clear. Report whatever goes through your mind. Pretend that you are a traveler, describing to someone beside you the changing views which you see outside the train window. (Ford and Urban, 1963, p. 168)

The alert psychotherapist notes the dominant themes in the client's narrative and attempts to interpret any symbolism that may represent disguised unconscious thoughts. The therapist also notes when the client shows **resistance** by acting uncomfortable, hesitating, changing the subject, or "forgetting" to attend sessions. Resistance indicates that painful topics are being approached and provides important clues to the root of the person's problems.

Another source of data concerning the unconscious is dreams. Because the ego defenses are more relaxed during sleep, the content of dreams often suggests the nature of the client's conflicts. The latent, or hidden, content of a dream is inferred from its manifest, or apparent, content. Similarly, hypnosis may be used to uncover the client's unconscious thoughts.

As psychotherapy progresses, the therapist begins interpreting free associations and dreams for the client, in order to increase the person's insight. The interpretations must come at the proper stage of analysis. The client

Insight psychotherapies attempt to bring to consciousness inner conflicts that may be causing psychological disturbances.

should be on the verge of his or her own discovery, so that the explanations will be accepted; if they are presented prematurely, the client may rebel, and his or her resistance will increase.

During psychoanalysis, the client generally forms a **transference neurosis,** transferring his or her feelings toward a dominant childhood figure—usually a parent—to the psychoanalyst. Depending on the nature of the childhood relationship, the feelings may be positive and loving, or negative and hostile. Transference is seen as essential for effective therapy; the psychoanalyst encourages its development by remaining a rather vague, shadowy figure seated behind the reclining client's head. Using the relationship that develops between client and therapist, the therapist can infer the childhood relationships that caused the conflicts to develop. However, the therapist must guard against the dangers of **countertransference,** which consists of the therapist's own feelings toward the client. All psychoanalysts must themselves receive a **training analysis** during their education, which permits them to understand their own conflicts and motivations, so as to avoid reacting inappropriately toward their clients.

According to Freud, therapists must not help their clients solve everyday problems. Solution of present problems is regarded by psychoanalysts as the easy way out, which should be avoided in the best interests of the client. (As we will see, most other types of therapists disagree with this belief.) In justifying their refusal to deal with their clients' present problems, psychoanalysts assert that the clients undoubtedly already received sympathy and advice from friends and family members; if such support was going to work, it already would have, and the clients would not have needed the services of a psychoanalyst. Instead, the clients must remain uncomfortable enough to be motivated to work on their repressed conflicts.

Evaluation

The scientific basis of psychoanalysis has not been established. As we saw in Chapter 15, the foundations of Freud's theory of personality remain unproved. But even though the theory cannot be confirmed, we should be able to assess the effectiveness of the psychoanalytical method—after all, it is results that count most.

However, it is difficult to evaluate the effectiveness of psychoanalysis, because only a small proportion of people with mental disorders qualify for this method of treatment. They must be intelligent, articulate individuals who are motivated enough to spend three or more hours a week for several years working hard to uncover unconscious conflicts. In addition, they must be able to afford the psychoanalyst's fees, which are high. (Psychoanalysts maintain that it is in the interests of clients to make a financial sacrifice, because doing so encourages them to take the procedure seriously.) These qualifications rule out most psychotics, as well as people who lack the time or money to devote to such a long-term project. Furthermore, many who enter psychoanalysis become dissatisfied with their progress and leave; in other cases the therapist encourages a client to leave, if he or she decides that the client is not cooperating fully. Thus, those who actually complete a course of psychoanalysis do not constitute a random sample, and we cannot conclude that psychoanalysis works just because a high percentage of this group is happy with the results. Those who have dropped out are not counted.

Another problem in evaluating psychoanalysis is the difficulty of explicitly defining the changes that are being sought in the client. For example, one of the goals is to lift unconscious repressions, but how can the therapist determine when this goal has been achieved? Perhaps a client's insight into his or her behavior demonstrates success. But some critics have argued that insight is no more than a client's acceptance of the therapist's belief system (Bandura, 1969). In fact one critic (Levy, 1963) has asserted that the unconscious does not exist—that it is merely a disagreement between therapist and client about the causes of the client's behavior.

Yet another problem in evaluating psychoanalysis is that psychoanalysts have a way to "explain" their failures: they can blame them on the client. If the client appears to accept an insight into his or her behavior but the behavior does not change, the insight is said to be merely "intellectual." This escape clause makes the argument for the importance of insight completely circular, and therefore illogical: If the client gets better, the improvement is due to insight, but if the client's behavior remains unchanged, real (as opposed to "intellectual")

Carl Rogers, the founder of client-centered therapy.

insight did not occur. An equivalent in logic would be to argue that wearing a charm (and sincerely believing in it) will cure cancer. If some people who wear the charm get better, then the charm obviously works; if other people who wear the charm die, then they obviously were not sincere believers.

According to Luborsky and Spence (1978), evaluations of the results of psychoanalysis suggest that the method does not work very well with severe mental disorders, such as schizophrenia. This finding is to be expected, because psychoanalysis is based on verbalization and rationality, which is not possible with extremely disturbed people. The method achieves better results with people who have anxiety disorders. Success appears to be best with highly educated clients.

Some clinicians have objected to the techniques used by psychoanalysts to encourage transference neurosis. For example, Wachtel (1977) asserts that by remaining a vague, shadowy figure and refusing to respond to the client's pleas for guidance, the psychoanalyst causes frustration. The client then acts "childish" because of the psychoanalyst's behavior, not necessarily because of deep-seated unresolved conflicts that stem from experiences during childhood.

Many psychiatrists today practice a form of therapy that is based on psychoanalytical principles but that does not require clients to embark on a full-fledged program of intensive psychoanalysis over several years. These practitioners have in fact adopted an eclectic approach to treatment, discussed later in this chapter.

Client-Centered Therapy

Description

Client-centered therapy was developed by Carl Rogers, an American psychologist. Rogers believed that people are basically good and that they all possess an innate drive toward self-actualization. Problems occur when people's concept of the **ideal self** begins to differ substantially from their concept of the **real self.** This discrepancy occurs when people fail to pay attention to their own internal evaluations of their self-concept, accepting the evaluations of others instead. The faulty self-concept inevitably conflicts with experience, and the person becomes dissatisfied. Rogers asserted that the therapist must provide an environment of **unconditional positive regard** for the client; that is, the therapist must totally and unconditionally accept the client and approve of him or her as a person. In such an environment, a client will follow his or her own instincts for goodness and will become a self-actualizing person without any psychological disturbances.

The primary objective of Rogers's therapeutic approach is to help the client pay attention to his or her own feelings, so that these innate tendencies toward goodness can emerge. Only by using these feelings as guides can the person move toward a life-style that will be most gratifying for him or her as an individual.

The first requirement is that the therapist provide an atmosphere of unconditional positive regard, so that the client can come to believe that his or her feelings are worthwhile and important. Once the client begins to pay attention to these feelings, a self-healing process begins. The therapist must be not only warm and friendly but also empathetic; he or she must use this empathy to try to help the client articulate these feelings. For example, a client usually has difficulty at first in expressing feelings verbally. The therapist tries to understand the feelings underlying the client's confused state and help the client put them into words. Through this process the client learns to understand and heed his or her own drive toward self-actualization and goodness. Mental health automatically comes with an awareness of his or her own feelings; adaptive behaviors will then replace maladaptive ones. According to Rogers, the therapist should not manipulate events but should create conditions under which the client can make his or her own decisions independently. The following interaction illustrates this process:

> ALICE: I was thinking about this business of standards. I somehow developed a sort of knack, I guess, of—well—habit—of trying to make people feel at ease around me, or to make things go along smoothly. . . .
>
> COUNSELOR: In other words, what you did was always in the direction of trying to keep things smooth and to make other people feel better and to smooth the situation.
>
> ALICE: Yes. I think that's what it was. Now the reason why I did it probably was—I mean, not that I was a good little Samaritan going around making other people happy, but that was probably the role that felt easiest for me to play. I'd been doing it around the home so much. I just didn't stand up for my own convictions, until I don't know whether I have any convictions to stand up for.
>
> COUNSELOR: You feel that for a long time you've been playing the role of kind of smoothing out the frictions or differences or what not. . . .
>
> ALICE: M-hum.
>
> COUNSELOR: Rather than having any opinion or reaction of your own in the situation. Is that it?
>
> ALICE: That's it. Or that I haven't been really honestly being myself, or actually knowing what my real self is, and that I've been just playing a sort of false role. Whatever role no one else was playing, and that needed to be played at the time, I'd try to fill it in. (Rogers, 1951, pp. 152–153)

According to Rogers, a good therapist is a spontaneous, open, authentic person who shows no phoniness or professional facade. A good therapist is self-disclosing and candid, which encourages the client to act in a similar fashion. (As we will see, behavior therapies and cognitive behavior therapies also rely heavily on the principle of *modeling*, or presenting a good example for the client to emulate.) Besides demonstrating unconditional positive regard, the therapist must truly understand how the client feels and show this empathy effectively.

Evaluation

Unlike many other clinicians, who prefer to rely on their own judgments concerning the effectiveness of their techniques, Rogers himself stimulated a considerable amount of research on the effectiveness of client-centered therapy. He recorded therapeutic sessions so that various techniques could be evaluated. One researcher, Charles Truax (1966), obtained permission from Rogers (and his clients) to record some therapy sessions, and he classified the statements made by the clients into several categories. One of the categories included statements of improving mental health, such as "I'm feeling better lately" or "I don't feel as depressed as I used to." After each of the patient's statements, Truax noted Rogers's reaction, to see whether he gave a positive response. Typical positive responses were "Oh, really? Tell me more" or "Uh-huh. That's nice" or just a friendly "Mm." Truax found that of the eight categories of client statements, only those that indicated progress were regularly followed by a positive response from Rogers. Not surprisingly, during their therapy the clients made more and more statements indicating progress.

This experiment attests to the power of social reinforcement and its occurrence in unexpected places. Rogers was an effective and conscientious psychotherapist, but he had not intended to single out and reinforce his clients' realistic expressions of progress in therapy. (Of course, he did not uncritically reinforce exaggerated or unrealistic positive statements.) This finding does not discredit client-centered therapy. Rogers simply adopted a very effective strategy for altering a person's behavior. He used to refer to his therapy as *nondirective*; however, when he realized that he was reinforcing positive statements, he stopped referring to it as nondirective, because it obviously was not.

Davison and Neale (1982) point out an apparent shortcoming of client-centered therapy. Rogers assumed that once a person begins to heed his or her own feelings, maladaptive behaviors will automatically cease. But this assumption has by no means been proved. For example, once a person with a severe feeling of inferiority acknowledges that feeling, he or she may withdraw from the company of other people and hence never learn the social skills that we all develop through interactions with others. Even if therapy did improve the person's self-concept, he or she would still have problems in society. As Davison and Neale observe, a good psychotherapist must help people develop social skills as well as to gain a better self-image; changes must occur in both behavior and self-concept to produce a notable improvement.

One other limitation requires mention. Like psychoanalysis, client-centered therapy is not appropriate for serious problems such as psychoses; it is most effective for people who are motivated enough to want to change and who are intelligent enough to be able to gain some insight concerning their problems. In addition, Rogers's model of humans as being basically good may be wrong. For example, we might question whether a person who has already exhibited signs of an antisocial personality disorder should be provided with unconditional positive regard.

In defense of client-centered therapy, the method is much more affordable and less time-consuming than traditional psychoanalysis. Most ordinary, decent neurotic people would probably enjoy and profit from talking about their problems with a person as sympathetic as Carl Rogers. Although his theoretical formulation of human behavior is unlikely to have a lasting influence on the science of psychology, his insights into the dynamics of the client-therapist relationship have had a major impact on the field of psychotherapy.

- How were mental disorders treated in the past? How did psychotherapy come about?
- What is psychoanalysis? Why is it difficult to evaluate scientifically?
- How would you describe client-centered therapy?

BEHAVIOR THERAPY

Insight psychotherapies are based on the assumption that understanding leads to behavioral change: once a person gains insight into the causes of his or her maladaptive behavior, that behavior will cease and will be replaced by adaptive behavior. However, insight is often *not* followed by behavioral change. In addition, some insight psychotherapies (particularly psychoanalysis) insist on explaining present difficulties as the result of conflicts dating from childhood. Behaviorally oriented therapists have decided that it is better to focus on a person's maladaptive behavior than to speculate on its causes. The *behavior itself* is the problem, and not the historical reasons for its development. Consequently, the goal is to change the behavior by whatever means are found to be most effective.

Practitioners of behavior therapy employ a variety of techniques based on the principles of classical and instrumental conditioning (defined and described in Chapter 6). The emphasis in classical conditioning is on stimuli that elicit new responses that are contrary to the old, maladaptive ones. In instrumental conditioning (also called *operant conditioning*), the

Behavior therapists have found that carefully exposing a person to a feared situation is particularly effective for treating phobic disorders, such as fear of flying.

emphasis is on the responses made; adaptive responses are selectively reinforced, and maladaptive ones are ignored or punished.

The fact that behavior therapy is based on the results of experimental research does not make this approach easier to use, nor does it require less sensitivity or clinical experience on the part of the therapist. A successful behavior therapist must be able to determine what behaviors and emotional reactions need to be changed, find out what stimuli can serve as effective reinforcers, and successfully alter the client's environment in a way that produces desirable changes. Many skeptical insight therapists have tried behavioral methods and claimed that "rewards didn't work." Perhaps they never found effective reinforcers, or the procedures they followed were inadequate. Perhaps their clients derived more reinforcement from making the therapist look foolish than from experiencing the "reinforcing" effects of the stimuli that they were expected to respond to. In any event, empirical research has proved the effectiveness of the techniques described in this section.

Classical Conditioning

Systematic Desensitization

One technique of behavior therapy has been especially successful in eliminating some kinds of fears and phobias. This technique, **systematic desensitization,** was developed by Joseph Wolpe, of the Temple University School of Medicine. Its goal is to remove the unpleasant emotional response and replace it with an incompatible one—relaxation.

First, the client is trained to achieve complete relaxation. The essential task is to learn to respond quickly to suggestions to feel relaxed and peaceful, so that these suggestions can elicit a relaxation response. Second, the client and therapist construct a hierarchy of anxiety-related stimuli. Table 17.1 presents a hierarchy constructed with a subject who had an intense fear of taking examinations. The situations provoking least fear are at the top.

Finally, the conditional stimuli (fear-eliciting situations) are paired with stimuli that elicit the learned relaxation response. For example, a person with a fear of taking exams is instructed to relax, and then to imagine entering a classroom to begin a new course. If the

TABLE 17.1

Desensitization hierarchy for test anxiety

Fear Rating	Hierarchy Item
0	Beginning a new course
10	Hearing an instructor announce a small quiz two weeks hence
25	Having a professor urge you personally to do well on an exam
40	Trying to decide how to study for an exam
45	Reviewing the material you know should be studied—listing study to do
50	Hearing an instructor remind the class of a quiz one week hence
65	Hearing an instructor announce a major exam in three weeks and its importance
70	Standing alone in the hall before an exam
75	Hearing an instructor announce a major exam in one week
80	Getting an exam back in class
80	Anticipating getting back a graded exam later that day
80	Thinking about being scared and anxious regarding a specific exam
85	Talking to several students about an exam right before taking it
85	Studying with fellow students several days before an exam
90	Hearing some "pearls" from another student which you doubt you'll remember, while studying a group
90	Cramming while alone in the library right before an exam
90	Thinking about being anxious over schoolwork in general
95	Thinking about not keeping up in other subjects while preparing for an exam
95	Talking with several students about an exam immediately after
100	Thinking about being generally inadequately prepared
100	Thinking about not being adequately prepared for a particular exam
100	Studying the night before a big exam

Note: 0 = total relaxation; 100 = maximum tension. From Kanfer, F.H., and Phillips, J.S. *Learning Foundations of Behavior Therapy.* New York: John Wiley & Sons, 1970.

client reports no anxiety, he or she is instructed to move to the next item and imagine hearing the professor announce a small quiz two weeks hence; and so on. Whenever the client begins feeling anxious, he or she signals to the therapist with some predetermined gesture—say, by raising a finger. The therapist instructs the client to relax and, if necessary, describes a less threatening scene. The client is not permitted to feel severe anxiety at any time. Gradually, over a series of sessions (the average is around eleven), the client is able to get through the entire list, vicariously experiencing even the most feared encounters.

Systematic desensitization is a very successful technique for people who have a specific phobia (as opposed to generalized fear and anxiety). Because this technique always has a specific goal, it is possible to assess its success or failure objectively. Of course, the therapist must first be sure that the client's anxiety is actually inappropriate. For example, a student's test anxiety may be realistic, reflecting the fact that the student does not prepare well for examinations. In such a case, therapeutic efforts should first be aimed at helping the student develop better study skills. Perhaps if the student learns to study more effectively, the test anxiety will disappear.

Scientific evaluations of systematic desensitization have been positive, and several experiments have found that all the elements of the procedure are necessary for its success. For example, a person will not get rid of a phobia merely by participating in relaxation training or by constructing hierarchies of fear-producing situations; only *pairings* of the anxiety-producing stimuli with instructions to relax will reduce the fear. One testimonial to this relation comes from a study by Johnson and Sechrest (1968), which attempted to reduce the fear of taking examinations in a group of college students. Students who underwent systematic desensitization received significantly higher grades on their final examination in a psychology course than did groups of control subjects who were also taking the course but who received either no treatment or relaxation training alone.

Systematic desensitization usually, but not always, involves imaginary encounters with the feared object or situation. In some cases the therapist arranges **in vivo** ("live") encounters. For example, a fear of snakes or spiders will be

Through the technique of aversive classical conditioning, many people can be assisted in their attempts to give up undesirable habits.

desensitized by actually approaching these animals. Similarly, a social phobia will be desensitized by having to talk in front of a group of strangers. The therapist generally begins systematic desensitization in the usual manner and then moves to actual encounters after progress has been made with imaginary ones. According to Wilson and O'Leary (1978), in vivo desensitization is almost always more effective and long-lasting than vicarious desensitization.

Aversive Classical Conditioning

Sometimes people are attracted by stimuli that most of us would ignore, and they engage in maladaptive behavior as a result of this attraction. Fetishes (such as sexual attraction to women's shoes) are the most striking examples. The technique of **aversive classical conditioning** attempts to establish an unpleasant response (such as a feeling of fear or disgust) to the object that produces the undesired behavior. For example, a person with a fetish for women's shoes might be given painful electrical shocks while viewing color slides of women's shoes. Besides fetishism, aversive classical conditioning has been used to treat drinking, smoking, transvestism, exhibitionism, and overeating. This technique has been shown to be moderately effective (Kanfer and Phillips,

1970). However, because the method involves pain or nausea, the client's participation must be voluntary, and the method should be employed only if other approaches fail or are impractical.

- What is behavior therapy? How does it differ from insight therapies?
- How would you describe systematic desensitization and aversive classical conditioning?

Instrumental Conditioning

Reinforcement of Adaptive Behaviors

Behavioral techniques are often used to alter the behavior of mentally retarded or emotionally disturbed people who are difficult to communicate with. Isaacs, Thomas, and Goldiamond (1960) reported the case of a forty-year-old man with schizophrenia who had been admitted to a hospital nineteen years previously and had not spoken one word to anyone during those years. A therapist decided to use instrumental conditioning to try to get him to speak once again. After observing the patient for a while, the therapist discovered that he loved chewing gum. The therapist would hold up a stick of gum and, when the patient looked at it, would give it to him. Soon he began paying attention to the therapist and would look at the piece of gum as soon as it was brought out.

Next, the therapist held up a piece of gum, waited until the patient moved his lips, and immediately reinforced the movement. Next, reinforcement was delivered only after the patient made a sound. Once the patient was reliably making a sound whenever the stick of gum was held up, the therapist held one up and said "Say 'gum.'" After a few minutes the patient finally said "gum"—his first word in nineteen years. Six weeks after the training had begun, the patient said, "Gum, please," adding the extra word on his own, and soon thereafter began talking with the therapist. The behavioral method worked where others had failed. (You may recall from Chapter 6 that the technique used to train a complex behavior is called *shaping*.)

Punishment of Maladaptive Behaviors

In general, punishment is not nearly so good a training method as positive reinforcement. For one thing, the person who is being punished may learn to fear or dislike the person who administers the punishment. If this person is the therapist, such an occurrence will probably interfere with other aspects of therapy. Second, there is a tendency to *overgeneralize*—to avoid performing a whole class of responses related to the one that is specifically being punished. For example, a child might not tell her father any more lies after being punished for doing so, but she might also stop sharing her fantasies with him. Unfortunately, it is usually easier to punish a response than it is to figure out how to reinforce other responses that will replace the undesirable one. And when we are angry, we often find that it is satisfying (reinforcing) to punish someone.

However, in some therapeutic situations, especially those in which the undesirable response is clearly harmful to the client, punishment is the most effective technique for eliminating an undesirable behavior. Cowart and Whaley (1971) reported the case of an emotionally disturbed child who persisted in self-mutilation. He banged his head against the floor until it was a swollen mass of cuts and bruises. As a result, he had to be restrained in his crib in a hospital for the mentally retarded. Obviously, the consequences of such confinement are serious for a child's development. After conventional techniques had failed, the therapist attached a pair of wires to the child's leg and placed him in a room with a padded floor. The child immediately began battering his head against the floor, and the therapist administered an electrical shock through the wires. The shock, which was certainly less damaging than the blows to the head, stopped the child short. He seemed more startled than anything else. He started banging his head against the floor again and received another shock. After very few repetitions of this sequence, the boy stopped his self-mutilation and could safely be let out of his crib.

Covert Reinforcement and Punishment

Sometimes the appropriate response need not actually be performed in the presence of the therapist but can be practiced vicariously.

Instead of receiving an actual reinforcer or punisher after performing an actual behavior, the client imagines that he or she is performing a desirable or undesirable behavior and then imagines receiving an appetitive or aversive stimulus. For example, Wisocki (1970) described the use of vicarious punishment in the treatment of a clothes-folding compulsion in a twenty-seven-year-old woman. Her ritual involved the following behaviors:

> (a) Ends of clothes brought together; (b) wrinkles smoothed out; (c) item folded carefully once; (d) item unfolded and smoothed over again; (e) folded neatly a second time (this process might be carried out several times until she was satisfied as to the lack of wrinkles); (f) carried to a dresser drawer across the room (each item carried individually); (g) drawer opened and item carefully placed on appropriate pile of clothing. If it became wrinkled at this point, it was refolded. (It was also sometimes necessary to refold the entire pile of clothes.) (h) drawer closed; (i) drawer opened to check neatness; (j) drawer closed; (k) patient turns attention to next item. (p. 235)

Wisocki had the woman imagine various disgusting scenes, in an attempt to make the ritual become aversive to her. According to Wisocki's report, vicarious punishment seems to have succeeded in ending the client's compulsion for clothes folding. However, because the woman wanted to do her own housework, therapy also had to establish a new set of behaviors. To do this, Wisocki employed vicarious reinforcement. For example, after helping her client establish an aversion to compulsive clothes folding, she had the woman imagine herself doing the job without being perfectionistic, allowing a few wrinkles to develop in the folded clothes. Next, she established that the client very much enjoyed practicing ballet, sipping sweet tea, eating Italian food, golfing, walking in a forest, completing a difficult job, being praised, having people seek her out for company, and being with happy people. The client was to imagine herself enjoying one of these reinforcers whenever the therapist said "Reinforcement." A typical training session went as follows:

> Relax and imagine that you are in the laundry room, standing in front of the day's laundry. You think to yourself that you'll really have to hurry folding these clothes so that you can go shopping with a friend ("Reinforcement"). You impatiently shove the clothes to one side ("Reinforcement").

> You take the next item, fold it quickly and it's a little wrinkled, but you put it on top of the other things ("Reinforcement"). (p. 236)

After a total of eight two-hour sessions, the client became much more efficient in her housework. Not only clothes folding but also other activities such as bed making and washing dishes took much less time. As long as one year later, the client remained satisfied with her improved performance.

■ How are reinforcement and punishment used in instrumental therapy procedures? What are the drawbacks and ethical problems with aversive techniques?
■ How is covert reinforcement used in instrumental behavior therapy?

Modeling

To change the behavior of a laboratory animal, an experimenter must either reinforce certain behaviors that are already present or shape a new one. In some cases, these methods appear to be the only ways to effect changes in humans, as with the schizophrenic patient who was induced to talk by rewards of chewing gum. However, even in this case the therapist did not simply wait until the patient spontaneously uttered a g sound. Instead, the therapist said, "Say 'gum.'" He provided a *model* for the patient to follow.

Humans (and many other animals) have the ability to learn without directly experiencing an event. As we have already seen, people can experience reinforcement and punishment vicariously. They can also imitate the behavior of other people, watching what they do and, if the conditions are appropriate, performing the same behavior. This capability provides the basis for the technique of modeling. Behavior therapists have found that clients can make much better progress when they have access to a model providing samples of successful behaviors to imitate. Bandura (1971) described a modeling session with people who had a phobic fear of snakes:

> The therapist himself performed the fearless behavior at each step and gradually led subjects into touching, stroking, and then holding the snake's

Modeling can be used to successfully eliminate fears. By imitating the behavior of someone fearlessly handling a snake, a person with a fear of snakes can learn to approach a snake with little or no fear.

body with gloved and bare hands while the experimenter held the snake securely by head and tail. If a subject was unable to touch the snake following ample demonstration, she was asked to place her hand on the experimenter's and to move her hand down gradually until it touched the snake's body. After subjects no longer felt any apprehension about touching the snake under these secure conditions, anxieties about contact with the snake's head area and entwining tail were extinguished. The therapist again performed the tasks fearlessly, and then he and the subject performed the responses jointly; as subjects became less fearful, the experimenter gradually reduced his participation and control over the snake, until eventually subjects were able to hold the snake in their laps without assistance, to let the snake loose in the room and retrieve it, and to let it crawl freely over their bodies. Progress through the graded approach tasks was paced according to the subjects' apprehensiveness. When they reported being able to perform one activity with little or no fear, they were eased into a more difficult interaction. (p. 680)

This treatment eliminated fear of snakes in 92 percent of the subjects who participated.

There are probably several reasons for the success of the modeling technique. Subjects learn to make new responses by imitating those of the therapist and are reinforced for doing so. When they observe a confident person approaching and touching a feared object without showing any signs of emotional distress, they probably experience a vicarious extinction of

their own emotional responses. In fact, Bandura (1971) reports that, "having successfully overcome a phobia that had plagued them for most of their lives, subjects reported increased confidence that they could cope effectively with other fear-provoking events" (p. 684), including their reaction to encounters with other people.

Modeling has been used to establish new behaviors as well as eliminate fears. For example, Lazarus (1971) uses **behavior rehearsal,** in which the therapist demonstrates how to handle a particular kind of interaction with other people. Clients practice the interaction, sometimes with the aid of a videotape machine, and acquire a repertoire of responses that they can use in real-life encounters with other people.

Token Economies

The instrumental conditioning approach has been used on a large scale with generally good success in institutions that house people with serious problems, such as schizophrenia or severe mental retardation. In such institutions, residents are often asked to do chores, both to keep operating costs low and to engage them in active participation in their environment. In some instances, other specific behaviors are also targeted as desirable and therapeutic, such as helping residents who have more severe problems. To promote these behaviors, therapists have designed **token economies.**

The principle is extremely simple. A list of tasks is compiled, and residents receive tokens as rewards for performing the tasks. Later they can exchange these tokens for snacks, other desired articles, or various privileges. Thus, the tokens become conditioned reinforcers for desirable and appropriate behaviors. Figure 17.5 shows the strong effects of the contingencies of a pay scale used in a token economy established by Ayllon and Azrin (1968). The amount of time spent performing the desirable behaviors was high when the reinforcement contingencies were imposed, and low when they were not.

A comprehensive experiment by Paul and Lentz (1977) clearly demonstrated the effectiveness of a token economy. The patients had severe, chronic schizophrenia and had been in the hospital for years. Some of them screamed wordlessly, some were mute and withdrawn, and some were violent. The experimenters set up a token economy designed to teach social skills such as self-grooming, good mealtime behavior, participation in classes, and socialization during free periods. The program lasted four and one-half years. By the end of the treatment, more than 10 percent of the patients in the token economy had been discharged, but none of the control patients given routine treatment had been able to leave. In addition, many of the patients from the token economy ward were able to leave the hospital for community-based facilities such as halfway houses. These patients fared much better than control patients who were also moved to the facilities in the community; more than 90 percent of the patients from the token economy ward were able to remain at these facilities during the eighteen-month follow-up period. The patients were not "cured" of their schizophrenia, but they obviously led much less disturbed lives.

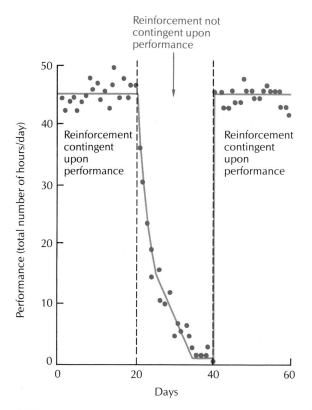

FIGURE 17.5

The effects of a token economy system of reinforcement on performance of a group of patients on specified chores. (From Ayllon, T., and Azrin, N. *The Token Economy: A Motivational System for Therapy and Rehabilitation.* New York: Appleton-Century-Crofts, 1968. By permission Prentice-Hall, Englewood Cliffs, N.J.)

Although token economies are based on a simple principle, they are very difficult to implement. A mental institution includes patients, caretakers, housekeeping staff, and professional staff. If a token economy is to be effective, all staff members who deal with residents must learn how the system is to work; ideally, they should also understand and agree with its underlying principles. A token economy can easily be sabotaged by a few people who believe that the system is foolish, wrong, or in some way threatening to themselves. If these obstacles can be overcome, token economies work very well.

Evaluation of Behavior Therapy

Psychotherapists with traditional orientations have criticized behavior therapy for its focus on the symptoms of a psychological problem, to the exclusion of its roots. Some psychoanalysts even argue that the treatment of symptoms is dangerous; in their view, the removal of one symptom of an intrapsychic conflict will simply produce another, perhaps more serious, symptom. This hypothetical process is called **symptom substitution.**

However, there is little evidence that symptom substitution occurs. It is true that many people's behavioral problems are caused by conditions that existed in the past and often these problems become self-perpetuating. Yet behavior therapy can, in many cases, eliminate the problem behavior without delving into the surrounding issues. For example, a child may (for one reason or another) begin wetting the bed. The nightly awakening irritates the parents, who must change the bedclothes and the child's pajamas. The disturbance often disrupts family relationships. The child develops feelings of guilt and insecurity and, as a result, wets the bed more often. Instead of analyzing the sources of family conflict, a therapist who uses behavior therapy would install a device in the child's bed that rings a bell when he or she begins to urinate. The child awakens and goes to the bathroom to urinate and soon ceases to wet the bed. The elimination of bedwetting causes rapid improvement in the child's self-esteem and in the entire family relationship. Symptom substitution does not appear to occur (Baker, 1969).

A criticism with real substance is that behaviors learned under one set of conditions may fail to occur in different environments; that is, the behavioral change may not generalize to other situations. This problem is especially acute in the treatment of alcohol addiction; addicts may abstain from drinking under laboratory conditions but go on a binge as soon as they are released.

Behavior therapists have designed specific methods to ensure that positive behavioral change generalizes to situations outside the clinic. These methods include intermittent reinforcement, self-observation, and recruiting of other people to serve as "therapists." As we saw in Chapter 6, intermittent reinforcement increases resistance to extinction. Thus, it is more effective not to reinforce every desirable response the client makes but to reinforce desirable responses intermittently.

Behavior therapy often employs methods of self-control. Although it may seem paradoxical that a person can reinforce or punish his or her own behavior, clients can indeed be taught methods to alter their own behavior or to maintain the behavioral changes accomplished in the clinic (Mahoney and Thoresen, 1974; Reese, 1978). To punish unwanted behaviors— say, smoking or picking an argument with a coworker—a client can make a contract with the therapist to send money to an organization he or she despises whenever the behavior occurs. To reinforce desirable behaviors, the client can treat himself or herself to an enjoyable activity, such as a telephone conversation with a friend or a snack (assuming that the client is not trying to eliminate a habit of overeating). The client and therapist help define the desirable and undesirable behaviors, set criteria for measuring them, and decide on the schedule of reinforcement or punishment that will be applied. As progress is made, the criteria and schedules are adjusted until the client's goals are met. The client may also be advised by the therapist to change his or her environment to eliminate discriminative stimuli that have in the past been present while the client performed the maladaptive behavior. For example, a person who habitually has had a cigarette with a cup of coffee after dinner should forego the cup of coffee (the discriminative stimulus) for a while if he or she is trying to quit smoking.

There are some situations in which behavior therapy should not be used. For example, a person who is involuntarily confined to an institution should not be subjected to aversive techniques unless he or she clearly wants to participate or unless the benefits far outweigh the discomfort, as in the case of the child who stopped battering his head against the floor after he had received a few mild electrical shocks for doing so. The decision to use aversive techniques must not rest only with people who are directly in charge of the patients, lest the procedures eventually be used merely for the sake of convenience. The decision must involve a committee containing people who serve as advocates for the patients.

In other situations, behavior therapy may not be appropriate because it raises unanswerable ethical issues. For example, a person may come to a therapist because his homosexuality causes him great anguish. The client asks for help and is willing to undergo whatever treatment is necessary; no coercion is involved. The therapist faces the dilemma of whether to embark on a course of treatment in which aversive stimuli are associated with other males or whether to try to help the client accept his sexual orientation and develop a better self-image. If the homosexuality is deep-seated, behavior therapy may simply make the client shun *all* sexual stimuli. It is not enough to learn the techniques of behavior therapy; one must also learn to recognize the circumstances in which these techniques are appropriate.

■ How can modeling be used in behavior therapy?
■ What are token economies? Why are they difficult to implement?
■ How would you evaluate behavior therapy?

COGNITIVE BEHAVIOR THERAPY

Subsequent to the development of behavior therapy a group of behavior therapists have begun to adopt strategies based on cognitive models of human behavior. The focus of this

Albert Ellis, the founder of rational-emotive therapy.

method, called **cognitive behavior therapy,** is on behavioral change. Like behavior therapists—and unlike most insight psychotherapists—cognitive behavior therapists are not particularly interested in events that occurred in the client's childhood. They are interested in the here and now, and in altering the client's behavior so that it becomes more functional. Although they employ many methods that are used by behavior therapists, they believe that when behaviors change, they do so because of changes in cognitive processes.

Rational-Emotive Therapy

Description

The first form of cognitive behavior therapy, called **rational-emotive therapy,** was developed in the 1950s by Albert Ellis, a clinical psychologist. In contrast to the other forms of cognitive behavior therapy, rational-emotive therapy did not grow out of the tradition of be-

havior therapy. For many years, Ellis was regarded as being outside the mainstream of psychotherapy, but now his methods are being practiced by a substantial number of therapists. Like Carl Rogers, Ellis asserts that psychological problems are the result of faulty cognitions; therapy is therefore aimed at changing people's beliefs. But unlike Rogers, who believes that people will naturally abandon their irrational beliefs and adopt rational ones if given an environment of unconditional positive regard, Ellis is highly directive and confrontational. He tells his clients what they are doing wrong and how they should change.

According to Ellis and his followers, emotions are the products of cognition. A *significant activating event (A)* is followed by a highly charged *emotional consequence (C)*, but it is not correct to say that A has caused C. Rather C is a result of the person's *belief system (B)*. Therefore, inappropriate emotions (such as depression, guilt, and anxiety) can be abolished only if a change occurs in the person's beliefs and perceptions. It is the task of the rational-emotive therapist to dispute the person's beliefs and to convince him or her that they are inappropriate.

The prevailing principle in rational-emotive theory is that the universe is logical and rational; the appropriate means of understanding it is the scientific method of controlled observation. Magic and superstition have no place in the belief system of a healthy, rational person. Therefore, the therapist attempts to get the client to describe his or her irrational beliefs, so that these beliefs can be challenged and defeated. As Ellis puts it, the rational-emotive therapist is "an exposing and nonsense-annihilating scientist" (1979, p. 187).

Rational-emotive theory asserts that people have the capacity for rational understanding and thus possess the resources for personal growth. Unfortunately, they also have the capacity for self-delusion and acceptance of irrational beliefs. Rational-emotive therapy seeks to rid people of illogical and counterproductive tendencies. In this process, called **cognitive restructuring,** the person's faulty cognitions—including their misperceptions of events in the world and the incorrect assumptions they make about their own needs—are changed by the therapeutic process. Several types of faulty cognitions receive special emphasis: the tendency to perceive a desirable event as an absolute necessity, the need to be better than everyone else, and the perception of failure as a disaster. If a person avoids social gatherings because he or she is afraid that someone else will not like or approve of him or her, a therapist would say something like this:

> Suppose that the worst happens. He hates you. He finds that you are a real jerk. You would say to yourself, "I *can't stand* that! It is absolutely *awful* that he doesn't like me! Because I can't make him like me I am a *worthless person!*" But that is not true. Actually, it is undesirable that he does not like you. It would be much nicer if he did. Being liked is definitely better than not being liked. But it is illogical and unproductive to perceive the rejection as a disaster.

Although rational-emotive therapy is much more directive than client-centered therapy, there are some similarities. Just as Rogers emphasizes unconditional positive regard, Ellis and his followers attempt to engender a feeling of **full acceptance** in their clients. They teach that self-blame is the core of emotional disturbance, and that it is possible for people to learn to stop continuously rating their own personal worth and measuring themselves against an impossible standard. They emphasize that people will be happier if they can learn to see failures as unfortunate events, not as disastrous ones that confirm the lack of their own worth. Unlike a Rogerian therapist, a rational-emotive therapist will vigorously argue with his or her client, attacking beliefs that the therapist regards as foolish and illogical. This approach also differs from the client-centered approach in that the therapist does not need to be especially empathetic in order to be an effective teacher and guide.

Unlike psychoanalysis, which seeks the source of a person's psychological problems in traumatic childhood experiences, rational-emotive therapy does not require the client to reconstruct and relive the original traumatic experiences. The emphasis is on the here and now. It may be useful to discuss some early experiences in order to uncover and correct the client's beliefs, but focusing on past misfortunes will only harm the client so long as faulty cognitive systems are interpreting these events. The only way to improvement is through a restructuring of these systems.

Rational-emotive theory also differs from psychoanalytic theory in denying the existence of an entity called *the unconscious*. Instead, it relies on brief, incisive questioning by the therapist to make the client aware of the reasons for some of his or her behaviors. In fact, the therapist often ridicules the client's irrational beliefs, in an attempt to get him or her to reject them. Transference is neither necessary nor desirable.

Evaluation

Rational-emotive therapy has appeal and potential usefulness for those who can enjoy and profit from intellectual teaching and argumentation. The people who are likely to benefit most from this form of therapy are those who are self-demanding and who feel guilty for not living up to their own standards of perfection. People with severe thought disorders, such as schizophrenia and the affective psychoses, are unlikely to respond to an intellectual analysis of their problems.

Research on rational-emotive therapy has shown that the results for some types of psychological problems appear to be good. For example, Brandsma, Maultsby, and Welsh (1978) found that rational-emotive therapy was as effective as insight therapy (and more effective than control procedures or participation in Alcoholics Anonymous) in the treatment of alcoholism. In contrast, Emmelkamp, Kuipers, and Eggeraat (1978) found that rational-emotive therapy was relatively ineffective in treating agoraphobia, whereas in vivo desensitization produced substantial improvement. Emmelkamp and colleagues suggested that a disorder such as agoraphobia, which evokes strong arousal and activity of the autonomic nervous system, cannot effectively be treated by purely cognitive methods.

Rational-emotive therapy has received considerable attention, and many therapists who adopt an eclectic approach use some of its techniques with some of their clients. In its advocacy of rationality and its eschewal of superstition, the theory can be seen as a systematized form of a common-sense approach to living. However, most other psychotherapists disagree with Ellis's denial of the importance of empathy in the relationship between therapist and client.

Methods Using a Combined Approach

Description

Rational-emotive therapy consists primarily of conversations between therapist and client. In contrast, most cognitive behavior therapists combine cognitive and behavioral methods. That is, they use all the methods I described in the section on behavior therapy, but they attempt to change their client's private behavior—the behavior going on in their client's head—as well as his or her public behavior. For example, Albert Bandura uses modeling to change people's overt behavior, such as their willingness to approach snakes, but he also attempts to change their thoughts and perceptions.

We saw that when behavior therapy successfully reduces people's fear of specific objects, the people usually report that their fear of other objects and situations also decreases. Bandura (1977) asserts that the reason for this generalized reduction in fear is the development of a cognitive concept he calls **self-efficacy.** By reducing a specific type of fear, behavior therapy enables a person to perform behaviors that he or she previously found impossible to do. The experience raises the person's evaluation of his or her self-efficacy—the degree to which the person is able to cope with a difficult situation. Thus, when the person encounters other situations that have caused trouble, he or she is much more willing to attempt acts previously avoided and, indeed, finds it possible to perform them. As you can see, Bandura's notion of self-efficacy is related to that of self-concept, which was discussed in Chapter 15.

Many cognitive behavior therapists employ behavioral methods to change a particular form of private behavior, referred to as **self-talk.** Most of us silently "talk" to ourselves as we go about our daily activities, especially when we are working on a complex task that can be guided by verbal rules.

Some cognitive behavior therapists have developed specific methods to alter people's self-talk in order to improve their psychological functioning. For example, Donald Meichenbaum (1977) developed a method that involves training clients to become aware of their own maladaptive self-statements. Once this training is done, the therapist models appropriate behavior while saying aloud accompanying self-

Albert Bandura, a pioneer in the use of modeling and imitation in cognitive behavior therapy.

talk that the clients can use to guide their own behavior. The clients then practice both the behavior and the verbalizations. For example, a client may find that a particular task produces so much anxiety that he or she cannot do it. By having the client perform the task while verbalizing the details of each step, Meichenbaum helps the client avoid thinking about possible failure. The client therefore becomes more likely to complete the task successfully.

Evaluation

Although cognitive behavior therapists believe in the importance of unobservable constructs such as feelings, thoughts, and perceptions, they do not believe that good therapeutic results can be achieved by focusing on cognitions alone. They, like their behaviorist colleagues, insist that it is not enough to have their clients introspect and analyze their thought patterns. Instead, therapists must assist clients to change their behavior. Behavioral changes cause cognitive changes; for example, when a client observes that he or she is now engaging in fewer maladaptive behaviors and more adaptive behaviors, the client's self-perceptions are bound to change as a result. But cognitive behavior therapists say that therapy can be even more effective when specific attention is paid to cognitions as well as behaviors.

It is probably impossible to prove or disprove such assertions. After all, cognitions are not directly observable but must be inferred from people's behavior. If changing people's self-talk helps them function more effectively, we can conclude that the therapeutic method works. From a practical point of view, it might not really matter *why* the method works.

Whether behavioral methods are therapeutic because they change cognitive structure will undoubtedly continue to be a matter of debate between behaviorists and cognitivists. In a practical sense, because both types of therapists are firmly committed to using behavioral methodology and to evaluating their results empirically, it probably does not matter which group is correct.

Because cognitive behavior therapists talk about unobservable cognitive processes, it is important to point out the differences between

them and insight therapists, who also deal with unobservable processes. As Beck (1976) notes, unlike insight therapists, cognitive behavior therapists concern themselves with conscious thought processes, not unconscious motives. They are also more interested in the present determinants of the client's thoughts and behaviors, rather than his or her past history. And because they come from the tradition of experimental psychology, they use rigorous empirical methods to evaluate the effectiveness of their techniques and to infer the nature and existence of cognitive processes.

GROUP PSYCHOTHERAPY

Description

Group psychotherapy became common during World War II, when the stresses of combat produced psychological problems in many of the members of the armed forces, and the demand for psychotherapists greatly exceeded the supply. What began as an economic necessity became an institution, once the effectiveness of group treatment was recognized.

Because most psychological problems involve interactions with other people, it is often worthwhile to treat these problems in a group setting. Such a setting permits the therapist to observe and interpret actual interactions without having to rely on clients' descriptions, which may be selective or faulty. Furthermore, a group can bring social pressure to bear on the behaviors of its members; if a person receives comments about his or her behavior from all the members of a group, the message is often more convincing than if a psychotherapist delivers the same comments in a private session. Finally, the process of seeking the causes of maladaptive behavior in other people often helps a person gain insight into his or her own problems.

The structure of the group session varies widely. Some sessions are little more than lectures, in which the therapist presents information about a problem that is common to all members of the group, followed by discussion. For example, in a case involving a person with

For some problems, group therapy can be an effective alternative to individual psychotherapy.

severe mental or physical illness the therapist explains to family members the nature, treatment, and possible outcomes of the disorder, then answers questions and allows people to share their feelings about what the illness has done to their family. Other groups are simply efficient ways to treat several clients at the same time; for example, systematic desensitization is often done in groups. But most types of group therapy involve interactions among the participants.

Psychodrama

In 1931, Jacob Moreno developed a form of structured group therapy called **psychodrama,** in which clients are asked to act out some of their problems by pretending that they are members of the cast of a play (Moreno, 1959). Some clients assume the role of actor while others serve as the audience. The therapist serves as director, commenting on the actors' performances and keeping the "plot" moving in a useful direction. If possible, the therapy takes place on an actual stage.

One of the techniques developed as a part of psychodrama is **mirroring,** in which one member of the group is asked to act out a particular maladaptive pattern of behavior that is displayed by another member. The object of this exercise is to help the person whose behavior is being mirrored to see himself or herself as others do, and therefore to gain insight that will facilitate change. In group therapy sessions today, videotape recordings are often made of clients' interactions with each other, in order to "mirror" precisely what other people see.

So far, no research has specifically evaluated the effectiveness of psychodrama.

Family Therapy

Family therapy has recently become an important technique for clinical psychologists. Very often, it is not enough to deal with the problems of an individual. People are the products of their environment, and the structure of a person's family is a crucial part of that environment. It is frequently impossible to help an unhappy person without also restructuring his or her relationship with other family members.

Family therapy is based on the premise that it is difficult to help one member of the family without examining the interactions within the whole family.

In many cases, a family therapist meets with all the members of a client's family and analyzes the ways in which individuals interact with each other. The therapist attempts to get family members to talk to each other instead of addressing all comments and questions to him or her. As much as possible, the family therapist tries to observe the data about the interactions—how individuals sit in relation to each other, who interrupts whom, who looks at whom before speaking—in order to infer the nature of the interrelationships within the family. For example, there may be barriers between certain family members; perhaps a father is unable to communicate with one of his children. Or two or more family members may be so "enmeshed" that they cannot function independently; they constantly seek each other's approval and, through overdependence, make each other miserable.

Salvador Minuchin (1974), a psychiatrist, has devised an approach called **structural family therapy.** He observes a family's interactions and draws simple diagrams of the relationships that he infers from the behavior of the family members. He identifies the counterproductive relationships and attempts to restructure the family in more adaptive ways by replacing pathological interactions with more effective, functional ones. He suggests that perhaps all members of the family must change if the client is to make real improvement.

In this approach, the therapist gets family members to "actualize" their transactional patterns—that is, to act out their everyday relationships—so that the pathological interactions will show themselves. Restructuring techniques include forming temporary alliances between the therapist and one or more of the family members, increasing tension in order to trigger changes in unstable structures, assigning explicit tasks and homework to family members (for example, making them interact with other members), and providing general support, education, and guidance. Sometimes the therapist visits the family at home. For example, if a child in a family refuses to eat, the therapist will visit during mealtime, in order to see the problem acted out as explicitly as possible.

The basic premise of family therapy seems sound: effective treatment of a person's problems often involves making changes in an important part of that person's environment—namely, his or her family. However, there is no clearly defined theory or set of procedures to help family therapists effect these changes, nor are there clear guidelines for assessing them. Until a more explicit and formal method has been developed, the effectiveness of family therapy is likely to depend on the skill and personality of the individual practitioner.

Group Behavior Therapy

Although most types of group therapy involve interactions among members of the group, at least one form of behavior therapy has lent itself to the treatment of noninteracting individuals in groups: systematic desensitization. As we saw, this technique involves imagining a series of increasingly threatening situations while remaining as relaxed as possible. Many behavior therapists (for example, Lazarus, 1961; Nawas, Fishman, and Pucel, 1970) have successfully performed systematic desensitization by assembling groups of people with the same type of phobia and providing them with group treatment.

As we saw earlier, therapists often attempt to help their clients develop more productive social behaviors by modeling the behaviors for them and having the clients copy and practice these behaviors. Obviously, social behaviors involve interactions among people, and a group provides an excellent setting for a behavior therapist to teach clients how to recognize adaptive and maladaptive interactions and to practice the adaptive ones. For example, Lewinsohn, Weinstein, and Alper (1970) have used behavioral techniques to teach groups of depressed patients behaviors that would be likely to win them social reinforcement from other people.

Evaluation

A bewildering variety of group therapies have been developed. In some groups, members are asked to lead blindfolded partners around, to develop trust; people meet in the nude, to establish openness and to eliminate hypocrisy and the trappings of status that we convey by our mode of dress; people vent their anger and hostility in emotional confrontations; groups meet in long marathon sessions with the assumption that fatigue will weaken defenses and permit people to encounter their real selves—the list could go on indefinitely. Each method has its adherents, but there is little objective evidence about the effectiveness of these techniques. However, methods with established effectiveness that have been adapted for use in groups, such as systematic desensitization and behavior therapy, continue to be effective. Other methods of group therapy have proved to be fads and are declining in popularity. But because it is clear that much can be accomplished in groups that cannot be accomplished in private sessions, future research will undoubtedly lead to more effective ways of treating people's psychological problems in groups.

■ What is rational-emotive therapy?
■ How would you describe cognitive behavior therapies and therapies that use a combined approach?
■ How would you describe and evaluate group psychotherapies?

BIOLOGICAL TREATMENTS

As we saw in Chapter 16, an important method for treating the symptoms of schizophrenia and the affective psychoses is medication. Besides drug therapy, there are two other forms of biological treatment: electroconvulsive therapy and psychosurgery.

Drug Therapy

Antipsychotic Drugs

Antipsychotic drugs have had a profound effect on the treatment of schizophrenia. Although they do not "cure" schizophrenia, they reduce the severity of its most prominent positive symptoms—delusions and hallucinations—apparently by blocking dopamine receptors in the brain. Pharmacological stimulation of these neurons with drugs such as amphetamine produces symptoms of schizophrenia, and inhibition with the antipsychotic drugs reduces these symptoms. Presumably, overactivity of these synapses is an important factor in the development of schizophrenia. Although dopamine-secreting neurons are located in several parts of the brain, most researchers believe that the ones involved in the symptoms of schizophrenia are those located in the hypothalamus, cerebral cortex, and parts of the limbic system near the front of the brain.

A different system of dopamine-secreting neurons in the brain is involved in control of movement. Occasionally, this system of neurons degenerates spontaneously in older people, producing Parkinson's disease. Symptoms of this disorder include tremors, muscular rigidity, loss of balance, difficulty in initiating a movement, and impaired breathing that makes speech indistinct. In extreme cases the person is bedridden.

The major problem with the antipsychotic drugs is that they do not discriminate between these two systems of dopamine-secreting neurons; the drugs interfere with the activity of both the circuit involved in the symptoms of schizophrenia and the motor circuit. Consequently, a patient being treated for schizophrenia often shows a disturbance in movement control and other symptoms of Parkinson's disease. One of these symptoms, loss of facial expression, can have serious consequences, because it is sometimes misdiagnosed as a recurrence of one of the symptoms of schizophrenia, lack of affect (Snyder, 1974). A resulting increase in dosage to counteract the presumed recurrence makes the problem worse. In fact, these motor side effects are usually temporary and can be controlled by adjusting the dosage of the medication.

A related problem is that certain other symptoms of motor impairment sometimes do not appear until after several years of medication. Symptoms of **tardive dyskinesia** (*tardive* means "late-developing"; *dyskinesia* refers to a disturbance in movement) include facial grimacing and involuntary movements of the tongue, mouth, and neck. Severely affected patients have difficulty talking, and occasionally the movements interfere with breathing. The symptoms can temporarily be alleviated by an *increase* in dosage, which only serves to increase and perpetuate the patient's dependence

Researchers are continually working to discover drugs that may be helpful in treating certain psychological disorders.

on the medication (Baldessarini and Tarsy, 1980). This side effect argues forcefully for the necessity of careful monitoring of patients' symptoms and for restriction of antipsychotic medication to the minimum effective dosage.

Clinicians and researchers continue to hope for the development of antipsychotic drugs that will affect only the dopamine neurons that are involved in the symptoms of schizophrenia and that will not interfere with the neurons that are involved in the control of movement. Because the biochemistry of these two types of neurons differs slightly, there is some basis for this hope.

Antidepressant Drugs

The uses of the antidepressant drugs—the tricyclic antidepressants and lithium carbonate—were discussed in Chapter 16. As we saw, the tricyclic antidepressant drugs are most effective in the treatment of major depression, while lithium carbonate is most effective in the treatment of bipolar disorders or simple mania. Patients' manic symptoms usually decrease as soon as their blood level of lithium reaches a therapeutic level (Gerbino, Oleshansky, and Gershon, 1978). In bipolar disorder, once the manic phase is eliminated, the depressed phase does not return. People with bipolar disorder have remained free of their symptoms for years, as long as they continue taking lithium carbonate. This drug appears to be remarkably free of side effects, but an overdose is toxic. Therefore, the patient's blood level of lithium should be monitored regularly.

Unlike lithium carbonate, the tricyclic antidepressant drugs only work on a short-term basis. They are useful in treating episodes of severe depression, but the evidence suggests that they are not useful when taken on a long-term basis. In general, the tricyclic antidepressant drugs should be used when there is a family history of severe depression or when the person exhibits psychotic symptoms, lethargy, agitation, severe insomnia, expressions of feelings of hopelessness, or signs of suicidal tendencies (Reda, 1984). Once the severity of the symptoms subsides, psychotherapy should also be instituted.

A study by DiMascio, Weissman, Prusoff, Neu, Zwilling, and Klerman (1979) found that psychotherapy and the administration of a tricyclic antidepressant drug had independent therapeutic effects in the treatment of acute depression. The drug primarily improved sleep and appetite disturbances, whereas psychotherapy primarily improved mood, suicidal thoughts, ability to work, and apathy. Thus, the best results were obtained by simultaneous use of both drugs and psychotherapy.

We also saw in Chapter 16 that a common side effect of some drugs used to treat high blood pressure is depression. Thus it should not be surprising that the principal side effect of the tricyclic antidepressant drugs is elevated blood pressure (hypertension). This effect makes treatment of a depressed person with high blood pressure a difficult problem. On the one hand, a patient with high blood pressure stands a good chance of suffering a heart attack or stroke. On the other hand, for many people, major depression makes life not worth living and may lead to suicide.

Besides being effective in treating depression, the tricyclic antidepressant drugs have also been used successfully to treat several anxiety disorders, including panic disorder, obsessive compulsive disorder, and agoraphobia (Marks, 1969; Klein and Rabkin, 1981; Klein, Zitrin, Woerner, and Ross, 1983). The drugs appear to reduce the incidence of panic attacks, including those that accompany severe agoraphobia, and they also reduce obsessions and compulsions. In addition, propranolol, a drug used to treat irregularities in heart rhythm, has proved helpful in reducing the changes in heart rate that accompany panic attacks (Granville-Grossman and Turner, 1966). The tricyclic antidepressant drugs do not reduce the anticipatory anxiety that the patient feels between panic attacks; this symptom can be reduced by antianxiety drugs, described in the very next section.

Although the tricyclic antidepressants and other drugs are useful in alleviating the symptoms of certain anxiety disorders, they do not "cure" any of these conditions. Because the disorders are at least partly heritable, as we saw in Chapter 16, they may thus have some biological causes at their root; yet the most permanent and long-lasting treatment is still behavior therapy. The drugs may be very useful in reducing the patients' symptoms so that they can participate effectively in therapy, but they do not provide a long-term solution.

Antianxiety Drugs

Antianxiety drugs, better known as tranquilizers, are the most prescribed of all drugs. Each year, North Americans consume many tons of drugs such as diazepam (Valium) and chlordiazepoxide (Librium) to combat the most common symptom of neurosis: anxiety. People with neuroses (or tendencies toward them) are especially prone to drug dependency in their search for a crutch to help them. Because some busy physicians find it easier to give a patient a prescription than to try to find out what is causing the anxiety, people rarely have trouble obtaining these drugs. If necessary, people hooked on tranquilizers will shop around until they find a physician who will oblige them.

Antianxiety drugs undoubtedly serve a useful purpose in helping people cope with transient crises. They are also effective in reducing the withdrawal symptoms of alcohol and opiate addictions. Sometimes they are used as antidotes for overdoses of stimulant drugs. And as we just saw, they can be used in conjunction with the tricyclic antidepressant drugs to reduce the anticipatory anxiety suffered by people with panic disorder or with agoraphobia accompanied by panic attacks. However, there is no "disease state" that is alleviated by the antianxiety medications. Chronic, long-term use of tranquilizers is probably not in anyone's best interest (Baldessarini, 1977).

Electroconvulsive Therapy

Electroconvulsive therapy (ECT) involves applying a pair of metal electrodes to a person's head and then passing a brief surge of electric current through them. The jolt produces a storm of electrical activity in the brain (a seizure) that renders the person unconscious. The wild firing of the neurons that control movement produces convulsions—muscular rigidity and trembling, followed by rhythmic movements of the head, trunk, and limbs. After a few minutes, the person falls into a stuporous sleep. Today, patients are anesthetized and temporarily paralyzed before the current is turned on. This procedure eliminates the convulsion but not the seizure, which is what delivers the therapeutic effect. (See Figure 17.6.)

Electroconvulsive therapy has a bad reputation among many clinicians because it has been

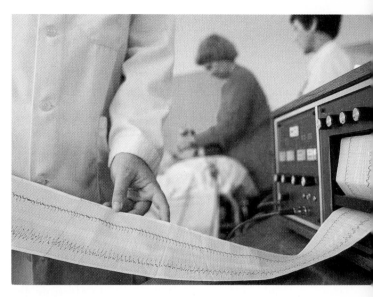

FIGURE 17.6

While some studies have shown electroconvulsive therapy to be effective in treating depression, it remains a potentially dangerous method of treatment.

used to treat disorders such as schizophrenia, on which it has no useful effects, and because patients have received excessive numbers of ECT treatments—as many as hundreds. Originally, ECT was thought to alleviate the symptoms of schizophrenia, because schizophrenic people who also had epilepsy often appeared to improve just after a seizure. Subsequent research has shown that ECT has little or no effect on the symptoms of schizophrenia. However, it has been shown to be singularly effective in treating severe depression (Baldessarini, 1977). Although no one knows for certain why ECT alleviates depression, it is possible that it does so by reducing REM sleep. As we saw in Chapter 16, people with major depression engage in abnormally large amounts of REM sleep, and REM-sleep deprivation is an effective antidepressant therapy.

A case report by Fink (1976) illustrates the response of a depressed patient to a course of ECT. A forty-four-year-old widow had been hospitalized for three months for severe depression. A course of three ECT treatments per week was prescribed for her by her therapist's supervisor. Unknown to her therapist (a trainee), the first twelve treatments were subthreshold; that is, the intensity of the electrical current was too low to produce seizures. (The treatments could be regarded as placebo treatments.) Although both the patient and therapist expected the woman to show some improvement, none was seen. In the next fourteen treatments, the current was raised to a sufficient level to produce seizures. After five actual seizures, both the patient and therapist noticed an improvement. The woman began to complain less about various physical symptoms, to participate in hospital activities, and to make more positive statements about her mood. She became easier to talk with, and the therapist's notes of their conversations immediately proliferated. The fact that these responses occurred only after several actual seizures suggests that improvement stemmed from the biological treatment and not simply from the therapist's or patient's expectations.

Some patients with affective psychoses do not respond to the antidepressant drugs, but a substantial percentage of these patients improve after a few sessions of ECT. Because antidepressant medications are generally slow-acting, taking ten days to two weeks for their therapeutic effects to begin, severe cases of depression are often treated with a brief course of ECT to reduce the symptoms right away. The patients are then maintained on the antidepressant drug. Electroconvulsive therapy is also useful in treating pregnant women with severe depression; because the procedure does not involve long-term administration of drugs, the danger to the fetus is minimized (Goodwin and Guze, 1984). Given that a depressed person runs a 15 percent chance of dying by suicide, the use of ECT may be justified in such cases.

The second criticism of ECT, concerning the dangers inherent in repeated treatment, is quite true. An excessive number of ECT treatments will produce permanent loss of memory (Squire, 1974) and probably also cognitive deficits. Thus, although a prolonged series of treatments is not necessary to achieve therapeutic results, it is likely that even a small number of treatments causes at least some permanent brain damage. Therefore, the potential benefits of ECT must be weighed against its potential damage. Electroconvulsive therapy must be used only when the patient's symptoms justify it. Because ECT undoubtedly achieves its effects through the biochemical consequences of

the seizure, pharmacologists may discover new drugs that can produce its rapid therapeutic effects without its deleterious ones. Once this breakthrough occurs, ECT can be discarded.

Psychosurgery

One form of treatment for mental disorders is even more controversial than electroconvulsive therapy. Psychosurgery is the treatment of a mental disorder, in the absence of obvious organic damage, by means of brain surgery. (Note that brain surgery to remove a tumor or diseased neural tissue or to repair a damaged blood vessel is *not* psychosurgery, and there is no controversy about these procedures.)

Psychosurgical treatment has no scientific basis, and it produces permanent, irreversible brain damage. Together, these facts form a convincing argument for banning the procedures, and in fact some jurisdictions in the United States have done so. However, although it has not proved effective in reducing or eliminating violent behavior, as was originally hoped, there is some evidence that psychosurgery has greatly improved the lives of mentally disturbed people who were formerly desperate for relief. This evidence has apparently been strong enough to convince even former critics. For example, in an excellent and influential book, Valenstein (1973) concluded that psychosurgical procedures were generally very poorly evaluated; few surgeons made careful measurements of their patients' symptoms before and after an operation, and the emphasis was often on manageability, not on actual remission of symptoms. However, a more recent report by a commission composed of experts, including Valenstein and other skeptics (National Commission for the Protection of Human Subjects of Biomedical and Behavioral Research, 1977), has drawn much more favorable conclusions about psychosurgery.

Psychosurgery was first performed in 1935, as an experimental procedure to investigate brain functions. Carlyle Jacobsen and two colleagues had been attempting to train a chimpanzee to perform a task that required the animal to note the presence of food, wait for a predetermined period, and then locate the food. One chimpanzee, Becky, did not take well to this task; she appeared to be "neurotic." The experimenters reversed her behavior by performing a **prefrontal lobotomy.** This procedure disconnects the frontmost portion of the brain, effectively eliminating its functions, which appear to include some related to emotional reactions.

Egas Moniz, a Portuguese psychiatrist, noted the similarity between Becky's behavior and that of people with mental disorders. He persuaded Almeida Lina, a neurosurgeon, to try the procedure on a human patient, and the first operation was performed in November 1935. Moniz himself supervised only about one hundred prefrontal lobotomies and wanted to wait for an evaluation of long-term results before recommending the procedure for more patients. (Ironically, a patient who had received a lobotomy later shot Moniz, and the bullet lodged in his spine, causing paralysis of the lower part of his body.) In 1949 Moniz received a Nobel Prize "for his discovery of the therapeutic value of prefrontal [lobotomy] in certain psychoses."

The award by the Nobel Committee was definitely premature; the procedure was found to have serious side effects, such as apathy and severe blunting of emotions, intellectual impairments, and deficits in judgment and planning. Nevertheless, the procedure was soon in common use for a variety of conditions, most of which were not improved by the surgery. It is estimated that approximately 40,000 prefrontal lobotomies were performed in the United States alone.

The development of antipsychotic drugs and the increasing attention to the serious side effects of prefrontal lobotomy led to a sharp decline in the use of this procedure during the 1950s. Today it is no longer performed.

A few surgeons have continued to refine the technique of psychosurgery and now perform a procedure called a **cingulectomy,** which involves cutting the **cingulum bundle,** a small bundle of nerve fibers that connects the prefrontal cortex with parts of the limbic system. According to the National Commission for the Protection of Human Subjects of Biomedical and Behavioral Research (1977), these more restricted operations do not appear to produce the intellectual impairments or changes in personality that often occurred after prefrontal

lobotomies. In fact, people's IQ test scores frequently improve after surgery, because their other problems are alleviated and they can devote more attention to the task at hand. The only reliable negative finding is an impairment in patients' ability to change their strategy in a problem-solving task. Another possible result is a mild, temporary blunting of affect.

Cingulectomies have been shown to be effective in helping people who suffer from severe compulsions. Tippin and Henn (1982) reported on five cases of people with obsessive compulsive disorder who received this form of surgery. Although the patients had had the disorder for between six and twenty years, all showed improvement. One was fully recovered; three were "much improved"; one was "improved."

According to the National Commission for the Protection of Human Subjects of Biomedical and Behavioral Research (1977), cingulectomy appears to be of most value in the treatment of affective disorders and compulsions; it does not substantially curtail thought disturbances. The report stresses the importance of carefully evaluating each case. In one flagrantly inadequate evaluation, a surgeon noted that the surgery produced "no or little changes in intellect and discriminative ability," using as the only criterion the patient's ability to knit after the operation (Winter, 1972). Surgeons should not be expected to be able to perform a psychological evaluation.

I must stress that if psychosurgery is ever used, it should be used only as a last resort, and never on a patient who cannot assent to treatment. The effects of psychosurgery are permanent; there is no way to reverse a brain lesion. Perhaps more effective behavioral techniques and new drug treatments will eventually make psychosurgical procedures obsolete.

- What are the effects and side effects of antipsychotic drugs?
- What drugs are used to treat major depression and anxiety? What are their effects and usefulness?
- What are the benefits and drawbacks of electroconvulsive therapy?
- Which disorders have been treated with psychosurgery? What are the benefits and drawbacks of psychosurgery?

Some studies indicate that people will be most likely to benefit from psychotherapy when they perceive the therapist to be similar to themselves.

ECLECTIC TREATMENT

In my description of the various kinds of psychotherapies, I may have given the impression that practitioners usually employ only one approach. They may be psychoanalysts, client-centered therapists, behavior therapists, cognitive behavior therapists, rational-emotive therapists, group psychotherapists, family therapists, or physicians who prescribe drugs. In fact, some psychotherapists do describe themselves in these terms. But the majority of clinical psychologists probably describe their own therapeutic preference as eclectic.

Eclectic (from the Greek *eklegein*, "to single out") means "choosing what appears to be the best from diverse sources, systems, or styles" (*American Heritage Dictionary*, 1975). The eclectic clinical psychologist attempts to learn what is good about each of many different approaches. If a client seems to be avoiding discussion of some painful childhood events that may still be affecting his or her behavior, the therapist may use hypnosis or free association to uncover these memories and try to work them out. For a client with a simple, isolated phobia, the therapist may use systematic desensitization to alleviate the problem. If the

problem seems to involve interactions with other family members, the therapist may meet with the entire family. If the client seems to be too self-critical, the therapist may use a cognitive approach to change his or her beliefs about what is necessary and desirable. For a client who appears to be suicidal, the therapist may consult a psychiatrist for electroconvulsive therapy or antidepressant drug treatment.

The average person who visits a clinical psychologist for help with a problem will probably not be able to identify the therapist's theoretical orientation, because the therapist will most likely adopt the technique that he or she believes is best suited to the client's problem.

EVALUATION OF THERAPIES AND THERAPISTS

Several factors make it extremely difficult to evaluate the effectiveness of a particular form of therapy or an individual therapist. One is the problem of *measurement*. It is difficult to measure a person's dysfunction. There are no easily applied, commonly agreed-upon criteria for mental health. Thus, it is usually not possible to make valid before-and-after measurements.

Ethics also sometimes prevent clinicians from using a purely scientific method of evaluation, which requires that experimental and control groups be constituted in equivalent ways. Leaving a person who appears to be suicidal untreated, so that comparisons can be made with similar people who receive therapy, presents risks that almost all therapists would consider unacceptable.

Self-selection involves clients' initial choices of a certain therapeutic approach. The resulting impossibility of establishing either a stable sample population or a control group also makes it difficult to compare the effectiveness of various kinds of therapies. Many patients change therapists or leave therapy altogether. What conclusions can we make about the effectiveness of the therapy by looking only at the progress made by the clients who remain?

Yet another problem with scientific evaluation of psychotherapy is the question of an appropriate *control group*. You may recall from Chapter 1 that the effects of therapeutic drugs must be determined through comparison with the effects of innocuous sugar pills, to be sure that the improvement has not occurred merely because the patient *thinks* that the pill has done some good. Placebo effects can also occur in psychotherapy; the person knows that he or she is being treated and gets better because he or she believes that the treatment should lead to improvement. Most studies that evaluate psychotherapeutic techniques do not include control groups for placebo effects. To do so, the investigator would have to design "mock therapy" sessions, during which the therapist does nothing therapeutic but convinces the patient that therapy is taking place; obviously, this goal is not easily achieved.

In a pioneering paper on psychotherapeutic evaluation, Eysenck (1952) examined nineteen studies assessing the effectiveness of psychotherapy. He reported that of the people who remained in psychoanalysis as long as their therapists thought they should, 66 percent showed improvement. Similarly, 64 percent of patients treated eclectically showed an improvement. However, 72 percent of patients who were treated only custodially in institutions (receiving no psychotherapy) showed improvement. In other words, people got better just as fast by themselves as they did in therapy. This was obviously not a favorable finding for psychotherapy.

Subsequent studies were not much more favorable. Some investigators (including Eysenck) concluded that it is unethical to charge a person for psychotherapy, because there is little scientific evidence that it is effective. Others say that the problems involved in performing scientific research are so great that we must abandon the attempt to evaluate therapies; validation of the effectiveness of therapy must rely on the therapist's clinical judgment. Many forms of therapy have never been evaluated objectively, because their practitioners are convinced that the method works and reject objective confirmation as unnecessary.

Several more recent studies have compared the effectiveness of insight psychotherapies, behavior therapies, and drug treatments. The most comprehensive review was performed by Smith, Glass, and Miller (1980). The authors used a technique called **meta-analysis,** devised by Glass, McGaw, and Smith (1981). This procedure provides a statistical method for estimating the magnitude of experimental effects reported by published studies.

Smith and her colleagues found 475 studies that provided enough information to be analyzed. The overwhelming majority of the therapies being evaluated achieved significant positive results. Only 9 percent of the measures indicated that the people being treated got worse, indicating that the therapies were rarely harmful. Some studies included groups that received placebo therapy. In studies that evaluated psychotherapy, placebo therapy typically consisted of relaxation training without any attempt to address a patient's particular problems. In studies that evaluated drugs, placebos were simply inert pills or injections. Many of the studies demonstrated a significant placebo effect. Thus, when people believe they are receiving therapeutic attention, they tend to show some improvement.

In comparisons of insight therapies and behavior therapies, Smith and her colleagues found that behavior therapies produced consistently better results. However, the comparison is difficult to make directly, because studies of the two approaches tended to measure the outcomes in different ways. The authors found that in treatment of both psychoses and neuroses, psychotherapy combined with drug therapy was more effective than either approach by itself. The authors concluded, "Psychotherapy is beneficial, consistently so and in many different ways. Its benefits are on a par with other expensive and ambitious interventions, such as schooling and medicine. The benefits of psychotherapy are not permanent, but then little is" (Smith, Glass, and Miller, 1980, pp. 183–188).

When examining the relative effectiveness of therapies against a broad range of disorders, no one therapy emerges as superior. Perhaps as a consequence, researchers studying the outcome of psychotherapy have increasingly turned their attention to more specific questions (Gomes-Schwartz, Hadley, and Strupp, 1978). Rather than asking the global question of whether psychotherapy is effective, researchers are asking what treatments are most effective with what problems, for what people, and under what conditions. They are finding that some therapies may be more effective for treating certain disorders.

For example, cognitive therapy seems to be superior to drug treatment in reducing the symptoms of depression (Rush et al. 1982). In a comparison of cognitive and behavioral treat-

A therapist's ability to express warmth, understanding, and empathy is an important determinant of therapeutic outcome.

ments for depression, researchers found that patients treated with cognitive methods report a greater initial improvement, but by the end of treatment no differences are apparent (Gardner and Oei, 1981). Anxiety disorders such as agoraphobia appear to respond best to behavioral methods of treatment that expose the person to the feared situation (Barlow and Wolfe, 1981). Direct exposure is more effective than imaginary exposure (Barlow and Beck, 1984).

An interesting study by Luborsky, Chandler, Auerbach, Cohen, and Bachrach (1971) investigated the factors that influence the outcome of a course of psychotherapy. They examined patient variables, treatment variables, and therapist variables. The important *patient variables* were psychological health at the beginning of the therapy, adequacy of personality, the patient's motivation for change, level of intelligence, level of anxiety (more anxious patients tended to do better), level of education, and socioeconomic status. Some of the variables seem to be self-confirming; if you are in fairly good psychological shape to begin with, you have a better chance of improving. In addition, if you are well educated and have adequate social and financial resources, your condition will probably improve. The finding that anxiety is a good sign probably indicates a motivation to improve.

The only significant *treatment variable* was the number of sessions of therapy. No one type of therapy appeared to be better than another. However, because a larger number of sessions causes the treatment to extend over a longer period of time, we cannot assume that the treatments themselves were responsible for the improvement; perhaps the mere passage of time was all that was necessary.

Several *therapist variables* were significant. These variables were the number of years the therapist had been practicing, similarity in the personality of therapist and client, and the ability of the therapist to communicate empathy to the client. The finding that the more experienced therapists had more success with their clients is very encouraging; it suggests that therapists learn something from their years of experience, which in turn implies that *there is something to learn.* Thus, we have reason to believe that the process of psychotherapy is not futile.

The fact that the therapist's ability to express empathy is a significant variable has suggested to several investigators (such as Fix and Haffke, 1976) that a therapist's most important function is to change the client's thoughts and behaviors by social reinforcement. You will recall that Truax (1966) found that Carl Rogers was inadvertently reinforcing statements from his clients that indicated improvement. Therapists who demonstrate warmth and understanding are most successful in reinforcing desirable statements and behaviors in their patients. Cold, uninvolved therapists simply have less impact. Truax and Carkhuff (1964) have distinguished between effective and ineffective therapists in the following way:

Patients whose therapists offered a high level of unconditional positive warmth, self-congruence or genuineness, and accurate empathetic understanding showed significant positive personality and behavioral change on a wide variety of indices, and . . . patients whose therapists offered relatively low levels of these conditions during therapy exhibited significant deterioration in personality and behavioral functioning. (pp. 130–131)

Several studies have suggested that the ability to form understanding, warm, and empathetic relationships is one of the most important traits that distinguish an effective therapist from an ineffective one. For example, Strupp and Hadley (1979) enlisted a group of college professors on the basis of their reputations as warm, trustworthy, empathetic individuals. The professors, from the departments of English, history, mathematics, and philosophy, were asked to hold weekly sessions to counsel students with psychological difficulties. Another group of students were assigned to professional psychotherapists, both psychologists and psychiatrists, and a third group received no treatment at all. Most of the students showed moderate depression or anxiety.

Although there was much variability, with some individual students showing substantial improvement, students who met with the professors did as well as those who met with the professional therapists. Both groups did significantly better than the control subjects who received no treatment. These results suggest that sympathy and understanding are the most important ingredients in the psychotherapeutic process, at least for treatment of mild neuroses. In such cases, therapists' theories of how mental disorders should be treated may be less important than their ability to establish a warm, understanding relationship with their clients.

■ How would you describe the eclectic approach to psychotherapy?
■ What are the four major difficulties encountered in evaluating psychotherapy?
■ What conclusions can be drawn from the research on the effectiveness of psychotherapy as a treatment?

Are you really ready, or are you just trying to stop me from building my tennis court?
Drawing by Hamilton; © 1987

CHAPTER SUMMARY

1. Insight psychotherapies are based primarily on conversation between therapist and client. The oldest form, psychoanalysis, was devised by Freud and attempts to resolve the inner conflicts of the client's psyche by bringing to consciousness his or her unconscious drives and the defenses that have been established against them. Insight is believed to be the primary source of healing.

2. Client-centered therapy is based on the premise that people are basically healthy and good, and that their problems result from faulty learning. Instead of evaluating themselves in terms of their own self-concepts, they judge themselves by other people's standards. This tendency is rectified by providing an environment of unconditional positive regard, in which clients can find their own way to mental health.

3. Behavior therapists attempt to use the principles of classical and instrumental (operant) conditioning to modify behavior: to eliminate fears or replace maladaptive behaviors with adaptive ones. Systematic desensitization uses classical conditioning procedures to condition the response of relaxation to stimuli that were previously fear producing. In contrast, aversive classical conditioning attempts to condition an unpleasant response to a stimulus with which the client is preoccupied, such as a fetish.

4. Token economies arrange contingencies in the environment of people who reside in institutions; in this case, the system of payment and reward is obvious to the participants. But not all instances of reinforcement and punishment are overt; they can also be vicarious. With the guidance of therapists, people can imagine their own behavior with its consequent reinforcement or punishment. Modeling has been used as an important adjunct to instrumental conditioning; therapists who use this effective technique provide specific examples of the desirable behaviors.

5. With the exception of rational-emotive therapy, cognitive behavior therapies grew out of the tradition of behavior therapy. These ther-

apies attempt to measure and change behavior, but they also pay attention to unobservable cognitive processes. Rational-emotive therapy is also based on the assumption that people's psychological problems stem from faulty cognitions, but its practitioners use many forms of persuasion, including ridicule, to get people to abandon these cognitions in favor of logical and healthy ones. Relief from distress is achieved by changing the belief system, not by reliving the past.

Most cognitive behavior therapists pay more attention to thinking and private verbal behavior than their behaviorist colleagues are likely to do. For example, Bandura concentrates on changes in self-efficacy as well as changes in behavior.

6. Group therapy has developed in response to the belief that certain problems can be treated more efficiently, and more effectively, in group settings. Practitioners of psychodrama, family therapy, and some forms of group behavior therapy observe people's interactions with others and attempt to help them learn how to establish more effective ones.

7. Biological treatments for mental disorders include drugs, electroconvulsive therapy, and psychosurgery. Research has shown that treatment of the positive symptoms of schizophrenia with antipsychotic drugs, of major depression with the tricyclic antidepressant drugs, and of bipolar disorder with lithium carbonate are the most effective ways to alleviate the symptoms of these disorders. Although electroconvulsive therapy is an effective treatment for depression, its use should be reserved for cases in which rapid relief is critical, because the seizures may produce brain damage. The most controversial treatment, psychosurgery, is rarely performed today. Its only presently accepted use, in the form of cingulectomy, is for the treatment of crippling compulsions that cannot be reduced by more conventional means of treatment.

8. The effectiveness of many traditional types of psychotherapy is difficult to assess. Outcomes are difficult to measure objectively, ethical considerations make it hard to establish control groups for some types of disorders, and self-selection and dropouts make it impossible to compare randomly selected groups of subjects. However, what research there is now suggests that some forms of psychotherapy—particularly behavior therapy and cognitive behavior therapy—are effective. The effectiveness of drug therapy is somewhat easier to demonstrate, because experimenters can construct double-blind studies with placebos. Several experiments assessing both drug treatment and psychotherapy have found that a combined approach is the most beneficial.

9. The most important characteristic of a good psychotherapist appears to be the ability to form a warm, understanding relationship with a client. The importance of this characteristic may derive from the fact that the client grows to care about such a person's opinions, which makes it possible for the therapist to administer social reinforcement. In addition, the client is more likely to be willing to model his or her behavior on the behavior of such a therapist.

KEY TERMS

antianxiety drugs "Tranquilizers," which reduce anxiety. The most common include chlordiazepoxide (Librium) and diazepam (Valium).

antipsychotic drugs Drugs used to eliminate or reduce the positive symptoms of schizophrenia, including hallucinations, delusions, and thought disorders; examples include chlorpromazine (Thorazine) and haloperidol (Haldol). The drugs apparently work by blocking dopamine receptors in the brain.

aversive classical conditioning A technique that attempts to establish an unpleasant response (such as a feeling of fear or disgust) to the object that produces the undesired behavior.

behavior rehearsal A technique in which the therapist demonstrates how to handle a particular kind of interaction with other people.

cingulectomy A technique of psychosurgery in which the cingulum bundle of the brain is cut.

cingulum bundle A small bundle of the nerve fibers that connects the prefrontal cortex with parts of the limbic system.

client-centered therapy Carl Rogers's therapeutic method of treating mental disorders and disturbances of adjustment by providing unconditional positive regard for the client, which permits the person's natural tendency to become healthy and productive to express itself.

cognitive behavior therapy A method for treating abnormal behavior and mental disorders; similar to behavior therapy but emphasizes unobservable cognitive processes as well as directly observable behaviors.

cognitive restructuring A process of rational-emotive therapy in which a person's faulty cognitions are changed.

countertransference The therapist's own feelings toward the client.

eclectic therapy An approach to psychotherapy that is not based on a single theory or method but which attempts to employ a variety of methods, depending on the nature of the client and the client's problems.

free association The method of psychoanalysis in which the client in encouraged to say whatever comes to his or her mind; presumably, the statements will express deep-seated anxieties and conflicts.

full acceptance In rational-emotive therapy, the desired state for the client, similar to unconditional positive regard.

ideal self A person's concept of a desired state which may differ from the real self.

insight psychotherapy A general approach to treating mental disorders in which the patient is helped to understand the causes of his or her maladaptive behaviors, especially those that occurred in the remote past; such understanding is presumed to lead to improvement.

in vivo method A form of behavior therapy in which the client's fear of an object or situation is desensitized by gradual exposure to that object or situation.

meta-analysis Statistical method for estimating the magnitude of experimental effects reported by published studies.

mirroring A technique of psychodrama in which one member of the group acts out a maladaptive pattern of behavior that is displayed by another member.

prefrontal lobotomy A surgical procedure that disconnects parts of the frontal lobe from the rest of the brain, with the intention of alleviating severe anxiety or severe, chronic pain; not currently employed.

psychoanalysis The first formal psychotherapeutic procedure in which a person's mind is analyzed.

psychodrama A form of structured group therapy in which the clients are asked to act out some of their problems by pretending to be members of the cast of a play.

rational-emotive therapy Developed by Albert Ellis, a cognitive behavior therapy that did not develop from behavior therapy, it seeks to cognitively restructure a person's belief system, not analyzing the client's past.

real self A person's self-concept, as opposed to the ideal self.

resistance A stage that a client goes through with his or her therapist indicating the approach of painful topics.

self-efficacy Belief in the ability to control one's own situation; an important feature of Bandura's method of cognitive behavior therapy.

self-talk A form of private behavior in which a person verbalizes each step of a desired behavior in order to accomplish a task.

structural family therapy Treatment in which counterproductive family relationships are restructured in more adaptive ways to insure the best environment for the individual client.

symptom substitution The hypothesis that if a maladaptive behavior is eliminated (for example, by contingent punishment or by reinforcement of competing behaviors), then the causes of the behavior will remain and will produce another maladaptive behavior.

systematic desensitization A technique of behavior therapy to eliminate some neurotic fears and phobias by removing the unpleasant emotional response produced by the feared object or situation and replacing it with a relaxation response.

tardive dyskinesia A serious movement disorder that can occur when a person has been treated with antipsychotic drugs for an extended period.

token economy A scheme within an institution whereby residents' adaptive behaviors are regularly reinforced, and maladaptive behaviors are punished or not reinforced; the typical medium of reinforcement consists of tokens that can be exchanged for desirable commodities or special privileges.

training analysis Part of a psychoanalyst's education that permits understanding of his or her own conflicts and motivations.

transference neurosis During psychoanalysis, a neurotic attachment that forms when the client transfers his or her feelings toward a dominant childhood figure—usually a parent—to the psychoanalyst.

unconditional positive regard According to Rogers, the nonjudgmental attitude that a therapist should express toward the client.

References

Abelson, R.P. Are attitudes necessary? In *Attitudes, Conflict, and Social Change*, edited by B.T. King and E. McGinnies. New York: Academic Press, 1972.

Adams, C.H., and Sherer, M. Sex role orientation and psychological adjustment: Comparison of MMPI profiles among college women and housewives. *Journal of Personality Assessment*, 1982, *46*, 607–613.

Adams, D.B., Gold, A.R., and Burt, A.D. Rise in female-initiated sexual activity at ovulation and its suppression by oral contraceptives. *New England Journal of Medicine*, 1978, *299*, 1145–1150.

Adams, G.R., and Huston, T.L. Social perception of middle-aged persons varying in physical attractiveness. *Developmental Psychology*, 1975, *11*, 657–658.

Aiken, L.R. *Psychological Testing and Assessment* (4th ed.). Boston: Allyn and Bacon, 1982.

Ainsworth, M.D.S. *Infancy in Uganda: Infant Care and the Growth of Love*. Baltimore: Johns Hopkins University Press, 1967.

Ainsworth, M.D.S. The development of infant-mother attachment. In *Review of Child Development Research* (vol. 3), edited by B.M. Caldwell and H.R. Ricciuti. Chicago: University of Chicago Press, 1973.

Allen, M.G. Twin studies of affective illness. *Archives of General Psychiatry*, 1976, *33*, 1476–1478.

Allison, T., and Chichetti, D. Sleep in mammals: Ecological and constitutional correlates. *Science*, 1976, *194*, 732–734.

Ammon, P.R., The perception of grammatical relations in sentences: A methodological exploration. *Journal of Verbal Learning and Verbal Behavior*, 1968, *7*, 869–875.

Amoore, J.E. *Molecular Basis of Odor*. Springfield, Ill.: Charles C Thomas, 1970.

Angrist, B.J., Rotrosen, J., and Gershon, S. Positive and negative symptoms in schizophrenia—differential response to amphetamine and neuroleptics. *Psychopharmacology*, 1980, *72*, 17–19.

Anonymous. An autobiography of a schizophrenic experience. *Journal of Abnormal and Social Psychology*, 1955, *51*, 677–689.

Anonymous. Effects of sexual activity on beard growth in man. *Nature*, 1970, *226*, 869–870.

Antill, J.K. Sex role complementarity versus similarity in married couples. *Journal of Personality and Social Psychology*, 1983, *45*, 145–155.

Appleton, T., Clifton, R., and Goldberg, S. The development of behavioral competence in infancy. In *Review of Child Development* (vol. 4), edited by F.D. Horowitz. Chicago: University of Chicago Press, 1975.

Arenberg, D. Cognition and aging: Verbal learning, memory, and problem solving. In *The Psychology of Adult Development and Aging*, edited by C. Eisdorfer and M.P. Lawton. Washington, D.C.: American Psychological Association, 1973.

Arkin, R.M., and Baumgardner, A.H. Self-presentation and self-evaluation: Processes of self-control and social control. In *Public Self and Private Self*, edited by R. Baumeister. New York: Springer-Verlag, 1986.

Arkin, R., Cooper, H., and Kolditz, T. A statistical review of the literature concerning the self-serving attribution bias in interpersonal influence situations. *Journal of Personality*, 1980, *48*, 435–448.

Aronson, E. Personal communication, 1975, cited by Nisbett, R.E., and Wilson, T.D. Telling more than we can know: Verbal reports on mental processes. *Psychological Review*, 1977, *84*, 231–259.

Aronson, E., and Mills, J. The effects of severity of initiation on liking for a group. *Journal of Abnormal and Social Psychology*, 1959, *59*, 177–181.

Asch, S.E. Effects of group pressure upon the modification and distortion of judgment. In *Groups, Leadership, and Men*, edited by H. Guetzkow. Pittsburgh: Carnegie, 1951.

Astrup, C., and Noreik, K. *Functional Psychoses: Diagnostic and Prognostic Models*. Springfield, Ill.: Charles C Thomas, 1966.

Ayllon, T., and Azrin, N.H. *The Token Economy: A Motivational System for Therapy and Rehabilitation*. Englewood Cliffs, N.J.: Prentice-Hall, 1968.

Azrin, N.H. Aggressive responses of paired animals. Paper presented at Symposium of the Walter Reed Institute of Research, Washington, D.C., April 1964.

Baddeley, A.D. A three-minute reasoning test based on grammatical transformation. *Psychonomic Science*, 1968, *10*, 341–342.

Baer, D.M., Peterson, R.F., and Sherman, J.A. Development of imitation by reinforcing behavioral similarity to a model. *Journal of the Experimental Analysis of Behavior*, 1967, *10*, 405–416.

Baker, B.L. Symptom treatment and symptom substitution in enuresis. *Journal of Abnormal Psychology*, 1969, *74*, 42–49.

Baldessarini, R.J. *Chemotherapy in Psychiatry*. Cambridge, Mass.: Harvard University Press, 1977.

Baldessarini, R.J., and Tarsy, D. Dopamine and the pathophysiology of dyskinesias induced by antipsychotic drugs. *Annual Review of Neuroscience*, 1980, *3*, 23–41.

Ball, K., and Sekuler, R. A specific and enduring improvement in visual motion discrimination. *Science*, 1982, *218*, 697–698.

Baltes, P., and Schaie, K. Aging and IQ: The myth of the twilight years. *Psychology Today*, October 1974, 35–38.

Bandura, A. *Principles of Behavior Modification*. New York: Holt, Rinehart and Winston, 1969.

Bandura, A. Psychotherapy based upon modeling

principles. In *Handbook of Psychotherapy and Behavior Change*, edited by A.E. Bergin and S.L. Garfield. New York: John Wiley & Sons, 1971.

Bandura, A. *Aggression: A Social Learning Analysis.* Englewood Cliffs, N.J.: Prentice-Hall, 1973.

Bandura, A. Self-efficacy: Toward a unifying theory of behavioral change. *Psychological Review,* 1977a, *84,* 191–215.

Bandura, A. *Social Learning Theory.* Englewood Cliffs, N.J.: Prentice-Hall, 1977b.

Bandura, A., and Mischel, W. Modification of self-imposed delay of reward through exposure to live and symbolic models. *Journal of Personality and Social Psychology,* 1965, *2,* 698–705.

Banks, M.S., Aslin, R.N., and Letson, R.D. Sensitive period for the development of human binocular vision. *Science,* 1975, *190,* 675–677.

Banks, W.P., and Barber, G. Color information in iconic memory. *Psychological Review,* 1977, *84,* 536–546.

Barber, T.X. *Hypnosis: A Scientific Approach.* New York: Van Nostrand Reinhold, 1969.

Barber, T.X. Responding to 'hypnotic' suggestions: An introspective report. *American Journal of Clinical Hypnosis,* 1975, *18,* 6–22.

Barber, T.X. Suggested ("hypnotic") behavior: The trance paradigm versus an alternative paradigm. In *Hypnosis: Developments in Research and New Perspectives,* edited by E. Fromm and R.E. Shor. Chicago: Aldine Press, 1979.

Barclay, C.D., Cutting, J.E., and Kozlowski, L.T. Temporal and spatial factors in gait perception that influence gender recognition. *Perception and Psychophysics,* 1978, *23,* 145–152.

Barlow, D.H., and Beck, J.G. The psychosocial treatment of anxiety disorders: Current status, future directions. In *Psychotherapy Research: Where Are We and Where Should We Go?* edited by J.B.W. Williams and R.L. Spitzer. New York: Guilford, 1984.

Barlow, D.H., and Wolfe, B.E. Behavioral approaches to anxiety disorders: A report on the NIMH-SUNY Albany research conference. *Journal of Consulting and Clinical Psychology,* 1981, *49,* 448–454.

Bartlett, F.C. *Remembering: An Experimental and Social Study.* Cambridge, England: Cambridge University Press, 1932.

Bassoff, E.S., and Glass, G.V. The relationship between sex roles and mental health: A meta-analysis of twenty-six studies. *Counseling Psychologist,* 1982, *10,* 105–112.

Beck, A.T. *Depression: Clinical, Experimental, and Theoretical Aspects.* New York: Harper & Row, 1967.

Beck, A.T. *Cognitive Therapy and the Emotional Disorders.* New York: International Universities Press, 1976.

Beckman, L. Effects of students' performance on teachers' and observers' attributions of causality. *Journal of Educational Psychology,* 1970, *61,* 75–82.

Bell, A.P., and Weinberg, M.S. *Homosexualities: A Study of Diversity among Men and Women.* New York: Simon & Schuster, 1978.

Bell, A.P., Weinberg, M.S., and Hammersmith, S.K. *Sexual Preference: Its Development in Men and Women.* Bloomington: Indiana University Press, 1981.

Bell, S.M., and Ainsworth, M.D. Infant crying and maternal responsiveness. *Child Development,* 1972, *43,* 1171–1190.

Bellugi, U., and Klima, E.S. The roots of language in the sign talk of the deaf. *Psychology Today,* June 1972, 61–76.

Bem, D.J. Self-perception theory. In *Advances in Experimental Social Psychology* (vol. 6), edited by L. Berkowitz. New York: Academic Press, 1972.

Bem, D., and Allen, A. On predicting some of the people some of the time: The search for cross-situational consistencies in behavior. *Psychological Review,* 1974, *81,* 506–520.

Bem, D.J., and Funder, D.C. Predicting more of the people more of the time: Assessing the personality of situations. *Psychological Review,* 1978, *85,* 485–501.

Bem, S.L. The measurement of psychological androgyny. *Journal of Consulting and Clinical Psychology,* 1974, *42,* 155–162.

Bem, S.L. On the utility of alternative procedures for assessing psychological androgyny. *Journal of Consulting and Clinical Psychology,* 1977, *45,* 196–205.

Bem, S.L. Gender schema theory: A cognitive account of sex typing. *Psychological Review,* 1981, *88,* 354–364.

Bem, S.L. Androgyny and gender schema theory: A conceptual and empirical investigation. *Nebraska Symposium on Motivation,* 1985, *32,* 179–226.

Benton, C., Hernandez, A., Schmidt, A., Schmitz, M., Stone, A., & Weiner, B. Is hostility linked with affiliation among males and with achievement among females? A critique of Pollak and Gilligan. *Journal of Personality and Social Psychology,* 1983, *45,* 1167–1171.

Berger, S.M. Conditioning through vicarious instigation. *Psychological Review,* 1962, *69,* 450–466.

Berkman, L.F., and Syme, S.L. Social networks, host resistance, and morality: A nine-year follow-up study of Almeda County residents. *American Journal of Epidemiology,* 1979, *109,* 186–204.

Berkowitz, L. Whatever happened to the frustration-aggression hypothesis? *American Behavioral Scientist,* 1978, *21,* 691–708.

Berkowitz, L., and Frodi, A. Stimulus characteristics that can enhance or decrease aggression. *Aggressive Behavior,* 1977, *3,* 1–15.

Berlyne, D.E. Motivational problems raised by exploratory and epistemic behavior. In *Psychology: A Study of a Science* (vol. 5), edited by S. Koch. New York: McGraw-Hill, 1966.

Bermant, G., and Davidson, J.M. *Biological Bases of Sexual Behavior.* New York: Harper & Row, 1974.

Bernstein, I. Learned taste aversion in children receiving chemotherapy. *Science,* 1978, *200,* 1302–1303.

Berscheid, E., Dion, K., Walster, E., and Walster, G.W. Physical attractiveness and dating choice: A test of the matching hypothesis. *Journal of Experi-*

mental *Social Psychology*, 1971, *7*, 173–189.

Bieber, I., Dain, H.J., Dince, P.R., Drellich, M.G., Grand, H.G., Gundlach, R.H., Kremer, M.W., Rifkin, A.H., Wilbur, C.B., and Bieber, T.B. *Homosexuality: A Psychoanalytic Study*. New York: Basic Books, 1962.

Binet, A., and Henri, V. La psychologie individuelle. *Année Psychologique*, 1896, *2*, 411–465.

Birren, J.E., and Morrison, D.F. Analysis of the WISC subtests in relation to age and education. *Journal of Gerontology*, 1961, *16*, 363–369.

Bleuler, E. *Dementia Praecox or the Group of Schizophrenias*. New York: International University Press, 1911/1950.

Bloom, L. *Language Development: Form and Function in Emerging Grammars*. Cambridge, Mass.: MIT Press, 1970.

Boisen, A.T. *Out of the Depths*. New York: Harper & Row, 1960.

Bolles, R.C. Species-specific defense reactions and avoidance learning. *Psychological Review*, 1970, *77*, 32–48.

Bookmiller, M.N., and Bowen, G.L. *Textbook of Obstetrics and Obstetric Nursing* (5th ed.). Philadelphia: W.B. Saunders, 1967.

Booth, D.A., Mather, P., and Fuller, J. Starch content of ordinary foods associatively conditions human appetite and satiation, indexed by intake and eating pleasantness of starch-paired flavours. *Appetite*, 1982, *3*, 163–184.

Botwinick, J., and Storandt, M. *Memory, Related Functions and Age*. Springfield, Ill.: Charles C Thomas, 1974.

Bower, G.H., and Clark, M.C. Narrative stories as mediators for serial learning. *Psychonomic Science*, 1969, *14*, 181–182.

Boynton, R.M. *Human Color Vision*. New York: Holt, Rinehart and Winston, 1979.

Brady, J.P., and Lind, D.L. Experimental analysis of hysterical blindness. *Archives of General Psychiatry*, 1961, *4*, 331–359.

Brandsma, J.M., Maultsby, M.C., and Welsh, R. *Self-help Techniques in the Treatment of Alcoholism*. Unpublished manuscript cited by Wilson, G.T., and O'Leary, K.D. *Principles of Behavior Therapy*. Englewood Cliffs, N.J.: Prentice-Hall, 1978.

Braver, S.L., Linder, D.E., Corwin, T.T., and Cialdini, R.B. Some conditions that affect admissions of attitude change. *Journal of Experimental Social Psychology*, 1977, *13*, 565–576.

Brehm, S.S., and Brehm, J.W. *Psychological Reactance: A Theory of Freedom and Control*. New York: Academic Press, 1981.

Brehm, S.S., and Weintraub, M. Physical barriers and psychological reactance: 2-year-old's responses to threats to freedom. *Journal of Personality and Social Psychology*, 1977, *35*, 830–836.

Breland, K., and Breland, M. The misbehavior of organisms. *American Psychologist*, 1961, *16*, 661–664.

Broca, P. Remarques sur le siège de la faculté du langage articulé, suivies d'une observation d'aphémie (perte de la parole). *Bulletin de la Société Anatomique* (Paris), 1861, *36*, 330–357.

Brown, R. *A First Language: The Early Stages*. Cambridge, Mass.: Harvard University Press, 1973.

Brown, R., and Bellugi, U. Three processes in the child's acquisition of syntax. *Harvard Education Review*, 1964, *34*, 133–151.

Brown, R., Cazden, C., and Bellugi, U. The child's grammar from I to III. In *The 1967 Minnesota Symposium on Child Psychology*, edited by J.P. Hill. Minneapolis: University of Minnesota Press, 1969.

Brown, R., and Fraser, C. The acquisition of syntax. *Monographs of the Society for Research in Child Development*, 1964, *29*, 43–79.

Brown, P.L., and Jenkins, H.M. Autoshaping of the pigeon's key-peck. *Journal of the Experimental Analysis of Behavior*, 1968, *11*, 1–8.

Broxton, J.A. A test of interpersonal attraction predictions derived from balance theory. *Journal of Abnormal and Social Psychology*, 1963, *66*, 394–397.

Buck, R.W. Nonverbal communication of affect in children. *Journal of Personality and Social Psychology*, 1975, *31*, 644–653.

Buck, R.W. Nonverbal communication accuracy in preschool children: Relationships with personality and skin conductance. *Journal of Personality and Social Psychology*, 1977, *33*, 225–236.

Burt, C. The concept of consciousness. *British Journal of Psychology*, 1962, *53*, 229–242.

Buss, A.H. Social rewards and personality. *Journal of Personality and Social Psychology*, 1983, *44*, 553–563.

Byrne, D., and Nelson, D. Attraction as a linear function of proportion of positive reinforcements. *Journal of Personality and Social Psychology*, 1965, *1*, 659–663.

Byrne, D., and Rhamey, R. Magnitude of positive and negative reinforcements as a determinant of attraction. *Journal of Personality and Social Psychology*, 1965, *2*, 884–889.

Cadoret, R.J. Psychopathology in adopted-away offspring of biologic parents with antisocial behavior. *Archives of General Psychiatry*, 1978, *35*, 176–184.

Campbell, R., and Dodd, B. Hearing by eye. *Quarterly Journal of Experimental Psychology*, 1980, *32*, 85–99.

Campos, J.J., Langer, A., and Krowitz, A. Cardiac responses on the visual cliff in prelocomotor human infants. *Science*, 1970, *170*, 196–197.

Canestrari, R.B. The effects of commonality on paired associate learning in two age groups. *Journal of Genetic Psychology*, 1966, *108*, 3–7.

Cannon, W.B. The James-Lange theory of emotions: A critical examination and an alternative. *American Journal of Psychology*, 1927, *39*, 106–124.

Cannon, W.B., and Washburn, A.L. An explanation of hunger. *American Journal of Physiology*, 1912, *29*, 444–454.

Carlsmith, J.M., and Gross, A.E. Some effects of guilt on compliance. *Journal of Personality and Social Psychology*, 1969, *11*, 240–244.

Carpenter, P.A., and Just, M.A. Sentence comprehension: A psychologistic processing model of verification. *Psychological Review*, 1975, *82*, 45–73.

Cassel, J. The relation of the urban environment to health: Implications for prevention. *Mount Sinai Journal of Medicine*, 1973, *40*, 539–550.

Catania, A.C., and Sagvolden, T. Preference for free choice over forced choice in pigeons. *Journal of the Experimental Analysis of Behavior*, 1980, *34*, 77–86.

Cattell, R.B. *Description and Measurement of Personality*. New York: World Books, 1946.

Cattell, R.B. *Abilities: Their Structure, Growth, and Action*. Boston: Houghton Mifflin, 1971.

Cavanaugh, J.R., and McGoldrick, J.B. *Fundamental Psychiatry*. Milwaukee: Brice, 1966.

Center for Disease Control. *Ten Leading Causes of Death in the United States, 1977*. Washington, D.C.: Government Printing Office, 1980.

Chapin, F.S. *Experimental Designs in Sociological Research*. New York: Harper, 1947.

Cheek, J.M., and Buss, A.H. Shyness and sociability. *Journal of Personality and Social Psychology*, 1981, *41*, 330–339.

Chen, J.S., and Amsel, A. Learned persistence at 11–12 days but not at 10–11 days in infant rats. *Developmental Psychobiology*, 1980a, *13*, 481–492.

Chen, J.S., and Amsel, A. Retention under changed-reward conditions of persistence learned by infant rats. *Developmental Psychobiology*, 1980b, *13*, 469–480.

Cherry, E.C. Some experiments on the recognition of speech, with one and with two ears. *Journal of the Acoustical Society of America*, 1953, *25*, 975–979.

Chiesi, H.L., Spilich, G.J., and Voss, J.F. Acquisition of domain-related information in relation to high and low domain knowledge. *Journal of Verbal Learning and Verbal Behavior*, 1979, *18*, 257–273.

Chomsky, N. *Syntactic Structure*. The Hague: Mouton Publishers, 1957.

Chomsky, N. *Aspects of the Theory of Syntax*. Cambridge, Mass.: MIT Press, 1965.

Christiansen, K.O. Crime in a Danish twin population. *Acta Geneticae Medicae et Gemellologiae*, 1970, *19*, 323–326.

Cialdini, R.B. *Influence: How and Why People Agree to Things*. New York: William Morrow, 1984.

Cialdini, R.B., and Ascani, K. Test of a concession procedure for inducing verbal, behavioral, and further compliance with a request to give blood. *Journal of Applied Psychology*, 1976, *61*, 295–300.

Cialdini, R.B., Borden, R.J., Thorne, A., Walker, M.R., Freeman, S., and Sloan, L.R. Basking in reflected glory: Three (football) field studies. *Journal of Personality and Social Psychology*, 1976, *34*, 366–375.

Cialdini, R.B., Braver, S.L., and Lewis, S.K. Attributional bias and the easily persuaded others. *Journal of Personality and Social Psychology*, 1974, *30*, 613–637.

Cialdini, R.B., and Mirels, H. Sense of personal control and attributions about yielding and resisting persuasion targets. *Journal of Personality and Social Psychology*, 1976, *33*, 395–402.

Clark, H.H., and Haviland, S.E. Comprehension and the given-new contract. In *Discourse Production and Comprehension*, edited by R.O. Freedle. Norwood, N.J.: Ablex Publishing, 1977.

Clark, K.B. *Dark Ghetto. Dilemmas of Social Power*. New York: Harper & Row, 1965.

Clark, R.D., and Word, L.E. Where is the apathetic bystander? Situational characteristics of the emergency. *Journal of Personality and Social Psychology*, 1974, *29*, 279–287.

Cleckley, H. *The Mask of Sanity*. St. Louis: C.V. Mosby, 1976.

Clemens, L.G. Influence of prenatal litter composition on mounting behavior of female rats. *American Zoologist*, 1971, *11*, 617–618.

Cloninger, C.R., and Guze, S.B. Psychiatric illness in the families of female criminals: A study of 288 first-degree relatives. *British Journal of Psychiatry*, 1973, *122*, 697–703.

Cohen, M., and Davis, N. *Medication Errors: Causes and Prevention*. Philadelphia: G.F. Stickley, 1981.

Coleman, J.C. *Abnormal Psychology and Modern Life* (5th ed.). Glenview, Ill.: Scott, Foresman, 1976.

Condry, J.C., and Ross, D.F. Sex and aggression: The influence of gender label on the perception of aggression in children. *Child Development*, 1985, *56*, 225–233.

Conner, R.L., and Levine, S. Hormonal influences on aggressive behaviour. In *Aggressive Behaviour*, edited by S. Garattine and E.B. Sigg. New York: John Wiley & Sons, 1969.

Conrad, R. Acoustic confusions in immediate memory. *British Journal of Psychology*, 1964, *55*, 75–83.

Cook, E.P. *Psychological Adjustment*. Elmsford, NY: Pergamon Press, 1985.

Cooper, J., Zanna, M.P., and Taves, P.A. Arousal as a necessary condition for attitude change following induced compliance. *Journal of Personality and Social Psychology*, 1978, *36*, 1101–1106.

Cooper, R.M., and Zubek, J.P. Effects of enriched and restricted early environments on the learning ability of bright and dull rats. *Canadian Journal of Psychology*, 1958, *12*, 159–164.

Corkin, S., Sullivan, E.V., Twitchell, T.E., and Grove, E. The amnesic patient H.M.: Clinical observations and test performance 28 years after operation. *Society for Neuroscience Abstracts*, 1981, *7*, 235.

Coryell, W. A blind family history study of Briquet's syndrome. Further validation of the diagnosis. *Archives of General Psychiatry*, 1980, *37*, 1266–1269.

Cottrell, N.B., Wack, D.L., Sekerak, G.J., and Rittle, R.H. Social facilitation of dominant responses by the presence of an audience and the mere presence of others. *Journal of Personality and Social Psychology*, 1968, *9*, 245–250.

Cowart, J., and Whaley, D. Punishment of self-mutilation behavior. Unpublished manuscript cited by Whaley, D.L., and Malott, R.W. *Elementary Principles of Behavior*. New York: Appleton-Century-Crofts, 1971.

Craik, F.I.M., and Lockhart, R.S. Levels of processing: A framework for memory research. *Journal of Verbal Learning and Verbal Behavior,* 1972, *11,* 671–684.

Craik, F.I.M., and Tulving, E. Depth of processing and the retention of words in episodic memory. *Journal of Experimental Psychology: General,* 1975, *104,* 268–294.

Cromer, R. The development of temporal reference during the acquisition of language. Ph.D. dissertation, Harvard University, 1968.

Cromwell, R.J., Butterfield, E.C., Brayfield, F.M., and Curry, J.C. *Acute Myocardial Infarction: Reaction and Recovery.* St. Louis: Mosby, 1977.

Crow, T.J. Molecular pathology of schizophrenia: More than one disease process? *British Medical Journal,* 1980, *280,* 66–68.

Crow, T.J., Cross, A.G., Johnstone, E.C., and Owen, F. Two syndromes in schizophrenia and their pathogenesis. In *Schizophrenia As a Brain Disease,* edited by F.A. Henn and G.A. Nasrallah. New York: Oxford University Press, 1982.

Crowe, R.R., Pauls, D.L., Slymen, D.J., and Noyes, R. A family study of anxiety neurosis. *Archives of General Psychiatry,* 1980, *37,* 77–79.

Croyle, R.T., and Cooper, J. Dissonance arousal: Physiological evidence. *Journal of Personality and Social Psychology,* 1983, *45,* 782–791.

Dale, P.S. *Language Development: Structure and Function* (2nd ed.). New York: Holt, Rinehart and Winston, 1976.

Daneman, M., and Carpenter, P.A. Individual differences in working memory and reading. *Journal of Verbal Learning and Verbal Behavior,* 1980, *19,* 450–466.

Daniels, D., and Plomin, R. Origins of individual differences in infant shyness. *Developmental Psychology,* 1985, *21,* 118–121.

Darley, J.M., and Latané, B. Bystander intervention in emergencies: Diffusion of responsibility. *Journal of Personality and Social Psychology,* 1968, *8,* 377–383.

Darwin, C. *The Expression of the Emotions in Man and Animals.* Chicago: University of Chicago Press, 1872/1965.

Darwin, C.J., Turvey, M.T., and Crowder, R.G. An auditory analogue of the Sperling partial report procedure: Evidence for brief auditory storage. *Cognitive Psychology,* 1972, *3,* 255–267.

Dashiell, J.F. Experimental studies of the influence of social situations on the behavior of individual human adults. In *A Handbook of Social Psychology,* edited by C. Murcheson. Worcester, Mass.: Clark University Press, 1935.

Datan, N., Rodeheaver, D., and Hughes, F. Adult development and aging. *Annual Review of Psychology,* 1987, *38,* 153–180.

Davidson, J.M., Camargo, C.A., and Smith, E.R. Effects of androgen on sexual behavior in hypogonadal men. *Journal of Clinical Endocrinology and Metabolism,* 1979, *48,* 955–958.

Davis, J.D., and Campbell, C.S. Peripheral control of meal size in the rat: Effect of sham feeding on meal size and drinking rats. *Journal of Comparative and Physiological Psychology,* 1973, *83,* 379–387.

Davis, J.M. A two-factor theory of schizophrenia. *Journal of Psychiatric Research,* 1974, *11,* 25–30.

Davison, G.C., and Neale, J.M. *Abnormal Psychology: An Experimental Clinical Approach.* New York: John Wiley & Sons, 1974.

Davison, G.C., and Neale, J.M. *Abnormal Psychology: An Experimental Clinical Approach* (3rd ed.). New York: John Wiley & Sons, 1982.

Day, R.S. Fusion in dichotic listening. Unpublished doctoral dissertation, Stanford University, 1968.

Day, R.S. Temporal order judgments in speech: Are individuals language-bound or stimulus-bound? *Haskins Laboratories Status Report,* 1970, *SR-21/22,* 71–87.

Deci, E.L. Effects of externally mediated rewards on intrinsic motivation. *Journal of Personality and Social Psychology,* 1971, *18,* 105–115.

Deci, E.L. *Intrinsic Motivation.* New York: Plenum Press, 1975.

deGroot, A.D. *Thought and Choice in Chess.* The Hague: Mouton Publishers, 1965.

Dekaban, A. *Neurology of Early Childhood.* Baltimore: Williams & Wilkins, 1970.

de Lacoste-Utamsing, C., and Holloway, R.L. Sexual dimorphism in the human corpus callosum. *Science,* 1982, *216,* 1431–1432.

Dement, W.C. *Some Must Watch While Some Must Sleep.* San Francisco: W.H. Freeman, 1974.

Dennis, W. Causes of retardation among institutional children: Iran. *Journal of Genetic Psychology,* 1960, *96,* 47–59.

Deutsch, J.A., Young, W.G., and Kalogeris, T.J. The stomach signals satiety. *Science,* 1978, *201,* 165–167.

deVilliers, P.A. Imagery and theme in recall of connected discourse. *Journal of Experimental Psychology,* 1974, *103,* 263–268.

deVilliers, J.G., and deVilliers, P.A. *Language Acquisition.* Cambridge, Mass.: Harvard University Press, 1978.

Diamond, M. Sexual identity, monozygotic twins reared in discordant sex roles and a BBC follow-up. *Archives of Sexual Behavior,* 1982, *11,* 181–186.

DiMascio, A., Weissman, M.M., Prusoff, B.A., Neu, C., Zwilling, M., and Klerman, G.L. Differential symptom reduction by drugs and psychotherapy in acute depression. *Archives of General Psychiatry,* 1979, *36,* 1450–1456.

Dimond, S.J., and Farrington, L. Emotional response to films shown to the right or left hemisphere of the brain measured by heart rate. *Acta Psychologica,* 1977, *41,* 255–260.

Dimond, S.J., Farrington, L., and Johnson, P. Differing emotional response from right and left hemispheres. *Nature,* 1976, *201,* 690–692.

Dion, K., Berscheid, E., and Walster, E. What is beautiful is good. *Journal of Personality and Social Psychology,* 1972, *24,* 285–290.

Dollard, J., Doob, L., Miller, N., Mowrer, O., and Sears, R. *Frustration and Aggression.* New Haven, Conn.: Yale University Press, 1939.

Donahoe, J.W., Crowley, M.A., Millard, W.J., and Stickney, K.A. A unified principle of reinforcement: Some implications for matching. In *Quantitative Analyses of Behavior: 2. Matching and Maximizing Accounts*, edited by M.L. Commons, R.J. Herrnstein, and H. Rachlin. New York: Ballinger, 1982.

Drabman, R.S., Spitalnik, R., and O'Leary, K.D. Teaching self-control to disruptive children. *Journal of Abnormal Psychology*, 1973, *82*, 10–16.

Drucker-Colín, R.R., and Spanis, C.W. Is there a sleep transmitter? *Progress in Neurobiology*, 1976, *6*, 1–22.

Dutton, D.G., and Aron, A.P. Some evidence for heightened sexual attraction under conditions of high anxiety. *Journal of Personality and Social Psychology*, 1974, *30*, 510–517.

D'Zurilla, T. Recall efficiency and mediating cognitive events in "experimental repression." *Journal of Personality and Social Psychology*, 1965, *1*, 253–257.

Eagly, A.H., and Himmelfarb, S. Attitudes and opinions. *Annual Review of Psychology*, 1978, *29*, 517–554.

Ebel, R.L. The social consequences of educational testing. In *Testing Problems in Perspective*, edited by A. Anastasi. Washington, D.C.: American Council on Education, 1966.

Efran, M.G., and Patterson, E.W.J. The politics of appearance. Unpublished manuscript, 1976, cited by Cialdini, R.B. *Influence: How and Why People Agree to Things*. New York: William Morrow, 1984.

Eibl-Eibesfeld, I. *The Biology of Peace and War*. New York: Viking Press, 1980.

Eimas, P.D., Siqueland, E.R., Jusczyk, P., and Vigorito, J. Speech perception in infants. *Science*, 1971, *171*, 303–306.

Einstein, G.O., and Hunt, R.R. Levels of processing and organization: Additive effects of individual-item and relational processing. *Journal of Experimental Psychology: Human Learning and Memory*, 1980, *6*, 588–598.

Ekman, P. *Darwin and Facial Expression: A Century of Research in Review*. New York: Academic Press, 1973.

Ekman, P. *The Face of Man: Expressions of Universal Emotions in a New Guinea Village*. New York: Garland STPM Press, 1980.

Ekman, P., and Friesen, W.V. Nonverbal leakage and clues to deception. *Psychiatry*, 1969, *32*, 88–105.

Ekman, P., and Friesen, W.V. Constants across cultures in the face and emotion. *Journal of Personality and Social Psychology*, 1971, *17*, 124–129.

Ekman, P., and Friesen, W.V. Detecting deception from body or face. *Journal of Personality and Social Psychology*, 1974, *29*, 288–298.

Ekman, P., and Friesen, W.V. *Unmasking the Face*. Englewood Cliffs, N.J.: Prentice-Hall, 1975.

Ekman, P., Friesen, W.V., and Ellsworth, P. *Emotion in the Human Face: Guidelines for Research and a Review of Findings*. New York: Pergamon Press, 1972.

Ekman, P., Levenson, R.W., and Friesen, W.V. Auto-

nomic nervous system activity distinguished between emotions. *Science*, 1983, *211*, 1208–1210.

Ellenberger, H.F. The story of "Anna O": A critical review with new data. *Journal of the History of the Behavioral Sciences*, 1972, *8*, 267–279.

Ellis, A. Rational-emotive therapy. In *Current Psychotherapies* (2nd ed.), edited by R.J. Corsini. Itasca, Ill.: Peacock, 1979.

Emmelkamp, P.M.G., Kuipers, A.C.M., and Eggeraat, J.B. Cognitive modification versus prolonged exposure *in vivo*: A comparison with agoraphobics as subjects. *Behaviour Research and Therapy*, 1978, *16*, 33–42.

Epstein, S. Traits are alive and well. In *Personality at the Crossroads: Current Issues in Interactional Psychology*, edited by D. Magnusson and N.S. Endler. Hillsdale, N.J.: Lawrence Erlbaum Associates, 1977.

Eriksen, C.W., and Collins, J.F. Some temporal characteristics of visual pattern perception. *Journal of Experimental Psychology*, 1967, *74*, 476–484.

Evans, R.B. Childhood parental relationships of homosexual men. *Journal of Consulting and Clinical Psychology*, 1969, *33*, 129–135.

Eysenck, H.J. The effects of psychotherapy: An evaluation. *Journal of Consulting Psychology*, 1952, *16*, 319–324.

Eysenck, H.J. *Personality, Genetics, and Behavior*. New York: Praeger, 1982.

Eysenck, H.J., and Rachman, S. *The Causes and Cures of Neurosis: An Introduction to Modern Behavior Therapy Based on Learning Theory and the Principles of Conditioning*. San Diego: Knapp, 1965.

Fantz, R.L. The origin of form-perception. *Scientific American*, 1961, *204*, 66–72.

Feldman, R.D. *Whatever Happened to the Quiz Kids?* Chicago: Chicago Review Press, 1982.

Feshbach, S., and Singer, R.D. *Television and Aggression*. San Francisco: Jossey-Bass, 1971.

Festinger, L. *A theory of cognitive dissonance*. Stanford: Stanford University Press, 1957.

Festinger, L., and Carlsmith, J.M. Cognitive consequences of forced compliance. *Journal of Abnormal and Social Psychology*, 1959, *58*, 203–210.

Field, T. Individual differences in the expressivity of neonates and young infants. In *Development of Nonverbal Behavior in Children*, edited by R.S. Feldman. New York: Springer-Verlag, 1982.

Field, T., Woodson, R., Greenberg, R., and Cohen, D. Discrimination and imitation of facial expressions in neonates. *Science*, 1982, *218*, 179–181.

Fillenbaum, S. Pragmatic normalization: Further results for some conjunctive and disjunctive sentences. *Journal of Experimental Psychology*, 1974a, *102*, 574–578.

Fillenbaum, S. Or: Some uses. *Journal of Experimental Psychology*, 1974b, *103*, 913–921.

Fink, M. Presidential address: Brain function, verbal behavior, and psychotherapy. In *Evaluation of Psychological Therapies: Psychotherapies, Behavior Therapies, Drug Therapies, and Their Interactions*, edited by R.L. Spitzer and D.F. Klein. Baltimore: Johns Hopkins University Press, 1976.

Fix, A.J., and Haffke, E.A. *Basic Psychological Therapies: Comparative Effectiveness.* New York: Human Sciences Press, 1976.

Fodor, J.A., and Garrett, M.F. Some syntactic determinants of sentential complexity. *Perception and Psychophysics,* 1967, *2,* 289–296.

Foley, V.D. Family therapy. In *Current Psychotherapies* (2nd ed.), edited by R.J. Corsini. Itasca, Ill.: Peacock, 1979.

Ford, D.H., and Urban, H.B. *Systems of Psychotherapy: A Comparative Study.* New York: John Wiley & Sons, 1963.

Fouts, R.S. Chimpanzee language and elephant tails: A theoretical synthesis. In *Language in Primates: Perspectives and Implications,* edited by J. de Luce and H.T. Wilder. New York: Springer-Verlag, 1983.

Fouts, R.S., Hirsch, A., and Fouts, D. Cultural transmission of a human language in a chimpanzee mother/infant relationship. In *Psychological Perspectives: Child Nurturance Series* (vol. III), edited by H.E. Fitzgerald, J.A. Mullins, and P. Page. New York: Plenum Press, 1983.

Frandsen, A.N., and Holder, J.R. Spatial visualization in solving complex verbal problems. *Journal of Psychology,* 1969, *73,* 229–233.

Freedman, J.L., and Fraser, S.C. Compliance without pressure: The foot-in-the-door technique. *Journal of Personality and Social Psychology,* 1966, *4,* 195–203.

Freud, S. Some psychological consequences of the anatomical distinction between the sexes. In *Collected Papers of Sigmund Freud* (vol. 5), edited by E. Jones. New York: Basic Books, 1959. (Originally published 1925.)

Freud, S. The passing of the Oedipus complex. In *Collected Papers of Sigmund Freud* (vol. 5), edited by E. Jones. New York: Basic Books, 1959. (Originally published 1924.)

Friedman, M., and Rosenman, R.H. Association of specific overt behavior patterns with blood and cardiovascular findings—blood cholesterol level, blood clotting time, incidence of arcus senilis, and clinical coronary artery disease. *Journal of the American Medical Association,* 1959, *162,* 1286–1296.

Friesen, W.V. Cultural differences in facial expression in a social situation: An experimental test of the concept of display rules. Unpublished doctoral dissertation, University of California, San Francisco, 1972.

Fromkin, V. *Speech Errors As Linguistic Evidence.* The Hague: Mouton Publishers, 1973.

Fromm, E. *Escape from Freedom,* New York: Holt, Rinehart and Winston, 1941.

Fuhrman, W., Rahe, D.F., and Hartup, W.W. Rehabilitation of socially withdrawn preschool children through mixed-age and same-age socialization. *Child Development,* 1979, *50,* 915–922.

Fuller, R.G.C., and Sheehy-Skeffington, A. Effects of group laughter on responses to humorous materials: A replication and extension. *Psychological Reports,* 1974, *35,* 531–534.

Galaburda, A., and Kemper, T.L. Observations cited by Geschwind, N. Specializations of the human brain. *Scientific American,* 1979, *241,* 180–199.

Garcia, J., and Koelling, R.A. The relation of cue to consequence in avoidance learning. *Psychonomic Science,* 1966, *4,* 123–124.

Gardiner, J.M., Craik, F.I.M., and Birtwistle, J. Retrieval cues and release from proactive inhibition. *Journal of Verbal Learning and Verbal Behavior,* 1972, *11,* 778–783.

Gardner, D.B., Hawkes, G.R., and Burchinal, L.B. Noncontinuous mothering in infancy and development in later childhood. *Child Development,* 1961, *32,* 225–234.

Gardner, H. *Frames of Mind.* New York: Basic Books, 1983.

Gardner, P., and Oei, T.P. Depression and self-esteem: An investigation that used behavioral and cognitive approaches to the treatment of clinically depressed clients. *Journal of Clinical Psychology,* 1981, *37,* 128–135.

Gardner, R.A., and Gardner, B.T. Teaching sign language to a chimpanzee. *Science,* 1969, *165,* 664–672.

Gardner, R.A., and Gardner, B.T. Early signs of language in child and chimpanzee. *Science,* 1975, *187,* 752–753.

Gardner, R.A., and Gardner, B.T. Comparative psychology and language acquisition. *Annals of the New York Academy of Sciences,* 1978, *309,* 37–76.

Garrity, L.I. Electromyography: A review of the current status of subvocal speech research. *Memory and Cognition,* 1977, *5,* 615–622.

Gazzaniga, M.S. *The Bisected Brain.* New York: Appleton-Century-Crofts, 1970.

Gazzaniga, M.S., and LeDoux, J.E. *The Integrated Mind.* New York: Plenum Press, 1978.

Geen, R.G., Stonner, D., and Shope, G.L. The facilitation of aggression by aggression: A study in response inhibition and disinhibition. *Journal of Personality and Social Psychology,* 1975, *31,* 721–726.

Geller, D.M., Goodstein, L., Silver, M., and Sternberg, W.C. On being ignored: The effects of the violation of implicit rules of social interaction. *Sociometry,* 1974, *37,* 541–556.

Gelman, R. Logical capacity of very young children: Number invariance rules. *Child Development,* 1972, *43,* 75–90.

Gerbino, L., Oleshansky, M., and Gershon, S. Clinical use and mode of action of lithium. In *Psychopharmacology: A Generation of Progress,* edited by M.A. Lipton, A. DiMascio, and K.F. Killam. New York: Raven Press, 1978.

Geschwind, N., Quadfasel, F.A., and Segarra, J.M. Isolation of the speech area. *Neuropsychologia,* 1968, *6,* 327–340.

Gibson, E.J., and Walk, R.R. The "visual cliff." *Scientific American,* 1960, *202,* 2–9.

Gilligan, C. *In a different voice: Psychological theory and women's development.* Cambridge, Mass. Harvard University Press, 1982.

Gladwin, T. *East is a Big Bird.* Cambridge, Mass.: Harvard University Press, 1970.

Glanzer, M., and Cunitz, A.R. Two storage mechanisms in free recall. *Journal of Verbal Learning and Verbal Behavior*, 1966, *5*, 351–360.

Glass, G.V., McGaw, B., and Smith, M.L. *Meta-analysis in Social Research*. Beverly Hills, Calif.: Sage Publications, 1981.

Glickman, S. E., and Schiff, B.B. A biological theory of reinforcement. *Psychological Review*, 1967, *74*, 81–109.

Goldblatt, P.B., Moore, M.E., and Stunkard, A.J. Social factors in obesity. *Journal of the American Medical Association*, 1968, *21*, 1455–1470.

Goldfarb, W. Emotional and intellectual consequences of psychological deprivation in infancy: A reevaluation. In *Psychopathology of Childhood*, edited by P.H. Hoch and J. Zubin. New York: Grune & Stratton, 1955.

Goldin-Meadow, S., and Feldman, H. The development of language-like communication without a language model. *Science*, 1977, *197*, 401–403.

Goldsmith, H.H., and Gottesman, I.I. Origins of variation in behavioral style: A longitudinal study of temperament in young twins. *Child Development*, 1981, *52*, 91–103.

Gomes-Schwartz, B., Hadley, S.W., and Strupp, H.H. Individual psychotherapy and behavior therapy. *Annual Review of Psychology*, 1978, *29*, 435–471.

Goodglass, H. Agrammatism. In *Studies in Neurolinguistics*, edited by H. Whitaker and H.A. Whitaker. New York: Academic Press, 1976.

Goodwin, D.W. *Phobias: The Facts*. London: Oxford University Press, 1983.

Goodwin, D.W., and Guze, S.B. *Psychiatric Diagnosis* (3rd ed.). New York: Oxford University Press, 1984.

Goodwin, F.K., Wirz-Justice, A., and Wehr, T.A., Evidence that the pathophysiology of depression and the mechanisms of action of antidepressant drugs both involve alterations in circadian rhythms. In *Typical and Atypical Antidepressants: Clinical Practice*, edited by E. Costa and G. Racagni. New York: Raven Press, 1982.

Gould, R.L. *Transformations*. New York: Simon and Schuster, 1978.

Goy, R.W., and Goldfoot, D.A. Hormonal influences on sexually dimorhic behavior. In *Handbook of Physiology* (section 7, vol. 2, part I), edited by R.O. Green. Washington, D.C.: American Physiological Society, 1973.

Goy, R.W., and McEwen, B.S. *Sexual Differentiation of the Brain*. Cambridge, Mass.: MIT Press, 1980.

Granick, S. Comparative analysis of psychotic depressives with matched normals on some untimed verbal intelligence tests. *Journal of Consulting Psychology*, 1963, *27*, 439–443.

Granville-Grossman, K.L., and Turner, P. The effect of propranolol on anxiety. *Lancet*, 1966, *1*, 788–790.

Graves, A.J. Attainment of conservation of mass, weight and volume in minimally educated adults. *Developmental Psychology*, 1972, *7*, 223.

Greenberg, R., Pillard, R., and Pearlman, C. The effect of dream (stage REM) deprivation on adaptation to stress. *Psychosomatic Medicine*, 1972, *34*, 257–262.

Gregory, W.L. Locus of control for positive and negative outcomes. *Journal of Personality and Social Psychology*, 1978, *36*, 840–849.

Griffith, J.D., Cavanaugh, J., Held, N.N., and Oates, J.A. Dextroamphetamine: Evaluation of psychotomimetic properties in man. *Archives of General Psychiatry*, 1972, *26*, 97–100.

Griffiths, M., and Payne, P.R. Energy expenditure in small children of obese and non-obese mothers. *Nature*, 1976, *260*, 698–700.

Gross, C.G., Rocha-Miranda, C.E., and Bender, D.B. Visual properties of neurons in inferotemporal cortex of the macaque. *Journal of Neurophysiology*, 1972, *35*, 96–111.

Grove, W.M., Andreasen, N.C., McDonald-Scott, P., Keller, M.B., and Shapiro, R.W. Reliability studies of psychiatric diagnosis. *Archives of General Psychiatry*, 1981, *38*, 408–413.

Gur, R.C., and Sackheim, H.A. Self-deception: A concept in search of a phenomenon. *Journal of Personality and Social Psychology*, 1979, *37*, 147–169.

Guyote, M.J., and Sternberg, R.J. A transitive-chain theory of syllogistic reasoning. *Cognitive Psychology*, 1981, *13*, 461–525.

Guze, S.B., and Robins, E. Suicide and primary affective disorders. *British Journal of Psychiatry*, 1970, *117*, 437–438.

Guze, S.B., Wolfgram, E.D., McKinney, J.K., and Cantwell, D.P. Psychiatric illness in the families of convicted criminals. A study of 519 first-degree relatives. *Disorders of the Nervous System*, 1967, *28*, 651–659.

Guze, S.B., Woodruff, R.A., and Clayton, P.J. Secondary affective disorder: A study of 95 cases. *Psychological Medicine*, 1971, *1*, 426–428.

Hafeiz, H.B. Hysterical conversion: A prognostic study. *British Journal of Psychiatry*, 1980, *136*, 548–551.

Haith, M.M. Infrared television recording and measurement of ocular behavior in the human infant. *American Psychologist*, 1969, *24*, 279–283.

Haith, M.M. Visual competence in early infancy. In *Handbook of Sensory Physiology* (vol. 8), edited by R. Held, H. Leibowitz, and H.-L. Teuber. New York: Springer-Verlag, 1976.

Hall, C.S., and Lindzey, G. *Theories of Personality* (3d ed.). New York: John Wiley & Sons, 1978.

Hall, E.T. *The Hidden Dimension*. New York: Doubleday, 1966.

Hare, R.D. Acquisition and generalization of a conditioned-fear response in psychopathic and non-psychopathic criminals. *Journal of Psychology*, 1965a, *59*, 367–370.

Hare, R.D. Temporal gradient of fear arousal in psychopaths. *Journal of Abnormal Psychology*, 1965b, *70*, 442–445.

Harkins, S.G., Petty, R.E. Effects of task difficulty and task uniqueness on social loafing. *Journal of Personality and Social Psychology*, 1982, *43*, 1214–1229.

Harlow, H. *Learning to Love*. New York: J. Aronson, 1974.

Harris, E.L., Noyes, R., Crowe, R.R., and Chaudhry,

D.R. A family study of agoraphobia: Report of a pilot study. *Archives of General Psychiatry*, 1983, *40*, 1065–1070.

Hayes, C. *The Ape in Our House*. London: Gollancz, 1952.

Hebb, D.O. *The Organization of Behaviour*. New York: Wiley-Interscience, 1949.

Hebb, D.O. Drives and the C.N.S. (conceptual nervous system). *Psychological Review*, 1955, *62*, 243–254.

Hebb, D.O., Lambert, W.E., and Tucker, G.R. A DMZ in the language war. *Psychology Today*, April 1973, 55–62.

Hecht, S., and Schlaer, S. An adaptometer for measuring human dark adaptation. *Journal of the Optical Society of America*, 1938, *28*, 269–275.

Heider, F. *The Psychology of Interpersonal Relations*. New York: John Wiley & Sons, 1958.

Henderson, D., and Gillespie, R.D. *A Textbook of Psychiatry for Students and Practitioners*. London: Oxford University Press, 1950.

Henderson, N.D. Human behavior genetics. *Annual Review of Psychology*, 1982, *33*, 403–440.

Herrnstein, R.J., and Loveland, D.H. Complex visual concept in the pigeon. *Science*, 1964, *146*, 549–551.

Heston, L.L., and Shields, J.S. Homosexuality in twins: A family study and a registry study. *Archives of General Psychiatry*, 1968, *18*, 149–160.

Hilgard, E.R. A neodissociation interpretation of pain reduction in hypnosis. *Psychological Review*, 1973, *80*, 396–411.

Hilgard, E.R. *Divided Consciousness: Multiple Controls in Human Thought and Action*. New York: Wiley-Interscience, 1977.

Hilgard, E.R. Divided consciousness in hypnosis: The implications of the hidden observer. In *Hypnosis: Developments in Research and New Perspectives*, edited by E. Fromm and R.E. Shor. Chicago: Aldine Press, 1979.

Hilgard, E.R., Hilgard, J.R., Macdonald, H., Morgan, A. H., and Johnson, L.S. Covert pain in hypnotic analgesia: Its reality as tested by the real-simulator design. *Journal of Abnormal Psychology*, 1978, *87*, 655–663.

Hirsch, H.V.B., and Spinelli, D.N. Modification of the distribution of receptive field orientation in cats by selective visual exposure during development. *Experimental Brain Research*, 1971, *13*, 509–527.

Hirsch, J., and Knittle, J.L. Cellularity of obese and non-obese human adipose tissue. *Federation Proceedings*, 1970, *29*, 1516–1521.

Hoffman, F.G. *A Handbook on Drug and Alcohol Abuse*. New York: Oxford University Press, 1975.

Hofling, C.K. *Textbook of Psychiatry for Medical Practice*. Philadelphia: J.B. Lippincott, 1963.

Hohman, G.W. Some effects of spinal cord lesions on experienced emotional feelings. *Psychophysiology*, 1966, *3*, 143–156.

Honig, W.K., Boneau, C.A., Burstein, K.R., and Pennypacker, H.C. Positive and negative generalization gradients obtained after equivalent training conditions. *Journal of Comparative and Physio-logical Psychology*, 1963, *56*, 111–116.

Horn, J.L. Organization of abilities and the development of intelligence. *Psychological Review*, 1968, *75*, 242–259.

Horn, J.L. Human abilities: A review of research and theory in the early 1970s. *Annual Review of Psychology*, 1976, *27*, 437–485.

Horn, J.L. Human ability systems. In *Life Span Development*, (vol. 1), edited by P.B. Baltes. New York: Academic Press, 1978.

Horn, J.L., and Cattell, R.B. Refinement and test of the theory of fluid and crystallized ability intelligences. *Journal of Educational Psychology*, 1966, *57*, 253–270.

Horner, M.S. Toward an understanding of achievement-related conflicts in women. *Journal of Social Issues*, 1972, *28*, 157–175.

Horney, K. *Neurotic Personality of Our Times*. New York: Norton, 1937.

Horney, K. *Our Inner Conflicts*. New York: Norton, 1945.

Horton, D.L., and Mills, C.B. Human learning and memory. *Annual Review of Psychology*, 1984, *35*, 361–394.

Hubel, D.H., and Wiesel, T.N. The period of susceptibility to the physiological effects of unilateral eye closure in kittens. *Journal of Physiology* (London), 1970, *206*, 419–436.

Hubel, D.H., and Wiesel, T.N. Functional architecture of macaque monkey visual cortex. *Proceedings of the Royal Society of London, Series B*, 1977, *198*, 1–59.

Hubel, D.H., and Wiesel, T.N. Brain mechanisms of vision. *Scientific American*, 1979, *241*, 150–162.

Hull, C.L. *Principles of Behavior*. New York: Appleton-Century-Crofts, 1943.

Hunt, E. Verbal ability. In *Human Abilities: An Information-Processing Approach*, edited by R.J. Sternberg. New York: W.H. Freeman, 1985.

Hunt, E., Lunneborg, C., and Lewis, J. What does it mean to be high verbal? *Cognitive Psychology*, 1975, *7*, 194–227.

Hyde, T.S., and Jenkins, J.J. The differential effects of incidental tasks on the organization of recall of a list of highly associated words. *Journal of Experimental Psychology*, 1969, *82*, 472–481.

Inglefinger, F.J. The late effects of total and subtotal gastrectomy. *New England Journal of Medicine*, 1944, *231*, 321–327.

Isaacs, W., Thomas, J., and Goldiamond, I. Application of operant conditioning to reinstate verbal behavior in psychotics. *Journal of Speech and Hearing Disorders*, 1960, *25*, 8–12.

Isaacson, R.L. Relations between achievement, text anxiety, and curricular choices. *Journal of Abnormal and Social Psychology*, 1964, *68*, 447–452.

Izard, C.E. *The Face of Emotion*. New York: Appleton-Century-Crofts, 1971.

Jackson, D.N., and Paunonen, S.V. Personality structure and assessment. *Annual Review of Psychology*, 1980, *31*, 503–551.

Jacobsen, C.F., Wolf, J.B., and Jackson, T.A. An experimental analysis of the functions of the frontal association areas in primates. *Journal of Nervous and Mental Disease*, 1935, *82*, 1–14.

James, W. What is an emotion? *Mind*, 1884, *9*, 188–205.

James, W. *Principles of Psychology*. New York: Henry Holt, 1890.

James, W.P.T., and Trayhurn, P. Thermogenesis and obesity. *British Medical Bulletin*, 1981, *37*, 43–48.

Jenkins, R.L. Classification of behavior problems of children. *American Journal of Psychiatry*, 1969, *125*, 1032–1039.

Jensen, A.R. How much can we boost IQ and scholastic achievement? *Harvard Educational Review*, 1969, *39*, 1–123.

Jensen, A.R. The nature of the black-white difference on various psychometric tests: Spearman's hypothesis. *The Behavioral and Brain Sciences*, 1985, *8*, 193–263.

Johansson, G. Visual perception of biological motion and a model for its analysis. *Perception and Psychophysics*, 1973, *14*, 201–211.

Johnson, M.K., Kim, J.K., and Risse, G. Do alcoholic Korsakoff's syndrome patients acquire affective reactions? *Journal of Experimental Psychology: Learning, Memory, and Cognition*, 1985, *11*, 22–36.

Johnson, S.B., and Sechrest, L. Comparison of desensitization and progressive relaxation in treating test anxiety. *Journal of Consulting and Clinical Psychology*, 1968, *32*, 280–286.

Johnson, T.J., Feigenbaum, R., and Weiby, M. Some determinants and consequences of the teacher's perception of causation. *Journal of Experimental Psychology*, 1964, *55*, 237–246.

Johnson-Laird, P.N. Deductive reasoning ability. In *Human Abilities: An Information-Processing Approach*, edited by R.J. Sternberg. New York: W.H. Freeman, 1985.

Johnstone, E.C., Crow, T.J., Frith, C.D., Stevens, M., Kreel, L., and Husband, J. The dementia of dementia praecox. *Acta Psychiatrica Scandinavica*, 1978, *57*, 305–324.

Jones, A.P., and Friedman, M.I. Obesity and adipocyte abnormalities in offspring of rats undernourished during pregnancy. *Science*, 1982, *215*, 1515–1519.

Jones, E.E., and Davis, K.E. From acts to dispositions: The attribution process in person perceptions. In *Advances in Experimental Social Psychology* (vol. 2), edited by L. Berkowitz. New York: Academic Press, 1965.

Jones, E.E., and Nisbett, R.E. The actor and observer: Divergent perceptions of the causes of behavior. In *Attribution: Perceiving the Causes of Behavior*, edited by E.E. Jones, D.E. Kamouse, H.H. Kelley, R.E. Nisbett, S. Valins, and B. Weiner. Morristown, N.J.: General Learning Press, 1971.

Jones, H.E., and Bayley, N. The Berkeley growth study. *Child Development*, 1941, *12*, 167–173.

Jones, W.H., Chernovetz, M.E., and Hansson, R.D. The enigma of androgyny: Differential implications for masculinity and femininity? *Journal of Consulting and Clinical Psychology*, 1978, *46*, 298–313.

Jost, A. Embryonic sexual differentiation. In *Her-maphroditism, Genital Anomalies and Related Endocrine Disorders*, (2nd ed.). Baltimore: Williams & Wilkins, 1969.

Jouvet, M. The role of monoamines and acetylcholine-containing neurons in the regulation of the sleep-waking cycle. *Ergebnisse der Physiologie*, 1972, *64*, 166–307.

Julesz, B. Texture and visual perception. *Scientific American*, 1965, *212*, 38–48.

Jung, C.G. The theory of psychoanalysis. In *Collected Works* (vol. 4). Princeton: Princeton University Press, 1961. (First German edition, 1913.)

Jung, C.G. The structure of the unconscious. In *Collected Works* (vol. 7). Princeton: Princeton University Press, 1953. (First German edition, 1916a.)

Jung, C.G. Psychological types. In *Collected Works* (vol. 6). Princeton: Princeton University Press, 1971. (First German edition, 1921.)

Kallman, F.J. Comparative twin study on the genetic aspects of male homosexuality. *Journal of Nervous and Mental Disease*, 1952, *115*, 283–298.

Kanfer, F.H., and Phillips, J.S. *Learning Foundations of Behavior Therapy*. New York: John Wiley & Sons, 1970.

Kaplan, E.L., and Kaplan, G.A. The prelinguistic child. In *Human Development and Cognitive Processes*, edited by J. Eliot. New York: Holt, Rinehart and Winston, 1970.

Karabenick, S.A., and Srull, T.K. Effects of personality and situational variation in locus of control on cheating: Determinants of the congruence effect. *Journal of Personality*, 1978, *46*, 72–95.

Kastenbaum, R., and Costa, P.T. Psychological perspectives on death. *Annual Review of Psychology*, 1977, *28*, 225–249.

Katz, D. *The World of Colour*. London: Kegan Paul, Trench, Trubner, 1935.

Kaufman, A.S., Kamphaus, R.W., and Kaufman, N.L. The Kaufman assessment battery for children (K-ABC). In *Major Psychological Assessment Instruments*, edited by C.S. Newmark. Boston: Allyn and Bacon, 1985.

Kaufman, A.S., and Kaufman, N.L. *K-ABC Administration and Scoring Manual*. Circle Pines, Minn.: American Guidance Service, 1983a.

Kaufman, A.S., and Kaufman, N.L. *K-ABC Interpretative Manual*. Circle Pines, Minn.: American Guidance Service, 1983b.

Kelley, H.H. Attribution theory in social psychology. In *Nebraska Symposium on Motivation* (vol. 15), edited by D. Levine. Lincoln: University of Nebraska Press, 1967.

Kelley, H.H. Attribution theory in social interaction. In *Attribution: Perceiving the Causes of Behavior*, edited by E.E. Jones, D.E. Kamouse, H.H. Kelley, R.E. Nisbett, S. Valins, and B. Weiner. Morristown, N.J.: General Learning Press, 1971.

Kelley, H.H. The process of causal attribution. *American Psychologist*, 1973, *28*, 107–128.

Kenrick, D.T., and Cialdini, R.B. Romantic attraction: Misattribution versus reinforcement explanations. *Journal of Personality and Social Psychology*, 1977, *35*, 381–391.

Keppel, G., and Underwood, B.J. Proactive inhibition in short-term retention of single items. *Journal of Verbal Learning and Verbal Behavior*, 1962, *1*, 153–161.

Kertesz, A. Personal communication, 1980.

Kertesz, A. Anatomy of jargon. In *Jargonaphasia*, edited by J. Brown. New York: Academic Press, 1981.

Kety, S.S., Rosenthal, D., Wender, P.H., and Schulsinger, F. The types and prevalence of mental illness in the biological and adoptive families of adopted schizophrenics. In *The Transmission of Schizophrenia*, edited by D. Rosenthal and S.S. Kety. Elmsford, N.Y.: Pergamon Press, 1968.

Kiang, N.Y.-S. *Discharge Patterns of Single Nerve Fibers in the Cat's Auditory Nerve*. Cambridge, Mass.: MIT Press, 1965.

Kihlstrom, J.F. Hypnosis. *Annual Review of Psychology*, 1985, *36*, 385–418.

Klaus, M.H., Jerauld, R., Krieger, N.C., McAlpine, W., Steffa, M., and Kennell, J.H. Maternal attachment: Importance of the first postpartum days. *New England Journal of Medicine*, 1972, *286*, 460–463.

Klein, D.F., and Howard, A. *Psychiatric Case Studies: Treatment, Drugs, and Outcome*. Baltimore: Williams & Wilkins, 1972.

Klein, D.F., and Rabkin, J.G. *Anxiety: New Research and Changing Concepts*. New York: Raven Press, 1981.

Klein, D.F., Zitrin, C.M., Woerner, M.G., and Ross, D.C. Treatment of phobias. II. Behavior therapy and supportive psychotherapy: Are there any specific ingredients? *Archives of General Psychiatry*, 1983, *40*, 139–145.

Klineberg, O. Emotional expression in Chinese literature. *Journal of Abnormal and Social Psychology*, 1938, *33*, 517–520.

Klopfer, P.H., Adams, D.K., and Klopfer, M.S. Maternal "imprinting" in goats. *Proceedings of the National Academy of Sciences, U.S.A.*, 1964, *52*, 911–914.

Knittle, J.L., and Hirsch, J. Effect of early nutrition on the development of rat epididymal fat pads: Cellularity and metabolism. *Journal of Clinical Investigation*, 1968, *47*, 2001–2098.

Knox, R.E., and Inkster, J.A. Postdecision dissonance at post time. *Journal of Personality and Social Psychology*, 1968, *8*, 310–323.

Koch, J.L.A. *Leitfaden der Psychiatrie*, (2nd ed.). Ravensberg, Austria: Dorn, 1889.

Kogan, N. *Categorizing and Conceptualizing Styles in Younger and Older Adults, RB-73*. Princeton, N.J.: Educational Testing Service, 1973.

Kohlberg, L. A cognitive-developmental analysis of children's sex-role concepts and attitudes. In *The Development of Sex Differences*, edited by E.E. Maccoby, Stanford, CA: Stanford University Press, 1966.

Kohlberg, L. Stage and sequence: The cognitive-developmental approach to socialization. In *Handbook of Socialization: Theory and Research*, ed. D.A. Goslin. Boston: Houghton Mifflin, 1969.

Kohlberg, L. The Philosophy of Moral Development: Essays on Moral Development (vol. I). San Francisco: Harper and Row, 1981.

Kolb, B., and Whishaw, I.Q. *Fundamentals of Human Neuropsychology*. New York: W.H. Freeman, 1985.

Kosslyn, S.M. Scanning visual images: Some structural implications. *Perception and Psychophysics*, 1973, *14*, 90–94.

Kosslyn, S.M. Evidence for analogue representation. Paper presented at the Conference on Theoretical Issues in Natural Language Processing, Massachusetts Institute of Technology, Cambridge, Mass., July 1975.

Kovner, R., and Stamm, J.S. Disruption of short-term visual memory by electrical stimulation of inferotemporal cortex in the monkey. *Journal of Comparative and Physiological Psychology*, 1972, *81*, 163–172.

Kozlowski, L.T., and Cutting, J.E. Recognizing the sex of a walker from a dynamic point-light display. *Perception and Psychophysics*, 1977, *21*, 575–580.

Kraines, S.H. *The Therapy of the Neuroses and Psychoses* (3rd ed.). Philadelphia: Lea & Febiger, 1948.

Krantz, D.S., Grunberg, N.E., and Baum, A. Health psychology. *Annual Review of Psychology*, 1985, *36*, 349–383.

Kraut, R.E., and Johnston, R. Social and emotional messages of smiling: An ethological approach. *Journal of Personality and Social Psychology*, 1979, *37*, 1539–1553.

Kroll, N.E.A., Parks, T., Parkinson, S.R., Bieber, S.L., and Johnson, A.L. Short-term memory while shadowing: Recall of visually and of aurally presented letters. *Journal of Experimental Psychology*, 1970, *85*, 220–224.

Kubler-Ross, E. *On Death and Dying*. New York: Macmillan, 1969.

Kulka, R.A., and Kessler, J.R. Is justice really blind? The effect of litigant physical attractiveness on judicial judgment. *Journal of Applied Social Psychology*, 1978, *4*, 336–381.

Kupfer, D.J. REM latency: A psychobiologic marker for primary depressive disease. *Biological Psychiatry*, 1976, *11*, 159–174.

Lacey, J.I., and Lacey, B.C. The law of initial value in the longitudinal study of autonomic constitution: Reproducibility of autonomic response patterns over a four-year interval. *Annals of the New York Academy of Sciences*, 1962, *98*, 1257–1290.

Lair, C.V., Moon, W.H., and Kausler, D.H. Associative interference in the paired-associate learning of middle-aged and old subjects. *Developmental Psychology*, 1969, *1*, 548–552.

Lamm, H., and Sauer, C. Discussion-induced shift toward higher demands in negotiation. *European Journal of Social Psychology*, 1974, *4*, 85–88.

Lange, C.G. *Über Gemüthsbewegungen*. Leipzig, East Germany: T. Thomas, 1887.

Langer, E.J. The illusion of control. *Journal of Personality and Social Psychology*, 1975, *32*, 311–328.

Lansman, M., Donaldson, G., Hunt, E., and Yantis, S. Ability factors and cognitive processes. *Intelligence*, 1983, *6*, 347–386.

Lao, R.C. Internal-external control and competent and innovative behavior among Negro college students. *Journal of Personality and Social Psychology*, 1970, *14*, 263–270.

LaPiere, R.T. Attitudes and actions. *Social Forces*, 1934, *13*, 230–237.

Latané, B., Williams, K., and Harkins, S. Many hands make light the work: The causes and consequences of social loafing. *Journal of Personality and Social Psychology*, 1979, *37*, 823–832.

Lau, R.R., and Russell, D. Attributions in the sports pages. *Journal of Personality and Social Psychology*, 1980, *39*, 29–38.

Laurence, J.R., and Perry, C. Hypnotically created memory among highly hypnotizable subjects. *Science*, 1983, *222*, 523–524.

Lazarus, A.A. Group therapy of phobic disorders by systematic desensitization. *Journal of Abnormal and Social Psychology*, 1961, *63*, 504–510.

Lazarus, A.A. *Behavior Therapy and Beyond*. New York: McGraw-Hill, 1971.

Lazarus, R.S. Thoughts on the relations between emotion and cognition. In *Approaches to Emotion*, edited by K.R. Scherer and P. Ekman. Hillsdale, N.J.: Lawrence Erlbaum Associates, 1984.

Leech, S., and Witte, K.L. Paired-associate learning in elderly adults as related to pacing and incentive conditions. *Developmental Psychology*, 1971, *5*, 180.

Lefkowitz, M.M., Eron, L.D., Walder, L.O., and Heusmann, L.R. *Growing Up to Be Violent: A Longitudinal Study of the Development of Aggression*. New York: Pergamon Press, 1977.

Leon, G.R. *Case Histories of Deviant Behavior* (2nd ed.). Boston: Allyn and Bacon, 1977.

Lepper, M.R., Greene, D., and Nisbett, R.E. Undermining children's intrinsic interest with extrinsic rewards: A test of the "overjustification" hypothesis. *Journal of Personality and Social Psychology*, 1973, *28*, 129–137.

Levy, L.H. *Psychological Interpretation*. New York: Holt, Rinehart and Winston, 1963.

Levy, W.B., and Steward, O. Temporal contiguity requirements for long-term associative potentiation/depression in the hippocampus. *Neuroscience*, 1983, *8*, 791–797.

Lewinsohn, P.H., Weinstein, M., and Alper, T. A behavioral approach to the group treatment of depressed persons: A methodological contribution. *Journal of Clinical Psychology*, 1970, *26*, 525–532.

Lewis, M., and Goldberg, S. Perceptual-cognitive development in infancy: A generalized expectancy model as a function of mother-infant interaction. *Merrill-Palmer Quarterly*, 1969, *15*, 81–100.

Ley, R.G., and Bryden, M.P. Hemispheric differences in processing emotions and faces. *Brain and Language*, 1979, *7*, 127–138.

Lincoln, J.S., McCormick, D.A., and Thompson, R.F. Ipsilateral lesions prevent learning of the classically conditioned nictitating membrane eyelid response. *Brain Research*, 1982, *242*, 190–193.

Lipton, S. Dissociated personality: A case report. *Psychiatric Quarterly*, 1943, *17*, 35–36.

Lisker, L., and Abramson, A. The voicing dimension: Some experiments in comparative phonetics. *Proceedings of Sixth International Congress of Phonetic Sciences, Prague, 1967*. Prague: Academia, 1970.

Loeb, A., Beck, A.T., Diggory, J.C., and Tuthill, R. The effects of success and failure on mood, motivation and performance as a function of predetermined level of depression. Unpublished manuscript, University of Pennsylvania, 1966.

Loehlin, J.C., and Nichols, R.C. *Heredity, Environment, and Personality: A Study of 850 Sets of Twins*. Austin: University of Texas Press, 1976.

Loftus, E.F., and Zanni, G. Eyewitness testimony: The influence of the wording of a question. *Bulletin of the Psychonomic Society*, 1975, *5*, 86–88.

Logan, F.A. Decision making by rats: Delay versus amount of reward. *Journal of Comparative and Physiological Psychology*, 1965, *59*, 1–12.

Loomis, W.F. Skin pigment regulation of vitamin-D biosynthesis in man. *Science*, 1967, *157*, 501–506.

Lorenz, K. Companionship in bird life. In *Instinctive Behavior*, edited by C.H. Schiller. New York: International Universities Press, 1957.

Lorenz, K. *On Aggression*. New York: Harcourt Brace Jovanovich, 1966.

Lubinski, D., Tellegen, A., and Butcher, J.N. The relationship between androgyny and subjective indicators of emotional well-being. *Journal of Personality and Social Psychology*, 1981, *40*, 722–730.

Luborsky, L., Chandler, M., Auerbach, A.H., Cohen, J., and Bachrach, H.M. Factors influencing the outcome of psychotherapy: A review of quantitative research. *Psychological Bulletin*, 1971, *75*, 145–185.

Luborsky, L., and Spence, D.P. Quantitative research on psychoanalytic therapy. In *Handbook of Psychotherapy and Behavior Change: An Empirical Analysis*, (2nd ed.). New York: John Wiley & Sons, 1978.

Maccoby, E.E., and Jacklin, C.N. *The Psychology of Sex Differences*. Stanford: Stanford University Press, 1974.

MacDonald, J., and McGurk, H. Visual influences on speech perception processes. *Perception and Psychophysics*, 1978, *24*, 253–257.

Magni, F., Moruzzi, G., Rossi, G.F., and Zanchetti, A. EEG arousal following inactivation of the lower brain stem by selective injection of barbiturate into the vertebral circulation. *Archives Italiennes de Biologie*, 1959, *97*, 33–46.

Mahoney, M.J., and Thoresen, C.E. *Self-control: Power to the Person*. Monterey, Calif.: Brooks/Cole, 1974.

Maier, S.F., and Seligman, M.E. Learned helplessness: Theory and evidence. *Journal of Experimental Psychology: General*, 1976, *105*, 3–46.

Margolin, D.I., Friedrich, F.J., and Carlson, N.R. Visual agnosia-optic aphasia: Continuum or dichotomy? Paper presented at the Meeting of the International Neuropsychology Society, 1985.

Margolin, D.I., Marcel, A.J., and Carlson, N.R. Common mechanisms in dysnomia and post-semantic surface dyslexia: Processing deficits and selective attention. In *Surface Dyslexia: Neuropsychological and Cognitive Studies of Phonological Reading.* London: Lawrence Erlbaum, 1985.

Mark, V.H., Sweet, W.H., and Ervin, F.R. The effect of amygdalotomy on violent behavior in patients with temporal lobe epilepsy. In *Psychosurgery*, edited by E. Hitchcock, L. Laitinen, and K. Vaernet. Springfield, Ill.: Charles C Thomas, 1972.

Marks, I.M. *Fears and Phobias.* New York: Academic Press, 1969.

Marler, P. Animal communication: Affect or cognition? In *Approaches to Emotion*, edited by K.R. Scherer and P. Ekman. Hillsdale, N.J.: Lawrence Erlbaum Associates, 1984.

Martens, R. Palmar sweating and the presence of an audience. *Journal of Experimental Social Psychology*, 1969, *5*, 371–374.

Maslow, A. *Toward a psychology of being* (2nd ed.) Princeton, N.J.: Van Nostrand Reinhold, 1968.

Maslow, A.H. *Motivation and Personality* (2nd ed.) New York: Harper and Row, 1970.

Masters, W.H., and Johnson, V.E. *Human Sexual Response.* Boston: Little, Brown, 1966.

Masters, W.H., and Johnson, V.E. *Homosexuality in Perspective.* Boston: Little, Brown, 1979.

Matarazzo, J.D. *Wechsler's Measurement and Appraisal of Adult Intelligence* (5th ed.). Baltimore: Williams & Wilkins, 1972.

Matheny, A.P., Wilson, R.S., Dolan, A.B., and Krantz, J.Z. Behavioral contrasts in twinships: stability and patterns of differences in childhood. *Child Development*, 1981, *52*, 579–588.

Matthews, K.A. Assessment of Type A, anger, and hostility in epidemiological studies of cardiovascular disease. In Ostfeld, A., and Eaker, E. *Measuring Psychosocial Variables in Epidemiologic Studies of Cardiovascular Disease.* Bethesda, Md.: National Institutes of Health, 1984.

Mayer, J. Regulation of energy intake and the body weight: The glucostatic theory and the lipostatic hypothesis. *Annals of the New York Academy of Science*, 1955a, *63*, 15–43.

Mayer, J. The role of exercise and activity in weight control. In *Weight Control: A Collection of Papers Presented at the Weight Control Symposium*, edited by E.S. Eppright, P. Swanson, and C.A. Iverson. Ames: Iowa State College Press, 1955b.

Mazis, M.B. Antipollution measures and psychological reactance theory: A field experiment. *Journal of Personality and Social Psychology*, 1975, *31*, 654–666.

Mazis, M.B., Settle, R.B., and Leslie, D.C. Elimination of phosphate detergents and psychological reactance. *Journal of Marketing Research*, 1973, *10*, 390–395.

McClelland, D.C., Atkinson, J.W., Clark, R.W., and Lowell, E.L. *The Achievement Motive.* New York: Appleton-Century-Crofts, 1953.

McClintock, M.K., and Adler, N.T. The role of the female during copulation in wild and domestic Norway rats *(Rattus norvegicus). Behaviour*, 1978, *67*, 67–96.

McCrae, R.R., and Costa, P.T. *Emerging Lives, Enduring Dispositions: Personality in Adulthood.* Boston: Little, Brown, 1984.

McGhie, A., and Chapman, J.S. Disorders of attention and perception in early schizophrenia. *British Journal of Medical Psychology*, 1961, *34*, 103–116.

McKay, D.C. Aspects of the theory of comprehension, memory and attention. *Quarterly Journal of Experimental Psychology*, 1973, *25*, 22–40.

McNeill, D. *The Acquisition of Language: The Study of Developmental Psycholinguistics.* New York: Harper & Row, 1970.

McReynolds, W.T. Learned helplessness as a schedule-shift effect. *Journal of Research in Personality*, 1980, *14*, 139–157.

Meichenbaum, D.H. *Cognitive-behavior Modification.* New York: Plenum Press, 1977.

Mézey, A.G., and Cohen, S.I. The effect of depressive illness on time judgment and time experience. *Journal of Neurology, Neurosurgery, and Psychiatry*, 1961, *24*, 269–270.

Miles, H.L. Apes and language: The search for communicative competence. In *Language in Primates: Perspectives and Implications*, edited by J. de Luce and H.T. Wilder. New York: Springer-Verlag, 1983.

Milgram, S. Behavioral study of obedience. *Journal of Abnormal and Social Psychology*, 1963, *67*, 371–378.

Milgram, S. *Obedience to Authority.* New York: Harper & Row, 1974.

Millenson, J.R. *Principles of Behavioral Analysis.* New York: Macmillan, 1967.

Miller, G.A. The magical number seven plus or minus two: Some limits on our capacity for processing information. *Psychological Review*, 1956, *63*, 81–97.

Miller, G.A., and Nicely, P. An analysis of perceptual confusions among some English consonants. *Journal of the Acoustical Society of America*, 1955, *27*, 338–352.

Miller, G.A., and Taylor, W.G. The perception of repeated bursts of noise. *Journal of the Acoustical Society of America*, 1948, *20*, 171–182.

Miller, N.E. Behavioral medicine: Symbiosis between laboratory and clinic. *Annual Review of Psychology*, 1983, *34*, 1–31.

Miller, R.E., Banks, J., and Kuwahara, H. The communication of affects in monkeys: Cooperative reward conditioning. *Journal of Genetic Psychology*, 1966, *108*, 121–134.

Miller, R.E., Banks, J., and Ogawa, N. Role of facial expression in "cooperative-avoidance conditioning" in monkeys. *Journal of Abnormal and Social Psychology*, 1963, *67*, 24–30.

Miller, R.E., Caul, W.F., and Mirsky, I.A. Communication of affects between feral and socially isolated monkeys. *Journal of Personality and Social Psychology*, 1967, *7*, 231–239.

Miller, R.E., Murphy, J.V., and Mirsky, I.A. Nonverbal communication of affect. *Journal of Clinical Psychology*, 1959, *15*, 155–158.

Miller, R.J., Hennessy, R.T., and Leibowitz, H.W. The effect of hypnotic ablation of the background on the magnitude of the Ponzo perspective illusion.

International Journal of Clinical and Experimental Hypnosis, 1973, *21*, 180–191.

Miller, W., and Ervin-Tripp, S.M. The development of grammar in child language. In *The Acquisition of Language. Monographs of the Society for Research in Child Development*, edited by U. Bellugi and R. Brown, 1964, *29* (serial no. 92), 9–34.

Miller, W.R., Rosellini, R.A., and Seligman, M.E.P. Learned helplessness and depression. In *Psychopathology: Experimental Models*, edited by J.D. Maser and M.E.P. Seligman. San Francisco: W.H. Freeman, 1977.

Milner, B. Memory and the temporal regions of the brain. In *Biology of Memory*, edited by K.H. Pribram and D.E. Broadbent. New York: Academic Press, 1970.

Minuchin, S. *Families & Family Therapy*. Cambridge, Mass.: Harvard University Press, 1974.

Mischel, W. *Personality and Assessment*. New York: John Wiley & Sons, 1968.

Mischel, W. Sex-typing and socialization. In *Carmichael's Manual of Child Psychology* (vol. 2), edited by P.H. Mussen. New York: John Wiley & Sons, 1970.

Mischel, W. Toward a cognitive social learning reconceptualization of personality. *Psychological Review*, 1973, *80*, 252–283.

Mischel, W. *Introduction to Personality* (2nd ed.). New York: Holt, Rinehart, and Winston, 1976.

Mischel, W. The interaction of person and situation. In *Personality at the Crossroads: Current Issues in Interactional Psychology*, edited by D. Magnusson and N.S. Endler. Hillsdale, N.J.: Lawrence Erlbaum Associates, 1977.

Mischel, W. On the interface of cognition and personality: Beyond the person-situation debate. *American Psychologist*, 1979, *34*, 740–754.

Money, J., and Ehrhardt, A. *Man & Woman, Boy & Girl*. Baltimore: Johns Hopkins University Press, 1972.

Money, J., and Tucker, P. *Sexual Signatures: On Being a Man or a Woman*. Boston: Little, Brown, 1975.

Moore, B.R. The role of directed Pavlovian reactions in simple instrumental learning in the pigeon. In *Constraints on Learning*, edited by R.A. Hinde and J. Stevenson-Hinde. New York: Academic Press, 1973.

Moreno, J.L. Psychodrama. In *American Handbook of Psychiatry* (vol. 2), edited by S. Arieti. New York: Basic Books, 1959.

Moss, C.S. *Hypnosis in Perspective*. New York: Macmillan, 1965.

Mowrer, O.H. *Learning Theory and Symbolic Processes*. New York: John Wiley & Sons, 1960.

Moyer, K.E. *The Psychobiology of Aggression*. New York: Harper & Row, 1976.

Murray, H.A. Techniques for a systematic investigation of fantasy. *Journal of Psychology*, 1936, *3*, 115–143.

Murray, H.A. *Explorations in Personality*. New York: Oxford University Press, 1938.

Nafe, J.P., and Wagoner, K.S. The nature of pressure adaptation. *Journal of General Psychology*, 1941, *25*, 323–351.

Nathans, J., Piantanida, T.P., Eddy, R.I., Shows, T.B., and Hogness, D.S. Molecular genetics of inherited variations in human color vision. *Science*, 1986, *232*, 203–210.

National Commission for the Protection of Human Subjects of Biomedical and Behavioral Research. *Report and Recommendations: Psychosurgery*. Washington, D.C.: U.S. Government Printing Office, 1977.

Nawas, M.M., Fishman, S.T., and Pucel, J.C. The standardized desensitization program applicable to group and individual treatment. *Behaviour Research and Therapy*, 1970, *6*, 63–68.

Neisser, U. Selective reading: A method for the study of visual attention. Paper presented at the Nineteenth International Congress of Psychology, London, 1969.

Neisser, U., and Becklen, R. Selective looking: Attending to visually specified events. *Cognitive Psychology*, 1975, *7*, 480–494.

Nisbett, R.E., and Schachter, S. Cognitive manipulation of pain. *Journal of Experimental Social Psychology*, 1966, *2*, 227–236.

Nisbett, R.E., and Wilson, T.D. Telling more than we can know: Verbal reports on mental processes. *Psychological Review*, 1977, *84*, 231–259.

Noirot, E. Selective priming of maternal responses by auditory and olfactory cues from mouse pups. *Developmental Psychobiology*, 1972, *5*, 371–387.

Novak, M.A., and Harlow, H.F. Social recovery of monkeys isolated for the first year of life: 1. Rehabilitation and therapy. *Developmental Psychology*, 1975, *11*, 453–465.

Oakley, A. *Sex, Gender and Society*. New York: Harper & Row, 1972.

Olds, J. Commentary. In *Brain Stimulation and Motivation*, edited by E.S. Valenstein. Glenview, Ill.: Scott, Foresman, 1973.

Oller, D.K., Wieman, L.A., Doyle, W.J., and Ross, C. Infant babbling and speech. *Journal of Child Language*, 1976, *3*, 1–11.

Olton, D.S., Collison, C., and Werz, M.A. Spatial memory and radial arm maze performance in rats. *Learning and Motivation*, 1977, *8*, 289–314.

Olton, D.S., and Papas, B.C. Spatial memory and hippocampal function. *Neuropsychologia*, 1979, *17*, 669–682.

Olton, D.S., and Samuelson, R.J. Remembrance of places past: Spatial memory in rats. *Journal of Experimental Psychology: Animal Behavior Processes*, 1976, *2*, 97–116.

Orlofsky, J.L., and Windle, M.I. Sex-role orientation, behavioral adaptability, and personal adjustment. *Sex Roles*, 1978, *4*, 801–811.

Orne, M.T. The nature of hypnosis: Artifact and essence. *Journal of Abnormal and Social Psychology*, 1959, *58*, 277–299.

Overmeier, J.B., and Seligman, M.E.P. Effects of inescapable shock upon subsequent escape and avoidance responding. *Journal of Comparative and Physiological Psychology*, 1967, *63*, 28–33.

Palmer, J.C., MacLeod, C. M., Hunt, E., and Davidson, J. Information processing correlates of reading: An individual differences analysis. *Journal of Memory and Language*, 1985, *24*, 59–88.

Parke, R.D., and Collmer, C.W. Child abuse: An interdisciplinary analysis. In *Review of Child Development Research* (vol. 5), edited by E.M. Hetherington. Chicago: University of Chicago Press, 1975.

Patterson, F.G., and Linden, E. *The Education of Koko.* New York: Holt, Rinehart, and Winston, 1981.

Pattie, F.A. The genuineness of hypnotically produced anesthesia of the skin. *American Journal of Psychology*, 1937, *49*, 435–443.

Paul, G.L., and Lentz, R.J. *Psychosocial Treatment of Chronic Mental Patients: Milieu versus Social Learning Program.* Cambridge, Mass.: Harvard University Press, 1977.

Pavlov, I.P. *Conditioned Reflexes.* New York: Oxford University Press, 1927.

People v. Kempinski, No. W80CF 352 (Circuit Court, 12th District, Will County, Illinois, 21 October 1980).

Persky, H., Lief, H.I., Strauss, D., Miller, W.R., and O'Brien, C.P. Plasma testosterone level and sexual behavior of couples. *Archives of Sexual Behavior*, 1978, *7*, 157–173.

Pervin, L.A. *Personality: Theory, Assessment, and Research.* New York: John Wiley & Sons, 1975.

Peterson, L.R., and Peterson, M.J. Short-term retention of individual verbal items. *Journal of Experimental Psychology*, 1959, *58*, 193–198.

Petty, R.E., and Cacioppo, J.T. Issue involvement as a moderator of the effects on attitude of advertising content and context. *Advances in Consumer Research*, 1981, *8*, 20–24.

Petty, R.E., Cacioppo, J.T., and Goldman, R. Personal involvement as a determinant of argument-based persuasion. *Journal of Personality and Social Psychology*, 1981, *41*, 847–855.

Petty, R.E., Harkins, S.G., and Williams, K.D. The effects of group diffusion of cognitive effort on attitudes: An information processing view. *Journal of Personality and Social Psychology*, 1980, *38*, 81–92.

Phares, E.J. *Clinical Psychology: Concepts, Methods, and Profession.* Homewood, Ill.: Dorsey Press, 1979.

Piaget, J. *The Origins of Intelligence in Children*, translated by M. Cook: New York: International Universities Press, 1952.

Piaget, J. *The Early Growth of Logic in the Child*, translated by E.A. Lunzer and D. Pappert. London: Routledge & Kegan Paul, 1964.

Pierrel, R., and Sherman, J.G. Barnabus, the rat with college training. *Brown Alumni Monthly*, February 1963, 8–12.

Plutchik, R. *The Emotions: Facts, Theories and a New Model.* New York: Random House, 1962.

Plutchik, R. *Emotion: A Psychoevolutionary Synthesis.* New York: Harper & Row, 1980.

Pollack, I., and Pickett, J.M. Intelligibility of excerpts from fluent speech: Auditory vs. structural context. *Journal of Verbal Learning and Verbal Behavior*, 1964, *3*, 79–84.

Pollak, S., & Gilligan, C. Images of violence in Thematic Apperception Test stories. *Journal of Personality and Social Psychology*, 1982, *42*, 159–167.

Pollak, S., & Gilligan, C. Differing about differences: The incidence and interpretation of violent fantasies in women and men. *Journal of Personality and Social Psychology*, 1983, *45*, 1172–1175.

Pollak, S., & Gilligan, C. Killing the messenger. *Journal of Personality and Social Psychology*, 1985, *48*, 374–375.

Posner, M.I., Boies, S.J., Eichelman, W.H., and Taylor, R.L. Retention of visual and name codes of single letters. *Journal of Experimental Psychology*, 1969, *79* (number 1, part 2).

Premack, D. Reinforcement theory. In *Nebraska Symposium on Motivation*, edited by D. Levine. Lincoln: University of Nebraska Press, 1965.

Premack, D. Language and intelligence in ape and man. *American Scientist*, 1976, *64*, 674–683.

Prichard, J.C. *A Treatise on Insanity and Other Disorders Affecting the Mind.* London: Sherwood, Gilbert, and Piper, 1835.

Provence, S., and Lipton, R.C. *Infants in Institutions.* New York: International Universities Press, 1962.

Purtell, J.J., Robins, E., and Cohen, M.E. Observations on clinical aspects of hysteria. *Journal of the American Medical Association*, 1951, *146*, 902–909.

Quattrone, G.A., and Tversky, A. Causal versus diagnostic contingencies: On self-deception and on the voter's illusion. *Journal of Personality and Social Psychology*, 1984, *46*, 237–248.

Quay, H.C. Psychopathic personality as pathological stimulus seeking. *American Journal of Psychiatry*, 1965, *122*, 180–183.

Rachman, S., and Hodgson, R.J. Experimentally-induced "sexual fetishism": Replication and development. *Psychological Record*, 1968, *18*, 25–27.

Ravelli, G.-P., Stein, Z.A., and Susser, M.W. Obesity in young men after famine exposure in utero and early infancy. *New England Journal of Medicine*, 1976, *295*, 349–353.

Reese, E.P. *Human Operant Behavior* (2nd ed.). Dubuque, Ia.: W.C. Brown, 1978.

Regan, D.T. Effects of a favor and liking on compliance. *Journal of Experimental Social Psychology*, 1971, *7*, 627–639.

Regan, D.T., and Fazio, R.H. On the consistency between attitudes and behavior: Look to the method of attitude formation. *Journal of Experimental Social Psychology*, 1977, *13*, 28–45.

Reiser, M., and Nielson, M. Investigative hypnosis: A developing specialty. *American Journal of Clinical Hypnosis*, 1980, *23*, 75–83.

Review Panel. Coronary-prone behavior and coronary heart disease: A critical review. *Circulation*, 1981, *673*, 1199–1215.

Reynolds, A.G., and Flagg, P.W. *Cognitive Psychol-*

ogy, (2nd ed.). Boston: Little, Brown, 1983.

Rheingold, H.L. The effect of a strange environment on the behavior of infants. In *Determinants of Infant Behaviour* (vol. 4), edited by B.M. Foss. London: Methuen, 1969.

Rheingold, H.L., and Eckerman, C.O. The infant separates himself from his mother. *Science*, 1970, *168*, 78–83.

Rideout, B. Non-REM sleep as a source of learning deficits induced by REM sleep deprivation. *Physiology and Behavior*, 1979, *22*, 1043–1047.

Riegel, K.P., Riegel, R.M., and Meyer, G. A study of the drop-out rates in longitudinal research on aging and the prediction of death. *Journal of Personality and Social Psychology*, 1967, *4*, 342–348.

Riesen, A.H. Sensory deprivation: Facts in search of a theory. *Journal of Nervous and Mental Disease*, 1961, *132*, 21–25.

Riggs, L.A., Ratliff, F., Cornsweet, J.C., and Cornsweet, T.N. The disappearance of steadily fixated visual test objects. *Journal of the Optical Society of America*, 1953, *43*, 495–501.

Ritchey, G.H., and Beal, C.R. Image detail and recall: Evidence for within-item elaboration. *Journal of Experimental Psychology: Human Learning and Memory*, 1980, *6*, 66–76.

Ritchie, D.E., and Phares, E.J. Attitude change as a function of internal-external control and communicator status. *Journal of Personality*, 1969, *37*, 429–443.

Rittle, R.H. Changes in helping behavior: Self- versus situational perceptions as mediators of the foot-in-the-door effect. *Personality and Social Psychology Bulletin*, 1981, *7*, 431–437.

Robbins, L.N., Helzer, J.E., Weissman, M.M., Orvaschel, H., Gruenberg, E., Burke, J.D., and Regier, D.A. Lifetime prevalence of specific psychiatric disorders in three sites. *Archives of General Psychiatry*, 1984, *41*, 949–958.

Rogers, C.R. *Client-centered Therapy*. Boston: Houghton Mifflin, 1951.

Rogers, C.R. *On Becoming a Person*. Boston: Houghton Mifflin, 1961.

Rogers, C.R. *A Way of Being*. Boston: Houghton Mifflin, 1980.

Rolls, E.T. Feeding and reward. In *The Neural Basis of Feeding and Reward*, edited by B.G. Hobel and D. Novin. Brunswick, Maine: Haer Institute, 1982.

Rose, G.A., and Williams, R.T. Metabolic studies of large and small eaters. *British Journal of Nutrition*, 1961, *15*, 1–9.

Rose, R.J., Harris, E.L., Christian, J.C., and Nance, W.E. Genetic variance in non-verbal intelligence: Data from the kinships of identical twins. *Science*, 1979, *205*, 1153–1155.

Rose, R.M., Bourne, P.G., Poe, R.O., Mougey, E.H., Collins, D.R., and Mason, J.W., Androgen responses to stress. II. Excretion of testosterone, epitestosterone, androsterone, and etiocholanolone during basic combat training and under threat of attack. *Psychosomatic Medicine*, 1969, *31*, 418–436.

Rosenblatt, J.S. and Aronson, L.R. The decline of sexual behavior in male cats after castration with special reference to the role of prior sexual experience. *Behaviour*, 1958, *12*, 285–338.

Rosenfield, M.E., and Moore, J.W. Red nucleus lesions disrupt the classically conditioned membrane response in rabbits. *Behavioural Brain Research*, 1983, *10*, 393–398.

Rosenhan, D.L. On being sane in insane places. *Science*, 1973, *179*, 250–258.

Rosenthal, A.M. *Thirty-eight Witnesses*. New York: McGraw-Hill, 1964.

Rosenthal, D. *Genetic Theory and Abnormal Behavior*. New York: McGraw-Hill, 1970.

Ross, E.D. The aprosodias: Functional-anatomic organization of the affective components of language in the right hemisphere. *Archives of Neurology*, 1981, *38*, 561–569.

Ross, L. The intuitive psychologist and his shortcomings: Distortions in the attribution process. In *Advances in Experimental Social Psychology*, edited by L. Berkowitz. New York: Academic Press, 1977.

Ross, L.D., Amabile, T.M., and Steinmetz, J.L. Social roles, social control, and biases in social-perception processes. *Journal of Personality and Social Psychology*, 1977, *35*, 485–494.

Ross, L.D., Bierbrauer, G., and Polly, S. Attribution of educational outcomes by professional and nonprofessional instructors. *Journal of Personality and Social Psychology*, 1974, *29*, 609–618.

Ross, L.D., Greene, D., and House, P. The "false consensus effect": An egocentric bias in social perception and attribution processes. *Journal of Experimental Social Psychology*, 1977, *13*, 279–301.

Rothbaum, F., Weisz, J.R., and Snyder, S.S. Changing the world and changing the self: A two-process model of perceived control. *Journal of Personality and Social Psychology*, 1982, *42*, 5–37.

Rotter, J.B. Generalized expectancies for internal versus external control of reinforcement. *Psychological Monographs*, 1966, *80* (number 609).

Rounsaville, B.J., Harding, P.S., and Weissman, M.M. Single case study. Briquet's syndrome in a man. *Journal of Nervous and Mental Disease*, 1979, *167*, 364–367.

Rubin, Z. *Liking and Loving: An Invitation to Social Psychology*. New York: Holt, Rinehart and Winston, 1973.

Rundus, D., and Atkinson, R.C. Rehearsal procedures in free recall: A procedure for direct observation. *Journal of Verbal Learning and Verbal Behavior*, 1970, *9*, 99–105.

Rush, A.J., Beck, A.T., Kovacs, M., Weissenberger, J., and Hollon, S.D. Comparison of the effects of cognitive therapy and pharacotherapy on hopelessness and self-concept. *American Journal of Psychiatry*, 1982, *139*, 862–866.

Russek, M. Hepatic receptors and the neurophysiological mechanisms controlling feed behavior. In *Neurosciences Research* (vol. 4), edited by S. Ehrenpreis. New York: Academic Press, 1971.

Ryback, R.S., and Lewis, O.F. Effects of prolonged bed rest on EEG sleep patterns in young, healthy volunteers. *Electroencephalography and Clinical Neurophysiology*, 1971, *31*, 395–399.

Sachs, J.S. Recognition memory for syntactic and semantic aspects of connected discourse. *Perception and Psychophysics*, 1967, *2*, 437–442.

Sackett, G.P. Innate mechanisms, rearing conditions, and a theory of early experience effects in primates. In *Miami Symposium on the Prediction of Behavior, 1968*, edited by M.R. Jones. Coral Gables, Fla.: University of Miami Press, 1970.

Sackheim, H.A., Paulus, D., and Weiman, A.L. Classroom seating and hypnotic susceptibility. *Journal of Abnormal Psychology*, 1979, *88*, 81–84.

Saegert, S.C., Swap, W., and Zajonc, R.B. Exposure, context, and interpersonal attraction. *Journal of Personality and Social Psychology*, 1973, *25*, 234–242.

Safer, M., and Leventhal, H. Ear differences in evaluating emotional tones of voice and verbal content. *Journal of Experimental Psychology: Human Perception and Performance*, 1977, *3*, 75–82.

Saffran, E.M., Schwartz, M.F., and Marin, O.S.M. Evidence from aphasia: Isolating the components of a production model. In *Language Production*, edited by B. Butterworth. London: Academic Press, 1980.

Salapatek, P. Pattern perception in early infancy. In *Infant Perception: From Sensation to Cognition* (vol. 1), edited by L.B. Cohen and P. Salapatek. New York: Academic Press, 1975.

Salmon, U.J., and Geist, S.H. Effect of androgens upon libido in women. *Journal of Clinical Endocrinology and Metabolism*, 1943, *172*, 374–377.

Sarason, S.B., and Mandler, G. Some correlates of test anxiety. *Journal of Abnormal and Social Psychology*, 1952, *47*, 810–817.

Scarr, S., and Weinberg, R.A. IQ test performance of black children adopted by white families. *American psychologist*, 1976, *31*, 726–739.

Schachter, S. The interaction of cognitive and physiological determinants of emotional state. In *Psychobiological Approaches to Social Behavior*, edited by P.H. Liederman and D. Shapiro. Stanford, Calif.: Stanford University Press, 1964.

Schachter, S., and Singer, J.E. Cognitive, social and physiological determinants of emotional state. *Psychological Review*, 1962, *69*, 379–399.

Schank, R., and Abelson, R.P. *Scripts, Plans, Goals, and Understanding*. Hillsdale, N.J.: Lawrence Erlbaum Associates, 1977.

Scherschlicht, R., Polc, P., Schneeberger, J., Steiner, M., and Haefely, W. Selective suppression of rapid eye movement sleep (REMS) in cats by typical and atypical antidepressants. In *Typical and Atypical Antidepressants: Molecular Mechanisms*, edited by E. Costa and G. Racagni. New York: Raven Press, 1982.

Schiano, D.J., and Watkins, M.J. Speech-like coding of pictures in short-term memory. *Memory and Cognition*, 1981, *9*, 110–114.

Schmauk, F.J. Punishment, arousal, and avoidance learning in sociopaths. *Journal of Abnormal Psychology*, 1970, *122*, 509–522.

Schmidt, G., and Sigusch, V. Sex differences in responses to psychosexual stimulation by films and slides. *Journal of Sex Research*, 1970, *44*, 229–237.

Schoedel, J., Frederickson, W.A., and Knight, J.M. An extrapolation of the physical attractiveness and sex variables within the Byrne attraction paradigm. *Memory and Cognition*, 1975, *3*, 527–530.

Schofield, J.W. Effects of norms, public disclosure, and need for approval on volunteering behavior consistent with attitudes. *Journal of Personality and Social Psychology*, 1975, *31*, 1126–1133.

Schon, M., and Sutherland, A.M. The role of hormones in human behavior. III. Changes in female sexuality after hypophysectomy. *Journal of Clinical Endocrinology and Metabolism*, 1960, *20*, 833–841.

Schwartz, M.F., Saffran, E.M., and Marin, O.S.M. The word order problem in agrammatism. I. Comprehension. *Brain and Language*, 1980, *10*, 249–262.

Scoville, W.B., and Milner, B. Loss of recent memory after bilateral hippocampal lesions. *Journal of Neurology, Neurosurgery and Psychiatry*, 1957, *20*, 11–21.

Scribner, S. Modes of thinking and ways of speaking: Culture and logic reconsidered. In *Thinking: Readings in Cognitive Science*, edited by P.N. Johnson-Laird and P.C. Wason. Cambridge, England: Cambridge University Press, 1977.

Sechehaye, M. *Autobiography of a Schizophrenic Girl*. New York: Grune & Stratton, 1951.

Seligman, M.E.P. *Helplessness*. San Franciso: W.H. Freeman, 1975.

Selye, H. *The Stress of Life*. New York: McGraw-Hill, 1956.

Sem-Jacobsen, C.W. *Depth-electrographic Stimulation of the Human Brain and Behavior*. Springfield, Ill.: Charles C Thomas, 1968.

Shanan, J. Personality types and culture in later adulthood. *Contributions in Human Development* (vol. 12), Basel: Karger (Monograph), 1985.

Shand, M.A., and Klima, E.S. Nonauditory suffix effects in congenitally deaf signers of American Sign Language. *Journal of Experimental Psychology: Human Learning and Memory*, 1981, *7*, 464–474.

Shapiro, C.M., Bortz, R., Mitchell, D., Bartel, P., and Jooste, P. Slow-wave sleep: A recovery period after exercise. *Science*, 1982, *214*, 1253–1254.

Shatz, M., and Gelman, R. The development of communication skills: Modifications in the speech of young children as a function of listener. *Monographs of the Society for Research in Child Development*, 1973, *38* (Serial no. 152).

Sheehan, P.W., and Perry, C.W. *Methodologies of Hypnosis: A Critical Appraisal of Contemporary Paradigms of Hypnosis*. Hillsdale, N.J.: Lawrence Erlbaum Associates, 1976.

Sheffield, F.D., Wulff, J.J., and Backer, R. Reward

value of copulation without sex drive reduction. *Journal of Comparative and Physiological Psychology*, 1951, *44*, 3–8.

Shipley, E.F., Smith, C.S., and Gleitman, L.R. A study in the acquisition of language: Free responses to commands. *Language*, 1969, *45*, 322–342.

Shirley, M.M. The first two years: A study of 25 babies. Vol. I: Postural and locomotor development. In *Institute of Child Welfare Monographs* (series no. 6). Minneapolis: University of Minnesota Press, 1933.

Siegelman, M. Parental background of male homosexuals and heterosexuals. *Archives of Sexual Behavior*, 1974, *3*, 3–18.

Sigusch, V., Schmidt, G., Reinfeld, A., and Wiedemann-Sutor, I. Psychosexual stimulation: Sex differences. *Journal of Sex Research*, 1970, *6*, 10–24.

Sims, E.A.H., and Horton, E.S. Endocrine and metabolic adaptation to obesity and starvation. *American Journal of Clinical Nutrition*, 1968, *21*, 1455–1470.

Skinner, B.F. Superstition in the pigeon. *Journal of Experimental Psychology*, 1948, *38*, 168–172.

Skinner, B.F. *Verbal Behavior*. Englewood Cliffs, N.J.: Prentice-Hall, 1957.

Skinner, B.F. *About Behaviorism*. New York: Vintage Books, 1974.

Slater, B., and Shields, J. Genetical aspects of anxiety. *British Journal of Psychiatry Special Publication No. 3, Studies of Anxiety*. Ashford, Kent: Headley Bros., 1969.

Slobin, D.I. The acquisition of Russian as a native language. In *The Genesis of Language*, edited by F. Smith and G.A. Miller. Cambridge, Mass.: MIT Press, 1966.

Smith, G.H., and Engel, R. Influence of a female model on perceived characteristics of an automobile. *Proceedings of the 76th Annual Convention of the American Psychological Association*, 1968, *3*, 681–682.

Smith, M.L., Glass, G.V., and Miller, T.I. *Benefits of Psychotherapy*. Baltimore: Johns Hopkins University Press, 1980.

Snow, C.E. Mothers' speech to children learning language. *Child Development*, 1972a, *43*, 549–565.

Snow, C.E. Young children's responses to adult sentences of varying complexity. Paper presented at the Third International Congress of Applied Linguistics, Copenhagen, August, 1972b.

Snyder, S.H. *Madness and the Brain*. New York: McGraw-Hill, 1974.

Solomon, R.C. *The Passions*. Garden City, N.Y.: Anchor Press/Doubleday, 1976.

Spanos, N.P., Gwynn, M.I., and Stam, H.J. Instructional demands and ratings of overt and hidden pain during hypnotic analgesia. *Journal of Abnormal Psychology*, 1983, *92*, 479–488.

Spearman, C. *The Abilities of Man*. London: Macmillan, 1927.

Spence, K.W. A theory of emotionally based drive (D) and its relation to performance in simple learning situations. *American Psychologist*, 1958, *13*, 131–141.

Sperling, G.A. The information available in brief visual presentation. *Psychological Monographs*, 1960, *74* (no. 498).

Sperry, R.W. Brain bisection and consciousness. In *Brain and Conscious Experience*, edited by J. Eccles. New York: Springer-Verlag, 1966.

Spiro, R.J. Remembering information from text: The "state of schema" approach. In *Schooling and the Acquisition of Knowledge*, edited by R.C. Anderson, R.J. Spiro, and W.E. Montague. Hillsdale, N.J.: Lawrence Erlbaum Associates, 1977.

Spiro, R.J. Accommodative reconstruction in prose recall. *Journal of Verbal Learning and Verbal Behavior*, 1980, *19*, 84–95.

Spitzer, R.L. On pseudoscience in science, logic in remission, and psychiatric diagnosis: A critique of Rosenhan's "On being sane in insane places." *Journal of Abnormal Psychology*, 1975, *84*, 442–452.

Squire, L.R. Stable impairment in remote memory following electroconvulsive therapy. *Neuropsychologia*, 1974, *13*, 51–58.

Squire, L.R. The neuropsychology of human memory. *Annual Review of Neuroscience*, 1982, *5*, 241–273.

Stapp, J., Fulcher, R., Nelson, S.D., Pallak, M.S., and Wicherski, M. The employment of recent doctorate recipients in psychology: 1975 through 1978. *American Psychologist*, 1981, *36*, 1211–1254.

Stebbins, W.C., Miller, J.M., Johnsson, L.-G., and Hawkins, J.E. Ototoxic hearing loss and cochlear pathology in the monkey. *Annals of Otology, Rhinology, and Laryngology*, 1969, *78*, 1007–1026.

Steele, C.M., and Liu, T.J. Making the dissonance act unreflective of self: Dissonance avoidance and the expectancy of a value-affirming response. *Personality and Social Psychology Bulletin*, 1981, *7*, 393–397.

Steele, C.M., Southwick, L.L., and Critchlow, B. Dissonance and alcohol: Drinking your troubles away. *Journal of Personality and Social Psychology*, 1981, *41*, 831–846.

Stein, B.S., and Bransford, J.D. Constraints on effective elaboration: Effects of precision and subject generation. *Journal of Verbal Learning and Verbal Behavior*, 1979, *18*, 769–777.

Stein, L., and Ray, O.S. Brain stimulation reward "thresholds" self-determined in rat. *Psychopharmacologia*, 1960, *1*, 251–256.

Stern, J.A., Brown, M., Ulett, G.A., and Sletten, I. A comparison of hypnosis, acupuncture, morphine, Valium, aspirin, and placebo in the management of experimentally induced pain. In *Hypnosis and Relaxation: Modern Verification of an Old Equation*. New York: Wiley-Interscience, 1977.

Stern, W. *The Psychological Methods of Testing Intelligence*. Baltimore: Warwick and York, 1914.

Sternbach, P.A. *Pain: A Psychophysiological Analysis*. New York: Academic Press, 1968.

Sternberg, R.J. *Beyond IQ: A Triarchic Theory of Human Intelligence*. Cambridge, England: Cambridge University Press, 1985.

Stevens, J.R. Neurology and neuropathology of schizophrenia. In *Schizophrenia As a Brain Disease*, edited by F.A. Henn and G.A. Nasrallah. New York: Oxford University Press, 1982a.

Stevens, J.R. Neuropathology of schizophrenia. *Archives of General Psychiatry*, 1982b, *39*, 1131–1139.

Sticht, T.G. *Reading for Working: A Functional Literary Anthology*. Alexandria, Va.: Human Resources Research Organization, 1975.

Stirnimann, F. Ueber das farbempfinden Neugeborener. *Annales Paediatrici*, 1944, *163*, 1–25.

Stokoe, W.C. Apes who sign and critics who don't. In *Language in Primates: Perspectives and Implications*, edited by J. de Luce and H.T. Wilder. New York: Springer-Verlag, 1983.

Stone, S. Psychiatry through the ages. *Journal of Abnormal and Social Psychology*, 1937, *32*, 131–160.

Strickland, B.R. Individual differences in verbal conditioning, extinction, and awareness. *Journal of Personality*, 1970, *38*, 364–378.

Strupp, H.H. and Hadley, S.W. Specific vs nonspecific factors in psychotherapy. *Archives of General Psychiatry*, 1979, *36*, 1125–1136.

Stunkard, A.S., and Burt, V. Obesity and the body image: II. Age at onset of disturbances in the body image. *American Journal of Psychiatry*, 1967, *123*, 1443–1447.

Suinn, R.M. Intervention with Type A behaviors. *Journal of Consulting and Clinical Psychology*, 1982, *50*, 797–803.

Suomi, S.J., and Harlow, H.F. Social rehabilitation of isolate-reared monkeys. *Developmental Psychology*, 1972, *6*, 487–496.

Svejda, M.J., Campos, J.J., and Emde, R.N. Mother-infant "bonding": Failure to generalize. *Child Development*, 1980, *51*, 775–779.

Swann, W.B. Quest for accuracy in person perception: A matter of pragmatics. *Psychological Review*, 1984, *91*, 457–477.

Swann, W.B., and Hill, C.A. When our identities are mistaken: Reaffirming self-conceptions through social interaction. *Journal of Personality and Social Psychology*, 1982, *43*, 59–66.

Swann, W.B., and Pittman, T.S. Initiating play activity of children: The moderating influence of verbal cues on intrinsic motivation. *Child Development*, 1977, *48*, 1128–1132.

Taube, S.L., Kirstein, L.S., Sweeney, D.R., Heninger, G.R., and Maas, J.W. Urinary 3-methoxy-4-hydroxyphenyleneglycol and psychiatric diagnosis. *American Journal of Psychiatry*, 1978, *135*, 78–82.

Terrace, H.S., Petitto, L.A., Sanders, R.J., and Bever, T.G. Can an ape create a sentence? *Science*, 1979, *206*, 891–902.

Thoresen, C.E., Freeman, M., Gill, J.K., and Ulmer, D. Recurrent coronary prevention project: Some preliminary findings. *Acta Medica Scandanavica Suppli.*, 1982, *660*, 172–192.

Thorndike, E.L. *The Elements of Psychology*. New York: Seiler, 1905.

Thurstone, L.L. *Primary Mental Abilities*. Chicago: The University of Chicago Press, 1938.

Tippin, J., and Henn, F.A. Modified leukotomy in the treatment of intractable obsessional neurosis. *American Journal of Psychiatry*, 1982, *139*, 1601–1603.

Tomkins, S.S. *Affect, Imagery, and Consciousness*. Vol. 1: *The Positive Affects*. New York: Springer-Verlag, 1962.

Tomkins, S.S. *Affect, Imagery, and Consciousness*. Vol. 2: *The Negative Affects*. New York: Springer-Verlag, 1963.

Tomkins, S.S. *Affect, Imagery, and Consciousness*. Vol. 3: *Cognition and Affect*. New York: Springer-Verlag, 1982.

Torrey, E.F., Torrey, B.B., and Peterson, M.R. Seasonality of schizophrenic births in the United States. *Archives of General Psychiatry*, 1977, *34*, 1065–1070.

Torrey, E.F., Yolken, R.H., and Winfrey, C.J. Cytomegalovirus antibody in cerebrospinal fluid of schizophrenic patients detected by enzyme immunoassay. *Science*, 1982, *216*, 892–894.

Tourney, G. Hormones and homosexuality. In *Homosexual Behavior*, edited by J. Marmor. New York: Basic Books, 1980.

Träskmann, L., Åsberg, M., Bertilsson, L., and Sjöstrand, L. Monoamine metabolites on CSF and suicidal behavior. *Archives of General Psychiatry*, 1981, *38*, 631–636.

Trehub, S.E. The discrimination of foreign speech contrasts by infants and adults. *Child Development*, 1976, *47*, 466–472.

Treisman, A.M. Contextual cues in selective listening. *Quarterly Journal of Experimental Psychology*, 1960, *12*, 242–248.

Triplett, N. The dynamogenic factors in pacemaking and competition. *American Journal of Psychology*, 1897, *9*, 507–533.

Tronick, E., Als, H., Adamson, L., Wise, S., and Brazelton, T.B. The infant's response to entrapment between contradictory messages in face-to-face interaction. *Journal of the American Academy of Child Psychiatry*, 1978, *17*, 1–13.

Truax, C.B. Reinforcement and nonreinforcement in Rogerian psychotherapy. *Journal of Abnormal Psychology*, 1966, *71*, 1–9.

Truax, C.B., and Carkhuff, R.R. Significant developments in psychotherapy research. In *Progress in Clinical Psychology*, edited by L.E. Abt and B.F. Reiss. New York: Grune & Stratton, 1964.

Tryon, R.C. Genetic differences in maze learning in rats. *Yearbook of the National Society for Studies in Education*, 1940, *39*, 111–119.

Tulving, E. Episodic and semantic memory. In *Organization of Memory*, edited by E. Tulving and W. Donaldson. New York: Academic Press, 1972.

Turner, S. The life and times of a pickle packer. *Boston Sunday Globe*, January 8, 1978, pp. 10–22.

Tyson, W. Personal communication, 1980.

Ullman, L.P., and Krasner, L. *Psychological Approach to Abnormal Behavior*. Englewood Cliffs, N.J.: Prentice-Hall, 1969.

Valenstein, E.S. *Brain Control*. New York: John Wiley & Sons, 1973.

Valenstein, E.S. *The Psychosurgery Debate: Scientific, Legal, and Ethical Perspectives*. San Francisco: W.H. Freeman, 1980.

Van de Castle and Smith, 1971. Personal communication cited by Money, J., and Ehrhardt, A.A. *Man & Woman, Boy & Girl*. Baltimore: Johns Hopkins University Press, 1972.

Vernon, P.E. *Intelligence: Heredity and Environment*. San Francisco: W.H. Freeman, 1979.

Vogel, G.W., Vogel, F., McAbee, R.S., and Thurmond, A.G. Improvement of depression by REM sleep deprivation. *Archives of General Psychiatry*, 1980, *37*, 247–253.

von Békésy, G. *Experiments in Hearing*. New York: McGraw-Hill, 1960.

Von Wright, J.M., Anderson, K., and Stenman, U. Generalization of conditioned GSRs in dichotic listening. In *Attention and Performance*, Vol. V, edited by P.M.A. Rabbitt and S. Dornic. London: Academic Press, 1975.

Wachtel, P. *Psychoanalysis and Behavior Therapy: Toward an Integration*. New York: Basic Books, 1977.

Wada, J.A., Clarke, R., and Hamm, A. Cerebral hemispheric asymmetry in humans: Cortical speech zones in 100 adults and 100 infant brains. *Archives of Neurology*, 1975, *32*, 239–246.

Wagner, R.K., and Sternberg, R.J. Executive control of reading, 1983. Cited by Sternberg, R.J. *Beyond IQ: A Triarchic Theory of Human Intelligence*. Cambridge, England: Cambridge University Press, 1985.

Walraven, P.L. A closer look at the tritanopic convergence point. *Vision Research*, 1974, *14*, 1339–1343.

Walster, E., Aronson, V., Abrahams, D., and Rottman, L. Importance of physical attractiveness in dating behavior. *Journal of Personality and Social Psychology*, 1966, *4*, 508–516.

Walster, E., and Berscheid, E. Adrenaline makes the heart grow fonder. *Psychology Today*, June 1971, 47–62.

Warren, J., and Hunt, E. Cognitive processing in children with Prader-Willi syndrome. In *Prader-Willi Syndrome*, edited by V.A. Holme, S.J. Sulzbacher, and P.L. Pipes. Baltimore, Md.: University Park Press, 1981.

Warren, R.M. Perceptual restoration of missing speech sounds. *Science*, 1967, *167*, 392–393.

Warren, R.M., and Warren, R.P. Auditory illusions and confusions. *Scientific American*, 1970, *223*, 30–36.

Warrington, E.K., and Shallice, T. Neuropsychological evidence of visual storage in short-term memory tests. *Quarterly Journal of Experimental Psychology*, 1972, *24*, 30–40.

Watson, J.B. *Behaviorism* (rev. ed.). New York: W.W. Norton, 1930.

Watson, J.S. Smiling, cooing, and the "game." *Merrill-Palmer Quarterly*, 1973, *18*, 323–339.

Watson, J.S., and Ramey, C.T. Reactions to responsive contingent stimulation in early infancy. *Merrill-Palmer Quarterly*, 1972, *18*, 219–227.

Watt, N.F., and Lubansky, A.W. Childhood roots of schizophrenia. *Journal of Consulting and Clinical Psychology*, 1976, *44*, 363–375.

Waxenberg, S.E., Drellich, M.G., and Sutherland, A.M. The role of hormones in human behavior: I. Changes in female sexuality after adrenalectomy. *Journal of Clinical Endocrinology and Metabolism*, 1959, *19*, 193–202.

Webb, W.B. *Sleep: The Gentle Tyrant*. Englewood Cliffs, N.J.: Prentice-Hall, 1975.

Webb, W.B., and Cartwright, R.D. Sleep and dreams. *Annual Review of Psychology*, 1978, *29*, 223–252.

Weigel, R.H., Vernon, D.T.A., and Tognacci, L.N. Specificity of the attitude as a determinant of attitude-behavior congruence. *Journal of Personality and Social Psychology*, 1974, *30*, 724–728.

Weinberger, D.R., Bigelow, L.B., Kleinman, J.E., Klein, S.T., Rosenblatt, J.E., and Wyatt, R.J. Cerebral ventricular enlargement in chronic schizophrenia: An association with poor response to treatment. *Archives of General Psychiatry*, 1980, *37*, 11–13.

Weinberger, D.R., and Wyatt, J.R. Brain morphology in schizophrenia: *In vivo* studies. In *Schizophrenia As a Brain Disease*, edited by F.A. Henn and G.A. Nasrallah. New York: Oxford University Press, 1982.

Weiner, B., Stone, A., Schmitz, M., Schmidt, A., Hernandez, A., & Benton, C. Compounding the errors: A reply to Pollak and Gilligan. *Journal of Personality and Social Psychology*, 1983, *45*, 1176–1178.

Weiss, J.M. Effects of coping responses on stress. *Journal of Comparative and Physiological Psychology*, 1968, *65*, 251–260.

Weiss, J.M. Somatic effects of predictable and unpredictable shock. *Psychosomatic Medicine*, 1970, *32*, 397–408.

Weiss, J.M. Effects of punishing the coping response (conflict) on stress pathology in rats. *Journal of Comparative and Physiological Psychology*, 1971, *77*, 14–21.

Wernicke, K. *Der Aphasische Symptomenkomplex*. Breslau, Poland: Cohn & Weigert, 1874.

Wertheimer, M. Psychomotor co-ordination of auditory-visual space at birth. *Science*, 1961, *134*, 1692.

Westwood, G. *A Minority: Report on the Life of the Male Homosexual in Great Britain*. London: Longmans, Green, 1960.

Whitehead, R.G., Rowland, M.G.M., Hutton, M., Prentice, A.M., Müller, E., and Paul, A. Factors influencing lactation performance in rural Gambian mothers. *Lancet*, 1978, *2*, 178–181.

Whitley, B.E. Sex role orientation and self-esteem: A critical meta-analytic review. *Journal of Personality and Social Psychology*, 1983, *44*, 765–778.

Whitlock, F.A. The aetiology of hysteria. *Acta Psychiatrica Scandinavica*, 1967, *43*, 144–162.

Wickens, D.D. Characteristics of word encoding. In

Coding Processes in Human Memory, edited by A.W. Melton and E. Martin. Washington, D.C.: Winston, 1972.

Wicker, A.W. Attitudes versus actions: The relationship of verbal and overt behavioral responses to attitude objects. *Journal of Social Issues*, 1969, *25*, 41–78.

Wieman, L.A. The stress pattern of early child language. Unpublished doctoral dissertation, University of Washington, 1974.

Williams, F.E. *Orokaiva Society*. Oxford, England: Clarendon Press, 1930.

Williams, K., Harkins, S., and Latané, B. Identifiability as a deterrent to social loafing: Two cheering experiments. *Journal of Personality and Social Psychology*, 1981, *40*, 303–311.

Wilson, G.T., and O'Leary, K.D. *Principles of Behavior Therapy*. Englewood Cliffs, N.J.: Prentice-Hall, 1978.

Wilson, P.R. The perceptual distortion of height as a function of ascribed academic status. *Journal of Social Psychology*, 1968, *74*, 97–102.

Winter, A. Depression and intractable pain treated by modified prefrontal lobotomy. *Journal of Medical Sociology*, 1972, *69*, 757–759.

Wisocki, P.A. Treatment of obsessive compulsive behavior by the application of covert sensitization and covert reinforcement: A case report. *Journal of Behavior Therapy and Experimental Psychiatry*, 1970, *1*, 233–239.

Woerner, P.L., and Guze, S.B. A family and marital study of hysteria. *British Journal of Psychiatry*, 1968, *114*, 161–168.

Wolff, P.H. Observations on the early development of smiling. In *Determinants of Infant Behaviour* (vol. 2), edited by B.M. Foss. London: Methuen, 1963.

Wolff, P.H. *The Causes, Controls and Organization of Behavior in the Neonate*. New York: International Universities Press, 1966.

Wolff, P.H. Crying and vocalization in early infancy. In *Determinants of Infant Behaviour* (vol. 4), edited by B.M. Foss. London: Methuen, 1969.

Woodruff, G., Premack, D., and Kennel, K. Conservation of liquid and solid quantity by the chimpanzee. *Science*, 1978, *202*, 991–994.

Woodruff, R.A., Guze, S.B., and Clayton, P.J. Anxiety neurosis among psychiatric outpatients. *Comprehensive Psychiatry*, 1972, *13*, 165–170.

Woodworth, R.S., and Schlosberg, H. *Experimental Psychology*. New York: Holt, Rinehart and Winston, 1954.

Zajonc, R.B. Social facilitation. *Science*, 1965, *149*, 269–274.

Zajonc, R.B. Attitudinal effects of mere exposure. *Journal of Personality and Social Psychology Monograph Supplement*, 1968, *9*, 1–27.

Zajonc, R.B. On primacy of affect. In *Approaches to Emotion*, edited by K.R. Scherer and P. Ekman. Hillsdale, N.J.: Lawrence Erlbaum Associates, 1984.

Zajonc, R.B., and Sales, S.M. Social facilitation of dominant and subordinate responses. *Journal of Experimental Social Psychology*, 1966, *2*, 160–168.

Zubin, J., and Barrera, S.E. Effect of electric convulsive therapy on memory. *Proceedings of the Society for Experimental Biology and Medicine*, 1941, *48*, 596–597.

Zuger, B. Monozygotic twins discordant for homosexuality: Report of a pair and significance of the phenomenon. *Comprehensive Psychiatry*, 1976, *17*, 661–669.

Name Index

Subject Index

Note: **Boldface** page numbers show the location of defined Key Terms.

573

Photo Researchers; page 124 (bottom) Petit Format/Nestle/ Science Source/Photo Researchers; page 126 © Michal Heron 1981/Woodfin Camp & Associates; page 128 Julie O'Neil/The Picture Cube; page 130 Nancy Rader; page 132 Yves DeBraine/Black Star; page 133 (left, center, right) Hazel Hankin; page 135 Richard Hutchings/Photo Researchers; page 139 Claudia Parks/The Stock Market; page 140 (left) Richard Dunoff/The Stock Market; page 144 Nina Leen/*Life Magazine*, © Time Inc.; page 145 © John Troha 1984/Black Star.

Chapter 5

Page 153 Rebecca Collette/Archive Pictures, Inc.; page 155 © Tom Sobolik 1985/Black Star; page 156 © Donna Ferrato 1985/Visions; page 157 (top) Jill Freedman/Archive Pictures, Inc.; page 157 (bottom) Index Stock International; page 158 © Jeffrey W. Myers 1985/The Stock Market; page 159 John Iacono/*Sports Illustrated*, Time, Inc.; page 160 © Kenneth Rogers 1985/Black Star; page 161 Roy Morsch/ The Stock Market; page 163 Bernholtz/The Stock Market; page 165 Andy Caulfield/The Image Bank; page 169 Peter Howe/Visions; page 171 Dennis Brack/Black Star; page 172 Carl Mydans/Black Star.

Chapter 6

Page 182 Naoki Okamoto/Black Star; page 187 Peter B. Kaplan; page 189 Dan McCoy/Rainbow; page 190 Mark Greenberg; page 191 © Richard Wood 1981/Taurus Photos; page 193 Reuters/Bettmann Newsphotos; page 194 Sepp Seitz/Woodfin Camp & Associates; page 197 Chuck O'Rear/Woodfin Camp & Associates; page 203 © Ed Kashi 1987; page 201 © Janice Rubin 1987/Black Star; page 204 Erika Stone/Peter Arnold, Inc.

Chapter 7

Page 212 © Christopher Morris 1985/Black Star; page 213 J.W. Myers/Stock Boston; page 216 © J. Berndt 1983/The Picture Cube; page 221 Pam Hasegawa/Taurus Photos; page 227 A. Tannenbaum/Sygma; page 229 Focus on Sports; page 230 © Eric Kroll 1984/Taurus Photos; page 232 Michal Heron/Monkmeyer Press Photo Service, Inc.; page 235 © Barbara Kirk 1986/The Stock Market.

Chapter 8

Page 242 Mary Ellen Mark/Archive Pictures, Inc.; page 243 Sal DiMarco/Black Star; page 245 © Susan Leavines/Photo Researchers; page 247 © Bob Shaw 1987/The Stock Market; page 249 Francis Miller, Life Magazine © 1963 Time, Inc.; page 250 Suzanne Szasz; page 253 Barbara Kirk/The Stock Market; page 255 Whitney Lane/The Image Bank; page 256 © Blair Seitz 1985/Photo Researchers; page 257 © Sonya Jacobs 1987/The Stock Market; page 259 © Hazel Hankin 1984; page 263 Alan Carey/The Image Works; page 265, 266 Photos Courtesy of R.A. and B.T. Gardner; page 246 © Richard Stack 1980/Black Star.

Chapter 9

Page 272 Lew Merrim/Monkmeyer Press Photo Service; page 277 © Eiji Miyazawa 1983/Black Star; page 279

© James S. Douglass 1987/Photo Group; page 281 Roy Morsch/The Stock Market; page 282 © Lewis Portnoy 1984/The Stock Market; page 284 © Richard Howard 1983/Black Star; page 285 by Permission of The Folger Shakespeare Library; page 287 Dennis Brack/Black Star; page 288 © James Balog 1983/Black Star; page 289 © Andy Levin 1987; page 290 Bill Pierce/Rainbow; page 291 © Michal Heron 1985/Monkmeyer Press Photo Service; page 293 (left) New York Public Library Picture Collection; page 293 (right) Leonard Andrews Collection/Sygma; page 296 Jed Share/The Stock Market.

Chapter 10

Page 313 © Richard Nowitz 1984/Black Star; page 314 Mimi Forsyth/Monkmeyer Press Photo Service, Inc.; page 320 © Ed Kashi 1987; page 323 © Bob Krist 1987/Black Star; page 325 The Bettmann Archive; page 328 © Ed Kashi 1985.

Chapter 11

Page 336 © 1985 Jose Fernandez 1985/Woodfin Camp & Associates; page 338 © Michael Putnam/Peter Arnold, Inc.; page 339 Jerry Irwin/Black Star; page 340 Joe McNally/Wheeler Pictures; page 342 © Andy Levin 1987; page 343 Steve Smith/Wheeler Pictures; page 350 © Michal Heron 1984/Woodfin Camp & Associates; page 352 Michael Melford/Wheeler Pictures; page 354 © Daniel Simon 1987/Gamma-Liaison; page 357 Holly Stein/Focus West.

Chapter 12

Page 363 Phototheque; page 367 (right) © Dennis Brack 1981/Black Star; page 369 Diana Walker/Gamma-Liaison; page 371 © Jerry Mesmer 1986/Folio, Inc.; page 372 Hugh Rogers/Monkmeyer Press Photo Service, Inc.; page 374 © David Burnett 1981/Contact Press Images/Woodfin Camp & Associates; page 375 Gale Zucker/Stock Boston; page 381 © Lew Long 1986/The Stock Market.

Chapter 13

Page 390 © Andy Levin 1987; page 391 UPI/Bettmann Newsphotos; page 394 © Charles Gupton 1985/The Stock Market; page 396 © Bill Pierce 1984/Sygma; page 397 Guido Alberto Rossi/The Image Bank; page 403 Coco McCoy/Rainbow; page 405 Diana Walker/Gamma-Liaison; page 408 Created by Bette Klegon President, Park Place Group Advertising, Inc.

Chapter 14

Page 414 © Sepp Seitz 1983/Woodfin Camp & Associates; page 416 Martin Bell/Archive Pictures, Inc.; page 417 © Andy Levin 1987; page 419 Roy Morsch/The Stock Market; page 421 John Coletti/Stock Boston; page 422 © Chuck Fishman 1986/Woodfin Camp & Associates; page 427 © David Marie 1987/Folio, Inc.; page 430 T. Campion/ Sygma; page 432 Peter Menzel/Wheeler Pictures; page 435 Peter Glass/Monkmeyer Press Photo Service; page 436 Henley and Savage/The Stock Market.

…einberg/The Picture Cube; page 443 Abi-…/Archive Pictures, Inc.; page 449 Ben Sim-…e Stock Market; page 450 Ted Horowitz/The …k Market; page 452 © Stephanie Maze 1985/Woodfin Camp & Associates; page 455 © Andy Levin 1987; page 456 Historical Pictures Service Chicago; page 457 Jeff Jacobson/Archive Pictures, Inc.; page 459 (left) Ben Simmons/The Stock Market; page 459 (right) Henley and Savage/The Stock Market; page 466 Stan Goldblatt/Photo Researchers; page 467 © 1943 by the President and Fellows of Harvard College; © 1971 by Henry A. Murray.

Chapter 16

Page 478 Eric Staller/Archive Pictures, Inc.; page 481 Art Resource; page 483 © Ed Lettau 1984/Photo Researchers; page 486 The Bettmann Archive; page 489 © Sam Gross 1986; page 490 Dan McCoy/Rainbow; page 491 UPI/Bettmann Newsphotos; page 494 Professor Ord Matek; page 495 Bill Binzen/Photo Researchers; page 498 Mel DiGiacomo/The Image Bank; page 502 (both) © Dan McCoy 1981/Black Star; page 503 Joe McNally/Wheeler Pictures; page 504 © Joel Gordon 1978.

Chapter 17

Page 512 (both) Culver Pictures, Inc.; page 513 Historical Pictures Service Chicago; page 514 Art Resource; page 515 (top) © Sam Gross 1986; page 515 (bottom) Susan Rosenberg/Photo Researchers; page 517 Michael Rougler/*Life Magazine*, © Time, Inc.; page 519 © Rick Friedman 1985/Black Star; page 521 John Chiasson/Gamma-Liaison; page 524 Dan McCoy/Rainbow; page 527 Dr. Albert Ellis; page 529 Ed Kashi 1986; page 530 Joan Menschenfreund/The Stock Market; page 531 © Ed Kashi 1984; page 533 © Dick Durrance II 1984/Woodfin Camp & Associates;

page 535 © Will McIntyre 1982/Photo Researchers; page 538 © John Madere 1984; page 540 © Bohdan Hrynewych/Stock Boston.

Chapter Openings

Chapter 1 ©Helen Marcus 1982/Photo Researchers
Chapter 2 ©Howard Sochurek 1984/Woodfin Camp & Associates
Chapter 3 Eric Meola/The Image Bank
Chapter 4 ©Tim Davis 1982/Photo Researchers
Chapter 5 ©Craig Aurness 1979/Woodfin Camp & Associates
Chapter 6 ©Andy Levin 1987
Chapter 7 ©David Frank 1987/The Stock Market
Chapter 8 Steve Dunwell/The Image Bank
Chapter 9 Mark Godfrey/Archive Pictures, Inc.
Chapter 10 Michael DeCamp/The Image Bank
Chapter 11 Michael Melford/The Image Bank
Chapter 12 Janeart/The Image Bank
Chapter 13 Jimmy Rodnick/The Stock Market
Chapter 14 C. Simonpietri/Sygma
Chapter 15 Chris Sorensen/The Stock Market
Chapter 16 Art Resource
Chapter 17 Mitchell Funk/The Image Bank

Part Openings

Part A Brownie Harris
Part A Case © 1984 Dennis Brack/Black Star
Part B Roger Ressmeyer
Part B Case © 1987 Dahlgren/The Stock Market
Part C Focus West
Part C Case LDG Productions/The Image Bank
Part D Larry Downing/Woodfin Camp
Part D Case David Brownell/The Image Bank
Part E © 1987 Sobel/Klonsky/The Image Bank
Part E Case Mel DiGiacomo/The Image Bank